THE PLASTIDS

THE PLASTIDS
Their Chemistry, Structure, Growth and Inheritance

JOHN T. O. KIRK
DEPARTMENT OF BIOCHEMISTRY,
UNIVERSITY OF WALES, ABERYSTWYTH

RICHARD A. E. TILNEY-BASSETT
DEPARTMENT OF GENETICS,
UNIVERSITY OF WALES, SWANSEA

W. H. FREEMAN AND COMPANY
London and San Francisco

The Frontispiece

By permission from 'Untersuchungen über die Chlorophyllkörper und die ihnen homologen Gebilde', A. F. W. Schimper (1885), *Jahrbücher f. wiss. Botan.*, pp. 1–247, Verlag von Gebrüder Borntraeger, Berlin.

Translator's note: The word 'leucoplast,' which we do not use in this book, is used by Schimper to refer to any plastid which is colourless. The word 'grana' is applied by Schimper, not only to particles within the chloroplast (its present-day usage), but also to grains of carotenoid within chromoplasts. No caption to Fig. 44 appears in the original.—J.T.O.K.

Fig. 1. *Phajus grandifolius*. Leucoplasts with rod-shaped protein-crystals in the epidermis of the tuber

Fig. 2. *P. grandifolius*. Chloroplasts with colourless protein-crystal in the periderm of the tuber

Fig. 3. *P. grandifolius*. Round chloroplast with enclosed crystal in the cortex of the tuber. The grainy appearance is due to the presence of oil-droplets

Fig. 4. *P. grandifolius*. Leucoplasts and cell nucleus in the parenchyma of the root

Fig. 5. *P. grandifolius*. Chloroplasts of a greening root

Fig. 6. *P. grandifolius*. Leucoplast with starch grain in the root

Fig. 7. *Maxillaria triangularis*. Leucoplasts with protein-crystals in the epidermis of a perianth-leaf of the flower-bud

Fig. 8. *M. triangularis*. Chromoplasts of the epidermis of a perianth-petal of the mature flower. The pigment-containing stroma incompletely covers the colourless protein-crystal

Fig. 9. *Colchicum autumnale*. Cell nucleus with crystal-containing leucoplasts in the leaf epidermis

Fig. 10. *Cerinthe minor*. Chloroplasts with protein-crystals in the epidermis of the stem

Fig. 11. *C. glabra*. Chloroplasts with large protein-crystals in the epidermis of an old stem

Fig. 12. *Goodyera pubescens*. Leucoplasts with protein-crystal in the leaf epidermis; *a*, larger leucoplast in another cell of the same leaf

Fig. 13. *G. pubescens*. Chloroplasts in the leaf mesophyll with protein-crystals. The grana are very distinct

Fig. 14. *Monotropa hypopithys*. Leucoplast protein-crystals in the parenchyma of the flower

Fig. 15. *Neottia nidus-avis*. Cell nucleus and leucoplasts, the latter with protein-crystals, in the centre of the stem

Fig. 16. *N. nidus-avis*. Chromoplasts with protein- and pigment-crystals in the upper part of the stem

Fig. 17. *N. nidus-avis*. Chromoplasts with pigment-crystals and also protein crystals, in the flower

Fig. 18. *Chrysanthemum phoeniceum*. Chromoplasts of the inside layer of the tubular flower. Colourless protein-crystals and yellow grana

Contents

Foreword

To us it seems obvious that animals are more complicated than plants. Being animals ourselves we are bound to notice that we have done better and gone further than the plants we feed upon. It was therefore natural enough for people to argue that a model of heredity and variation which sufficed for animals should serve for plants and even leave room to spare.

There were other reasons for this confidence in 1930. Fifty years or more of breeding experiment and microscopic study had been spent on the job. Both plants and animals had been pressed into service. The model showed how chromosomes propagated themselves in the individual and distributed themselves in the population, maintained and modified their character in evolution, and by their activities in the nucleus controlled the life of the cell and the organism. What more could be wanted?

So far as animals were concerned at that time no more was wanted. But in plants it was known that the chromosomes were not enough. Something outside the nucleus was somehow and sometimes escaping from its control. Something was demonstrating an awkward disobedience to the laws of Mendel and Morgan. This something could not always be seen and named. But in certain experiments it showed itself to lie in, or go with, or actually to be, the green pigment-producing organs of the cell, the plastids.

Slowly in the years following 1930, it became clear that the plastids in all green plants propagate themselves everlastingly just as the nucleus does. But they do so on their own. Not for them are mitosis and meiosis. Not for them indeed is sexual reproduction in any ordinary sense. In genetics and physiology and therefore in evolution they are little worlds of their own. Or, as we may say, little principalities within the biological kingdom.

Soon also it began to appear that, in animals as well as in plants, other kinds of heredity existed outside the nucleus. Such heredity must depend on invisible corpuscles to which the plastids would provide a visible clue. Thus the plastids of plants introduced us to methods and principles common to a new world of plant and animal studies. They did so simply because the differences between green and white leaves were the first to declare their properties. They declared themselves in a way that the naked untrained eye had been able to see for over three hundred years; and in a way that we can now understand.

Such is the new world that John Kirk and Richard Tilney-Bassett have set out to show us in this book. They have worked together. If they have done so it is not so much because the study of plastids is too big for one man to grasp. Rather it is because the world of plastids is expanding too rapidly and in too many directions for one man to sort out the new material day by day. With the nucleus, breeding and microscopy had to be set in one yoke. Now, with the plastids, chemistry and electron microscopy must be harnessed to the same yoke. The attempt to manage this *quadriga* is notable in itself. For if it succeeds, as I believe it does, one man will in due course be able to grapple with what now takes the strength of two.

We are still, to be sure, far from having digested the chromosome theory of heredity. Its problems still cause discomfort. Some may turn pale when they are told so soon that they must for their own health and well-being absorb yet another elaborate confection. This, however, is the wrong way of looking at the matter. What Kirk and Tilney-Bassett give us now may indeed make each of the compartments of biology heavier. Separately, genetics and physiology, cytology and biochemistry may become harder to bear. But biology as a whole will be made lighter. Biology as a unit will become easier. And it is as a piece of biology that I want to recommend this book.

September 1966   CDD

Preface

PLASTIDS are of fundamental importance in the living world. Life on this planet is maintained largely by the energy trapped in the green plastids, or chloroplasts, of land plants and the corresponding green, red, and brown plastids of the aquatic algae, including the very important phytoplankton of the sea. Starch, the main source of carbohydrate in the diet of humans and many other animals is formed by plastids; chloroplasts are probably the main source of protein for herbivorous, and hence ultimately for carnivorous, animals; and certain vitamins and essential fatty acids are also derived from plastids.

In addition to their immense practical importance plastids are of extreme interest to the biologist, for it is the possession of these organelles which perhaps more than anything else distinguishes plants from animals. The elucidation of the intricacies of plastid fine structure has been, and still is, a rich field for exploration by the electron microscopists. The far-reaching concept of the extra-nuclear inheritance of certain cell organelles in both the plant and animal kingdoms developed out of the classic studies of plastid behaviour; the continued study of their inheritance remains just as important today. Research on their physiological function and growth has lately gained such momentum that it is now one of the most important fields in plant biochemistry.

In the past, investigations on plastids have been concentrated rather towards the physiological side, especially into the problems of photosynthesis and related topics. Consequently, books on the physiological aspects have appeared with some regularity, and it has not been too difficult to be reasonably well informed about the current state of the subject. By contrast it seems that no book has ever been written on plastids as interesting objects in themselves, apart from their functional aspects; their chemistry, structure, formation, and inheritance have been somewhat neglected. Over the years so many important papers have been published in this field that it is becoming increasingly difficult to digest all the relevant material. Moreover, review papers, helpful though they are, inevitably leave out many interesting and significant observations which consequently become buried deeper and deeper in the literature. A second problem, especially in regard to inheritance studies, is that much of the extensive German work has never been adequately reported in the English-language scientific literature, presumably owing to the sheer bulk of the work coupled with the difficulties of translation.

Clearly, there is a great need for a comprehensive and up-to-date account of the state of our knowledge in this subject. This book is an attempt to satisfy this need: to bring together, and if possible, to relate, findings from genetics, biochemistry, and electron microscopy, in order to give an overall picture of the biology of plastids. In particular, it was felt that the time had come when some of the curious features of plastid inheritance could tentatively be given a biochemical meaning. Many of the early observations which had become lost from view in the older literature have been brought together, and it has often been possible to suggest likely explanations, in the light of our present knowledge, where previously these were lacking. We have also given a fairly detailed account of much of the German research in this field, and hope in this way to draw attention to findings with which many English-speaking workers are not familiar.

The book is divided into three main parts. The first (J.T.O.K.) defines and describes the different kinds of plastid, with particular reference to their chemistry, structure, and function and introduces the concept of plastid autonomy. The second (R.A.E.T.-B.) is concerned with plastids and inheritance. It begins with an introductory classification of the variegated plants which have been so valuable in furthering our knowledge of plastid inheritance, and which are considered fully in the following chapters. These include chapters on gene and chromosome control of plastid behaviour; on chimeras; and on the recognition, inheritance and behaviour firstly, of different types of mutant plastid and secondly, of different types of normal plastid. The third part (J.T.O.K.) deals with the biochemistry of plastid inheritance and growth, and describes work on the nature of the genetic material of the plastid, the genetic control of plastid formation, the biosynthetic capabilities of plastids, the growth and differentiation of plastids, and the effect of various inhibitors on these processes.

The book is written primarily for the benefit of research workers in this and related fields, and for university teachers who wish to give courses on plastid biochemistry or genetics. Postgraduate and honours students in biochemistry or botany should also be able to make use of the book. Some of the material in it has already been given in lectures to honours students of botany in Oxford, and of biochemistry in Aberystwyth. The extensive information on variegated plants we hope will make it a useful addition to the reference shelves of botanic garden libraries.

We wish to thank Professor C. D. Darlington, F.R.S., in whose department this book was mainly written, for his help and encouragement throughout. Indeed, the book may be said to have had its origin in lectures which at Professor Darlington's request we gave in Oxford early in 1963: in the ensuing three years we have attempted to expand

and develop the original ideas and provide a comprehensive account of the important recent developments in this field. One of us (R.A.E.T.-B.), wishes to acknowledge his special debt to Professor Darlington for introducing him, as a research student, to the fascinating study of plastids and variegated plants. Mr J. K. Burras, N.D.H., has also been a continual source of encouragement, and has given much of his time to discussing many interesting aspects of the fine collection of about three hundred variegated plants that he has helped Professor Darlington to develop in the Oxford Botanic Garden. In 1961 Dr Tilney-Bassett was able to make a short visit to a number of departments in Germany and one in Sweden in which plastid researches were in progress. He is grateful for the hospitality he was given and the opportunity for fruitful talks. A second, longer visit, this time to the Botany Department at Cologne University from November 1964 to September 1965 was made possible by the kindness of Professor W. Menke and the financial assistance of a scholarship from the Alexander von Humboldt Foundation for which he is again most grateful. These visits were of great value in helping him to become acquainted with the extensive researches into plastids by many German workers.

We would particularly like to thank Dr G. B. Bouck, Dr P. Döbel, Dr E. Gantt, Professor T. W. Goodwin, Mr A. D. Greenwood, Dr B. E. S. Gunning, Dr R. Hagemann, Professor J. Heslop-Harrison, Dr B. E. Juniper, Professor I. Manton, Professor W. Menke, Dr P. Michaelis, Dr A. Nougarède, Dr R. B. Park, Professor K. Steffen, Dr W. Stubbe, Mr D. M. Thomas, Dr W. Wehrmeyer, Professor T. E. Weier, and Professor D. von Wettstein, who have so kindly allowed us to reproduce tables and figures from their published and unpublished work, or have lent us original photographs and electron-micrographs; the details of these are individually acknowledged in the main text.

Finally we would especially like to express our gratitude to our wives for all their help, both practical and moral, during the long and arduous task of preparing this book.

John T. O. Kirk   Richard A. E. Tilney-Bassett
Aberystwyth   Swansea

August, 1966

List of Abbreviations

ACP   Acyl carrier protein
ADP   Adenosine diphosphate
A/G ratio   Molar ratio of adenine to guanine
ALA δ-Aminolaevulinic acid
AMP   Adenosine monophosphate
ATP   Adenosine triphosphate
CoA   Coenzyme A
CTP   Cytidine triphosphate
DNA   Deoxyribonucleic acid
DPIP   2,6-Dichlorophenol-indophenol
EPR   Electron paramagnetic resonance
FAD   Flavin adenine dinucleotide
GC content   (Guanine + Cytosine) content
GTP   Guanosine triphosphate
$h\nu$ One quantum of light
NAD   Nicotinamide adenine dinucleotide
NADP   Nicotinamide adenine dinucleotide phosphate
OD   Optical density
Pi   Orthophosphate
P_r 660 mμ-absorbing form of phytochrome
P_{fr} 730 mμ-absorbing form of phytochrome
PP   Pyrophosphate
RNA   Ribonucleic acid
S   Svedberg unit
UDPG   Uridinediphosphoglucose
UTP   Uridine triphosphate

CHAPTER I

The Chemistry, Structure, and Function of Plastids

I.1. Introduction

PLANT and animal cells are fundamentally very similar. They both have a nucleus, mitochondria, Golgi bodies, endoplasmic reticulum, ribosomes and a bounding membrane. However, as well as all these structures, plant cells contain another class of organelles, the plastids. Plastids exist in a number of different forms, with different functions. These different forms are all referred to as 'plastids' because they are all, to some extent, interconvertible: that is, any kind of plastid can be shown to change into, or be formed from, one or more other kinds of plastid. All the bodies referred to as 'plastids' are related to each other in this way. In general, all the plastids in a given plant cell will be of the same type. In the more complex multicellular plants the form taken by the plastids of a cell is determined by the tissue in which the cell is located. In this chapter we shall discuss the chemistry, structure, and function of the different types of plastid, so far as these are known. We shall also examine the concept of the autonomy and continuity of plastids, derived from the cytological studies of Schimper, Meyer, and others.

I.2. The Chloroplast

I.2.i. OCCURRENCE, DISCOVERY, AND ISOLATION OF CHLOROPLASTS

The chloroplast is the best studied of the plastids, and was the first to be discovered. In higher plants chloroplasts present the appearance of lens-shaped green bodies usually 4–6 μ in diameter. Most of the chloroplasts of the plant are found in the leaves, in the palisade and spongy mesophyll cells (Fig. I.1), and the guard cells of the epidermis (in many plant species the chloroplasts of the other epidermal cells are incompletely developed). Chloroplasts are also found in the outer cells of the stem, but are absent from the meristematic (i.e. dividing, undifferentiated) cells of the shoot, and from the root. The average palisade cell of

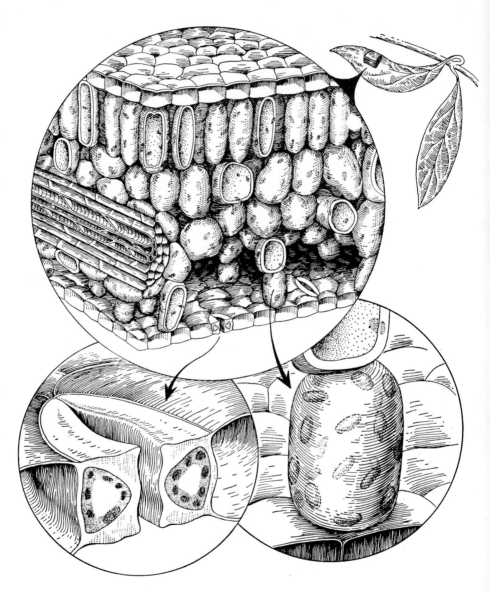

Fig. I.i. *Between the upper and lower epidermis of the leaf lie the cells of the mesophyll and the vascular tissues. Interspersed between the parenchymatous cells of the mesophyll are intercellular air spaces which lead, through the stomata, to the exterior (from Bonner and Galston,* Principles of Plant Physiology, *1952, W. H. Freeman and Company, San Francisco)*

Ricinus communis contains about thirty-six chloroplasts, and the spongy mesophyll cell about twenty[91]. This implies a total of 495,200 chloroplasts per square millimetre of leaf, 18 per cent of these being in the spongy mesophyll cells. The chloroplasts are found within the cytoplasm, usually around the periphery, closely appressed to the cytoplasmic membrane. In the palisade cells the chloroplasts may be so numerous as to form an almost continuous layer. In the algae, chloroplasts may be green, brown, or red in colour, and sometimes have very bizarre shapes (see I.2.iii.c). The brown and red plastids of the *Phaeophyta* and *Rhodophyta* are sometimes referred to as phaeoplasts and rhodoplasts, respectively. However, both these kinds of plastids contain chlorophyll (the green colour of which is masked by other pigments), and have the same physiological function as the chloroplasts of green plants, so we shall refer to them as 'chloroplasts'. In the more complex multicellular algae chloroplasts may be absent from the rhizoids, sexual organs, and apical cells[88,24], but are present throughout the rest of the thallus.

The first person to record seeing chloroplasts was the seventeenth-century plant anatomist Nehemiah Grew. He speaks of the air acting on 'the acid and sulphurous parts of plants for the production of their verdure; that is they all strike together into a green precipitate'. Ingen-Housz (1779) showed that only the green parts of plants (the parts containing chloroplasts) had the ability 'to correct bad air' (to remove carbon dioxide and evolve oxygen), and then only in sunlight. Von Mohl (1837) observed starch grains within the chloroplast. Sachs (1887) was able to demonstrate that these starch grains were the direct product of the assimilation of carbon dioxide in the light. Thus, before the end of the nineteenth century the existence and the essential function of the chloroplast were well established.

For a detailed study of the chemistry and function of chloroplasts, it was essential that the bodies be isolated. Noack (1927) showed that if spinach leaves were ground with water and the extract was centrifuged, chloroplasts were deposited. The first extensive studies on isolated chloroplasts were those of Menke (1938) and Granick (1938). Menke isolated the chloroplasts by centrifugation of, or addition of ammonium sulphate to, an aqueous extract of spinach leaves. Granick also used centrifugation and included 0·5M glucose in his isolation medium to preserve the semipermeable membrane of the chloroplast intact. The most common procedure now in use for chloroplast isolation is based on this early work, and involves disintegrating leaf tissue in a medium containing sucrose, sodium chloride, or other solutes (usually buffered in the region of pH 7) and collecting the fraction which sediments when the homogenate is centrifuged at 500–1000 *g* for 10–15 minutes (see, for instance, ref. 116).

For many purposes, particularly certain photosynthetic studies, differential centrifugation of chloroplasts is quite a satisfactory method of preparation. However, when it is desired to reduce contamination by other cell constituents to the absolute minimum, methods which take advantage of the differences in density of the chloroplasts and other organelles are preferable. Jagendorf (1955) obtained very pure chloroplasts by mixing a crude chloroplast preparation with a dense solution of sucrose and glycerol, and centrifuging at 100,000 g: most of the chloroplasts, being less dense than the medium, floated to the top. Chloroplasts isolated by differential centrifugation are always liable to be contaminated to a slight extent by mitochondria. James and Das (1957) showed that broad-bean leaf chloroplasts could be obtained free of such contamination if the crude chloroplast preparation was placed on top of a density gradient consisting of two dense layers of a solution of glycerol and sucrose, and then centrifuged at 1000 g for 12 minutes. The densities of the layers were chosen so that chloroplasts could travel down through the upper layer, ending up at the interface, whereas mitochondria remained at the top of the upper layer. Chloroplasts prepared by differential centrifugation tend to be seriously contaminated by nuclei and nuclear fragments. This type of contamination can also be minimized by using density gradient centrifugation. However, it is essential in this case to carry out the preparation at high centrifugal fields: broad-bean chloroplasts isolated by density gradient centrifugation at 2000 g appeared to have a DNA content of about 2 per cent of the dry weight, but this could be reduced to about 0·15 per cent simply by carrying out the centrifugation at 76,000 g[129].

It has been known for some years that isolated chloroplasts are leaky: if a suspension of chloroplasts is allowed to stand for, say, 30 minutes and the chloroplasts are then spun down, the supernatant will be found to contain protein. The true seriousness of the situation was not revealed, however, until electron micrographs were taken of isolated chloroplasts. Kahn and von Wettstein (1961) and Jacobi and Perner (1961) showed that in preparations isolated by differential centrifugation in aqueous media, many, and sometimes most, of the chloroplasts had completely lost their outer membrane, and with it virtually all the electron dense material (mainly protein) of the stroma (see I.2.iii.a for an explanation of this term). Curiously enough, such chloroplasts look more or less normal in the optical microscope, which may explain why this situation remained undiscovered for so long. The loss of the outer membrane and soluble contents of the chloroplast is probably due to the violent methods used for disintegration of the leaves. If the leaves are broken very gently, chloroplast preparations in which most of the outer membranes remain intact may be obtained, but the yields are small[141]. Intact chloroplasts appear to be more dense than those which have lost their outer membrane. This difference may be utilized to separate the two kinds of chloroplasts—if a crude chloroplast preparation from broad-bean leaves is layered onto 46 per cent (w/v) sucrose (M/15 phosphate, pH 7·3) and centrifuged, the broken chloroplasts remain at the top of this layer but the intact ones pass through[142]. To obtain the maximum proportion of intact chloroplasts in aqueous media, Perner (1965) recommends that isolation be carried out in 0·6M sucrose, 0·01M pyrophosphate, pH 7·8. To avoid loss of photosynthetic ability, isolation should be carried out at a pH value in the region of 8·0, rather than in the region of 6·0: at the lower pH value enzymic hydrolysis of chloroplast galactolipids (I.2.ii.b) takes place[219] and the linolenic acid liberated inhibits photosynthetic electron transport[160].

A general method of preventing the leaking of water-soluble constituents from organelles is to isolate these in non-aqueous solvents, in which the hydrophilic substances are not soluble. This is a method which was first devised by Behrens for the isolation of nuclei. It has now been applied to chloroplasts by a number of workers[95,243,19,233]. The procedure used is to freeze-dry the leaves, and then to homogenize them in petrol ether. The chloroplasts are centrifuged down, and then purified further by centrifugation in petrol ether/carbon tetrachloride mixtures of suitable densities. Chloroplasts prepared in this way can be seen in electron micrographs to have lost their outer membrane but retained their stroma materials; by comparison with these non-aqueous chloroplasts, chloroplasts isolated in aqueous media appear to lose 67–85 per cent of their water-soluble protein (calculated from the results of Heber and Tyszkiewicz, 1962). This technique has been much used to investigate which enzymes are actually present in the chloroplast (see I.2.iv.d). Although leaching of water-soluble materials is prevented by this technique, there is probably some loss of lipids; however, according to Biggins and Park (1964) this amounts to not more than 5 per cent of the dry weight of the chloroplast.

I.2.ii. CHEMICAL COMPOSITION OF CHLOROPLASTS

I.2.ii.a. *Protein content and overall composition*

Chloroplasts are the major protein-bearing bodies of the leaf: Stocking and Ongun (1962) found that chloroplasts of tobacco or bean leaves contain about 75 per cent of the total leaf nitrogen. Various values have been reported for the protein content of isolated chloroplasts (see review by Thomas, 1960). However, most of these values were obtained with chloroplasts prepared from leaves disintegrated in distilled water: such chloroplasts would have lost virtually all the water-soluble proteins of the stroma. Consequently, the values reported for protein content of these chloroplasts will be too low, and the values for the content of other components too high. However, it is possible to make rough corrections to these values by making use of the results of Heber and Tyszkiewicz on the water-soluble-protein content of chloroplasts isolated in non-aqueous media. For non-aqueously-isolated chloroplasts of *Spinacia oleracea* the ratio of water-soluble to water-insoluble protein was 1·22. It seems likely that this is a good estimate of the ratio of soluble to insoluble protein in the chloroplast *in vivo*. For spinach chloroplasts isolated by centrifugation in distilled water, Menke (1938) found a protein content of 47·7 per cent: Comar (1942) obtained a number of values, a typical one being 52·5 per cent. The mean of these two estimates is about 50 per cent, which we may take to be the protein content of spinach chloroplasts which have lost nearly all their water-soluble protein. Thus, 100 g of chloroplasts isolated in this way have the following composition:

$$50 \text{ g insoluble protein} + 50 \text{ g non-protein material}$$
$$= 100 \text{ g chloroplasts}$$

However, these same chloroplasts *in vivo* would also contain $(50 \times 1 \cdot 22)$ g, i.e. 61 g, water-soluble protein, and so would have the following composition:
50 g insoluble protein + 61 g soluble protein

$$+ 50 \text{ g non-protein material}$$
$$= 161 \text{ g chloroplasts}$$

Consequently, the total protein content of chloroplasts which have not lost their soluble protein is $111/161 \times 100$ per cent, i.e. 69 per cent. To correct the values for the contents of the various non-protein materials we divide by 1·61. The effect of loss of other water-soluble components, such as sugar phosphates, salts, nucleic acids, etc., on the dry weight of chloroplast preparations has been ignored, since this will be small compared to the effect of loss of soluble protein.

Table I.1 gives data on the overall chemical composition of spinach chloroplasts: both the observed values (obtained with chloroplasts isolated in distilled water) and values corrected for loss of soluble protein are given.

The corrected values for protein content of spinach chloroplasts given in Table I.1 are in good agreement with values recently obtained by Nickel[174] for chloroplasts of *Antirrhinum majus* isolated by techniques which avoid loss of soluble proteins. Structural (water-insoluble) and stroma (water-soluble) proteins constituted 30 per cent and 42 per cent, respectively, of the chloroplast dry weight, as determined with chloroplasts isolated in non-aqueous media. The dry weight of one chloroplast was calculated to be $20 \cdot 1 \times 10^{-12}$ g. *Antirrhinum* chloroplasts isolated

TABLE 1.1. OVERALL CHEMICAL COMPOSITION OF SPINACH CHLOROPLASTS

Component	Percentage of dry weight of chloroplasts			
	Values for chloroplasts isolated in water		Values corrected for loss of soluble protein	
Total protein	50		69	
Water-insoluble protein		50		31
Water-soluble protein		0		38
Total lipid	34		21	
Chlorophyll		8·0		5·0
Carotenoids		1·1		0·7
RNA	—		1·0–7·5	
DNA	—		0·02–0.1	
Carbohydrate (starch, etc.)	Variable			

See the appropriate sections for references.

from freeze-dried leaves, without the use of liquids, had a structural protein content of 32 per cent. The calculated dry weight of a chloroplast prepared by this technique was $26·6 \times 10^{-12}$ g.

One of the major components of the water-soluble protein of the chloroplasts is the so-called Fraction I protein. This is a large protein[54] with a molecular weight in the region of 515,000–564,000[262,258]. There is some evidence that it is a glycoprotein containing galactose and arabinose, with glucose, rhamnose, and ribose or xylose as minor components[1]. It is confined to the chloroplasts[153] and constitutes 27–36 per cent of the water-soluble protein of the chloroplasts[98]. Most of the water-insoluble protein of the chloroplasts is probably the protein of the lamellae (see I.2.iii). Electron microscope studies on Fraction I protein from Chinese cabbage leaves show cubical particles often with a central depression, the side of the cube being 120 Å long[92a]. The cube appears to be composed of about twenty-four subunits, three along each edge, and one in the centre of each of four faces. The subunits have a diameter of 20–30 Å. Data on the amino-acid composition and number of tryptic peptides of the Chinese cabbage Fraction I protein indicate that it consists of twenty-four identical subunits, each of molecular weight 22,500[211d].

Criddle[40,39] has obtained a protein fraction from chloroplasts of spinach which he believes to be the lamellar structural protein. It is homogeneous on electrophoresis and in the analytical ultracentrifuge ($S_{20,w} = 2·3$ S at infinite dilution) and its molecular weight is 25,000. The amino-acid composition of this protein is shown in Table I.2. It appears to have one N-terminal amino acid molecule—aspartic—per mole of protein, suggesting that it is a single polypeptide chain. *In vitro*, it appears to be able to bind one mole of chlorophyll per mole of protein. *In vivo*, there is a higher ratio of chlorophyll to structural protein; whether all (or indeed any) of this is bound to the protein is not known. This protein constitutes about 40 per cent of the total chloroplast protein.

Only a few other chloroplast proteins have been obtained in any degree of purity. Davenport and Hill (1952) purified cytochrome f from leaves of parsley (*Petroselinum sativum*). It is an acidic protein with an isoelectric point of pH 4·7. Sedimentation and diffusion measurements indicate a molecular weight of 110,000. There appear to be two haem groups per molecule. The oxidation reduction potential (E_0') at pH 7 is $+0·365$ volts: the cytochrome is slowly autoxidizable. The α band of the absorption spectrum of the reduced form (room temperature) is at 554·5 mμ. Katoh (1960) has obtained a cytochrome of the f type from the red alga, *Porphyra tenera*. This has a molecular weight of 13,600, with one haem group per molecule. Like the parsley cytochrome f it is acidic (isoelectric point pH 3·5) and has a high redox potential ($E_0' = +0·355$ V at pH 7). The α band of the reduced form is at 553 mμ. The f type cytochrome (cytochrome-552) from *Euglena gracilis* has a molecular weight (measured by sedimentation–diffusion methods) of about 17,000 with one haem group per molecule, an isoelectric point of about pH 5·5 and a redox potential of $+0·370$ V at pH 7, the α band of the reduced form being at 552 mμ[209a,285a]. The other chloroplast cytochrome of higher plants, cytochrome b_6, has not yet been purified. Its redox potential (E_0') is $-0·030$ V and the α band of the reduced form is at 563 mμ[104a]. Unlike cytochrome f, b_6 is rapidly autoxidizable. The ratio, b_6/f in spinach chloroplasts is about 1·3[104a]. The molar ratio of chlorophyll to cytochrome f in higher plants, or of chlorophyll to cytochrome-552 in *E. gracilis* is 300–400 to 1[46a,285a]. Biggins and Park (1965) have obtained a preparation of spinach chloroplast lamellar protein which is similar in its physicochemical properties to Criddle's preparation. The Biggins and Park preparation consists mainly of non-haem protein but includes cytochromes f and b_6 in approximately equimolar amounts. The cytochromes appear to sediment together with the bulk of the protein, suggesting that they are of about the same molecular weight (*ca.* 22,000) as the structural protein: this finding is surprising since Davenport and Hill (1952) obtained a molecular weight of 110,000 for purified cytochrome f from parsley.

The copper-containing chloroplast protein, plastocyanin, has been purified from higher plant leaves by Katoh and his co-workers[125b]. It is an acidic protein (isoelectric point less than pH 4). Sedimentation and diffusion data indicate a molecular weight of 21,000. It appears to contain about 200 amino-acid residues and a small amount of carbohydrate. The copper content is 0·58 per cent indicating the presence of two atoms of copper per molecule: these copper atoms appear to be bound to the protein through the sulphydryl groups of cysteine. In its oxidized form plastocyanin is deep blue in colour, having absorption maxima at 460, 597, and 770 mμ. The reduced form is colourless, having no absorption in the visible or far-red regions. The redox potential (E_0') is +0·370 V at pH 7: the reduced form is not autoxidizable. In spinach chloroplasts there are about 600 chlorophyll molecules per molecule of plastocyanin, i.e. about 300 chlorophyll molecules per atom of copper in plastocyanin: as mentioned above, the molar ratio of chlorophyll to cytochrome f is also about 300.

Ferredoxin, the iron-containing, non-haem protein of chloroplasts has been purified from higher plant leaves. Sedimentation and diffusion data indicate a molecular weight of 12,200[13a]. The oxidized form of the protein is reddish-brown in colour, having absorption maxima at 330, 420, and 465 mμ (in addition to the usual peak at 277 mμ)[61a]. Ferredoxin contains 0·88 per cent Fe, corresponding to two atoms of

TABLE 1.2. AMINO ACID COMPOSITION OF PURIFIED LAMELLAR STRUCTURAL PROTEIN FROM SPINACH CHLOROPLASTS

By permission, from Criddle, R. S. (1965).
Symposium on Biochemistry of Chloroplasts
Ed., T. W. Goodwin. Academic Press, London

	Moles % of amino acids	Moles amino acid per mole of protein, molecular weight 25,000
Aspartic	13·95	31·1
Threonine	3·74	8·4
Serine	5·47	12·2
Proline	5·14	11·5
Glutamic	13·08	29·2
Glycine	9·02	20·2
Alanine	10·40	7·5
Valine	7·43	16·6
Cystine	—	—
Methionine	0·15	0·33
Isoleucine	6·61	14·8
Leucine	11·38	25·4
Tyrosine	0·71	1·6
Phenylalanine	0·23	0·5
Lysine	8·17	18·3
Histidine	2·12	4·7
Arginine	1·04	2·3
Tryptophan	—	—
Cysteic	1·32	2·95

Fe per molecule[13a]. The protein also appears to contain sulphur in a labile form (not due to cysteine residues) which is liberated as hydrogen sulphide on acidification: the ratio of labile sulphur to iron is approximately $1 \cdot 0$[61a]. Ferredoxin is an acidic protein, containing relatively large amounts of aspartic and glutamic acids, and low amounts of the basic amino acids. Spinach ferredoxin contains one residue of tryptophan per molecule, while parsley ferredoxin contains none[61a]. Ferredoxin from spinach leaves has a very negative redox potential ($E_0' = -0 \cdot 432$ V at pH $7 \cdot 55$) and is rapidly autoxidizable: on reduction of the oxidized form the colour becomes paler, due to a marked fall in absorbance at the 420 and 465 mμ peaks[253a]. The molar ratio of chlorophyll to ferredoxin in spinach chloroplasts is about 400[253a].

The enzyme, ferredoxin–NADP reductase (also known as transhydrogenase, NADPH$_2$ diaphorase, and NADPH$_2$–cytochrome f reductase) of spinach chloroplasts has a molecular weight of 40,000–45,000: it is a flavoprotein, containing one mole of FAD per mole of protein[230,286a].

I.2.ii.b. *Overall lipid composition of chloroplasts*

The total lipid content of spinach chloroplasts isolated by centrifugation in water was found by Menke (1938) to be $30 \cdot 8$ per cent of the dry weight. Comar (1942) found up to $36 \cdot 7$ per cent total lipid in spinach chloroplasts prepared in a similar manner. Therefore 34 per cent of the dry weight is probably a fair estimate of the total lipid content (this includes pigments) of spinach chloroplasts which have lost most of their soluble protein. Applying the correction discussed in the previous section, we arrive at a figure of 21 per cent for the total lipid content of spinach chloroplasts which have not lost their soluble protein. This is in good agreement with the values obtained by Nickel[174] for *Antirrhinum* chloroplasts: the value of lipid content obtained from aqueously isolated chloroplasts, after correction, was 20 per cent; the value obtained for chloroplasts isolated without the use of liquids was 22 per cent.

The lipid fraction of chloroplasts includes a very large number of different compounds. The relative amounts of the known lipid components of the spinach chloroplast calculated from the results of various workers are shown in Table I.3.

Quantitatively the most important lipids are the two galactosyl diglycerides. Between them they constitute about 40 per cent by weight of the total lipid (Table I.3). They are found only in the chloroplast[279]. The nature of the fatty acids in the diglyceride moiety depends on the source from which the lipids are isolated[196]: in the case of alfalfa 95 per cent of the monogalactosyl diglyceride fatty acid, and 82 per cent of the digalactosyl diglyceride fatty acid is linolenic (18 C atoms, 3 double bonds: or in shorthand notation, 18:3). The remainder

TABLE 1.3. RELATIVE AMOUNTS OF DIFFERENT LIPIDS
IN SPINACH CHLOROPLASTS

(*Modelled on Lichtenthaler and Park, 1963*)

Number of lipid molecules per 100 molecules of chlorophyll	*Percentage by weight of total lipids*		

100 chlorophyll[1]
    70 chlorophyll *a*
    30 chlorophyll *b*
	20·8		

21·6 carotenoid[1]
    6 β-carotene
    10·2 lutein + zeaxanthin (mostly lutein)
    2·8 violaxanthin
    2·6 neoxanthin
	2·8		

22·1 quinone and related compounds
    11·5 plastoquinone A[2]
    2·1 plastoquinone B[2]
    2·1 plastoquinone C + plastoquinone D[2]
    0·2 plastoquinone E[3]
    1·3 plastochromanol-8[10]
    1·9 α-tocopherol[1]
    1·2 α-tocopherylquinone[2]
    0·03 β-tocopherylquinone + γ-tocopherylquinone[2]
    1·6 vitamin K_1[4]
    0·2 vitamin K (but not K_1)[5]
	3·3		

50·6 phospholipid[6]
    23·0 phosphatidyl glycerol
    18·0 phosphatidyl choline
    5·7 phosphatidyl inositol
    2·9 phosphatidyl ethanolamine
    1·0 phosphatidic acid
	9·1		

234 glycolipid[7]
    150 monogalactosyl diglyceride
    63 digalactosyl diglyceride
    21 sulpholipid
	44·3	26·8
		13·4
		4·1	

24·6 sterols[8]	2·2		
2·9 prenols: probably about 90% prenols -11 and -12[9]	0·5		
Unidentified lipids[11]	17·0		

[1] Lichtenthaler and Calvin (1964)
[2] Henninger and Crane (1963)
[3] Henninger, Barr, Wood, and Crane (1965)
[4] Henninger, Dilley, and Crane (1963)
[5] McKenna, Henninger, and Crane (1964)
[6] Wintermans (1960)
[7] Wintermans (1963)
[8] Menke and Jacob (1942). Number of molecules calculated on assumption that the average molecular weight is equal to the molecular weight of cholesterol (see text)
[9] Wellburn and Hemming (1965)—horse-chestnut chloroplasts
[10] Dunphy, Whittle and Pennock (1965)—*Polygonum* chloroplasts
[11] Lichtenthaler and Park (1963)

is mainly palmitic (16 C atoms, no double bonds: 16:0). The galactosyl diglycerides from *Chlorella pyrenoidosa* have a very different fatty-acid composition[196]: the fatty acids of the monogalactosyl diglyceride consist of 40·5 per cent 18:1 and only 26·8 per cent 18:3 (linolenic); the digalactosyl diglyceride has similar fatty acids, 36·8 per cent 18:1 and 27·0 per cent 18:3. The structures of the galactosyl diglycerides are shown in Fig. I.2(a) and (b): for simplicity it is assumed that linolenic is the only fatty acid present. Another carbohydrate-containing lipid present in chloroplasts (4 per cent of total lipid—Table I.3) is the sulpholipid discovered by Benson, Daniel and Wiser (1959). This is confined to the chloroplasts[46b] and nearly all of it is found in the lamellar fraction[229a]. When isolated from alfalfa its fatty acids are made up of about half palmitic and half linolenic acids; when isolated from *Chlorella pyrenoidosa* its fatty-acid composition is 67·5 per cent palmitic, 18·3 per cent of an 18:1 acid, and only 9·8 per cent linolenic[196]. Its structure (assuming one molecule of palmitic acid and one of linolenic) is shown in Fig. I.2(c); the sugar present is a sulphonic acid derivative of 6-deoxyglucose.

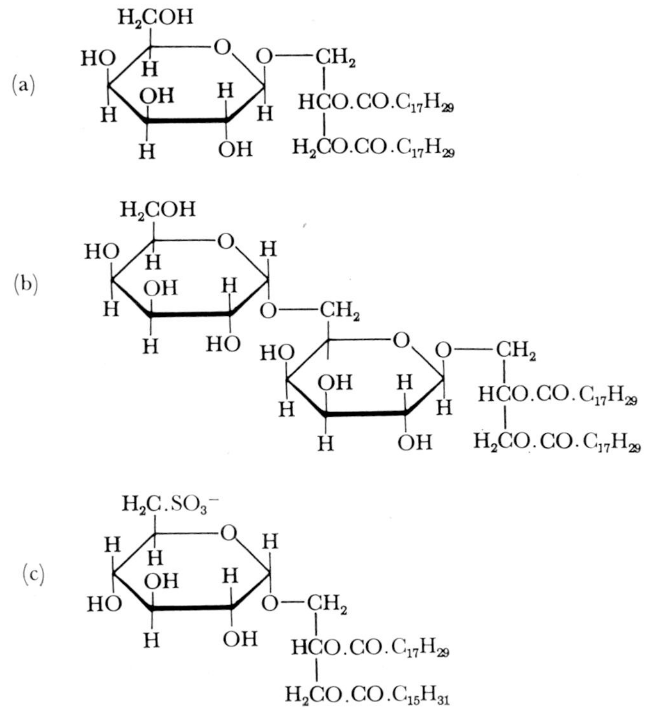

FIG. I.2. *Chloroplast glycolipids (see Benson, 1964). (a) Monogalactosyl diglyceride; (b) Digalactosyl diglyceride; (c) Plant sulpholipid*

Chloroplasts contain large amounts of fatty acids, combined in various forms (galactolipids, phospholipids, etc.) and possibly free as well. Crombie (1958) found that fatty acids (free and combined) made up about 44 per cent by weight of the total lipid of chloroplasts of *Vicia faba*. The major fatty acid in higher plant chloroplasts is lino-lenic[41,48,284]. Most of the linolenic acid is found in the galactolipids (see above). Table I.4 presents the fatty-acid composition of chloro-plasts of three higher plant species. It was recently shown[285] that arachidonic acid (20:4), previously thought to occur only in animals, was present in the chloroplasts of three species of moss, and three out of four species of fern, but not in the chloroplasts of any of the gymno-sperms (three species) or angiosperms (six species) tested.

TABLE I.4. FATTY ACID COMPOSITION OF HIGHER
PLANT CHLOROPLASTS

(*See Crombie, 1958; Wolf, Coniglio and Davis, 1962*)

| Fatty Acid | | % by wt. of Total Fatty Acid | | |
Name	C atoms: No. of double bonds	Vicia faba	Acer negundo	Spinach
Capric	10:0	—	—	Trace
Dodecenoic	12:1	—	—	Trace
Myristic	14:0	—	2·4	Trace
Palmitic	16:0	7·4	12·6	11·2
Palmitolcic	16:1	11·8	11·0	3·5
Hexadecadienoic	16:2	—	—	Trace
Hexadecatrienoic	16:3	—	—	10·8
Stearic	18:0	1·2	2·4	Trace
Oleic	18:1	5·2	10·6	1·1
Linoleic	18:2	2·6	3·8	4·6
Linolenic	18:3	72·0	61·1	68·9
Eicosenoic	20:1 ⎫			
Long-chain unsaturated	⎬	1·4	0·5	—
(as Docosenoic)	22:1 ⎭			
Long-chain saturated	(as 22:0)	1·2	—	—

Another important group of chloroplast lipids are the phospho-lipids[279]. These make up about 9 per cent of the total chloroplast lipid (Table I.3). Their structures are shown in Fig. I.3. At least half the phosphatidyl glycerol of the leaf cell is found in the chloroplasts[279]: the other phospholipids (apart from phosphatidic acid, which may be an artefact anyway) exist mainly in other parts of the cell. Phosphatidyl glycerol from spinach leaves has 31·7 per cent of its fatty acids in the form of a *trans*-hexadecenoic acid which is not found in the other lipids: 1-linolenoyl-2-*trans*-Δ^3-hexadecenoyl-glycero-3-phosphoryl-1'-glycerol constitutes about 50 per cent of the total phosphatidyl glycerol[93,49].

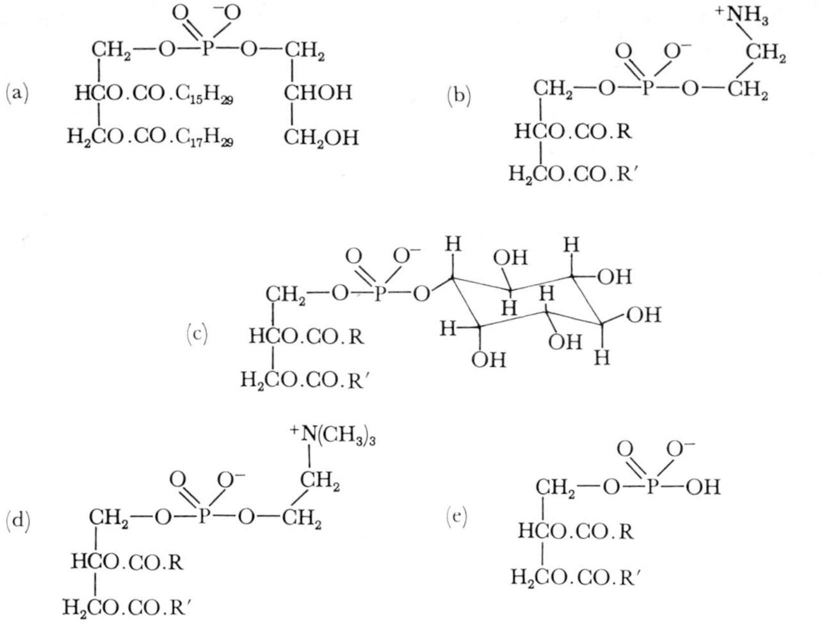

FIG. I.3. *Chloroplast phospholipids (see Wintermans, 1960; Benson 1964; van Deenen and Haverkate, 1965). (a) Phosphatidyl glycerol; (b) Phosphatidyl ethanolamine; (c) Phosphatidyl inositol; (d) Phosphatidyl choline; (e) Phosphatidic acid*

Chloroplasts contain several different kinds of quinone[21,102,162,101]. Together they constitute about 3 per cent by weight of the total chloroplast lipid (Table I.3). The structures of some of these are shown in Fig. I.4. Plastoquinone B has two hydrogen atoms less than plasto-quinone A, the additional unsaturation being located in the second isoprene unit from the quinone ring. Plastoquinone C may be a hydroxylated form of plastoquinone A, or a hydrated form of plasto-quinone B. Plastoquinone D appears to be an isomer of plasto-quinone C[44a]. Plastoquinone, α-tocopherol, α-tocopherylquinone, and vitamin K_1 appear to be confined to the chloroplast[241,50,259,44]. In young leaves of *Vicia faba* not less than 95 per cent of the plastoquinone A and α-tocopherylquinone of the chloroplasts are confined to the lamellae[31a]. Chloroplasts of leaves of *Polygonum cuspidatum* contain, as well as plastoquinone A (plastoquinone-9), the closely related (see Fig. I.4) compound plastochromanol-8[53] in an amount corresponding to about one-sixteenth of the total plastoquinone content. On the basis of examination of a number of plant species Threlfall, Griffiths, and Goodwin (1965) suggest that there are three types of chloroplast quinone pattern: (1) (basic) consisting of vitamin K_1, plastoquinone A, and α-tocopherol, e.g. maize, barley, and *Euglena*; (2) basic plus plasto-quinones C and D, e.g. tobacco; (3) basic plus plastoquinones B, C, and D, e.g. spinach, lucerne, nettle, *Ulva*, and *Polysiphonia*. The quinone composition of chloroplasts can vary according to the time of year at which the plants are grown: the plastoquinone-C content of young leaves of *Vicia faba* was found to be maximal for plants grown in early summer, but was very low, or zero, in plants grown in the winter[31]. The ratio of α-tocopheryl quinone to chlorophyll, on the other hand, was relatively constant whatever time of year the plants were grown.

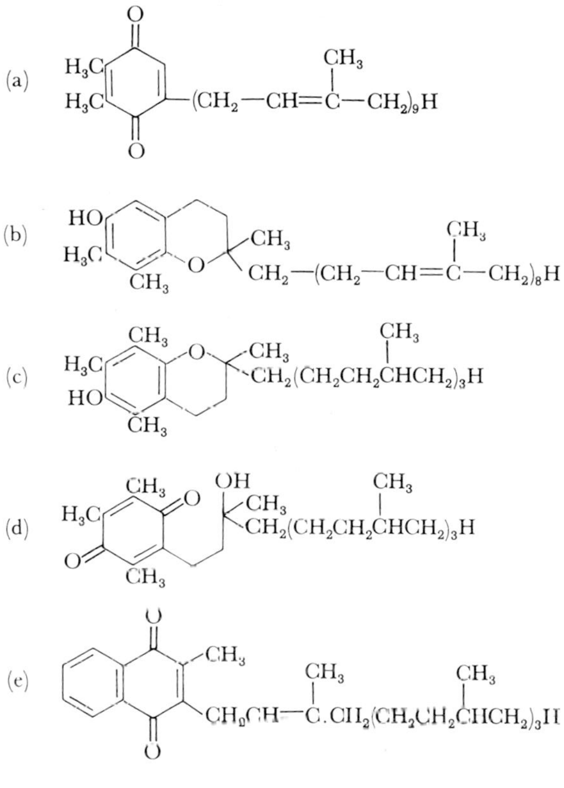

FIG. I.4. *Some chloroplast quinones and related compounds.* (a) *Plastoquinone A;* (h) *Plasto- chromanol-8;* (c) α-*Tocopherol;* (d) α-*Tocopherylquinone;* (e) *Vitamin K₁*

Menke and Jacob (1942) reported that 1·82–2·53 per cent of the lipids of spinach chloroplasts consisted of sterols. Zill and Harmon (1962) also claim to have found sterols in spinach chloroplasts, but no quantitative data are given. Nichols (1963) was unable to find any sterols in lettuce chloroplasts, but recently Mercer and Treharne (1965) have detected significant amounts of sterol (*ca.* 0·5 per cent of the dry weight) in *Phaseolus* chloroplasts, even though these were isolated in organic solvents: about 80 per cent of this sterol consisted of a component tentatively identified as cholesterol (Fig. I.5). The presence of sterol esters as well as sterols in chloroplasts has been reported for *Sapium sebiferum*[107] and *Beta vulgaris*[6]. The number of sterol molecules given in Table I.3 has been calculated on the assumption that these have about the same molecular weight as cholesterol.

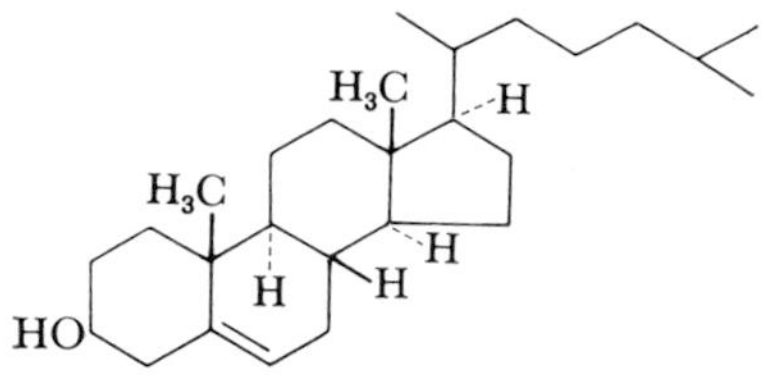

FIG. I.5. *Cholesterol*

Stevenson, Hemming, and Morton (1963) have shown that tobacco chloroplasts contain the isoprenoid alcohol, solanesol. At least 85 per cent of the solanesol of the leaf cell is found in the chloroplasts. Other isoprenoid alcohols with various numbers of isoprene units, have now been found in chloroplasts. Wellburn and Hemming (1965) have suggested 'prenol', followed by a number to indicate the number of isoprene units, as the general name for compounds of this type. In horse-chestnut (*Aesculus hippocastanum*) leaf chloroplasts, 'castaprenols' (and solanesol) constitute 0·5 per cent of the total lipids[272]: the castaprenols are mainly confined to chloroplasts. The presence of these compounds has not yet been demonstrated in spinach chloroplasts but it seems unlikely that they would be absent. In *Beta vulgaris*, which is a member of the same family (*Chenopodiaceae*) as spinach, 1·3 per cent of the prenol fraction had 9 isoprene residues, 3·3 per cent had 10, 51·5 per cent had 11, 42·6 per cent had 12, and 1·3 per cent had 13[272]. The structures of solanesol and castaprenol-12 are shown in Fig. I.6.

(a) $CH_3C=CHCH_2—(CH_2C=CHCH_2)_8OH$
  $\overset{|}{CH_3}$ ... $\overset{|}{CH_3}$
  cis, trans   all *trans*

(b) $CH_3C=CHCH_2—(CH_2C=CHCH_2)_{10}—CH_2C=CHCH_2OH$
  cis, trans   6 *cis* : 4 *trans*   *trans*

FIG. I.6. *Chloroplast isoprenoid alcohols (Stevenson et al., 1963; Wellburn, and Hemming 1965). (a) Solanesol; (b) Castaprenol-12*

About 83 per cent of the chloroplast lipids can be accounted for in terms of known constituents[150]: the remaining 17 per cent probably includes free fatty acids, phytol, chlorophyll and carotenoid precursors and breakdown products, and perhaps some as yet undiscovered lipids.

I.2.ii.c. *The chlorophylls*

The most important chloroplast pigments are the chlorophylls, to which green plants owe their colour. These occur only in the chloroplasts, and appear to be confined to the lamellae. All plants (other than those which do not have the ability to photosynthesize) have chlorophyll *a*. Most groups of plants have, in addition, chlorophyll *b*, *c*, or *d*. The distribution of the chlorophylls amongst the different plant groups is shown in Table I.5. A curious exception to the generalization that all photosynthetic higher plants contain chlorophyll *b* is the saprophytic orchid, *Neottia nidus-avis*: this apparently has chlorophyll *a* and large amounts of carotenoids, but no chlorophyll *b* (Shibata, quoted by French, 1960).

TABLE I.5. DISTRIBUTION OF CHLOROPHYLLS AMONGST DIFFERENT GROUPS OF PLANTS

(See Allen, French, and Brown, 1960; Holt, 1965)

Plant Group	Chlorophyll			
	a	*b*	*c*	*d*
Vascular plants, pteridophytes, bryophytes	+	+	−	−
Algae				
Chlorophyta	+	+	−	−
Euglenophyta	+	l	−	−
Chrysophyta				
Chrysophyceae	+	−	±	−
Xanthophyceae	+	−	−	−
Bacillariophyceae	+	−	+	−
Pyrrophyta	+	·	+	−
Phaeophyta	+	−	+	−
Cryptophyta	+	−	+	−
Rhodophyta	+	−	−	±
Cyanophyta	+	−	−	−

Michel Welwerz, Sironval, and Goedheer (1965) claimed that in extracts of *Chlorella* they could detect, by paper chromatography, three chlorophyll *a* components—a_1, a_2, and a_3. The a_3 band they found to be contaminated with another chlorophyll pigment which, on the basis of its spectroscopic and fluorescence properties, they believe to be similar to chlorophyll *d*. Since it has been generally believed until now that green algae and higher plants contain only one molecular species of chlorophyll *a* and one of chlorophyll *b*, it would seem highly desirable

2—P.

that further investigations should be carried out to determine whether all three of these chlorophyll a-like pigments, and the chlorophyll d-like pigment, really exist *in vivo*, or whether some of them are artefacts, perhaps produced by degradation of chlorophyll a during the isolation procedure.

Chlorophylls a and b constitute about 8 per cent of the dry weight of spinach chloroplasts isolated in water[166]; the chlorophyll content of spinach chloroplasts which had not lost their water-soluble protein would therefore be about 5 per cent. Wilstätter and Stoll (1913) found that the ratio of chlorophyll a to chlorophyll b in several different higher plants varied from 2·05 to 3·52. Plants which naturally grow in light of high intensity tend to have a higher ratio of chlorophyll a to b than plants which grow in light of low intensity: alpine plants, for instance, have been reported to have an a/b ratio of 5·5, and shade plants to have an a/b ratio of 2·6[223, 224, 226]. There is some evidence that algae in the *Chlorophyta* tend to have lower chlorophyll a to b ratios than higher plants; for instance, the a/b ratio is reported to be 1·3 for *Ulva lactuca*[278]. For the other chlorophyll b-containing algal group, the *Euglenophyta*, little evidence is available: however, for *Euglena gracilis* the a/b ratio appears to be, if anything, higher than that found in higher plants— it is 4·1 in cells grown at high light intensity and 7·2 in cells grown at low light intensity[27]. The structures of chlorophylls a and b are shown in Fig. I.7. It will be seen that the chlorophylls are porphyrins—conju-

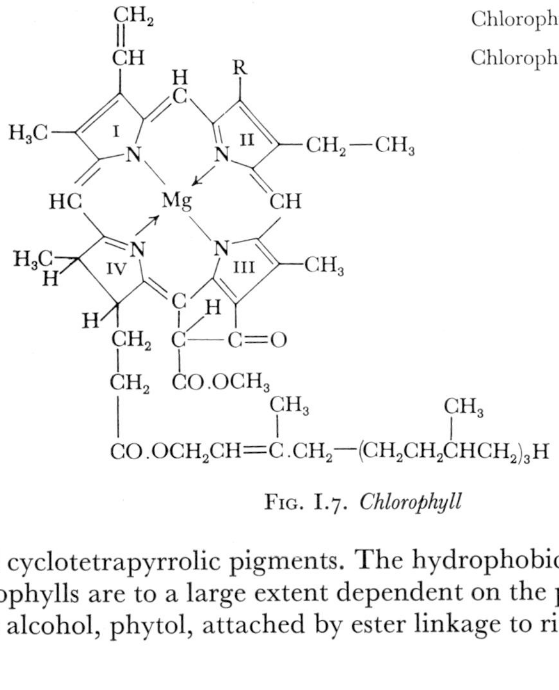

Chlorophyll a.   R = CH_3
Chlorophyll b.   R = CHO

FIG. I.7. *Chlorophyll*

gated cyclotetrapyrrolic pigments. The hydrophobic properties of these chlorophylls are to a large extent dependent on the presence of the long chain alcohol, phytol, attached by ester linkage to ring IV. Chlorophyll

c occurs in certain groups of algae (Table I.5). It may be present in an amount, relative to chlorophyll a, comparable to the amount of chlorophyll b in higher plants. For instance, in *Sphaleromantis* sp. and *Isochrysis galbana* (*Chrysophyceae*) the chlorophyll a/c ratios are 3·6 and 2·6 respectively[119]. The structure of chlorophyll c is still unknown. It apparently lacks phytol[80]. Chlorophyll d, which has been found only in certain red algae[246], has a structure similar to that of chlorophyll a, except that the vinyl group on ring I is replaced by a formyl (—CHO) group[110].

The absorption spectra of the chlorophylls are somewhat different according to whether they are measured *in vivo* or *in vitro*. The long wavelength absorption maximum of chlorophyll a is at 662 mμ in ether solution[235]: in the living leaf, however, this band is at about 677 mμ[228]. The explanation for the different position of the peak *in vivo* is not known: the shift may be due to aggregation of chlorophyll molecules, or to formation of complexes with protein, to changes in dielectric constant of the surrounding environment, or to a combination of more than one of these factors.

Some evidence for the existence of a protein-chlorophyll complex *in vivo* is provided by the fact that a soluble protein-chlorophyll complex may be isolated from spinach chloroplasts by a procedure involving treatment with the non-ionic detergent Triton X-100[121, 122]. The protein appears to have a molecular weight of about 11,600, and to have six molecules of chlorophyll associated with it. Its long wavelength absorption maximum is at 671 mμ. Not more than 3–5 per cent of the total chlorophyll a of the chloroplasts can be isolated in this form, and it is thought[121] to be a unique state of chlorophyll present *in vivo*. Ogawa, Obata, and Shibata (1966) have found that when spinach chloroplasts solubilized with the detergent sodium dodecyl sulphate are subjected to polyacrylamide gel electrophoresis at pH 10·3, three pigmented bands move towards the anode. Band III is just a mixture of pigments, but bands I and II also contain protein. The relative amounts of the chlorophylls and of the carotenoids, are different in I and II (see below). A soluble chlorophyll protein or -lipoprotein complex has also been extracted from spinach chloroplasts with 30 per cent acetone[255]. The proportion of leaf chlorophyll which can be extracted with petrol ether has been used[159] as a measure of the proportion which exists in the free form, not bound to protein. In the normal leaf only 5–8 per cent of the chlorophyll was extractable. After brief heat treatment the fraction of the chlorophyll which could be extracted with petrol increased to 50–80 per cent: this was attributed to heat-denaturation of the protein binding the chlorophyll. The extractibility of chlorophyll b increases less on heat treatment than does the extractibility of chlorophyll a[59]: this has been taken to indicate that chlorophyll *b* is more strongly bound to protein than chlorophyll *a*, possibly as a result of hydrogen bonding to the —CHO group. Godnev and Ossipova (1947) have suggested that the link between chlorophyll and protein involves binding between the pyrrole N atoms of the chlorophyll and the free carboxyl groups of the protein. Weier and Benson (1965), on the other hand, have suggested that there is hydrophobic bonding between the phytol and the chains of the chloroplast structural protein. In view of the ease with which chlorophyll may be extracted with the more polar organic solvents such as ethanol or acetone, it seems unlikely that there is any covalent bonding between chlorophyll and protein.

The absorption spectrum of chlorophyll *a* seen in the living cell is due to a mixture of different forms of this pigment. All plants appear to have a form of chlorophyll *a* with an absorption peak at about 670 mμ and another with a peak at about 683 mμ; the algae *Euglena gracilis* and *Ochromonas danica* also have a type of chlorophyll *a* with a peak at 695 mμ (see Smith and French, 1963; Brown, 1963; and French, 1965 for a discussion of these problems). Cederstrand, Rabinowitch, and Govindjee (1966) have concluded, on the basis of measurements on algae and on higher plant chloroplasts, that the relative heights of the two main chlorophyll *a* bands vary only from 0·7 to 0·9, the 668 mμ (i.e. approximately 670 mμ) band always being weaker than the 683 mμ band. Thomas, Kleinen Hammans, and Arnolds (1965) have concluded, from studies on weak shoulders on the red absorption band of chlorophyll *a in vivo*, that there are at least six forms of chlorophyll *a* in the living cell.

Other kinds of physical measurements also indicate that chlorophyll *a* exists in more than one form in the chloroplast. Studies on the degree of polarization of the chlorophyll fluorescence in spinach chloroplasts and in *Chlorella* indicate that most of the chlorophyll (that is, chlorophyll *a* 672) has an orientation that is little different from random[76]. However Sauer and Calvin (1962), on the basis of measurements of electric dichroism (the anisotropy of optical absorption induced by an electric field) of spinach chloroplast fragments at different wavelengths, have concluded that while the bulk of the chlorophyll (and carotenoid) molecules are unoriented, there is a small proportion of the chlorophyll *a* molecules (about 5 per cent of the total) which are highly oriented, perhaps in groups of about ten molecules. The evidence for this was that the dichroic ratio (ratio of the absorbance for light polarized with its electric vector parallel to the electric field vector, to the absorbance for light polarized with its electric vector perpendicular to the field vector) was only slightly more than unity (1·03–1·10) throughout most of the spectrum, but rose sharply to a peak (1·25) at 695 mμ. The position of the peak indicates that the oriented form of chlorophyll *a* has its absorption maximum at 695 mμ. By sensitive spectrophotometry, Kok[131] discovered a form of chlorophyll *a* which was very rapidly, but reversibly bleached (that is, absorbance decreased) in the light. This has its absorption peak at about 700 mμ, and is commonly referred to either as P700 or chlorophyll a_I. It constitutes only about 0·1 per cent of the total chlorophyll a[281].

Some degree of success in the actual physical separation of chloroplast fractions containing the different forms of chlorophyll has been achieved. With the help of the detergent sodium dodecyl sulphate, lipoprotein fractions enriched for chlorophyll *a* 672, or chlorophyll *a* 683, have been obtained from tobacco chloroplasts[29]. Spinach chloroplasts have been separated by digitonin treatment into two fractions, one having a chlorophyll *a* to *b* ratio of about 6, the other having an *a* to *b* ratio of about 2[22]. Pigment-protein band II separated electrophoretically from spinach chloroplast extract[198a] has a chlorophyll *a/b* ratio of 1·9; it contains violaxanthin and neoxanthin. Pigment-protein band I has a chlorophyll *a/b* ratio of 7·0 and contains no violaxanthin or neoxanthin. These fractions with a high *a/b* ratio may possibly be derived from the particle responsible for System I in photo-

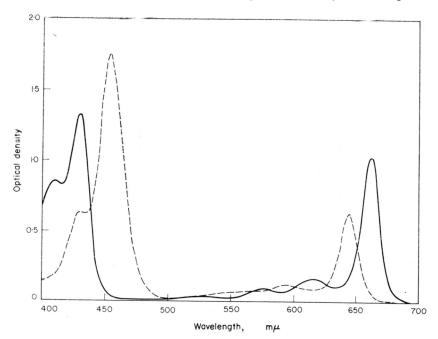

Fig. I.8. *Absorption spectra of chlorophylls in ether. These spectra are those which chlorophyll* a *and chlorophyll* b *have when dissolved at 10 μg/ml in diethyl ether. They have been calculated from the data given by French, C. S. (1960). Encycl. Plant Phys. V.1. Ed., W. Ruhland. Springer-Verlag, Berlin, pp. 252–297*

Chlorophyll a ——————   *Chlorophyll* b --------

synthesis; the low *a/b* fractions may be derived from the particle responsible for System II (I.2.iv.b).

The absorption spectra of chlorophylls *a* and *b* in ether are shown in Fig. I.8, and of broad-bean chloroplasts suspended in glycerol in Fig. I.9.

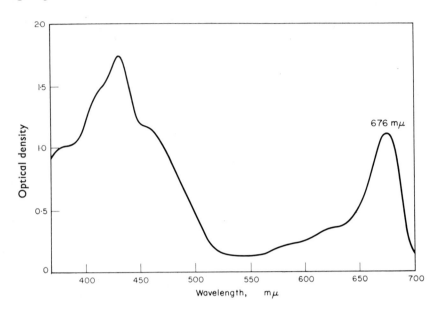

FIG. I.9. *Absorption spectrum of chloroplast pigments* in situ *(Kirk, J. T. O. and Sutton, J., unpublished). Broad-bean leaf chloroplasts isolated in o·5M sucrose/o·05M phosphate, pH 7·0, and resuspended in glycerol for determination of absorption spectrum with Unicam SP 800 spectrophotometer (second sample position)*

I.2.ii.d. *The carotenoids*

All photosynthetic plants contain carotenoids in their chloroplasts. There are far more known carotenoids than there are chlorophylls. The distribution of chloroplast carotenoids amongst different plant groups is shown in Table I.6: it will be noted that β-carotene is present in all except the *Cryptophyta*. Lichtenthaler and Calvin (1964) give the ratio (by weight) of chlorophylls to carotenoids in spinach chloroplasts as 7·5. Assuming the chlorophyll content of spinach chloroplasts isolated in water to be 8·0 per cent of the dry weight (I.2.ii.c) we may calculate the total carotenoid content to be 1·1 per cent of the dry weight: correcting for loss of water-soluble protein, we arrive at a figure of about o·7 per cent. The carotenoids of the green cell are, like the chlorophylls, confined to the chloroplast: they probably exist mainly in the lamellae.

The major carotenoids, and their relative amounts, found in spinach leaf chloroplasts are listed in Table I.3. The ratio, by weight, of

By permission, from Goodwin, T. W. (1965). In Chemistry and Biochemistry of Plant Pigments. Ed., T. W. Goodwin, Academic Press, London.

(+ = present; − = absent; ? possibly present in traces)

	Chlorophyta		Chrysophyta			Phaeophyta	Rhodophyta	Pyrrophyta	Euglenophyta	Archephyta	Cryptophyta
	Charophyceae[b]	Chlorophyceae	Xanthophyceae (Heterokontae)	Bacillariophyceae (Diatomophyceae)	Chrysophyceae	(Phaeophyceae)	(Rhodophyceae)	(Dinophyceae)	(Euglenineae)	(Cyanophyceae)	(Cryptophyceae)
Carotenes											
α-Carotene	−	+	−	−	−	−	+	−	−	−	+
β-Carotene	+	+	+	+	+	+	+	+	+	+	+
γ-Carotene	+	+[c]	−	−	−	−	−	−	−	−	−
ε-Carotene	−	?[d]	−	+	−	−	−	−	−	+	−
Flavacene	−	−	−	−	−	−	−	−	−	−	−
Xanthophylls											
Echinenone	−	−	−	−	−	+?	+	−	+	+?	−
Lutein	+	+	−[g]	−	−	+?	+	−	+	−	−
Zeaxanthin	+	+	+?	−	−	+?	+?	−	−	+	+[i]
Violaxanthin	+	+	−	−	−	+?	−?	−	+	−	−
Flavoxanthin	−	−	−	−	−	−	?	−	−	−	−
Neoxanthin	+	+	+?	−	−	−	−	−	+	−	−
Antheraxanthin	−	−	−	−	−	−	−	−	+	−	−
Fucoxanthin	−	−	−	+	+	+?	−	−	−	−	+
Diatoxanthin	−	−	−	+	+	−	−	−	−	−	−
Diadinoxanthin	−	−	−	+	+	−	−	−	+	−	−
Dinoxanthin	−	−	−	−	−	−	−	+	−	−	−
Peridinin	−	−	−	−	−	−	−	+	−	−	−
Myxoxanthophyll	−	−	−	−	−	−	−	+	−	+	−
Siphonaxanthin	−	+[e]	−	−	−	−	−	−	−	+	−
Astaxanthin	−	+[f]	−	−	−	−	−	−	+[h]	−	−
Oscillaxanthin	−	−	−	−	−	−	−	−	−	+[h]	−

[a] No information exists on the carotenoids of the Chloromonadophyta (Chloromonadineae).
[b] Only one species (Chara fragilis) studied; lycopene also reported present.
[c] Present in traces in some species.
[d] Present in one marine species.
[e] The main pigments of the Siphonales.
[f] The main extra-plastidic pigment (haematochrome) of some encysted flagellates.
[g] Unknown xanthophylls possibly related to zeaxanthin present in most species.
[h] Not present in every species.
[i] The pigment present may be diatoxanthin.

xanthophylls to carotene is 2·8. Some plants also contain substantial amounts of α-carotene—up to about the amount of β-carotene[154]. Leaf chloroplasts of other higher plants have very similar carotenoid composition to the one given in Table I.3: the same is true of chloroplasts in tissues other than leaves—the major carotenoids of green (unripe) *Capsicum annuum* fruit are lutein (40·8 per cent), neoxanthin (15·1 per cent), violaxanthin (13·8 per cent), and β-carotene (13·4 per cent)[43]. About 40 per cent of the carotenoid of barley leaves can be extracted with petrol ether; it is thought that the remaining 60 per cent

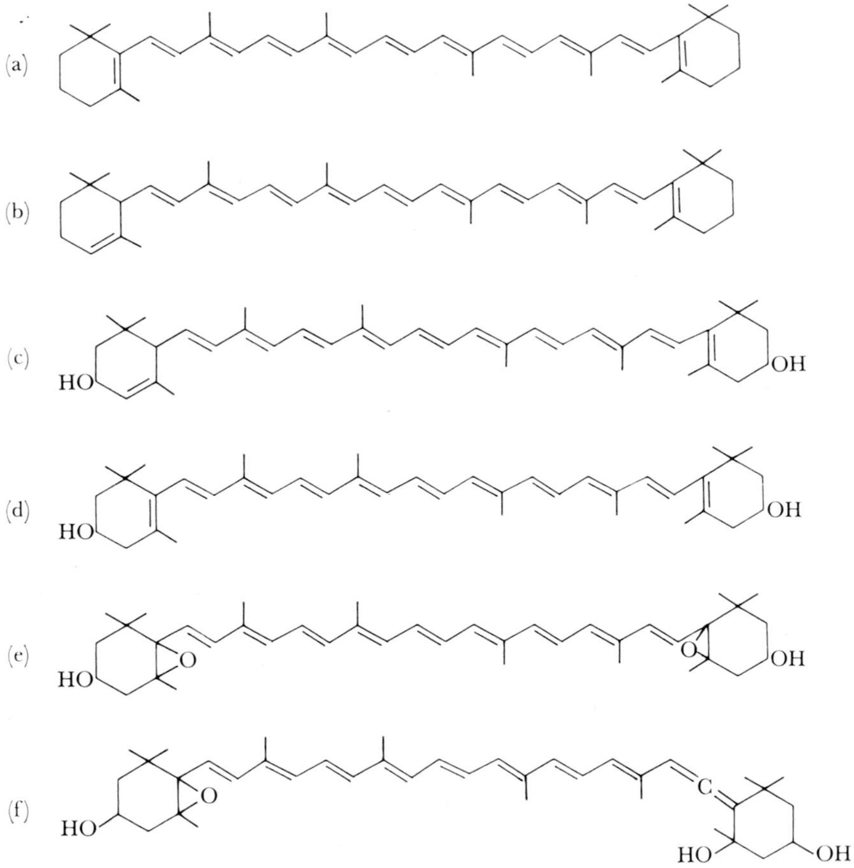

Fig. I.10. *Chloroplast carotenoids*

(a) *β-Carotene*	(b) *α-Carotene*	(c) *Lutein*
(d) *Zeaxanthin*	(e) *Violaxanthin*	(f) *Neoxanthin*

Structures (a)–(e) from Davies, B. H. *in* The Chemistry and Biochemistry of Plant Pigments. Ed., T. W. Goodwin, *Academic Press, London, 1965, pp. 489–532. Structure (f) from Weedon, B. C. L. in* Phytochemical Group Symposium on Terpenoids in Plants (Aberystwyth, 1966). *Academic Press, London (in press)*

is bound, in some way, to protein[59]. As in the case of chlorophyll, the proportion of extractable carotenoid increases (by *ca.* 100 per cent) on heat treatment. The rapid and complete extraction of chloroplast carotenoids with polar organic solvents (ethanol, acetone) would seem to preclude any covalent linkage between carotenoid and protein. Structurally the carotenoids are long-chain (C_{40}) isoprenoid compounds with a long series of conjugated double bonds which is responsible for their characteristic colours (yellow, orange, or red). The structures of chloroplast carotenoids are shown in Fig. I.10. The absorption spectrum of β-carotene is shown in Fig. I.11.

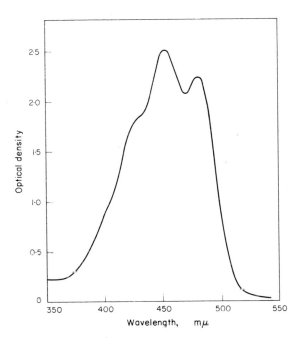

FIG. I.11. *Absorption spectrum of β-carotene in petrol (Thomas, D. M., unpublished). The values on the optical density scale have been calculated for a solution containing 10 μg β-carotene/ml, assuming $E^{1\%}_{1cm}$ at 451 mμ to be 2505 (Goodwin, T. W. in Modern Methods of Plant Analysis, III Eds. K. Paech and M. V. Tracey. Springer-Verlag, Berlin, 1955, p. 272)*

I.2.ii.e. *The biliproteins*

The biliproteins are chloroplast pigments which are found only in certain algae, the *Rhodophyta*, the *Cryptophyta*, and the *Cyanophyta* (see Haxo and O'hEocha, 1960; O'hEocha, 1965a). They are localized in the chloroplasts, but their exact situation within the chloroplasts is not known. The red alga *Ceramium rubrum* contains 1·6–1·9 per cent (of the dry weight) biliproteins in the early spring, and about half this amount later in the spring[138, 143] If, therefore we take 1·3 per cent as being a representative value for the biliprotein content of this alga, and 0·345 per cent of the dry weight as a representative value for its chlorophyll *a* content[225], we arrive at a biliprotein/chlorophyll *a* weight ratio of 3·8. If we go on to assume that, apart from the presence of biliproteins and the absence of chlorophyll *b*, the chloroplasts of this alga have, very approximately, the same chemical composition as spinach chloroplasts, then we can calculate their biliprotein content to be in the region of 12 per cent of the dry weight (this is for chloroplasts which retain their water-soluble proteins).

Chemically, these pigments are proteins with a chromophore group attached. Comprehensive accounts of their chemistry will be found in reviews by O'hEocha (1965a; 1965b). Unlike the other chloroplast pigments they are soluble in water. At least twelve biliproteins are known to exist[199]. The biliproteins which occur in the red algae (*Rhodophyta*) are R-phycoerythrin and B-phycoerythrin, which are red, and R-phycocyanin, C-phycocyanin, and allophycocyanin which are blue. C-phycocyanin and allophycocyanin are also found in *Cyanidium caldarium*, which is of uncertain taxonomic position. In the *Cyanophyta* (which we shall include, for completeness, despite the fact that they lack chloroplasts), C-phycoerythrin, C-phycocyanin, and allophyco-cyanin occur. In the *Cryptophyta* six more biliproteins are found: three of the phycoerythrin type, and three of the phycocyanin type[199]. The number of different biliproteins in a given algal species varies from one to three. Red algae usually contain one phyco-erythrin and one or two phycocyanins: cryptomonads contain either a phycoerythrin or a phycocyanin as their major biliprotein, but phyco-erythrin-containing species may contain small quantities of phyco-cyanin[200]. The molecular weights of R-phycoerythrin and R-phycocyanin have been determined in Svedberg's laboratory to be 291,000 and 273,000 respectively[57]. The compounds which form the chromophores of the biliproteins are known as the phycobilins. These are open chain tetrapyrrole compounds firmly (probably covalently) bound to the proteins; the details of their structures are still unknown. O'Carra, O'hEocha, and Carroll (1964) have suggested that the chromophore of phycoerythrin (phycoerythrobilin) has the structure shown in Fig. I.12. There appear to be a large number of chromo-

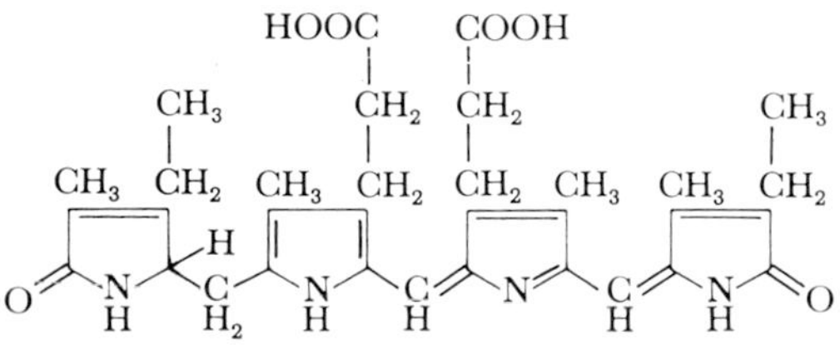

FIG. I.12. *A possible structure for phycoerythrobilin—chromophore of phycoerythrin (O'Carra, O'hEocha, and Carroll, 1964)*

phoric groups per molecule of biliprotein. There may be one or two kinds of chromophore present in a single biliprotein. O'Carra (1962) has estimated that C-phycoerythrin contains about twenty-five phycoerythrobilin residues per unit of molecular weight 226,000; that R-phycoerythrin contains about twenty-five phycoerythrobilin and twelve phycourobilin residues per unit of molecular weight 291,000; that C-phycocyanin contains about twenty-two phycocyanobilin

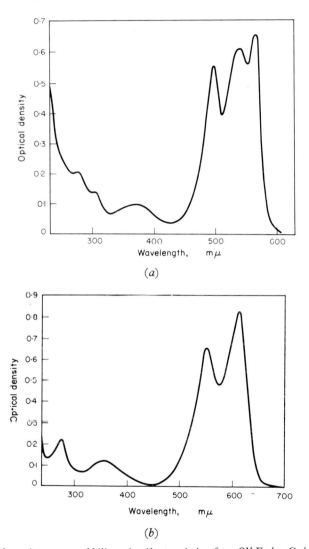

Fig. I.13. *Absorption spectra of biliproteins (by permission from O'hEocha, C. in* Chemistry and Biochemistry of Plant Pigments. *Ed. T. W. Goodwin, Academic Press, London, 1965, pp. 175–196.) (a) R-phycoerythrin from* Ceramium rubrum *(pH 6–7); (b) R-phycocyanin from* Porphyra laciniata *(pH 6–7)*

residues per unit of molecular weight 276,000; and that R-phycocyanin contains about twenty-two phycocyanobilin and eight phycoerythrobilin residues per unit of molecular weight 273,000. In C-phycocyanin the chromophores amount to about 5 per cent by weight of the biliprotein. The large number of chromophore groups per molecular weight unit suggests that the biliprotein molecules may be built up of many protein sub-units.

The absorption spectra of R-phycoerythrin and R-phycocyanin are shown in Fig. I.13.

I.2.ii.f. *Other chloroplast constituents*

When chloroplasts are isolated in aqueous media a large proportion of their salts, and other low molecular weight constituents leach out, so that analyses of the mineral composition of chloroplasts prepared in this way are unreliable. Stocking and Ongun (1962) found that tobacco chloroplasts isolated in non-aqueous media, to prevent leaching, contained 51 per cent of the sodium, 55 per cent of the potassium, 72 per cent of the magnesium, and 63 per cent of the calcium of the whole leaf. For comparison, chloroplasts isolated in aqueous media had only 0·5 per cent of the potassium, 5 per cent of the magnesium, and 3·3 per cent of the calcium of the whole leaf. The iron in the chloroplasts apparently does not leach out as readily as the other minerals: spinach chloroplasts isolated in water contained 82 per cent of the total iron of the leaf[151]. Iron constituted 0·05 per cent of the dry weight of the chloroplasts; correcting for loss of soluble protein, we arrive at a figure of about 0·03 per cent of the dry weight. Warburg (1949) found that washed spinach chloroplast fragments contained 0·016 per cent manganese (dry weight) and 0·0068 per cent zinc.

The carbohydrate of the chloroplast (apart from the galactolipids) consists, in the case of higher plants and green algae, mainly of starch, and the various sugar phosphates that are intermediates in the CO_2 fixation cycle (see I.2.iv.c). Starch usually contains about 75 per cent amylopectin and 25 per cent amylose. Amylopectin is an α-D-($1 \rightarrow 4$)-linked glucan with α-D-($1 \rightarrow 6$)-linked branch points. Amylose is an unbranched α-D-($1 \rightarrow 4$)-linked glucan.

In algal groups other than the *Chlorophyta* the insoluble end-products of photosynthetic CO_2 fixation may be substances other than starch[163]. These include Floridean starch (a glucan containing α-D-($1 \rightarrow 4$), α - D-($1 \rightarrow 6$), and α -D-($1 \rightarrow 3$) links) in some *Rhodophyta*, laminarin (a β-D-($1 \rightarrow 3$)-linked glucan with occasional β-D-($1 \rightarrow 6$) links, and containing 2 per cent mannitol) in certain *Phaeophyta*, paramylon (a β-D-($1 \rightarrow 3$)-linked glucan) in the *Euglenophyta*, and leucosin (a β-D-($1 \rightarrow 3$)-linked glucan) in several *Chrysophyta*. Cells of the

Xanthophyceae are reputed to contain an oil as their storage material in place of starch[35]. The polysaccharide grains in cells of the *Cryptophyta* and *Pyrrophyta* are sometimes referred to as starch grains by microscopists, but I am not aware of chemical evidence for this. The granules of these photosynthetic products occur inside the chloroplasts in the *Chlorophyta*, and outside in the other groups of algae (I.2.iii.c). The carbohydrate content of the chloroplasts depends upon the metabolic state of the cell, and can be reduced almost to zero by keeping the plant in the dark, so that starch is oxidized in respiration. The figures given in Table I.1 for chemical composition of chloroplasts are calculated on the assumption that the starch content is very low.

The problem of the presence of nucleic acids in chloroplasts is discussed in detail in Chapter X.

I.2.ii.g. *Chemical composition of chloroplast lamellae and globules*

The chloroplast consists of a system of membranes (lamellae) embedded in a surrounding matrix (see I.2.iii). Park and Pon (1963) obtained highly purified preparations of lamellar fragments from spinach chloroplasts. This lamellar material consisted of about 52 per cent lipid and 48 per cent protein, and also contained 0·035 per cent iron, 0·005 per cent manganese, and 0·02 per cent copper. The ratio of total lipid to chlorophyll in these preparations was about 4.6. In chloroplasts the lipid/chlorophyll ratio is about 4·2 (Table I.1). Since the lamellae contain certainly most (and probably all) of the chlorophyll of the chloroplast, they must also contain most of the lipid. However, they do not contain all the lipid since some of this is found in the osmiophilic globules (I.2.iii) of the chloroplast[7, 6]. In chloroplasts of *Beta vulgaris* about 89 per cent of the globule material is lipid; the globules contain about one tenth of the total lipid of the chloroplast. This includes the carotenoid precursors phytoene (75 per cent of the total amount in the leaf), phytofluene, and ζ-carotene, but not β-carotene, and 40–50 per cent of the total plastoquinone of the chloroplast. Galactolipids, phospholipids, sulpholipids, sterols, and sterol esters occur in similar relative proportions in globules and lamellae, but two unknown lipids have been found to be present in globules but not in lamellae[6]. The distribution of plastoquinone between lamellae and globules may vary with the age of the leaf: in chloroplasts from four-week-old horse-chestnut leaves, the plastoquinone was found mainly in the lamellae; as the leaves got older, a higher proportion was found in the globules—50 per cent at 12 weeks, and 80 per cent at 28 weeks[272]. Most of the castraprenol in these horse-chestnut chloroplasts was found in the globules, but there was some in the lamellar fraction. In chloroplasts of *Beta vulgaris* a solanesol-like alcohol was found to be equally distributed between the globules and the lamellae[272].

I.2.iii. ULTRASTRUCTURE OF CHLOROPLASTS

I.2.iii.a. *Chloroplasts of vascular plants*

The typical higher-plant chloroplast is shaped like a lens: the lens may be bi-convex, plano-convex, or concavo-convex. Seen at right angles to its plane, the chloroplast is circular or elliptical in outline. In 200 plant species studied by Möbius (1920) the long diameter of the chloroplast varied from 3 to 10 μ: 75 per cent of the chloroplasts measured were 4–6 μ long and 50 per cent were 5 μ.

The chloroplast is bounded by a membrane. In electron micrographs, this sometimes appears as a single electron-dense line, and sometimes as two dense lines separating a clear space (Fig. I.14), the whole unit being about 300 Å thick[269]. Most workers consider the chloroplast envelope to be a double membrane. According to Heslop-Harrison (1963), each of the two membranes constituting the envelope is of the 'unit membrane' type, i.e. at high resolution, in $KMnO_4$-fixed material, each of these membranes can be seen to consist of two dense lines, *ca.* 20 Å thick, enclosing a lighter space, *ca.* 10 Å wide.

In electron micrographs of sections, chloroplasts can be seen to be filled with a slightly electron-dense, somewhat granular, matrix: this is referred to as the 'stroma'. Embedded within the stroma is a complex system of membranes[239, 145]: these membranes are often referred to as the 'lamellae' of the chloroplast. The complex appearance of these structures can be explained by the supposition that they are composed of large numbers of membrane-bounded sacs. Each sac is completely flattened so that the opposite sides of the sac are close together presenting, in section, the appearance shown in Fig. I.14; i.e. the sac looks like a pair of parallel membranes joined at each end. Menke (1962) has coined the word 'thylakoid' for these flattened sacs (from θυλακοειδής —'sack-like'), but they are often referred to as 'discs'[217]. The thylakoids occur in regular, closely-packed stacks. Seen from above these stacks are roughly circular and so might be likened to piles of pennies. It is believed that these thylakoid stacks seen with the electron microscope, correspond to the minute particles that can just be resolved within the chloroplast by the optical microscope. These particles were referred to by microscopists as 'grana' (singular 'granum'). The grana are about 3000–6000 Å in diameter, and there may be 40–60 grana per chloroplast[83, 145]. There may be anything from 2 to 100 thylakoids in a granum. Most of the thylakoids in a granum extend beyond the edge of the granum. That part of a thylakoid extending into the stroma is often referred to as a 'stroma lamella'. Along one side of a granum, seen in section, about every other thylakoid continues into the stroma. Many of the thylakoids which do not continue into the stroma on one

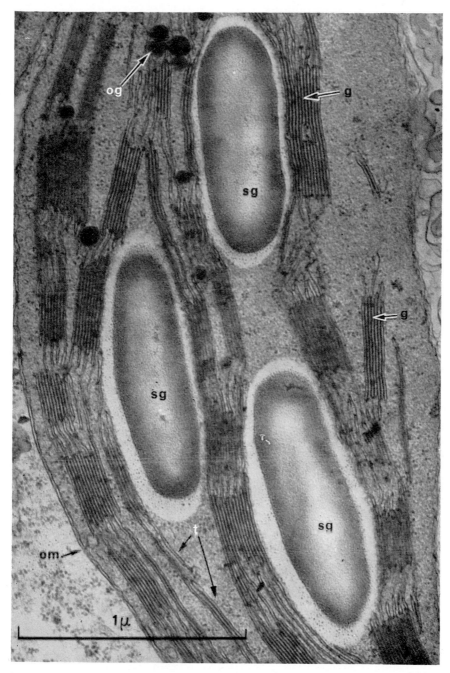

FIG. I.14. *A higher plant chloroplast (Juniper, B. E., unpublished).* Peperomia *leaf. Glutaraldehyde–OsO_4 fixation.* om—*outer membrane.* g—*granum.* t—*single thylakoids in stroma.* og—*osmiophilic globules.* sg—*starch grains*

side of the granum will do so on the other side. Some thylakoids can be seen to continue beyond the edge of the granum on both sides; a few thylakoids do not appear (at least in section) to extend beyond the edge of the granum on either side. Some of the thylakoids which extend into the stroma just come to an end, but most of them continue on into an adjoining granum, and perhaps into other grana as well. It appears likely that all the different grana in a chloroplast are connected up in this way.

Sections, of course, only give a two-dimensional picture of the arrangement of membranes. Various attempts have been made to infer the three-dimensional arrangement from these two-dimensional pictures. The simplest model is that proposed by Eriksson, Kahn, Walles, and von Wettstein (1961), in which some of the thylakoids are represented as flat sheets extending through a large part of the chloroplast, intersecting a number of grana (Fig. I.15). Weier, Thomson, Stocking,

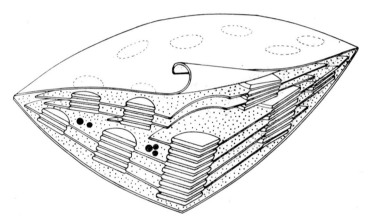

Fig. I.15. *Three-dimensional model of higher plant chloroplast. By permission from Eriksson, G., Kahn, A., Walles, B. and von Wettstein, D. (1961).* Ber. Deut. Bot. Ges. **74**, *221–232*

and Drever (1963) propose a much more complicated model in which different grana are connected together by a ramifying network of flattened tubules, joining the thylakoids in one granum to the thylakoids of others (Fig. I.16). A thylakoid apparently extending into the stroma is thought, in fact, to correspond to a section through one of the tubules joining one granum to another. It was found by Weier and Thomson (1962b) that sections through grana of tobacco chloroplasts occasionally show what appear to be two adjacent thylakoids in the granum opening into a single thylakoid in the stroma. Heslop-Harrison (1963) has observed a similar arrangement in sections of hemp chloroplasts, and to explain these findings has suggested that the relationship between the

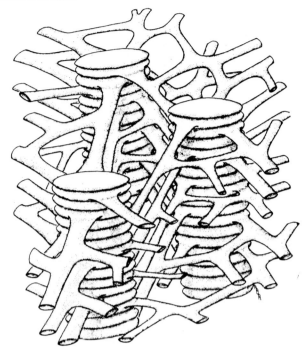

FIG. I.16. *Three-dimensional model of grana with interconnecting fretwork system in higher plant chloroplast. By permission from Weier, T. E., Stocking, C. R., Thomson, W. W. and Drever, H. (1963).* J. Ultrastruct. Res. *8, 122–143*

membranes of the stroma and those of the grana is as indicated in Fig. I.17. Here, one stroma lamella is shown connected to six thylakoids in the granum. According to this model, the different thylakoids in a granum are not separate closed sacs, but are all continuous with each

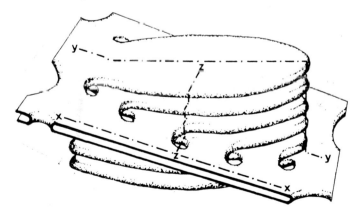

FIG. I.17. *An interpretation of the relationship between part of a granum and one fretted stroma lamella. By permission from Heslop-Harrison, J. (1963).* Planta *60, 243–260*

3—P.

other. Since the different grana are also connected together by these stroma lamellae, it would also follow that the lamellar system constitutes a single, enormously complex, membrane-enclosed cavity, separate and distinct from the stroma. Wehrmeyer (1964) has suggested a somewhat similar model (Fig. I.18).

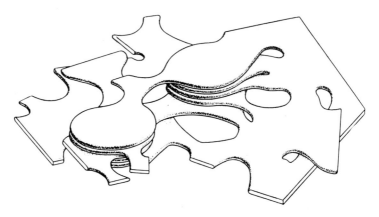

Fig. I.18. *Three-dimensional model of grana with inter-granal connections. By permission from Wehrmeyer, W. (1964). Planta 63, 13–30*

The evidence available, at the moment, does not permit a decision as to which of these models is nearest to the truth.

Another very prominent feature of chloroplasts are the starch grains (Fig. I.14). These will probably be completely absent if the plant has been kept in the dark for, say, 24 hours, but will certainly be present in chloroplasts of leaves which have been photosynthesizing for a few hours. They are roughly ellipsoidal in shape, and the length can be anything up to about 1·5 μ. They lie in the stroma, usually with grana close on either side. There are likely to be one to four starch grains per chloroplast. In the stroma of chloroplasts of oat leaves fixed in glutaraldehyde-OsO_4, Gunning (1965a) has observed a structure he refers to as a 'stromacentre': this has the appearance of a mass of tightly, but regularly, packed fibrils. Such a stromacentre (actually in an etioplast) may be seen in Fig. I.37. Stromacentres have not yet been observed in any plant other than *Avena sativa*.

In sections of osmium-fixed chloroplasts, strongly stained globules can be seen, 500–2700 Å in diameter[147, 7]. These are generally referred to as 'osmiophilic globules'. The numbers are very variable. There might be as few as six, or as many as thirty or more, visible in one section. The number per chloroplast is likely to run into the hundreds. They usually occur very close to grana (Fig. I.14), and indeed the thylakoid membranes sometimes appear to run right into them.

Much smaller granules, 150–200 Å in diameter, can also be seen in the stroma; these are thought to be ribosomes (see X.3). With appropriate fixation techniques, minute fibrils, *ca.* 25 Å in diameter, may be seen in certain regions of the stroma; these are thought to be DNA (see X.3).

Price, Martinez, and Warmke (1966) have observed, within some of the chloroplasts of coconut palm leaves, membrane-bounded sacs containing rhomboidal crystalline bodies, *ca.* 1 μ across. These can be seen to be made up of particles, of diameter about 120 Å, in a close hexagonal packing.

The general picture of chloroplast structure described above has been derived from work on angiosperms. However, the mesophyll chloroplasts of other vascular plants turn out to have essentially the same type of structure. This has been shown for chloroplasts of spruce (a gymnosperm)[273] and for chloroplasts of the pteridophytes *Psilotrum triquetrum*[252], *Isoetes howellii*[209], and *Matteuccia struthiopteris* (Gantt and Arnott (1963)—see Fig. XIV.7). The chloroplasts of *Psilotrum triquetrum* are rather elongated ellipsoids with a principal axis of 13 μ and a short axis of 3-6 μ. According to Mühlethaler (1955) one primitive pteridophyte, *Selaginella*, does not have grana, but just has thylakoids extending through the length of the plastid. However, Gerola and Dassu (1960) and McHale (1965) report that well-differentiated grana can be observed in the chloroplasts of wild plants of *Selaginella* but not in those of plants grown in the greenhouse at low light intensities.

Leaf cells other than mesophyll cells may have chloroplasts with a somewhat different structure. For instance, in corn leaves, the parenchyma sheath cells which surround each vascular bundle contain chloroplasts without grana[108]. The thylakoids, usually single, extend the full length of the chloroplast. In the epidermal cells of leaves of many plants the plastids never develop into chloroplasts at all. The guard cells of the epidermis of grasses have partially-differentiated chloroplasts containing a few scattered single thylakoids, and occasional stacks of two or three thylakoids; fully developed grana are absent[30]. The plastids of the root-hair cells of *Azolla imbricata* are partially differentiated chloroplasts with small stacks of up to about four thylakoids; these plastids have a double-membraned sheath, similar in appearance to endoplasmic reticulum, close to the plastid outer membrane, and going most, but generally not all, the way round[126]. A similar sheath of endoplasmic reticulum has been observed around the plastids in the companion cells of the phloem of *Acer*, and in the cells lining the resin canal of *Pinus*[286]: in this case the sheathing endoplasmic reticulum is thought to be connected directly to the nuclear envelope and to the cytoplasmic endoplasmic reticulum.

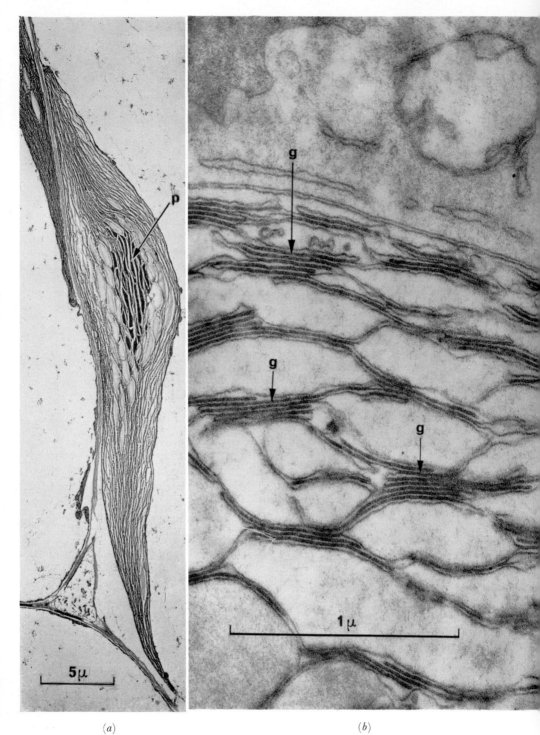

(a)   (b)

FIG. I.19. *Chloroplast of* Anthoceros. *By permission from Manton, I. (1962).* J. Exp. Bot.
13, *325–333.* (a) *A whole chloroplast.* p—*pyrenoid;* (b) *Part of an older plastid from the
sub-epidermis.* g—*granum*

I.2.iii.b. *Chloroplasts of bryophytes*

Little electron microscopy has been carried out on the chloroplasts of bryophytes. The plant which has been studied most from this point of view is the liverwort *Anthoceros*[169, 157, 277]. This has large chloroplasts (40 μ long) bounded by a double membrane (Fig. I.19). The thylakoids often occur in small stacks, somewhat similar to the grana of the higher plant chloroplast, with up to about eight thylakoids in a stack. *Anthoceros* may not be typical in that, unlike those of many other bryophytes, its chloroplasts contain a pyrenoid. Pyrenoids are found in many algal chloroplasts (see I.2.iii.c) but are absent from those of higher plants. In the light microscope they appear as dense, roughly spherical bodies, usually surrounded by starch grains. In electron micrographs[169] the pyrenoid of the *Anthoceros* chloroplast appears as a large (perhaps *ca.* 4–8 μ long), irregularly shaped region of a fairly uniformly granular appearance. It is bounded by a single membrane which, here and there, invaginates deeply into it so that, in section, it has the appearance of being divided into compartments.

I.2.iii.c. *Algal chloroplasts*

In our consideration of algal chloroplasts we shall not be dealing with blue-green algae. These do not have chloroplasts; their photosynthetic apparatus consists of thylakoids lying free in the cytoplasm. These organisms are probably better included amongst the photosynthetic bacteria.

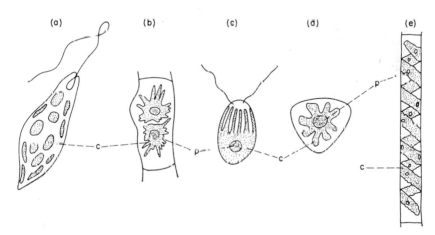

FIG. I.20. *Some algal chloroplasts.* (*a*) Euglena gracilis; (*b*) Zygnema stellinum; (*c*) Chlamydomonas Kleinii; (*d*) Staurastrum Kjelmanni; (*e*) Spirogyra *sp.* c—*chloroplast*, p—*pyrenoid*.

(*b*)–(*e*) *after West, G. S.* (*1904*). The British Freshwater Algae. *Cambridge University Press.*

In the algae, chloroplasts show an enormous variation in size, shape, and number. There may be only one chloroplast per cell, as in *Chlamydomonas*, or there may be 100 or more, as in certain *Euglena* species. They may be lens-shaped (*Euglena*), spiral-shaped (*Spirogyra*), star-shaped (*Zygnema*), in the form of an irregular network (*Oedogonium*), or various other shapes (Fig. I.20). Usually, algal chloroplasts are found just underneath the cell membrane.

It appears to be generally true that algal chloroplasts, like higher plant chloroplasts, are bounded by a double membrane 120–150 Å wide[70]. A possible exception is *Cyanidium caldarium* (uncertain taxonomic position, possibly *Rhodophyta*), which is reported to have only a single membrane[213]. They also possess osmiophilic globules. In section they all appear to have thylakoids. However, the manner in which the thylakoids are arranged differs from one type of alga to another. We shall consider the main different types of chloroplast in turn, in order of increasing complexity.

The algae with the simplest type of chloroplast are the red algae (*Rhodophyta*). These appear, in section, to have single thylakoids (Figs. I.21 and XIV.8) lying separately in the stroma, roughly parallel to each other[26, 25]. The length of these may be anything up to half, or more, of that of the chloroplast. Here and there, the thylakoids may open up to form apparently empty vesicles (Fig. XIV.8). A number of thylakoids may form a line, perhaps extending the full length of the chloroplast. Just within the limiting membrane a thylakoid, or line of thylakoids can be seen to pass all the way round the plastid. With certain fixation procedures, particles, about 320 Å in diameter (Fig. I.21b) can be seen distributed along each of the outer surfaces of a thylakoid[86, 67]: these might possibly contain biliproteins. Only the more primitive members of the *Rhodophyta* have pyrenoids in their chloroplasts. The pyrenoid contains a dense matrix material which is traversed by a number of widely separated single thylakoids[26, 183, 71]. The two membranes of the thylakoids are sometimes more widely separated within the pyrenoid than they are in the rest of the chloroplast. In the *Rhodophyta* the polysaccharide grains (Floridean starch) occur outside the chloroplast.

The next simplest type of chloroplast is that found in the *Cryptophyta*. These have thylakoids in pairs (Fig. I.22), the members of each pair being closely appressed together[70]. The individual thylakoid pairs are sometimes fairly widely separated from each other, and in other places come close together. The thylakoid pairs run along the length of the chloroplast, many of them being almost as long as the chloroplast itself. The pyrenoid in *Cryptomonas* is a large, dense body within the chloroplast membrane. Polysaccharide grains can be seen outside the chloroplast, lying closely against the part of the chloroplast membrane

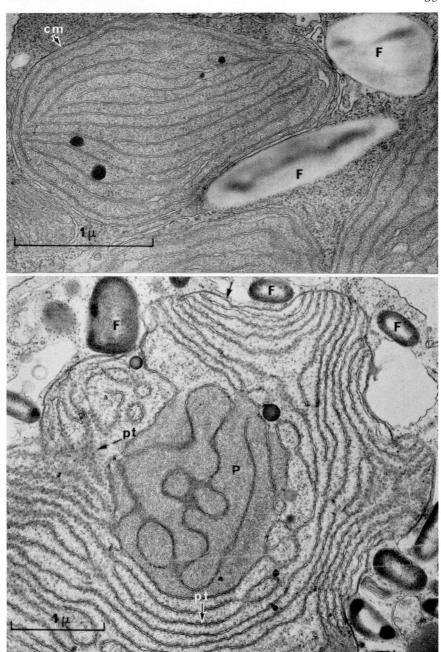

FIG. I.21. *Chloroplasts of red algae with single thylakoids (Greenwood, A. D., unpublished).*
Glutaraldehyde fixation.
  (a) (*Top*) Ceramium sp. F—*Floridean starch.* cm—*chloroplast membrane.*
  (b) (*Bottom*) Porphyridium cruentum. P—*pyrenoid.* pt—*particles along surface of the*
thylakoids. F—*Floridean starch*

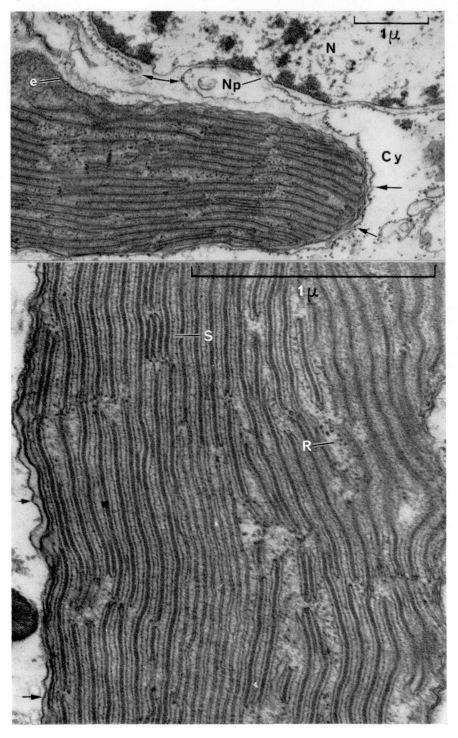

which covers the pyrenoid[71]. The pyrenoid does not appear to be traversed by thylakoids. In *Cryptomonas* and *Rhodomonas* the plastid is surrounded by an outer double-membraned envelope which lies outside the usual chloroplast double membrane[72]. The polysaccharide grains occur between the chloroplast membrane and this outer double membrane. At the borders of the area where the chloroplast lies adjacent to the nucleus, this outer envelope is continuous with a double-membraned outfolding of the outer nuclear membrane. Thus, the entire chloroplast lies within a double-membraned sac, one wall of which is the nuclear envelope.

The most common type of chloroplast structure amongst the algae is that in which the whole length of the chloroplast is traversed by sheets, appearing in cross-section as bands consisting of three thylakoids closely appressed together. This is the type of structure commonly found in chloroplasts of members of the *Chrysophyta*, *Pyrrophyta*, *Phaeophyta*, *Euglenophyta*, and *Chloromonadales*[148, 18, 70, 86]. Most of the bands within such a chloroplast will be of the three-thylakoid type (Fig. I.23), but occasional bands with two, four, five, or six thylakoids may be seen. Sometimes a thylakoid may terminate before it reaches the end of the band. Thus, the band can be three thylakoids thick over part of its length, and two thylakoids thick over another part. Occasionally thylakoids may be seen which appear to leave one band and join another. Except in the case of the *Euglenophyta*, it appears that there is one band (the 'girdle lamella'—Fig. I.23b) which travels almost right round the other bands, underneath the chloroplast membrane. Greenwood (1964), on the basis of serial sections, has suggested that the

---

FIG. 1.22. *Chloroplasts of* Cryptophyta *with thylakoids in pairs* (*Greenwood, A. D., unpublished*). OsO_4 *fixation.*

(*Top*) Cryptomonas. N—*nucleus.* Np—*nuclear pore.* Cy—*cytoplasm.* e—*chloroplast membrane. Section shows a place (spanned by double-headed arrow) where the outer nuclear membrane, reflexed to left and right, is continuous with the outer membrane investing the chloroplast. To the right this membrane (note attached ribosomes) can be followed round the margin of the chloroplast and for some distance along its outer face. It continues (out of the picture) unbroken, to return to the nucleus at its left-hand point of flexure (left point of double arrow). The space bounded by this membrane and another membrane internal to it which also surrounds the plastid is continuous with the perinuclear space, being therefore morphologically part of the endoplasmic reticulum system. The stroma of the plastid is immediately covered by its own pair of membranes (seen at e). The total of four investing membranes can be seen at the right-hand margin (arrows). The central pair of these membranes are set widely apart over the nuclear face of the plastid but are normally in close contact or fusion on the outer face.*

(*Bottom*) Cryptomonas. S—*stacked thylakoids.* R—*ribosome-like particles in stroma. The lamellae consist mainly of pairs of thylakoids. Members of a pair may terminate together or separately or extend to become one of another pair. Single thylakoids or groups of adjacent thylakoids (e.g. mid and bottom centre) may remain unassociated for part of their extent. Two or more lamellae sometimes make contact for short distances, sometimes forming granum-like stacks. Ribosome-like stroma particles can be distinguished.*

The fused central pair of membranes referred to above can be seen as the thick central line in the chloroplast covering membranes (arrows on left)

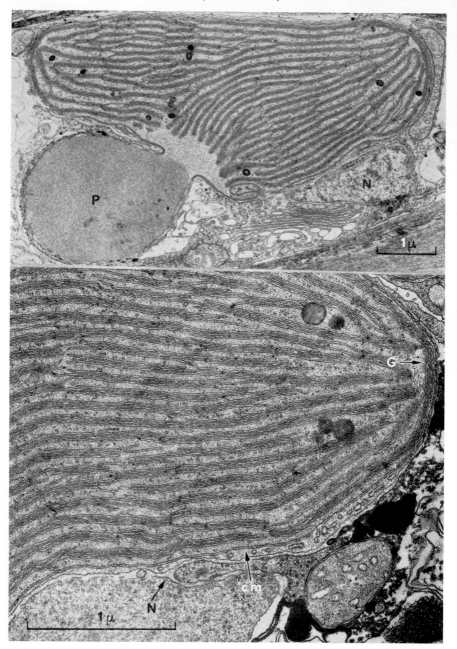

FIG. I.23. *Chloroplasts of brown algae with thylakoids in groups of three (Greenwood, A. D., unpublished). Glutaraldehyde fixation. (a)* Scytosiphon lomentaria. *P—stalked pyrenoid. N—nucleus; (b)* Scytosiphon lomentaria. *G—the 'girdle' compound lamella. N—nucleus, with arrow pointing to the junction between the double membrane of the nucleus and the double, membraned envelope which surrounds the chloroplast outside the chloroplast double membrane. cm—chloroplast membrane*

thylakoids are not isolated from each other as they appear to be in sections, but that there is, in fact, one elaborate, continuous double-membraned structure. Pyrenoids are often, but not invariably, present in those algal chloroplasts of the three-thylakoid-band types. In the species studied so far[207, 208, 71, 111, 157] the pyrenoid has been found, by electron microscopy, to be a region containing a characteristic dense matrix material. Amongst the *Chrysophyta* pyrenoids are common in the *Chrysophyceae* and *Bacillariophyceae* but are present in only a few members of the *Xanthophyceae*. It appears to be generally true of the *Chrysophyta* that the pyrenoid is traversed by a number of thylakoid bands, continuous with those of the rest of the chloroplast. Out of six species of diatom (*Bacillariophyceae*) which have been examined[52], five species had chloroplasts in which the pyrenoid was bounded by a single membrane. In these five species the pyrenoid was traversed by only one or two thylakoid bands. In the species without a pyrenoid membrane, the pyrenoid was crossed by several thylakoid bands[52]. In some of these different kinds of algae, the bands contain the same number of thylakoids within the pyrenoid as they do outside it: in others the three-thylakoid bands are reduced to one- or two-thylakoid bands where they cross the pyrenoid, i.e. one or two of the thylakoids terminate at the pyrenoid border. Amongst the *Pyrrophyta*, *Amphidinium carteri* has three-thylakoid bands traversing the pyrenoid. In the *Euglenophyta* (*Euglena gracilis*) the bands are reduced from three (or sometimes four) thylakoids to two thylakoids where they cross the pyrenoid[71]. It appears to be usually the case, in all these algae, that within the pyrenoid the thylakoids are somewhat distended. Pyrenoids are present in the chloroplasts of some members of the *Phaeophyta*. These pyrenoids, like those in the *Cryptophyta*, are apparently not traversed by thylakoids[71]. In some members of the *Phaeophyta*, for instance *Chorda filum* and *Scytosiphon lomentaria*, the pyrenoid protrudes from the chloroplast (Fig. I.23b and I.24) and is closely capped, outside the chloroplast, by a dilated sac[25].

It seems to be generally true of these algae with the three-thylakoid bands in their chloroplasts that the polysaccharide end-product of photosynthesis accumulates outside the plastid. In *Ochromonas danica* (*Chrysophyta*) the polysaccharide, leucosin, occurs in a single large granule, just outside the chloroplast double membrane, and flanked by lobes of the chloroplast[73]. In *Amphidinium carteri* (*Pyrrophyta*), large polysaccharide grains are found as shells lying outside the chloroplast, but closely appressed against it in the region of the pyrenoid[71]. Some smaller grains occur scattered in the cytoplasm. *Pylaiella littoralis* (*Phaeophyta*) also has a shell of material which may be polysaccharide (laminarin?) lying closely against the outside of the chloroplast in the region of the pyrenoid[71]. In cells of the *Euglenophyta* grains of the

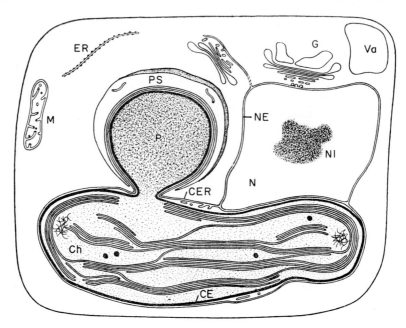

FIG. I.24. *Diagram of a hypothetical brown algal cell. Reprinted by permission of The Rockefeller University Press from Bouck, G. B.,* J. Cell Biol., *August 1965,* **26**, *No. 2, 523–537.* CE—*chloroplast envelope.* CER—*chloroplast endoplasmic reticulum which can be seen, in* Chorda filum, *at least, to be continuous with the nuclear envelope* (NE). P—*pyrenoid.* PS—*pyrenoid sac; a distinct and often dilated envelope which may contain reserve carbohydrates synthesized and/or polymerized within the pyrenoid.* N—*nucleus*

polysaccharide paramylon may be seen free in the cytoplasm, or closely appressed against the outside of a chloroplast (Fig. I.25).

The chloroplasts of *Ochromonas danica*, and at least two other members of the *Chrysophyta*, as well as having the usual chloroplast double membrane are also (like the chloroplasts of the *Cryptophyta*) enclosed within a double-membraned envelope, which is an outfolding of the outer nuclear membrane. Each of the chloroplasts of *Olisthodiscus*, another member of the *Chrysophyta*, is surrounded by an extra double-membraned envelope (outside the chloroplast double membrane) but in this case no connection with the nuclear envelope has been found[72]. Amongst the *Phaeophyta*, *Chorda filum* and *Scytosiphon lomentaria* have, outside the usual chloroplast envelope, another double-membraned envelope, continuous with the nuclear envelope (Figs. I.23b and I.24): this passes between the chloroplast envelope and the pyrenoid sac. In certain other *Phaeophyta*, *Giffordia*, and *Fucus*, there is also an extra envelope outside the chloroplast, but no connections with the nuclear envelope have yet been seen[25]. Bouck (1965) suggests that this outer envelope, which he calls the 'chloroplast endoplasmic reticulum', may be a structural channelling system for transport of carbohydrate reserves.

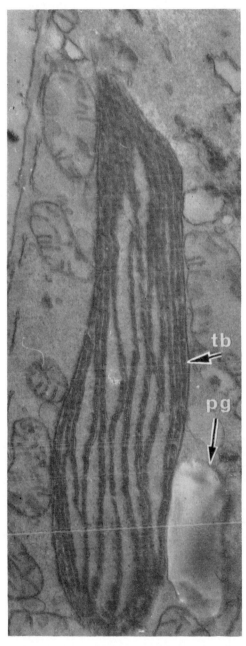

FIG. I.25. *Chloroplast of* Euglena gracilis (*Kirk, J. T. O. and Juniper, B. E., unpublished*). pg—*paramylon granule.* tb—*thylakoid bands, each consisting of three thylakoids*

The algal chloroplasts with the most complicated type of internal structure are found amongst the *Chlorophyta*. Like the other algae, these have long thylakoids, usually extending from one end of the chloroplast to the other[2, 178, 217]. In some of these algae, for instance, *Chlorella pyrenoidosa*[177], the thylakoids are organized into fairly regular bands, usually with three thylakoids per band, but sometimes as many as seven. However, in many other green algae there is little suggestion of regular bands; the thylakoids come together and move apart in a rather irregular manner. In the chloroplast of *Chlamydomonas reinhardi* there may be anything from two to eight thylakoids associated together at any one point[217]. In *Nitella*[178], all the 40–100 thylakoids may exist as one single band or stack, occupying most of the volume of the chloroplast. The lamellar organization in the chloroplast of the desmid *Micrasterias rotata* approaches that of the higher plant chloroplast with well-defined, apparently cylindrical, stacks of anything up to fifty or so thylakoids, some of the thylakoids extending beyond the edge of one stack, through the stroma, and into another stack[51]. These thylakoid stacks are very similar to the grana of the higher plant chloroplast. Again, in the chloroplast of *Acetabularia*, the thylakoids are arranged in much the same way as in a higher plant chloroplast, with stacks containing up to about eleven thylakoids, with some thylakoids extending from one granum to another[38]. In the chloroplast of *Carteria*, Lembi and Lang (1965) have observed structures which they refer to as 'pseudograna'. In section these look as if a single thylakoid in the stroma has opened out to several times its normal width and then filled up the space in between by folding in and out to form something rather similar to a stack of thylakoids (Fig. I.26). There may be as many as eleven of these infoldings.

Fig. I.26. *Appearance, in section, of a 'pseudo-granum' in a chloroplast of* Carteria. (*Drawn on the basis of the electron micrographs of Lembi and Lang, 1965*)

Chloroplasts of members of the *Chlorophyta* normally contain pyrenoids. In electron micrographs the pyrenoid region can be seen to contain a dense matrix material which, according to Gibbs (1962e) appears to consist of tightly packed fibrils, about 60 Å in diameter. In many, but not all, cases the pyrenoid is traversed by thylakoids continuous with those of the rest of the chloroplast[146, 74]. In *Pyramimonas* and *Spirogyra* a number of single thylakoids cross the pyrenoid. In *Chaetomorpha linum* and *Rhizoclonium tortuosum* a single central thylakoid divides the pyrenoid into two hemispheres. In *Chlamydomonas moewusii* two-thylakoid bands extend into the pyrenoid, but very often they extend only a short distance, not right across the pyrenoid. In *Scenedesmus quadricauda* no thylakoids are seen within the pyrenoid. As was observed for other types of algae (see above) the membranes of a thylakoid are more widely spaced where it crosses the pyrenoid than in the rest of the chloroplast. The pyrenoids of the chloroplasts of the *Chlorophyta* are surrounded by a shell of starch grains lying within the chloroplast membrane. The presence of polysaccharide grains within the chloroplast rather than outside is a feature that the *Chlorophyta* share with higher plants, but in which they differ from all the other groups of algae.

In certain green algae a red eye-spot may occur within the chloroplast. In the case of *Chlamydomonas reinhardi* the eye-spot (Fig. I.27) is a

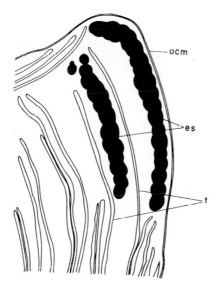

FIG. I.27. *Appearance, in section, of the eye-spot region of the chloroplast of* Chlamydomonas reinhardi. (*Drawn on the basis of one of the electron micrographs of Sager and Palade, 1957*). es—*layers of granules, seen in side view.* t—*thylakoids.* ocm —*outer chloroplast membrane*

defined region of the chloroplast, consisting of two, or sometimes three, plates of closely packed osmiophilic granules in a constant location near the periphery of the chloroplast, roughly parallel to the chloroplast surface[217].

I.2.iii.d. *Molecular structure of the thylakoid*

In high resolution electron micrographs of $KMnO_4$-fixed material the membrane of the thylakoid appears to be of the unit membrane[212] type, both in algal[177] and higher plant[104] chloroplasts. In the case of the higher plant chloroplast the membrane appears to be about 50–75 Å thick overall, and consists of two outer dense layers, 20–25 Å thick, and an inner light space 10–25 Å thick. The space within the thylakoid is 35–65 Å across. The space between adjacent thylakoids within a granum is 20–25 Å. The overall thickness of a thylakoid, then, is 135–215 Å. If we add to this the distance between thylakoids we arrive at a value of 155–240 Å for the space allotted to each thylakoid along the axis of the granum.

Some recent electron microscope studies at very high resolution have cast more light on the detailed structure of the thylakoid membrane. Weier and his co-workers[268, 267] have found that in leaf material from various higher plants, fixed in glutaraldehyde and $KMnO_4$, the thylakoid membrane can be seen to consist of spherical subunits, having a light core, about 37 Å in diameter, and a dark rim, about 28 Å wide (Fig. I.28). Similar results have been obtained by Hohl and Hepton (1965)

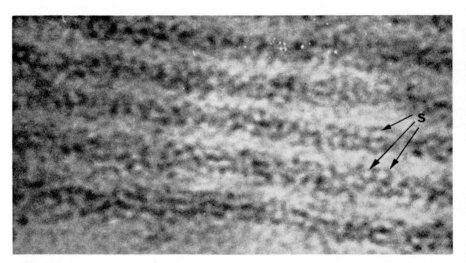

FIG. I.28. *Subunits of thylakoid membrane in* Aspidistra *granum. By permission, from Weier, T. E., Engelbrecht, A. H. P., Harrison, A. and Risley, E. B. (1965). J. Ultrastruct. Res. 3, 92–111. Glutaraldehyde–KMnO$_4$ fixation.* s—*subunits*

for the chloroplasts of fruitlets of immature pineapple fruit: the thylakoid membrane was reported to be composed of globular subunits, 75 Å in diameter, comprising a core, about 35 Å in diameter, surrounded by an electron-dense layer, about 20 Å thick. The thylakoid appears to have the same substructure whether it is inside or outside a granum. It is presumably the combination of the light core and the dark rim of these subunits that gives the unit membrane type of appearance at lower resolution.

These electron-microscope studies on thylakoid structure have been carried out on sections of chloroplasts. Other information can be gained by examination of specimens prepared in different ways. Park and Biggins (1964) and Park (1965) have obtained pictures of metal-shadowed fragments of grana in which it appears that one surface of the thylakoid membrane is covered with a layer of particles, these particles being about 160–185 Å long, 155 Å wide, and 100 Å thick. The name 'quantasome' has been coined for these particles. Each quantasome appears to consist of four subunits *ca.* 90 Å in diameter. The quantasomes are normally in a fairly random array, but sometimes occur in straight lines, and occasionally may be seen to form a regular two-dimensional arrangement (Fig. I.29). The quantasomes were originally thought to be on the inside of the thylakoid, but more recent work[203a] suggests that they are on the outside. There is some evidence that on the inside surface of the thylakoid there are single 90 Å particles.

FIG. I.29. *Quantasomes. By permission, from Park, R. B. and Biggins, J. (1964).* Science **144**, *1009–1011 (frontispiece of issue of 22 May. Copyright 1964 by the American Association for the Advancement of Science). Chromium-shadowed spinach chloroplast thylakoid showing quantasomes (each appearing to consist of four subunits)*

A type of structure somewhat similar to that described by Park and Biggins has been deduced by Mühlethaler and his co-workers[188, 189a] on the basis of electron microscope studies on freeze-etched material. He reports that on the outer surface of the thylakoid there are approximately rectangular particles 120 Å wide; these are composed of four subunits of diameter 60 Å. The 120 Å particles are in a regular crystalline array near the centre of the thylakoid, but are more scattered towards the edge. The particles are embedded, 20 Å deep, in a fairly uniform layer 40 Å thick, which Mühlethaler believes to consist of lipid. On the inside surface of the thylakoid, that is on the other surface of the 40 Å layer, there appear to be single particles, about the same diameter, 60 Å, as the subunits of the 120 Å particles on the outer surface of the thylakoid: these particles on the inside are also thought to be embedded 20 Å deep into the 40 Å layer, and therefore may possibly be touching the particles on the outside. To explain the unit membrane appearance seen in sections of $KMnO_4$-fixed material, Mühlethaler suggests that the particles consist of protein and that on treatment with the fixative the molecules unravel and spread out, giving rise to a protein layer on either side of the 40 Å, supposedly lipid, layer.

Kreutz and Menke[137, 132, 133, 134, 135, 171, 172] have used small-angle X-ray scattering to study the structure of the thylakoid. To determine the X-ray scattering properties of the thylakoids in the living cell, the scattering curve of leaves of a yellow mutant (without chloroplasts) of *Antirrhinum majus* was subtracted from that of normal green leaves of this plant. The calculated difference-scattering curve was presumed to represent the scattering due to the thylakoids alone. By one-dimensional Fourier analysis the distribution of electron-density difference along a line normal to the plane of the thylakoid was calculated (Fig. I.30). The results indicated that the thylakoid is built up of a number of layers symmetrically disposed in pairs about a central, aqueous layer. The chemical nature of the material in each layer was deduced from the observed electron densities obtained in these experiments and in experi-

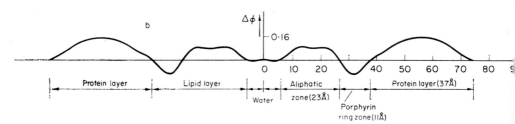

Fig. I.30. *Electron density-difference (see text) for a chloroplast thylakoid of living cells of* Antirrhinum majus, *along a line normal to the plane of the thylakoid. By permission, from Kreutz, W. (1964). Z. Naturforsch.* **19b**, *441–446*

ments with dried chloroplasts. In the centre of the thylakoid it appears that there is a layer of water about 8 Å thick; on either side of this there is a layer of aliphatic lipid 23 Å thick; outside each lipid layer there is a layer 11 Å thick, thought to contain the porphyrin rings of the chlorophylls, and outside each porphyrin layer there is a layer of protein 37 Å thick. Fig. I.31 shows a diagrammatic representation of a model of the

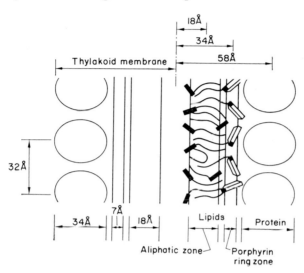

Fig. I.31. *Diagrammatic representation of the substructure of the thylakoid membrane, in cross-section. By permission, from Kreutz, W. (1964). Z. Naturforsch. **19b**, 441–446*

thylakoid (in cross-section) designed to explain the X-ray scattering results[134]. The overall thickness of the thylakoid, according to this model, is about 150 Å, which agrees with the lower estimates from electron microscopy.

The scattering curves also suggest that there is a periodicity within the plane of the protein layer. The periodicity could be explained on the assumption that the protein layer consisted of an aggregation of two-dimensional crystallites, each one consisting of 16–32 lattice points. The crystallites might be arranged regularly with 'amorphous' interspaces, or irregularly in a fluid-like structure. The protein particles at the lattice points appear to have a diameter (parallel to the plane of the crystallite) of about 27 Å, and are considered to form a quadratic lattice, the distance between the centres of adjacent particles being 32–45 Å. Fig. I.32 shows one such two-dimensional crystallite with sixteen lattice points. Kreutz (1965b) believes that these protein particles are joined together in pairs to form dumbbell-like, or bone-like structures. One such 16-point crystallite, which one can regard as approximately a square of side about 150 Å, is thought to correspond to one of the 'quantasomes' seen in the electron micrographs of Park and Biggins (1964). X-ray studies on air-dried or lipid-extracted chloroplasts indicate the presence of a lattice of only four lattice-points instead of sixteen: this suggests that the 16-point crystallite consists of four subunits (as shown in Fig. I.32) into which it can disaggregate. In this connection it is interesting that the quantasome, in electron micrographs, also appears to consist of four subunits. Recent X-ray studies by Kreutz and Weber (1966) suggest that each protein particle consists of an upper and a lower layer containing most of the protein, and a layer in between consisting mainly of water.

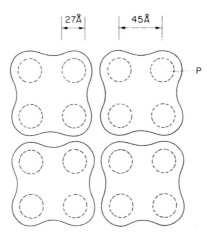

FIG. I.32. *Possible structure of quantasome, based on X-ray evidence (adapted from Kreutz, 1965a). Two-dimensional crystallite with sixteen lattice points. At each lattice point there is a particle of thylakoid structural protein—*p

The models of thylakoid membrane structure derived from X-ray diffraction studies and from electron microscopy of metal-shadowed and freeze-etched preparations, have certain features in common. Both imply that the thylakoid membrane has on its outer surface, units ('crystallites', 'quantasomes'), roughly 120–150 Å square, each unit being made up of four subunits. The X-ray work appears to give more precise indications as to the relative positions of the different chemical components of the membrane: as we have seen, Kreutz and Menke have concluded that the protein molecules form the outer surface of the thylakoid, with the porphyrin rings and the lipids forming other layers inside this. However, in contradiction to Kreutz and Menke's conclusion that the protein particles are present on the outer surface, Mühlethaler, on the basis of the electron microscope evidence, believes that there are protein particles both on the outside and on the inside of the thylakoid membrane.

Yet another model has been put forward by Weier and Benson (1965), based, in part, on the particulate substructure of the thylakoid membrane as seen in electron micrographs of sections of $KMnO_4$-fixed material. They propose that the membrane consists of a two-dimensional array of globular protein subunits. To fit this model in with the observations of Park and Biggins, they suggest that the globular protein subunits correspond to the subunits of the quantasome. They further suggest that the molecules of the protein are of a relatively hydrophobic nature and that the hydrocarbon chains of the chlorophylls, carotenoids, and various lipids are buried within the protein molecules, where they are bound by hydrophobic association with the hydrophobic internal structure of the lamellar protein. The ionic and carbohydrate moieties of the phospholipids and glycolipids, and the hydrophilic regions of the protein are thought to be on the periphery of the protein subunit. The porphyrin part of the chlorophyll is thought to be mainly in the region where the outer surface of one thylakoid is appressed against the outside surface of the next thylakoid in the granum. Some of the chlorophyll molecules, however, are thought to be entirely within the protein subunits, and it is supposed that this will be the normal situation of the chlorophyll in chloroplasts with separate, isolated thylakoids such as those of red algae. The cytochromes are thought to be also embedded within the protein subunits, and to be associated with these special chlorophyll molecules.

The Weier and Benson model differs from that of Kreutz and Menke in that, whereas in the former the lipids and proteins are represented as being closely interwoven in one layer, in the latter the protein and lipid are thought to exist mainly as distinct layers side by side. Furthermore, whereas Weier and Benson propose (as also suggested by von Wettstein, 1961) that the porphyrin rings of the chlorophyll molecules are mainly on the outside surface of the thylakoid, Kreutz and Menke believe that the porphyrin rings form a layer within the thylakoid membrane, between the protein layer and the lipid layer. The Mühlethaler model, with its lipid layer with protein molecules on either side, is equally inconsistent with the Weier and Benson model.

In view of the existence of these distinct, and mutually inconsistent, models, each having some evidence in its favour, it is clear that at the moment we can say relatively little with certainty about the molecular structure of the thylakoid.

I.2.iii.e. *Usefulness of the thylakoid concept*

The concept of the thylakoid, a flattened, membrane-bounded sac, is very helpful for the purpose of talking about, and interpreting, chloroplast structure as seen in electron micrographs of sections. In any given section of a chloroplast many apparently distinct thylakoids can be seen, and indeed the thylakoids were originally thought of as being quite independent, each representing a separate, membrane-bounded space. However, Manton (1962) believes that in the case of the *Anthoceros* chloroplast the concept of separate thylakoids is incompatible with the electron microscope evidence: she interprets the internal structure of this chloroplast as being the result of growth and folding of one membrane which is ultimately derived from invaginations protruded into the stroma from the innermost layer of the plastid wall. And, as discussed above, it has been suggested both for higher plant[104] and certain algal[85, 86] chloroplasts, that the lamellar system constitutes a single, membrane-enclosed cavity, separate and distinct from the stroma. These views of chloroplast structure are by no means established, but if further work confirms them, the thylakoid concept must either be given up altogether, or modified. In view of its linguistic usefulness it might be better simply to modify it; that is, the lamellar system would still be regarded as being composed of a number of membrane-bounded sacs, but it would be understood that the sacs were all in communication with one another. However, these matters cannot, of course, be decided until it is clear which view of chloroplast structure is nearer the truth.

I.2.iv. FUNCTION OF CHLOROPLASTS

I.2.iv.a. *The overall photosynthetic process*

The function of the chloroplast is to trap light energy and use it for the conversion of atmospheric carbon dioxide to carbohydrate which the cell can then metabolize in the usual way. Thus the chloroplast provides the cell with all the energy and carbon that it needs. No attempt will be made here to discuss in detail the photosynthetic process that takes place in the chloroplast, because this is a subject on which there are many excellent reviews available[211b, 106, 124, 65]. I shall merely give a brief account of some of the current views on the mechanism by which light energy is trapped and carbon dioxide fixed. It should be emphasized that there are divergences of opinion as to the details of the photosynthetic mechanism. The reaction sequences I describe are reasonably typical of those being considered by workers in this field, but for a critical analysis of theories of photosynthesis the reader should consult the specialized reviews.

The photosynthetic process can be divided into two parts, the light reaction and the dark reaction. In the light reaction hydrogen is withdrawn from water and passed along a series of hydrogen carriers to NADP, so that $NADPH_2$ is formed and oxygen is liberated. Associated with this hydrogen (or electron) transport there is a conversion of ADP and inorganic phosphate to ATP, one ATP molecule being formed for every two electrons transferred, or molecule of NADP reduced. The energy for both these highly endergonic processes—the removal of hydrogen from water and the formation of ATP—comes from the light absorbed by the chloroplast. Thus we may represent the light reaction by the equation

$$H_2O + NADP \xrightarrow{\sim 4h\nu} \tfrac{1}{2}O_2 + NADPH_2$$
$$ADP + P_i \quad ATP$$

In the presence of suitable cofactors, such as flavin mononucleotide or vitamin K_3, light energy can be used to promote ATP formation without the concomitant reduction of NADP.

In the dark reaction, the $NADPH_2$ produced in the light reaction is used to reduce CO_2 to the level of carbohydrate. This is also an endergonic process, and the energy required to drive it comes in part from the breakdown of the ATP produced in the light reaction. The dark reaction might be represented by the equation

$$CO_2 + 2\ NADPH_2 \longrightarrow (CH_2O) + H_2O + 2\ NADP$$
$$3\ ATP \quad 3\ ADP + 3\ P_i$$

I.2.iv.b. *Light reactions*

In the case of the chloroplasts of higher plants and green algae (*Chlorophyta* and *Euglenophyta*) the light reaction is brought about by light absorbed by chlorophyll *a*, chlorophyll *b*, and carotenoids. The reaction scheme outlined here is based on the work of many people (see reviews): the particular formulation chosen largely follows that used by Witt, Muller, Rumberg, and their co-workers[281, 282]. It is thought that a particular form of chlorophyll *a*, chlorophyll a_I, which represents only about 0·1 per cent of the total chlorophyll present (and which has an absorption band at *ca.* 700 mμ), is raised to an excited state by this absorbed light energy. In the excited state, chlorophyll a_I becomes a powerful reducing agent and can lose an electron to some unknown acceptor in the chloroplast (Light Reaction I). This unknown electron acceptor is sometimes given the symbol Z. It is supposed that the reduced form of Z, termed Z^-, transfers an electron to an iron-containing protein, ferredoxin; ferredoxin reduces a flavoprotein, and the flavoprotein reduces NADP, yielding $NADPH_2$. However, we are now left with positively charged chlorophyll a_I which, since chlorophyll is not actually used up in photosynthesis, must be restored to its original state. The electrons for this come ultimately from water, via another series to electron carriers. Since water is a very stable compound, the removal of electrons, or hydrogen, from it requires energy. This energy is thought to be provided by absorption of light in a second, light-driven step (light reaction II). The light energy, absorbed by various pigments, is thought to be eventually received by another form of chlorophyll a— chlorophyll a_{II}. The excited chlorophyll a_{II}, in some way which is not understood, brings about transference of one electron from a compound Y (the chemical identity of which is unknown) to plastoquinone. The energy in the excited chlorophyll a_{II} is required at this stage because the redox potential of Y is much more positive than that of plasto-quinone, and so the reduction cannot take place spontaneously—it requires energy to drive it. The reduced plastoquinone can spontaneously transfer electrons to cytochrome f by a route which probably involves the electron carriers plastocyanin and cytochrome b_6 (the details of this part of the pathway are obscure). The reduced cytochrome f molecules can then transfer electrons to the positively charged chloro-phyll a_I molecules, restoring them to their original state. The reaction sequence is not yet complete because we are still left with oxidized compound Y. This is believed to be such a strong oxidizing agent that it can remove hydrogen from water, thus liberating oxygen.

The possible sequence of electron transport steps between H_2O and NADP is summarized in Fig. I.33. It must be understood that this reaction mechanism is far from being completely established, but it seems likely that it is at least the right sort of reaction mechanism. The formation of ATP from ADP and P_i is thought to be coupled to an electron transport step somewhere between plastoquinone and cyto-chrome f.

The pigments and electron transport components primarily concerned with light reaction I are referred to as System I; those primarily con-cerned with light reaction II are referred to as System II. If, as current theories suggest, the pigments (primary pigments) which take a direct part in the chemistry of electron transport, chlorophyll a_I and chlorophyll a_{II}, represent only a very small proportion of the total pigments present, then the question arises as to what is the function of the remaining pigment. It seems likely that these secondary pigments, the carotenoids and the remainder of the chlorophylls a and b, function by absorbing radiant energy and transferring it to the primary pigments. Thus the primary pigments may be activated either directly by absorbing light energy, or indirectly by energy transfer from the secondary pigments. I am using the phrase 'secondary pig-ments' because the more commonly used phrase 'accessory pigments' is currently used in the literature in two different ways: it may refer to any pigment which does not take a direct part in the chemistry of elcctron transport (secondary pigment), or it may be used (as in the phrase 'accessory pigment system') of any of that set of pigments concerned in light reaction II (that is, the light reaction not involving

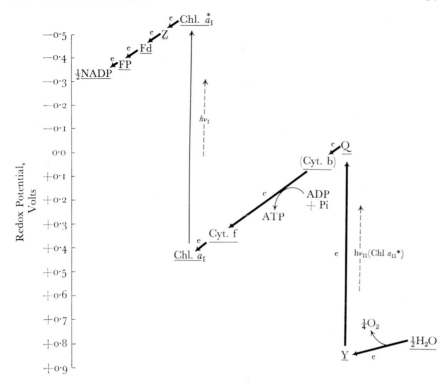

FIG. I.33. *The chloroplast electron transport system (adapted from Witt* et al., *1963, 1965).* FP—*flavoprotein (transhydrogenase).* Fd—*ferredoxin.* Chl—*chlorophyll.* Cyt—*cytochrome.* Q—*plastoquinone.* hv_I—*light absorbed by pigments of system I.* hv_{II}—*light absorbed by pigments of system II.* e—*electron*

chlorophyll a_I). It is thought[34a] that in *Chlorella* a large proportion of the 668 mμ-absorbing form of chlorophyll *a* belongs, together with a large proportion of chlorophyll *b*, to System II, while a large part of the 683 mμ-absorbing form of chlorophyll *a* must be identified with System I, although some of it probably belongs to System II.

In chloroplasts of algae other than green algae, chlorophyll *b* is absent, and other pigments, such as chlorophylls *c* or *d*, or the biliproteins, may be present. In such cases the details of the electron transport steps of photosynthesis are likely to be somewhat different. However, it is probably generally true that there are two light reactions, and that the processes which take place are fundamentally similar. The biliproteins, or other pigments replacing chlorophyll *b*, may act as secondary pigments collecting light energy to be used in light reaction II.

Chloroplasts, whether isolated or in the living cell, undergo volume changes in the light[202, 201, 113, 288, 203]. The characteristic response is shrinkage but, under some circumstances, swelling may occur. These volume changes are linked, in some way which is not understood, to the light-induced electron transport and phosphorylation processes which we have discussed in this section. It has also been shown that isolated spinach chloroplasts can carry out a light-dependent uptake of calcium, phosphate, and sodium (but not potassium) ions: there is some evidence that calcium uptake and phosphate uptake may be, at least in part, linked[194a].

Chloroplasts may be involved in a light-dependent assimilation of nitrate. Spinach chloroplasts contain a flavoprotein which catalyses the reduction of nitrate to nitrite in the presence of grana in the light: the electrons for this reduction can be passed to the nitrate reductase from the chloroplast NADP reductase[152a]. Ramirez, Del Campo, Paneque, and Losada (1966) have reported the presence of another enzyme in spinach chloroplasts, which will reduce nitrite to ammonia in the presence of grana plus ferredoxin in the light. It appears that ferredoxin is the immediate electron donor for this nitrite reductase. The reduction of nitrite is coupled with the formation of stoichiometric amounts of O_2 and ATP. Thus, photoreduction of nitrate and nitrite may provide the cell with a way of making ATP that is not coupled to the reduction of NADP. The nitrite reductase appears not to be a flavoprotein.

I.2.iv.c. *Dark reactions*

The dark reactions of photosynthesis, in which CO_2 is converted to carbohydrate are shown in Fig. I.34. The enzymes involved are also listed. This reaction scheme has emerged to a large extent from the work of Calvin and his co-workers (see for example, Bassham and Calvin, 1957). It may possibly be that this pathway is not exactly true in every detail (see Stiller, 1962), but most workers consider it to be fundamentally correct.

The cycle is somewhat involved and needs several turns to produce one molecule of hexose. To understand the overall effect of the dark reactions let us consider the fate of six molecules of carbon dioxide. These react with six molecules of ribulose diphosphate (C_5) to give twelve molecules of phosphoglyceric acid (C_3). The phosphoglyceric acid is, with the help of ATP and $NADPH_2$, converted to triose phosphate. For simplicity, we can regard the twelve molecules of triose phosphate (C_3) as being converted to six molecules of hexose phosphate (C_6). One of these molecules of hexose can be removed for starch formation, leaving five hexose phosphate molecules. The five hexose phosphate molecules can then be rearranged to form six pentose phosphate (C_5) molecules. The six pentose phosphate molecules are then, with the help of ATP, converted to six molecules of ribulose

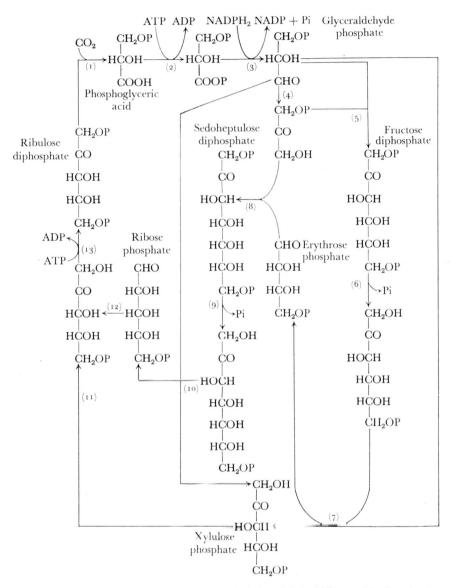

FIG. I.34. *The Calvin-Benson CO_2 fixation cycle (adapted from Stiller, 1962). P—phosphate group. P_i—inorganic phosphate.*
The enzymes involved in each step are: (1) carboxydismutase; (2) 3-phosphoglyceric acid kinase; (3) glyceraldehyde-3-phosphate dehydrogenase; (4) triose phosphate isomerase; (5) fructose diphosphate aldolase; (6) fructose diphosphate phosphatase; (7) transketolase; (8) aldolase; (9) sedoheptulose diphosphate phosphatase; (10) transketolase; (11) ribulose-5-phosphate epimerase; (12) phosphoriboisomerase; (13) ribulose-5-phosphate kinase

diphosphate and so the cycle is completed, with six molecules of CO_2 having been converted to hexose. The process might be summarized as in Fig. I.35. The CO_2 fixation cycle shown in Fig. I.34 was derived from studies on algae in the *Chlorophyta*, and on higher plants. There is as yet insufficient evidence to say whether the reaction sequence is the same in all algae.

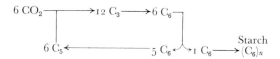

FIG. I.35. *Summary of photosynthetic CO_2 fixation cycle*

During photosynthesis with $^{14}CO_2$, radioactivity is rapidly incorporated into the galactolipids of the chloroplast. It appears that there is an active exchange of the galactose residues with the intermediates of the CO_2 reduction cycle[60]. The function of these galactolipids is not known; since they are present in large amounts they may possibly serve as a carbohydrate reservoir.

I.2.iv.d. *Location of the light and dark reactions*

Although it might be expected on general grounds that the enzymes of photosynthesis would be located in the chloroplast, it is only in recent years that firm evidence for this has been obtained. Much of the evidence has come from the use of the non-aqueous procedure for the isolation of chloroplasts. As we saw previously (I.2.i) the use of this procedure prevents leakage of proteins from the chloroplast. By means of this technique it has been shown that higher plant chloroplasts contain most, and possibly all, of the carboxydismutase, NADP-requiring triose phosphate dehydrogenase, and alkaline fructose-1,6-diphosphatase activities of the cell[234,97,232]. Use of the non-aqueous procedure indicates that about two-thirds of the aldolase activity and half the phosphorylase activity of the leaf cell are in the chloroplasts[96,243]. Non-aqueous chloroplasts of *Vicia faba* possess sucrose synthetase, as indicated by the formation of sucrose from uridine-diphosphoglucose and fructose[20b]. Chloroplasts of sugar cane and of spinach also have an enzyme which catalyses the formation of sucrose phosphate from uridinediphosphoglucose and fructose-6-phosphate[91a]. Doi, Doi, and Nikuni (1966) have isolated a soluble enzyme from spinach chloroplasts which transfers glucosyl residues from adenosine-diphosphoglucose to the α-1,4-glucan, amylopectin, which is one of the components of starch.

As far as the electron transport components of photosynthesis are concerned the photosynthetic pigments occur only in the chloroplasts, and there is evidence that cytochromes f and b_6[105,45] and plasto-quinone[50] in leaves are also confined to the chloroplasts.

The non-aqueous technique has been extended by Smillie (1963) to the study of intracellular enzyme distribution in cells of *Euglena gracilis*. The results (Table I.7) show that, despite the fact that the end-product of photosynthesis (paramylon) accumulates outside the chloro-plasts in this alga, at least four of the twelve or so enzymes involved in CO_2 fixation are confined to the chloroplasts; another five are present both in the chloroplasts and in other parts of the cell. Also, in agreement with the higher plant work, two cytochromes, b_6 and *Euglena* cyto-chrome-552, are confined to the chloroplast, and so is ferredoxin. Most, and probably all, of the plastoquinone of the *Euglena* cell is located in the chloroplast[259]. In algae, as in higher plants, the photosynthetic pigments occur only in the chloroplasts.

If higher plant chloroplasts are disrupted by sonication and then subjected to high speed centrifugation (up to 145,000 g for 30 minutes), virtually all the pigments, i.e. chlorophylls and carotenoids, are found in the pellet. When this green pellet is examined by electron micro-scopy[206] it can be seen to consist of thylakoids and thylakoid frag-ments. Thus, it appears that the light-absorbing components of the photosynthetic mechanism occur in the thylakoids. Two of the haem-containing electron-transfer components of the chloroplast, cyto-chromes f and b_6, are also confined to the thylakoid regions[118]. Plastocyanin appears to be mainly associated with the thylakoids[125b]. Plastoquinone is present both in the thylakoids and in the osmiophilic globules[7]. The flavoprotein which transfers hydrogen from ferredoxin to NADP appears to be fairly firmly bound to the insoluble fraction of the chloroplasts[128,230,16] and is, therefore, probably in the thyla-koids. However, ferredoxin itself appears to be rather readily released into solution from isolated chloroplasts[5,230]: its whereabouts in the chloroplast of the living cell is, therefore, somewhat uncertain. The fact that it reduces the thylakoid-bound flavoprotein would suggest that ferredoxin itself is normally bound to the thylakoids; it may be that this binding is rather weak. However, it seems fair to conclude, on the basis of chemical evidence, that most of the known components of the light reactions are present, wholly or partly, in the thylakoids. This is con-firmed by the fact that the insoluble, chlorophyll-containing fraction of the chloroplast (i.e. the thylakoid fraction), if supplemented with ferredoxin, will carry out the complete light reaction; the reduction of NADP, liberation of oxygen from water, and formation of ATP[218,5]. Even in the absence of ferredoxin the purified thylakoid fraction will carry out photophosphorylation with flavin mononucleotide or vitamin K_3 as catalysts[190].

The straw-coloured supernatant left over after high-speed centrifugation of the disrupted chloroplasts appears to consist largely of soluble proteins. About 27–36 per cent of this protein apparently is Fraction I protein[98] and it also contains 90–96 per cent of the carboxydismutase

TABLE I.7. INTRACELLULAR DISTRIBUTION OF CERTAIN ENZYMES IN AUTOTROPHICALLY GROWN CELLS OF *EUGLENA GRACILIS*

(Adapted from Smillie, R. M., Evans, W. R. and Lyman, H. (1963) Brookhaven Symp. Biol. **16**, *88–107)*

Enzymes which are, or may be concerned with photosynthetic electron transport:	
Cytochrome b_6	*a*
Cytochrome-552	*a*
Ferredoxin	*a*
NADPH$_2$ cytochrome *c* reductase	*b*
NADPH$_2$ diaphorase	*b*
Transhydrogenase	*b*
Adenylate kinase	*b*
Enzymes of photosynthetic CO_2 fixation cycle:	
Carboxydismutase	*a*
3-phosphoglycerate kinase	*b*
NADP-glyceraldehyde phosphate dehydrogenase	*a*
Triose phosphate isomerase	*b*
Fructose diphosphate aldolase	*b*
Alkaline fructosediphosphatase	*a*
Transketolase	*b*
Phosphopentoisomerase	*b*
Ribulokinase	*a*
Other enzymes:	
Phosphohexoisomerase	*c*
Phosphofructokinase	*c*
Phosphoglycerate mutase	*c*
Enolase	*c*
Pyruvate kinase	*c*
Phosphoglucomutase	*c*
Neutral fructosediphosphatase	*c*
UDPG pyrophosphorylase	*c*
Transaldolase	*c*
Glucose-6-phosphate dehydrogenase	*c*
6-Phosphogluconate dehydrogenase	*c*
Isocitrate dehydrogenase	*c*
Malate dehydrogenase	*c*
Malic enzyme	*c*
Glutathione reductase	*c*
NADH$_2$-cytochrome *c* reductase	*c*
NADH$_2$-glyoxylate reductase	*c*
NADPH$_2$-glyoxylate reductase	*c*
Ribonuclease	*c*
Pyrophosphatase	*b*

a Enzyme confined to the chloroplasts.
b Enzyme occurring both inside and outside chloroplasts.
c All or most of enzyme occurring outside chloroplasts.

activity of the chloroplast[205]. Trebst, Tsujimoto, and Arnon (1958) showed that if this chlorophyll-free supernatant is supplied with $NADPH_2$ and ATP (either added directly or formed by a preliminary incubation with the thylakoid fraction) it will fix $^{14}CO_2$ into the various phosphorylated intermediates of the CO_2 fixation cycle. Since the pellet obtained on high-speed centrifugation of disrupted chloroplasts appears to contain all the thylakoid fraction of the chloroplasts, and little else, it seems likely that the proteins of the supernatant come mainly from the stroma region of the chloroplast.

To summarize current views on the location of the reactions of photosynthesis: it is believed that the light reactions, the production of energy in the form of ATP and reducing power in the form of $NADPH_2$, occur in, or on, the thylakoids: the dark reactions, the conversion of carbon dioxide to carbohydrate, take place in the stroma.

I.3. The Proplastid

'Proplastid' is the word used for the small, colourless or pale green, undifferentiated plastids which occur in the meristematic (dividing) cells of the shoot and root. Nothing is known of their chemistry since they have never been isolated.

In the shoot meristem there are 7–20 proplastids per cell[181]. They are usually roughly ellipsoidal or spherical in shape, but may be amoeboid: they are generally $1 \cdot 0 – 1 \cdot 5 \mu$ long and perhaps about $0 \cdot 7 \mu$ thick[100]. They have relatively little internal structure: in electron micrographs (Fig. I.36) they can be seen to be bounded by a double membrane and to contain a fairly homogeneous matrix into which extend occasional invaginations, sometimes possibly tubular, from the inner plastid membrane[139, 32, 274, 189]. They may also contain one or two isolated vesicles and thylakoids, or, in seedlings germinated in the light, occasional stacks of about four thylakoids[139, 167].

In the meristematic region of the root cap there may be 20–40 proplastids per cell[120]. These have a similar structure to the shoot proplastids: a few isolated vesicles, an occasional invagination from the inner membrane, and perhaps one or two thylakoid-like structures[34, 276]. Sometimes these proplastids contain small starch grains.

Proplastids are not confined to vascular plants: they may also be found in the apical cells of the more complex, multicellular algae, such as *Lomentaria baileyana*[24] (Fig. XIV.8).

It is usually considered that the main function of proplastids is to act as the precursors of the more differentiated types of plastid, such as the chloroplast, etioplast, or amyloplast. The formation of these other plastids from proplastids is discussed in Chapters XIII and XIV.

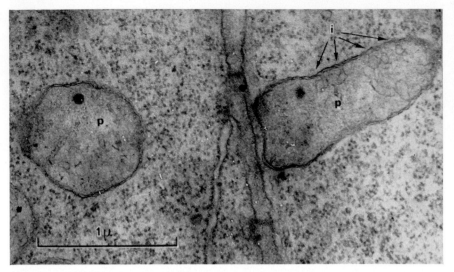

Fig. I.36. *Proplastids in leaf meristem of* Nicotiana tabacum (*von Wettstein, D., un-published*). *Glutaraldehyde–OsO₄ fixation. p—proplastid. i—invaginations from inner plastid membrane*

Whether proplastids have any biochemical function in their own right is not known. It seems not unlikely that they might play some important role in the carbohydrate metabolism of the meristematic cells.

I.4. The Etioplast

I.4.i. DEFINITION OF THE ETIOPLAST

'Etioplast' is the name which I suggest should be applied to those plastids which are formed in the leaf cells of plants grown entirely in the dark. The prefix 'etio-' is used because these plastids are characteristic of etiolated leaves (see XIII.7). They are often referred to as 'proplastids', but I suggest that this nomenclature is misleading because these plastids are not structureless, undifferentiated bodies as are the proplastids, but have a definite and complicated internal structure. Indeed they are formed by differentiation from proplastids (see XIII.7).

I.4.ii. COMPOSITION OF THE ETIOPLAST

A certain amount of work has been carried out on the chemical composition of etioplasts. Plastids have been isolated from leaves of dark-grown *Phaseolus vulgaris* by grinding the leaves in buffered sucrose, and, after a centrifugation at 270 g for three minutes, centrifuging the supernatant at 1500 g for six minutes. This pellet contained most of the plastids[164]: these had a dry weight of $3 \cdot 2 – 3 \cdot 6 \times 10^{-12}$ g per plastid. The etioplasts have a nitrogen content which is about 8·4 per cent of their dry weight. Lipid and nucleic acid N might account for about 1 per cent of this 8·4 per cent, and so the protein N content is probably in the region of 7 per cent of the dry weight, indicating a protein content of about 46 per cent.

The lipid content is about 20 per cent of the dry weight (which is about the same as that of spinach chloroplasts). Wallace and Newman (1965) have reported some data on the composition of these lipids. The phospholipid content of *Phaseolus vulgaris* etioplasts (in micromoles per kg wet weight of plastids) is about half that in *Phaseolus* chloroplasts. If, in these chloroplasts, phospholipids form 9 per cent of the total lipid (as in spinach chloroplasts—Table I.3), then in the etioplasts the phospholipids might be expected to constitute about 4·5 per cent of the total lipid. The mono- and di-galactosyl glyceride content of the etioplasts (in micromoles per kg wet weight) is about one-eighth of that of the chloroplasts. If the galactosyl glycerides form about 40 per cent of the total lipid of the chloroplast (as in spinach chloroplasts—Table I.3), then in the etioplasts, galactosyl glycerides might be expected to form about 5 per cent of the total lipid. The fatty acids of the etioplasts consist (moles per cent) of 15 per cent linolenic (18:3), 15 per cent linoleic (18:2), 15 per cent oleic (18:1), 11 per cent stearic (18:0), 5 per cent palmitoleic (16:1), 34 per cent palmitic (16:0), 4 per cent myristic (14:0), and 2 per cent dodecanoic (12:0). This fatty-acid composition is quite different from that of the *Phaseolus* chloroplasts which have much more linolenic acid (61 per cent—compare with 69 per cent in spinach chloroplasts) and correspondingly less of the other fatty acids (4 per cent linoleic, 5 per cent oleic, 3 per cent stearic, 5 per cent palmitoleic, 18 per cent palmitic, 2 per cent myristic, and 1 per cent dodecanoic).

The lipid fraction will also include a certain amount of pigments. Etiolated leaves of *Phaseolus vulgaris* contain about one-third as much carotenoid, per g dry weight, as similar leaves which have been allowed to form chloroplasts in the light[78]. Thus we might expect the amount of carotenoid in an etioplast to be up to one-third that in a chloroplast. The dry weight of a *Phaseolus* etioplast will be in the region of half that of the chloroplast which can be formed from it[164] and so we can calculate that if the carotenoid content of a chloroplast is about 0·7 per cent of the dry weight (Table I.1) the carotenoid content of an etioplast might be of the order of 0·5 per cent of the dry weight. The carotenoids of the etioplast include far more xanthophyll than carotene, the xanthophyll/carotene ratio being between 7 and 14[58, 9, 245] as opposed to a ratio of about 2 in chloroplasts. In etiolated maize seedlings lutein was found

5—P.

to be the major carotenoid (*ca.* 50 per cent) with violaxanthin, flavo-xanthin, β-carotene, and neo-β-carotene being present in much smaller amounts in the order listed[127]. In leaves of etiolated *Phaseolus vulgaris*[78] the carotenoids present were neoxanthin (50 per cent), lutein (38 per cent), and β-carotene (11 per cent). In dark-grown wheat seedlings[283] lutein was the major component, with neoxanthin, lutein epoxide, neozeaxanthin, violaxanthin, and β-carotene being also present. The lipids will also include protochlorophyll (protochlorophyllide and proto-chlorophyllide ester, mainly the former—see XIII.5), and a similar calculation to that made for carotenoids (assuming that the amount of protochlorophyll in an etioplast is approximately 1/300 the amount of chlorophyll in a chloroplast) suggests that the protochlorophyll content of an etioplast may be in the region of 0·03 per cent of the dry weight. It must be understood that these calculations of the carotenoid and protochlorophyll contents of etioplasts are approximate in the extreme, and can give no more than an estimate of the order of magni-tude of these quantities.

Etioplasts contain RNA, and almost certainly DNA (see Chapter X for a more detailed discussion). Values reported for their RNA content are 9·0 per cent of the dry weight in the case of rye etioplasts[253], 6·3 per cent in the case of wheat[253], and 7·2 per cent in the case of pea[231]. As far as DNA is concerned it seems likely that an etioplast would con-tain the same amount of DNA as a chloroplast. Representative values for a higher plant chloroplast are about $2\cdot0-5\cdot6 \times 10^{-15}$ g DNA (see X.7). Assuming the dry weight of the etioplast to be $3\cdot2-3\cdot6 \times 10^{-12}$ g[164] we arrive at a figure of about 0·1 per cent of the dry weight for the DNA content of an etioplast.

Etioplasts may also contain appreciable amounts of starch[164].

I.4.iii. STRUCTURE OF THE ETIOPLAST

Etioplasts are usually irregularly ellipsoidal in shape. In leaves of dark-grown *Phaseolus vulgaris* they have a diameter of about 3 μ[164]. The etioplast is bounded by a double membrane. The plastid is filled with a fairly homogeneous matrix, or stroma, and contains usually one, but possibly up to four, crystalline centres (Fig. I.37). These crystalline centres (sometimes called Heitz-Leyon crystals, or prolamellar bodies) were first discovered by Heitz (1954) and Leyon (1954b). Their appearance in section suggests that they consist of a three-dimensional cubic lattice of inter-connected tubules[273, 274, 263, 90]. Around the periphery of the crystalline centre extending into the stroma, are a few lamellae, similar in appearance to thylakoids. These lamellae appear to be continuous with the tubules of the crystalline centre. Where there is more than one

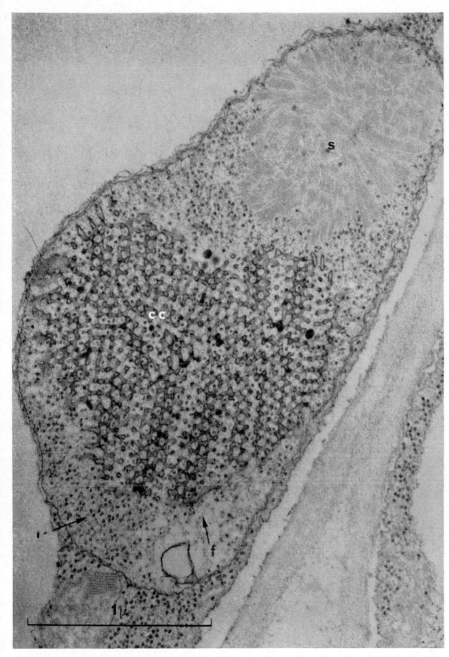

FIG. I.37. *Etioplast in a dark-grown oat leaf. By permission, from Gunning, B. E. S. (1965).* Protoplasma 55, 111–130. cc—*crystalline centre.* s—*stromacentre.* r—*ribosome-like particles.* f—25Å *fibrils*

crystalline centre in an etioplast, lamellae may extend from one crystalline centre to another.

Gunning (1965b) has analysed the structure of the crystalline centre of the oat leaf etioplast in detail, using glutaraldehyde–osmium fixation: this appears to be particularly effective at preserving fine structure. He has shown that where three tubules (one in each axis of the lattice) meet and fuse at the corners of each unit cell of the lattice, the membranes are smoothly confluent so that any two adjacent tubules lying at right angles to one another in one plane contain a quadrant of a circle. That is, in face view, the unit cell appears as a circle, of diameter 380 Å, bounded by tubule membrane, rather than as a square. The drawing in Fig. I.38 shows the probable arrangement, in three dimensions, of the tubules of the crystalline centre: the region of the crystal-

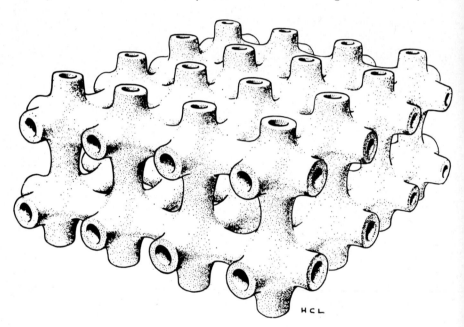

FIG. I.38. *Three-dimensional representation of the membrane system of the crystalline centre of an oat etioplast. By permission, from Gunning, B. E. S. (1965). Protoplasma, 55, 111–130*

line centre portrayed in this figure includes a sheet of nine unit cells (3 × 3), these being delimited by thirty-two (2 × 4 × 4) six-armed nodal units of the tubule system[90]. The external diameter of a tubule at its narrowest point, half-way along the edge of a unit cell, is 210 Å. The membrane, which is of the three-layered unit membrane type, is 50–60 Å thick, so the internal diameter of a tubule is about 100 Å. The unit cells of the crystalline centre are continuous with the stroma of the etioplast. In uranyl acetate-stained sections the stroma can be seen to contain large numbers of particles similar in size and appearance to ribosomes (Fig. I.37): furthermore, there is a single ribosome-like particle in the middle of each unit cell of the crystalline centre[90]. Gunning suggests that these ribosome-like particles in the crystalline centre are, in fact, responsible for maintaining the tubules in their crystalline lattice form (see XIII.7). The stroma of the etioplast of the oat leaf also contains fibres, similar to DNA fibres, and a stromacentre (Fig. I.37) of the type also observed in the oat chloroplast (see I.2.iii.a). The osmiophilic globules of the oat etioplast occur either within or round the periphery of the crystalline centre. The crystal lattice is somewhat disturbed in the region of these globules.

This three-dimensional cubic lattice of interconnected tubules is probably the normal structure of the etioplast crystalline centre in most higher plants (see Gunning, 1965b, for a review of the literature on this). However, in certain plastids in *Elodea canadensis*, Menke (1960b) has described crystalline centres which appear to be made up of bundles of tubules. The tubules may be straight, lightly corrugated, or helically coiled. They are packed hexagonally, and do not appear to be interconnected.

The plastids of etiolated leaves can be shown by light microscopy to contain up to five small granules. These granules show a red fluorescence[251, 81, 23] indicating that they contain the protochlorophyll of the etioplast: they are yellowish in colour, suggesting that they also contain the carotenoids[81]. These granules are probably the crystalline centres, or prolamellar bodies, seen in electron micrographs of etioplasts.

I.4.iv. FUNCTION OF THE ETIOPLAST

The etioplast has the ability rapidly to transform itself into a chloroplast on exposure to light (XIII). It seems, therefore, reasonable to suppose that the main, or one of the main, functions of the etioplast is to act as a readily convertible chloroplast precursor. It is possible that it may also have some function concerned with carbohydrate metabolism.

I.4.v. PLASTIDS OF DARK-GROWN ALGAE

The great majority of algae form chloroplasts in the dark (XIII.2). Amongst those which do not, *Euglena gracilis* and *Ochromonas danica* have been studied by electron microscopy. The dark-grown cells of *E. gracilis* contain at least twenty, and probably about thirty, plastids[55]. These are very irregularly ellipsoidal in shape, and are about 1 μ across. They are bounded by a double membrane and show little internal structure other than a few ribosome-like particles[15]. Dark-grown cells of *Ochromonas danica* contain only one plastid: this has a double membrane, and is usually seen to contain just a few small vesicles, a single thylakoid, and a large number of ribosome-like particles[73].

It is not easy to decide which term to apply to these plastids. The fact that they are formed in cells grown in the dark would suggest that 'etioplast' might be the appropriate word. However, they do not have crystalline centres, and, in terms of structure, are much more similar to higher plant proplastids than to higher plant etioplasts. We shall, therefore, refer to the plastids of dark-grown cells of *Euglena gracilis* and *Ochromonas danica* as proplastids.

Plastids of dark-grown cells of *E. gracilis* have a markedly different fatty-acid composition from the chloroplasts of the green cells[215]. As may be seen from the data in Table I.8, nearly half the fatty acid of the proplastids consists of arachidonic acid $(20:4)$ and other highly unsaturated C_{20} acids, and there are only small amounts $(0–2\cdot5$ per cent) of unsaturated C_{16} and C_{18} acids. The chloroplasts contain a substantial amount of C_{20} polyunsaturated acids, but much less $(14$ per cent) than do the proplastids: also the chloroplasts contain much more of the C_{16} and C_{18} di- and tri-unsaturated acids than do the proplastids.

TABLE I.8. FATTY ACID COMPOSITION OF PLASTID FRACTIONS FROM GREEN AND ETIOLATED CELLS OF *EUGLENA GRACILIS*

(Calculated from results of Rosenberg, Pecker, and Moschides, 1965)

| | Fatty acid | % by weight of total fatty acid | |
Carbon atoms	Number of double bonds	Chloroplasts	'Proplastids'
13	0	1·5	3·0
14	0	4·0	3·5
15	0	2·0	3·0
16	0	8·0	6·0
16	1	5·5	1·5
16	2	7·0	—
16	3	14·5	—
17	0	2·0	1·5
17	1	5·5	2·5
18	0	—	1·0
18	1	2.5	2.5
18	2	8·0	0·5
18	3	12·5	1·0
19	1	1·5	—
19	2	—	1·5
19	4 and more	—	5·0
20	2	3·5	3·0
20	4 and more	14·0	48·0
21	4 and more	—	2·0
22	4 and more	—	10·5

I.5. The Amyloplast

An amyloplast is a mature plastid, most of the internal volume of which is filled with starch. Such plastids are found in the differentiated cells of the root, particularly the root cap; they are also generally found in storage tissues, such as cotyledons, endosperm, and tubers. There may be just one very large starch grain, as in the amyloplasts of the potato tuber, or there may be a number (perhaps as many as eight or so) of tightly packed starch grains, as in the amyloplasts of the root cap (Fig. I.39). The amyloplast is bounded by a double membrane. In the case of the potato tuber, the starch grain may grow so large that the membrane is ruptured. Apart from the starch grain, the amyloplasts appear to contain just the usual, apparently structureless, stroma. The starch grain of the potato amyloplast appears to be made up of a series of concentric layers. From polarized light studies, Frey-Wyssling (1953) has concluded that the chains of starch molecules lie approximately parallel, and extend from one concentric layer outward to the next concentric layer. He also suggests that each concentric layer is at its most dense in its inner region, and becomes less dense (more hydrated) towards its outer region.

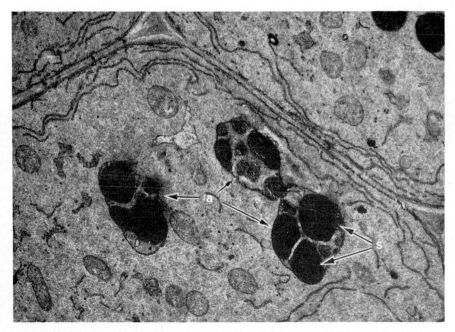

FIG. I.39. *Amyloplasts of maize root cap cell (Juniper, B. E., unpublished). Glutaraldehyde–KMnO₄ fixation. a—amyloplasts. s—starch grains*

No data on the chemical composition of amyloplasts are available, since these plastids have not been isolated. However, it seems reasonable to suppose that if they were isolated, they would be found to consist mainly of starch.

The function of amyloplasts in storage tissues is, presumably, to synthesize starch as a reserve when carbohydrates are available in excess, and then to break their starch down to free sugars or sugar derivatives when the plant is in need of carbohydrate again. The amyloplasts of the root cap may have a totally different function. It has been suggested that they may be an essential part of the mechanism of graviperception in roots[191]. Because of their high density, they are amongst the first cellular organelles to adjust their positions within the cell when the orientation of the cell with respect to the direction of the gravitational field is changed. Hence, they do at least have physical properties which might lend themselves to a graviperception system.

I.6. The Chromoplast

I.6.i. DEFINITION OF THE CHROMOPLAST

'Chromoplast' is the term used for those carotenoid-containing plastids responsible for the yellow, orange, or red colour of many fruits and flower petals, and certain roots. They are of extremely wide occurrence. Probably most orange, red, or yellow fruits owe their colour to carotenoids, present in chromoplasts—typical examples are capsicums, tomatoes, rose hips, and berries of *Sorbus*. Well-known examples of flowers which owe their colour to chromoplasts are *Ranunculus*, *Lilium tigrinum*, and *Tropaeolum*. For extensive lists of fruits or flowers in which the colour is due to the presence of carotenoids (and hence chromoplasts) the reader should consult the books by Karrer and Jücker (1951) and Goodwin (1952). Examples of roots which contain chromoplasts are the carrot and the sweet potato.

I.6.ii. COMPOSITION OF CHROMOPLASTS

Some types of chromoplast may be isolated by the same methods as are used for chloroplasts (I.2.i). However, a proportion of the chromoplasts of carrot appear to be less dense than water since they float up, rather than down, on high-speed centrifugation[250]. Little work has been done on the overall chemical composition of isolated chromoplasts. For carrot chromoplasts, Straus (1954) found an average total lipid content of 72 per cent of the dry weight: this included 20–56 per cent (of the chromoplast dry weight) of carotene, and 10–16 per cent of phospho-lipid. The chromoplasts also contained about 16 per cent protein, and 0·5 per cent RNA, and yielded an amount of ash equivalent to 4·5 per cent of the dry weight.

A great deal of work has been done on the carotenoid composition of the pigmented tissues which contain chromoplasts. Since the carotenoids of such tissues are confined to the chromoplasts, the data will also apply to the chromoplasts themselves. There are usually one to six major carotenoid components, and sometimes a large number of minor components, as can be seen from the data for *Capsicum annuum*, shown in Table I.9. The carotenoid composition of tomato chromoplasts is somewhat simpler: lycopene accounts for about 87 per cent, β-carotene

TABLE I.9. THE CAROTENOID COMPOSITION OF CHROMOPLASTS OF RED *CAPSICUM ANNUUM* FRUIT

(From the data of Curl, 1962)

Carotenoid	percentage of total
Capsanthin	34·7
β-carotene	11·6
Violaxanthin	9·9
Cryptoxanthin	6·7
Capsorubin	6·4
Cryptocapsin	4·3
Zeaxanthin	2·3
Capsolutein	2·3
Hydroxycapsolutein	1·9
Phytoene	1·7
Antheraxanthin	1·6
Mutatoxanthins	1·6
ζ-Carotene	1·5
Capsolutein-5,6-epoxide	1·5
Phytofluene	1·1
Hydroxy-α-carotene	1·0
Hydroxycapsolutein-5,6-epoxide	1·0
Carbonyl	1·0
Luteoxanthins	0·9
Capsanthin-5,6-epoxide	0·9
Neoxanthin	0·7
Tetrahydrocapsorubin	0·7
P-482, diol	0·6
Cryptoflavin-like	0·5
Hydroxycapsanthin-like	0·5
Hydroxy-α-carotene-like	0·4
Capsolutein-5,8-epoxide	0·4
Capsochrome	0·3
Mutatochrome-like	0·3
α-Carotene	0.2
Trolliflor-like	0·1

for 7 per cent, phytofluene for 3 per cent, and there may also be traces of ζ-carotene[155]. The carotenoid make-up of chromoplasts is very much more varied than that of chloroplasts. Any, or all, of the typical chloroplast carotenoids may be found in chromoplasts, but there is a large number of chromoplast carotenoids which are not found in chloroplasts. Typical examples are capsanthin (Fig. I.40(a)) which occurs almost exclusively in the chromoplasts of red peppers, and lycopene (Fig. I.40(b)) which is the major carotenoid of the chromoplasts of the tomato and many other red fruits. The xanthophylls of

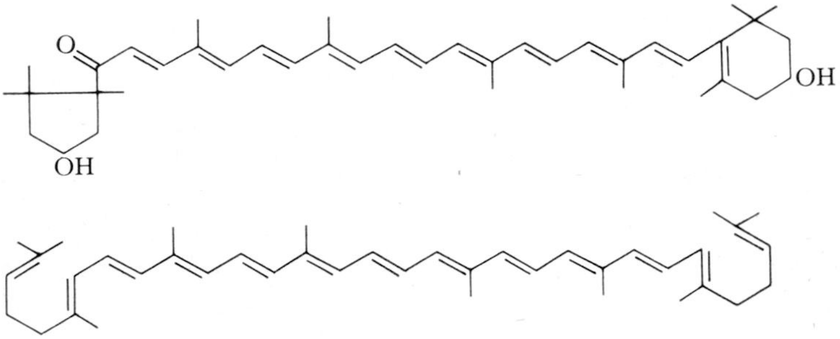

Fig. I.40. *Chromoplast carotenoids.* (a) *Capsanthin.* (b) *Lycopene.* (*Structures from Davies, B. H. in* The Chemistry and Biochemistry of Plant Pigments. *Ed., T. W. Goodwin, Academic Press, London, 1965, pp. 489–532*)

chromoplasts are usually esterified with fatty acids whereas the xanthophylls of chloroplasts usually have their hydroxyls free. For instance, in the fruits of *Physalis*, zeaxanthin occurs as the dipalmitate. A detailed account of the carotenoids of flowers, fruits, and roots may be found in Karrer and Jücker (1951) and Goodwin (1952).

I.6.iii. STRUCTURE OF THE CHROMOPLAST

Chromoplasts have an extremely varied morphology (see the frontispiece). They tend to be roughly the same size as chloroplasts: this is not surprising since they are often derived from chloroplasts (see XIV.5.ii). They may, as in fruit of *Solanum dulcamara* or *Physalis*, have the same, roughly ellipsoidal, shape as a chloroplast, or they may be spindle-shaped, as in *Sorbus* berries or rose hips: sometimes the spindle may be bifurcated so that the plastid has three sharp points. Many chromoplasts have an irregular, amoeboidal shape[237]: in the epidermis of flower petals of *Lilium tigrinum*, or the orange-red berries of *Convallaria majalis*, the amoeboid chromoplasts are long (∼ 10 μ) and thin, and appear, under the light microscope, to contain up to seventeen or so large globules of pigment, fairly widely separated, and one to three vacuoles; in the lower epidermis of petals of *Tagetes patula* the chromoplasts are more rounded and less

amoeboid. In some plants the chromoplasts may have a highly crystalline appearance, either long needle-shaped crystals being observed as
in the tomato, or a mixture of needle-shaped crystals, flat polygonal
plates, and spiral bodies built round starch grains, as in the carrot.
The crystals in the carrot can be up to 40 μ long[14]. Two types of
chromoplast ultrastructure have so far been recognized with the electron microscope. In the simpler kind (Fig. I.41) found in petals of

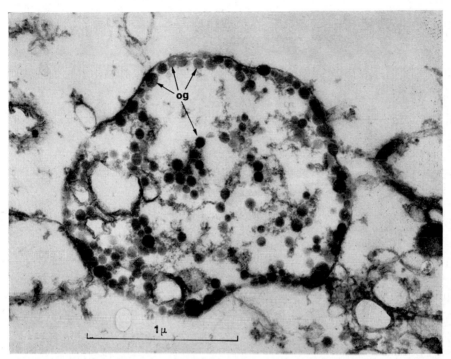

FIG. I.41. *Chromoplast of yellow petal of* Spartium junceum (*Nougarède, A., unpublished*)
OsO_4 *fixation.* og—*osmiophilic globules*

Ranunculus repens, Chrysanthemum segetum, Aloe plicatilis, or *Spartium junceum,*
and which may be typical of carotenoid-containing flower petals, the
only observable structures within the plastids are homogeneous osmiophilic globuli, which are up to 1500 Å in diameter[63, 33, 140, 195]. The
carotenoids are presumably located in these globuli. In the more
complicated type, found in fruit of *Capsicum annuum* and *Solanum capsicastrum*[64, 238, 130] the plastid contains a large number of fibres, mostly
150–450 Å in diameter. Frey-Wyssling and Kreutzer (1958b) suggest
that these fibres contain carotenoid complexed with protein. Fig. I.42
shows these fibres in a chromoplast of red *Capsicum annuum* fruit.
Occasionally a fibre may be seen to have, either at the end, or some-

where in the middle, a swelling up to about 1000 Å in diameter (see XIV for possible relation of these to osmiophilic globules). On close examination (Fig. I.42) the fibres appear to have faint longitudinal striations. The length of the fibres is somewhat difficult to ascertain since they are rather closely packed together, and also they are liable to pass out of the section. However, fibres can be seen with lengths up to about 1·4 µ (14,000 Å). The chromoplast may contain large numbers of osmiophilic globules as well as the fibres. It seems likely that the carotenoids are present both in the fibres and in the globules.

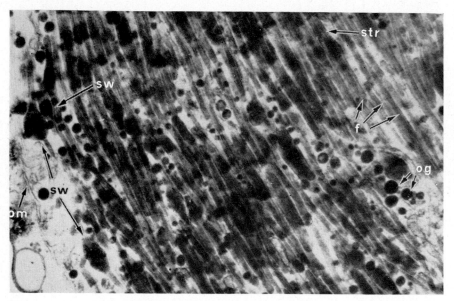

FIG. I.42. *Part of Chromoplast of red fruit of* Capsicum annuum (*Kirk, J. T. O. and Juniper, B. E., 1964, unpublished*). *Glutaraldehyde–OsO₄ fixation. f—fibres. og—osmiophilic globules. sw—swellings on fibres. str—striations along fibres. om—outer membrane of chromoplast*

Not all fruit chromoplasts contain these fibrous structures: as well as the red *Capsicum* fruit, at least three other colour varieties of *Capsicum* exist—orange, yellow, and white—the chromoplasts of which have structures rather more of the flower petal type[130]. The orange fruit have only about 3 per cent of the carotenoid content of the red fruit, and the chromoplasts contain no fibres, but contain a large number of osmiophilic globules aggregated together in anything up to five clumps: these chromoplasts also contain what appear in section as long tubules, or double-membraned sheets, which may extend most of the way round the chromoplast. The yellow fruit have about the same carotenoid content as the orange fruit (although the carotenoid composition is different) and the chromoplasts have much the same structure as the orange chromoplasts (Fig. I.43). The white fruit contain no carotenoids at all: the plastids have no fibres, but do possess osmiophilic globules and the tubules or double-membraned sheets: however, the globules (which presumably contain unsaturated lipids other than

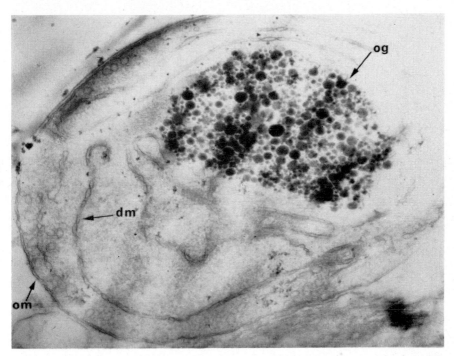

FIG. I.43. *Chromoplast of a yellow fruit of* Capsicum annuum (*Kirk, J. T. O. and Juniper, B. E., 1964, unpublished*). *Glutaraldehyde–OsO₄ fixation.* og—*osmiophilic globules.* om—*outer membrane.* dm—*double membraned structure*

carotenoids) are not aggregated together (Fig. I.44) as they are in the orange and yellow chromoplasts. Other fruit chromoplasts of the non-fibrous type are found in the navel orange: these chromoplasts are irregular in shape, contain many large osmiophilic globuli, some starch grains, and a small amount of membranous material[257]. Chromoplasts, like other plastids, are bounded by a double membrane (Fig. I.42).

The ultrastructure of the crystalline type of chromoplast, as found in the tomato or the carrot, remains to be elucidated. A type of plastid which may be regarded both as a chloroplast and a chromoplast has been observed in leaves of *Selaginella helvetica* which have turned red[68]; these plastids possess a large number of carotenoid-containing droplets, responsible for the red colour, and also have a normal system of chlorophyll-containing lamellae and grana. Also, red pigment (presumably

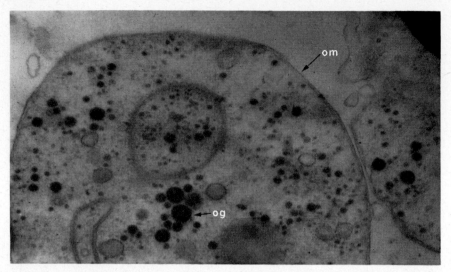

FIG. I.44. *Part of a plastid of a white fruit of* Capsicum annuum (*Kirk, J. T. O. and Juniper, B. E., 1964, unpublished*). *Glutaraldehyde–OsO₄ fixation. og—osmiophilic globules. om—outer membrane*

carotenoid) droplets appear in leaf chloroplasts of *Thuja ericoides* in the winter (see frontispiece).

I.6.iv. FUNCTIONS OF CHROMOPLASTS

No physiological function is known for any of the different types of chromoplast. It seems plausible that the main, and perhaps the only, function of fruit and flower chromoplasts is, by means of their bright colours, to attract animals. In the case of fruit, the useful consequences of this are that the animals, particularly birds, are likely to eat the fruit, and hence distribute the seed over a wide area. In the case of flowers, it is, no doubt, insects which are attracted and which, as a consequence, bring about cross-pollination.

It is more difficult to think of a function for the chromoplasts of roots, such as those of the carrot. There is no reason, in principle, why the accumulated carotenoids should not be used as a reserve product, as a source of carbon and energy. However, there does not appear to be any evidence that the carrot plant uses them in this way. It may be that these chromoplasts serve no useful purpose; that they represent an abnormal situation produced, perhaps as a result of a mutation in one of the genes concerned with carotenoid formation, which has been selected out and propagated by man. This idea is perhaps supported by the fact that the root of the wild carrot does not contain chromoplasts.

I.7. Other Plastid Types

There exist certain kinds of plastid which cannot conveniently be included in the classes dealt with so far.

In some angiosperms, plastids largely filled with oil may be seen. These oil-containing plastids are known as 'elaioplasts'[227]. They may often be found in the epidermal cells of plants of the monocotyledonous families *Liliaceae*, *Amaryllidaceae*, and *Orchidaceae*. It is not known whether they have any function. It may be that some of them, at least, are merely senescent chloroplasts[82].

Manuel (1936) has described what may be a different kind of lipid-accumulating plastid. In many cacti, particularly *Echinocereus procumbens*, she found plastids with one to five large lipid globules, often nearly completely filling the plastid. On various histochemical grounds, for instance the Liebermann reaction, she concluded that these globules consisted of esterified sterols, and for this reason referred to these plastids as 'sterinochloroplasts'. These 'sterinochloroplasts' were found in the epidermal and subepidermal layers. Since there is some degree of uncertainty about whether chloroplasts contain sterols (I.2.ii.b) it would be extremely interesting to know the true nature of the lipid globules in these cactus plastids. In this connection it is interesting that recent electron microscopical observations have shown cactus chloroplasts to be almost filled with osmiophilic globules[69]. The function of 'sterinochloroplasts' is not known.

In the epidermal cells of *Helleborus corsicus*, colourless plastid-like bodies containing large amounts of protein may be seen[92]. In the roots of the orchid, *Phajus wallichii*, plastids containing bundles of fine fibrils of what is thought to be protein have been observed[33]: in some places where the fibrils are closely aligned together striations can be seen running transversely across the bundles of fibrils, suggesting that the fibrils are composed of subunits. These 'proteoplasts' also contain starch grains, which is confirmatory evidence that the bodies are indeed plastids: they also contain a tubular structure, rather similar in appearance to the crystalline centre of an etioplast. Similar protein-containing bodies have been observed in seeds: for instance, Morton and Raison (1963) have described protein bodies, 0·5–20 μ in diameter in sections of wheat endosperm. These protein bodies appear to have an outer membrane, and to contain ribosomes and a reticular network. However, in the case of these organelles in endosperm it has not yet been demonstrated that they are plastids (e.g. by showing that they are derived from proplastids or other plastids, or that they form starch), and so it seems questionable whether a term such as 'proteoplast', which implies that they are a form of plastid, should be used. Until there is evidence that they are plastids, it might be better to refer to them just as 'protein bodies'. Schimper (1885) observed structures that he believed to be protein crystals in plastids from various plants (see frontispiece).

I.8. The Autonomy and Continuity of Plastids

The concept of the autonomy and continuity of plastids was, to a large extent, founded on the fact that, in the algae, chloroplasts can be seen to divide and to be transmitted to the daughter cells during cell division (see Guilliermond, 1941). For instance, Strasburger (1882; 1884) was able to follow the division of the single chloroplast in living *Spirogyra* during cell division. Very recently, Green (1964) has succeeded in recording, by microcinephotography, division of chloroplasts in the alga, *Nitella*: in the film itself many chloroplasts can be seen to divide, and in the published still pictures from the film a population of eight plastids is shown to increase by division until the progeny number eighteen. Convincing electron micrographs of algal chloroplasts in the course of division have also been obtained in recent years (see XIV.1.vi and Fig. XIV.8(b)).

In the bryophyte *Anthoceros*, the chloroplast is transmitted by division from cell to cell[88, 47].

In the higher plants, similarly, chloroplasts have been seen to divide. In the lycopod *Isoetes* as the leaf cells mature the number of chloroplasts per cell increases greatly: this increase takes place by division of the chloroplasts[240]. Amongst the angiosperms, chloroplast division has been observed in *Elodea canadensis*[88], and Lance (1958) has obtained an electron micrograph of a chloroplast apparently in the course of division in *Chrysanthemum segetum* (Fig. XIV.6). However, in these higher plants it is not mature chloroplasts which are transmitted at cell division: as Schimper demonstrated, in the meristematic cells, instead of chloroplasts, undifferentiated proplastids are present, and these divide and are transmitted from cell to cell at division. In *Isoetes* each meristematic cell contains a single, colourless plastid (proplastid) closely appressed to the nucleus[240]. This plastid divides, and the two daughter plastids move round to opposite sides of the nucleus. Nuclear division then occurs, followed by cell division, so that two daughter cells, each containing a single plastid, are produced.

A proplastid, apparently dividing, can be seen in an electron micrograph by Buvat (1958) of a meristematic cell of *Elodea canadensis*.

The other important kinds of differentiated plastid, the amyloplast, the chromoplast, and the etioplast are formed, like the chloroplast, only in maturing non-dividing cells, and so probably do not get the chance of being transmitted at cell division. However, like the chloroplast, these are all derived ultimately from proplastids.

From the foregoing evidence, then, it appears that in vegetatively reproducing cells of lower and higher plants the plastids (either in the form of chloroplasts or proplastids) multiply by division and are transmitted from cell to cell.

In sexual reproduction the situation is sometimes more complex. Amongst the algae, in the *Conjugatae*, it appears that only the chloroplasts of the female parent are transmitted to the new individual. For instance, in *Rhynchonema*, the zygote at first contains two chloroplasts, one contributed by each gamete. Soon one of these chloroplasts (that contributed by the male parent) begins to turn yellow and to shrink; eventually it breaks up into small pieces. During the subsequent cell divisions, only the chloroplast of the female parent is transmitted[36]. Similarly, in *Hyalotheca dissiliens*, in the ripening zygote one of the two chloroplasts (one from each gamete) atrophies and disappears[211]. However, although some chloroplasts may be lost in sexual reproduction, the chloroplasts of the new individual are still derived from those of at least one of the parents.

The cytological evidence, then, on the whole supports the theory of Schimper (1883; 1885) and Meyer (1883) that plastids do not arise *de novo*, but are formed by division of pre-existing plastids, and are transmitted from cell to cell during vegetative or sexual reproduction. However, a theory has recently been put forward that plastids may not always arise from pre-existing plastids. Bell and Mühlethaler (1962) observed, by means of electron microscopy, that during maturation of the egg cell of the fern *Pteridium aquilinum* the plastids and mitochondria underwent certain structural changes; they became somewhat distended and vacuolate, and irregular in outline. These authors interpret the changes as representing degeneration of these organelles. At about the same time complex blebs, or evaginations of the nuclear membrane, projecting into the cytoplasm, appeared. On the basis of examination of serial sections of one of these blebs, Bell and Mühlethaler (1964) concluded that it was somewhat similar in structure to a mitochondrion. However, more recently, Bell (1964) has given it as his opinion that the bleb is perhaps more like a plastid than a mitochondrion. On the basis of these studies, these workers have suggested (see, for example, Bell, 1963) that during maturation of the egg cell, a whole generation of organelles is eliminated, and a new one arises *de novo* from the nucleus; this takes place by the formation of evaginations from the nuclear membrane which become detached and develop into new plastids and mitochondria.

The question raised by this work, that is, whether plastids always arise from other plastids, or whether they are formed from the nucleus in the egg cell and from other plastids only during vegetative multiplication, is clearly of the most fundamental importance. Have Bell and

6—P.

Mühlethaler supplied us with good reasons for rejecting the classical theory that plastids never arise *de novo*? My own opinion is that they have not. The changes in the plastids of the egg cell, which Bell and Mühlethaler refer to as 'degeneration', could equally well represent an internal reorganization of the plastids in preparation for the rapid multiplication of plastids that will take place when the egg is fertilized and the embryo begins to develop. That is, the changes may be due to a 'dedifferentiation' from the chloroplast stage of development back to the proplastid stage. At every stage in the maturation of the egg cell (as seen, for instance, in the electron micrographs of Bell and Mühlethaler, 1962) there are bodies present which could reasonably be regarded as proplastids; that is, at no stage can it be said that the egg cell has lost its plastids. In this connection it is worthy of note that Menke and Fricke (1964) have studied maturation of the egg cell of another fern, *Dryopteris filix mas*, and have been unable to observe an elimination and *de novo* formation of plastids and mitochondria: both types of organelle were found to be present at all stages of development of the egg cell. Diers (1965) was also unable to observe degenerating mitochondria or plastids in the growing archegonium of the liverwort, *Sphaerocarpus donnellii*. With regard to the evaginations from the nuclear membrane, these have, in general, little or no internal structure. One such evagination was identified by Bell and Mühlethaler (1964) as a mitochondrion, or possibly a plastid[11], but this identification was based only on the presence of what appeared to be a short length of double membrane or a pair of small vesicles inside the evagination: this does not, I would suggest, provide a sufficient basis for regarding this evagination as being either a mitochondrion or a plastid.

It should be emphasized that these considerations do not disprove the theory of Bell and Mühlethaler. However, I believe that they do rob it of much of its plausibility. On the basis of the evidence available at the moment, then, I see no good reason for rejecting the view that plastids always arise from existing plastids, and are never formed *de novo*.

However, we must not deduce from this alone that plastids are autonomous bodies, replicating themselves quite independently of the nucleus and the rest of the cell. Indeed, the *cytological* continuity of plastids is entirely consistent with their being completely dependent on the nucleus: it could be, for instance, that all the information required for the formation of plastid materials was stored in the nucleus; that the plastid substance was synthesized under nuclear control. The division of a plastid could then represent a response to some kind of physical stress which built up as the plastid increased in size: the apparent absence of *de novo* formation of plastids could perhaps be explained if, for some reason, it is easier to add more material to an existing membranous structure than to start a completely new one. It must be understood, therefore, that the cytological continuity of the plastids is a necessary, but by no means a sufficient, condition for the theory that plastids are autonomous organelles which, at least in part, control their own formation. The evidence which, in addition to the cytological evidence, has led to this concept, has come from genetic studies, which have shown that plastids can inherit certain characteristics in a manner quite independent of nuclear inheritance. This evidence is dealt with in the next section of the book (Chapters II–IX).

REFERENCES

1. AKAZAWA, T., SAIO, K. & SUGIYAMA, N. (1965). *Biochem. Biophys. Res. Comm.* **20**, 114–119
2. ALBERTSSON, P. A. & LEYON, H. (1954). *Exp. Cell. Res.* **7**, 288
3. ALLEN, M. B., FRENCH, C. S. & BROWN, J. S. (1960). In *Comparative Biochemistry of Photoreactive Systems.* Ed. M. B. Allen, Academic Press, New York, pp. 33–52
4. ARNON, D. I. In *Symposium on Biochemistry of Chloroplasts (Aberystwyth, 1965).* Ed., T. W. Goodwin. Academic Press, London (in press)
5. ARNON, D. I., WHATLEY, F. R. & ALLEN, M. B. (1957). *Nature, Lond.* **180**, 182–185
6. BAILEY, J. L., THORNBER, J. P. & WHYBORN, A. G. In *Symposium on Biochemistry of Chloroplasts (Aberystwyth, 1965).* Ed., T. W. Goodwin. Academic Press, London (in press)
7. BAILEY, J. L., WHYBORN, A. G., GREENWOOD, A. D., LEECH, R. M. & WILLIAMS, J. P. (1963). *Biochem. J.* **88**, 27P
8. BASSHAM, J. A. & CALVIN, M. (1957). *The path of carbon in photosynthesis.* Prentice Hall Inc., New Jersey
9. BECK, W. A. (1937). *Plant Phys.* **12**, 885–886
10. BELL, P. R. (1963). *J. Linn. Soc.* **58**, 353–359
11. BELL, P. R. (1964). Paper presented at 10th Internat. Bot. Congr. Edinburgh
12. BELL, P. R. & MÜHLETHALER, K. (1962). *J. Ultrastruct. Res.* **7**, 452–466
13. BELL, P. R. & MÜHLETHALER, K. (1964). *J. Cell Biol.* **20**, 235–248
13a. BENDALL, D. S., GREGORY, R. P. F. & HILL, R. (1963). *Biochem. J.* **88**, 29P–30P
14. BEN-SHAUL, Y. & KLEIN, S. (1965). *Bot. Gaz.* **126**, 79–85
15. BEN-SHAUL, Y., SCHIFF, J. A. & EPSTEIN, H. T. (1964). *Plant Phys.* **39**, 231–240
16. BENSON, A. A. (1964). *Ann. Rev. Plant Phys.* **15**, 1–16
17. BENSON, A. A., DANIEL, H. & WISER, R. (1959). *Proc. Natl. Acad. Sci.* **45**, 1582–1587
18. BERKALOFF, C. (1961). *Compt. Rend. Acad. Sci.* **252**, 2747
19. BIGGINS, J. & PARK, R. B. (1961). *Bio-organic Chem. Quart. Rep.* UCRL-9900, 39–43
20. BIGGINS, J. & PARK, R. B. (1964). *Nature, Lond.* **203**, 425–426
20a. BIGGINS, J. & PARK, R. B. (1965). *Plant Phys.* **40**, 1109–1115
20b. BIRD, I. F. & STOCKING, C. R. (1964). *1st Meeting Fed. Europ. Biochem. Socs.* 56–57
21. BISHOP, N. I. (1959). *Proc. Natl. Acad. Sci.* **45**, 1696–1702
22. BOARDMAN, N. K. & ANDERSON, J. M. (1964). *Nature, Lond.* **203**, 166–167
23. BOARDMAN, N. K. & WILDMAN, S. G. (1962). *Biochim. Biophys. Acta.* **59**, 222–224
24. BOUCK, G. B. (1962). *J. Cell Biol.* **12**, 553–569

25. BOUCK, G. B. (1965). *J. Cell Biol.* **26**, 523–537
26. BRODY, M. & VATTER, A. E. (1959). *J. Biophys. Biochem. Cytol.* **5**, 289
27. BROWN, J. S. (1960). *Carneg. Inst. Wash. Yearbook.* **59**, 330
28. BROWN, J. S. (1963). *Photochem. & Photobiol.* **2**, 159–173
29. BROWN, J. S. & DURANTON, J. G. (1964). *Biochim. Biophys. Acta.* **79**, 209–211
30. BROWN, W. V. & JOHNSON, SR. C. (1962). *Am. J. Bot.* **49**, 110–115
31. BUCKE, C. & HALLAWAY, M. In *Symposium on Biochemistry of Chloroplasts* (*Aberystwyth*, 1965). Ed. T. W. Goodwin. Academic Press, London (in press)
31a. BUCKE, C., LEECH, R. M., HALLAWAY, M. & MORTON, R. A. (1966). *Biochim. Biophys. Acta.* **112**, 19–34
32. BUVAT, R. (1958). *Ann. des. Sci. Nat.* 11e *Ser.* (*Bot.*) **19**, 121–161
33. BUVAT, R. (1963). *Internat. Rev. Cytol.* **14**, 41–155
34. CAPORALI, L. (1959). *Ann. des. Sci. Nat.* 11e *Ser.* (*Bot.*). **20**, 215–247
34a. CEDERSTRAND, C. N., RABINOWITCH, E. & GOVINDJEE. (1966). *Biochim. Biophys. Acta.* (in press)
35. CHAPMAN, V. J. (1941). *An introduction to the study of algae.* Cambridge University Press, Cambridge
36. CHMIELEVSKY, V. (1890). *Bot. Zeit.* **48**, 773–780
37. COMAR, C. L. (1942). *Bot. Gaz.* **104**, 122–127
38. CRAWLEY, J. C. W. (1964). *Exp. Cell. Res.* **35**, 497–506
39. CRIDDLE, R. S. In *Symposium on Biochemistry of Chloroplasts* (*Aberystwyth*, 1965). Ed., T. W. Goodwin, Academic Press, London (in press)
40. CRIDDLE, R. S. & PARK, L. (1964). *Biochem. Biophys. Res. Commun.* **17**, 74–79
41. CROMBIE, W. M. (1958). *J. Exp. Bot.* **9**, 254–261
42. CURL, A. L. (1962). *J. Agric. Food Chem.* **10**, 504–509
43. CURL, A. L. (1964). *J. Agric. Food. Chem.* **12**, 522–524
44. DAM, H. (1942). *Adv. Enz.* **2**, 285–324
44a. DAS, B. C., LOURASMAA, M., TENDILLE, C. & LEDERER, E. (1965). *Biochim. Biophys. Res. Commun.* **21**, 318–322
45. DAVENPORT, H. E. (1952). *Nature, Lond.* **170**, 1112–1113
46. DAVENPORT, H. E. (1963). *Nature, Lond.* **199**, 151–153
46a. DAVENPORT, H. E. & HILL, R. (1952). *Proc. Roy. Soc. B.* **139**, 327–345
46b. DAVIES, W. H., MERCER, E. I. & GOODWIN, T. W. (1965). *Phytochem.* **4**, 741–749
47. DAVIS, B. M. (1899). *Bot. Gaz.* **28**, 89–109
48. DEBUCH, H. (1961). *Z. Naturforsch.* **16b**, 246–248
49. VAN DEENEN, L. L. M. & HAVERKATE, F. In *Symposium on Biochemistry of Chloroplasts* (*Aberystwyth*, 1965). Ed. T. W. Goodwin. Academic Press, London (in press)
49a. DIERS, L. (1965). *Planta.* **66**, 165–190
50. DILLEY, R. A. & CRANE, F. L. (1963). *Plant Phys.* **38**, 452–456
50a. DOI, A., DOI, K. & NIKUNI, Z. (1966). *Biochim. Biophys. Acta.* **113**, 312–320
51. DRAWERT, H. & MIX, M. (1961). *Planta.* **56**, 648–665
52. DRUM, R. W. & PANKRATZ, H. S. (1964). *Am. J. Bot.* **51**, 405–418
53. DUNPHY, P. J., WHITTLE, R. J. & PENNOCK, J. F. In *Symposium on Biochemistry of Chloroplasts* (*Aberystwyth*, 1965). Ed. T. W. Goodwin. Academic Press, London (in press)
54. EGGMAN, L., SINGER, S. J. & WILDMAN, S. G. (1953). *J. Biol. Chem.* **205**, 969
55. EPSTEIN, H. T. & SCHIFF, J. A. (1961). *J. Protozool.* **8**, 427–432
56. ERIKSSON, G., KAHN, A., WALLES, B. & VON WETTSTEIN, D. (1961). *Ber. Deut. Bot. Ges.* **74**, 221–232
57. ERIKSSON-QUENSEL, I. (1938). *Biochem. J.* **32**, 585–589
58. VON EULER, H. & HELLSTROM, A. (1929). *Z. Phys. Chem.* **183**, 177–183

59. FALUDI-DANIEL, A., NAGY, A., GYURJAN, I. & FALUDI, B. (1965). *Photochem. & Photobiol.* **4**, 359–367

60. FERRARI, R. A. & BENSON, A. A. (1961). *Arch. Biochem. Biophys.* **93**, 185–192

61. FRENCH, C. S. In *Symposium on Biochemistry of Chloroplasts (Aberystwyth, 1965)*. Ed., T. W. Goodwin. Academic Press, London (in press)

61a. FRY, K. T. & SAN PIETRO, A. (1963). In *Photosynthetic Mechanisms of Green Plants*, NAS-NRC Publ. No. 1145. Washington, pp. 252–261

62. FREY-WYSSLING, A. (1953). *Submicroscopic morphology of cytoplasm.* 2nd ed. Elsevier, Houston, Texas

63. FREY-WYSSLING, A. & KREUTZER, E. (1958a). *Planta.* **51**, 104–114

64. FREY-WYSSLING, A. & KREUTZER, E. (1958b). *J. Ultrastruct. Res.* **1**, 397–411

65. GAFFRON, H. (1960). Chapter 4 in *Plant Physiology* Vol. IB. Ed., F. C. Steward. Academic Press, New York, pp. 3–277

66. GANTT, E. & ARNOTT, H. J. (1963). *J. Cell Biol.* **19**, 446–448

67. GANTT, E. & CONTI, S. F. (1965). *J. Cell Biol.* **26**, 365–381

68. GEROLA, F. M., DASSU, G. & CRISTOFORI, F. (1960). *Atti. accad. nazl. Lincei Classe sci. fis. mat. e nat.* (7) **28**, 73–76

69. GENEROSOVA, I. P. (1965). *Chloroplast Ultrastructure.* Academy of Sciences, S.S.S.R. Moscow. Quoted by (6)

70. GIBBS, S. P. (1962a). *J. Ultrastruct. Res.* **7**, 418–435

71. GIBBS, S. P. (1962b). *J. Ultrastruct. Res.* **7**, 247–261

72. GIBBS, S. P. (1962c). *J. Cell Biol.* **14**, 433–444

73. GIBBS, S. P. (1962d). *J. Cell Biol.* **15**, 343–361

74. GIBBS, S. P. (1962e). *J. Ultrastruct. Res.* **7**, 262–272

75. GODNEV, T. H. & OSSIPOVA, O. P. (1947). *Dokl. Akad. Nauk. S.S.S.R.* **57**, 161. Quoted by (59)

76. GOEDHEER, J. C. In *Symposium on Biochemistry of Chloroplasts (Aberystwyth, 1965)*. Ed., T. W. Goodwin. Academic Press, London (in press)

77. GOODWIN, T. W. (1952). *The comparative biochemistry of the carotenoids.* Chapman & Hall, London

78. GOODWIN, T. W. & PHAGPOLNGARM, S. (1960). *Biochem. J.* **76**, 197–199

79. GRANICK, S. (1938). *Am. J. Bot.* **25**, 558–561

80. GRANICK, S. (1949). *J. Biol. Chem.* **170**, 505

81. GRANICK, S. (1961a). *Proc. 5th Internat. Congr. Biochem. VI*, 176–186

82. GRANICK, S. (1961b). In *The Cell*. II. Eds., J. Brachet & A. E. Mirsky. Academic Press, New York, pp. 489–602

83. GRANICK, S. & PORTER, K. R. (1947). *Am. J. Bot.* **34**, 545–550

84. GREEN, P. B. (1964). *Am. J. Bot.* **51**, 334–342

85. GREENWOOD, A. D. (1963). Paper presented at Royal Microscopical Society Symposium on Botanical Applications of Electron Microscopy, Oxford

86. GREENWOOD, A. D. (1964). *Abstracts, 10th Internat. Bot. Congr. Edinburgh*, 212–213

87. GREW, N. (1682). *The anatomy of plants, with an idea of a philosophical history of plants.* London. Quoted by (152)

88. GUILLIERMOND, L. (1941). *The cytoplasm of the plant cell.* Transl. by L. R. Atkinson. Chronica Botanica Co., Waltham, Mass.

89. GUNNING, B. E. S. (1965a). *J. Cell Biol.* **24**, 79–93

90. GUNNING, B. E. S. (1965b). *Protoplasma.* **55**, 111–130

91. HABERLANDT, G. (1914). *Physiological Plant Anatomy.* Macmillan, New York

91a. HAQ, S. & HASSID, W. Z. (1965). *Plant Phys.* **40**, 591–594

92. HARTEL, O. & THALER, I. (1953). *Protoplasma* **42**, 417

92a. HASELKORN, R., FERNANDEZ-MORAN, H., KIERAS, F. J. & VAN BRUGGEN, E. F. J. (1965). *Science*, **150**, 1598–1601

93. HAVERKATE, F. & VAN DEENEN, L. L. M. (1965). *Biochim. Biophys. Acta.* **106**, 78–92

94. HAXO, F. T. & O'HEOCHA. C. (1960). In *Encycl. Plant Phys.* V.I. Ed., W. Ruhland, Springer-Verlag, Berlin, pp. 497–510

95. HEBER, U. (1957). *Ber. Deut. Bot. Ges.* **70**, 371–382

96. HEBER, U. (1960). *Z. Naturforsch.* **15b**, 100–109

97. HEBER, U., PON, N. G. & HEBER, M. (1963). *Plant Phys.* **38**, 355–360

98. HEBER, U. & TYSZKIEWICZ, E. (1962). *J. Exp. Bot.* **13**, 185–200

99. HEITZ, E. (1953). *Exp. Cell. Res.* **7**, 606–608

100. HEITZ, E. & MALY, R. (1953). *Z. Naturforsch.* **8b**, 243–249

101. HENNINGER, M. D., BARR, R., WOOD, P. M. & CRANE, F. L. (1965). *Plant Phys.* **40**, xxix

102. HENNINGER, M. D. & CRANE, F. L. (1963). *Biochemistry.* **2**, 1168–1171

103. HENNINGER, M. D., DILLEY, R. A. & CRANE, F. L. (1963). *Biochem. Biophys. Res. Commun.* **10**, 237–242

104. HESLOP-HARRISON, J. (1963). *Planta.* **60**, 243–260

104a. HILL, R. & BONNER, W. D. (1961). In *Light and Life.* Eds. W. D. McElroy & B. Glass. Johns Hopkins Press, Baltimore, pp. 424–435

105. HILL, R. & SCARISBRICK, R. (1951). *New Phytol.* **50**, 98

106. HILL, R. & WHITTINGHAM, C. P. (1957). *Photosynthesis.* 2nd ed. Methuen, London

107. HIRAYAMA, O. (1965). *J. Biochem.* **57**, 581–589

108. HODGE, A. J., McLEAN, J. D. & MERCER, F. V. (1955). *J. Biophys. Biochem. Cytol.* **1**, 605–614

109. HOHL, H. R. & HEPTON, A. (1965). *J. Ultrastruct. Res.* **12**, 542–546

110. HOLT, A. S. (1965). Chapter 1 in *Chemistry and Biochemistry of Plant Pigments.* Ed., T. W. Goodwin. Academic Press, London, pp. 3–28

111. HOVASSE, R. & JOYON, L. (1960). *Rev. Algol.* **5**, 66–83

112. INGEN-HOUSZ, J. (1779). *Experiments upon vegetables, discovering their great power of purifying common air in the sunshine and of injuring it in the shade and at night.* London. Quoted by (152)

113. ITOH, M., IZAWA, S. & SHIBATA, K. (1963). *Biochim. Biophys. Acta.* **66**, 319

114. JACOBI, G. & PERNER, E. (1961). *Flora* **150**, 209–226

115. JAGENDORF, A. T. (1955). *Plant Phys.* **30**, 138

116. JAGENDORF, A. T. & WILDMAN, S. G. (1954). *Plant Phys.* **29**, 270–279

117. JAMES, W. O. & DAS, V. R. (1957). *New Phytol.* **56**, 325–343

118. JAMES, W. O. & LEECH, R. M. (1960). *Endeavour* **19**, 108–114

119. JEFFREY, S. W. (1961). *Biochem. J.* **80**, 336–342

120. JUNIPER, B. E. & CLOWES, F. A. L. (1965). *Nature, Lond.* **208**, 864–865

121. KAHN, J. S. & BANNISTER, T. T. (1965). *Photochem. & Photobiol.* **4**, 27–32

122. KAHN, J. S. & CHANG, I. C. (1965). *Photochem. & Photobiol.* **4**, 733–738

123. KAHN, A. & VON WETTSTEIN, D. (1961). *J. Ultrastruct. Res.* **5**, 557–574

124. KAMEN, M. D. (1963). *Primary Processes in Photosynthesis.* Academic Press, New York

125. KARRER, P. & JÜCKER, E. (1951). *Carotenoids.* Elsevier, London

125a. KATOH, S. (1960). *Plant and Cell Physiol.* **1**, 91–98

125b. KATOH, S. & TAKAMIYA, A. (1963). In *Photosynthetic Mechanisms of Green Plants.* NAS-NRC Publ. No. 1145. Washington, pp. 262–272

126. KAWAMATU, S. (1963). *Cytologia.* **28**, 12–20

127. KAY, R. E. & PHINNEY, B. (1956). *Plant Phys.* **31**, 226–231

128. KEISTER, D. L., SAN PIETRO, A. & STOLZENBACH, F. E. (1960). *J. Biol. Chem.* **231**, 2989–2996

129. KIRK, J. T. O. (1963). *Biochim. Biophys. Acta.* **76**, 417–424

130. KIRK, J. T. O. & JUNIPER, B. E. (1965). In *Symposium on Biochemistry of Chloroplasts* (*Aberystwyth*, 1965). Ed., T. W. Goodwin. Academic Press, London (in press)

131. KOK, B. & HOCH, G. (1963). In *La Photosynthese*. Editions du Centre National de la Recherche Scientifique, Paris. pp. 93–105

132. KREUTZ, W. (1963a). *Z. Naturforsch.* **18b**, 567–571

133. KREUTZ, W. (1963b). *Z. Naturforsch.* **18b**, 1098–1104

134. KREUTZ, W. (1964). *Z. Naturforsch.* **19b**, 441–446

135. KREUTZ, W. (1965a). *Nature, Lond.* **206**, 1358–1359

136. KREUTZ, W. (1965b). In *Symposium on Biochemistry of Chloroplasts* (*Aberystwyth*, 1965). Ed., T. W. Goodwin. Academic Press, London (in press)

137. KREUTZ, W. & MENKE, W. (1962). *Z. Naturforsch.* **17b**, 675–683

137a. KREUTZ, W. & WEBER, P. (1966). *Naturwiss.* **53**, 11–14

138. KYLIN, H. (1910). *Z. Phys. Chem.* **69**, 169–239

139. LANCE, A. (1958). *Ann. des. Sci. Nat.* 11e *Serie* (*Bot.*). **19**, 165–202

140. LANCE-NOUGARÈDE, A. (1960). *Compt. rend. acad. sci.* **250**, 173–175

141. LEECH, R. M. (1964). *Biochim. Biophys. Acta.* **79**, 637–639

142. LEECH, R. M. In *Symposium on Biochemistry of Chloroplasts* (*Aberystwyth*, 1965). Ed., T. W. Goodwin. Academic Press, London (in press)

143. LEMBERG, R. (1928). *Justus Liebigs Ann. Chem.* **461**, 46–89

144. LEMBI, C. A. & LANG, N. J. (1965). *Ann. J. Bot.* **52**, 464–477

145. LEYON, H. (1953). *Exp. Cell. Res.* **4**, 371–382

146. LEYON, H. (1954a). *Exp. Cell. Res.* **6**, 497–505

147. LEYON, H. (1954b). *Exp. Cell. Res.* **7**, 265–273, 609–611

148. LEYON, H. & VON WETTSTEIN, D. (1954). *Z. Naturforsch.* **9b**, 471–475

149. LICHTENTHALER, H. K. & CALVIN, M. (1964). *Biochim. Biophys. Acta.* **79**, 30–40

150. LICHTENTHALER, H. K. & PARK, R. B. (1963). *Nature, Lond.* **198**, 1070–1072

151. LIEBICH, H. (1941). *Z. Bot.* **38**, 129–157

152. LOOMIS, W. E. (1960). In *Encycl. Plant Phys.* V.1. Ed., W. Ruhland. Springer-Verlag, Berlin, pp. 85–114

152a. LOSADA, M., RAMIREZ, J. M., PANEQUE, A. & DEL CAMPO, F. F. (1965). *Biochim. Biophys. Acta.* **109**, 85

153. LYTTLETON, J. W. & TS'O, P. O. P. (1958). *Arch. Biochem. Biophys.* **73**, 120–126

154. MACKINNEY, G. (1935). *J. Biol. Chem.* **111**, 75

155. MACKINNEY, G. & JENKINS, J. A. (1952). *Proc. Natl. Acad. Sci.* **38**, 48–52

156. MANTON, I. (1962). *J. Exp. Bot.* **13**, 325–333

157. MANTON, I. & LEEDALE, G. F. (1961). *J. Marine Biol. Assoc.* (U.K.) **41**, 519–526

158. MANUEL, J. (1936). *Rev. Gen. Bot.* **48**, 49–79

159. MASLOVA, T. G. (1958). *Botan. Journ.* **13**, 103 Quoted by (59)

160. McCARTY, R. E. & JAGENDORF, A. T. (1965) *Plant Phys.* **40**, 725–735

161. McHALE, J. T. (1965). *Am. J. Bot.* **52**, 630

162. McKENNA, M., HENNINGER, M. D. & CRANE, F. L. (1964). *Nature, Lond.* **203**, 524–525

163. MEEUSE, B. J. D. (1962). In *Physiology and Biochemistry of Algae*. Ed., R. A. Lewin. Academic Press, New York, pp. 289–313

164. MEGO, J. L. & JAGENDORF, A. T. (1961). *Biochim. Biophys. Acta.* **53**, 237–254

165. MENKE, W. (1938). *Z. Bot.* **32**, 273–295

166. MENKE, W. (1940). *Z. Phys. Chem.* **263**, 100–103

167. MENKE, W. (1960a). *Z. Naturforsch.* **15b**, 479–482

168. MENKE, W. (1960b). *Z. Naturforsch.* **15b**, 800–804

169. MENKE, W. (1961). *Z. Naturforsch.* **16b**, 334–336

170. MENKE, W. (1962). *Ann. Rev. Plant Phys.* **13**, 27–44

171.   MENKE, W. (1963). In *Photosynthesis Mechanisms in Green Plants*. Publication 1145. National Academy of Sciences—National Research Council, Washington, pp. 537–544

172.   MENKE, W. (1964). *Ber. Deut. Bot. Ges.* **77**, 340–354

173.   MENKE, W. (1965a). *Z. Naturforsch.* **20b**, 802–805

174.   MENKE, W. (1965b). In *Symposium on Biochemistry of Chloroplasts* (*Aberystwyth*, 1965). Ed., T. W. Goodwin. Academic Press, London (in press)

175.   MENKE, W. & FRICKE, B. (1964). *Z. Naturforsch.* **19b**, 520–524

176.   MENKE, W. & JACOB, E. (1942). *Z. Phys. Chem.* **272**, 227–231

177.   MERCER, F. V., BOGORAD, L. & MULLENS, R. (1962). *J. Cell Biol.* **13**, 393–403

178.   MERCER, F. V., HODGE, A. J., HOPE, A. B. & McLEAN, J. D. (1955). *Austr. J. Biol. Sci.* **8**, 1–18

179.   MERCER, E. I. & TREHARNE, K. J. In *Symposium on Biochemistry of Chloroplasts* (*Aberystwyth*, 1965). Ed., T. W. Goodwin. Academic Press, London (in press)

180.   MEYER, A. (1883). *Bot. Zeit.* **41**, 489–498, 505–514, 525–531

181.   MICHAELIS, P. (1958). *Planta* **51**, 600

182.   MICHEL-WOLWERZ, M. R., SIRONVAL, C. & GOEDHEER, J. C. (1965). *Biochim. Biophys. Acta.* **94**, 584–585

183.   MITRAKOS, K. (1960). *Protoplasma* **52**, 611

184.   MÖBIUS, M. (1920). *Ber. Deut. Bot. Ges.* **38**, 224

185.   VON MOHL, H. (1837). *Untersuchungen über die anatomischen Verhältnisse des Chlorophylls*. Diss., W. Michler. Univ. Tubingen. Quoted by (152).

186.   MORTON, R. K. & RAISON, J. K. (1963). *Nature, Lond.* **200**, 429–433

187.   MÜHLETHALER, K. (1955). *Int. Rev. Cytol.* **4**, 197–220.

188.   MÜHLETHALER, K. In *Symposium on Biochemistry of Chloroplasts* (*Aberystwyth*, 1965). Ed., T. W. Goodwin. Academic Press, London (in press)

189.   MÜHLETHALER, K. & FREY-WYSSLING, A. (1959). *J. Biophys. Biochem. Cytol.* **6**, 507–512

189a. MÜHLETHALER, K., MOOR, H. & SZARKOWSKI, J. W. (1965). *Planta* **67**, 305–323

190.   MULLER, H. R., STEERE, R. L. & ARNON, D. I. (unpublished). Quoted by D. I. Arnon in *Light and Life*. Eds., W. D. McElroy & B. Glass. Johns Hopkins Press, Baltimore, 1961, pp. 489–565

191.   NEMEC, B. (1900). *Ber. Deut. Bot. Ges.* **18**, 241–245

192.   NICHOLS, B. W. (1963). *Biochim. Biophys. Acta.* **70**, 417–422

193.   NICKEL, H. (1965). Quoted by (174)

194.   NOACK, R. (1927). *Biochem. Z.* **183**, 125

194a. NOBEL, P. S. & PACKER, L. (1965). *Plant Phys.* **40**, 633–640.

195.   NOUGARÈDE, A. (1964). *Compt. Rend. Acad. Sci.* **258**, 683–685.

196.   O'BRIEN, J. S. & BENSON, A. A. (1964). *J. Lipid Res.* **5**, 432–436

197.   O'CARRA, P. (1962). Doctoral Thesis, National University of Ireland. Quoted by (199)

198.   O'CARRA, P., O'hEOCHA, C. & CARROLL, D. M. (1964). *Biochemistry*, **3**, 1343–1350

198a. OGAWA, T., OBATA, F., & SHIBATA, K. (1966). *Biochim. Biophys. Acta.* **112**, 223–234

199.   O'hEOCHA, C. (1965a). In *Chemistry and Biochemistry of Plant Pigments*. Ed., T. W. Goodwin, Academic Press, London, pp. 175–196

200.   O'hEOCHA, C. (1965b). In *Symposium on Biochemistry of Chloroplasts* (*Aberystwyth*, 1965). Ed., T. W. Goodwin. Academic Press, London (in press)

201.   PACKER, L. In *Symposium on Biochemistry of Chloroplasts* (*Aberystwyth*, 1965). Ed., T. W. Goodwin. Academic Press, London (in press)

202.   PACKER, L. & MARCHANT, R. H. (1964). *J. Biol. Chem.* **239**, 2061–2069

203.   PACKER, L., SIEGENTHALER, P. & NOBEL, P. S. (1965). *J. Cell Biol.* **26**, 593–599

203a. PARK, R. B. (1965). *J. Cell Biol.* **27**, 151–161
204. PARK, R. B. & BIGGINS, J. (1964). *Science* **144**, 1009–1011
205. PARK, R. B. & PON, N. G. (1961). *J. Mol. Biol.* **3**, 1–10.
206. PARK, R. B. & PON, N. G. (1963). *J. Mol. Biol.* **6**, 105–114
207. PARKE, M., MANTON, I. & CLARKE, B. (1958). *J. Marine Biol. Assoc.* (U.K.) **37**, 209–228
208. PARKE, M., MANTON, I. & CLARKE, B. (1959). *J. Marine Biol. Assoc.* (U.K.) **38**, 169–188
209. PAOLILLO, D. J. (1962). *Am. J. Bot.* **49**, 590–598
209a. PERINI, F., KAMEN, M. D., & SCHIFF, J. A. (1964). *Biochim. Biophys. Acta.* **88**, 74–90
210. PERNER, E. (1965). *Planta* **66**, 44–64
211. POTTHOF, H. (1927). *Planta* **4**, 261–283
211a. PRICE, W. C., MARTINEZ, A. P. & WARMKE, H. E. (1966). *J. Ultrastruct. Res.* **14**, 618–621
211b. RABINOWITCH, E. *Photosynthesis and related Processes.* I (1945), II.1 (1951), II.2 (1956). Interscience Publishers, New York
211c. RAMIREZ, J. M., DEL CAMPO, F. F., PANEQUE, A. & LOSADA, M. (1966). *Biochim. Biophys. Acta.* **118**, 58–71.
211d. REES, M. W. Quoted by (92a)
212. ROBERTSON, J. D. (1959). *Biochem. Soc. Symp.* No. **16**, 3
213. ROSEN, W. G. & SIEGESMUND, K. A. (1961). *J. Biophys. Biochem. Cytol.* **9**, 910–914
214. ROSENBERG, A. (1963). *Biochemistry* **2**, 1148–1154
215. ROSENBERG, A., PECKER, M. & MOSCHIDES, E. (1965). *Biochemistry,* **4**, 680–685
216. VON SACHS, J. (1887). *Lectures on the Physiology of Plants.* Transl. by H. Marshall Ward. Clarendon Press, Oxford
217. SAGER, R. & PALADE, G. E. (1957). *J. Biophys. Biochem. Cytol.* **3**, 463–488
218. SAN PIETRO, A. & LANG, H. M. (1958). *J. Biol. Chem.* **231**, 211–229
219. SASTRY, M. C. & KATES, M. (1964). *Biochemistry.* **3**, 1280–1287
220. SAUER, K. & CALVIN, M. (1962). *J. Mol. Biol.* **4**, 451–466
221. SCHIMPER, A. F. W. (1883). *Bot. Zeit.* **41**, 105–112, 121–131, 137–146, 153–162
222. SCHIMPER, A. F. W. (1885). *Jahrb. f. wiss. Bot.* **16**, 1–247
223. SEYBOLD, A. & EGLE, K. (1938a). *Planta* **28**, 87–123
224. SEYBOLD, A. & EGLE, K. (1938b). *Planta* **29**, 114–118, 119–128
225. SEYBOLD, A. & EGLE, K. (1938c). *Jahrb. f. wiss. Bot.* **86**, 50–60
226. SEYBOLD, A. & EGLE, K. (1939). *Botan. Arch.* **40**, 560
227. SHARP, L. W. (1934). *Introduction to Cytology.* McGraw-Hill Book Company Inc., New York
228. SHIBATA, K. (1957). *J. Biochem.* **44**, 147–173
229. SHIBATA, K. (unpublished). Quoted by C. S. French. *Encycl. Plant Phys.* V.1. Ed., W. Ruhland. Springer-Verlag, Berlin, pp. 252–297
229a. SHIBUYA, I. & MARUO, B. (1965). *Nature, Lond.* **207**, 1096–1097
230. SHIN, M., TAGAWA, K. & ARNON, D. I. (1963). *Biochem. Z.* **338**, 84–96
231. SMILLIE, R. M. (1956). *Austr. J. Biol. Sci.* **9**, 339–346
232. SMILLIE, R. M. (1960). *Nature, Lond.* **187**, 1024–1025
233. SMILLIE, R. M. (1963). *Can. J. Bot.* **41**, 123–154
234. SMILLIE, R. M. & FULLER, R. C. (1959). *Plant Phys.* **34**, 651
235. SMITH, J. H. C. & BENITEZ, A. (1955). In *Modern Methods of Plant Analysis* IV. Eds., K. Paech & M. V. Tracey. Springer-Verlag, Berlin, pp. 143–196
236. SMITH, J. H. C. & FRENCH, C. S. (1963). *Ann. Rev. Plant Phys.* **14**, 181–224
237. STEFFEN, K. (1964). *Planta* **60**, 506–522
238. STEFFEN, K. & WALTER, F. (1958). *Planta* **50**, 640–670

239. STEINMANN, E. (1952). *Exp. Cell. Res.* **3**, 367
240. STEWART, W. N. (1948). *Bot. Gaz.* **110**, 281–300
241. STEVENSON, J., HEMMING, F. W. & MORTON, R. A. (1963). *Biochem. J.* **88**, 52–56
242. STILLER, M. (1962). *Ann. Rev. Plant Phys.* **13**, 151–170
243. STOCKING, C. R. (1959). *Plant Phys.* **34**, 56–61
244. STOCKING, C. R. & ONGUN, A. (1962). *Am. J. Bot.* **49**, 284–290
245. STRAIN, H. H. (1938). *Plant Phys.* **13**, 413–418
246. STRAIN, H. H. (1958). *Chloroplast pigments and chromatographic analysis.* Pennsylvania State University Press, Pennsylvania.
247. STRASBURGER, E. (1882). *Arch. f. Mikr. Anat.* **21**, 476–590. Quoted by (88)
248. STRASBURGER, E. (1884). *Das botanische Praktikum.* 1. Aufl. Jena. Quoted by (88)
249. STRAUS, W. (1954). *Exp. Cell. Res.* **6**, 392–402
250. STRAUS, W. (1956). *Exp. Cell. Res.* **11**, 289–296
251. STRUGGER, S. & KRIGER, L. (1960). *Protoplasma* **52**, 230–246
252. SUN, C. N. (1961). *Am. J. Bot.* **48**, 311–315
253. SZARKOWSKI, J. W. & GOLASZEWSKI, T. (1961). *Naturwiss.* **48**, 457
253a. TAGAWA, T. & ARNON, D. I. (1962). *Nature, Lond.* **195**, 537–543
254. THOMAS, J. B. (1960). In *Encycl. Plant Phys.* V.1. Ed., W. Ruhland. Springer-Verlag, Berlin
255. THOMAS, J. B. & BARTELS, C. T. In *Symposium on Biochemistry of Chloroplasts* (*Aberystwyth*, 1965). Ed., T. W. Goodwin. Academic Press, London (in press)
256. THOMAS, J. B., KLEINEN HAMMANS, J. W. & ARNOLDS, W. J. (1965). *Biochim. Biophys. Acta.* **102**, 324–332
257. THOMPSON, W. W. (1965). *Am. J. Bot.* **52**, 622
258. THORNBER, J. P., RIDLEY, S. M. & BAILEY, J. L. In *Symposium on Biochemistry of Chloroplasts* (*Aberystwyth*, 1965). Ed., T. W. Goodwin. Academic Press, London (in press)
259. THRELFALL, D. R. & GOODWIN, T. W. (1964). *Biochem. J.* **90**, 40P
260. THRELFALL, D. R., GRIFFITHS, W. T. & GOODWIN, T. W. (1965). *Biochim. Biophys. Acta.* **102**, 614–618
261. TREBST, A. V., TSUJIMOTO, H. Y. & ARNON, D. I. (1958). *Nature, Lond.* **182**, 351–355
262. TROWN, P. W. (1965). *Biochemistry* **4**, 908–918
263. VIRGIN, H. I., KAHN, A. & VON WETTSTEIN, D. (1963). *Photochem. & Photobiol.* **2**, 83–91
264. WALLACE, J. W. & NEWMAN, D. W. (1965). *Phytochem.* **4**, 43–47
265. WARBURG, O. (1949). *Heavy Metal prosthetic Groups and enzyme action.* Oxford University Press, Oxford
266. WEHRMEYER, W. (1964). *Planta* **63**, 13–30
267. WEIER, T. E. & BENSON, A. A. In *Symposium on Biochemistry of Chloroplasts* (*Aberystwyth*, 1965). Ed., T. W. Goodwin. Academic Press, London (in press)
268. WEIER, T. E., ENGELBRECHT, A. H. P., HARRISON, A. & RISLEY, E. B. (1965). *J. Ultrastruct. Res.* **3**, 92–111
269. WEIER, T. E. & THOMPSON, W. W. (1962a). *Am. J. Bot.* **49**, 807–820
270. WEIER, T. E. & THOMSON, W. W. (1962b). *J. Cell Biol.* **13**, 89–108
271. WEIER, T. E., STOCKING, C. R., THOMSON, W. W. & DREVER, H. (1963). *J. Ultrastruct. Res.* **8**, 122–143
272. WELLBURN, A. R. & HEMMING, F. W. In *Symposium on Biochemistry of Chloroplasts* (*Aberystwyth*, 1965). Ed., T. W. Goodwin. Academic Press, London (in press)
273. VON WETTSTEIN, D. (1959a). *Brookhaven Symp. in Biol.* **11**, 138–159
274. VON WETTSTEIN, D. (1959b). In *Developmental Cytology.* Ed., D. Rudnick. Ronald Press, New York, pp. 123–160

275. VON WETTSTEIN, D. (1961). *Can. J. Bot.* **39**, 1537–1546
276. WHALEY, W. G., MOLLENHAUER, H. H. & LEECH, J. H. (1960). *Am. J. Bot.* **47**, 401–419
277. WILSENACH, R. (1963). *J. Cell Biol.* **18**, 419–428
278. WILSTÄTTER, R. & STOLL, A. (1913). *Untersuchungen über das Chlorophyll.* Springer, Berlin
279. WINTERMANS, J. F. G. M. (1960). *Biochim. Biophys. Acta.* **44**, 49–54
280. WINTERMANS, J. F. G. M. (1963). In *La Photosynthese.* Editions du Centre National de la Recherche Scientifique, Paris, pp. 381–385
281. WITT, H. T., MÜLLER, A. & RUMBERG, B. (1963). In *La Photosynthese.* Editions du Centre National de la Recherche Scientifique, Paris, pp. 43–73
282. WITT, H. T., RUMBERG, B., SCHMIDT-MENDE, P., SIGGEL, U., SKERRA, B., VATER, J. & WEIKARD, J. (1965). *Angew. Chem.* (English edition) **4**, 799–819
283. WOLF, F. T. (1963). *Plant Phys.* **38**, 649–652
284. WOLF, F. T., CONIGLIO, J. G. & DAVIS, J. T. (1962). *Plant Phys.* **37**, 83–85
285. WOLF, F. T., CONIGLIO, J. G. & BRIDGES, R. B. In *Symposium on Biochemistry of Chloroplasts* (*Aberystwyth*, 1965). Ed., T. W. Goodwin. Academic Press, London (in press)
285a. WOLKEN, J. J. & GROSS, J. A. (1963). *J. Protozool.* **10**, 189–195
286. WOODING, F. B. P. & NORTHCOTE, D. H. (1965). *Am. J. Bot.* **52**, 526–531
286a. ZANETTI, G. & FORTI, G. (1966). *J. Biol. Chem.* **241**, 279–285
287. ZILL, L. P. & HARMON, E. A. (1962). *Biochim. Biophys. Acta.* **57**, 573–583
288. ZURZYCKI, J. In *Symposium on Biochemistry of Chloroplasts* (*Aberystwyth*, 1965). Ed., T. W. Goodwin. Academic Press, London (in press)

CHAPTER II

Plastids and Variegation

II.1. Introduction

ALMOST everything we know about plastid genetics has come from studying variegation in seed bearing plants. Hence it is very difficult, and certainly most unsatisfactory, to talk about plastid genetics without at the same time talking about variegated plants. Clearly then we must begin by defining what these are, and how best we can classify them.

II.2. Definition of Variegated Plants

Any plant which develops patches of different colours in the vegetative parts may be said to be variegated. Within this definition, the immense variety of variegated plants that we find in our botanic and pleasure gardens, as well as the variety of ornamental plants that we take into our homes, together form a very heterogeneous group. Many of these have never been studied at all, and others have received only superficial attention. But what of the few that we do know something about? Among these we find some variegations which are to be immediately discarded from further discussion because the variegation is not inheritable. These include variegations caused by infectious diseases, particularly virus diseases as found in *Abutilon striatum*, and variegations caused by the environment as, for instance, soil mineral deficiency (see Chapter XV for an account of the effects of nutritional deficiencies on plastid growth). More often the variegation is inherited, and it is this kind that we must now consider.

Among inheritable variegations are red leaf markings such as are found in a variety of forms of *Coleus* and the common white clover. These markings are due to variegation in the anthocyanin pigments and have nothing to do with the plastids. They must therefore also be discarded from our further consideration. In short, we are interested in plants which may be defined as variegated because they differ from related individuals, races or species in having a non-uniform development of chlorophyll or related pigments as between plastids, cells or tissues of their leaves, bracts or fruits under normal conditions of nutrition, temperature, and illumination.

II.3. False Variegation

The variegation of many plants, which appears at first sight to be caused by the non-uniform development of chlorophyll, in fact turns out to be due to special features of the leaf cells and tissues producing a false variegation (Fig. II.1).

FIG. II.1. *Single leaves illustrating false variegations from four unrelated species of flowering plants. Left to right:* Lamium maculatum, Zebrina pendula, Pulmonaria saccharatum, *and* Pilea cadierei

II.3.i. SUB-EPIDERMAL BLISTER FORMATIONS

The frequently grown herbs, *Pulmonaria saccharatum, Lamium maculatum, Begonia maculata,* and a number of others, all have air blisters beneath the upper epidermis of their leaves producing greyish-white markings against the otherwise green background. The houseplant *Pilea cadierei* normally has air blisters too, but a sport with no air blisters has arisen in the Oxford botanic garden (Burras, personal communication). Four different forms have been recognized in *Cyclamen persicum*[9, 10]. Each form is controlled by a separate allele of a multiple allelic series. The alleles determine whether the air pockets are peripheral (Z_p), medial (Z_m), basal (z), or completely absent (Z_v). In combination with one another the alleles exhibit the following order of dominance: $Z_p > Z_v > Z_m > z$.

II.3.ii. MODIFIED EPIDERMAL STRUCTURE

The false variegation in *Collinsia bicolor* is not due to a chlorophyll character, but to the structure of the epidermis which, according to Hiorth (1930, 1931), affects the total reflection of the light. If the epidermis is removed the leaf area beneath is uniformly green. It is represented by a number of forms, each controlled by a different allele of a multiple allelic series as follows:

F^f The cotyledons have white veins and no spots. The leaves have large white spots scattered over the surface, the veins are not white.

F^z The cotyledons have white veins and no spots. The leaves have white veins except for the green midrib, there are no spots.

F^a The cotyledons have white veins and no spots. The leaves are wholly green.

F^s The cotyledons are covered in numerous small white spots, the veins are not white. The first leaves have several white spots but later leaves are mostly without spots, the veins are not white.

F^p The cotyledons and leaves are both variegated with several little white spots, their veins are not white.

f^o The homozygous recessive. The cotyledons and leaves are completely green.

Unlike the cyclamen, the unmarked form of *Collinsia* is recessive to all others. Moreover, the other alleles are not dominant to one another, instead, in some combinations, the phenotypes of the two alleles of a heterozygote can be expressed together. For example, the combination F^sF^f produces plants in which the cotyledons have both white veins and white spots; the leaves too are spotted.

II.3.iii. DISORGANIZATION OF PALISADE MESOPHYLL CELLS

The best known leaf variegations, which are clearly false, are the polymorphic V-shaped leaf markings found in the common white clover,

Trifolium repens, and in other related species[2, 3, 4]. Like *Collinsia* and *Cyclamen*, the many forms are controlled by the different alleles of a multiple allelic series. In heterozygotes some alleles are dominant in certain combinations, but with other combinations the phenotypes of both alleles are expressed together; the individual phenotypes have been described often enough and need not be repeated here. The manner in which the markings are achieved is not entirely clear, except that the development of the palisade mesophyll cells appears to be disorganized in localized regions of the leaf, as determined by the geno-typic constitution. According to Davies (1963) the paler areas of the patterns are due to the palisade cells being smaller, shorter and more irregularly shaped, and with more intercellular spaces than the adjacent cells. Williams (1964), on the other hand, is of the opinion that the marks are due to a special group of palisade cells in which the plastids are either absent, or else present in low concentration.

Other examples of false variegation are described by Hara (1957).

II.4. Non Cell Lineage Variegation

Let us now look at the truly variegated plants. We find that we still have a very heterogeneous assortment which must be split up into smaller and more homogeneous groupings. The most striking difference among them is that in some, the contrasting areas follow cell lineages. By this is meant that if, for example, the variegated leaf consists of a white area on an otherwise normal green background, then all the cells comprising the white area have a common cell origin, each cell being a descendant by successive cell divisions of the initial cell in which the change from green to white first took place. The remaining variegated plants are not of this kind. In these the contrasting coloured areas do not show any relationship to the pattern of leaf cell division. The pre-sence of a cell lineage pattern is highly indicative of a mutation, although the possibility of such an effect being due to a physiological change cannot be entirely ruled out in some cases. A non cell lineage pattern, on the other hand, is definitely not due to mutation for this would necessitate a sudden genetic change in thousands or millions of individual cells in highly localized areas and after cell division had ceased, an impossible assumption. Thus non cell lineage patterns are clearly due to physiological changes occurring during leaf development. The distinction between non cell lineage and cell lineage variegation is therefore not just a convenient morphological grouping, it reflects a really fundamental difference between the causes of variegation.

The non cell lineage variegations occur in a large and heterogeneous collection of plants which have been so little studied that it is scarcely possible at present to separate them on basic physiological differences, although this has been done for some members of the Araceae[1], but without any knowledge of the genetical control. The scheme adopted for breaking down this jumble into manageable groups is therefore based on more obvious morphological features; hence it must be regarded as a tentative classification to be improved upon in the light of future knowledge.

II.4.i. FIGURATIVE PATTERNS

In many different variegated species, races or individuals, every leaf produces an almost identical leaf marking under uniform environmental conditions, because the pattern of variegation is fixed by the physiological conditions which control plastid development and differentiation in the cells and tissues. Examples of these highly uniform and stable markings may be conveniently grouped together under the general term 'figurative patterns'. To give an indication of the varying types of figurative pattern the following subgroupings are suggested:

(1) *Marginal patterns or pseudochimeras*: The decorative leaves of the greenhouse plant *Acalypha wilkesiana* have narrow white margins, while the bracts have conspicuous white margins in the annual *Euphorbia marginata*. These white margins produce a pattern resembling, and often confused with, the white-margined leaves of many periclinal chimeras (for a discussion of the different types of chimera see Chapter VI). The white margins to the leaves of these pseudochimeras are, however, much more regular in outline and, unlike the true chimeras, they are absolutely stable in development owing to their dependence upon a physiological reaction with the plastids and not, as in true chimeras, upon the variable tissue contributions of a particular germ layer. Thus it is owing to the action of the same genotype that in the green part chlorophyll is formed and in the white part it is not; the plastid phenotype evidently varies in development and differentiation.

(2) *Diffuse spots*: Decorative plants are frequently chosen as much for the beauty of their leaves as for their flowers or fruit. Among such plants are those with yellowish-white spots or blotches on the leaves such as occur on the leaves of the widely grown Japanese spotted laurel, *Aucuba japonica*. Individual shrubs vary from those with only a few small spots on some leaves to others with spots so numerous or so large that they frequently run together. Sometimes the spots coalesce to such an extent that almost the whole leaf becomes yellow, especially as it ages. One form has a single and very large blotch in the centre of each leaf. These spots and blotches, large or small, clearly do not follow cell lineages. On the contrary, they tend to be roughly circular, as if each

was caused by an agent diffusing outwards in all directions from the spot centre. The appearance of these spots is therefore similar to ring spots caused by many virus infections and consequently the variegation is often thought to be symptomatic of an unknown virus disease. Experimental evidence does not support this view. Firstly, the character is seed transmitted since natural seed from a moderately spotted plant gives seedlings varying from weakly to intensely spotted. Secondly, the spotting character is not transmitted to a green plant either by sap inoculation or by grafting. Another garden plant that is often thought to be infected with a virus is the yellow spotted form of *Ligularia tussilaginea*, but Burras (personal communication) has found the spotting to be seed transmitted suggesting that in this example too the spotted character is probably inheritable.

(3) *Prominent veins*: Vein clearing is a common symptom of many virus infections[11], but examples are also known in which the veins become unusually prominent owing to an inheritable factor. The veins may become prominent either owing to the loss of chlorophyll from the interveinal spaces thereby highlighting the normal coloured area around the veins, or alternatively the tissue around the veins may change colour while the interveinal spaces remain normal.

(4) *Stripes and bands*: Monocotyledons frequently possess lanceolate leaves in which the veins run parallel to the longitudinal axis. Consequently any figurative pattern in which the veinal and interveinal areas differ in colour results in an overall striping. Alternatively colour differences may develop in zones at right angles to the longitudinal axis giving rise to transverse bands.

II.4.ii. GENERAL CHLOROSIS

In contrast to the regular markings found in figurative patterns, some other non cell lineage variegations are highly erratic. This happens when there is a localized, or more often widespread and irregular loss of chlorophyll during growth, so that affected parts of the plant develop a chlorotic appearance. In extreme cases the chlorosis behaves like a disease and gradually kills off the plant. The variegated appearance results from the contrast between affected and unaffected cells and tissues.

II.5. Cell Lineage Variegation

In contrast to non cell lineage variegations which have been little studied, many cell lineage variegations have been intensively investigated. Now a cell lineage variegation implies that the normal leaf colouration, say green, and the abnormal colouration, say white, differ from one another not only phenotypically, but genotypically. This is because the change has arisen by mutation (this view is questioned in III.3.iv). The type of mutation determines the character of the variegation it gives rise to and thereby forms a natural basis for classification. As we shall see, mutations may occur in the nucleus or in the plastids, they may occur singly or repeatedly in the life of an individual, and they may alter the plastid phenotype from green to white or from white to green. Moreover, in some plants, the final variegation may be due to one kind of behaviour being superimposed on another. On the basis of these differences in mutation, and its consequences, we are able to divide cell lineage variegations into a number of smaller groups, which we will now briefly refer to before discussing them in much greater detail in later chapters.

II.5.i. MOSAIC AND STRIPED PATTERNS

Among dicotyledons, many variegated plants possess an irregular distribution of green and white areas in their leaves which have been variously described as mosaiced, marbled, mottled, flecked or simply variegated. The most frequently used varietal names are variegata, marmorata, and maculata, but this does not mean that all plants bearing these names necessarily belong here. Among monocotyledons with lanceolate leaves the cell lineages run parallel to the longitudinal axis so that the leaves appear striped, and frequently the plants acquire the varietal name striata. The variegated leaves consist of normal green areas interspersed with white flecks and sectors or stripes of various shapes and sizes; within the white areas additional islands of green are commonly found. The green islands in some plants are few and large so that the variegation appears coarse; in other plants the islands are so numerous and so small that the white areas appear to be dusted with green. Between these extremes of coarse and fine variegation many intermediate types are found. When the white area of a leaf, or of a plant, is small in comparison to the green area, the leaf or plant is described as slightly, faintly, or weakly variegated. When the white area is large compared with the green area, the leaf or plant is said to be strongly or intensely variegated. The intermediate condition is moderately variegated. The two extreme conditions are when a genotypically variegated plant remains phenotypically green throughout development or, at the opposite end of the scale, when a germinating seedling is completely white and dies without further development.

Although the variegation of these plants is most probably due to a genetic instability of the nuclei or plastids, they are commonly regarded as pattern variegations. This is because, in spite of the clear distinction between them and figurative patterns, they are nevertheless, for the most part stable both in their development and in their true breeding. This stability stems from the fact that the mutations which produce the variegation are restricted to the leaves and do not seem to affect either the primary initial cells of the growing-point or the germ cells of the flowering shoots. Thus the breeding behaviour is not complicated by the mutations going on in the leaves during development. Consequently the breeding behaviour of these cell lineage variegated plants is similar to the non cell lineage variegated plants, and for this reason the two can be conveniently grouped together under the general heading of variegation caused by stable pattern genes, which we will discuss further in Chapter III.

II.5.ii. MUTABLE NUCLEAR GENES

All nuclear genes, detectable by crossing experiments, occasionally mutate from one allele to an alternative allele. The two or more alleles of a gene do not always mutate with the same low frequency; on the contrary, some genes have one or more alleles with a very high mutation frequency and so we call them mutable genes. The normal allele of a gene is necessary to produce a healthy plant whereas the alternative allele often has a detrimental effect; this is especially true of genes participating in plastid development in which the normal allele is generally dominant and its alternative alleles recessive in their effects. Among variegated plants a number of cases have been described in which, during development, a recessive allele repeatedly mutates to a dominant allele. Because these mutations are marked by the plastid phenotype changing from a chlorophyll deficient colouring back to green, they are called back-mutations. Conversely, repeated mutations changing the plastid phenotype from green to white can be called forward mutations.

The back-mutations form a homogeneous group of variegated plants which will be discussed in the first part of Chapter IV. On the other hand, variegated plants classified by mutation from green to white form a heterogeneous group which include chromosome abnormalities discussed in Chapter V, gene-induced plastid mutation discussed in Chapter VIII, and forward gene mutations. Examples of recurrent forward nuclear gene mutation are rare and in variegated plants the only known example is in a tomato which has been carefully investigated by Hagemann, whose work, which he calls somatic gene conversion, will be described in the second part of Chapter IV.

II.5.iii. CHROMOSOME ABNORMALITIES

Occasionally variegated plants have been observed, in which the few, or numerous but simple, cell lineages without sorting-out (the meaning of the term sorting-out is explained in Chapter VI) indicate a nuclear rather than a plastid mutation as the cause of variegation. The variegation of a few such plants has been shown to be due to the loss of chromosome fragments or even whole chromosomes. Proof that the variegation results from somatic loss of part of the chromosome complement is obtained by cytological analysis which distinguishes the type of variegation from the alternative possibility of nuclear gene mutation. The two alternative explanations cannot be distinguished simply on outward appearance; nonetheless, as we shall see when these plants are considered in Chapter V, the appearance coupled with breeding experiments can give a strong indication of a variegation caused by a chromosomal upset.

II.5.iv. CHIMERAS

A plant composed of tissues of two or more genetically distinct types of cell may be called a chimera. This definition, however, would encompass all our cell lineage types of variegation, because these plants all consist of at least two types of cell, cells produced before and cells produced after mutation. Instead, in this book, the term chimera will be restricted to the condition in which the two or more types of cell are separated into tissue layers in such a way as to give a characteristic structure. Two main types of chimera structure can be recognized: firstly, the sectorial chimera, in which the distinct tissues are arranged in cross sections just as in the sectors of a circle, and secondly, the periclinal chimera, in which the distinct tissues are arranged in concentric layers so that one tissue layer covers another just as a glove covers a hand.

We are concerned with variegated chimeras but, of course, plants can also be chimerical in respect of other differences such as may occur in cell structure, chromosome number or anthocyanin pigmentation for example. Among variegated plants, a typical sectorial chimera is predominantly green with a white sector running up one side of the shoot parallel to the axis. The leaves are green, white or also sectorial depending upon the relationship of their origin with the sectorially divided variegated shoot. A typical periclinal chimera produces leaves with a white skin over a green core or vice versa; superficially the leaves appear to have a white margin and a green centre, or else a green margin and a white centre respectively. A fuller description of these chimeras will be given in Chapter VI.

II.5.v. SORTING-OUT VARIEGATION

In higher plants there are usually many plastids within each cell, and since each plastid contains its own genetic material (see Chapter X for a discussion on the genetic material of the plastids), a mutation can occur in just one plastid at a time. Such a mutation gives rise to a mixed cell containing one mutant plastid among many unchanged plastids. During subsequent cell divisions both normal and mutant plastids multiply by division and pass randomly into the daughter cells. Consequently, starting with a mixed cell, some daughter cells will obtain normal plastids, some mutant plastids, and some will obtain both types of plastid just as in the mixed starting cell. This process of separation or segregation of two types of plastid has been termed sorting-out, and since there are usually many plastids in each cell, a complete sorting-out of the two types of plastid until there are no more mixed cells left in the meristematic tissue must inevitably take many cell divisions. The process of sorting-out is therefore gradual. When variegation first appears after plastid mutation the leaves are finely mosaiced or striped, but gradually the variegation becomes coarser in each successive leaf until finally the growing-point becomes pure green, or pure white or sometimes chimerical, when sorting-out is complete. Hence the process of sorting-out creates its own characteristic multiple cell lineage pattern of variegation which will be discussed fully in parts of Chapter VI and particularly in Chapters VII and VIII.

II.5.vi. HYBRID VARIEGATION

As we shall see in Chapter IX, the term hybrid variegation refers not to the appearance of a group of variegated plants, but to the method in which they are produced—by crossing certain green plants. Once produced, plants of this group appear and behave outwardly like typical sorting-out plants. Only when the genetical and physiological behaviour of their two types of plastid is compared with the behaviour of the plastids of a spontaneously occurring sorting-out plant, does the difference between them become apparent. Hence, although it is wrong to classify them in a group of their own on the basis of their variegation pattern, we must take into account our knowledge of their behaviour, which coupled with the very important studies that have been made on them, fully justifies their treatment in a chapter of their own.

Our outline classification of variegated plants is now complete, and we have a rough idea of the main types of variegation. Now we must get down to the serious business of examining each of these groups more closely. Our object must be to find out just what genetic information is available about them. The reader will then be in a position to judge where the gaps in our knowledge are greatest, and perhaps even be stimulated to tackle some of these interesting problems in the future.

REFERENCES

1.   BERGDOLT, B. (1955). *Z. Bot.* **43**, 309–340
2.   BREWBAKER, J. L. (1955). *J. Hered.* **46**, 115–123
3.   BREWBAKER, J. L. & CARNAHAN, H. L. (1956). *J. Hered.* **47**, 103–104
4.   CARNAHAN, H. L., HILL, H. D., HANSON, A. A. & BROWN, K. G. (1955). *J. Hered.* **46**, 109–114
5.   DAVIES, W. E. (1963). From *Teaching Genetics*, 94–98. Eds., C. D. Darlington & A. D. Bradshaw. Oliver and Boyd, Edinburgh and London
6.   HARA, N. (1957). *Jap. J. Bot.* **16**, 86–101
7.   HIORTH, G. (1930). *Z. Vererbungsl.* **55**, 127–144
8.   HIORTH, G. (1931). *Z. Vererbungsl.* **59**, 236–269
9.   SEYFFERT, W. (1955). *Report XIV Int. Horticultural Congress.* 929–937
10. SEYFFERT, W. (1957). *Gartenwelt*, **57**, 57–58
11. SMITH, K. M. (1957). *A textbook of plant virus diseases.* 2nd ed. J. and A. Churchill Ltd, London
12. WILLIAMS, W. (1964). *Genetical principles and plant breeding.* Botanical Monographs 5. Ed., W. O. James. Blackwell Scientific Publications, Oxford

CHAPTER III

Stable Pattern Genes

III.1. Figurative Patterns

Variegated plants with figurative patterns are those with highly
uniform and stable markings under normal environmental conditions
(Table III.1), which are caused by a physiological reaction with the
plastids and not by mutation. The markings therefore do not follow
cell lineages (see also Chapter II).

TABLE III.1. EXAMPLES OF HIGHER PLANTS WITH
FIGURATIVE OR CHLOROTIC VARIEGATED-LEAF
PATTERNS

Plant and form and pattern type	Genetic control	Authors	Dates
Marginal patterns			
Antirrhinum majus			
albomarginata (alma)	recessive	Schick, Stubbe	1932
Coleus blumei	Purple > green > pattern	Boye, Rife	1938
	P > p^g > p	Boye	1941
	Intense colour > dilute		
	I > i		
Lunaria annua albomarginata	recessive	Correns	1909a
Primula malacoides			
albomarginata	recessive	Correns	1931a,b
Diffuse spots			
Coleus hybridus	spotted probably dominant	Schwarz	1908
	to unmarked	Correns	1931a,b
Gossypium hirsutum			
mottled (mt)	recessive	Lewis	1960
Phaseolus vulgaris	incomplete dominance	Parker	1933
Zea mays piebald (pb)	recessive (4 genes)	Demerec	1926
polkadot (pk)	recessive	Eyster	1924
yellow fleck (yf)	recessive	Eyster	1934
Prominent veins			
Lycopersicum esculentum			
chloronerva (chln)	recessive	Böhme, Scholz	1960
		Scholz, Böhme	1961
		Scholz	1964

TABLE III.1—*Continued*

Plant and form and pattern type	Genetic control	Authors	Dates
Stripes and bands			
Zea mays argentia (ar)	recessive	Eyster	1933
green stripe (gs)	recessive	Emerson	1912
		Lindstrom	1918
yellow stripe (ys)	recessive	Beadle	1929
zebra striping (zb)	recessive (4 genes)	Demerec	1921
		Stroman	1924
		Hayes	1932
Restricted chlorosis			
Zea mays white sheath (ws)	recessive (3 genes)	Kempton	1921
		Clark	1932
white base leaf (wl)	recessive	Stroman	1924
		Carver	1927
pale midrib (pm)	recessive	Brink	1935
Tissue degeneration			
Viola arvensis	recessive	Kristofferson	1923
Zea mays dead leaf margin (dl)	recessive	Kempton	1923
Unrestricted chlorosis			
Lycopersicum esculentum ghost (gh)	recessive	Rick, Thompson and Brauer	1959
Vicia faba	incomplete dominance	Darlington	1929

III.1.i. MARGINAL PATTERNS OR PSEUDOCHIMERAS

A plant with white-margined leaves that was not typical of the species was first described by Correns (1909a) in the biennial *Lunaria annua*. The variegation is expressed only when the plant is homozygous for a recessive mutant gene and, unlike *Acalypha* and *Euphorbia* (see II.4.i), the margin is not a pure white band but an irregular, flecked border. The green and white areas of the border are sharply separated from each other but the flecks are so fine that the border has the appearance of a fine mosaic. The width of the border varies among individuals. The cotyledons are believed to be always green but the phenotype of the first leaves appears to be dependent upon the environmental conditions at the time. When seeds germinate out of doors towards the end of winter the first leaves are often intensely variegated, but if these seedlings are now placed in a greenhouse their next leaves are green, and seedlings which have germinated in the warmer days of spring are for some time indistinguishable from normal. It seems as if the expression of variegation in young seedlings is emphasized by low and retarded by high temperatures. The stage of growth also appears to be important. The rosette stage is usually only weakly or not at all variegated, whereas the leaves of the upright flowering shoot of the second year's growth are intensely variegated forming a wide border to every leaf.

A similar example of a white-margined plant produced by the action of a recessive mutant gene when homozygous occurs in *Primula malacoides*[17, 18]. Each new leaf of the rosette has a clear but irregular, flecked fringe with sharp borders between the green and white areas. The symptom of variegation becomes progressively more distinct as one's eye moves from the old and outermost leaves of the rosette towards the new and innermost leaves; the bracts and sepals are also variegated. The offspring from selfing, as in *Lunaria*, are variable and show all grades of variegation from weakly to intensely variegated.

A recessive albomarginata (alma) mutant of *Antirrhinum majus*[57] developed greenish-yellow cotyledons with white hypocotyls. The cotyledons gradually developed a white region at their base, and the first and all subsequent leaves developing during the summer were white-margined. The cotyledons and leaves were slower in growth than normal and were more pointed; the adult plants did not flower.

The colour of the leaves in *Coleus blumei* is partially determined by a triple allelic series of genes[7, 8]. The leaves are purple (P), green (p^g), or patterned (p). A second gene determines whether the chlorophyll coloration, which is masked by the purple colour when present, is an intense blue green (I) or a dilute yellow green colour (i). The leaf pattern allele is recessive to the purple- and green-determining alleles; it is therefore expressed only when homozygous, and it causes the leaf to become differentiated into a light marginal region surrounding a darker centre. Depending upon the allele present at the second locus the pseudochimera pattern is either intense or dilute.

In contrast to the white-margined leaves, the pattern gene in the cabbage[43] develops a marginate phenotype similar to some green-over-white periclinal chimeras. The leaves have green margins and white centres, individual plants varying in the relative sizes of the two regions. Alternatively, instead of regarding these leaves as pseudochimeras, they may also be thought of as having a large central blotch, which brings us to our next group.

III.1.ii. DIFFUSE SPOTS

One form of *Coleus hybridus* which is frequently grown in the summer as a bedding plant, appears somewhat like a chimera because the centre part of the leaf is yellowish-white and the outer part green. The border between the two zones is jagged owing to the white tissue extending further into the green tissue along the veins than between them. In addition, there are small, unconnected yellowish-white spots between the green lobes of the leaf margin. According to Schwarz (1928) the white tissue results from the action of a hormone which causes chlorophyll loss from the cells under its influence. The hormone is developed in the vascular bundles and diffuses from there into the mesophyll. The process is reversible, and secondary greening can occur under the right conditions of nutrition and a high average temperature. On selfing, the variegation breeds true but does not always reproduce the original pattern. Correns (1931a, b) found a wide variety of phenotypes among the seedlings. Some had the original basic pattern, but varied in the size of the white zone from those with only a narrow strip along the midrib to those with the typical large white blotch. In others the basic pattern was no longer recognizable; instead the variegation was expressed as few or numerous small spots widely scattered over the leaf area; these spots were often mere pinpricks of white. Sometimes the spots were concentrated along the midrib and main veins, sometimes they were found only around the midrib where they tended to run together. In yet other seedlings the white areas were so fine and so frequent that the leaves appeared as if dusted with a white powder. Reciprocal crosses between a true-breeding, green *Coleus* and a true-breeding variegated plant produced two green offspring among over fifty variegated. The wide range in the variegated phenotype from scarcely to intensely variegated suggested that the two green seedlings represented one extreme of the variegated phenotype and not a genotypically distinct class. In the F_2 generation, seedlings derived from the variegated F_1 plants segregated in ratios approximately equal to 3 variegated: 1 green, but with rather more than the expected number of green assuming it is a true monohybrid ratio. Again, some of these green seedlings might have belonged to the genotypically variegated class, their wrong classification biasing the ratios. At all events the results strongly suggest that variegation is controlled by the action of a dominant gene. This nuclear gene is presumably further modified by other genes to give the wide range of patterns and intensities of variegation, or these variations may result from the action of different alleles of a multiple allelic series, a possibility that waits to be investigated.

The presence of numerous, small yellow spots on the primary and compound leaves is not a typical character of the bean, *Phaseolus vulgaris*. Nevertheless Parker (1933) found this character to be partially dominant. He found that the diffuse spots on the leaves of some plants were so numerous that irregular yellow patches were formed; these intensely spotted plants turned out to be homozygous for the mutant gene. Other plants had fewer spots with no appreciable coalescing; these moderately spotted plants turned out to be heterozygous for the mutant gene. Evidently a double dose of the mutant allele induced spotting far more frequently than a single dose. At first Parker had suspected that the beans were infected with a virus disease, but negative results from grafting and inoculation experiments, as well as the observed Mendelian segregations in the F_2 and F_3 generations, proved this hypothesis to be without foundation.

Besides plants in which leaf spotting is characteristic of the species or is controlled by the action of a gene with a dominant effect, there are other examples in which the nuclear gene responsible is recessive in effect acting only when homozygous. Several types of recessive spotting have been described in *Zea mays*. Piebald seedlings (pb) have irregular white or yellowish spots on their leaves devoid of chlorophyll[24]. The spots are extremely variable in size, shape and position. Four different genes are known to produce a piebald phenotype—pb_1, pb_2, pb_3, and pb_4. Each gene behaves as a simple Mendelian recessive; the two genes pb_2 and pb_3 act as duplicate genes. The phenotype of piebald-4 is particularly prominent and develops blotches both on the seedlings and on the mature plants. Polkadot leaves (pk) develop at about the time when the tassel emerges[26]. At first, the green leaves lose their chlorophyll from the interveinal spaces so that the leaf appears to have a yellow lamina with green veins. Chlorophyll degeneration then affects the veins as well so that the green vein stripes become interrupted to form a series of green dots on a yellow background. Yellow fleck (yf) is described as a polkadot pattern which consists of yellow dots on an otherwise green leaf[28]. It can be recognized only in the seedling leaves. Other spotted leaves mentioned without further description by Eyster are dotted leaf (dt) and chloroblotch (cb).

Besides these maize types, a recessive spotted mutant termed mottled (mt) has been described in cotton, *Gossypium hirsutum*[45]. Small pale-green areas are produced at random over the leaves. Since the total area of normal green tissue is always greater than the light-green area, the character is not particularly conspicuous.

III.1.iii. PROMINENT VEINS

Descriptions of various types of patterns, and analyses of their genetical behaviour, form the necessary initial stages of getting to understand these variegations. But, of course, it leaves many questions still unanswered, and in most of our examples the lack of further experimentation means that there is, at present, nothing more to be said. A most interesting exception is found in the experiments of Böhme and Scholz (1960) with a mutant tomato, *Lycopersicum esculentum*. These workers describe a recessive mutant in which a chlorophyll defect called chloronerva (chln) first appears shortly after seed germination during the formation of the leaves. The area between the veins is yellowish-white, while the area immediately surrounding the veins is green. Thus the leaves are characterized by a green network of veins on a yellowish-white background. Besides this prominent vein pattern, root development is seriously inhibited, overall growth in size is much reduced, and finally no flowers are formed at all. Now these workers had the fore-thought to graft chloronerva plants as stock or scion on to normal green plants, and this produced a marked overall improvement in the growth of the mutant which now flowered and set seed. This 'normalization' was shown to be phenotypic and not genotypic because the seed germi-nated to give wholly chloronerva offspring; furthermore the chloronerva character was reversible and reappeared during later stages of growth. It thus appeared as if the temporary curing of the chloronerva malady was due to a substance able to diffuse through the graft union from the healthy to the defective partner. This supposition was fully substanti-ated by further experiments in which a partial normalization was achieved by infiltrating into the mutant plants water-soluble extracts from normal plants. Further tests[59] showed that a partial phenotypic normalization could be induced by grafting with different species of the genera *Lycopersicum, Solanum, Nicotiana,* and *Datura* both as stock or scion. And also partial normalization could be achieved by spraying the leaves with water-soluble extracts from different *Lycopersicum* species and from *Medicago sativa* and *Malva verticillata.* Clearly the normalizing factor was a substance of widespread occurrence and not specific to tomato alone. Also, it was a substance that could be analysed more precisely. It turned out to be heat stable, soluble in water and alcohol, but insoluble in typical organic solvents. And from paper and ion-exchange chromatographic analysis, it appears to be basically a peptide containing glycine, serine, and glutamic acid[58]. Hence the pleiotropic effects associated with the chloronerva mutant presumably result from a block in a metabolic pathway which can be partially cured by the artificial addition of a water-soluble peptide. The actual peptide and the metabolic pathway it is associated with is still unknown. (The reader is referred to Chapter XI for further examples of the genetic control of plastid biochemistry.) The lesson for us is to recognize the possibility that other variegations may be due to similar blocks and perhaps they also could be analysed a great deal more thoroughly using a similar biochemical approach.

III.1.iv. STRIPES AND BANDS

Green stripe (gs) of maize consists of uniform longitudinal streaks of light green on a normal green background caused by a deficiency in the chlorophyll content of the interveinal regions of the leaf blade[25,46]. Yellow stripe (ys) is similar, but the interveinal spaces are yellow instead of pale green[5]. It is thought that the striping is caused by defects in iron metabolism (see XI.6). Argentia (ar) consists of a very fine striping due to the development of chlorophyll in the cells adjacent to the vascular bundles and its partial absence from all interveinal cells[27]. At first the seedlings may be white, but chlorophyll development, beginning at the tips and bases of the leaves, spreads rapidly along the midrib to all the veins. Its expression is strongly influenced by temperature. At 10°C there is an almost complete inhibition of chlorophyll so that the seedlings are almost white. Between 15 and 22°C the argentia pattern is clearly expressed, while above 25°C the plants are frequently normal green.

Zebra striping-1 (zb_1) begins as yellowish-green dots caused by the loss of chlorophyll from the leaves of apparently normal seedlings[23]. The numerous dots are so arranged as to form more or less irregular transverse bands. The dots gradually enlarge and coalesce to form a continuous yellow band clearly seen in the mature plant. Zebra striping-2 (zb_2) is similar but the phenotype of this gene is unrecognizable in the mature plant[64]. Zebra striping-4 (zb_4) is again only distinguishable before the plant reaches maturity[29]; moreover, it appears to be dependent upon fluctuating temperatures for its expression. The presumed zebra striping-3 does not seem to have been described. Besides these examples from maize, zebra striping is also well known in the ornamental grass, *Miscanthus sinensis*.

At the time, the main object in studying these maize mutants was for their value as markers in building up linkage maps of the chromosomes. Consequently we still know little about these patterns. Nevertheless, it is felt that these almost forgotten examples are worth remembering, if only because of the challenge that they must continue to present until such time as the causes of their differing patterns have been unravelled.

III.2. General Chlorosis

Plants, in which there occurs during growth an irregular loss or absence of chlorophyll, which is not caused by mutation and yet does not produce any characteristic leaf marking, may be loosely defined as chlorotic variegated plants.

III.2.i. RESTRICTED CHLOROSIS

A number of recessive mutant genes have been described in maize which prevent the normal development of chlorophyll, not all over, but in particular regions. One such mutation is called white sheath (ws) because the leaf sheaths and husks fail to develop chlorophyll and so remain white[40]. The chlorosis is slow to set in and does not usually begin before the tenth leaf is formed, although in extreme cases it begins in the sheath of the fourth leaf and also extends into the base of the leaf. Two additional recessive genes, white sheath-2 (ws₂) and white sheath-3 (ws₃), produce a similar phenotype[11]. White base leaf (wl) is a mutation which can be recognized in the seedling stage but which also gradually becomes more apparent during growth[10, 64]. At first, the leaf sheaths and the base of the leaves are nearly white but as the plant approaches maturity the chlorosis at the leaf base slowly extends into the leaf blade giving the leaf a mottled appearance. The recessive gene pale midrib (pm) causes a reduction in the amount of chlorophyll along the midrib of the leaf and also in the leaf sheath[9].

III.2.ii. TISSUE DEGENERATION

Localized loss of chlorophyll from leaves is sometimes accompanied by, and probably caused by, the death of the tissue. The recessive mutant gene in *Zea mays* called dead leaf margin (dl) begins to be expressed in the margins of leaves developing between the ear shoot and the tassel[41]. The margins, instead of developing normal green mesophyll, develop a dead tissue of varying width depending upon the intensity of expression. Owing to the absence of chlorophyll from the dead tissue it appears white so that the leaf as a whole looks somewhat like a white-margined chimera.

Destruction of tissue proceeds even further in a mutant of *Viola arvensis*[42]. Chlorosis sometimes begins with the formation of white spots in the cotyledons but more often the spots first appear later in development. Spots begin to develop with the dying of solitary or small groups of palisade cells accompanied by a loss of chlorophyll; they soon cease to be recognizable as cell destruction proceeds. Destruction is often so considerable that the tissue simply falls away from the leaf until only the midrib remains. The damage becomes increasingly widespread as the plant ages but curiously it does not affect the stem or the leaf stalks. The plant really does appear to be seriously diseased but crossing experiments clearly showed that a single recessive gene and not a pathogen was responsible.

III.2.iii. UNRESTRICTED CHLOROSIS

Chlorosis was found by Darlington (1929) to affect all normally green organs in a variegated mutant of the broad bean, *Vicia faba*. Seedlings were, at first, scarcely distinguishable from green, but by the sixth node their stems began to lose chlorophyll, and by the eighth node stems and leaf petioles turned permanently white. Finally, the leaves lost their chlorophyll, beginning around the midrib and veins and gradually spreading to the margins until they too were completely white. At this stage the plants threw up shoots from the base. These usually had white stems but their leaves were much less regular in their development than those of the main shoot; they began white and turned variegated, or began green, turned white, and then turned green again as if there was a relationship between the bleaching effect at the growing-point and the amount of chlorophyll produced in the growth that had just taken place. The young pod was slightly greenish but as it grew it rapidly lost chlorophyll until only the sutures remained green. On pure white shoots pure white pods were obtained. Nevertheless, according to Darlington, the cotyledons of the developing seeds were always green showing that their colour was not adversely affected by their genetical constitution. This presumably referred to their colour before ripening, since the cotyledons of 'albino' seedlings were chlorotic at germination. The environment, probably because of differences in light intensity or duration, modified the expression of variegation. Thus by sowing in midsummer the young plants developed variegation very early and it lasted until the autumn when the leaves began to turn green again. By sowing in late autumn the growth of plants in the greenhouse was indistinguishable from that of normal green plants except for the development of the pod, which bleached as in summer though more gradually.

When selfed or crossed amongst themselves, the variegated broad-bean plants set seed, which germinated to give green, variegated and 'albino' offspring in a Mendelian ratio of 1:2:1 showing that variegated plants were heterozygous for the mutant gene. This was confirmed by the fact that the green and 'albino' plants were true-breeding. In summer the so-called 'albino' seedlings died without further development, but when raised in December a few of them developed enough chlorophyll to support their growth until maturity when they set a few seeds. A rather small number of observations showed a bias in the Mendelian segregation towards more than the expected number of green offspring from green nodes, and more than the expected number of variegated offspring from variegated nodes, which suggested a maternal influence on the inheritance.

An equally striking example of variegation caused by a progressive absence of chlorophyll is to be found in the 'ghost' tomato. Breeding experiments, which included selfing, reciprocal crosses, and back crosses clearly show that the mutant ghost (gh) is controlled by the action of a homozygous recessive gene. Moreover, Rick, Thompson, and Brauer (1959) also found that the disease-like character could not be transmitted either by inoculation or by grafting, thus confirming that the chlorosis is not caused by a virus infection. (See XI.3.ii for an account of the effects of this gene on plastid carotenoids.) On germination the cotyledons are smaller than normal and are frequently pale green with paler blotches. In the first true leaves the lack of chlorophyll becomes more conspicuous since plants vary from those with almost completely green leaves, to others which are almost completely white. The distribution of green and white areas in the leaves shows no apparent pattern. The proportion of leaves or parts of leaves developing without chlorophyll increases in the second leaf stage and by the third leaf stage the shoot tips of most plants are completely without chlorophyll; thereafter many plants slowly die off. A few plants remain variegated until the flowering stage. When the absence of chlorophyll is over 99 per cent complete it produces a white coloration, but more rarely a yellow coloration is produced in which 5 per cent of the normal chlorophyll content remains. A few chloroplasts present in occasional cells in the stems, petioles and leaves account for the 5 per cent chlorophyll content in the yellow phase. These white or yellow phases are fairly stable but they do occasionally change from one to the other, and very rarely they revert briefly to green. In plants in which the change from green to white or yellow is slow to take place, one frequently finds green areas surrounded by areas of white or yellow; these green areas are much rarer in seedlings which have changed rapidly. On the stems and leaf petioles the green tissue appears as elongate strands as if derived by cell lineages from one or more primordial cells that possessed chloroplasts. On the leaves the green tissues develop as swollen masses of large, undifferentiated cells well lined with chloroplasts and conforming neither to palisade nor to spongy mesophyll tissue. Furthermore, they appear to be islands of green as if they had arisen *de novo* because no connections of green tissue could be traced between them and the remaining regions of the green phase. Nevertheless, they may possibly have arisen from cells having a very small number of normal chloroplasts.

Anatomically the leaves are drastically modified in the white and yellow phases: the leaves are much smaller than normal and are strongly folded, the epidermal cells are larger than normal and assume irregular shapes and the epidermal hairs are concentrated in groups, the internal parenchyma is not differentiated into palisade and spongy mesophyll tissue and finally the vascular tissue is more abundant than normal. The high degree of distortion found in these leaves suggests that the tissues probably develop in a near-normal fashion in the early stages of leaf differentiation but the usual coordination between cells and tissues breaks down during the subsequent period of leaf expansion. Stems, petioles, flowers, and fruit are much less modified. Flowers developing in the white phase are very small and scarcely open but flowers developing in the yellow or green phase are nearly normal; in all phases a high proportion of the pollen is aborted. The fruits are invariably white or yellow even when developed on a green shoot although these occasionally have one or more green stripes. Thus the gradient towards chlorophyll absence is finally almost total in fruit development. On ripening the white or yellow fruits turn bright yellow and the green stripes red. The seed set is higher in fruits produced by the green and yellow phase than in fruits produced by the white phase. The viable seeds germinate normally.

Since there is such a wide variation in the ghost gene's expression, Rick, Thompson, and Brauer endeavoured to test whether there is any evidence of genetical differences between green, yellow, and white phases. They found that selfed seed from striped, or yellow or white fruit gave only ghost offspring of very similar range of expression suggesting there was no genetical difference between the tissues. This observation also suggests that the green sectors occurring in the fruit, and therefore presumably the green islands in the leaves, are not caused by either nuclear or plastid mutation. But this result may simply mean that mutation never occurs in the germ track. They were also unable to select lines of different degrees of expression again suggesting that the ghost gene expression was not being modified by any other genes. The reason for the changes thus remains a mystery. But the observation that plants respond to the environment by growing best between the late spring and early autumn, leads to the suggestion that slight alterations in the environment might be an important factor in determining whether a tissue should be white, or yellow or green. It is evident that the difference between remaining white or developing chlorophyll must be controlled by a delicately balanced system which waits to be discovered. It is finally interesting to note that whereas the ghost plants of *Lycopersicum* tend to develop more green tissue in the summer than in the winter, the response of the variegated *Vicia* was just the opposite. It would indeed be rash to assume that the mechanism of chlorophyll loss is the same in the two plants.

III.3. Mosaic and Striped Patterns

Plants, in which the variegated areas follow cell lineages, but in which the probable mutations causing the variegation do not seem to affect the growing-point initials or germ cells, may be loosely grouped together as mosaic and striped patterned variegations (see also Chapter II). The many plants that have been described contain among them types

8—P.

TABLE III.2. EXAMPLES OF HIGHER PLANTS WITH CELL LINEAGE MOSAIC AND STRIPED VARIEGATION PATTERNS

Plant and form	Mendelian ratios: F_2 segregation ($g = green$)	Authors	Dates
	Monohybrid ratios		
Antirrhinum majus gilvostriata (gilv)	3 g:1 gilvostriata	Scherz	1927
Barbarea vulgaris variegata	3 g:1 variegata (deficit)	Dahlgren	1921
		Andersson	1924
		Tilney-Bassett	1963c
Capsicum annuum variegata	3 g:1 variegata	Imai	1938
bushy variegated (bv)	3 g:1 bushy variegated	Cook	1962
marbled (m)	3 g:1 marbled	Lippert, Bergh, Cook	1964
Gossypium hirsutum mosaic leaf (ml)	3 g:1 mosaic leaf	Lippert, Bergh, Cook	1964
Oryza sativa striped	3 g:1 striped	Lewis	1958
Pelargonium zonale variegata	3 g:1 variegata	Morinaga	1932
Petunia hybrida albomutabilis	3 g:1 albomutabilis (deficit)	Imai	1936a
Pharbitis nil deficient (df)	3 g:1 deficient	Correns	1936
		Imai	1925, 30b
		Miyake, Imai	1934
Polygonum orientale variegata	3 g:1 variegata (deficit)	Imai	1934a
Salpiglossis sinuata variegata	3 g:1 variegata	Dale, Rees-Leonard	1939
Taraxacum platycarpum variegata	3 g:1 variegata (deficit)	Iinuma	1941
Tropaeolum majus albopulvereum	3 g:1 albopulvereum	Correns	1920
		Rasmuson	1920
		Moffett	1936
		Imai	1937a
Vitis vinifera variegata	3 g:1 variegata	Rasmuson	1917
Zea mays argostripe (ag)	3 g:1 argostripe	Eyster	1934
fine-streaked (fi)	3 g:1 fine-streaked	Anderson	1922
fine-stripe (f)	3 g:1 fine-stripe	Lindstrom	1918

japonica (j)	3 g : 1 japonica	Emerson	1912
		Miles	1915
lineate (li)	3 g : 1 lineate	Lindstrom	1918
striped auricle (sa)	3 g : 1 striped auricle (2 genes)	Collins, Kempton	1920
		Eyster	1934
	Dihybrid ratios		
Capsella bursa pastoris albovariabilis	15 g : 1 albovariabilis	Correns	1919a
Pharbitis nil albomarmorata	3 g : 1 albomarmorata	Correns	1920
variegata (v)	3 g : 1 variegata	Imai	1925
variegated-reduced (v-r)	3 variegata : 1 variegated-reduced	Miyake, Imai	1934
	12 g : 3 variegata : 1 variegated-reduced	Imai	1936b, 37a
Phaseolus vulgaris variegata	3 g : 1 variegata	Zaumeyer	1938, 42
	15 g : 1 variegata		
Plantago major asiatica variegata	3 g : 1 variegata	Ikeno	1917, 27
	15 g : 1 variegata		
	Trihybrid ratios		
Phaseolus vulgaris variegata	3 g : 1 variegata	Wade	1941
	9 g : 7 variegata		
	27 g : 37 variegata		
	Sex-linkage		
Melandrium album × *rubrum* variegata	7 g : 1 variegata (♀s 3 g : 1 v)	Winge	1931
	15 g : 1 variegata (♀ 7 g : 1 v)		
	63 g : 1 variegata (♀ 31 g : 1 v)		
	Multiple allelic series		
Capsicum annuum variegated mottled (vg^m) variegated virescent (vg^v)	vg$^+$ > vg^m > vg^v	Lippert, Bergh, Cook	1964

Fig. III.1. *Single leaves illustrating mosaic patterned variegations. Left,* Tropaeolum majus; *right,* Barbarea vulgaris

showing distinctive patterns of behaviour, which deserve our attention, and merit their separate classification (Fig. III.1).

III.3.i. PERMANENT MOSAICS

A number of variegated plants have been described (Table III.2) in which we observe in the leaves, or parts of the leaves, of young plants, a sharp separation between green and mosaic regions. This separation is clearly due to a cell lineage difference; hence we may assume that a mutation has taken place causing a change in the phenotype from green to mosaic. This may be called the primary mutation. Within the mosaic area we find a confusing mixture of green and white tissues. Exactly what is happening is not clear, but this will be discussed later. First we must describe the development of variegation in more detail.

III.3.i.a. *Standard types*

The cotyledons of potentially variegated plants vary from completely green to, exceptionally, completely white. Seedlings with little green tissue frequently die without developing further. Green seedlings

usually develop variegation in the first few leaves but occasional seedlings may show no sign of variegation until as late as the flowering stage
and, in some species, a few remain phenotypically green throughout
their life. Generally speaking, the later the first appearance of variegation, the weaker it is during subsequent development. Mature plants
therefore show a wide variation in the phenotypic expression from
weakly to strongly variegated but, whatever the intensity, the variegation becomes a permanent feature of the plant. Whether or not the
variegation is equally stable under all light and temperature regimes is
impossible to say since there appear to have been no adequate experiments made to test this point. Besides the green leaves produced before
variegation develops, additional green leaves are sometimes sporadically produced throughout development. In *Gossypium hirsutum*, *Pharbitis
nil* 'deficient', and *Phaseolus vulgaris* individual leaves are frequently
green and many others contain only a sector of variegation as if they
were sectorial chimeras for green and mosaic. As the result of the
development of variegation in one layer but not in another, periclinal
leaves and even periclinal shoots are sometimes produced by *Pharbitis
nil* 'variegata', *Plantago major*, *Capsicum annuum*, and *Pelargonium zonale*
in addition to the occasional pure green leaf in *Pharbitis* and *Pelargonium*.
Strictly speaking, the white skin usually has a few small green islands
and the green core an occasional white sector or fleck, but the overall
periclinal structure is clearly recognizable. White leaves also occur
sometimes but they are never pure since they always contain one or
more small green islands.

Variegation in *Barbarea vulgaris* begins, as in other plants, in the
cotyledons, or in the first, second, or third leaf, seemingly quite randomly[65]. Yet gradually, as the plant grows, the variegation pattern
changes. Instead of a random distribution of green and mosaic areas,
a characteristic pseudochimera pattern develops with a yellowish-white,
speckled margin and a green centre. Occasionally, this pattern is
reversed so that the margin is green and the centre mosaic. Generally
speaking, individuals in which the variegation is late to develop are
weakly variegated; conversely, early developers tend to be intensely
variegated. When the pseudochimera pattern develops in weakly variegated plants the green centre tends to be wide and the mosaic margin
narrow, whereas in strongly variegated plants the green centre is
narrow and the margin wide. These observations have recently been
confirmed and extended by Scheel (1965), who has now shown
experimentally that the pattern of variegation cannot be related to any
unusual behaviour in the anatomical development of the leaves. In
particular, periclinal divisions in the dermatogen cannot be held
responsible for the abundant sprinkling of green cells scattered in the
white tissues.

During leaf development white tissues often expand less than green which causes variegated leaves to be frequently wrinkled, crumpled or twisted. Sectorial leaves are especially prone to twisting but species differ in the extent to which they are affected. In *Phaseolus* some variegated plants were so badly affected that Zaumeyer at first thought they might be infected with a virus disease. Intensely variegated seedlings died, and the survivors were frequently stunted with distorted leaves and pods and shortened internodes; a few plants were even reduced to rosettes. More moderately variegated plants were not so badly affected. Generally speaking seed set in weakly and moderately variegated plants is good, but intensely variegated plants are usually too feeble to flower well, if at all, and the seed set is correspondingly poor. When a variegated streak affects the flowers of *Gossypium* the anthers within the area wither and fail to dehisce, but this is an exceptional and not a common effect of variegation. In the 'deficient' form of *Pharbitis* the flower is sometimes deformed, and the petals are striped white. Thus in some plants the primary mutation produces not only mosaics but it is also pleiotropic in its effect, and interferes with flower pigmentation and even with the overall morphological structure of the whole plant.

The inheritance of the variegation is mendelian, and the species that have been studied are grouped in Table III.2 according to their F_2 segregation, with the exception of *Capsicum annuum* in which the interest of the multiple allelic series is pointed out. In several instances the proportion of green seedlings obtained was higher than expected for the mono- or dihybrid ratio. There is, however, no reason to doubt the validity of the ratios since the deficit of variegated offspring can probably be traced to the poorer viability of variegated embryos, or the poorer germination of variegated seeds as has been shown in the case of *Barbarea vulgaris*[65]. Furthermore, the monohybrid ratios have sometimes been supported by backcrosses between the heterozygous green F_1 and the homozygous recessive variegated to give the expected 1 green:1 variegated ratio, and sometimes the observations have been carried through to, and confirmed by, the F_3 generation. Alternatively, the ratios may sometimes be biased towards green owing to a few of the genotypically variegated seedlings developing as phenotypically green plants; indeed, this was proved to occur in *Capsella bursa pastoris* 'albovariabilis'.

Correns (1919a) discovered that by selfing weakly variegated *Capsella* plants he obtained more phenotypically green offspring than when he selfed intensely variegated plants. Similarly, from the same individual plant, the greener a branch was, the more green offspring there were and the fewer moderately or intensely variegated. Conversely, intensely variegated plants or branches produced more moderate and intensely variegated seedlings and fewer or no phenotypically green. By continued selection Correns was able to obtain almost true-breeding green lines even though the plants still contained the variegated genotype. Nevertheless, by selection in the opposite direction he was able to return from the predominantly green back to the almost true-breeding variegated condition showing that the intermediate steps in the selection were not fixed. The correlation between the colour of the offspring and the colour of the mother plant clearly demonstrates a maternal influence on the inheritance reminding us of the apparent maternal influence on the inheritance of variegation found by Darlington in *Vicia faba* (III.2.iii). Occasionally some green seedlings also arose by back-mutation of the recessive gene to the normal allele since on selfing they proved to be heterozygous. Numerous variegated *Phaseolus* plants died before flowering and consequently Zaumeyer (1938, 1942) could only obtain seed from the more vigorous, weakly variegated plants. These did not breed true and gave many phenotypically green as well as variegated offspring. Again this might be the result of a maternal influence, but Zaumeyer believed that many variegated plants carried inhibitors of variegation, possibly in the heterozygous condition, so that in their progeny the variegated phenotype was often suppressed.

The variegated form of *Pharbitis nil* is particularly interesting. The coarse mosaic of the leaves is caused by a single recessive gene when homozygous, and seedlings from selfing the green F_1 heterozygotes segregate in the typical 3:1 ratio. But this pattern can be modified by a second recessive gene to give a fine variegation termed 'variegated-reduced', in which the green islands in the white area are much smaller and more numerous than in the 'variegated' form. When both recessive genes are present, the F_2 offspring from selfing a heterozygous green plant segregate in a ratio of 12 green:3 variegated:1 variegated-reduced indicating the influence of a suppressor gene showing dominant epistasis. In other words, only if the dominant gene for normal green is absent so that the plant is potentially variegated can it then be modified by a second recessive gene when homozygous to give variegated-reduced.

III.3.i.b. *Sex linkage in* Melandrium

Variegation in the dioecious *Melandrium* arose in the fourth generation after a cross between a female *M. rubrum* and a male *M. album*. Winge's investigations (1931) showed that almost all variegated plants were females owing to the Y chromosome of the male inhibiting variegation; occasionally he found a very weak variegation in the male owing to the Y inhibitor not being perfectly epistatic. Three more genes inhibiting variegation, which he called L, M, and O, were found in the autosomes. Hence plants were variegated only when they had the genotypic constitution llmmooXX. Crosses between green males and green or variegated females resulted in the offspring segregating into green and variegated seedlings in 7:1, 15:1, or 63:1 ratios, which may be illustrated as follows:

(1) 7:1 ratio:

Cross	Variegated female		Green male
	llmmooXX	×	llMmOoXY

Expected segregation for each gene pair			Expected frequency
+ Inhibitor		− Inhibitor	without inhibitor
1 Mm	:	1 mm	1/2
1 Oo	:	1 oo	1/2
1 XY	:	1 XX	1/2

Chance of obtaining llmmooXX = $1/2 \times 1/2 \times 1/2 = 1/8$
Therefore expected segregation of male
and female   = 7 green:1 variegated
Therefore segregation of the female alone   = 3 green:1 variegated
    Winge obtained a total segregation of 506 green:54 variegated and a female segregation of 269 green:54 variegated.

(2) 15:1 ratio:

Cross	Green female		Green male
	LlMmOoXX	×	llmmooXY

Expected segregation for each gene pair			Expected frequency
+ Inhibitor		− Inhibitor	without inhibitor
1 Ll	:	1 ll	1/2
1 Mm	:	1 mm	1/2
1 Oo	:	1 oo	1/2
1 XY	:	1 XX	1/2

Chance of obtaining llmmooXX = $1/2 \times 1/2 \times 1/2 \times 1/2 = 1/16$
Therefore expected segregation of male and
female   = 15 green:1 variegated
Therefore segregation of the female alone   = 7 green:1 variegated
    Winge obtained a total segregation of 2331 green:127 variegated and a female segregation of 1089 green:127 variegated.

(3) 63:1 ratio:

Cross	Green female		Green male
	LlMmOoXX	×	llMmOoXY

Expected segregation for each gene pair			Expected frequency
+ Inhibitor		− Inhibitor	without inhibitor
1 Ll	:	1 ll	1/2
3 M_	:	1 mm	1/4
3 O_	:	1 oo	1/4
1 XY	:	1 XX	1/2

Chance of obtaining llmmooXX $= 1/2 \times 1/4 \times 1/4 \times 1/2 = 1/64$
Therefore expected segregation of male and
  female $= 63$ green : 1 variegated
Therefore segregation of the female alone $= 31$ green : 1 variegated

Winge obtained a total segregation of 2153 green : 43 variegated. In all crosses there is a deficit of male seedlings which Winge does not explain. The deficit of variegated seedlings is at least partly due to the occurrence of occasional phenotypically green plants among the genotypically variegated females.

III.3.i.c. *Extra-nuclear control of gametic lethality in* Vicia faba

As the result of a series of experiments, which need not be discussed in detail, Sirks (1931a, b; 1938) came to the conclusion that the normal green 'typica' colour of the leaves of *Vicia faba* depended, among other things, upon the presence of a dominant gene A, which was epistatic to certain other genes affecting leaf coloration. In the absence of A, that is in aa plants homozygous for the recessive allele, a second gene C was able to express itself. Now the gene C consisted of a multiple allelic series which produced a corresponding series of phenotypes as follows:

$C_3 =$ 'subtypica' gave a green leaf colour, brighter than typica.
$C_2 =$ 'semichlorina' gave a more yellowish-green leaf colour.
$C_1 =$ 'chlorina' gave a yellow-green leaf colour
  $c =$ 'albino' gave a colourless leaf.

These alleles together formed a series in the following order of decreasing dominance: $C_3 > C_2 > C_1 > c$.

In addition to the C gene, a second gene V, producing a variegated phenotype, also expressed itself only in homozygous aa individuals. Furthermore, the variegated phenotype, which consisted of chlorina coloured leaves in which spots of subtypica or semichlorina were dispersed, was expressed with the C_3 and C_2 alleles of the C gene but not with the C_1 and c alleles.

Plants which were heterozygous for the variegation sometimes possessed apparently wholly subtypica or semichlorina as well as variegated shoots. Breeding tests suggested to Sirks that although the two shoots differed in phenotype, they were genotypically identical. Thus it appeared that the difference between the chlorina background and the subtypica, and presumably also the semichlorina spots on variegated leaves was phenotypic. Hence the variegation must have been physiologically controlled and not due to mutation. This conclusion was further supported as the result of testing the genotype of subtypica individuals derived from variegated parents. The tests showed that the subtypica plants were in fact heterozygous, Vv, for the variegation gene and not homozygous recessive, vv. They were therefore genotypically variegated and only phenotypically subtypica. A possible explanation of the phenomenon is that the V allele acts as a partial inhibitor of the subtypica phenotype, the degree of inhibition depending upon the number of V alleles present as follows:

VV never allows full development of subtypica.

Vv sometimes allows full development of subtypica in shoots and seedlings.

vv always allows full development of subtypica.

This explanation is, however, somewhat premature for the breeding experiments in fact only show that there is no mutation at the V locus. They may suggest that the chlorina and subtypica areas of variegated plants are genotypically identical, but they do not prove this, for the chlorina phenotype was never actually tested. Moreover, Sirks' reason for believing them to be genetically identical depended on the unstated assumption that the change in phenotype was in the direction chlorina $\rightarrow$ subtypica, owing to the occurrence of subtypica spots on a chlorina background. Yet the direction of change could equally well be in the opposite direction, namely from subtypica to chlorina, in which case the subtypica spots, shoots or seedlings would represent an absence of change. Now a change in the direction subtypica $\rightarrow$ chlorina need not be a physiological change; it could equally well be a mutational change in which the V allele induces the mutation of C_3 or C_2 to C_1. The effect of the V allele in inducing mutation would then appear to be additive as follows:

vv allows C_3 and C_2 to remain perfectly stable.

Vv causes irregular mutation of C_3 and C_2 to C_1 so that unchanged subtypica and semichlorina shoots and seedlings are sometimes produced.

VV always causes regular mutation of C_3 and C_2 to C_1 so that all shoots and seedlings are variegated.

Unfortunately the experiments needed to distinguish between the alternative explanations of the causes of variegation were not made.

Segregation at the variegation locus, when heterozygous, is naturally expected to produce offspring in the ratio of 1 VV:2 Vv:1 vv according to the normal behaviour of the chromosomes at meiosis, as is indeed found in *Vicia faba*. This expectation was fully confirmed by selfing or intercrossing F_1 plants which had the typica phenotype, yet were heterozygous at the variegation locus. In the absence of the dominant gene A, the typica phenotype is replaced by the variegata phenotype in heterozygous Vv individuals, except for a few subtypica or semi-chlorina plants. As we have already mentioned, some of the heterozygous variegated plants develop subtypica shoots as well as variegated shoots. On selfing, both types of shoot gave variegated and subtypica offspring. But their proportions, and the further analysis of these offspring, showed that the segregation from the two types of shoot was quite different as follows:

Variegated shoots: The variegated offspring from variegated shoots were either true-breeding VV homozygotes or segregating Vv heterozygotes. The heterozygotes sometimes developed into variegated plants with one or more wholly subtypica shoots. The non-variegated plants were phenotypically subtypica, but genotypically they were also Vv heterozygotes. The ratio of VV homozygotes:Vv heterozygotes was 1:1. The expected vv homozygotes were not found.

Non-variegated shoots: The variegated offspring from non-variegated shoots were all Vv heterozygotes, sometimes with wholly variegated and sometimes with subtypica shoots. The non-variegated, subtypica offspring were true-breeding vv homozygotes. The ratio of Vv heterozygotes to vv homozygotes was 1:1. The expected VV homozygotes were not found.

Thus Sirks found that the variegated shoots produce no vv homozygotes and the non-variegated shoots produce no VV homozygotes. Clearly these expected homozygotes must have been eliminated in some way. They might have been eliminated during embryo development, but this seems improbable because we would then expect a 1:2 ratio of the viable homozygote:the heterozygote. Instead the observed 1:1 ratio strongly suggests, as Sirks believed, that one of the alternative alleles is eliminated at the gametic stage, which may be shown schematically as follows:

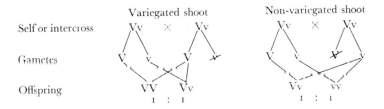

	Variegated shoot	Non-variegated shoot
Self or intercross	Vv × Vv	Vv × Vv
Gametes	V v V v	V v V v
Offspring	VV Vv	Vv vv
	1 : 1	1 : 1

Whether the shoots are variegated or not, the genotype of Vv plants, at least at the V/v locus, is the same. Hence Sirks concluded that the presence or absence of gametic lethality must depend upon an extranuclear factor, which he suggested was in the cytoplasm, but it could equally well be in the plastids or mitochondria for all we know. In typica cytoplasm the segregation is normal 1 VV:2 Vv:1 vv, whereas in variegata cytoplasm all v gametes are eliminated by one of the sexes, and in subtypica cytoplasm all V gametes are eliminated by one of the sexes. In which of the sexes the gametes were eliminated was not determined.

III.3.i.d. *Physiologically controlled cell lineage variegation in* Lastraea atrata?

Variegation in the sporophytes of the fern *Lastraea atrata* consists of a mixture of green tissue, with normal chloroplasts, and white tissue, with smaller pale green plastids. The white areas occur in sharp stripes or sectors running from the midrib to the margin of the pinnae. Entirely green or entirely white pinnae are rare, and entire fronds of only one colour are never found. Sori are produced on both green and white pinnae, or parts of pinnae, and it is therefore possible to collect spores derived from one sporangium developed solely in the white zone, or solely in the green zone. Yet when these spores germinate they produce only green gametophytes; white or variegated gametophytes are never produced. The green gametophytes, for their part, give only variegated sporophytes. Within each sporangium Andersson-Kottö (1930; 1931) found thirty-two spores instead of the more usual number for ferns of sixty-four. Of these, some were normal in size and some small, but only the normal ones germinated. These imperfections, however, were common to both green and white sporangia; hence there is no reason to think that they were connected with variegation. On the contrary, the imperfections in spore development were found to be due to an abortive meiotic division resulting in dyads with an unreduced chromosome number, instead of tetrads. The germinating gametophytes were therefore of the same ploidy as the sporophytes. Sex organs were rarely found on the gametophytes, and the sporophytes developed asexually, without the fusion of gametes, from purely vegetative cells. The alternation of generations may be illustrated schematically as follows:

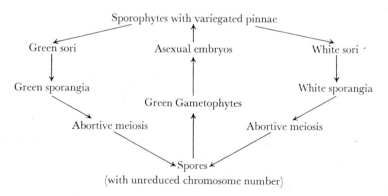

Hence we have in *Lastraea atrata* the remarkable situation of the alternation of variegation in the sporophyte and its absence from the gametophyte. And this occurs in spite of the fact that all gametophytes and their following sporophytes are genetically identical. Thus just as the genotype controls the differentiation of the sporophyte from the gametophyte, so it allows the development of variegation at one stage of the life cycle and inhibits it at another.

A second remarkable feature is that the green and white tissues of the variegated sporophytes behave as if they are genetically identical, yet the really sharp divisions between green and white areas, as well as the sectorial or striped shape of the white areas, make it almost certain that these are cell lineage variegations. Can it be that these cell lineages are caused by physiological differences between green and white areas? Can it be possible for cell lineage patterns to occur in which the difference between green and white areas is phenotypic, but not genotypic? These questions must clearly be given serious consideration, for if we assume, as we have done in the past, that a cell lineage can only occur as a result of mutation, then in *Lastraea* we must also assume that the mutation from green to white in the sporophyte is completely reversible in the formation of the spores, and why should this happen? On present information these questions must be left open; perhaps a new investigation would lead to an answer, and certainly it would be useful to have the observations confirmed.

It is perhaps worth mentioning that Andersson-Kottö (1930; 1931) also made intensive studies of another interesting variegated fern, *Polystichum angulare*, which can probably be classified as a kind of pattern or mutating variegation. Unfortunately, nearly all her breeding results are presented as ratios instead of actual numbers of offspring, thus making it difficult to follow her observations and impossible to judge her conclusions.

III.3.ii. STRIPED LINEAGES

We have already mentioned examples of striped variegation in maize that do not follow cell lineages (III.1.iv) Now we must mention a few that do appear to follow cell lineages. *Zea mays japonica* (j), the ornamental maize, contains broad yellow or white cell lineage stripes alternating with green[25, 46, 48]. The two types are caused by the action of a second gene in which the white stripe is dominant to the yellow (l). Argostripe (ag) is conspicuous throughout development[28]. The seedlings vary from almost pure white to a mixture of fine and coarse longitudinal white stripes following cell lineages. A few of the whitest seedlings die. Fine stripe (f) germinates as a virescent seedling[46]. As the plants grow the virescence becomes replaced by fine stripes which appear to follow cell lineages. The stripes become narrower and more numerous towards the leaf margins. Fine streaked (fi) consists of narrow light streaks on the leaf blades[1]. The streaks are sometimes prominent but they are usually limited to a few faint streaks. They may follow cell lineages. Lineate (li) consists of a very fine striping first appearing on about the tenth leaf[12]. The stripes are very narrow and closely spaced giving the leaves an overall greyish appearance. Striped auricle$_1$ (sa$_1$) and striped auricle$_2$ (sa$_2$) contain stripes which are limited almost entirely to the sheaths and auricles[28]. They appear to follow cell lineages, but this is not always very clear in the published photographs so this interpretation could be wrong both for this example and some of the other examples mentioned. In each case the striping is controlled by the action of recessive mutant genes when homozygous.

III.3.iii. TRANSITORY MOSAICS

The cotyledons of *Petunia hybrida* 'albomutabilis' are always green, but variegation appears on the first pair of foliage leaves. Individual leaves vary from those with occasional small white flecks to leaves with large white or mosaic sectors. The mosaic areas do not expand as much as the green which causes the leaves to be crumpled and distorted. The second pair of leaves tend to be more intensely variegated than the first pair. Subsequently, later leaves become progressively less intensely variegated and eventually all new leaves on the main shoot are green. Only in extreme cases are variegated leaves produced right up to the time of flowering. In *Phaseolus vulgaris*, Wade (1941) found that the variegation rarely occurred in the primary leaves, but any trifoliate leaves produced up to flowering time might show it. After flowering, the variegation in old leaves tended to become less distinct, and only rarely did any new leaves show it. The variegation in these two plants is evidently of a transitory nature. In *Petunia* it is also periodical for side branches arising from the green phase are often variegated. According to Correns (1936), the periodicity was not affected by changes in the genotype, but the degree of variegation and the length of the variegated phase was. He found that strongly variegated plants gave more intensely variegated offspring than weakly variegated offspring, and the variegated phase lasted longer.

Variegation in *Petunia* is controlled by a single recessive gene when homozygous. It is not entirely true-breeding because on intercrossing the self-sterile plants a few green offspring arise as well as variegated; the green offspring turn out to be heterozygous and must therefore arise by back-mutation. Correns found that he obtained more hetero-zygous green offspring from intercrossing weakly, than from inter-crossing strongly variegated plants, which suggests that the mutation frequency was modified by the polygenes that reduced the variegation intensity. These back-mutations to green appear to be restricted to the germ track because there is no evidence of the formation of genotypic-ally heterozygous green branches. The F_2 seedlings from selfing hetero-zygous green *Phaseolus* plants segregate in three different ratios namely, 3 green: 1 variegated, 9 green: 7 variegated, and 27 green: 37 variegated, owing to one recessive gene, or the complementary action of two reces-sive genes, or the complementary action of three recessive genes respectively. These genes have a cumulative effect upon the degree of variegation. The average variegation intensity is greatest when all three recessive genes are present, less when two genes are present, and least when the variegation is induced by only one gene. Another example of a transitory mosaic variegation, which has not been studied genetically, occurs in the common ivy, *Hedera helix*. In one variegated variety the young leaves are always variegated, but as they age they green up until eventually the original mosaic can no longer be recognized.

III.3.iv. POSSIBLE CAUSES OF MOSAIC AND STRIPED PATTERNS

Whether a plant is variegated or not is dependent upon the presence or absence of the appropriate genotype. Firstly, one, two or more recessive genes in the homozygous condition determine whether the variegated phenotype is expressed or not, and secondly, it is probable that many other genes with small effects modify the variegation expres-sion. The variegation intensity of the maternal parent may also influence the variegation intensity of the offspring in some cases. But how can we account for the actual pattern of variegation? The straightforward answer is that we do not know. Nevertheless suggestions have been made which are worth considering.

It is generally believed that mosaic and striped patterns which follow cell lineages are caused by nuclear or plastid gene mutation, whereas non cell lineage patterns are caused by a physiological effect. It is therefore important to be certain whether the variegation is a cell lineage or non cell lineage type and this is not always clear, as in some of the striped varieties of maize. In the fern *Lastraea alrata* the variega-tion appeared to be following cell lineages, and yet it was not possible to confirm the assumed mutations; either the mutation was fully reversible during spore formation, or the cell lineage was caused by a physiological change, or perhaps it was not a cell lineage variegation at all. In *Barbarea vulgaris* we observed cell lineage differences between green and mosaic areas, but within the mosaic area it is doubtful. The very impermanence of the transitory mosaics suggests that a physio-logical explanation is more likely than a mutational one, and yet leaves sectorial for green and mosaic areas have been observed; but perhaps even this is not a true indication of a cell lineage mutation? An important observation of Correns strongly emphasizes a physiological explanation for *Capsella bursa pastoris*. He found that embryos segregating in the F_2 generation from crosses between 'albovariabilis' and 'typica' were always more or less green and never variegated. When the seeds ripen the chloroplasts in the cotyledons lose their chlorophyll and regain it during germination. Correns found that the cotyledons which were wholly green in the embryo often became mosaiced in the germinating seedling; this surely could not be a mutation phenomenon. Since the plastids have proved themselves capable of developing into chloroplasts in the embryo, they are evidently being inhibited in some way in the seedlings. A possible explanation for the occurrence of sectorial leaves, which does not necessitate a mutational difference between the two halves might be as follows. In the early stages the gene inducing variegation is not working, thus accounting for the fact that the cotyledons and first leaves are often green. When the gene begins to become effective its action is at first sporadic so that variegation is produced in one cell lineage but not in another. This gives rise to small flecks or large sectors depending upon the moment or position in leaf development at which the gene action becomes operative. In extreme cases, the whole of one half of a leaf is affected and becomes variegated, while the other half, because it is derived from a different cell lineage, remains green. Gradually, in permanent mosaics, the gene becomes operative continuously and all leaves are variegated while, in transitory mosaic plants, the gene becomes operative for only a limited period of development. In *Capsella* the gene appears to be turned off during the development of the chloroplasts in the cotyledons of the embryo, whereas it appears to become turned on when the plastids of the same cells fail to become green for the second time at germination.

The more conventional explanations of mosaic and striped patterns are firmly rooted in the mutation hypotheses. Imai (1936a, b; 1937a) considered that white areas are caused by gene-induced plastid mutation, which he refers to as exomutation of the plastids (see Chapter VIII.6 for a detailed account of gene-induced plastid mutations). He then assumes that green flecks appearing within the white areas are caused by localized automutation of the mutant white plastids back to green (see Chapter VIII.7 for other examples of unstable plastids). Dale and Rees-Leonard (1939) do not think that the plastids mutate because they observed no sorting-out; however, this is not necessarily a valid objection. When a plastid mutates spontaneously a mixed cell results containing both normal and mutant plastids. But when plastids mutate under the control of a particular genotype it is possible that all the plastids of a cell could mutate together so that there would be no plastid sorting-out pattern to observe. Another possibility is that interaction between normal and mutant plastids of a mixed cell could occur in such a way as to obscure the usual sorting-out pattern (see Chapter VII.3 for further details on the masking of mixed cells). As an alternative to the plastid mutation hypothesis, Dale and Rees-Leonard suggest that the white areas of *Salpiglossis sinuata* are caused by a mutable gene or a pattern gene giving an unstable phenotype, while the green flecks on the white sectors arise from a chance arrangement of the green to white change. In coarse mosaics in which the green flecks are rare, a chance arrangement of green and white cells may appear as a reasonable explanation, but it could hardly account for fine mosaics in which the green flecks are frequently very numerous. Hence the mutable gene hypothesis, like the mutable plastid hypothesis, has to assume that there are two mutations, firstly, from green to white, and secondly, from white back to green.

Thus the variegation in mosaic and striped patterns is either caused by a physiological effect, or by nuclear, or by plastid mutation. At the moment we are doubtful as to how to distinguish between them. It is possible that one type of mechanism is responsible for the variegation pattern of all our examples (Table III.2), but it is also possible that all three types may be involved in different cases. Clearly we must still keep an open mind on the subject.

REFERENCES

1. ANDERSON, E. G. (1922). *J. Hered.* **13**, 91–93
2. ANDERSSON, I. (1924). *J. Genet.* **14**, 185–195
3. ANDERSSON-KOTTÖ, I. (1930). *Z. Vererbungsl.* **56**, 115–201
4. ANDERSSON-KOTTÖ, I. (1931). *Bibliogr. genet.* **8**, 269–294
5. BEADLE, G. W. (1929). *Amer. Nat.* **63**, 189–192
6. BÖHME, H. & SCHOLZ, G. (1960). *Die Kulturpflanze* **8**, 93–109
7. BOYE, C. L. (1941). *J. Genet.* **42**, 191–196
8. BOYE, C. L. & RIFE, D. C. (1938). *J. Hered.* **29**, 55–60
9. BRINK, R. A. (1935). *J. Hered.* **26**, 249–251
10. CARVER, W. A. (1927). *Genetics* **12**, 415–440
11. CLARK, F. H. (1932). *J. Hered.* **23**, 235–237
12. COLLINS, G. N. & KEMPTON, J. H. (1920). *J. Hered.* **11**, 2–6
13. COOK, A. A. (1962). *Proc. Amer. Soc. Hort. Sci.* **81**, 390–395
14. CORRENS, C. (1909a). *Z. Vererbungsl.* **1**, 291–329
15. CORRENS, C. (1919a). *S.B. preuss. Akad. Wiss.* 585–610
16. CORRENS, C. (1920). *S.B. preuss. Akad. Wiss.* 212–240
17. CORRENS, C. (1931a). *S.B. preuss. Akad. Wiss.* 203–231
18. CORRENS, C. (1931b). *Z. Vererbungsl.* **59**, 274–280
19. CORRENS, C., Edited KAPPERT, H. (1936). *S.B. preuss. Akad. Wiss.* 3–21
20. DAHLGREN, K. V. O. (1921). *Hereditas* **2**, 88–98
21. DALE, E. E. & REES-LEONARD, O. L. (1939). *Genetics* **24**, 356–367
22. DARLINGTON, C. D. (1929). *J. Genet.* **21**, 161–168
23. DEMEREC, M. (1921). *J. Hered.* **12**, 406–407
24. DEMEREC (I, M.926). *J. Hered.* **17**, 301–306

25. EMERSON, R. A. (1912). *Rep. Neb. agric. Exp. Sta.* **25**, 85–109
26. EYSTER, W. H. (1924). *J. Hered.* **15**, 397–400
27. EYSTER, W. H. (1933). *Plant Phys.* **8**, 105–121
28. EYSTER, W. H. (1934). *Bibliogr. genet.* **11**, 187–392
29. HAYES, H. K. (1932). *J. Hered.* **23**, 415–419
30. IINUMA, Y. (1941). *Jap. J. Genet.* **17**, 229–230
31. IKENO, S. (1917). *Genetics* **2**, 390–416
32. IKENO, S. (1927). *Bibliogr. genet.* **3**, 313–353
33. IMAI, Y. (1925). *Bot. Gaz.* **80**, 276–287
34. IMAI, Y. (1930b). *Genetica* **12**, 297–318
35. IMAI, Y. (1934a). *J. Genet.* **29**, 145–151
36. IMAI, Y. (1936a). *J. Genet.* **33**, 169–195
37. IMAI, Y. (1936b). *Z. Vererbungsl.* **71**, 61–83
38. IMAI, Y. (1937a). *Cytologia, Fujii Jubilee* **2**, 934–947
39. IMAI, Y. (1938). *J. Genet.* **35**, 375–382
40. KEMPTON, J. H. (1921). *J. Hered.* **12**, 224–226
41. KEMPTON, J. H. (1923). *J. Hered.* **14**, 349–353
42. KRISTOFFERSON, K. B. (1923). *Hereditas* **4**, 251–289
43. KRISTOFFERSON, K. B. (1924). *Hereditas* **5**, 297–364
44. LEWIS, C. F. (1958). *J. Hered.* **49**, 267–271
45. LEWIS, C. F. (1960). *J. Hered.* **51**, 209–212
46. LINDSTROM, E. W. (1918). *Mem. Cornell agric. Exp. Sta.* **13**
47. LIPPERT, L. F., BERGH, B. O. & COOK, A. A. (1964). *J. Hered.* **55**, 79–83
48. MILES, F. C. (1915). *J. Genet.* **4**, 193–214
49. MIYAKE, K. & IMAI, Y. (1934). *J. Coll. Agric. Tokyo* **13**, 27–44
50. MOFFETT, A. A. (1936). *J. Genet.* **33**, 151–161
51. MORINAGA, T. (1932). *Bot. Mag. Tokyo* **46**, 202–207
52. PARKER, M. C. (1933). *J. Hered.* **24**, 481–486
53. RASMUSON, H. (1917). *Z. Vererbungsl.* **17**, 1–52
54. RASMUSON, H. (1920). *Hereditas* **1**, 270–276
55. RICK, C. M., THOMPSON, A. E. & BRAUER, O. (1959). *Amer. J. Bot.* **46**, 1–11
55a. SCHEEL, H. (1965). *Z. Pflanzenz.* **54**, 225–246
56. SCHERZ, W. (1927). *Z. Vererbungsl.* **45**, 1–40
57. SCHICK, R. & STUBBE, H. (1932). *Z. Vererbungsl.* **62**, 249–290
58. SCHOLZ, G. (1964). *Flora* **154**, 589–597
59. SCHOLZ, G. & BÖHME, H. (1961). *Die Kulturpflanze* **9**, 181–191
60. SCHWARZ, W. (1928). *Planta* **5**, 660–680
61. SIRKS, M. J. (1931a). *Genetica* **13**, 209–631
62. SIRKS, M. J. (1931b). *Proc. Acad. Sci. Amst.* **34**, 1340–1346
63. SIRKS, M. J. (1938). *Bot. Rev.* **4**, 113–131
64. STROMAN, G. N. (1924). *Genetics* **9**, 493–512
65. TILNEY-BASSETT, R. A. E. (1963c). *Heredity* **18**, 543–545
66. WADE, B. L. (1941). *J. agric. Res.* **63**, 661–669
67. WINGE, Ø. (1931). *Hereditas* **15**, 126–165
68. ZAUMEYER, W. J. (1938). *Phytopathology* **28**, 520–522
69. ZAUMEYER, W. J. (1942). *J. agric. Res.* **64**, 119–127

CHAPTER IV

Mutable Nuclear Genes

IV.1. Back-Mutations

CELL lineage variegations are said to be caused by back-mutations whenever a recessive allele of a nuclear gene mutates to a dominant allele, so that the plastid phenotype changes from a chlorophyll deficient colouring back to green (see Chapter II).

IV.1.i. DEVELOPMENTAL BEHAVIOUR

When looking at a new variegated plant it is always helpful to know any features by which one can quickly classify it. Accordingly, variegation caused by repeated back-mutation of a recessive gene is recognized visually by one or more of the following characteristics:

(1) Variegated leaves have green flecks or sectors of varying size on a chlorophyll deficient or, more simply, a white background (Fig. IV.1).

(2) Early mutations in one or more layers of the growing-point sometimes produce green-variegated sectorial and mericlinal shoots. These in turn can give rise to stable green shoots and periclinal shoots in which the leaves have a variegated skin surrounding a green core or vice versa.

(3) Variegated plants do not always breed true but may also produce lethal white and viable green seedlings; the green seedlings produce no variegated leaves during subsequent development.

When mutations are restricted to the leaves or the germ track as sometimes happens, the second of the above characteristics is not possible but all three may occur with mutations not restricted to these tissues. In practice, even with these unlocalized mutations, pure green shoots arise only or more often when:

(1) Mutations occur early in development rather than late.
(2) Mutations are frequent rather than rare.
(3) The shoot apical growing-point has a few initial cells rather than many.
(4) Lateral buds develop from a small sector of the main shoot rather than from a large sector.

FIG. IV.1. *Single leaves illustrating the repeated back-mutation of a recessive nuclear gene resulting in a cell lineage change in the plastid phenotype from chlorophyll deficient to normal green. Notice particularly the difference between the two plants in the frequency and size of the green areas. Left,* Mirabilis jalapa; *right,* Ballota nigra

(5) Plants produce side shoots frequently rather than rarely.

(6) Plants have a long vegetative phase rather than a short one.

In short, the plant's mode of development is important as well as the mutability of the gene.

White seedlings are often produced by plants when the gene has a low mutation frequency early in development. In some cases, however, the cotyledons are not pure white and observation under the binocular microscope reveals extremely small green flecks comprising only a few cells each. Such small green areas in *Ballota nigra* are insufficient to support further growth so that seedlings with a really white background completely lacking in chlorophyll die. In *Mirabilis jalapa* and *Zea mays* (Table IV.1), on the other hand, the background chlorophyll deficiency is pale green and there is enough chlorophyll to support further development.

In order to understand the origin of green seedlings it is essential fully to appreciate the genetic constitution of these variegated plants. Wherever a recessive allele back-mutates to the normal allele the genotype of that cell and all its later cell descendants are no longer homozygous but heterozygous for that locus, which now contains in a diploid

TABLE IV.1. EXAMPLES OF VARIEGATION CAUSED BY THE REPEATED BACK-MUTATION OF A RECESSIVE GENE

Plant and form	Approximate appearance and behaviour				Authors	Dates
	Ground colour and viability: V	Green and periclinal shoots	Green areas on leaves Size, frequency	Seedlings from selfing		
Antirrhinum majus						
albostriata (stri)	White	Occasional	Variable, many	? + V	Baur	1924
bicolor (bic)	Yellow-white	Occasional	Large, few	? + V	Kuckuck, Schick	1930
flavostriata (flast)	Golden	Frequent	Large, many	G + V	" "	"
marmorata (marm)	White	None	Large, many	V	" "	"
Aquilegia vulgaris variegata	Yellow-green V	None	Large, few	G + V	Baur	1911a, 12
Avena sativa yellow-striped	Yellow	?	Large, ?	G + V	Christie	1922
Ballota nigra variegata	Yellow-white	Frequent	Variable, many	G + V ± W	Tilney-Bassett	unpub.
Epilobium parviflorum marmorata	White	?	Variable, many	? + V	Michaelis	1957a
Mirabilis jalapa variegata	Pale green V	Occasional	Large, few	G + V ± W	Correns	1909a, 10
Oryza sativa white-striped	White	Occasional	Large, ?	G + V ± W	Mitra; Mitra, Ganguli	1932; 1934
Pharbitis nil						
yellowy (ye)	Yellow-green V	Frequent	Large, few	G + V	Imai	1934b
yellow-inconstant (yi)	Yellow V	Frequent	Variable, few	G + V ± W	Miyake, Imai; Imai	1934; 1926, 27, 30a, 34b, 36b
xanthic (x)	Yellow	None	Small, few	V + W	Miyake, Imai; Miyazawa; Miyake, Imai	1934; 1929, 32; 1934
Zea mays						
pale green mutable (pg^m)	Pale green V	None	Variable, many	G + V ± W	Peterson	1953, 58, 60
pale green mottled (pg^{mo})	Pale green V	None	Variable, many	G + V	Peterson	1960

plant one allele dominant and one allele recessive in its effect. The back-mutation is accompanied by a change in the phenotype of the plastids from white to green. As a result of such frequent back-mutations the plant is genotypically heterogeneous and consists of a mosaic of homozygous recessive white areas intermingled with heterozygous normal green areas. The individual's overall appearance is therefore variegated. The mosaic shoots developed in plants with unlocalized mutations eventually give rise to mosaic inflorescences and hence to mosaic germ tracks. Consequently, some gametes possess a nucleus with the recessive allele and others possess the dominant allele. When both pollen and egg contain the recessive allele the embryo is homozygous recessive for the gene and the resulting seedling white, or it may become variegated. When one gamete contains the recessive allele and the other the dominant allele the embryo is heterozygous for the gene and the resulting seedling green. When both gametes contain the dominant allele the embryo is homozygous dominant for the gene and the resulting seedling is again green. Green seedlings may also be produced by back-mutation occurring very early in the development of a homozygous recessive embryo. Among the green seedlings produced by selfing a variegated plant, we must therefore expect to obtain a few true-breeding green plants as well as many segregating. This expectation, and consequently the whole explanation of the origin of green seedlings, was admirably confirmed by Correns (1909a, 1910) and Baur (1924) both of whom obtained true-breeding and segregating green plants from selfing a variegated *Mirabilis* and *Antirrhinum* respectively.

In no two individuals of a particular form is the pattern of variegation exactly alike. Nevertheless, the overall variegation pattern of all the individuals of one form is frequently quite distinct from that of another. These differences arise from the limitless combinations of the position or timing and the frequency of mutation throughout development. In addition, differences of cell ontogeny, especially of the leaves, will also bring about differences in the variegation patterns. At one extreme we find (Table IV.1) plants such as *Antirrhinum majus* flavo-striata, *Ballota nigra* variegata (Fig. IV.1) and *Pharbitis nil* yellowy and yellow-inconstant in which early mutations give rise to frequent green and periclinal shoots and, on selfing, to green seedlings. Intermediate examples are *Antirrhinum majus* albostriata and bicolor and *Mirabilis jalapa* variegata (Fig. IV.1) which occasionally develop pure green growing-points and also give rise to a few green seedlings. *Avena sativa* yellow-striped and *Zea mays* pale green mutable and pale green mottled produce green seedlings on selfing as well as variegated, but no green shoots have been reported from their tillers. An entirely localized mutation pattern is found in *Antirrhinum majus* marmorata which is completely true to type; even though the marmorata mutations are restricted to the leaves the green sectors are large showing that mutation must be limited to a fairly early period in leaf development. At the furthest extreme we find the flecking in *Pharbitis nil* xanthic to be not only restricted to the leaves but also so infrequent that most selfed seedlings have pure yellow cotyledons which die without ever producing green flecks at all. Moreover, even when the cotyledons are variegated the area of the green flecks is frequently too small and provides too little chlorophyll to promote the growth of any foliage leaves.

Plants with mutations restricted to the leaves are, of course, similar to pattern variegations (see Chapter III) in their true-breeding behaviour. They are distinguished as belonging to the mutable gene group because the direction of mutation is quite clearly from white to green. The cotyledons especially are always white or variegated whereas in pattern variegations the cotyledons are frequently green and the variegation only develops later. Furthermore, the green areas of the mutating variegation are not secondarily flecked with white as is often the case with pattern variegations. The white-striped leaves of *Oryza sativa* were considered by Mitra and Ganguli (1934) to be caused by a pattern gene, but their results clearly indicate that they were dealing with a mutable gene or genes; since the background leaf colour is white the rice plant would have been more accurately called green-stripe rice. The yellow-stripe oat, *Avena sativa*, was not understood by Christie (1922) who believed his selfing results indicated sorting-out of plastids. This interpretation was plainly wrong since, on selfing, a number of green families segregated into green and variegated offspring with a significant fit to a monohybrid ratio. The description of his material and the high proportion of green seedlings obtained from selfing variegated plants, suggest that he too had failed to recognize the behaviour of a mutable gene.

IV.1.ii. MUTATION MECHANISMS

Most authors have been content to describe the behaviour of their variegated plants without delving into the problem of the mutation mechanism. An early step in this direction was made by Imai (1936b) with the simple suggestion that the yellowy, yellow-inconstant, and xanthic forms of *Pharbitis nil* carried automutable genes, mutating without help from other genes, which frequently altered to the constant normal allele. This explanation was in keeping with the single gene system suggested by the observed monohybrid ratios but it is too simple for plants in which the dihybrid ratio shows that at least two genes are involved (Table IV.2). The intensive investigations of Peterson (1953, 1958, 1960) into the pale green mutable system in *Zea mays* has now

TABLE IV.2. EXAMPLES OF MONO- AND DIHYBRID RATIOS SHOWING SEGREGATION OF MUTABLE NUCLEAR GENES RESPONSIBLE FOR VARIEGATION AS LISTED IN TABLE IV.1.

Plant	Monohybrid ratios (g = green)	Dihybrid ratios (g = green)
Antirrhinum majus	3 g:1 albostriata 3 g:1 bicolor 3 g:1 flavostriata 3 g:1 marmorata 3 g:1 yellow-striped	
Avena sativa	3 g:1 marmorata	
Epilobium parviflorum	3 g:1 yellowy	
Pharbitis nil	3 g:1 xanthic	
Aquilegia vulgaris	3 g:1 variegata 3 variegata:1 yellowish-g (chlorina)	Failure to give expected 12:3:1 ratio attributed to close linkage
Ballota nigra	Ratios not clear but segregation into: green and variegated and green and white	Segregation into green, variegated and white gave 12:3:1 ratio in two families but not in a third
Mirabilis jalapa	3 g:1 variegata 3 variegata:1 pale-g (chlorina)	12 g:3 variegata:1 pale-g
Oryza sativa	3 g:1 white-striped 3 white-striped:1 white	12 g:3 white-striped:1 white
Zea mays	3 g:1 pale-g stable 3 g:1 pale-g mutable 3 pale-g mutable:1 pale-g stable 3 g:1 pale-g mottled 3 pale-g stable:1 pale-g mottled	12 g:3 pale-g mutable:1 pale-g stable $Pg > pg^m > pg^s > pg^{mo}$ But $pg^m = pg^s$ + Enhancer
Pharbitis nil	3 g:1 yellow 3 g:1 yellow-inconstant 3 yellow-inconstant:1 yellow	$Y > yi > y$ But relationship of yi to y may be the same as pg^m to pg^s in Zea mays

given us a much clearer insight into the possible mutation mechanisms. It will be as well, therefore, to discuss his experiments in detail, especially as his most important paper (1960) is difficult to follow without a close acquaintance with the interpretation of breeding experiments.

IV.1.ii.a. *Pale green mutable system in* Zea mays

To explain the pale green mutable system of maize (Tables IV.1 and 2) Peterson (1960) put forward the hypothesis that there are two components as follows:

(1) *I*, a factor which inhibits the expression of the normal green allele, Pg, and causes the pale phenotype to be expressed (pg^s); it is located at the Pg locus.

(2) *En*, a factor called enhancer which causes the removal of *I*. The removal of *I* stops the inhibition of the normal green allele and thereby causes the back-mutation of pg → Pg resulting in a green stripe. In the absence of *En* the pale green seedlings are stable (pg^s), in the presence of *En* the pale green seedlings are mutable (pg^m).

Enhancer segregating independently of the pale green locus: Peterson has shown that enhancer can be located on a chromosome independent of the pale green locus, by the following breeding experiments:

(1) Selfing the F_1 heterozygotes with the constitution *En*/+, +/pg gave a modified dihybrid ratio of 12 green:3 pale green mutable:1 pale green stable (Table IV.2). The full details of the dihybrid segregation are illustrated in the checkerboard (Fig. IV.2). The modified dihybrid ratio indicates that a factor controlling the mutability of pale green (pg)

♂ ／ ♀	+, +	En, +	En, pg	+, pg
+, +	+/+, +/+ (Pg)	+/En, +/+ (Pg)	+/En, +/pg (Pg)	+/+, +/pg (Pg)
En, +	En/+, +/+ (Pg)	En/En, +/+ (Pg)	En/En, +/pg (Pg)	En/+, +/pg (Pg)
En, pg	En/+, pg/+ (Pg)	En/En, pg/+ (Pg)	En/En, pg/pg (pg^m)	En/+, pg/pg (pg^m)
+, pg	+/+, pg/+ (Pg)	+/En, pg/+ (Pg)	+/En, pg/pg (pg^m)	+/+, pg/pg (pg^s)

FIG. IV.2. F_2 *segregation in a modified dihybrid ratio of* 12 *green* (Pg):3 *pale green mutable* (pg^m):1 *pale green stable* (pg^s) *after selfing the* F_1 *heterozygote* En/+, +/pg. *The genotypes of the* F_1 *gametes are shown in the left hand margin and across the top of the figure; the sixteen rectangles in the centre show the genotypic constitution of the* F_2 *progeny.*

is segregating independently of it. When the factor is present pg is mutable (pg^m), when absent pg is stable (pg^s).

(2) Crossing the F_1 heterozygote $En/+$, $+/pg$ with a normal line

Gametes	+, +	En, +	En, pg	+, pg
+, +	$+/+$, $+/+$ (Pg)	$+/En$, $+/+$ (Pg)	$+/En$, $+/pg$ (Pg)	$+/+$, $+/pg$ (Pg)

Fig. IV.3. *Green plants of four different genotypes obtained by crossing the heterozygote $En/+$, $+/pg$ with a normal line $+/+$, $+/+$.*

$+/+$, $+/+$ gave all green offspring of four different genotypes (Fig. IV.3). When these green plants were selfed half bred true, a quarter segregated in a ratio of 12 green : 3 pale green mutable : 1 pale green stable and a quarter segregated in a ratio of 3 green : 1 pale green stable as follows:

$$1 \quad +/+, \; +/+ \; \rightarrow \text{Green}$$
$$1 \quad +/En, \; +/+ \; \rightarrow \text{Green}$$
$$1 \quad +/En, \; +/pg \; \rightarrow 12 \; Pg : 3 \; pg^m : 1 \; pg^s$$
$$1 \quad +/+, \; +/pg \; \rightarrow 3 \; Pg : 1 \; pg^s$$

The 1 : 1 ratio of the two classes of segregating families shows that one half of the pg-containing gametes of the F_1 plants possessed *En* and one half did not.

(3) Further confirmation of *En* segregating independently of pg was obtained by Peterson when he selfed the F_2 green plants the genotypes of which are shown in the checkerboard (Fig. IV.2). The F_3 progeny were as follows:

$+/+$, $+/+$; $En/+$, $+/+$; $+/En$, $+/+$ and En/En, $+/+$ gave only green F_3

$+/En$, $+/pg$; $+/En$, $pg/+$; $En/+$, $+/pg$ and $En/+$, $pg/+$ gave 12 $Pg : 3 \; pg^m : 1 \; pg^s$

$+/+$, $+/pg$ and $+/+$, $pg/+$ gave 3 $Pg : 1 \; pg^s$
En/En, $pg/+$ and En/En, $+/pg$ gave 3 $Pg : 1 \; pg^m$

Peterson's data agreed with the above F_3 segregation which thereby confirmed the F_2 data and hence the independent segregation of enhancer, *En*. These experiments show conclusively that enhancer is situated on a chromosome independent of the pale green locus. It is therefore rather surprising to find that enhancer can also behave as though located next to the pale green locus.

Enhancer linked with the pale green locus: The F_1 heterozygote $En/+$, $+/pg$ that produced the ratio of 12 $Pg : 3 \; pg^m : 1 \; pg^s$ on selfing (Fig.

IV.2) originated from a cross between a heterozygous pale green mutable plant and a standard line, which may be shown schematically as follows:

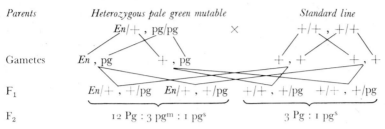

The same cross also produced a second F_1 heterozygote $+/+$, $+/pg$ and this, on selfing, produced offspring that segregated in a ratio of 3 green (Pg) : 1 pale green stable (pg^s). It is to be noticed that neither of these two F_1 heterozygotes segregates into green and pale green mutable. Nevertheless, out of a total of thirty-seven F_1 individuals that Peterson selfed, only eight families segregated as expected. The remaining twenty-nine families segregated in a ratio of approximately 3 green : 1 pale green mutable, plus an occasional pale green stable seedling. Thus the majority of F_2 plants are segregating in a monohybrid ratio and the dihybrid ratio is the exception. The simplest explanation for this monohybrid ratio is that enhancer is located next to the pale green locus or is a component of it $(\overline{pgEn})$ so that the mutability is apparently autonomously controlled, or as Imai suggested, the gene is automutable. The origin of the F_2 segregating into green and pale green mutable may be shown schematically as follows:

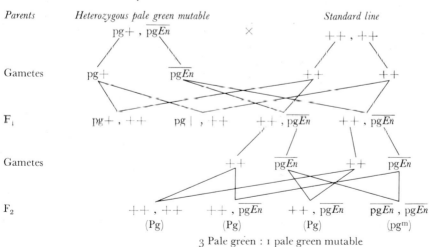

3 Pale green : 1 pale green mutable

The alternative possibility that the F_2 segregating into green and mutable progeny could be explained on the basis of independently assorting enhancers at two or three loci was investigated by Peterson with negative results. However, plants in which enhancer was duplicated at two different and independent loci were produced in an unrelated experiment.

IV.1.ii.b. *Automutation or induced mutation?*

To account for the very unusual behaviour of the same heterozygote segregating into both mono- and dihybrid ratios, it is necessary to assume that enhancer is a transposable factor which can be situated at the pale green locus on the same chromosome (autonomous control), or independently of it on a separate chromosome (independent control). This is a most useful concept for it enables one to suggest that the mutation mechanism is essentially the same throughout (see IV.1.iv for a further discussion on this subject). Thus it seems likely that the apparently automutable genes, mutating without help from other genes (that is, those with a monohybrid segregation, Table IV.2), are not really automutable but are in fact induced to mutate by an enhancer situated at a closely linked locus. On the other hand, in those plants with a dihybrid segregation (Table IV.2), mutations are recognized as being induced because of the independent segregation of the enhancer due to its position on an independent chromosome. In the intensely studied *Zea mays* apparent automutation and induced mutation have both been found, but in other mutable variegated plants different workers have observed either a linked enhancer with automutation, or an independent enhancer and induced mutation. The irregular segregation in *Ballota nigra* (Table IV.2) may, however, have been due to a change in the site of an enhancer from an independent to a linked position. Baur evidently had considerable foresight when he attributed the failure of *Aquilegia vulgaris* to produce a ratio of 12 green:3 variegated:1 pale green to close linkage.

The triple allelic series in the japanese morning glory, *Pharbitis nil*, namely green (Y), yellow-inconstant (yi) and yellow (y) can also be interpreted in a similar manner. It is possible that there could be two and not three alleles at the yellow locus, namely the wild type and the mutant. In the absence of enhancer the phenotype of the mutant is yellow, whereas in the presence of enhancer its phenotype is yellow-inconstant, which is variegated.

A second, less questionable, example of a third allele is pale green mottled (pg^{mo}) allelic to the pale green locus of *Zea mays*. It produces a variegation which consists of heavy, indistinctly outlined green stripes on a pale green ground owing to the repeated back-mutation of $pg^{mo} \rightarrow Pg$. Pale green mottled is recessive to pale green mutable and pale green stable. It appears to be automutable and the enhancer for the pale green mutable actually inhibits the expression of pale green mottled which is only fully expressed when enhancer is absent.

Since enhancer is transposable the question arises as to what extent its movement is reversible. In maize the occasional appearance of a green fleck on a pale green stable plant, and conversely of a stable sector on a mutable plant, support Peterson's suggestion that the transposition of enhancer from an autonomous to an independent locus is slightly reversible during development. On the other hand, the back-mutation of pale green to green, pg → Pg, does not appear to be reversible except with the low frequency of a non-mutable gene.

IV.1.iii. MUTABILITY

No two individuals of a mutable variegated plant ever have exactly similar mutation patterns, nevertheless, a general pattern of behaviour for a particular nuclear gene is clearly recognizable. From time to time the general pattern alters as a result of spontaneous internal genotypic changes. It can also be induced to alter by external changes in the environment. Few investigations into these changes have been made, but the available observations are full of interest and their further study would certainly be well rewarded. The mechanisms responsible for these changes may prove, in time, to be similar or identical to the mechanisms controlling similar alterations in anthocyanin variegations (see IV.1.iv).

IV.1.iii.a. *Genotypic changes*

What is probably the first observation of a somatic change in the genotype was made by Baur (1924) who states that a branch of *Antirrhinum majus* albostriata with a few green flecks produced late in development may suddenly produce a side shoot in which many large flecks are produced early in development. Similar spontaneous changes have been observed in *Ballota nigra* (Tilney-Bassett, unpublished) during the growth of which as many as four distinct variegated shoots have arisen (Fig. IV.4) as follows:

V 1 The original type of variegation which has many green flecks and sectors.
V 2 Few green flecks and mostly small green sectors.
V 3 Numerous green flecks and rarely any green sectors.
V 4 Few green flecks and few or no green sectors such that the leaf is almost white.

These variations have all arisen vegetatively from the original type of variegation in various combinations and frequencies. The cause of the

FIG. IV.4. *Examples of different types of variegation pattern in leaves of Ballota nigra, due to variations in the mutability of the mutable gene. Top row: left, green; right, the original type of variegation V 1; centre, a pair of leaves sectorial for green and the original type of variegation. Bottom row: three variations in the variegation pattern: left, V 2; centre, V 3; right, V 4*

changes is not known. Baur suggested that the two mutant alleles in a homozygous recessive *Antirrhinum* had a mutability independent of each other and that both were labile towards early or late mutation. This would appear to be too simple an explanation for the *Ballota* with its four different mutation patterns. It is possible that the four variants comprise a multiple allelic series, or changes may be occurring in different elements of a foreign control system causing modifications in the frequency and position of mutation in the recessive gene (see IV.1.iv). These suggestions remain to be investigated. Similar changes have been observed in breeding experiments (Table IV.3).

TABLE IV.3. FREQUENCIES OF DIFFERENT CLASSES OF SEEDLINGS OBTAINED FROM SELFING VARIEGATED PLANTS WITH MUTABLE NUCLEAR GENES AS LISTED IN TABLES IV.1 AND 2

Plant and form	Nos. and percentages of offspring			
	Green	Variegated plus white		Total
Ballota nigra variegata	(1) 109 70·8%	45 29·2%		154
	(2) 39 37·1	66 62·9		105
Avena sativa yellow-striped	104 37·7	172 62·3		276
Pharbitis nil yellowy	20 14·8	115 85·2		135
Mirabilis jalapa variegata	11 6·3	165 93·7		176
Oryza sativa white-striped	13 1·6	829 98·4		842
		Mosaics	*Y-inconstants*	
Pharbitis nil yellow-inconstant				
New line: y-inconstant-2: Imai	133 23·3	264 46·3%	173 30·4%	570
New line: y inconstant-2: Miyazawa	(1) 120 11·8	596 58·8	297 29·4	1019
New line: y-inconstant-2: Miyazawa	(2) 61 4·9	186 14·9	1001 80·2	1248
Old line: y-inconstant-1: Imai	120 5·2	212 9·3	1958 85·5	2290

The yellow-inconstant line of *Pharbitis nil* has been known for over a century in Japan as the Matsushima variegation. It was therefore particularly interesting when it again arose as a new mutation in the course of Miyazawa's experiments. Miyazawa (1929, 1932) studied the new line and found the inheritance to be similar to the old line. Imai (1934b) called the old line yellow-inconstant-1 and the new line yellow-inconstant-2. The new line gave a much higher proportion of green and mosaic plants after selfing than Imai's old line (Table IV.3). The mosaic plants are sectorial or periclinal chimeras for green and variegated, whereas in the pure yellow-inconstants the green flecks are localized in the leaves. Evidently the mutation frequencies at different stages of development in the two lines are not alike. Mutation is most frequent early in development in the new line and late in development in the old. One of the families of the new line of Miyazawa, yellow-inconstant-2, differed remarkably from the others. It appears to behave similarly to the yellow-inconstant-1 families of Imai; they are therefore bracketed in the table. Since all the yellow-inconstant-2 families are from the same stock one must presume that the remarkable divergence of one family has resulted from a new mutation, or from the segregation of a factor or factors responsible for determining the position and frequency of mutation in development. A similar phenomenon has been observed in *Ballota nigra* (Tilney-Bassett, unpublished). The original variegated stock produced about 71 per cent of green offspring on selfing, but in the one divergent family this proportion was reduced to 37 per cent (Table IV.3).

IV.1.iii.b. *Environmental changes*

The study of the effects of growing mutating variegated plants under different environmental conditions received little or no attention until Peterson (1958) investigated the influence of temperature differences on the pale green mutable system of maize. He grew plants at 16°C and 28°C and found a strikingly higher mutation rate among seedlings developing at the higher temperature. The difference ranged from an approximately fivefold increase in mutation frequency for the first leaf to more than a twelvefold increase for the third leaf. The differences between the leaves he related to differences in the number of cell divisions between the time of the initial stage of germination and the time of counting the flecks in the first, second, and third leaf respectively. The position of enhancer, whether linked or independent of the pale green locus, gave no differential response to the temperature treatments. The effect of temperature on the mutation rate can be considered in terms of a cell which contains competing mutagen and inhibitor systems, either one of which may be preferentially affected by an increase in temperature. Peterson suggested, therefore, that the effect of an increase in temperature might be to cause an increase in the rate at which enhancer removed the inhibitory material, thereby increasing the chance for the locus to mutate.

IV.1.iv. THE CONTROL OF GENE ACTION IN ANTHOCYANIN VARIEGATIONS

The work of Peterson, in particular, has been most useful in helping us to begin to formulate constructive suggestions as to the mechanisms governing the control of gene action in mutating variegations. The existence of similar kinds of mutating variegation in eight other, unrelated, genera comprising two monocotyledons and six dicotyledons suggests that the controlling mechanism or mechanisms responsible will be found to be widespread in higher plants. Furthermore, many similarities exist between the known behaviour of mutating variegations involving plastid pigments and mutating variegations involving the red anthocyanin pigments. Now anthocyanin variegations are not connected with the plastids so this book is not the place to review the extensive work on them. Nevertheless, it must be stressed that a great deal more is known about the anthocyanin variegations than about the plastid variegations; hence explanations given for the former can serve as working hypotheses for the latter.

Anthocyanin variegations, which are well known in cultivated and ornamental plants, occur in leaves, flowers, and fruits. Many papers have been written about them but among the most impressive results are those of Brink, McClintock, Rhoades, and others working with maize kernels. These workers have found substantial evidence for the existence of both simple and more complex regulatory systems, which often give rise to varying patterns of anthocyanin variegation in mature tissues. Briefly, they find that a number of different structural genes, including genes associated with anthocyanin synthesis, which are variously located in the chromosome complement, can become placed under the control of one of these regulatory systems. The basic regulatory system controlling the action of the structural gene consists of two elements, of as yet unknown constitution, foreign to the gene, one an operator-like element at the gene locus, and the other a regulator element which may also be sited at the gene locus or it may be located elsewhere in the chromosome complement. The structural gene comes under the control of the regulator system by the insertion of the foreign element at the locus of the gene. This foreign inserted element may be the regulator of the foreign control system or it may be the operator element that responds only to signals from the regulator. In the absence of the foreign element the recessive allele of the gene is stable, but in the presence of the element it is activated in a very characteristic way, as evidenced by the subsequent variegated patterns of gene expression that appear in the mature tissues of the maize plant and kernel. Insertion of the foreign element at a gene locus is due to its ability to move from one location in the chromosome complement and become inserted in another, as a consequence of which a number of different genes may from time to time come under the control of a single foreign system of controlling elements. Release of the gene from the control of the regulating system occurs when the foreign element moves away from the gene locus, a process which may result in the appearance of a new, stable allele of the gene. The gene expression may, however, become altered without release of the foreign element. The operator and regulator elements may also become modified and these changes in turn modify the expression of the gene.

For further details of these most interesting systems the reader is referred to the recent review paper by McClintock (1965), and to the earlier papers mentioned by her. Enough has already been said to make it clear that the pale green mutable system of plastid variegation described by Peterson is indeed very similar. His proposed factor I (see IV.1.ii.a) clearly corresponds to the operator and the factor En to the regulator of the foreign control system. Moreover, the regulator En, like the regulator controlling anthocyanin variegation, is mobile; it can occur either at the pg gene locus, or it may move to a site on another chromosome. The decisive evidence that finally clinched the connection between the control of gene action in the pale green mutable plastid variegation and in some anthocyanin variegations of maize came, however, when it was recently recognized that the enhancer (En) of Peterson was in fact the same regulator as the element called suppressor-mutator (Spm). This rather complex regulator was independently investigated by McClintock in connection with its control of the action of a number of other genes which, incidentally, were not limited simply to those associated with anthocyanin synthesis.

Hence the basic similarity in the mechanism of the control of gene action in plastid and anthocyanin mutating variegations of maize is confirmed. To go further than this is perhaps somewhat premature, nevertheless it now seems likely, on the limited evidence available, that similar regulatory systems will be found to control the mutating variegations found in other genera, and perhaps also be responsible for at least some of the pattern variegations discussed in Chapter III. The examples already available of either apparent automutation or induced mutation (see IV.1.ii.b) can certainly be fitted to the hypothesis of a transposable regulator. Moreover, observations in *Antirrhinum*, *Ballota*, and *Pharbitis* of changes in frequency and position of mutation occurring both in the germ line and during vegetative growth, are similarly paralleled by observations in anthocyanin variegations of maize. The time is clearly ripe to analyse some of these cases again in suitable material, especially now that we have the added advantage of a good working hypothesis to test.

IV.2. Somatic Gene Conversion

IV.2.i. ORIGIN OF THE SULFUREA MUTANT

During the course of X-irradiation experiments with the tomato, *Lycopersicum esculentum*, there arose in the X_2 generation of the variety Lukullus, a yellow-green variegated plant which, for several years before it was studied, was propagated by seed. The seedlings ranged from weakly to intensely yellow-green variegated and, in addition, a number of wholly green and wholly yellow seedlings were also produced.

Reciprocal crosses between a range of the variegated plants and the parent variety, Lukullus, were made by Hagemann (1958). All the F_1 seedlings had green cotyledons and in most of them the foliage leaves were also green. Unexpectedly, irrespective of the direction of the cross, a few had variegated foliage leaves. On selfing either the green or the variegated F_1 plants, the offspring segregated into green and yellow seedlings. These yellow mutant seedlings Hagemann called sulfurea (sulf) because of their sulphur colouring.

IV.2.ii. DEVELOPMENT OF SULFUREA MUTANTS

The sulfurea seedlings derived from green or variegated F_1 hetero-zygotes are homozygous recessive (sulf/sulf). Shortly after germination the sulfurea seedlings have yellow cotyledons with a greenish tinge. In the following days a distinct difference between the cotyledons of individual lines from different F_1 plants becomes apparent. They form two distinct groups as follows:

Group 1. Lethal, pure sulfurea seedlings (sulf[pura]): The cotyledons become pale yellow and the greenish tinge disappears. After 5–10 days the cotyledons die and hence the seedlings die. The seedlings can, how-ever, be kept alive by grafting on to a normal green tomato plant. Successful grafts develop yellow foliage leaves and eventually flower and fruit. Seedlings from these pure yellow foliage grafted plants are all yellow. They are therefore called sulfurea[pura] and are homozygous for this pure form of the sulfurea gene (sulf[pura]/sulf[pura]).

Group 2. Semilethal, variegated sulfurea seedlings (sulv[vag]): Most seedlings die at the cotyledon stage, as they did in group 1, but a small portion become stronger and during the first day they become greener and develop green spots. In many of these spotted seedlings the size of the green areas is not sufficient to keep the seedlings alive and they die; others remain alive and slowly grow. Many families give an almost continuous range from pure yellow to almost completely green seed-lings. The surviving seedlings develop foliage leaves with varying degrees of variegation and the greenest eventually flower and fruit. The seedlings can also be grafted and this produces yellow or variegated plants which are often greener and which grow more vigorously than the non-grafted plants. The variegation consists of green and greenish-yellow, yellowish-white or white areas. The variegated phenotype was recognized by Hagemann as a second type of mutant allele of the sul-furea locus, and in contrast to the first mutant allele, sulfurea[pura], he has called it sulfurea [variegata] (sulf[vag]) (Fig. IV.5).

The offspring of the variegated plants, whether grafted or not,

Fig. IV.5. *Cotyledons showing differences in the phenotypic expression of the sulfurea gene of* Lycopersicum esculentum. *Left sulf$^+$/sulf$^+$ or sulf$^+$/sulf^{vag} or sulf$^+$/sulf^{pura}, centre sulf^{vag}/sulf^{vag} or sulf^{vag}/sulf^{pura}, right sulf^{pura}/sulf^{pura}. This previously unpublished photograph has been kindly provided by Dr R. Hagemann*

ranged from various degrees of variegation to yellow, from surviving to lethal. All are homozygous for the sulfurea^{variegata} allele (sulf^{vag}/sulf^{vag}). On one occasion Hagemann obtained green seedlings, as well as yellow and variegated, from selfing sulfurea^{variegata} plants. This could have resulted from a back-mutation of sulf^{vag} → sulf$^+$, in which case it would seem probable that the green areas of sulfurea^{variegata} plants are due to similar back-mutations in the somatic cells, and not just to a general greening of cells, or both changes may occur.

IV.2.iii. DEVELOPMENT AND BEHAVIOUR OF SULFUREA HETEROZYGOTES

Green heterozygotes: When the green F$_1$ plants mentioned earlier were selfed, they produced seedlings showing a monohybrid segregation of 3 green : 1 yellow. This established that the green F$_1$ plants were heterozygous (sulf$^+$/sulf) and that the yellow or sulfurea seedlings were homozygous recessive (sulf/sulf).

Variegated heterozygotes: All the F$_1$ seedlings had green cotyledons and the majority had green foliage leaves, but in a few the foliage leaves were variegated. The variegation is not uniform. Sometimes most of a plant is pure green and only one or two shoots reveal a few yellow, yellowish-white or white flecks on the leaves. Other plants have more frequent yellow or white flecks and sectors of various sizes on a green background. Individual leaves are frequently sectorial chimeras with one side of the midrib green and the other flecked or wholly yellow. Yet other leaves are yellow-margined periclinal chimeras. In extreme cases a whole shoot is completely yellow. In short, the cell lineage pattern of variegation follows the course expected of green to yellow mutations occurring at various stages of cell division from early in the apical growing-point to late in leaf development.

When selfed, both the green and the variegated F_1 plants produced green and yellow seedlings in the phenotypic, monohybrid ratio of $3:1$, which is genotypically $1:2:1$. The majority of the F_2 green seedlings were green but again a few were variegated. Analysis of the F_3 generation showed that the one third of the green F_2 plants which were homozygous dominant (sulf$^+$/sulf$^+$) were true-breeding and never produced any variegation. The variegated leaves developed only among a portion of the two-thirds of the green F_2 plants that were heterozygous (sulf$^+$/sulf) for the sulfurea mutant.

More detailed selfing experiments with the variegated heterozygotes showed that individual families ranged in their segregation from a ratio of slightly over 3 green:1 yellow to considerably less than 1 green:1 yellow. Offspring from green branches of variegated heterozygotes gave a good 3:1 segregation. The deviations towards yellow arose only when seeds from variegated branches were sown. Thus Hagemann found that the greater the proportion of yellow to green areas in the parent shoot, the higher the proportion of yellow seedlings in the offspring. Moreover, in the extreme case of a pure yellow shoot, only yellow offspring were usually produced. These results plainly show the proportion of yellow offspring to be related to the degree of variegation in the parent, and in particular, to the shoots from which the fruit is collected. Since the yellow seedlings are homozygous recessive, it is therefore evident that the yellow areas of the variegated heterozygote are also homozygous recessive and they result from the mutation of the dominant sulf$^+$ allele to the recessive sulf allele. Consequently, the variegated plant is not a true heterozygote but is really a mosaic of heterozygous green areas (sulf$^+$/sulf) and homozygous yellow areas (sulf/sulf). Hence, should germ cells develop from a heterozygous cell lineage then all the gametes will be either sulf$^+$ or sulf, just as from a pure green heterozygote, but should germ cells develop from a homozygous recessive cell lineage then all the gametes must be sulf and on fertilization will give only homozygous recessive embryos which will germinate to give only yellow seedlings. There is no evidence to support the alternative possibility of selective fertilization against the normal allele to give the observed deviations from the monohybrid ratio.

IV.2.iv. MULTIPLE ALLELES OF SULFUREA

The sulfurea gene forms a multiple allelic series consisting of the normal allele sulf$^+$ and two groups of mutant alleles, the sulf^{pura} type and the sulf^{variegata} type. Reciprocal crosses between grafted sulf^{pura} and sulf^{variegata} plants produced variegated seedlings in the F_1 thereby demonstrating that sulf^{vag} is dominant over sulf^{pura}. Both alleles are recessive to the wild type, sulf$^+$. The dominance relationship is therefore sulf$^+$ > sulf^{vag} > sulf^{pura}. In addition, Hagemann (1961c) has mentioned the possibility of a third mutant allele, sulfurea^{virescens} (sulf^{vis}).

The sulfurea system is further complicated by the existence of several sulf^{pura} and sulf^{variegata} alleles. When homozygous, alleles from the two series are distinguishable by the presence or absence of variegated seedlings, but within each series further alleles are not distinguishable. This further division is only possible in the heterozygotes.

Distinct lines of F$_1$ heterozygotes are recognizable because of the different percentages of variegated heterozygotes that they give. In the sulf^{pura} group one finds alleles with all possible degrees of conversion activity varying between 0·5 per cent and 100 per cent, whereas in the sulf^{vag} group conversion activity rises to a maximum of 10 per cent. This means that a sulf^{pura} allele with 20 per cent conversion activity, which may be called sulf$^{pura\ 20\%}$, causes twenty plants in every hundred of the heterozygotes to become variegated in the foliage leaves.

It might be argued that there is really only one allele which is very variable in its activity. This does not seem to be the case, however, because from one year to the next the percentage frequency of variegation produced by a heterozygous line is often very constant. Nonetheless, on several occasions the heterozygous offspring of one plant, which arose from a family with low conversion activity, showed a high conversion activity; the offspring of other plants of the same line behaved as previously without any change in activity. It thus appears as if a new sulfurea allele had arisen by mutation from an allele of low conversion activity to an allele of high conversion activity. Alternatively, the same allele could be caused to increase or decrease in activity by the action of a modifying gene, but Hagemann says there is no supporting evidence for this whereas there is clearly good evidence for the occurrence of several sulf alleles.

Somatic mutations also occur from one series to another. Thus when sulf$^+$ is induced to mutate by an allele such as sulf$^{pura\ 90\%}$, the new allele is not necessarily another sulf$^{pura90\%}$, it could equally well be another sulf^{pura} allele with a different conversion activity or it could even be a sulf^{vag} allele. In fact, according to Hagemann (1961c), sulf^{vag} arises from the heterozygote sulf$^+$/sulf^{pura} more often than sulf^{pura} itself. We can now explain some of the differences which occur in the variegation pattern of the same plant, such as sudden changes from large sectors to small flecks, as due to the formation of alleles of both series and of varying conversion activity.

IV.2.v. CONVERSION MECHANISM

The mutation of sulf$^+$ to sulf is not the result of a highly mutable gene in the usual sense since sulf$^+$/sulf$^+$ homozygotes are perfectly stable even when they arise by segregation among the offspring of variegated heterozygotes. The mutation of sulf $^+$ in the heterozygote must therefore occur under the influence of the sulf allele already present. Such a directed mutation has been termed by Winkler (1930) a conversion, and in this particular instance where conversion occurs in the somatic tissues of the shoot extending into the germ track, Hagemann has called it somatic conversion.

One possible way in which the mutation might come about is by mitotic crossing-over. Should this indeed take place during some cell divisions then the heterozygous parent cell would give rise to two daughter cells, one of which would be homozygous dominant (sulf$^+$/ sulf$^+$) and the other homozygous recessive (sulf/sulf). Twin spots would therefore be formed, one yellow and one green. Phenotypically, however, the homozygous green spot would be indistinguishable from the heterozygous green background. Evidence for homozygous green areas must therefore be sought for by breeding experiments, and this Hagemann (1961b) has done. He realized that should there be homozygous dominant green areas arising by mitotic crossing-over, they must be as common as homozygous recessive yellow areas and must affect the genotype of the germ track just as frequently. Consequently, on selfing green shoots of variegated plants, one would expect to find deviations from the monohybrid segregation giving proportions of green offspring higher than the ratio of 3 green:1 yellow. Hagemann found no such deviations other than slight deviations which were always within the region of chance and therefore of no significance. Since no homozygous green areas could be found, not even in fruit which were sectorial for green and yellow, Hagemann concluded that somatic crossing-over could not be taking place. Hence the somatic conversion must be the result of genuine gene mutation in some as yet unknown manner.

Hybridization between sulf homozygotes of *Lycopersicum esculentum* and the closely related species *Lycopersicum pimpinellifolium* of the same subgenus Eulycopersicum had no effect on the conversion activity of the sulf allele present (Hagemann, 1961d); conversion stable sulf$^+$ alleles could not be found. On the other hand, in hybrids between sulf homozygotes of *Lycopersicum esculentum* and the more distantly related *Lycopersicum hirsutum* of the subgenus Eriopersicum, or in hybrids with *Solanum pennellii*, variegation seldom occurred; evidently in these hybrids the conversion activity was influenced by the hybrid genotype (Hagemann, 1965).

Further, as yet undisclosed, experiments have shown[11] that conversion is not controlled by a two-element system such as that found responsible for the mutating variegations of maize. Instead, Hagemann (oral communication) is now of the opinion that somatic conversion may be connected with the localization of the sulf gene at or near a heterochromatic region, or near the nucleolar organizer of one of the tomato chromosomes. These are certainly interesting suggestions.

Finally it should be mentioned that a number of workers have described instances of gene conversion in fungi, particularly *Neurospora* (Wagner and Mitchell, 1964), but it is not known whether this is basically the same phenomenon as somatic gene conversion in tomato. It also remains to be seen whether or not somatic conversion in the cruciata, or sepaloid petal, character of *Oenothera* (Renner, 1959) is again similar. Clearly there is still much to learn about these phenomena.

REFERENCES

1. Baur, E. (1911a). *Z. Vererbungsl.* **4**, 81–102
2. Baur, E. (1912). *Z. Vererbungsl.* **6**, 201–216
3. Baur, E. (1924). *Bibl. genet. Lpz.* **4**, 1–170
4. Christie, W. (1922). *Z. Vererbungsl.* **27**, 134–141
5. Correns, C. (1909a). *Z. Vererbungsl.* **1**, 291–329
6. Correns, C. (1910). *Ber. dt. bot. Ges.* **28**, 418–434
7. Hagemann, R. (1958). *Z. Vererbungsl.* **89**, 587–613
8. Hagemann, R. (1961b). *Biol. Zbl.* **80**, 477–478
9. Hagemann, R. (1961c). *Biol. Zbl.* **80**, 549–550
10. Hagemann, R. (1961d). *Biol. Zbl.* **80**, 717–719
11. Hagemann, R. (1965). *Genetics Today* **1**, 11–12
12. Imai, Y. (1926). *Bot. Mag. Tokyo* **40**, 226–235
13. Imai, Y. (1927). *J. Genet.* **17**, 329–348
14. Imai, Y. (1930a). *J. Genet.* **22**, 191–200
15. Imai, Y. (1934b). *J. Coll. Agric. Tokyo* **12**, 479–523
16. Imai, Y. (1936b). *Z. Vererbungsl.* **71**, 61–83
17. Kuckuck, H. & Schick, R. (1930). *Z. Vererbungsl.* **56**, 51–83
18. McClintock, B. (1965). *Brookhaven Symp. Biol.* **18**, 162–184
19. Michaelis, P. (1957a). *Protoplasma* **48**, 403–418
20. Mitra, S. K. (1932). *Curr. Sci.* **1**, 102–103
21. Mitra, S. K. & Ganguli, P. M. (1934). *Indian J. agric. Sci.* **4**, 537–545
22. Miyake, K. & Imai, Y. (1934). *J. Coll. Agric. Tokyo* **13**, 27–44
23. Miyazawa, B. (1929). *Jap. J. Genet.* **4**, 167–184
24. Miyazawa, B. (1932). *Bull. Miyazaki Coll. Agric. For.* **4**, 111–125
25. Peterson, P. A. (1953). *Rec. Genetics Soc. Am.* **22**, 92–93
26. Peterson, P. A. (1958). *J. Hered.* **49**, 120–124
27. Peterson, P. A. (1960). *Genetics* **45**, 115–133
28. Renner, O. (1959). *Heredity* **13**, 283–288
29. Wagner, R. P. & Mitchell, H. K. (1964). *Genetics and Metabolism*, 2nd ed. John Wiley and Sons Inc., New York–London–Sydney
30. Winkler, H. (1930). *Die Konversion der Gene*. Gustav Fischer, Jena

CHAPTER V

Chromosome Control

V.1. Diploids: Loss of Chromosome Fragments

V.1.i. GENE-INDUCED CHROMOSOME BREAKAGE

THE leaves of a variegated *Zea mays* were found by Beadle (1932) to be marked by fine longitudinal white streaks following cell lineages. Free-hand sections of living leaves show that the streaks are due either to a reduction in the number of plastids per cell, or to the absence of chlorophyll from them. In addition the plants are small, they are highly pollen- and egg-sterile and they possess an abnormal scarred endosperm in their seeds. Cytological observations show that these defects are caused by the sticking together of the chromosomes, a condition induced by a recessive gene (st) when homozygous. The meiotic divisions rarely approach normal. The chromosomes are usually very viscid and they appear to have to be mechanically torn apart during anaphase. When the two chromosome clumps move to opposite poles, they are frequently held together by chromatin bridges which stretch and break releasing broken-off chromosome fragments into the cytoplasm. The second meiotic division is also somewhat aberrant. In mitosis, the chromosome stickiness persists to some extent and many divisions are upset. Again one or two fragments are frequently broken off the chromosomes and subsequently lost in the following cell divisions, and even a whole chromosome may be lost in root tip mitoses. From this evidence, it seems almost certain that the white streaks are caused by losses during leaf mitoses of similar chromosome fragments containing genes needed for chloroplast development.

V.1.ii. ARTIFICIALLY INDUCED CHROMOSOME BREAKAGE

V.1.ii.a. *X-rays*

Among the progeny of *Zea mays* crosses, in which X-irradiated pollen was used, McClintock (1932, 1938) found two cases of a deficiency adjacent to the centromere region of chromosome V. In the first deficiency (Def. 1) about one-twentieth, and in the second deficiency

(Def. 2) about one-seventh of the chromosome length was deleted. The pieces deleted formed a smaller and a larger ring chromosome, R1 and R 2 respectively. In each case a section of the centromere was transferred to the ring chromosome, and a section retained by the deficient rod chromosome. Hence all four parts contained a functional centromere allowing each to participate successfully in cell division. By crossing the two types, plants were produced with both deficient rod chromosomes together with various combinations of ring chromosomes. During their development, these double-deficient plants tend to lose their ring chromosomes at cell division. Whenever both rings are lost, the subsequent cell lineage completely lacks a portion of the chromosome complement, which results in the immediate inhibition of chloroplast development and the corresponding appearance of a white streak on the leaf. Loss of the larger R 2 chromosome occurs more frequently than loss of the R 1 chromosome. Hence the pattern of white streaks varies with different complements of ring chromosomes as we shall now see.

The simplest variegation pattern arises in plants which are double deficient for the rod chromosome and contain only one ring chromosome, either R 1 or R 2. The ring chromosomes are lost with a regular frequency thus producing a uniform pattern of colourless streaks throughout the leaf area. The streaks are more numerous in R 2 than R 1 plants since the R 2 ring is lost more often than the R 1 ring chromosome. The white cells do not grow as well as adjacent green cells, hence there is often a certain amount of distortion and roughening of the leaf surface. Sometimes the tension between green and adjacent white cell lineages is so great that the tissues break apart and holes appear in the leaves. Plants with two similar ring chromosomes behave like the corresponding plants with only one ring chromosome, except that they have two rings to lose before a white streak appears. Accordingly, the streaks are fewer and somewhat less uniform in distribution. Again the double R 2 chromosome plants are more variegated than the double R 1 chromosome plants. The mixed double ring plants have fewer streaks than the two R 2 plants, but more than the two R 1 plants. Their white stripes are either of the R 2 type, when the R 1 chromosome is lost first, or of the R 1 type, when the R 2 chromosome is lost first. The three ring double-deficient plants produce few colourless streaks which are scattered here and there over the leaf surface. The two R 2 plus one R 1 plants are more streaked than the two R 1 plus one R 2 plants.

In addition to the variation in the variegated pattern, the plant size is also affected by the chromosome constitution in double-deficient plants. The greater the total amount of homozygous deficient tissue present, the smaller the plant. Thus the one R 2 double-deficient plants are smaller than the two R 2 plants, which in turn, are smaller than the R 1, R 2 plants. The three-ring plants are practically equal in size and vigour to plants with a normal chromosome constitution.

An example of variegation in the tomato, *Lycopersicum esculentum*, arose in the X_2 generation after bombarding seeds with X-rays. After selfing the variegated plant, Hagemann (1963) found that the germinating seedlings were green, variegated or yellow (Fig. V.1); the green seedlings themselves became variegated during their subsequent

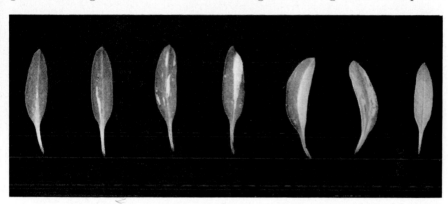

FIG. V.1. *Cotyledons of the unstable variegated line of Lycopersicum esculentum. Left, cotyledon pure green, phenotype similar to normal; right, cotyledon pure yellow yv^{ms}/yv^{ms} without fragments. All other cotyledons are variegated owing to the loss of the fragments during mitotic divisions; the yellow regions are yv^{ms}/yv^{ms} without fragments. All cotyledons, except the one at the extreme right, have the genetical constitution yv^{ms}/yv^{ms} + fragments. This previously unpublished photograph has been kindly provided by Dr R. Hagemann*

development. The variegated plants bear green leaves flecked or sectored with variable sized yellow lineages (Fig. V.2), and sometimes whole side-shoots are completely yellow. The viable yellow seedlings, which gradually become yellowish-green and even pale green in the greenhouse, develop flowers, but rarely set seed because their pollen is almost completely sterile; the yellow side branches of variegated plants behave similarly. Genetical tests show that the yellow phenotype is controlled by a recessive gene allelic to a previously described gene, yellow-virescent (yv). (See XI.2 for a discussion of the relationship between virescence and chloroplast ultrastructure in a barley mutant.) Since yellow-virescent plants are self fertile and the new mutant pollen sterile, Hagemann called it yellow virescent ^{masculosterilis} (yv^{ms}). Together with the wild type, the two genes form a triple allelic series with the dominance relationship $yv^+ > yv > yv^{ms}$.

Crosses between green and yellow plants, or yellow branches of variegated plants, gave wholly green offspring. On selfing the F_1 plants, the F_2 generation segregated into green and yellow offspring in a monohybrid ratio, except that there was a marked deficit of yellow

FIG. V.2. *Leaves of the unstable variegated line of* Lycopersicum esculentum, yv^{ms}/yv^{ms} + *fragments. This previously unpublished photograph has been kindly provided by Dr R. Hagemann*

seedlings. The F_3 generation confirmed the assumed monohybrid segregation. Similarly, crosses between green plants and variegated branches of variegated plants also produced wholly green offspring. But on selfing these F_1 plants, Hagemann obtained two types of segregation in the F_2 generation. Some families segregated into green and yellow offspring, while other families, in addition to green and yellow, also produced variegated offspring. Genetically, the two types of segregation can be explained by the assumption that the green parts of variegated plants contain a fourth allele, yellow-virescent[mutabilis] (yv^{mut}), which like the wild type allele allows the development of normal green chloroplasts, but it is mutable and during development regularly mutates to yv^{ms} thereby producing yellow lineages. Cytological examination, however, leads to quite a different explanation.

Variegated plants contain, in addition to twenty-four chromosomes, one or more chromosome fragments, whereas the yellow plants contain no fragments. During meiosis in variegated plants the fragments are either paired with a normal chromosome to form a bivalent or they form univalents. The fragments divide in first or second meiotic division. In both divisions they frequently lag which leads to the formation of pollen grain nuclei without a fragment. Similarly, the female often loses fragments in the formation of the egg. Quite clearly the variegated plants give rise to yellow plants by loss of their fragments.

The two types of F_2 segregation are therefore the result of two types of F_1 heterozygote. Heterozygotes with the constitution yv^+/yv^{ms} give rise to green and yellow offspring alone, while heterozygotes with the constitution $yv^+/yv^{ms} + 1$ or more fragments give rise to green, variegated and yellow offspring. The first cross may be shown schematically as follows:

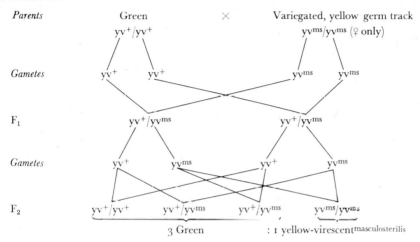

and the alternative cross as follows:

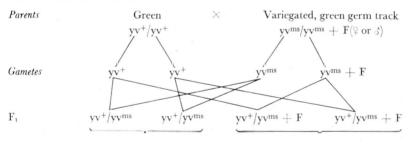

From the possible combinations between the four types of gamete the following genotypes can be expected in the F_2 generation:

Green: $yv^+/yv^+ + 2$ F; $yv^+/yv^+ + 1$ F; $yv^{\,l}/yv^{\,l}$; $yv^{\,l}/yv^{ms} + 2$ F; $yv^+/yv^{ms} + 1$ F; yv^+/yv^{ms}.

Variegated: $yv^{ms}/yv^{ms} + 2$ F; $yv^{ms}/yv^{ms} + 1$ F.

Yellow-virescent^{masculosterilis}: yv^{ms}/yv^{ms}.

The ratio of green:variegated plus yellow-virescent is $3:1$, but the proportion of variegated:yellow-virescent will depend upon the frequency with which the fragment chromosome is lost.

Thus the yellow plants have the constitution yv^{ms}/yv^{ms}, and the variegated plants the constitution $yv^{ms}/yv^{ms} + 1$ or more fragments, in which the fragment contains either the yv^+ allele, or a factor complementary with yv^{ms} enabling chlorophyll to develop fully and the pollen to be fertile. In the course of development, the fragments divide and pass into the daughter cells, but quite frequently cells are produced without a fragment owing to lagging of the fragment during the previous anaphase division of mitosis, or owing to both parts of a divided fragment entering the same daughter cell. Whenever cells arise without a fragment a yellow lineage appears since these cells are now homozygous yv^{ms}/yv^{ms}. The stage in development in which variegation begins, and the frequency of flecking or sectoring, is essentially dependent upon the number of fragments which exist in the zygote. Thus plants with two fragments will be slower to lose them than plants with only one fragment, they will therefore develop variegation later and it will be less frequent; they will also be less likely to lose both fragments at meiosis and hence will produce fewer yellow offspring.

Hagemann suggests that because his yellow-virescent plants are always male sterile, they are controlled by an allele (yv^{ms}) distinct from the previously described yellow-virescent plants which are male fertile (yv). The nature of the origin of his strain makes an alternative explanation perhaps more likely. The new mutant arose in the X_2 generation after seeds had been treated with X-rays. At the same time one or more chromosome fragments were found in the variegated plants, which gave rise to the male sterile yellow-virescent plants by loss of fragments. It is possible that the X-rays caused chromosome breakage resulting in the deletion of a portion of chromosome containing the wild type allele (yv^+) of the yellow-virescent locus, the deleted portion producing the chromosome fragment. As the result of recombination, the next generation then produced a plant which was homologous for the deletion and also contained the fragment. Whenever this fragment was lost, the yv^+ allele was lost with it, and the plastids were then unable to develop chlorophyll fully. Consequently, yellow lineages appeared in the leaves and yellow-virescent seedlings among the offspring. It is further possible that the deleted fragment contained other genes, including one having an important function in the development of male fertile flowers. Hence, whenever the fragment was lost from a plant homologous for the deletion, the gene for male fertility would always be lost together with the gene for full chlorophyll production. Consequently, yellow-virescent plants would always be male sterile in this particular line. In the previous yellow-virescent line, with a different origin, the closely linked male fertility gene was presumably not affected, and therefore these plants were always pollen fertile. Should this explanation in fact be the true one, then the third allele yv^{ms} would be as hypothetical as the suggested fourth allele yv^{mut}. Hence the locus would, in fact, contain only two true alleles, namely yv^+ and yv.

An example of X-ray induced variegation in the quick growing annual crucifer, *Arabidopsis thaliana* (Fig. V.3) regularly develops numerous white flecks and sectors of variable size standing out against the green background of the leaves (Tilney-Bassett and Burras, unpublished). The white cell lineages frequently occur in the growing-point, which often leads to the development of completely white

FIG. V.3. *A sample of variegated leaves from* Arabidopsis thaliana, *in which the white areas are believed to be due to the somatic loss of a chromosome fragment carrying genes essential for chloroplast development*

vegetative and flowering shoots. Owing to the complete absence of pigment, these all-white shoots grow very weakly, and the poorly developed flowers, which often fail to open, set no seed. However, it is possible that the more strongly developed white flowers of variegated shoots do set seed. Seed from the naturally self-pollinating flowers of variegated shoots, gives rise to widely varying proportions of green, variegated, and white offspring. Between families, the proportions of pure white seedlings, with white hypocotyls and white cotyledons, varies from a minimum of 10 per cent to an exceptional value of 82·5 per cent. The pure white seedlings die. The variegated seedlings have green hypocotyls, but the cotyledons are either pure white, variegated or green; when green the first and all subsequent leaves are variegated or white. The green seedlings also turn out to be genetically variegated since they all develop variegation during development; they form less than 10 per cent of all the offspring. Green shoots of variegated plants behave in the same way as the variegated shoots and give rise, on selfing, to temporary green, variegated and white seedlings; again there are more variegated plus white offspring than green.

Reciprocal crosses between true-breeding green plants and variegated plants give rise to pure green seedlings in the F_1 generation. In the F_2

the seedlings segregate into green and variegated plus white offspring in a Mendelian 3:1 ratio, albeit with a marked deficit of variegated plus white offspring. The assumed ratio is confirmed by the F_3 generation results.

The change from green to white is plainly not caused by a gene-induced plastid mutation because there are no variegated or white offspring from reciprocal crosses between variegated and green plants (see VIII.6 for an account of gene-induced plastid mutation). Hence we must look for a wholly nuclear explanation. The results are extremely similar to those of Hagemann with the variegated tomato, except that only one type of F_1 heterozygote was found in *Arabidopsis*; the F_2 segregation in a ratio of 3 green:1 white was not found. However, this can be explained by assuming that when green and variegated *Arabidopsis* plants were crossed, all the successful gametes from the variegated parent came from the green germ track and none from the white. Hence only one type of F_1 heterozygote was produced and not two as in the tomato. The *Arabidopsis* results can therefore be explained in the same way as the tomato results. Either the green to white change is caused by a mutable nuclear gene, or else by the loss of a chromosome fragment containing an essential factor for chloroplast development. Now the deficit of variegated and white seedlings from segregating families shows that there must be some selection against them. Since selfing results show that variegated and white embryos are perfectly capable of growing to maturity, and germination tests show that they germinate as well as green seeds, the selection is probably before fertilization, which means a gametic selection. On the basis of the mutable gene hypothesis it is difficult to see why there should be any selection at all. On the other hand, a gamete with a deleted chromosome and without the deleted chromosome fragment would be completely without a portion of the normal chromosome complement, which would be highly likely to put it at a disadvantage in competition with normal gametes, or with gametes containing a deleted chromosome plus the corresponding deleted chromosome fragment. Without going into further details, it can be deduced that such deficient gametes must indeed be produced if the fragment hypothesis is correct and fragments are lost at meiosis as well as during mitoses. Moreover, selection against them would lead to the observed deficit of variegated and white seedlings in the F_2 segregating families; it would also account for the absence of two types of F_1 heterozygote. Only cytological discovery of the fragments could prove the hypothesis, but this would be difficult to establish with the very small chromosomes of *Arabidopsis*. We must therefore content ourselves with the limited genetic evidence which favours the loss of a chromosome fragment, in the same manner as in the tomato, as the most likely explanation of the variegation.

V.1.ii.b. *Radioactive isotopes*

An earlier variegation in the tomato, *Lycopersicum esculentum*, which Lesley and Lesley (1961) called 'flaked' first appeared in the R_2 generation after soaking seeds in the radioactive isotope of phosphorus ^{32}P as phosphate solution. The cotyledons, stems, leaves, calyx, and fruit were all striped, sectored or flecked with numerous white areas of variable sizes and following cell lineages. The leaves and fruit are often somewhat distorted owing to the reduced growth of the white tissues; moreover, the palisade cells are replaced by colourless spongy parenchyma in white parts of the leaves. In addition, and quite independent of the white areas, there are glabrous patches in which the usual epidermal hairs are missing. As we shall soon see, the loss of a chromosome fragment is responsible for both changes, but the leaf colouring is a character of the germ layers L II and L III, whereas the presence or absence of epidermal hairs is a character of L I (see Chapter VI for the meaning of the terms L I, L II, and L III). The fertility of hairy variegated shoots is reduced and glabrous shoots are sterile. Grafting experiments showed that the variegation was not caused by a transmissible virus infection.

On selfing, flaked plants bred true. All flaked plants were found to contain twelve pairs of chromosomes plus one or two small fragment chromosomes. Reciprocal crosses between flaked and normal plants gave wholly normal F_1 offspring, usually with, but occasionally without, a fragment. Since all flaked plants have a fragment, and all F_1 plants from crossing normal and flaked are normal, it follows that flaked plants lack part of a normal chromosome. Hence, we may assume that the normal parts of flaked plants contain the fragment that is missing from the deficient chromosome, and the white areas arise whenever the fragment is lost during mitosis. In the epidermis, the loss of the fragment results in the failure of the epidermis to develop hairs. Evidently, the fragment contains genes, missing from the deficient chromosome, which control the development of green chloroplasts and the production of epidermal hairs, and are also necessary for the formation of viable gametes. In the F_2 generation, segregation in the ratio of 6 green:1 flaked offspring occurred from some F_1 families, but others gave only green seedlings. This difference is probably because some families are derived from green F_1 plants, which still contain the fragment in the germ track and can therefore give rise to flaked offspring, whereas families derived from plants in which the fragment has been lost produce gametes either with a deleted chromosome or a normal chromosome. But since the gametes with a deleted chromosome and no fragment are lethal, all the successful gametes have a normal chromosome and therefore do not give rise to flaked plants, hence all these offspring are green.

11—P.

V.1.iii. NATURALLY OCCURRING CHROMOSOME BREAKAGE?

Since the five cases of variegation caused by chromosome breakage so far discussed have all been induced, it is interesting to know whether or not any natural occurrences in diploids have been found. There appear to be no proven examples in the literature, but the variegation of *Nigella damascena*, described by Toxopeus (1927), may be such a case. Individual plants vary from almost completely green with only a few yellow flecks, to almost completely yellow. The leaves of typical variegated plants vary from pure green to pure yellow, but they are mostly variegated with various frequencies and sizes of yellow flecks and sectors against the green background. Every change from green to yellow is irreversible and each new yellow area develops as a simple cell lineage.

No selfing data were given. The variegation, however, is probably true-breeding since seedlings which begin green are said to become variegated during development, and there is no mention of the occurrence of pure yellow seedlings. Reciprocal crosses between green and variegated plants gave an all green F_1 from which the F_2 segregated in a ratio of 3 green : 1 variegated. The backcross between the green F_1 and the variegated gave a segregation of 1 green : 1 variegated. Evidently variegated behaves as a homozygous recessive. In addition, a second factor for yellow was described which gave an F_2 segregation of 3 green : 1 yellow, hence this factor also behaves as a recessive. If the yellow factor corresponds to the yellow of the variegated plants then there must be two types of F_1 heterozygote segregating either into green and variegated or into green and yellow. This behaviour would there-therefore be very similar to that found by Hagemann in the tomato, which suggests that the variegation in *Nigella* is also either due to a mutable gene or to the loss of a chromosome fragment. A better described example of presumed naturally occurring chromosome fragment or whole chromosome loss is later described for the tetraploid fern *Adiantum cuneatum*.

V.2. Polyploids: Loss of Whole Chromosomes

V.2.i. SESQUIDIPLOIDS

Following crosses between two tobacco species, *Nicotiana tabacum* $(n = 24)$ and *Nicotiana plumbaginifolia* $(n = 10)$, variegation sporadically occurred. This was particularly frequent in the sesquidiploid hybrid with two *tabacum* and one *plumbaginifolia* chromosome sets (tbc. tbc. pbg.). Moav and Cameron (1960) attributed the variegation to the breaking up of the *plumbaginifolia* genom into individual chromosomes, so that from time to time somatic loss of a *plumbaginifolia* chromosome carrying genes necessary for chlorophyll development occurred. This happened against a background of a pair of tabacum chromosomes which were homozygous for a recessive gene causing chlorophyll deficiency. Thus each time the appropriate *plumbaginifolia* chromosome was lost it gave rise to a white cell lineage producing white sectors in the otherwise green leaves.

V.2.ii. TETRAPLOIDS

A variegation that has not been investigated cytologically, yet may well be caused by abnormal chromosome behaviour, occurred in rice, *Oryza sativa*. Imai (1934c) found a line of rice that segregated in a ratio of 163 green:52 albino offspring. During the next three successive generations he obtained seventy families that gave a total segregation of 6773 green:2004 albino offspring, plus six additional seedlings which became variegated with a coarse white stripe or stripes on one or more adjacent leaves. Ten more families, with varying proportions of albino offspring, gave a total segregation of 1208 green:43 albino, plus two additional variegated plants. Finally, thirty families gave 2942 green offspring, plus three plants which became variegated.

Imai suggests that the first group of seventy families are segregating monogenically, while all the variegated plants, plus the albino seedlings from the second group arise by frequent sporadic mutation of the normal allele to its recessive allele. An alternative and more likely suggestion is that this is one of the Japanese autotetraploid races of rice. The apparently monogenic 3:1 segregation would then arise after selfing plants with the genotypic constitution Aaaa. The much smaller proportion of albinos in the second group would arise from selfing plants of constitution AAaa to give an autotetraploid 35:1 ratio, with which the observed results are in good agreement. Finally, the origin of variegation could be explained by the occasional loss during mitosis of the chromosome carrying the dominant A allele in plants of constitution Aaaa. Without the dominant gene the plants would be unable to develop green chloroplasts and so a colourless stripe is formed, which produces the variegated phenotype.

Variegation in *Adiantum cuneatum*, a species of maidenhair-fern, was investigated by Andersson (1923; 1931), but she was unable to discover its cause, and she could only make the loose suggestion that it might possibly be a matter of plastid inheritance. Her observations, however, strongly suggest that the variegation is caused by the loss of a chromosome or chromosome fragment; they do not suggest the behaviour of an abnormal plastid.

The sporophyte, which is the diploid generation developing into the adult fern, always becomes variegated during its growth. Individual pinnae on the frond are variegated with wedge-shaped white sectors or stripes following cell lineages, and occasionally a pinna is completely white, in which case it remains more or less underdeveloped. If a sorus develops on a variegated pinna, normal sporangia grow out of the green areas, but in the white areas they do not develop properly and fail to produce any spores. Individual sporangia originate entirely from single epidermal cells and give rise to sixty-four haploid spores by successive cell divisions including a meiotic reduction division. On germination, the spores from the green sporangia produce two kinds of prothallia, either with normal dark green chloroplasts, or with small pale green plastids which soon become white. The pale green prothallia soon die. The dark green prothallia grow normally, but sooner or later they all develop one or more white sectors following cell lineages. Hence all the viable gametophytes become variegated like the sporophytes. Archegonia and antheridia do not develop successfully on white areas of gametophytes. Hence the sporophytes arise from green areas; nevertheless white sporophytes may occasionally arise, probably due to the change to white occurring early in embryo development.

Altogether Andersson germinated 18,704 spores, of which 5875 developed into dark green prothallia and 12,829 developed into white prothallia. Thus about 69 per cent of the spores were of the white type, even though they were all derived from sporangia developing out of green and not white tissue. Within individual sporangia the proportion of green and white spores varied considerably from a minimum of two green and sixty-two white to a rare maximum of thirty-two green and thirty-two white. On no occasion did the number of green spores ever exceed the number of white. Environmental factors, and the degree of variegation of the parent fronds played no role in determining the ratios of green to white spores.

Adiantum cuneatum with $2n = 120$ chromosomes is probably a tetraploid since many species of this genus with $2n = 60$ chromosomes have half this number[13]. Nevertheless, the high frequency of white sectors in the sporophyte is more characteristic of a diploid plant; it may, of course be an allotetraploid and behave like a diploid. Without any cytological observations one cannot be too certain how the variegation arises, but the likely behaviour of a dicentric chromosome could account for all the results. Meiosis in the sporangium occurs at the last two cell divisions, that is after the sixteen cell stage, so that there are in fact sixteen separate meioses in one sporangium to give the sixty-four spores.

As we shall see there would certainly be one and often a pair of dicentric chromosomes present in the first meiotic division. Their likely behaviour could be expected to give rise to many spores lacking them, or containing only broken parts of them, thus accounting for the high proportion of white prothallia. Spores receiving a dicentric chromosome would develop into green prothallia, which in turn would occasionally lose the dicentric at mitosis owing to anaphase lagging and consequent loss, for instance, or to non-median breakage, thereby producing the white sectors of the gametophyte. Fertilization takes place only between gametes produced in green zones containing a dicentric, hence the young sporophytes would presumably contain a pair of dicentric chromosomes; these too would be liable to become lost one at a time during mitotic divisions, and so produce variegation in the sporophyte. Hence the fertile green cells would contain one or two dicentrics and the sterile white cells no dicentric chromosomes. If this variegated plant still exists, it would clearly be well worth while to examine it cytologically to check this hypothesis.

V.2.iii. HEXAPLOIDS

In the F_4 generation of a cross between the oats *Avena sativa gigantica* and *Avena fatua,* one family unexpectedly segregated in a ratio of 1 green: 6 albino offspring. In the following generations, after selfing the green plants, the abnormal 1:6 segregation is repeated. Each time about 14 per cent of the green plants become variegated, either early or late in development. Usually only one white sector is produced, but occasionally there are two independent sectors. The green shoots of variegated plants behave in the same way as green plants. On cytological examination, Philp (1935) found that the 1:6 type green plants had forty-one chromosomes instead of the normal hexaploid number of forty-two. During meiosis the odd chromosome is frequently lost owing to lagging, hence the pollen grain nucleus usually has only twenty instead of twenty-one chromosomes. It is quite likely that a similar loss occurs during female meiosis in the formation of the egg. Consequently, only a few progeny contain forty-one chromosomes and are green, while the majority contain forty chromosomes and are albino. Presumably the odd chromosome carries a gene or genes essential for chloroplast development. Philp suggested that the variegation in the 41-chromosome green plants is almost certainly the result of the occasional loss of the odd chromosome during mitosis.

The segregation in the progeny of 41-chromosome plants twice changed from the 1:6 type to a typical Mendelian ratio of 3 green: 1 white. Most of these green offspring were homozygous or heterozygous, were normal in vigour and meiosis, and contained only forty chromosomes; a few were of the original 41-chromosome type. Philp suggested that irregular disjunction, as a consequence of the sporadic multivalent formation, gave rise to a 41-chromosome plant with the sole dominant gene carried by the odd univalent. In its progeny 41-chromosome plants are green, 40-chromosome plants are albino. When the univalent pairs with one of the semi-homologous chromosomes of the hexaploid, however, this results in a change in the subsequent segregation from a 1:6 to a 3:1 ratio.

A few instances of variegation in the cotyledons and later leaves of seedlings of *Nicotiana otophora* were attributed by Gerstel (1960) to somatic instability. It is quite possible that other authors may have made similar observations in their material but without any further investigation. The mention of variegation in polyploids by some cytologists is, however, in reference to tissues containing cells differing in their chromosome complement and not to the phenomenon of plastid variegation. Hence these examples have been left out of the present account.

V.3. Other Phenomena

A character called striato-virescens (sv) first appeared in the F_5 generation after crosses between two varieties of wheat, *Triticum vulgare*. When the seeds are sown in the autumn, in New Zealand, the leaves are marked with alternating green and white longitudinal sectors. But when the tillers begin to elongate the white tissue turns green and becomes indistinguishable from normal. No symptoms of variegation appear when the seeds are sown in the spring, or in the winter under glass. Breeding experiments in the hexaploid gave a good fit with a ratio of 63 green: 1 striato-virescens showing that the variegation was caused by three recessive genes. Breeding and cytological evidence further showed that the mutant occurred suddenly and coincided with the appearance of a large inverted chromosome duplication. Frankel (1950) believed the duplication to be responsible, in some unknown way, for inducing mutation in all three genes at the same time.

V.4. Conclusions

A comparison between the few examples analysed shows that the loss of chromosome fragments from the diploids during mitosis is frequent, whereas the loss of whole chromosomes from the polyploids is rare, with the exception of *Adiantum*. Consequently, the diploids have many flecks and sectors and the polyploids only one or two.

Among the diploids, the two examples from *Zea mays* are special cases and there is nothing more to add, but the behaviour of the two tomatoes and *Arabidopsis* show interesting similarities and differences which are worth further discussion; *Nigella* may also be similar but it has been insufficiently studied for a useful comparison. In the tomatoes, cytological examination shows that the variegation is caused by the loss of a chromosome fragment. This is probably also the case in *Arabidopsis*, or it may be caused by the mutation of a mutable nuclear gene. However, there is as yet no precedent for the mutable gene hypothesis in the direction of green to white; this is in strong contrast to the many cases of mutable gene changes in the opposite direction (Chapter IV). Somatic gene conversion (Chapter IV) in the direction of green to white is, of course, quite another phenomenon.

On selfing the variegated yellow-virescent tomato of Hagemann and the variegated *Arabidopsis*, both produce respectively yellow and white seedlings as well as variegated, whereas the flaked tomato breeds true. The true breeding can be explained on the assumption that the male or female or both gametes are lethal when without a portion of the chromosome complement, owing to loss of the chromosome fragment, unless it is that no fragments are lost during meiosis. As a result all zygotes double-deficient for the deleted chromosome would contain at least one and maybe two chromosome fragments, which would probably become lost too late in embryo development to be able to give rise to a pure white seedling. By contrast, we may assume that gametes lacking a portion of the chromosome complement, corresponding to the missing fragment, are not lethal in the yellow-virescent tomato. Consequently some zygotes are regularly formed without fragments and these develop into yellow seedlings. It seems likely that the behaviour of *Arabidopsis* is similar (Table V.1). It might be objected that pure yellow and white shoots of the yellow-virescent tomato and *Arabidopsis* are sterile, or almost so. But this does not mean that their potential gametes are lethal when produced in the germ track of a fertile green shoot, as a result of the loss of the fragment during a meiotic division. Indeed they cannot be lethal in these circumstances or there would be no Mendelian F_2 segregation into green and yellow, or green and variegated plus yellow or white seedlings. None the less, the excess of green offspring in the F_2 segregation of both plants does indicate that the deficient gametes are somewhat selected against, especially in *Arabidopsis* in which there is no evidence of any zygotic selection.

Hence we may conclude that in cases of variegation caused by the loss of chromosome fragments in diploid plants, the genetic behaviour will be largely determined by the following factors:

(1) Whether fragments are lost at meiosis, thereby regularly producing some gametes without fragments.

TABLE V.I. SUMMARY OF THE PROBABLE BEHAVIOUR OF THREE DIPLOID PLANTS IN WHICH THE VARIEGATION IS CAUSED BY THE LOSS OF A CHROMOSOME FRAGMENT

Plant and form	Characteristics of variegated plants				Gametic fitness		Possible zygotes	Seedling colour
	Colour of shoot or sector	Flower fertility		Kind of gamete*	Survival	Selection against		
		Female	Male					
All three plants	Green	Fertile	Fertile	or (see below)	Viable	None	±	Green but unstable†
Lycopersicum esculentum yellow-virescent^masculosterilis	Yellow	Fertile	Sterile		Viable	Partial		Yellow
Arabidopsis thaliana	White	Sterile?	Sterile?		Viable	Partial		White
Lycopersicum esculentum flaked	White	Sterile	Sterile		Lethal	Complete	None	None

* Gametes contain normal haploid chromosome complement, except for one chromosome which is split into a deleted chromosome and the broken-off chromosome fragment

† Green becomes variegated during development by somatic loss of chromosome fragment; even white seedlings may arise if fragment is lost early enough in embryo development.

(2) Whether deficient gametes lacking a part of the normal chromosome complement are lethal or viable.

(3) Whether viable, deficient gametes are selected against in competition with gametes containing a normal chromosome complement.

(4) Whether there is any zygotic selection against embryos lacking a part of the normal chromosome complement.

The actual pattern of variegation during development will be determined both in diploids and in polyploids by the frequency of fragment or whole chromosome losses during cell division, and whether or not there is any tendency for the losses to be more frequent at some stages or times of development than at others.

REFERENCES

1. ANDERSSON, I. (1923). *J. Genet.* **13**, 1–11
2. ANDERSSON-KOTTÖ, I. (1931). *Bibliogr. genet.* **8**, 269–294
3. BEADLE, G. W. (1932). *Z. Vererbungsl.* **63**, 195–217
4. FRANKEL, O. H. (1950). *Heredity* **4**, 103–116
5. GERSTEL, D. U. (1960). *Genetics* **45**, 1723–1734
6. HAGEMANN, R. (1963). *Züchter* **33**, 282–284
7. IMAI, Y. (1934c). *Jap. J. Genet.* **10**, 89–90
8. LESLEY, J. W. & LESLEY, M. M. (1961). *Genetics* **46**, 831–844
9. McCLINTOCK, B. (1932). *Proc. nat. Acad. Sci., Wash.* **18**, 677–681
10. McCLINTOCK, B. (1938). *Genetics* **23**, 315–376
11. MOAV, R. & CAMERON, D. R. (1960). *Amer. J. Bot.* **47**, 87–93
12. PHILP, J. (1935). *J. Genet.* **30**, 267–302
13. ROY, R. P. & SINHA, R. P. (1961). *Caryologia* **14**, 413–428
14. TOXOPEUS, H. J. (1927). *Genetica* **9**, 341–441

CHAPTER VI

Chimeras

VI.1. The Chimera Hypothesis

AT THE beginning of the present century the thoughts of many botanists were concerned with the fundamental question raised by the graft-hybrid hypothesis: When two plants were grafted together, could there be a fusion of vegetative cells leading to the development of a vegetative or graft hybrid, in contrast to the normal formation of hybrids by the fusion of sexual cells? In an attempt to answer this question Winkler (1907) grafted together the two species *Solanum lycopersicum* and *Solanum nigrum*. In so doing he produced one plant which he recognized as not being a hybrid because the shoot was divided longitudinally into two halves; one half was composed of one parent, *S. lycopersicum*, and the other half of the second parent, *S. nigrum*. This plant which was composed of two genetically distinct types of tissue, he termed a chimera. Among variegated *Pelargonium* seedlings Baur (1909) found similar plants; one half of the axis had green leaves and the other half white leaves, and leaves which were half green half white were occasionally produced on the border of the two halves of the axis. These plants with a sectorially divided growing-point Baur called sectorial chimeras.

Other variegated *Pelargonium* seedlings developed leaves with white margins and green centres similar to the parental white-margined cultivars. Microscopical examination showed that the white tissue was not only present at the leaf margins but actually formed a continuous thin skin of colourless mesophyll cells completely enveloping a solid core of green mesophyll cells. Furthermore, selfing the white-margined plants gave only white seedlings proving that the white layer was continuous from the leaves back into the apical growing-point and into the flowers of the inflorescence where it formed the germ layer. Baur concluded that these plants were also chimeras, but with a periclinally and not a sectorially divided growing-point; he therefore called them periclinal chimeras.

The significance of Baur's hypothesis was immediately recognized because it agreed so well with the conclusions of the late nineteenth-century anatomists. They had found that the shoot growing-point of

170

higher plants was frequently constructed of two or three germ layers
which were superimposed one above the other like a series of cones from
which the body structure of the plant was derived. Thus Baur was able
to explain the chimeral structure met with in *Pelargonium* leaves by
assuming that the growing-points themselves were composite; that is the
pattern found in the leaf was a development of the layered structure
already present at the growing-point.

As the result of the publication of Baur's ideas, Winkler (1910)
decided that some of his experimental *Solanum* graft hybrids were really
periclinal chimeras. At the same time, the classical graft hybrid,
Laburnum adami, was shown to be a periclinal chimera by Buder (1910),
and Winkler (1910) was of the same opinion. Descriptions of a variety
of other examples soon followed and today chimeras are known to be of
widespread occurrence; especially frequent are the variegated-leaf
chimeras. How then do they arise?

VI.2. Origin of Variegated-leaf Chimeras

The vast majority of the hundreds of variegated-leaf chimeras known in
cultivation today have undoubtedly arisen by mutation; a few have
arisen by hybridization, but contrary to popular belief none have arisen
by grafting. Mutations sometimes occur repeatedly in the life of a plant
and in a sense such individuals are chimeras because they are composed
of two or more genetically distinct types of cell. But in practice, whether
the mutation occurs once or many times, the term chimera is seldom
used simply to describe a plant with two or more genetically distinct
types of cell, for which such terms as variegated, mosaiced, mottled, or
marbled suffice. Instead, the term chimera is mostly used to refer to the
condition in which the two or more types of cell are separated into tissue
layers in such a way as to give a characteristic sectorial or periclinal
structure (see also II.5.iv). The developmental period between the
original mutation and the subsequent chimera structure is the period of
sorting-out, and how this proceeds depends upon whether the mutation
site is in the nucleus or in a plastid.

VI.2.i. NUCLEAR MUTATION

Plantsmen often see examples of wild and cultivated plants in which a
spontaneous mutation has produced a white, or yellow, or pale green
sector in a solitary leaf, but these mutations are of no consequence to the
future development of the plant since they are lost as soon as the leaf
falls to the ground. When, however, a mutation occurs in the growing-

point, instead of being localized in the leaf, the consequences are quite different. Supposing, for example, a nuclear gene mutation causes a defect in chlorophyll development so that the plastids in cells of the shoot remain white instead of becoming green, then the mutation will be recognizable as a white sector running down one side of the plant away from the place of origin in a growing-point initial cell. The size of the sector will depend upon the developmental importance of the mutated cell in the group of initials comprising the growing-point. But whether the sector is wide or narrow, the plant as a whole may now be called a sectorial chimera since it consists of two genetically distinct tissues, the normal green and the mutant white, growing side by side parallel to the longitudinal axis.

Because the growing-point of most higher plants is constructed of two or three germ layers, usually only one of them is affected by a single mutation. Sometimes, however, a second or third layer becomes affected

FIG. VI.1. *Kinds of chimera:* (*1*) *Pure for first genetic type;* (*2*) *Sectorial chimera;* (*3*) *Pure for second genetic type;* (*4*) *Periclinal chimera;* (*5*) *Mericlinal chimera*

as the result of subsequent layer alterations, or simply because the mutation had occurred early in embryo development before the differentiation of the growing-point. If, for one of these reasons, the mutant cell lineage is present in all the germ layers of the affected area of the growing-point, the plant is a sectorial chimera for all layers (Fig. VI.1 (2)). But if, as is more often the case, the mutant white cell lineage is in only one germ layer, it must be immediately above or below one or two unchanged green layers, or between two green layers; the sector is therefore periclinal in relation to the other layers, and such plants are frequently referred to as mericlinal (Fig. VI.1 (5)) instead of sectorial chimeras.

In a mericlinal chimera the shoot is sectorial with one unchanged and one periclinal sector. Should a side shoot develop in the axil of a leaf on the border of the normal and mutant lineages, which is half green, half periclinal, it is again mericlinal like the parent axis. But a side shoot developing in the axil of a completely periclinal leaf is itself wholly periclinal (Fig. VI.1(4)). This development of a periclinal side shoot is most important for in one step a condition is attained which is far more stable than that of the only partially periclinal, parental growing-point. Occasionally the shoot on which the mutation arose itself becomes periclinal all over. This happens when successive divisions

TABLE VI.1. EXAMPLES OF NUCLEAR-DIFFERENTIAL CHIMERAS

Plant and form	Probable structure	Authors	Dates
	Sectorials		
Arabidopsis thaliana	w-G (dominant)	Röbbeln	1962
Capsicum annuum	w-G (recessive)	Deshpande	1939
Gossypium arboreum	y-G (recessive)	Nath	1955
Zea mays	w-G (recessive)	Garber, Hoover	1927
	Periclinals (All recessive mutations)		
Antirrhinum majus	GwG or wwG GyG or yyG GpG or ppG	Abel	1962
Arabis albida pseudoleucodermis chlorotidermis	GwG or wwG GpG or ppG	Correns	1919b
Coleus hybridus green-yellow green-yellow flecked yellow-green	GyG Gy^{s}G GGy	Beyer	1932
Glechoma hederacea	GwG or wwG	Correns	1919b
Melandrium album	GwG or wwG	Baur	1911a
Pelargonium zonale Crystal Palace Gem Golden Harem A Happy Thought	ggG ggG GGp	Tilney-Bassett	1963b

Key: G=unchanged green layer; g, p, y, y^s, and w=mutant golden, pale-green, yellow, unstable yellow, and white layers respectively.

of the mutant initial cell succeed in displacing the normal initials surrounding them in the same layer. But the reverse behaviour in which the mutant initial is displaced by the normal initials followed by the whole growing-point reverting to normal is more frequent. Thus since wholly periclinal shoots usually develop from the side branches of mericlinal shoots, plants which form few or no side branches are less likely to develop periclinal growing-points than plants which branch freely.

Variegated-leaf chimeras originating by nuclear mutations may be classed as nuclear-differential chimeras to distinguish them from plastid-differential chimeras originating by plastid mutation. In the literature reports of nuclear-differential chimeras are few (Table VI.1), whereas similar looking chlorophyll chimeras developed from the sorting-out of two types of plastid have been more commonly reported (see Chapters VII and VIII), but the majority of chimeras in cultivation have not been genetically tested. The nuclear-differential chlorophyll chimeras are, however, of only little interest to us since they have not been of any special value in studies of the genetic control of plastid biochemistry (see Chapter XI).

VI.2.ii. PLASTID MUTATION

The nuclear genom is localized in one body, the nucleus, containing the chromosomes which have a uniform and very precise mode of division. At each cell division the chromosomes replicate themselves exactly, divide into two identical portions and separate to form the new nucleus of each daughter cell. Only rarely do the nuclei of two daughter cells differ as a result of faulty division or gene mutation. By contrast, genetic, biochemical, and microscopic evidence has shown that the extra-nuclear genom is contained in at least two bodies, the plastids and the mitochondria. Each carries its own genetic information (see Chapter X for an account of the genetic material of the plastid) which is used directly for its reproduction in conjunction with nuclear gene products. The size and number of these particles differ very considerably between each other and between cells at different stages of development and in different tissues. Unlike the chromosomes, they possess no orderly mechanism for an equal separation at mitosis. Consequently, they probably normally separate at random during cell division, although one must allow for the possibility that they are not thoroughly mixed between divisions.

Whenever the genotype changes through the action of a mutable nuclear gene (Chapter IV), or through loss of a chromosome or chromosome fragment (Chapter V), a new simple cell lineage is initiated in which all subsequent cells are identical in respect of the new genotype.

If the new mutation prevents the development of chlorophyll and it occurs in the normally green shoot, then the new lineage is at once conspicuous by the appearance of a single white, or yellow, or even pale green sector (Fig. VI.2 right). Two independent mutations give two distinct white sectors, and still more frequent mutations give correspondingly more white lineages so that the final number of separate lineages is an exact measure of the observed mutation frequency. The

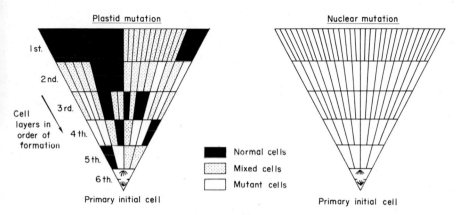

FIG. VI.2. *Comparison between the patterns of sorting-out following a single nuclear mutation right and a single plastid mutation left. The two-dimensional diagram represents a simpler situation than is found in practice in which cell division is usually three dimensional*

behaviour of the extra-nuclear particles is quite different. Each particle is a separate entity and spontaneous mutation in one has no genetic effect, and frequently no phenotypic effect, on the remaining particles of the now mixed cell. Because one mutant particle among so many normal particles is quite inconspicuous, the first signs of a mutation having occurred do not appear until many cell divisions later after the original mutant particle has sufficiently multiplied. During this intervening period the normal and mutant particles of the mixed cells sort-out from one another by the chance process of their distribution into the daughter cells at cell division. Thus, in the case of two types of plastid sorting-out from mixed cells, should a daughter cell have only normal plastids, then a purely green cell lineage will be recreated. Should a daughter cell have only mutant plastids, then a purely white cell lineage will be created. Should the daughter cell again be a mixed cell, it will be able to sort-out further into green or white or both types of lineage during its later divisions. Thus as the result of a single plastid mutation, there are within the primary cell lineage secondary, tertiary, and many more lineages until sorting-out of pure cells from mixed cells is complete (Fig. VI.2, left). Hence the overall effect of sorting-out of two types of plastid is to produce during the development of the plant a characteristic complex multiple cell lineage chequered pattern of green and white areas.

As a result of this sorting-out process, the palisade and spongy mesophyll cells of the leaf appear as various shades of green, depending upon the proportions of green to white plastids in the mixed cells, while the pure cells are green or white. Consequently these areas of the leaf appear to be very finely mosaiced in dicotyledons, or finely striped in monocotyledons (Fig. VI.3). This phase of frequent sorting-out,

FIG. VI.3. *Three leaves from* Coronilla varia *illustrating different stages in the sorting-out of green and white plastids following a single spontaneous plastid mutation. Individual leaflets are pure green or pure white, or they possess a fine or coarse mosaic of green and white cells*

characterized by the finely chequered mosaic or striping, lasts for many successive cell divisions but slowly, as sorting-out proceeds, the proportion of mixed cells decreases and the proportion of pure green and pure white cells increases. Accordingly, as the plant grows, the fine mosaic or striping becomes gradually replaced in successive leaves by an increasingly coarse mosaic or striping as the formation of new pure white or green lineages from the remaining mixed cells becomes an increasingly rare event. Finally the last vestige of the sorting-out mosaic becomes replaced by pure green and pure white cell lineages, from which development of pure green, pure white, sectorial, and periclinal growing-points now proceeds in precisely the same manner as already described for nuclear-differential chlorophyll chimeras.

Most plastid mutations are inviable on their own and their chlorophyll-deficient seedlings do not succeed in growing beyond the cotyledon stage. Fortunately, this drawback is overcome in chimeras because the mutant tissues get sufficient nourishment from the surrounding green tissues. Hence by forming chimeras, and in particular stable periclinal chimeras, the plastid mutations are preserved. Furthermore, when the plastid-differential chimeras contain the mutant plastids in the germ layer, L II, their behaviour in breeding experiments can be studied. Consequently such chimeras are of great value for analysing the behaviour of plastids in inheritance (see Chapter VIII).

VI.2.iii. HYBRIDIZATION

In the genera *Hypericum*, *Oenothera*, and *Pelargonium*, and probably in a number of other plants (see Chapters VIII and IX), the mutant and normal plastids are both transmitted by the pollen as well as by the eggs. As a result, hybridization between species or cultivars with white and species or cultivars with green germ layers can produce mixed zygotes containing both green and white plastids. During embryogenesis the plastids sort-out to give a number of variegated seedlings as well as green and white, and the variegated seedlings subsequently sort-out to give pure green, pure white, sectorial or periclinal growing-points. The formation of new variegated seedlings and subsequently chimeras by hybridization is, of course, not possible with the many plants whose plastids are transmitted solely by the female parent. In these cases, variegated seedlings occur only when sorting-out in the mother is incomplete so that some mixed eggs are produced containing both kinds of plastid (see VII.2.i).

Again in *Hypericum* and *Oenothera*, some variegated seedlings are frequently produced when two normally green species are crossed together. This is because the plastids of one species are able to develop into normal green chloroplasts with the hybrid nucleus, while the genetically different plastids of the second species remain white. Since in these genera the plastids are transmitted by both parents, hybridization results in the production of a mixed zygote, and during embryogenesis the green and white plastids sort-out in the usual manner to give some green, some white and some hybrid variegated seedlings, from which chimeras may subsequently develop (see Chapter IX).

VI.3. The Relationship between the Position of Mutation in Development and subsequent Chimera Formation

VI.3.i. MUTATIONS DURING EMBRYO DEVELOPMENT

As the result of spontaneous plastid mutation, mixed cells can originate at any stage of embryogenesis, or they may occur as mixed eggs owing to incomplete sorting-out in the mother, or as mixed zygotes through hybridization. The first division of the fertilized egg produces a two-celled embryo consisting of a basal and terminal cell; the basal cell gives rise to the suspensor and is no longer important for sorting-out. If the terminal cell is a mixed cell the subsequent sorting-out pattern will in most cases be reflected throughout the adult plant. But if the initial plastid mutation takes place later in embryogenesis the subsequent primary sorting-out lineage is less widespread.

The second successive division, which includes the first division of the terminal cell, is either transverse or vertical, depending upon the plant concerned[23]. After a transverse division, the upper cell farthest from the suspensor is the one which gives rise to the cotyledons and shoot, while the lower cell gives rise to the hypocotyl and roots. Hence a mutation in the upper cell will usually give rise to a sorting-out pattern reflected throughout the adult plant. But after a vertical division of the terminal cell, a mutation occurring in either daughter cell will subsequently show sorting-out only on that side of the developing shoot; the embryo and later the adult plant will therefore be sectorial for a pure green half and a sorting-out half. Up until the vertical division of the terminal cell all nuclear mutations give rise to wholly mutant lineages, but a mutation in one of the daughter cells would give rise to a green-white sectorial chimera. Mutations in cells giving rise to the root and hypocotyl regions are unimportant in the adult plant since we are only interested in the development of the chlorophyll chimeras of the shoot.

During the next two successive divisions, the third and fourth, the two terminal cells are split first into four and then into eight cells to produce an upper and a lower quadrant of four cells each. The lower quadrant produces the root and hypocotyl regions and the upper quadrant the cotyledons and shoot. A mutation in the lower group of cells is unimportant, but a nuclear or plastid mutation in one of the four upper cells will give rise to respectively a white mutant lineage or a sorting-out cell lineage encompassing the corresponding quarter sector of the shoot. Hence the adult shoot will probably develop into a sectorial chimera for approximately three-quarters green and one-quarter white or sorting-out. A good example of this kind of sectorial chimera has been illustrated in a variegated *Epilobium* by Bartels (1960).

After the fifth division new mutations give rise not to true sectorial chimeras but to mericlinal chimeras in which the mutant sector is actually periclinally divided. The fifth division divides each of the octant cells periclinally into an outer and an inner cell. The outer group give rise to the epidermis, L I, and the inner group to the remaining layers, L II and L III. Hence a mutation in any of the eight upper cells produces a mutant lineage that affects either L I, or the future L II and L III, but not all three layers together; it therefore gives rise to a periclinal mutant sector. At a later stage of development the separation between layers II and III takes place, unless there is no L III.

VI.3.ii. MUTATIONS IN THE SHOOT GROWING-POINT

Only before the second or third successive division of the embryo is it possible for a mutation to affect all the future cells of the shoot. After the second or third and before the fifth division a half or quarter sector can be affected. Finally after the fifth successive division, all mutations are restricted to one of the future germ layers so that only a mericlinal sector is affected. In the two- or three-layered growing-point of the shoot, chimeras arising from single mutations are always of the mericlinal kind, since a single mutation can occur in only one cell of only one layer, although sometimes a second or third layer becomes affected as the result of subsequent layer alterations.

Most monocotyledons are two layered, and in white-over-green or green-over-white periclinal chimeras of *Chlorophytum* and *Hosta* (Fig. VI.4) and many other genera it is clear that L I regularly produces the marginal mesophyll tissue of the leaf as well as the epidermis, while L II produces the central mesophyll tissue. Hence mutations in the growing-point of either layer are quickly revealed by the appearance of conspicuous white sectors in the leaves. Many dicotyledons, on the other hand, are three layered and the leaf mesophyll tissue is developed largely, and often entirely, from L II and L III, while L I produces just the epidermis. Hence a mutation in L II or L III is conspicuous by the sectoring it produces in the leaves, whereas a mutation in the unseen epidermis, L I, may pass quite unnoticed. The epidermis is said to be unseen because the plastids in its cells are too dispersed for their colour to be seen by the naked eye, although usually recognizable with the microscope[28]. Consequently chlorophyll mutations in the outer layer of either an embryo or the growing-point of an adult plant give periclinal chimeras with the structure WGG, which are frequently over-

Fig. VI.4. *A white-over-green, two-layered periclinal chimera of the monocotyledon* Hosta sieboldiana, *WG. The white margin is developed from L I and the green centre from L II*

looked, as are also chimeras with the reciprocal structure GWW. The letters G and W are used as abbreviations for green and white respectively; the letters WGG, for example, are therefore shorthand for white-green-green and refer to the character of the three germ layers of the growing-point from the outside to the inside, that is in the order L I, L II, L III.

Unfortunately, the failure to recognize the existence of a WGG periclinal or conversely of a GWW periclinal has sometimes been the cause of considerable trouble in chimera studies and has given rise to what are probably quite erroneous conclusions. This is because the rule that L I produces only the epidermis is not as perfect as some people have assumed. On the contrary, there are dicotyledons such as *Veronica gentianoides* albocincta, WG(G) (Fig. VI.5), and *Daphne odora* marginata, WGG, in which the white L I always contributes to the marginal mesophyll tissue. In *Spiraea japonica* bumalda, WGG, the white L I may produce only the epidermis, but it frequently divides periclinally to give marginal flecks and sectors. A bud variation of *Pelargonium zonale* Flower of Spring, with the structure WGG, also produces sporadic white flecks or sectors, which on a cutting that has previously

Fig. VI.5. *A white-over-green, two-layered periclinal chimera of the dicotyledon* Veronica gentianoides, *WG. The white margin is developed from L I and the green centre from L II*

Fig. VI.6. *The green-white-green mesochimera of the dicotyledon* Hydrangea hortensis, *GWG. The green marginal teeth, which are clearly separated from the green core L III by the white layer L II, arise by localized periclinal divisions in the epidermis L I during the leaf's development*

appeared perfectly green, can easily be mistaken for mutation. Flecks of mesophyll developed from the epidermis have also been recorded in many mesochimeras, GWG. In the GWG mesochimera and YWG trichimera of *Hydrangea hortensis*, for example, L I produces the mesophyll tissue of many of the marginal teeth in almost every leaf (Fig. VI.6). In the GWG *Abutilon striatum* the leaf tip is frequently green showing its development from L I (Fig. VI.7). In many GWG *Pelargonium zonale*

Fig. VI.7. *The green-white-green mesochimera of the dicotyledon* Abutilon striatum, *GWG. The green tip, which is clearly separated from the green core L III by the white layer L II, arises by localized periclinal divisions in the epidermis L I during the leaf's development*

cultivars L I frequently produces flecks of green mesophyll tissue in the otherwise white margin in the region of the leaf stalk, and in the cultivar Dolly Varden almost every leaf is flecked in this way (Fig. VI.8); occasionally flecks and sectors also occur elsewhere in the leaf. Quite frequently bud variations in chimeras give rise to white shoots and it is often assumed that these are pure, but my own observations[28] show that they often have a green epidermis so their real structure is GWW; this is sometimes confirmed by the appearance of green flecks developed from L I. Similar apparently white shoots can be produced directly by sorting-out in variegated embryos. Many other examples could be quoted[6, 28] which show that different species vary considerably in the frequency with which L I divides periclinally to produce flecks of mesophyll. Moreover, even within species there can be considerable

Fig. VI.8. *The green-white-green mesochimera of the dicotyledon* Pelargonium *zonale cultivar Dolly Varden, GWG. The green flecks at the base of the leaf near the petiole are derived from the epidermis L I by localized periclinal divisions during the leaf's development*

variation between cultivars. However, on the whole, flecks appear to be more frequent on the leaf margins than elsewhere, and on the margins they are often largely restricted to specific areas.

On two occasions, firstly by Imai (1936a) in *Pelargonium zonale,* and secondly by Michaelis (1957b) in *Epilobium hirsutum,* claims were made of the back-mutation of white plastids to green. This explanation was given for the unexpected appearance of green flecks in an otherwise white leaf area. In *Pelargonium* my own studies[28] make it clear that Imai was almost certainly dealing with a periclinal chimera with a genetically green epidermis, GWW. The *Epilobium* example has been criticized on similar grounds by Bergann (1962). Neither Imai nor Michaelis excluded the more likely possibility that the epidermis was genetically green and divided periclinally to produce the green flecks of mesophyll tissue. In *Epilobium,* the numerous small green flecks all within a sector on one half of the leaf suggest that the epidermis was in fact not pure green, but was at the finely mosaiced stage of sorting-out. Had these authors really appreciated the importance of the epidermis, they would have realized that their interpretations could not be accepted without indisputable proof that L I was not responsible for the occurrence of the green flecks.

VI.4. Permutations of Structure, Genotype, and Variation in Periclinal Chimeras

It is not the true purpose of this book to discuss at length the many interesting facets of chimera studies. But since a failure to recognize the full potentialities of the chimera structure of the growing-point of higher plants has resulted in numerous inexact descriptions, it is hoped that the following survey will help to correct this situation. Three main questions need to be considered:

(1) How many structural, growing-point arrangements of two- and three-layered periclinal chimeras are possible?

(2) How many genetic combinations result from the possible permutations of two or three genetic types with the different layers?

(3) What bud variations are possible from these periclinal chimeras?

These questions may be answered firstly in respect of a two-layered chimera, and secondly in respect of a three-layered chimera. For convenience in description the germ layers, of which only the inner can be more than one cell thick, have been termed L I, L II, and L III[27] from the outside to the inside. If a plant has a two-layered apex L III is missing. Also it is convenient to use the symbols A, B, and C to represent genetically distinct types as in the trichimeras of *Pelargonium zonale* Madame Salleron[7, 8] and *Euphorbia pulcherrima* Weissrand-Rosa[5], or just A and B where a chimera has only two genetic types which is the most commonly found situation.

VI.4.i. TWO-LAYERED CHIMERAS

A two-layered chimera has only two genetic types of tissue for which there are only two possible structural arrangements (Fig. VI.9), and only two genetic combinations[11]:

$$
\begin{array}{ccc}
\text{L I} & \text{II} & \text{Fig. VI.9} \\
\text{A} & \text{B} & 4 \\
\text{or} \quad \text{B} & \text{A} & 3
\end{array}
$$

Bud variations in a two-layered chimera are of two types (Fig. VI.10):

(1) L I duplicates, leaving L II behind, and a shoot is formed composed of only the genetic type of the skin:

$$
\begin{array}{ccccccc}
\text{L I} & \text{II} & & \text{L I} & \text{II} & & \text{Fig. VI.10} \\
\text{B} & \text{A} & \rightarrow & \text{B} & \text{B} & & 1
\end{array}
$$

(2) L II duplicates and perforates L I so that a shoot is formed composed of only the genetic type of the core:

$$
\begin{array}{ccccccc}
\text{L I} & \text{II} & & \text{L I} & \text{II} & & \text{Fig. VI.10} \\
\text{B} & \text{A} & \rightarrow & \text{A} & \text{A} & & 2
\end{array}
$$

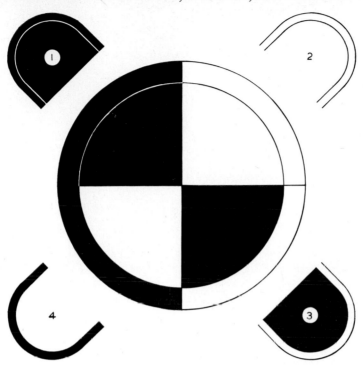

FIG. VI.9. *Two-layered chimera having only two possible structural arrangements:* (*1*) *Pure for first genetic type AA;* (*2*) *Pure for second genetic type BB;* (*3*) *Periclinal chimera BA;* (*4*) *Periclinal chimera AB. Black = A, white = B*

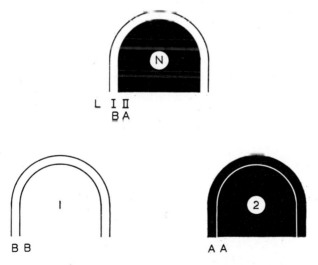

FIG. VI.10. *Possible bud variations in two-layered chimeras: N Periclinal chimera BA;* (*1*) *Pure for second genetic type BB;* (*2*) *Pure for first genetic type AA. Black = A, white = B*

The different types of two- and especially three-layered chlorophyll chimeras have been given a variety of names particularly by Imai (1934b; 1935a, b) and by Correns (1937); recently the most useful names for three-layered plastid-differential chimeras have been summarized by Hagemann (1964). Sometimes these names may be useful, but for most purposes the use of the two letters WG meaning a white-over-green two-layered plastid-differential chimera, for example, or wG for a nuclear-differential chimera is quite sufficient. Similarly for three-layered chimeras, a simple abbreviation is clearer than separate names for each type of structure.

VI.4.ii. THREE-LAYERED CHIMERAS

A three-layered chimera, whether it has two or three genetic types of tissue, has only six possible structural arrangements (Figs. VI.11 and 12):

	2 *Genetic types*				3 *Genetic types*		
L I	II	III	Fig. VI.11	L I	II	III	Fig. VI.12
A	A	B	8	A	B	C	1
A	B	A	2	A	C	B	4
B	A	A	5	B	A	C	2
B	B	A	6	B	C	A	5
B	A	B	4	C	A	B	3
A	B	B	7	C	B	A	6

In the three-layered chimera with two genetic types there are six different genetic combinations[8,12,18,21] corresponding to the six structural arrangements. From the three-layered chimera with three genetic types twenty-seven genetic combinations are obtainable; they include the three pure types and four groups of six structural arrangements[8,19]. These four groups comprise one, with three genetic types, and three with the three possible combinations of only two of these types together as follows:

One group 3 Genetic types (A B C)			Three groups, 2 Genetic types (A B)			(A C)			(B C)		
L I	II	III	L I	II	III	L I	II	III	L I	II	III
A	B	C	A	A	B	A	A	C	B	B	C
A	C	B	A	B	A	A	C	A	B	C	B
B	A	C	B	A	A	C	A	A	C	B	B
B	C	A	B	B	A	C	C	A	C	C	B
C	A	B	B	A	B	C	A	C	C	B	C
C	B	A	A	B	B	A	C	C	B	C	C

FIG. VI.11. *Three layered chimeras having only six possible structural arrangements with two genetic types of tissue, giving six genetic combinations; the two pure types are also shown: (1) Pure for first genetic type AAA; (2) Mesochimera ABA; (3) Pure for second genetic type BBB; (4) Mesochimera BAB; (5) Periclinal chimera BAA; (6) Periclinal chimera BBA; (7) Periclinal chimera ABB; (8) Periclinal chimera AAB. Black = A, white = B*

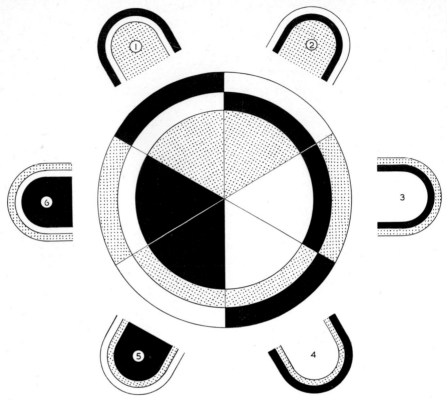

FIG. VI.12. *Three-layered chimeras having only six possible structural arrangements with three genetic types of tissue:* (*1*) *ABC;* (*2*) *BAC;* (*3*) *CAB;* (*4*) *ACB;* (*5*) *BCA;* (*6*) *CBA. Black = A, white = B, spotted = C*

Bud variations in each of the six different structural arrangements, whether there be two or three genetic types, occur in principle in nine different ways (Fig. VI.13). In each variation periclinal division in the cells of one layer, causing duplication of that layer, leads to displacement of the cells in the adjoining layer. This displacement is either a shifting of one layer further inward or outward, or else an outer layer is perforated by the duplicating layer. As the result of these bud variations, the chimeral structure alters to produce a growing-point with a new constitution. It is of great interest that these nine bud variations have been produced experimentally, firstly from the trichimera *Pelargonium zonale* Madame Salleron[7] and secondly from the trichimera *Euphorbia pulcherrima* Weissrand-Rosa[5]. In Madame Salleron L I is normal, green with long internodes, L II is white with long internodes, and L III is green but with short internodes. In Weissrand-Rosa L I can synthesize chlorophyll but not anthocyanin, L II can synthesize anthocyanin but not chlorophyll and the normal L III synthesizes both chlorophyll and

POSSIBLE VARIATIONS IN DEVELOPMENT OF A
THREE – LAYERED SHOOT APEX.

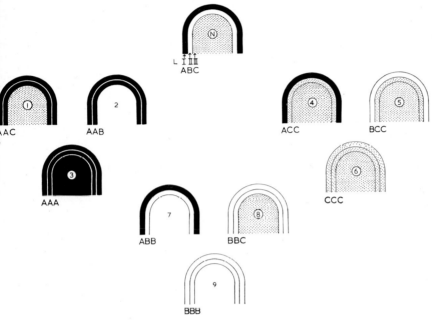

FIG. VI.13. *Possible bud variations in three-layered chimeras: N Periclinal chimera with three genetic types ABC; (1) Periclinal chimera AAC; (2) Periclinal chimera AAB; (3) Pure for first genetic type AAA; (4) Periclinal chimera ACC; (5) Periclinal chimera BCC; (6) Pure for third genetic type CCC; (7) Periclinal chimera ABB; (8) Periclinal chimera BBC; (9) Pure for second genetic type BBB. Black = A, white = B, spotted = C*

anthocyanin. In both these papers each of the nine bud variants from the trichimeras is described, and the layer changes giving rise to them are shown by a most instructive series of diagrams.

Less frequently a translocation of layers can take place, and by this means the twenty-four different genetic combinations plus the three pure types could be formed from one original trichimera. This has not yet been done, but Bergann and Bergann (1962) have illustrated the translocations BBC → BCB, ABC → ABA, and ABC → BAC which they have noted in their careful observations of Madame Salleron and its variants. External signs of these layer movements are shown by the breaking down of the periclinal arrangement of the layers followed by the development of a new layer arrangement indicating that one layer has been translocated in relation to the other layers, or sometimes two layers appear to have changed places. Internally, as shown by one of the diagrams from Bergann and Bergann's paper, these changes arise in two stages. Firstly, one of the three layers of the periclinal growing-point duplicates by periclinal divisions in a sector thereby making the growing-point as a whole mericlinal. Secondly, one or two layers of the original periclinal sector transgress sideways by anticlinal divisions thereby displacing the cells of the same layer in the new sector, or vice versa. In this way, by its sideways movement one layer slides above, or below another layer, or between two layers. It is necessary to stress, however, that layer movements of this kind appear to be rare, but they may be more frequent with experimental treatments of the growing-point than under natural conditions.

REFERENCES

1. ABEL, B. (1962). Z. Bot. **50**, 60–93
2. BARTELS, F. (1960). Flora **150**, 552–571
3. BAUR, E. (1909). Z. Vererbungsl. **1**, 330–351
4. BAUR, E. (1911a). Z. Vererbungsl. **4**, 81–102
5. BERGANN, F. (1961). Biol. Zbl. **80**, 403–412
6. BERGANN, F. (1962). Wiss. Z. Pädagogischen Hochschule Potsdam **7**, 75–85
7. BERGANN, F. & BERGANN, L. (1959). Züchter **29**, 361–374
8. BERGANN, F. & BERGANN, L. (1962). Züchter **32**, 110–119
9. BEYER, J. J. (1932). Genetica **14**, 279–318
10. BUDER, J. (1910). Ber. dt. bot. Ges. **28**, 188–192
11. CHODAT, R. (1919). C.R. Soc. Phys. Hist. nat. Genève **36**, 81–85
12. CLOWES, F. A. L. (1961). Apical Meristems. Botanical Monographs 2. Ed., W. O. James. Blackwell Scientific Publications, Oxford
13. CORRENS, C. (1919b). S.B. preuss. Akad. Wiss. 820–857
14. CORRENS, C. edited WETTSTEIN, F. v. (1937). Nicht mendelnde Vererbung. Gebrüder Borntraeger, Berlin
15. DESHPANDE, R. B. (1939). Curr. Sci. **8**, 313–314
16. GARBER, R. J. & HOOVER, M. M. (1927). J. Hered. **18**, 542–543
17. HAGEMANN, R. (1964). Plasmatische Vererbung. Genetik Grundlagen, Ergebnisse und Probleme in Einzeldarstellungen. Veb Gustav Fischer Verlag, Jena
18. IMAI, Y. (1934b). J. Coll. Agric. Tokyo **12**, 479–523
19. IMAI, Y. (1935a). J. Genet. **30**, 1–13
20. IMAI, Y. (1935b). J. Genet. **31**, 53–65
21. IMAI, Y. (1935c). Amer. Nat. **69**, 587–595
22. IMAI, Y. (1936a). J. Genet. **33**, 169–195
23. MAHESHWARI, P. (1950). An introduction to the embryology of angiosperms. McGraw-Hill Book Company, New York
24. MICHAELIS, P. (1957b). Planta **50**, 60–106
25. NATH, B. (1955). Nature Lond. **176**, 316
26. RÖBBELEN, G. (1962). Z. Vererbungsl. **93**, 25–34
27. SATINA, S. & BLAKESLEE, A. F. (1941). Amer. J. Bot. **28**, 862–871
28. TILNEY-BASSETT, R. A. E. (1963a). Heredity **18**, 265–285
29. TILNEY-BASSETT, R. A. E. (1963b). Heredity **18**, 485–504
30. WINKLER, H. (1907). Ber. dt. bot. Ges. **25**, 568–576
31. WINKLER, H. (1910). Ber. dt. bot. Ges. **28**, 116–118

CHAPTER VII

Recognition of Sorting-out

VII.1. Extra-nuclear versus Nuclear Inheritance

THE PROOF of the ability of a character to be inherited by particles outside the nucleus is based on the following three main criteria:

(1) Non-Mendelian inheritance.
(2) Reciprocal differences after reciprocal crosses.
(3) The sorting-out of genetic particles during development.

It is also important to be able to exclude false impressions of extra-nuclear inheritance. Let us now consider the meaning of each of these criteria.

VII.1.i. NON-MENDELIAN INHERITANCE

According to the Mendelian rules, we should expect reciprocal crosses between green and variegated parents to give solely green F_1 offspring which, on selfing, segregate into green and variegated F_2 seedlings in a monohybrid ratio, showing that variegation is caused by the action of a stable recessive gene (Chapter III). More complicated crosses involving two or three genes would again give a uniform F_1, but the F_2 would now segregate in a di- or tri-hybrid ratio respectively, showing that the genes are segregating independently from each other. Or the genes might not segregate independently owing to linkage. Or as in *Melandrium*, only the female offspring would be variegated owing to the action of sex-linked genes. Sometimes, however, variegated plants do not breed true owing to the action of mutable genes (Chapter IV), which are less predictable than stable genes, but which still follow the Mendelian rules. Finally, standard Mendelian behaviour can sometimes go completely astray owing to irregular chromosome behaviour (Chapter V). The control of variegation is none the less strictly nuclear. Only when the inheritance of a character cannot be explained in any of these ways should an extra-nuclear explanation be sought.

Reciprocal crosses between *Pelargonium zonale* plants with green germ layers and plants with white germ layers give green, variegated, and white offspring, whereas one would expect a uniform F_1 according to the Mendelian rule. Moreover, the green F_1 plants and the green shoots of variegated plants give no F_2 segregation; they are true-breeding. On selfing the chimeras with white germ layers and the white shoots of variegated plants, the few seedlings are white; they die shortly after germination. Evidently the green and white plastid characters are both true-breeding, yet, when crossed, instead of forming a hybrid they form a mixture of the two plastid types.

Two years before Baur (1909) made these observations, he had already demonstrated (1907) the Mendelian inheritance of golden or aurea leaved plants. He found that when golden plants were selfed, they segregated in a ratio of 1 green:2 golden, together with a few white seedlings. He concluded that the golden nuclear genotype was heterozygous, and the theoretical monohybrid segregation of 1 green:2 golden: 1 white had been disturbed by the inviability of most of the white embryos. Two years after his plastid experiments Baur was able to report (1911b) that the inheritance of flower colour had also followed Mendelian rules. In one pair of reciprocal crosses he had used a green plastid parent with red flowers and a white plastid parent with whitish flowers. All green F_1 plants, and both green and white branches of variegated plants, bore red flowers. The F_2 offspring segregated in relation to the flower colour in a monohybrid ratio of 3 red:1 white. These two examples, in which the inheritance of leaf and flower colour characters follows the Mendelian rule while the green and white plastid character of the same plants does not, clearly demonstrate that the plastid inheritance is not governed by the nucleus; its control must therefore be outside the nucleus, that is it is extra-nuclear.

VII.1.ii. RECIPROCAL DIFFERENCES AFTER RECIPROCAL CROSSES

Among the simpler algae are many isogamous species in which sexual reproduction involves the fusion of the whole of two morphologically identical cells. Other sexually reproducing algae and all higher plants are oogamous, in which a large motionless female cell is fertilized by a much smaller active male cell. With oogamous fertilization, since the large female egg is filled with food reserves, it does not necessarily follow that the contributions of cytoplasm and associated extra-nuclear particles are directly related to the respective sizes of the gametes. Nevertheless, breeding experiments show that these extra-nuclear genetic components of the cell are predominantly or exclusively transmitted by the female as a rule. Hence reciprocal crosses between two individuals differing in their extra-nuclear genotype invariably leads to reciprocal differences appearing in their F_1 progeny.

Several workers, interested in Baur's results, have repeated his famous *Pelargonium* crosses with their own material. Hagemann (1964) has tabulated their data and shown that almost all the crosses show a statistically very significant reciprocal difference. But even more striking reciprocal differences are shown by higher plants in which the male cell appears to transmit no extra-nuclear particles as Correns (1909a, b) discovered in a variegated *Mirabilis jalapa*. He found that green shoots on the variegated plant gave green offspring, white shoots gave white offspring and variegated shoots gave green, variegated, and white offspring. Furthermore, the type of offspring obtained from crossing was exactly the same as from selfing, for it was entirely dependent upon the colour of the female shoot; the pollen from different coloured shoots had absolutely no effect. The reciprocal differences following reciprocal crosses were therefore absolute, for the plastid character was plainly transmitted solely by the female parent. At the same time the behaviour of other characters, indeed of another type of variegation (see Chapter IV) followed the Mendelian rule.

These two examples, *Pelargonium* and *Mirabilis*, both independently discovered in Germany in 1909 and both the first examples of their kind, illustrate the two types of non-Mendelian inheritance, biparental and uniparental-maternal respectively. Thus with maternal inheritance, while green and white offspring can be derived by sorting-out from a variegated mother their two types of pure germ cells cannot again be recombined to form variegated offspring; with biparental inheritance they can be so recombined.

VII.1.ii.a. *False impressions*

Reciprocal differences between crosses are not always caused by the unequal transmission of extra-nuclear particles from the two sexes. Other phenomena exist among plants and animals which can give the same effect; these have been listed by Hagemann (1964) as follows:

(1) Apparent inheritance.
(2) Peculiarities in the manner of multiplication.
(3) Special cases of chromosomal inheritance.
(4) Predetermination.
(5) Dauermodification.

Fortunately, these phenomena are not all found among variegated plants, in which the most important difficulties are due to chromosome irregularities (Chapter V), apomixis, and virus infection. Apomictic

13—P.

plants produce their seeds without sexual fertilization; pollination may be necessary to stimulate development but there is no actual fusion of a male and female gamete prior to embryo formation. Consequently the offspring always resemble the female parent and the male has no influence. If this possibility is not eliminated by cytological examination or by the observation of the normal Mendelian inheritance of other characters, the symptoms of apomixis can be mistakenly diagnosed as the purely maternal inheritance of an extra-nuclear factor. Fortunately most cases of extra-nuclear inheritance in higher plants have been reported from species in which normal Mendelian inheritance has already been demonstrated by other workers in unrelated experiments, a fact, however, which is seldom referred to.

Many variegations are caused by virus infection, and many by an abnormal genotype, but the two cannot always be immediately distinguished from each other even by an experienced eye. Experiment is necessary. Frequently it is sufficient to determine that the variegation is not inherited to be certain that it is caused by a virus or another infective agent, or by poor nutrition. But sometimes viruses are transmitted either through the egg, or through the pollen, or through both parents. A variegated *Capsicum annuum* was found by Ikeno (1917) to be true-breeding, and to give wholly variegated offspring after reciprocal crosses with normal green plants. It appeared, at first, as if the variegation was caused by an extra-nuclear particle that was inherited through both parents. Later, Ikeno (1930) found that the variegation was also graft transmissible, showing that it was the behaviour of a virus that had given the false impression. Bearing this example in mind, it is particularly important that doubtful cases of nuclear or extra-nuclear inheritance of variegation should always be tested by grafting and by inoculation methods for the possibility of virus infection.

VII.1.iii. THE SORTING-OUT OF PLASTIDS DURING DEVELOPMENT

The sorting-out of plastids after a plastid mutation has already been described in detail (VI.2.ii), but the main phases may now be summarized as follows:

(1) A latent, invisible phase immediately after plastid mutation in which mutant plastids and mixed cells multiply before any pure white cells are produced.

(2) A fine mosaic or fine striping phase in which pure green and pure white cells are sorting-out from mixed cells.

(3) A coarse mosaic or coarse striping phase in which pure green and

pure white cells are sorting-out from mixed cells only occasionally, but in which pure tissues are sorting-out from pure cells.

(4) The final phase in which pure green or pure white shoots or green-white sectorial and periclinal shoots sort-out from pure tissues.

The overall effect of this phased plastid sorting-out is to produce what has been described as the characteristic complex multiple cell lineage chequered pattern, a pattern which is very distinct from the simple cell lineage produced by a spontaneous nuclear mutation (Fig. VII.1).

Fig. VII.1. *The characteristic complex multiple cell lineage chequered pattern caused by the sorting-out of green and white plastids is illustrated in a single leaf from* Epilobium hirsutum, *left. This is compared with the very different pattern of green flecks on a white background produced by the repeated mutation of a mutable gene illustrated in a single leaf from* Epilobium parviflorum, *right. The photos have been kindly provided by Dr P. Michaelis*

VII.2. Sorting-out in the Germ Cells

By flowering time different plants have quite naturally sorted-out to different degrees so that sometimes sorting-out in the growing-point is still in process and at other times it is complete. This is important for it determines the choice of shoots available for breeding experiments and consequently the kind of offspring obtained from them.

VII.2.i. RELATIONSHIP BETWEEN MOTHER AND OFFSPRING

By uniparental-maternal plastid transmission the type of offspring obtained from crossing or selfing is entirely dependent upon the colour of the female shoot. Hence when sorting-out is complete and the egg cells contain only green or only white plastids, then the offspring are pure green or pure white respectively. But many authors have also obtained variegated offspring, which were presumably derived from mixed cells, indicating that sorting-out was not complete (Table VIII.1). In support of the assumption that variegated offspring really do come from mixed eggs, and the green or white offspring from respectively green or white eggs, attention may be drawn to correlations between the degree of variegation of the shoot or flower or fruit parts and the frequency of green, variegated, and white offspring.

In a study of plastid-differential chimeras of *Chlorophytum elatum* and *comosum* and crosses between them, Collins (1922) found that seed produced on wholly green or white flowering shoots produced green or white seedlings respectively, but from coarsely striped flowering stems he also received a few variegated seedlings. These variegated seedlings grew into variegated plants which produced some finely striped stems. Collins noticed that seeds from these finely striped stems produced a much higher proportion of variegated offspring than from coarsely striped flowering stems. Thus the most variegated seedlings came from the most finely striped areas where we would logically expect to find the highest frequency of mixed cells and subsequently mixed eggs. Moreover, the colour of the seedlings showed a close correspondence to the colour of the seed capsule. In the composites *Senecio vulgaris* and *Taraxacum officinale* there are numerous seeds produced in each flowering head. Correns (1922) drew a plan of the seed distribution in several flowers of sorting-out plants, germinated the seed and then plotted the distribution of green, variegated, and white offspring according to the original position of each seed in the flower. He found that green and white seeds were often in large or small clusters on their own, but variegated seeds were always associated with neighbouring green and white seeds showing a similarity to the close association of mixed cells on the borders of green and white areas of the leaves. A similar correlation was found in the sorting-out of a maize plant by Anderson (1923) who noted that striped seedlings usually come from seeds obtained on or near the borders of areas giving only pale or only green seedlings. The examples of *Senecio* and *Zea* have been illustrated by Hagemann (1964). A few years later Demerec (1927) examining a second case of sorting-out in *Zea mays* found a decrease in the percentage of green offspring and a corresponding increase in the percentage of pale green and variegated offspring with an increase in the area of pale green tissue in the parent. Moreover, he found that the distribution of the three types of offspring with respect to their position on the ear was not random but that there was a tendency for like types to appear in patches suggesting that all the seeds from a common patch were derived from a common cell lineage. A similar correlation was established in *Sorghum* by Karper (1934), and several other workers have mentioned this relationship between mother and offspring in their own plants even though they have not always presented experimental data.

Thus in many examples of sorting-out variegation, allowing for the fact that sorting-out is also occurring in the formation of the egg, the character of the seedlings has been shown to correspond very closely with the pattern of sorting-out in the shoot, flower, and fruit parts. Moreover, where it has been tested, in no case has the correlation between mother and offspring not been found. Hence, so long as the frequency of variegated seedlings from sorting-out plants is well above the spontaneous mutation rate, there is no reason to doubt that they have come from mixed eggs. Since mixed eggs are mixed cells, the occurrence of variegated seedlings provides genetic evidence, which is equivalent in value to the cytological evidence, of the existence of such mixed cells. The cytological observation of mixed cells, which will be discussed later in this chapter, has been widely accepted as strong evidence that the original mutation occurred within the changed plastid itself and not within any other extra-nuclear particle; the genetic evidence surely permits the same conclusion. Clearly the two approaches, cytological and genetical, and the two observations, mixed cells and variegated seedlings, are complementary to each other, and indeed both have frequently been found together (Table VIII.1). It is therefore difficult to see the logic of the many authors who put their whole faith in the cytological observation while ignoring the genetic demonstration of mixed cells; both are valid.

VII.2.ii. PLASTID LETHALITY

Three spontaneously occurring variegated plants were described by Clausen (1927, 1930) in *Viola tricolor* and *arvensis* and a hybrid between the two. His descriptions and illustrations suggest that each was caused by the sorting-out of two kinds of plastid. Crosses between green and variegated shoots showed that the inheritance was non-Mendelian, and his limited data suggest that the plastids were transmitted only by the female parent (Table VIII.1). On selfing variegated shoots, the progeny consisted of green seedlings and variegated seedlings, which were said to have green cotyledons, but surprisingly no white seedlings. Clausen noticed that the undernourished white shoots, and white areas of variegated shoots, produced only a few poor seeds which failed to germinate. It therefore appears as if the absence of white seedlings from sorting-out in *Viola* is due to the particular lethality of the mutant white plastids. This is unusual, but it is not unique for mutant white plastids are frequently extremely lethal in *Pelargonium zonale*, and some cultivars never produce any white seedlings from selfing plants with white germ layers, even though numerous embryos begin to develop[64].

Many of the numerous sorting-out plants produced in *Epilobium hirsutum* by Michaelis (1958a, b) gave rise to variegated and white flowering shoots from which viable seeds were obtained. The seeds containing only white or, in some plants yellowish-green or pale green plastids germinated to give the corresponding coloured seedlings. But in a few plants the mutant plastids degenerated before the completion of leaf cell division. This degeneration was accompanied in pure white cells by the cessation of cell division, which caused serious anatomical disturbances owing to the stress between these cells and surrounding normal green cells. Seeds from white areas of such plants failed to germinate.

Clearly the effect of a plastid mutation may sometimes be sufficiently drastic to lead to the complete lethality of germ cells, embryos or seeds. It seems likely therefore, that other plastid mutations, although not leading to complete lethality, may nevertheless cause a serious reduction in fertility as indeed happens in *Pelargonium* (VIII.4). But unfortunately there is no further data on this point owing to the almost universal failure to realize the usefulness of fertility measurements in studies of sorting-out variegation. Should different plastid mutations in fact cause significant differences in their effects upon the fertility, this might prove to be a useful additional way of classifying or distinguishing them, besides raising important new questions to which such a finding would lead.

VII.2.iii. PLASTID VIABILITY

Sorting-out in the vast majority of plants observed leads to the development of pure green, pure white, green-white sectorial and periclinal shoots. The white cells and tissues are able to divide and grow quite normally so long as they receive sufficient nourishment from the supporting green tissue, whereas their corresponding white seedlings,

which lack the support of any green tissues, usually die at the cotyledon
stage. The mutant seedlings are not always completely lacking in pigment, they may be yellow, yellowish-green or pale green in different
examples: nevertheless, the absence of reports to the contrary suggests
that they usually die. In a sorting-out *Antirrhinum majus*, however,
Wild (1960) found one spontaneous mutant plastid type which is
definitely viable. The mutant cells and tissues are at first pale, but as
they age they become so green in the cool shaded greenhouse as to be
almost indistinguishable from normal. Wild found that the new virescent
mutant could be grown and propagated in the greenhouse, without any
support from normal green tissues, either by taking cuttings of virescent
shoots or from seed. In the garden, however, the strong light tended to
destroy both virescent cuttings and seedlings, especially when young.
In young leaves the mutant plastids are amoeboid in form, and a grana
structure is hardly recognizable; the plastids may even become completely vacuolized. As the leaves age, the tendency to degenerate is
replaced by a much improved development in which a good grana
structure appears and the plastids become almost normal green. (See
Chapters XIII and XIV for an account of the growth and differentiation of plastids.) As a result of this transition with ageing, many degenerative and developmental stages of the plastids can be found in
different cells of the same leaf and sometimes within the same cell.
The exceptional viability of this plastom mutant confers on it the
great advantage that it can be propagated in unlimited quantity
without any influence from neighbouring normal green tissue such as
might occur in chimeras. This makes it particularly ideal material for
biochemical studies on the manifold effects of the plastid mutation[51].
It will be interesting to see to what extent work in this direction in
Germany leads to a better understanding of the nature of plastom
mutations in general.

The viable *Antirrhinum* mutant may be the first to be used for biochemical analysis, but it is not the first to be recognized. A pale green
Hordeum vulgare plant was noticed growing among normal plants by
Robertson (1937), and selfed seed produced viable pale green offspring.
Seedlings from reciprocal crosses between pale and normal green plants
demonstrated a purely maternal inheritance (Table VIII.1). No mention of sorting-out was made, but this may have been complete at the
time of discovery. However, this is not so important, the main point
is that it was clearly an extra-nuclear mutant and the mutant barley
seedlings were able to grow into adult plants. Among a number of
gene-induced plastom mutants of *Nepeta cataria* Woods and DuBuy
(1951b) describe one as a viable yellow-green type. And Stubbe (oral
communication) possesses a pale green *Oenothera* plastom mutant which
is viable, even though it is not so green as some other plastom mutants

which survive only as chimeras. We shall see later (IX.5.iv) that the reason for differences in viability of plastom mutants is not necessarily related to their total chlorophyll content, but whether or not they are capable of photosynthesis.

VII.3. The Investigation of Mixed Cells

It is widely considered[55] that the best single evidence that sorting-out variegation results from a plastom mutation rather than a mutation in any other extra-nuclear genetic particle, is the cytological observation of mixed cells containing two morphologically distinct plastids (Fig. VII.2). Another mutant particle such as a mutant mitochondria,

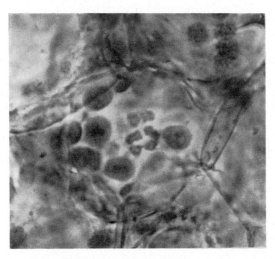

Fig. VII.2. *Phase contrast photomicrograph of a mixed cell from a sorting-out variegated plant of* Antirrhinum majus. *By permission, from Hagemann, R.* (*1960*). Die Kulturpflanze **8**, *168–184, figure 10, and Akademie-Verlag, Berlin*

would, it is argued, if it affected the plastids at all, affect all the plastids of the same cell more or less equally. Mixed cells have now been reported from one Monocotyledon and twelve Dicotyledon genera (Table VII.1). In four genera the plastids are transmitted by both parents in reciprocal crosses, in seven genera by the mother alone, and in two genera breeding experiments have not been made; in the tomato reciprocal crosses in *Lycopersicum esculentum* (Table VIII.1) showed the plastids to be maternally inherited, but mixed cells were observed by a different worker in another species, *Lycopersicum pimpinellifolium*. In many cases the mixed cells have been drawn or photographed from the light microscope, and even electron micrographs of mixed cells have

TABLE VII.1. LIST OF HIGHER PLANTS WITH SORTING-OUT VARIEGATIONS IN WHICH MIXED CELLS HAVE BEEN OBSERVED

Plant and mode of plastid inheritance	Authors	Dates
Uniparental-maternal		
Antirrhinum majus	Maly, Wild	1956
	Wild	1958, 60
	Hagemann	1960, 61, 64, 65
	Döbel, Hagemann	1963
	Döbel	1964
Arabidopsis thaliana	Röbbelen	1962
Epilobium hirsutum	Michaelis	1957–1965
Hosta japonica (Monocotyledon)	Yasui	1929
Nicotiana tabacum	Woods, DuBuy	1951a
	Burk, Stewart, Dermen	1964
	Wettstein, Eriksson	1965
Primula sinensis	Gregory	1915
Stellaria media	Funaoka	1924
Biparental		
Hypericum species crosses	Noack	1931b, 32b, 34
	Herbst	1935
Nepeta cataria	Woods, DuBuy	1951a, b
Oenothera species crosses	Krumbholz	1925
	Schötz	1954
	Stubbe	1957, 58
Pelargonium zonale	Hagemann	1964
Not determined		
Lycopersicum pimpinellifolium	Hagemann	1964
Senecio vulgaris	Funaoka	1924

been illustrated from *Antirrhinum majus* (Fig. VII.3) and *Nicotiana tabacum*, and mentioned from *Arabidopsis thaliana*. In all cases other data, where available, support these observations.

Mixed cells are to be expected and are found during the second phase of sorting-out in tissues where the leaf variegation is finely mosaiced or striped, but they may still occur occasionally in leaves in which sorting-out has reached the third phase. Sorting-out in variegated *Antirrhinum* seedlings, derived from mixed eggs, is fairly slow and Hagemann (1960) was able to find mixed cells throughout the foliage regions, including the cotyledons, leaves, bracts, and sepals. But in *Oenothera*, sorting-out from mixed zygotes is so rapid that mixed cells are only found in the cotyledons and first foliage leaves, or rarely later in development. In many plants the leaves are structurally less suitable for finding mixed cells than in other plants; in such cases the genetic demonstration of the existence of mixed cells may be easier to establish than the cytological demonstration. Indeed, the existence of mixed cells has been demon-

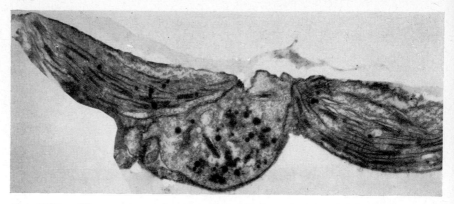

Fig. VII.3. *Electron micrograph of a mixed cell from a sorting-out variegated plant of* Antirrhinum majus. *Two normal plastids are situated on either side of a mutant plastid. By permission, from Döbel, P. (1964).* Zeitschrift für Vererbungslehre **95**, *226–235, figure 7, and Springer-Verlag, Berlin–Göttingen–Heidelberg*

strated genetically much more often than cytologically (Table VIII.1). Many authors, however, have not attempted to look for mixed cells, and even in suitable material the searcher may encounter a number of difficulties, either through the finding of apparent mixed cells where they are not expected, or through the masking of true mixed cells where they are expected.

Before discussing these difficulties, the following terms used by Michaelis to describe different types of cell in relation to the plastids should be mentioned:

(1) Heteroplasmonic cells are mixed cells containing at least two genetically distinct types of extra-nuclear particle of an undefined kind; the two types of particle could be plastids, or mitochondria, or some other extra-nuclear component. The corresponding pure cells are homoplasmonic.

(2) Heteroplastidic cells are cells containing at least two types of morphologically distinct plastids. The corresponding cells with all plastids morphologically alike are homoplastidic cells. These terms have also been adopted by some other workers[8].

(3) Heteroplastomatic cells are mixed cells containing at least two types of genetically distinct plastids. The corresponding pure cells are homoplastomatic.

It is, of course, possible for homoplastidic cells to be also hetero-plastomatic or vice versa.

(4) It is not clear whether the additional terms hetero- and homo-plasmatic are intended as synonyms of hetero- and homo-plasmonic, or whether they have the more useful function of defining the particles of the protoplasm outside the nucleus, plastids and mitochondria.

(5) Woods and DuBuy have used the similar terms hetero- and homo-chondric to define mixed and pure cells in relation to the mitochondria.

It remains to be seen to what extent these precise, but somewhat cumbersome terms, become generally adopted.

VII.3.i. TRANSITIONAL AND PSEUDO-MIXED CELLS

Observations of the development of normal plastids, or of the degeneration of mutant ones, show that even within the same cell plastids do not always change their form in perfect unison with each other. At times their morphological appearance can be so varied that the pure cells seem to contain two or more distinct types of plastid. Cells containing plastids at different stages of a transition from one morphological form to another have been called transitional cells, while cells which contain two or more morphologically distinct but genetically identical plastid forms without any apparent transition are best described as pseudo-mixed cells. But in practice the two terms appear to be used almost synonymously.

Plastids in various stages of development were found in the embryonic cells of normal maize plants by Randolph (1922), who pointed out that these stages could be mistaken for the presence of two kinds of plastid. In *Antirrhinum majus*, every possible degeneration stage of mutant white plastids was found, both between cells of a tissue and plastids of a cell, in white leaf sectors, whole white leaves and shoots, and the white margins of periclinal chimeras[32, 70]. Sometimes individual cells appeared to contain as many as three different kinds of plastid, which made it difficult to distinguish these transitional cells from the genuine mixed cells, except by a careful comparison of the grana structure of normal plastids; even then the distinction was difficult for as long as the degenerating plastids retained a good grana structure. Different rates of degeneration of mutant plastids have also been reported in several more plants by other workers. They include the chlorophyll deficient plastids from the hybrid variegated offspring of crosses between *Hypericum acutum × montanum*[48, 49], and between *Oenothera berteriana × odorata*[80], some gene-induced plastid mutants of *Nepeta cataria*[73], and spontaneous plastid mutants.

In several variegated *Epilobium* plants Michaelis (1957a) found pale golden green areas appearing in the middle of the white flecks during the summer. Individual cells in these areas contained both yellow-green and colourless plastids in various proportions. Nevertheless, these were not true mixed cells because with the yellowish-green cells plastids were clearly aligned in the regions of the veins and a typical sorting-out pattern was lacking. Moreover, the yellow-green plastids completely failed to appear in winter-sown variegated seedlings. Evidently such cells are pseudo-mixed cells in which the more or less sharp border between two plastid classes occurs through a physiological reaction of some kind. In some other plants restricted plastid division in individual sectors produced cells with fewer but correspondingly larger plastids. In certain developmental periods all cells contained an approximately equal low number of these giant plastids, in other periods pseudo-mixed cells occurred with normal and giant plastids in the same cell. It is probable that in these pseudo-mixed cells only some plastids were restricted in division so that two plastid sizes occurred within the same cell, giving the false impression of a mixed cell. Unfortunately the author does not make it clear whether these two interesting types of pseudo-mixed cells occurred in sorting-out variegated plants, or in pattern variegations, or in some other kind of variegation. The main problem is to distinguish real mixed cells from transitional or pseudo-mixed cells in sorting-out plants, which arise either by spontaneous plastid mutation or by hybridization. To make this distinction it is essential to have a thorough knowledge of the structure and behaviour of normal and mutant plastids in pure cells, and then to look for the mixed cells only in finely mosaiced or striped areas of the characteristic sorting-out pattern where they are most expected. It is also said that a large number of suspected mixed cells should be scored to obtain a frequency curve of the variation in the proportions of mutant to normal plastids. If the curve agrees statistically with the characteristic proportions predicted by the mathematical properties of sorting-out (discussed later in this chapter) it would prove that they were true mixed cells. In practice, however, such an ideal solution is extremely difficult to realize. Moreover, it is not certain that sorting-out proceeds in practice according to these purely theoretical predictions. Nevertheless daughter cells, if true mixed cells, will usually have similar mixture proportions, but such a relationship will not hold with pseudo-mixed cells.

VII.3.ii. PARTIAL OR COMPLETE MASKING OF MIXED CELLS

The presence of mixed cells is sometimes difficult or impossible to demonstrate, either because the tissue is too young or too old, or because substances diffusing within and between cells react upon the normal and mutant plastids in such a way as to smooth over their differences, as may be shown by a few examples.

VII.3.ii.a. *Normalization*

In a number of sorting-out plants of *Epilobium hirsutum* mixed cells could not be distinguished under the light microscope because the differences between normal green and slightly paler mutant plastids were so slight[39]. A similar difficulty would presumably occur in some *Oenothera* hybrids, if variegated seedlings were produced containing a mixture of normal green plastids and the more photo-stable deficient plastids, which are quite green except during their bleaching phase (see IX.5 for a detailed account of the physiological behaviour of *Oenothera* hybrids).

Mixed cells could be recognized in the young leaves of the original virescent *Antirrhinum* mutant mentioned earlier (VII.2.iii), but as the leaves aged the mutant plastids became extensively normal so that they could no longer be distinguished from normal plastids.

A highly unstable normalization occurs in the variable yellow-green, gene-induced plastid mutant of *Nepeta cataria*. In a young leaf the mutant plastids are yellow and vacuolate, but as the leaf matures, they often become more or less normal. Chlorophyll formation is encouraged by low light and an abundant supply of mineral nutrients. However, the pigment is not necessarily retained and the leaf may become yellow again and even necrotic, in which case the plastids become extremely vacuolized. Woods and DuBuy (1951b) further point out that the retention of pigment and the vacuolization of these abnormal plastids is so irregular that it varies not only between different parts of the same leaf, but even between different plastids within the same cell. Hence pure mutant cells may look like pseudo-mixed cells indistinguishable from true mixed cells.

VII.3.ii.b. *Degeneration*

Quite commonly among sorting-out variegations the mutant plastids begin to degenerate as soon as cell division has finished, or even earlier. They lose their pigmentation if any, their grana structure breaks down, their stroma becomes swollen and vacuolized, and finally they often coalesce into an incoherent heap, or completely disappear. Examples of this behaviour have been well described in *Antirrhinum*[23, 24, 32] and in *Epilobium*[39]. In some cases in *Epilobium* in which plastid degeneration started before the normal end of cell division, the cells themselves stopped dividing, when they contained only mutant plastids, which led to various degrees of cell and leaf distortion. In these examples mixed cells were often found in young leaves. In older leaves the mutant plastids may be completely absent, and the only indication of the previous existence of mixed cells is the presence of cells with exceptionally low numbers of green plastids.

VII.3.ii.c. *Inhibition*

Plastid degeneration sometimes begins even before the formation of a grana structure, owing to the early inhibition of plastid development.

Thus among the gene-induced plastid mutants of *Nepeta* were some, in which the development was sufficiently retarded that the plastids were reduced in size and without pigment, and in one example there was apparently no development at all[73]. Early plastid inhibition and degeneration has also been observed in *Epilobium*[39], and this led to the inhibition of the last successive cell divisions in pure mutant cells of the leaf[41, 42, 44]. The failure of one, two, or three successive cell divisions reduces the number of mutant cells by about one-half, one-quarter, and one-eighth respectively. As a result, the occurrence of large mutant white sectors in variegated leaves caused a narrowing of the leaves, asymmetrical leaf development, buckling, and general deformation of tissues. Similar but less conspicuous growth deformities occurred if normal and mutant tissues were periclinal to one another. The white palisade cells appeared more like spongy parenchyma and were sometimes stretched into tube shapes, or even torn apart. A strong inhibition of cell growth leading to considerable leaf distortion was also noticed in the *Nepeta* plastid inhibited tissues; it seems probable that cell division must have also been upset in this case.

Plastid growth and differentiation is inhibited in the bleaching phase of certain *Oenothera* hybrids (Chapter IX). When such hybrids are also variegated with normal harmonious green plastids, then it can be observed that poor division of the bleached plastids inhibits the division and expansion of the mutant cells within which they are situated[59]. Once again the asymmetrical leaf development and growth distortions provide a good external marker for the internal disturbances.

It seems likely that the inhibition and degeneration of mutant plastids is responsible for the many reports in the literature of the absence of plastids in white cells, especially as usually only mature tissues have been examined. Clearly, in all these cases, mixed cells can only be expected if sought when the leaf is very young before the mutant plastids have perished beyond recognition.

VII.3.ii.d. *Diffusion between cells*

According to Correns (1909a) the boundaries between green and white areas of the sorting-out *Mirabilis jalapa* were not sharp, but showed a gradation between the two colours. A similar boundary gradation was found in a sorting-out strain of maize[52], in which the transitional regions between green and yellow areas on striped plants contained, even within a single cell, plastids showing many intermediate sizes and depths of colour. Similar indistinct borders have been observed in some sorting-out variegations of *Epilobium*[36, 39, 42, 45]. It seems probable that these boundary gradations occur through substances which succeed in diffusing from one cell to a neighbouring cell and in so doing affect the plastids to such an extent as to make it impossible to recognize the true mixed cells. Whether the diffusible substance is produced by the white or by the green cells, or whether there is a reciprocal influence is undecided.

In a hybrid *Oenothera* containing yellowish-green mutant *suaveolens* plastids and pale non-harmonious *lamarckiana* plastids Stubbe (1958) observed some cells with normal green chloroplasts. Further analysis showed that these were *lamarckiana* plastids, which were always found immediately above or below cells containing yellowish-green *suaveolens* plastids. Stubbe therefore concluded that a transportable substance was diffusing in a vertical direction from cells containing *suaveolens* plastids to cells containing *lamarckiana* plastids, which enabled the *lamarckiana* plastids, that were normally pale with the *albicans-velans* genotype, to become green. (See Chapter IX for an explanation of the classification of *Oenothera* species and hybrids.) A similar partner induction was observed between neighbouring cells of different genetic constitution in a nuclear-differential *Antirrhinum* chimera[1].

VII.3.ii.e. *Diffusion within cells*

If it is possible for cells with one kind of plastid to be influenced by neighbouring cells containing another kind, then it is to be expected that a similar interaction will sometimes occur between the genetically different plastids of the same mixed cell. The postulated diffusible substance would not necessarily be different, it might simply be produced at a lower concentration so that it could affect plastids within the same cell, but be too weak to affect plastids of neighbouring cells. The nature of the interaction between normal green and mutant white plastids within the mixed cell could be one of several possibilities as follows:

(1) White plastids are completely dominant over green plastids in mixed cells so that the expected mixed cells cannot be recognized; the white plastids bleach or inhibit the development of the green plastids. Consequently the white cell lineages sometimes contain unrecognizable mixed cells in which the genetically green plastids are masked. But in the course of sorting-out during the successive cell divisions of leaf development, the hidden green plastids can give rise to pure cells in which they are again able to express themselves as normal green chloroplasts. Hence in the mature leaf green islands are found as part of the sorting-out pattern in the midst of white cell lineages.

Alternatively the white plastids may be only partially dominant over the green, in which case the proportions of green:white plastids found in mixed cells will depend on the strength of the bleaching action. Examples of both partial and complete dominance have been reported in *Epilobium* by Michaelis (1957a; 1958b; 1959; 1962a; 1963). In the example of partial dominance, all expected proportions of mixed cells were found except those containing less than 1–3 green plastids, which indicates that the threshold number for the dominance of white plastids over green was high, in other words the bleaching action was weak. One should point out, however, that it is not clear whether a sufficient number of mixed cells were examined to be certain that mixed cells with less than three green plastids were not overlooked.

(2) Green plastids are completely dominant over the white plastids so that mixed cells cannot be found; the green plastids aid the development of the white. The situation is the reciprocal of the above example when white plastids were dominant. Hence in the mature leaf white islands are found as part of the sorting-out pattern in the midst of green cell lineages. Again examples of this behaviour have been reported in *Epilobium*[36, 40, 45]. Alternatively, the green plastids could be only partially dominant, in which case they would aid the white plastids only when they were above the threshold number, below which mixed cells would be observable.

(3) Above a threshold value, when the green plastids are dominant over the white, they aid the development of the white plastids, which therefore appear green. But below the threshold value, when the white plastids are dominant over the green, they suppress the green plastids, which therefore appear white. Thus a balanced situation exists in which mixed cells are recognizable only at the centre of balance, if at all. Owing to the chance sorting-out during successive cell divisions the direction of the interaction sometimes becomes reversed so that a white island suddenly appears in an apparently green cell lineage, or conversely a green island suddenly appears in an apparently white cell lineage, as has indeed been observed in *Epilobium*[36, 42, 46] and possibly in *Nicotiana*[8].

In all three of the above kinds of interaction, although mixed cells are not found in mature leaves, they may in fact be recognizable in young leaves.

We are very largely indebted to Michaelis for his intensive investigations on numerous different examples of sorting-out variegation in *Epilobium* for much of our knowledge of the possible interactions between plastids in mixed cells, and the consequent sorting-out patterns. It is therefore to be hoped that these observations will serve as a model for other investigators so that we may learn to what extent the present findings can be confirmed by the behaviour of plastids in other sorting-out plants. For the moment, however, we can safely conclude that the finding of mixed cells is only to be expected if the genetically different plastids do not noticeably influence each other, either in one direction or reciprocally, although this difficulty may at least sometimes be overcome by studying young tissues. Hence if mixed cells are not found, it does not necessarily follow that the plastid itself has not mutated. In other words the failure to find mixed cells is not a proof of a non-plastom extra-nuclear mutation.

VII.4. The Mathematical Properties of Sorting-out

The mathematical properties governing the theoretical sorting-out from mixed cells of two types of extra-nuclear particle have been carefully analysed by Michaelis (1955a, b; 1956; 1959, 1961). Michaelis has produced mathematical formulae relating the numerical effects of one or more cell divisions on the subsequent proportions of two types of particle segregating into the daughter cells at random beginning with known starting ratios. Many examples with varying starting ratios and different total numbers of particles have been worked out by him, and he has abundantly illustrated his results with appropriate tables and curves to which the reader is referred. Here it is proposed not to burden the reader with such details but simply to summarize the principal conclusions. In the following summary, which is published by permission of Veb Gustav Fischer Verlag, Jena, and Dr R. Hagemann, and which is translated with only minor changes from Hagemann's most useful book *Plasmatische Vererbung*, it is proposed to use the illustration of two types of plastid, green and white, but the conclusions are equally applicable to other particles such as two types of mitochondria. In order to calculate what might happen to the two types of plastid during successive cell divisions Michaelis assumes that only two types of plastid exist in the cell, that they are randomly mixed before and separate randomly at cell division, at which stage their number is exactly halved, and that all plastids double again after cell division so that their total number per cell remains constant. Under these conditions the following mathematical properties are valid:

(1) The number of possible combinations of green and white plastids increases with increasing total numbers of plastids per cell ($2n$); the number of combinations equals $n + 1$.

(2) The frequency of the appearance of sorting-out decreases with increasing total numbers of plastids.

(3) The number of successive cell divisions which leads to an almost complete sorting-out (over 99 per cent) amounts to approximately $10n$.

(4) After the first cell division, the frequency of individual mixture combinations depends upon the mixture proportions of the starting cell. With increasing numbers of cell divisions, the frequency with which any combination appears always remains less than the frequency of the

starting mixture even though the percentage frequency of the starting mixture decreases with each successive cell division. The frequency values of mixture combinations approach one another more closely with each successive division. The stage when sorting-out is practically complete is solely dependent upon the total number of plastids per cell and not upon the proportions of the two types of plastid in the starting cell.

(5) After fully sorting-out, the two kinds of pure cell, the one with only green and the other with only white plastids, appear in the same proportion as the two types of plastid were mixed in the starting cell.

The moment at which the mutant particle is manifest depends upon: (a) whether it must first become completely sorted-out (compare the action of a recessive nuclear gene), (b) whether it must reach a certain proportion of mutant to normal particles, or (c) whether it is immediately manifest (compare the action of a dominant nuclear gene).

In many cases of plastid mutation, in which there is no interaction between mutant and normal plastids, the new mutant white plastid is immediately distinct from normal green plastids in the mixed cell. However, the presence of the white plastid remains invisible to the eye, but in theory not to the microscope, until after the latent period of sorting-out. In other cases where mutant and normal plastids interact, a manifestation of any of the suggested three kinds is possible.

The genetic particles, associated with their respective organelles, do not necessarily behave in the same way either in regard to their sorting-out or their manifestation. But on the assumption that they do follow the above mathematical laws, it is probable that only the plastids and possibly the mitochondria exist in sufficiently low numbers to have any chance of achieving complete sorting-out during the approximately one hundred successive cell divisions[35] needed for the complete development of the average annual plant. By contrast, other more numerous particles would take several generations before sorting-out was complete. Thus by comparing the observed sorting-out rates with the expected rate of sorting-out, it is possible to assess whether one is dealing with a plastid or another particle. Such an assessment supports the supposition that all the numerous examples of sorting-out variegation (Table VIII.1) are caused by the sorting-out of two kinds of plastid rather than by any other particle.

VII.5. Agreement between Observed and Expected Sorting-out

It has for a long time been believed that the proof that sorting-out variegation results from a plastom rather than from a non-plastom mutation is the cytological observation of mixed cells. To this Michaelis has added the rider that not only should mixed cells be found, but a large number of them should be scored, and the proportions of normal to mutant plastids should be found to be in agreement with the expected proportions predicted by the mathematical laws of sorting-out. The usefulness of the laws, however, depends upon the validity of the assumptions that the two types of plastid are randomly mixed before and separate randomly at cell division, at which stage their number is exactly halved, and that all plastids double again after cell division so that their total number per cell remains constant. It is therefore important to consider how far these assumptions are true.

VII.5.i. RANDOM MIXING

The extremely rapid sorting-out from mixed zygotes after hybridization in *Pelargonium* (Chapter VIII) is almost certainly due to the very poor mixing of plastids from the two sexes before the first division of the zygote and perhaps in one or two of the following divisions. It is equally clear that in many cases of spontaneous mutations, the sorting-out in the meristematic cells of the shoot growing-point is nothing like so rapid. Nevertheless, the movement of plastids and other particles, perhaps owing to the viscosity of the cytoplasm, may sometimes be sufficiently restricted to increase markedly their speed of sorting-out, indeed Michaelis (1965c) has found examples of such behaviour. For instance, after division each pair of daughter plastids may remain close together and hence tend to move into the same daughter cell at cell division. This would be especially likely to happen if plastid and cell division were synchronous, or if cell division followed immediately after plastid division. The apparent synchronous division of plastids, as found in *Epilobium* by Michaelis (1962c), makes it probable that daughter plastids would pass to the same daughter cell if cell division occurred at the same time or shortly afterwards.

In every case, since any tendency to reduce mixing must increase the speed of sorting-out, the calculated rates, based on the assumption of random mixing, must be considered as the slowest.

VII.5.ii. RANDOM SORTING-OUT

The pattern of the first few successive cell divisions in the development of an *Epilobium* leaf has been described by Michaelis (1957b; 1959; 1961) and Bartels (1960). They find that the two halves of a leaf, either side of the midrib, come from different cell lineages, whereas the adjacent halves of two adjacent leaves orientated at right angles to each other in the decussate leaf arrangement have a common origin. Hence adjacent half leaves are more often similarly variegated than the two longitudinal halves of the same leaf. The first division of the growing-point initial common to the adjacent half leaves separates the cell into two initials each leading to the development of one half leaf. Each of these two cells now divides to produce an inner and an outer cell, the inner cell gives rise to the basal part and the outer cell to the apical part of each half leaf, thus dividing the half leaf into two primary sectors. Occasionally, owing to the sorting-out of pure white cells from mixed cells, either the apical or the basal primary sector is pure white. Among the offspring of a sorting-out plant, Michaelis (1961) scored 148 white primary sectors of which 45·9 per cent were basal and 54·1 per cent apical. These two frequencies of sorting-out into daughter cells are sufficiently close to one another to suggest that at least at this stage of development sorting-out is random. During observations of the varie-gated mother of these seedlings, Michaelis divided the primary sectors longitudinally into an outer and an inner half to give a total of four quarter sectors, two apical and two basal. For each quarter he scored the number and area of the large and small white flecks. He obtained similar values in each quarter for both determinations again indicating a random distribution of the green and white plastids. Other sorting-out *Epilobium* plants apparently showed similar random distributions. Un-fortunately, the complicated and little known pattern of cell divisions in the development of higher plant leaves made it almost impossible to score the sorting-out into daughter cells at later stages of development. In other plants, while there has been no experimental evidence of random sorting-out, it must be said that there has also been no evidence to the contrary. An exception is the hypothesis of a one-sided wandering of white plastids in several cases of sorting-out in *Epilobium hirsutum*.

VII.5.iii. ONE-SIDED SORTING-OUT

On several occasions Michaelis has suggested the possibility of, and hinted at the existence of, a non-random or one-sided sorting-out in several spontaneous plastid mutants of *Epilobium* (1957a; 1958a, b; 1959; 1963). These have now been reported in detail (1961; 1965b). In the earlier paper he describes a plant in which most of the leaves had one or two white flecks on an otherwise green background, reaching a maximum of nine flecks on one leaf. The majority of these flecks occurred in the apical half of the leaf and usually on the margins. The variegation thus resembled that of a number of chimeras known to have a white L I and green L II and L III (see Chapter VI). Michaelis, however, explains this fleck distribution on the hypothesis that the greater part of the mutant plastids wandered into the apical cell during the first divisions of the initial cell for each half leaf, and into the marginal cells during later divisions parallel to the leaf margin. If green or white plastids really are able to move in a definite direction at such an early stage of development, then this would clearly have repercussions for the whole theory of the sorting-out of extra-nuclear particles. There are the following good reasons, however, for thinking that the observations provide convincing evidence, not of a one-sided plastid wandering, but of the sorting-out of a plastid mutant that arose in L I, and led to the development of a periclinal chimera having a genetically white epidermis, WGG; a possibility which was not considered:

(1) Mixed cells were found only in a small area of a basal axillary shoot in the tissue immediately under the epidermis. It seems probable that in these regions sorting-out was still in progress in L I, and by its duplication it occasionally gave rise to a small sorting-out area in L II tissue.

(2) In every case the white flecks were connected to the epidermis and were never found as isolated islands within the green mesophyll tissue. This is to be expected if their origin is from a genetically white epidermis but, bearing in mind that the leaves are several cell layers thick, it is astonishing to think that a one-sided plastid wandering could produce such an exact distribution.

(3) Many side shoots turned out to be white-over-green periclinal chimeras, but green-over-white periclinals were not observed. Michaelis considers this to be evidence for the wandering of white plastids into cells of the leaf surface and margin. It is more likely that the side shoots arose as bud variations from a main shoot with a genetically white epidermis, WGG → WWG; such a duplication of the epidermis is a common change among many chimeras either in the growing-point, or in the leaf, or in both positions[7, 63]. Moreover, green-over-white chimeras, GGW, would not be expected.

(4) Seedlings included, besides numerous green, a few white and variegated offspring. The frequency of variegated was close to the expectation for new mutations but may have come from sorting out. The white seedlings could have also arisen from a genetically white epidermis following layer alterations, again a not uncommon occurrence[63].

Unfortunately there is no report of epidermal strips having been examined to determine whether the plastids in the guard cells and other epidermal cells were green or white, or whether they were sometimes mixed cells. The presence of mixed cells, cells with white plastids, and leaves with only white cells in L I would have proved the chimeral explanation.

The suggestion that the higher frequency of white-over-green chimeras compared with green-over-white in *Oenothera*[59, 60] might also be due to a one-sided plastid wandering is without foundation, because the scoring method did not take into account possible changes during development, and the fact that white layers in three-layered chimeras are usually more stable in the L II position, as in GWG chimeras, than in the L III position, as in GGW chimeras, according to present observations of the many different chimeras in the collection at the Oxford Botanic Garden.

In his more recent paper Michaelis (1965b) explains and describes three types of sorting-out as follows:

(1) Plants with a typical random sorting-out pattern in which the leaves have the characteristic multiple cell lineage chequered pattern, but in which marginal and apical white flecks are lacking.

(2) Plants with a limited one-sided sorting-out, in which the leaves have the usual multiple cell lineage chequered pattern, and in which marginal and apical white flecks also appear.

(3) Plants with a perfect one-sided sorting-out, in which the leaves lack the usual multiple cell lineage pattern and possess only marginal and apical white flecks.

It seems more probable, however, that these are not three types of sorting-out, but merely the varying expression of sorting-out in different germ layers as follows:

(1) Sorting-out in L II and perhaps L III, but not L I. The type, therefore, has the periclinal structure GSG or GSS, where S represents a sorting-out layer.

(2) Sorting-out occurs in L I as well as L II and perhaps L III. The structure is therefore SSG or SSS. Or sorting-out may have given rise to a white L I, in which case the structure is WSG or WSS.

(3) Sorting-out occurs only in L I to give the periclinal structure SGG, or after sorting-out to give a white L I is complete, WGG.

Again there is no record of the possible character of L I having been taken into account before putting forward the hypothesis of a partial or complete one-sided sorting-out. Yet similar variegation patterns were observed in *Nicotiana* by Burk, Stewart, and Dermen (1964), who clearly demonstrated the importance of not forgetting the epidermis in the analysis of sorting-out.

Quite different evidence for one-sided sorting-out comes from the search for mixed cells. In a plant supposed to show partial one-sided sorting-out, mixed cells were found in the tip sector of young, 1–3 mm long leaves in which cell division was still taking place[46]. The white plastids could be distinguished from the normal at this stage, because they were of a type that degenerate early without developing chlorophyll. At least some of the mixed cells contained normal plastids distributed on the side furthest from the tip and the mutant plastids on the side nearest the left tip, thus clearly demonstrating a non-random distribution. It seems possible that the normal plastids may have moved in response to an external stimulus such as light, while the degenerating white plastids were unaffected. If the supposed movement occurred in mixed cells throughout the young leaf then it would clearly cause a non-random sorting-out as Michaelis suggests. Nevertheless this demonstration only affects the last one or two cell divisions; it is therefore no proof that sorting-out must have also been non-random at earlier stages. Indeed, had sorting-out been non-random in the first few cell divisions of leaf development, mixed cells would not be expected at such a late stage. Yet sorting-out would have had to be one-sided in the very earliest divisions in order to produce white flecks preferentially on the margins and in particular at the tip of the leaves. Hence the one-sided distribution of normal and mutant plastids in mixed cells towards the end of leaf cell division can hardly be correlated with the distribution of white flecks. In other words the cytological evidence of a one-sided distribution of plastids in mixed cells in the young leaf, even if its frequency could be shown to be statistically significant, can only be used as evidence for changes in the fine pattern of sorting-out in the course of the last cell divisions.

VII.5.iv. EVEN MULTIPLICATION

Interspecific crosses in *Oenothera* demonstrate that plastids from different species multiply at their own specific rates (see VIII.5). In sorting-out variegations, on the other hand, white plastids arise by a spontaneous mutation of normal green plastids so that the two plastid types are not only of the same species but are also derived from the same plant. There is therefore no reason why the white plastids should change their multiplication rate, unless the mutation actually affects the multiplication mechanism. Furthermore, since the original spontaneous mutant plastid forms only a small fraction of the total number of plastids in the cell, the chance of it ever sorting-out would be extremely unlikely if it multiplied more slowly than the normal plastids. That it does sort-out demonstrates that it can multiply quite successfully in mixed cells of the growing-point at least. It also seems unlikely that the mutant plastids multiply faster than the normal plastids, because sorting-out plants frequently produce mixed egg cells which are descendants of the original starting cell (Table VIII.1). It is highly improbable that mixed cells would be maintained over such a long growth period, perhaps 50–100 successive cell divisions, if one plastid type multiplied faster than the other. Indeed, whenever one type of plastid multiplies faster than the other in hybrid sorting-out variegations of *Oenothera*, it is difficult to find

mixed cells still existing beyond the first few leaves, even if the slower
multiplying plastids outnumber the faster in the original starting cell,
in this case the mixed zygote. Hence in most observed plants normal and
mutant plastids probably do multiply at the same rate.

Michaelis maintains that the proof of an even multiplication rate,
providing sorting-out is random, is that the proportions of green:white
flecks and sectors is the same as the proportions of normal:mutant
plastids in the starting cell. The proof of differences in multiplication
rate is that the proportions change even though sorting-out is random.
Unfortunately it is virtually impossible to determine the proportions in
the starting cell. Another method was therefore used by Hagemann
(1961). During sorting-out in *Antirrhinum* he scored the relative numbers
of green and pale plastids in a large number of mixed cells and plotted
a curve of the frequency of the various mixture proportions. He obtained
an almost normal curve in which the most frequent mixture contained
half green and half pale plastids, from which he concluded that the two
kinds of plastid were multiplying at similar rates. He believed that a
deviation of the curve towards a greater proportion of green or pale
would have indicated that the green or pale plastids respectively were
multiplying faster. Hagemann's curves, however, do not correspond to
the curves predicted by Michaelis in which the most frequent mixture
proportion should be equal to the starting mixture proportion. It seems
unlikely that the starting proportion after a spontaneous mutation
would be in a ratio of 1 green:1 pale plastid; it is much more likely
that there would be many more green than pale plastids. Hagemann
suggests that the difference between his determinations and the predicted curve may be caused by his scoring technique, but there may
also be other factors involved. It is therefore questionable whether he
has really demonstrated an even multiplication rate; nevertheless, it
does seem significant that he obtained similar curves for young foliage
leaves, bracts, and sepals, suggesting that there was no change in the
proportions of green to pale plastids during development.

In general, even if the multiplication rates are even, the total number
of plastids per cell may vary at different stages of development; an
increase in the total number will slow down the rate of sorting-out,
and conversely, a decrease will speed up the rate of sorting-out.

VII.6. Plastom or Non-plastom Mutation?

The intensive genetical investigations on biparentally transmitted,
sorting-out variegation in *Pelargonium* and *Oenothera* (Chapter VIII), as
well as on hybrid variegation in *Oenothera* (Chapter IX), has led to the

general acceptance that a white plastid differs from a green plastid owing to a plastom mutation within its own boundaries. This explanation for the existence of two kinds of plastid in sorting-out variegations has been less readily accepted for examples in which the plastids are inherited uniparental-maternally, and some workers are still doubtful or sceptical[22, 53, 54, 58, 65, 66, 67, 68, 71], but is this scepticism still justified?

The non-plastom concept was first put forward by Correns (1909a, b), who believed that a diseased cytoplasm was responsible for the sorting-out variegation in *Mirabilis jalapa*. He later (1922) modified this explanation with the suggestion that the abnormal cytoplasm was in a labile condition, which could change into a normal state that permitted plastid development or into a diseased state that prevented it. In other words, he postulated the existence of three heritable types of cytoplasm; normal, labile, and diseased. He did, however, accept the sorting-out of plastids hypothesis for *Pelargonium* (1928). Now if Correns is right, then within an individual cell the plastids should be either all green or all white. But if the sorting-out hypothesis is right, then mixed cells should occur with both types of morphologically distinct plastids within the same cell; moreover, the two types of plastid should most often occur in sister mixed cells in similar proportions, and the borders between green and white cell lineages should be sharp, or so it was thought. Thus since in several sorting-out plants mixed cells were not found and the borders were not sharp, Correns (1937) and later Rhoades (1946) maintained that at least in these cases the plastid itself had not mutated. At that time the absence of mixed cells may have been a valid objection in cases where they had been sought. But we now know, largely through the observations of Michaelis on *Epilobium*, that there are several ways in which the existence of mixed cells can be obscured, especially in mature leaves, whereas in young leaves of the same material they are still distinguishable. Moreover, the absence of sharp borders is presumably caused by the action of the same diffusible substance as obscures the presence of mixed cells. Hence the absence of mixed cells and sharp borders in the sorting-out variegation of any material observed to date (Table VIII.1) can no longer be regarded as evidence for the sorting-out of a non-plastom, mutant extra-nuclear particle.

In *Nicotiana*, mitochondria were found to degenerate as well as plastids, hence Wettstein and Eriksson (1965) took the view that it is just as possible to suggest that the mitochondria are mutant and affect the plastids, as it is to suggest that the plastids are mutant and affect the mitochondria. The observation certainly suggests that a diffusible substance from one organelle is capable of affecting the other, but it does not explain the presence of mixed cells observed with the electron microscope, unless one makes the further assumption that the cells contain two types of mitochondria and the mutant mitochondria only affect the plastids that are near to them; however, cells with mixed mitochondria were not observed. Furthermore, if the variegation is caused by the sorting-out of two kinds of mitochondria, this should be expressed in the variegation pattern, which was not considered. Now according to the mathematical properties, sorting-out should be nearing completion after $10n$ divisions, where n equals half the total number of plastids or mitochondria per cell. Estimates of the number of successive cell divisions required for almost complete sorting-out in *Epilobium*, show that the calculated number of particles required to give this speed of sorting-out is within the region of the number of plastids per cell[37, 40]. In addition, mathematical calculations can show approximately how many particles per cell would be required in order to give the observed frequency for the sorting-out of new white and new green cell lineages from mixed cell lineages, which may be counted by carefully scoring the leaves, a painstaking but not impossible task. Determinations of this kind in *Epilobium* again point to the plastids as the sorting-out particle. This does, however, depend on the assumption that in the development of the shoot the effective numbers of mitochondria per cell considerably outnumber the plastids; unfortunately such data for this region are lacking. With regard to *Nicotiana*, no attempts have yet been made to correlate the sorting-out pattern with any particle; hence the possibility that one is dealing with a mitochondriom rather than a plastom mutant remains speculative, but the precedent of *Epilobium* favours the plastom alternative.

Rhoades (1946) has suggested that a cell with a critical proportion of mutant extra-nuclear particles, mitochondria for example, might contain poorly developed plastids, while a cell with a higher proportion of normal particles might contain normally developed plastids. With such a sensitively balanced system, a small change in the number of one type of particle within a hidden mixed cell could produce a sufficiently large change in the proportion of the two types as to tip the balance towards allowing the development of green plastids and green cell lineages on the one hand, or white plastids and white cell lineages on the other hand. In this way, white and green cell lineages could appear as quickly as by the sorting-out of two types of plastid since it would not be necessary for a white cell to contain the mutant particle alone but only a preponderance of it. This hypothesis is essentially the same as Correns' explanation of a labile cytoplasm except that Correns considered the cytoplasm to be a homogeneous mass, whereas Rhoades found a particulate explanation more acceptable. This hypothesis thus attempts to explain the frequent occurrence of green and white sorting-out flecks in cases where mixed cells cannot be found, for in his more recent review, at least, Rhoades (1955) accepts the evidence of mixed cells as demonstrating the existence of a plastom mutant. A sorting-out pattern of this nature has indeed already been described in *Epilobium*, where it was assumed that a balanced situation existed between the plastids of a mixed cell. But among other plants, in which mixed cells were not found, we now know that we do not have enough information to know whether such a balanced situation existed or not; hence the idea of Rhoades cannot be used to explain historical observations in support of an argument against the sorting-out of plastids.

A hundred years ago Mendel deduced the laws of nuclear inheritance from breeding experiments without ever seeing the chromosomes. Today the genetic evidence for plastid inheritance is equally strong, and within the limits that they have been investigated, all examples of the sorting-out of green and white plastids, whether inherited by one or both parents, can be satisfactorily explained on the basis that the mutation affecting the plastid has occurred within its own body, a genuine plastom mutation. Furthermore, as shown in Chapter X, there is now a considerable body of biochemical evidence for the presence within plastids of deoxyribonucleic acid, which could act as the genetic material of the plastid, and within which plastom mutation could occur. As long as the objections to this theory are based on speculative hypotheses which lack sound experimental data to support them, there seems every justification for fully supporting the plastom rather than the non-plastom mutation concept.

REFERENCES

1. ABEL, B. (1962). *Z. Bot.* **50**, 60–93
2. ANDERSON, E. G. (1923). *Bot. Gaz.* **76**, 411–418
3. BARTELS, F. (1960). *Flora* **150**, 552–571
4. BAUR, E. (1907). *Ber. dt. bot. Ges.* **25**, 442–454
5. BAUR, E. (1909). *Z. Vererbungsl.* **1**, 330–351
6. BAUR, E. (1911b). *Einführung in die experimentelle Vererbungslehre* 1. Aufl. Gebrüder Borntraeger, Berlin
7. BERGANN, F. (1962). *Wiss. Z. Pädagogischen Hochschule Potsdam* **7**, 75–85
8. BURK, L. G., STEWART, R. N. & DERMEN, H. (1964). *Amer. J. Bot.* **51**, 713–724
9. CLAUSEN, J. (1927). *Hereditas* **9**, 245–256
10. CLAUSEN, J. (1930). *Hereditas* **13**, 342–356
11. COLLINS, E. J. (1922). *J. Genet.* **12**, 1–17
12. CORRENS, C. (1909a). *Z. Vererbungsl.* **1**, 291–329
13. CORRENS, C. (1909b). *Z. Vererbungsl.* **2**, 331–340
14. CORRENS, C. (1922). *S.B. preuss. Akad. Wiss.* 460–486
15. CORRENS, C. (1928). *Z. Vererbungsl.*, Suppl. Bd. **1**, 131–168
16. CORRENS, C. edited WETTSTEIN, F. v. (1937). *Nicht mendelnde Vererbung.* Gebrüder Borntraeger, Berlin
17. DEMEREC, M. (1927). *Bot. Gaz.* **84**, 139–155
18. DÖBEL, P. (1964). *Z. Vererbungsl.* **95**, 226–235
19. DÖBEL, P. & HAGEMANN, R. (1963). *Biol. Zbl.* **82**, 749–751
20. FUNAOKA, S. (1924). *Biol. Zbl.* **44**, 343–384

21. GREGORY, R. P. (1915). *J. Genet.* **4**, 305–321
22. GUSTAFSSON, Å. & WETTSTEIN, D. v. (1956). From *Handbuch der Pflanzenzüchtung* 2 Aufl., Bd. **1**, 612–699. Eds., H. Kappert & W. Rudorf. Paul Parey, Berlin-Hamburg
23. HAGEMANN, R. (1960). *Die Kulturpflanze* **8**, 168–184
24. HAGEMANN, R. (1961a). *Die Kulturpflanze* **9**, 163–170
25. HAGEMANN, R. (1964). *Plasmatische Vererbung.* Genetik Grundlagen, Ergebnisse und Probleme in Einzeldarstellungen. Veb Gustav Fischer Verlag, Jena
26. HAGEMANN, R. (1965). *Genetics Today* **3**, 613–625
27. HERBST, W. (1935). *Flora* **129**, 235–259
28. IKENO, S. (1917). *J. Genet.* **6**, 201–229
29. IKENO, S. (1930). *Planta* **11**, 359–367
30. KARPER, R. E. (1934). *J. Hered.* **25**, 49–54
31. KRUMBHOLZ, G. (1925). *Jena Z. Naturw.* **62**, 187–260
32. MALY, R. & WILD, A. (1956). *Z. Vererbungsl.* **87**, 493–496
33. MICHAELIS, P. (1955a). *Cytologia* **20**, 315–338
34. MICHAELIS, P. (1955b). *Züchter* **25**, 209–221
35. MICHAELIS, P. (1956). From *Handbuch der Pflanzenzüchtung* 2 Aufl., Bd. **1**, 140–175. Eds., H. Kappert & W. Rudorf. Paul Parey, Berlin-Hamburg
36. MICHAELIS, P. (1957a). *Protoplasma* **48**, 403–418
37. MICHAELIS, P. (1957b). *Planta* **50**, 60–106
38. MICHAELIS, P. (1958a). *Planta* **51**, 600–634
39. MICHAELIS, P. (1958b). *Planta* **51**, 722–756
40. MICHAELIS, P. (1959). *Proc. X. Int. Congr. Genet.* **1**, 375–385
41. MICHAELIS, P. (1961a). *Flora* **151**, 162–201
42. MICHAELIS, P. (1962a). *Biol. Zbl.* **81**, 91–128
43. MICHAELIS, P. (1962b). *Planta* **58**, 34–49
44. MICHAELIS, P. (1962c). *Protoplasma* **55**, 177–231
45. MICHAELIS, P. (1963). *Naturwiss.* **50**, 581–585
46. MICHAELIS, P. (1965b). *Z. Vererbungsl.* **96**, 1–12
47. MICHAELIS, P. (1965c). *Flora* **156**, 1–19
48. NOACK, K. L. (1931b). *Z. Vererbungsl.* **59**, 77–101
49. NOACK, K. L. (1932b). *Z. Vererbungsl.* **63**, 232–255
50. NOACK, K. L. (1934). *Z. Bot.* **28**, 1–71
51. RADUNZ, A. (1965). *Hoppe-Seyl. Z.* **341**, 192–203
52. RANDOLPH, L. F. (1922). *Bot. Gaz.* **73**, 337–375
53. RHOADES, M. M. (1946). *Cold Spr. Harb. Symp. quant. Biol.* **11**, 202–207
54. RHOADES, M. M. (1955). From *Handbuch der Pflanzenphysiologie* **1**, 19–57. Ed., W. Ruhland. Springer-Verlag, Berlin-Göttingen–Heidelberg
55. RÖBBELEN, G. (1961). *Fortschr. d. Bot.* **23**, 287–297
56. RÖBBELEN, G. (1962). *Z. Vererbungsl.* **93**, 25–34
57. ROBERTSON, D. W. (1937). *Genetics* **22**, 104–113
58. SAGER, R. & RYAN, F. J. (1961). *Cell heredity.* John Wiley and Sons Inc., New York and London
59. SCHÖTZ, F. (1954). *Planta* **43**, 182–240
60. SCHWEMMLE, J., HAUSTEIN, E., STURM, A. & BINDER, M. (1938). *Z. Vererbungsl.* **75**, 358–800
61. STUBBE, W. (1957). *Ber. dt. bot. Ges.* **70**, 221–226
62. STUBBE, W. (1958). *Z. Vererbungsl.* **89**, 189–203
63. TILNEY-BASSETT, R. A. E. (1963a). *Heredity* **18**, 265–285
64. TILNEY-BASSETT, R. A. E. (1963b). *Heredity* **18**, 485–504
65. WETTSTEIN, D. v. (1957a). *Exp. Cell. Res.* **12**, 427–506
66. WETTSTEIN, D. v. (1957b). *Hereditas* **43**, 303–317

67. WETTSTEIN, D. v. (1961). *Canad. J. Bot.* **39**, 1537–1545
68. WETTSTEIN, D. v. & ERIKSSON, G. (1965). *Genetics Today* **3**, 591–610
69. WILD, A. (1958). *Planta* **50**, 379–387
70. WILD, A. (1960). *Beitr. Biol. Pfl.* **35**, 137–175
71. WILKIE, D. (1964). *The cytoplasm in heredity.* Methuen's Monographs on Biological Subjects. Methuen and Company Ltd, London
72. WOODS, M. W. & DuBUY, H. G. (1951a). *Amer. J. Bot.* **38**, 419–434
73. WOODS, M. W. & DuBUY, H. G. (1951b). *J. Nat. Cancer Inst.* **11**, 1105–1151
74. YASUI, K. (1929). *Cytologia* **1**, 192–215

CHAPTER VIII

Inheritance of Sorting-out Variegation

VIII.1. Distinction between Uniparental-maternal and Biparental Plastid Inheritance

VIII.1.i. ALBOMACULATUS AND PARALBOMACULATUS

IN ORDER to distinguish plants in which the plastids are transmitted only by the mother from those in which the plastids are transmitted by both parents, Correns (1909a, b; 1919b; 1922; 1931a, b) introduced the terms status albomaculatus and status paralbomaculatus respectively. In my opinion these terms are cumbersome and not really necessary, but they have often been used, especially in the extensive German literature. Unfortunately, they have also led to some confusion.

The occurrence of green, variegated, and white offspring from sorting-out variegated parents is due to the transmission of green and white plastids by the female egg. But this does not tell us whether or not the pollen parent can also transmit the plastids. Hence this selfing experiment does not distinguish between albomaculatus and paralbomaculatus. Nevertheless, in the lists of de Haan (1933) and Correns (1937) a number of plants are classified as albomaculatus even though only selfing experiments were made, and these are not distinguished in any way from those cases in which the purely maternal plastid inheritance was demonstrated by crossing experiments. Furthermore, other examples have been given of supposed paralbomaculatus for which there is again little or no evidence, owing to quite inadequate crossing experiments. Consequently, the terms albomaculatus and paralbomaculatus as used in these tables are unreliable. It might be more satisfactory to use the simpler terms maculatus -a -um to describe plants with a sorting-out variegation, and to keep to the terms biparental and maternal when describing the inheritance. If it should be necessary to specify the colour of the chlorophyll-deficient plastids, the prefixes albo-, virido-, etc., could be added to give the terms

222

albomaculatus and viridomaculatus. But this would give no information on the inheritance of the sorting-out plastids, which would only be obtainable after suitable crossing experiments.

VIII.1.ii. INTERPRETATION OF RECIPROCAL CROSSES

Ideally, flowers borne on pure white shoots are crossed with flowers borne on pure green shoots. Or alternatively, white-over-green periclinal chimeras among three-layered dicotyledons and green-over-white periclinal chimeras among two-layered monocotyledons, with white germ layers, are usually a good substitute for white shoots. The following results are to be expected, in each case the female parent is written first:

Uniparental-maternal plastid transmission:
I a G × W → G offspring
  b W × G → W offspring
or
Biparental plastid transmission:
I a G × W → G + V ± W offspring
  b W × G → W + V ± G offspring

In practice, the results of these reciprocal crosses are sometimes confused because the green and white parental shoots are not always as homogeneous as they appear. For instance, the unseen epidermis of an apparently pure white shoot or of a white-over-green periclinal chimera is often genetically green and by layer alterations it can occasionally give rise to the germ cells[122]. Hence green offspring are occasionally, and sometimes, though rarely, frequently, produced by the apparently white mother. This could be mistakenly interpreted as arising from green plastids introduced by the male parent, or it could be misinterpreted as the back-mutation of the maternal white plastids to green. The two chimeras of *Hydrangea hortensis* (Table VIII.1), for example, gave green as well as white seedlings from the GWG chimera, and yellow as well as white seedlings from the YWG chimera. The marginal teeth of the leaves in these *Hydrangea* chimeras are frequently developed from the epidermis and so Chittenden (1926) recognized the origin of the green and yellow seedlings; the absence of variegated seedlings was also consistent with his conclusion that the inheritance of plastids was purely maternal.

Occasionally a few unexpected variegated seedlings are produced as well as white seedlings, as found by Correns (1909b) from crosses between apparently white and green shoots of *Mirabilis* (Table VIII.1). Again this is probably not a result of biparental plastid transmission, but rather because the white shoot was not completely pure. Since the *Mirabilis* was not a stable chimera, but was still sorting-out, it is highly likely that the few variegated seedlings came from a few unsuspected mixed cells still remaining in the growing-point of the female shoot, and which gave rise to the occasional mixed egg (see VII.2). It is also to be expected that a variegated seedling will occasionally be produced from a green embryo by a new mutation, which must also not be confused with biparental inheritance. Finally, there are some indications that in certain plants white plastids may occasionally mutate back to green and so give rise to a few unexpected seedlings (see VIII.7). In all these cases, biparental inheritance can only be inferred if the results of crossing differ significantly from the results of selfing.

Instead of the above crosses, reciprocal crosses have frequently been made before sorting-out is complete so that one of the parents is variegated; the following results are then to be expected:

Uniparental-maternal plastid transmission:

II *a* G × V → G offspring
 b V × G → ± G, ± V, ± W offspring (from sorting-out)
 c W × V → W offspring
 d V × W → ± G, ± V, ± W offspring (from sorting-out)

or

Biparental plastid transmission:

II *a* G × V → ± G, ± V, ± W offspring (from crossing)
 b V × G → ± G, ± V, ± W offspring (from sorting-out or crossing)
 c W × V → ± G, ± V, ± W offspring (from crossing)
 d V × W → ± G, ± V, ± W offspring (from sorting-out or crossing)

The above comparison shows that only the crosses G × V and W × V have any certainty in distinguishing between maternal and biparental transmission, because the reciprocal crosses could give the same result. But even these crosses might not be satisfactory for two reasons. Firstly, pollen from a variegated parent could all come from germ cells developed in a green or white sector so that the crosses are really G × G or W × W respectively. Secondly, even if the pollen from a variegated parent does contain both green and white types, it is still conceivable that one type of pollen might germinate quicker than the other so that the crosses are again really G × G or W × W respectively. Should either of these two events in fact occur the transmission will appear to be purely maternal. Hence the result is only really conclusive if biparental inheritance is demonstrated.

In many experiments the total number of offspring obtained from reciprocal crosses has been too few, for even in known cases of biparental inheritance, as in *Oenothera* and *Pelargonium*, the effective male contribution can sometimes be as little as 1–2 per cent or even lower. Evidently, if too few offspring are obtained there is a serious possibility of registering a maternal instead of a biparental inheritance.

VIII.2. Uniparental-maternal Transmission of Plastids

In the majority of sorting-out variegations, reciprocal crosses have shown that the plastids are transmitted only through the female parent; the male has no influence (Table VIII.1). In compiling this table a number of particularly doubtful cases mentioned in the earlier lists[27, 40] and also some later ones, in which crossing experiments were not made at all, or were in only one direction, or in which the numbers of offspring were very few indeed, have been ignored. To have included them would have been most misleading. Even with these precautions, several of the cases included cannot be regarded as definitely proven, in particular, because crosses were used which are open to the criticisms discussed above, or because of small numbers of offspring, or because in some cases the actual numbers of offspring were never published. Should the opportunity arise, confirmation of such cases by more exact methods would be welcome.

Fairly exhaustive demonstrations that the plastids were the cause of the sorting-out variegation, and not some other extra nuclear particle, have been made for *Epilobium*, and many of the sorting-out characteristics demonstrated in *Epilobium* have been found in other plants. Thus in all the examples given in the table, different phases of the characteristic multiple cell lineage chequered pattern have been described and often illustrated; moreover, the presence of mixed cells has frequently been demonstrated by either genetical or cytological or both methods (see Chapter VII for details of these). Where mixed cells were not found cytologically this is because they were not looked for or were masked. None the less, in most of these instances the production of variegated seedlings from sorting-out showed that mixed cells must have been present. When variegated seedlings were not obtained, or when they were particularly rare, this was because sorting-out of pure cells from mixed cells was complete before the formation of the germ cells. Where variegated seedlings were found they were invariably fewer than the green or white seedlings. Clearly sorting-out was largely completed, indicating a speed expected only from the sorting-out of two kinds of plastid.

TABLE VIII.1. LIST OF HIGHER PLANTS WITH UNIPARENTAL-MATERNAL TRANSMISSION OF THEIR PLASTIDS*

(See also sections VIII.6 and 7 for additional examples)

Plant	P	Demonstration mixed cells — Cytological observation	Inferred by breeding: seedlings	Type of cross	Ia G×W / IIa G×V — G	V	W	Ib W×G / IIb V×G — G	V	W	Authors	Dates
Dicotyledons												
Antirrhinum majus		—	G V W	IIa, b	G	—	—	4	—	12	Baur	1910, 11a, 30
	P	—	G V W	Ia, b	G	—	—	700	—	—	Scherz	1927
		Yes	—	Ia, b	7970	3	·4	∞	—	—	Gairdner, Haldane	1929
Arabidopsis thaliana		Yes	G V W	—	—	—	—	—	—	—	Maly, Wild	1956
			G V W	—	—	—	—	—	—	—	Wild	1958, 60
			—	—	—	—	—	—	—	—	Hagemann	1960, 61a, 64, 65
			—	—	—	—	—	—	—	—	Döbel, Hagemann	1963
		Yes	G V W	I, b	—	—	—	323	—	—	Röbbelen	1962
Arabis albida	P	—	—	Ia, b	466	—	—	254	—	—	Correns	1919b
Aubrietia graeca	P	—	—	Ia, b	75	—	—	14	—	—	Correns	1919b
Aubrietia purpurea	P	—	—	Ia, b	92	—	—	25	—	—	Correns	1919b
Beta vulgaris		—	—	Ia, b	G	—	—	W	—	—	Stehlik	1921
		—	—	—	—	—	—	—	—	—	Munerati	1928, 42
Capsicum annuum		—	G — W	Ia, b	277	—	—	1	—	21	Dale	1930
Curcurbita maxima		—	G V W	Ia, b	2021	—	—	281	—	—	Hutchins, Youngner	1952
Epilobium hirsutum (numerous mutants)		Yes	G V W	Ia, b	∞	—	—	∞	—	—	Michaelis	1935–1965
Hydrangea hortensis	P	—	—	Ia, b	G	—	—	383G / 54Y	—	216 / 104	Chittenden	1926
Lactuca sativa		—	—	Ia, b	G	—	—	W	—	—	Whitaker	1944
Lycopersicum esculentum (*Solanum lycopersicum*)	P	—	—	Ia, b	G	—	—	2500	—	—	Schlösser	1935
Mesembryanthemum cordifolium	P	—	—	Ia, b	21	—	—	12	—	—	Correns	1919b

Species	P	Types	Class	No.	Y	G	V	W	Sorting-out*	Author(s)	Date
Mimulus quinquevulnerus		G V W	IIa,b	94					—	Brozek	1923, 26
Mirabilis jalapa	P	G V W	Ia,b	1200		—	3	12	—	Correns	1909a, 09b
Nicotiana colossea		G V W	IIa,b	500		—	—	1830	Yes	Honing	1927
Nicotiana tabacum	P	G V —	Ia,b	287		31	131	83	—	Woods, DuBuy	1951a
		G V W	Ia,b	322		1	—	184	—	Burk, Grosso	1963
		G V W	Ia,b						Yes	Burk, Stewart, Dermen	1964
Petunia violacea		G V W	Ia,b	2235		—	—	1770	—	Wettstein, Eriksson	1965
		G V W	Ia,b			—	—	110	—	Terao, U	1929
Pharbitis nil		G V W	IIa,b	153		195	11	861	—	Pandey, Blaydes	1957
		G V —	Ia,b	442		—	—	24	—	Miyake, Imai	1935
				66					—	Imai	1936b
Pisum sativum		G V W	IIa,b	12		2	7	4	—	de Haan	1930
Primula sinensis		G V W	Ia,b	70		—	—	11	Yes	Gregory	1915
Primula vulgaris			Ia,b	32		—	—	120	—	Chattaway, Snow	1929
Stellaria media		G V W	Ia,b	100		—	—	49	Yes	Correns	1922, 31a, 31b
Trifolium pratense		G V W	IIa,b	83		35	25	11	—	Funaoka	1924
Viola tricolor		G V —	IIa,b	22		4	6	—	—	Nijdam	1932
									—	Clausen	1927, 30
Monocotyledons											
Avena sativa		G V W	IIa,b	43		—	6	12	—	Akerman	1933
Avena sativa × sterilis		G V W	IIa,b	26		34	18	—	—	Love, Craig	1936
Chlorophytum comosum × elatum	P	G V W	Ia,b	438	6	1	11	143	—	Collins	1922
Chlorophytum elatum	P	G V W	Ia,b	52	4	1	1	92	—	Pandey, Blaydes	1957
Hordeum vulgare			Ia,b	30		—	—	26	—	Robertson	1937
Hosta japonica	P	G V W	Ia,b	164					Yes	Yasui	1929
Sorghum vulgare		G V W	Ia,b	6		—	2	17	—	Karper	1934
Triticum vulgare		G V W	IIa,b	∞		—	—	7	—	Umar	1943
		G V W	a,b	10		—	—	27	—	Pao, Li	1946
Zea mays		G V W	Ia,b	∞					—	Randolph	1922
									—	Anderson	1923
		G V W	Ia,b						—	Demerec	1927
		G V W	Ia,b	16675		60	48	137	—	Zirkle	1929

* In each case at least a part of the typical sorting-out process has been described and/or illustrated.

Key: G = green, V = variegated, W = white, and Y = yellow germ cells or seedlings; W is used in the general sense to signify any mutant plastid type.

P = breeding experiments were made with stable periclinal chimeras. ∞ = numerous seedlings.

When an investigator began with a periclinal chimera, it was naturally impossible for him to record the phases of sorting-out. But we know that the formation of all non-nuclear-differential variegated chimeras is preceded by sorting-out (see VI.2); no other way has been discovered. There is therefore no reason, on our present knowledge, to regard these periclinals as anything more than the end product of the sorting-out of two kinds of plastid.

In conclusion, for every case of maternal transmission listed, there is positive evidence that the uniform chlorophyll deficiency is caused by a plastom mutation. In no case is there evidence to the contrary. Naturally, the best proof comes from the demonstration of every expected stage but this is often impossible. Thus, since the available observations of each plant fit so precisely into the respective phases of such a clearly recognizable pattern, the validity of the generalization that the variegation of all these plants is caused by two genetically and morphologically distinct plastids and not by differences in any other extra-nuclear particles, is very convincing.

The inheritance of unstable mutant plastids causing a heterogeneous chlorophyll deficiency, and of gene-induced plastom mutations, is discussed later in this chapter.

VIII.3. Biparental Transmission of Plastids

The biparental transmission of plastids was first demonstrated in *Pelargonium zonale* by Baur (1909) who made reciprocal crosses between plants with green and plants with white germ layers, from which he obtained green, variegated (Figs. VIII.1 and 2) and white offspring in various proportions (see VII.1). His results were confirmed by a number of workers[17, 51, 84, 85, 104, 126] whose data have recently been summarized briefly by Tilney-Bassett (1963b) and more fully by Hagemann (1964). Biparental inheritance of normal and spontaneously occurring defect mutant plastids has also been established in *Hypericum perforatum*[25] and *acutum*[87], and in numerous species of *Oenothera*, including species from the subgenus Euoenothera[95, 97, 98, 107, 108, 109] and the subgenus Raimannia[110, 111]. In a fourth genus *Nepeta*, the mutant plastids were gene-induced[135]; in addition there is some evidence for the biparental transmission of unstable mutant plastids in *Phaseolus* and *Borrago* to be discussed later in this chapter. Finally, there is evidence of further examples of biparental plastid transmission from hybrid variegation studies (see Chapter IX), which include both *Oenothera* and *Hypericum* species crosses. Thus in these two genera the biparental transmission of defect plastids has been confirmed by the

FIG. VIII.1. *Young variegated seedling of* Pelargonium zonale *obtained by crossing plants with green and plants with white germ layers owing to the biparental inheritance of the plastids*

biparental transmission of differential plastids (see IX.3 for the meaning of these terms).

In the three genera, *Hypericum, Oenothera,* and *Pelargonium,* the formation of variegated seedlings by hybridization, the characteristic sorting-out pattern, the rapidity of sorting-out and the finding of mixed cells all point to the sorting-out of two kinds of plastid in the manner first suggested by Baur (1909) to explain his *Pelargonium* results[123]; the explanation has now become universally accepted for these plants. But how do the two types of plastid, normal and mutant or green and white, behave in crossing experiments?

The numerous crosses between different and often unknown *Pelargonium* cultivars gave very variable results, so they cannot be compared too closely. But one fact that was clearly shown by all investigators is that reciprocal crosses do not give the expected reciprocal proportions of offspring. Instead, the majority of offspring are green, or occasionally variegated, but apart from a single exception the white are always in a minority. Hence there is an advantage of green plastids over white which is greater than the advantage of plastid transmission by the egg compared with transmission by the pollen. Consequently, the plastid inheritance is predominantly maternal in G × W crosses and predominantly paternal in W × G crosses. All experiments, from Baur to Imai, point to these observations, but they are completely lacking in

FIG. VIII.2. *Older variegated seedling of* Pelargonium zonale *(cf. Fig. VIII.1) in which the green and white cells have sorted-out to give a white-over-green periclinal chimera with a white germ layer L II. It is this type of chimera that is used for breeding experiments*

sound additional information to support possible explanations. This neglected problem has recently been taken up again and the new findings will be reported in this chapter.

The early experiments of Renner with mutant *Oenothera* plastids were also poorly planned, for some crosses were made by natural instead of controlled pollinations, which makes them unreliable, and other crosses are valueless because definite numbers of green, variegated, and white offspring were not given. Sometimes too his crosses were not reciprocal. His results do show, however, that green and white plastids are transmitted more successfully by the female than by the male parent. Thus, in contrast to *Pelargonium*, the direction of the cross is more important than the colour of the plastids in deciding the proportions of green, variegated, and white seedlings, or so it would appear. Nevertheless, as with *Pelargonium*, reciprocal crosses did not always give reciprocal proportions of offspring. Furthermore, the proportions of offspring from different crosses varied considerably, but the lack of any connection between crosses made it impossible to formulate any general explanation for these variations, until the problem was studied in much greater detail by Schötz, whose results will be discussed in this chapter.

Reciprocal crosses between green and variegated shoots of a sorting-out *Hypericum perforatum* showed that the plastid inheritance was bi-parental and probably predominantly maternal, but Correns' failure (1931a) to use plastids from pure white germ layers prevents a more precise estimate of the male and female contributions. In *Hypericum acutum* pure green and white germ layers were used for reciprocal crosses, from which Noack (1932b) obtained the following offspring:

$$G \times W \rightarrow 937 \text{ G}:626 \text{ V}: \ 5 \text{ W}$$
$$W \times G \rightarrow \ 20 \text{ G}: 554 \text{ V}:16 \text{ W}$$

Again we see that reciprocal crosses did not give reciprocal proportions of offspring, instead, as in *Pelargonium*, the green plastids were more successful than the white. The advantage of the green plastids is, however, much greater when they enter with the egg than with the pollen. Noack noticed the supremacy of the green plastids and suggested that this could be explained either by assuming that more green plastids were contributed to the fertilized egg than white, or by assuming that the green plastids multiplied faster than the white. Unfortunately, the suggestions have not been followed up by further experiment to choose between these hypotheses, or between them and other possible explanations.

VIII.4. Plastid Inheritance in Pelargonium Zonale

Breeding experiments between different cultivars of *Pelargonium zonale* have demonstrated the failure of reciprocal crosses to give reciprocal proportions of offspring, the almost constant supremacy of green plastids over white, irrespective of the direction of the cross, to the extent that white seedlings are usually few and sometimes completely absent, and the great variability of the results from different crosses. Alone these results do not explain themselves; hence in a search for an explanation Tilney-Bassett (1963b, 1964, 1965) has recently begun a new series of experiments.

VIII.4.i. FERTILITY

In a survey of twenty cultivars[123], including some with green and some with white germ layers, nine probable factors were found to contribute to the breakdown of fertility on selfing; these were male sterility; incompatibility; pollen tube, embryo, and germination failure; competition between ovules; gene and plastid lethality and environmental conditions. Male sterility and incompatibility made certain cultivars useless for further breeding experiments. The fertility of the most fertile selfed green plants was below 30 per cent, while the much lower fertility of selfed whites failed to reach even 3 per cent and was often nil. The fertility of reciprocal crosses between plants with green and plants with white germ layers usually lay somewhere between the fertilities of the parents.

In order to be able to separate possible effects of white plastids on fertility, the basic causes of fertility losses were investigated in more detail in material most suitable for crossing experiments. From the two GWG mesochimeras Flower of Spring and Dolly Varden pure green bud variants were isolated. Since these bud variants arose without any change in the nucleus, the green and chimera clones within each cultivar were isogenic; they differed from each other only in relation to the germ layer (L II), which possessed green or white plastids respectively. Hence one could assume that differences in the progenies and fertilities of selfs and crosses were dependent upon differences in the behaviour of the two types of plastid. The effect of the plastids on development could, therefore, be separated from the effects of the nucleus.

Macroscopic observations of ovule growth, and microscopic examination of serial sections, demonstrated a large pre-fertilization fertility loss caused by the existence of numerous under-developed shrivelled ovules that were quite incapable of becoming fertilized. In addition, a few apparently good ovules were not fertilized owing, presumably, to pollen tube failure. These two factors together ensured that in all selfs and crosses not more than 40 per cent of the ovules were fertilized. After fertilization, a high proportion of embryos died during development, due possibly to the effects of segregating lethal recessive genes following the selfing of the nucleus in all isogenic selfs and crosses. This post-fertilization loss dropped the fertility down to about 20 per cent in Flower of Spring and 27 per cent in Dolly Varden[125].

These fertility values for the selfed green clones represent the maximum fertilities to be expected in all selfs and crosses; they represent the fertilities achieved after all detrimental effects of the nucleus have had their toll. Any further lowering of the fertility following the introduction of white plastids must therefore be attributed to the white plastids, since the nucleus remains the same in these isogenic selfs and crosses. The extremely low fertility of W × W selfs showed that the white plastids do indeed affect the fertility. The Flower of Spring crosses, on the other hand, had a fertility which was only slightly lower than the selfed green. Evidently the lethal effects of the white plastids were greatly reduced by the presence of green plastids either in the embryo, or in the endo-sperm, or in both tissues. By contrast, the gradations in fertility shown by

Dolly Varden, if significant, suggested that its white plastids lowered the fertility even when green plastids were present, especially when the white plastids entered from the egg.

VIII.4.ii. SELECTION?

It was originally thought that the large falls in fertility probably facilitated a strong selection against white embryos. This would have accounted for the frequent deficit of white seedlings, which was particularly noticeable from W × G crosses (Table VIII.2) in which white seedlings were most expected owing to the assumed maternal predominance. But the finding[125] that the bulk of the fertility losses were common to all isogenic crosses, and that differences in fertility between reciprocal crosses and selfed green plants were slight, at least in Flower of Spring, made the selection hypothesis seem less likely. It was therefore fortunate that the nature of the embryo development enabled this hypothesis to be studied still further.

The young *Pelargonium* seed has a transparent wall enabling normal plastids in the rapidly growing embryo to develop into green chloroplasts, so that within ten days of pollination it is possible to see whether sorting-out of plastids is giving rise to green, white or variegated embryos. Now almost all embryos reach the stage of early cotyledon development before any lethal effects set in. Hence it is possible to compare counts of green, variegated, and white embryos at ten days, when there is almost no post-fertilization fertility drop, with counts of the seedlings, when all post-fertilization fertility losses are complete. The results of such a comparison from both crosses in Flower of Spring and Dolly Varden showed that the proportions of green, variegated, and white seedlings turn out to be of the same order as the proportions of the embryos: the green embryos and seedlings predominate. The predominance of green offspring in W × G crosses of both cultivars is therefore not the result of selection against white embryos during the post-fertilization fertility drop. Furthermore, the gradations in total fertility that were observed in Dolly Varden could not be explained by selective elimination of different numbers of white embryos. These findings are further supported by recent unpublished observations showing that the failure of many embryos to expand beyond the ten-day stage is quite independent of whether the embryos are green, white or variegated. Moreover, in the G × W Flower of Spring cross (Table VIII.2) numerous white embryos were in fact produced, and grew to maturity, and successfully germinated just as well as the green embryos. Yet if there is no significant selection against white embryos in reciprocal crosses, how is it that nearly all the white embryos of selfed white plants fail to reach the seedling stage?

Macroscopic observations of ovule growth, and microscopic examination of serial sections, show that self fertilization of Flower of Spring or Dolly Varden plants with white germ layers is practically as good as with green germ layers[125]. Yet the majority of white embryos from plants with white germ layers break down before the seeds are ripe, and most of those that do survive to maturity fail to germinate. Clearly these W × W embryos lack something that is present in the white embryos after G × W crosses. It seems not unlikely that the difference may lie in the endosperm, which could contain only abnormal mutant plastids in the W × W selfs, but would probably contain a majority of normal plastids in the G × W Flower of Spring cross, in which the white embryos were able to develop so successfully.

VIII.4.iii. PLASTID SUCCESS

The finding that white embryos produced by the two isogenic reciprocal crosses are not preferentially selected against during development means that the results from scoring seedlings are approximately similar to those from scoring embryos. Hence both sets of results may be used as a measure of plastid success. But since a similar comparison has not yet been made for non-isogenic intervarietal crosses, the overall plastid success of these can only be scored from seedling results. Hence, for the moment, the success of green and white plastids for all crosses is scored from seedling data (Table VIII.2).

In order to convert varying numbers of seedlings into actual plastid distributions it is assumed that each fertilized egg receives at least four plastids. A pure green seedling can therefore be said to represent four green plastids while a pure white seedling represents four white plastids. A variegated seedling, on the other hand, clearly has an effective plastid contribution from both parents and can therefore be said to represent three green and one white plastid when it is predominantly green, or conversely three white and one green plastid when it is predominantly white, and two green and two white plastids when the seedling is approximately half green half white. When this estimation was first made[125] each seedling was calculated on the basis of only two plastids. This had the disadvantage that all variegated seedlings were given equal value as if they were half green half white. But in fact that was not always the case. On the contrary, the majority of variegated seedlings were frequently almost all green, which ought to be allowed for. This has now been done to some extent by splitting the variegated seedlings into the above three classes; it would be still more accurate if variegated seedlings were split into even more groups, assuming that the fertilized egg actually contains many more than four plastids. However, this was not done; moreover, since the experiments were carried out under greenhouse conditions subject to day-to-day fluctua-

THE GRADATION IN THE SUCCESS OF GREEN AND WHITE PLASTIDS FROM AN ADVANTAGE THROUGH THE FEMALE TO AN ADVANTAGE THROUGH THE MALE PARENT

(Adapted from Tilney-Bassett, 1965)

Crosses (* = Green parent)	Nos. of seedlings			Per cent variegated seedlings	Nos. of plastids			Plastid distribution percentages		Per cent gradation in non-reciprocal plastid inheritance
	G	V	W		G	W	Total	Female	Male	
Crystal Palace Gem* G×W	67	4	—	5·7	280	4	284	98·6	1·4	Maternal advantage
×Dolly Varden W×G	44	43	—	49·4	272	76	348	21·8	78·2	20·4
Crystal Palace Gem* G×W	208	5	—	2·3	847	5	852	99·4	0·6	
×J. C. Mapping W×G	83	40	3	31·7	425	79	504	15·7	84·3	15·1
Dolly Varden G×W	78	27	4	24·8	370	66	436	84·9	15·1	Paternal advantage
isogenic W×G	36	13	—	26·5	171	25	196	12·8	87·2	2·3
Paul Crampel* G×W	276	76	28	20·0	1268	252	1520	83·4	16·6	
×F. of Spring W×G	121	30	2	19·5	548	64	612	10·4	89·6	6·2
Paul Crampel* G×W	12	11	11	32·4	70	66	136	51·5	48·5	
×Miss B-Coutts W×G	11	24	—	68·6	86	54	140	38·6	61·4	9·9
Flower of Spring G×W	104	14	73	7·4	451	313	764	59·0	41·0	
isogenic W×G	115	27	2	18·8	518	58	576	10·1	89·9	30·9
Paul Crampel* G×W	108	139	83	42·1	716	604	1320	54·2	45·8	
×Dolly Varden W×G	127	50	3	27·7	619	101	720	14·0	86·0	31·8

tions in light, temperature, and humidity, it is probable that the variations that would occur if the experiments were repeated would be sufficiently great to render a very accurate measure of the relative proportions of green and white tissue in variegated seedlings of little extra value.

In all crosses (Table VIII.2), more green plastids are distributed to the offspring than white. Hence the plastid inheritance is predominantly maternal in the G × W crosses and predominantly paternal in the W × G crosses. The proportion of green plastids is not the same in reciprocal crosses. In five sets of crosses, the proportion of green plastids is unexpectedly lower when they are transmitted by the female egg (G × W) than when they are transmitted with the male gamete (W × G); this was not found in the earlier crossing results of other workers. Evidently green plastids, and consequently white plastids, are most successful when they are transmitted by the pollen. By contrast, this behaviour is reversed in the two sets of intervarietal crosses with Crystal Palace Gem as the source of the green plastids. This time it agrees with the expectation and the results of other workers, since the green and white plastids are most successful when transmitted by their female parent. Each pair of crosses differs from the others in the extent to which its green or white plastids are inherited more successfully by the male than by the female or vice versa. Hence the crosses have been arranged in a series showing steps in the gradation from maternal advantage to paternal advantage. This gradation can conveniently be expressed in percentage values which are calculated by subtracting the lowest green or white plastid distribution from the highest green or white plastid distribution respectively. Providing green plastids are always more successful than white, the white plastid distribution can never go above 50 per cent, hence the theoretical range of the scale is from a maximum of 50 per cent female advantage to a maximum of 50 per cent male advantage. New crossing experiments now in progress, however, show that the numbers of white offspring can sometimes be more than the numbers of green in G × W crosses. Moreover, a single exception to this range occurred in one of Noack's reciprocal crosses, listed by Hagemann (1964). In this reciprocal cross the majority of offspring were green from the G × W cross and white from the W × G cross, which gave a maternal advantage of approximately 64 per cent.

VIII.4.iv. PLASTID TRANSMISSION

Measurements of the successful inheritance of green and white plastids are not necessarily related to the actual numbers of plastids transmitted by the male and female gametes. In the two isogenic crosses there is no significant preferential selection against white embryos, but there could be a strong selection against white plastids in mixed cells, which would be especially important in the zygote and the first few cells of the embryo. For instance, should the normal plastids be able to multiply rapidly, while the mutant plastids multiplied only slowly, then the mutant plastids would be quickly outnumbered by the normal, which would lead to the observed predominance of green embryos. Alternatively, there could be more green plastids because the numbers of plastids contributed might depend not only upon whether they are transmitted by a male or female gamete, but also whether they are green or white. The green plastids might multiply in the haplophase much more successfully than the white plastids, irrespective of their behaviour in the diplophase.

The seedling results (Table VIII.2) show a great variation in the proportions of variegated seedlings from different crosses. This could be due to differences in the total numbers of plastids sorting-out, or it could be due to better mixing of the plastids in some crosses than in others. In the isogenic Flower of Spring G × W cross the numerous white as well as green seedlings together with a very low proportion of variegated indicates that the total number of plastids in the mixed zygote must have been small or else they were very poorly mixed.

The advantage of transmission by the female parent in some crosses and by the male parent in other crosses, suggests that the position of the plastids in relation to the first division of the zygote could be important. Clearly there are many factors that could affect the plastids so as to end up with the varying results observed. It is further possible that different factors may operate in different crosses and more than one factor may act at a time. The exact analysis of the crossing results is therefore likely to be complicated. So far, the only factor that can certainly be eliminated as relatively insignificant is selection against white embryos, at least in the two isogenic crosses. More experiments will be needed before the importance of some of the other possible factors can be properly assessed.

VIII.5. Plastid Inheritance and Competition in Oenothera

VIII.5.i. VARYING SUCCESS OF CONSTANT WHITE PLASTIDS WITH DIFFERENT GREEN PLASTIDS

VIII.5.i.a. *Crossing experiments*

Among his *Oenothera* collection Renner possessed a small-flowered *O. hookeri* which contained, as the result of earlier crossing, the green plastids of *O. biennis*. A spontaneous mutation arose and produced a sorting-out plant containing mutated white *biennis* plastids, which gave rise to shoots with white germ layers. The plant served as a constant source of white plastids in a series of reciprocal crosses which Schötz (1954) made with different *Oenothera* species as a source of green plastids (Table VIII.3). Schötz found that the G × W crosses gave green and variegated offspring, while the reciprocal W × G crosses gave white and variegated offspring. This showed that the plastids were transmitted predominantly by the female parent, and the mutant white plastids were constant under all nuclear genoms; they were defect plastids. The crosses also showed that the same white plastids gave different proportions of variegated offspring with different green species. Hence the G × W crosses could be arranged in a series showing a steadily increasing proportion of variegated offspring. The reciprocal W × G crosses produced a similar series in which the crosses could be arranged in approximately the same order showing a decreasing proportion of variegated offspring.

A second source of white plastids arose by a spontaneous mutation in an *O. blandina* containing *O. lamarckiana* plastids. Schötz was therefore able to make a second series of crosses using the same range of species as the source of the green plastids, but with the mutant *lamarckiana* plastids serving as a different constant source of white plastids, although this time he was only able to make the cross in one direction, G × W. The crosses could again be arranged in a series showing a steadily increasing proportion of variegated offspring. But when the two sets of G × W crosses were compared, the proportion of variegated seedlings was almost always greater with white *lamarckiana* plastids than with white *biennis* plastids and the same green species. In other words, the transmission of green plastids by almost every species was less successful with the constant white *lamarckiana* plastids than with the constant white *biennis* plastids. It actually turned out that the plastids of these two species differed relatively little in their multiplication rates (to be discussed below). Had Schötz been fortunate enough to have used mutant plastids from say *O. hookeri* and *O. atrovirens* with the fastest and slowest plastid multiplication rates, he would have observed much greater differences.

VIII.5.i.b. *Variegation rating*

The variegated offspring varied from weakly to intensely variegated; in some crosses these seedlings were biased towards predominantly green, in others towards predominantly white. Hence the proportion of green : variegated or white : variegated offspring gave only an approximate estimate of the proportion of green : white plastids. To obtain a more accurate estimate, Schötz scored in twelve classes the fraction of white tissue in the cotyledons, and where possible in the first pair of leaves, in

FROM CROSSES BETWEEN A SERIES OF OENOTHERA SPECIES, USED AS A VARIABLE SOURCE OF GREEN PLASTIDS, AND TWO MUTANT PLANTS, USED AS A CONSTANT SOURCE OF WHITE PLASTIDS. THE GREEN SPECIES ARE ARRANGED IN THE TENTATIVE ORDER OF DECREASING PLASTID MULTIPLICATION RATES

(Adapted from Schötz, 1954)

Source of plastids		Nos. offspring			Per cent variegated	Variegation rating*	2nd Male	Nos. offspring			Per cent variegated	Variegation rating*
Female	1st Male	G	V	W				G	V	W		
Green × white crosses												
hookeri	× biennis	797	—	—	—	—	lamarckiana	380	65	—	14·7	0·25
lamarckiana	× „	555	14	—	2·5	0·14	„	376	140	—	27·2	1·31
bauri	× „	256	26	—	9·3	0·06	„	119	91	—	43·3	2·47
rubricaulis	× „	255	84	—	24·8	0·69	„	90	56	—	38·4	3·39
suaveolens	× „	264	71	—	21·1	1·34	„	105	117	—	52·6	7·23
biennis	× „	118	68	—	36·4	2·85	„	77	64	—	45·4	4·53
syrticola	× „	169	108	—	38·9	4·22	„	72	134	—	65·0	9·83
parviflora	× „	219	158	—	41·9	5·11	„	64	83	—	56·4	8·04
rubricuspis	× „	183	108	—	37·1	7·26	„	27	57	—	67·8	14·46
ammophila	× „	63	51	—	44·6	8·86	„	—	—		—	—
atrovirens	× „	148	344	—	69·9	15·69	„	27	51	—	65·3	22·10
White × green crosses												
biennis	× hookeri	—	12	76	13·5	93·36						
„	× lamarckiana	—	124	68	68·2	86·17						
„	× bauri	—	54	159	25·5	95·24						
„	× rubricaulis	—	34	55	38·2	—						
„	× suaveolens	—	8	52	13·3	—						
„	× biennis	—	11	45	20·5	—						
„	× syrticola	—	—	150	—	100·00						
„	× parviflora	—	1	65	1·5	99·97						
„	× rubricuspis	—	—	—	—	—						
„	× ammophila	—	—	204	—	100·00						
„	× atrovirens	—	—	207	—	100·00						

White × green crosses were not made with O. lamarckiana.

* Variegation rating = Scheckungswert of Schötz

each variegated seedling. Counting a pure green seedling as nought and
a pure white seedling as one, together with the sum of the fractions of
white tissue in the variegated seedlings, he was now able to obtain a
much better estimate of the percentage of white tissue in the sum of all
the seedlings of a cross. Accordingly each cross could be given a
variegation rating corresponding to the proportion of white tissue in the
offspring. When the G × W crosses were now arranged in order of
increasing variegation rating, they showed a close correspondence with
the first arrangement based on the percentage of variegated offspring
and only slight changes were necessary (Table VIII.3). Moreover, only
slight variations in the results of individual crosses over a three-year
period confirmed the constancy of this order. The order of the reciprocal
crosses still did not correspond so well. This was probably due to the
greater difficulties in scoring the white and variegated seedlings of the
W × G crosses compared with the green and variegated seedlings of the
G × W crosses. In addition, of the two genom complexes in some
Oenothera species, one is only viable in the pollen and the other in the
egg (Table IX.1); consequently the resulting hybrid nucleus with
O. hookeri was not always exactly the same in the reciprocal cross, and
the different nuclei have a modifying influence on the final proportions
of variegated seedlings and their intensities. Nevertheless, it was clear
that the green plastids which were most successful in competition with
the constant white plastids when transmitted by the female, were also
most successful when transmitted by the male. Similarly, green plastids
that were least successfully transmitted by the female were also least
successfully transmitted by the male parent. In between these two
groups were species whose plastids were of intermediate strength.

VIII.5.i.c. *Hypotheses*

Schötz considers that the variable success of the green plastids from
different species could be due to one of four possible causes as follows:
(1) The different degrees of variegation could be caused by the
different genotypes but a comparison of certain crosses showed that
this was in fact not the case. The hybrid *O. pictirubata* actually contained
the plastids of *O. atrovirens*, so that the two W × G crosses *O. hookeri* ×
O. atrovirens and *O. hookeri* × *O. pictirubata* which produced different
hybrid nuclei, *hookeri . flectens* and *hookeri . rubens* respectively, nevertheless contained the same plastids, the green plastids of *O. atrovirens* and the
white plastids of *O. biennis*. The two crosses gave a similar percentage of
variegated seedlings with a similar variegation rating. By contrast,
when two other crosses were compared, having the same nucleus,
hookeri . rubens, but different plastids (one had green *atrovirens* plus white
biennis plastids, and the other had green *biennis* plus white *biennis* plastids), then the percentage variegated seedlings and the variegation

rating were quite different. The comparison shows that a change of plastid has a much greater effect than a change of nucleus; hence the plastom is the controlling factor and not the genom, although the genom does have a modifying influence.

(2) The different degrees of variegation could be caused by different numbers of plastids coming from the pollen, but since in G × W crosses the pollen parent was always the same this meant that the egg cell must also contain different numbers of plastids. Counts of the numbers of plastids in the eggs of several species failed to reveal any significant differences, hence Schötz rejects this hypothesis.

(3) A third possibility is that different egg cells give varying degrees of resistance to the penetration of the plastids from the same pollen tube, and conversely the plastids from the pollen tubes of different species have varying powers of penetration into the same egg. Such a co-adaptation is indeed possible but it is difficult to see how it could account for the large differences that can arise in several crosses in which the nuclei are the same and only the plastids differ, unless the plastids themselves, or their associated cytoplasms, are responsible for the co-adaptation.

(4) The fourth, simplest, and most likely hypothesis is that the plastids of each species have their own rate of multiplication; a presumption that had already been made by Renner (1924, 1929). As a result of their individual speeds of multiplication one plastid, either the white or the green, multiplies faster than the other in the same mixed cell such that the number of plastids formed from the faster effectively decreases the number of plastids formed from the slower. In this way the two plastids compete with each other so long as they are together in mixed cells, yet each plastid type still has enough time for adequate multiplication before cell division in pure cells. Hence there is competition between different plastids in mixed cells, but not between the rates of division of different pure cells. Such a competitive multiplication is quite plausible because mixed cells certainly exist (Table VII.1) and the assumption that there is an upper limit to the number of plastids in a dividing cell is highly probable. Finally, the hypothesis is highly satisfactory for it explains the breeding results and their corresponding variegation ratings, and moreover it can be tested by further experiment.

VIII.5.ii. EVIDENCE FOR COMPETITIVE PLASTID MULTIPLICATION

VIII.5.ii.a. *Genetical confirmation*

Schötz realized that if the competitive plastid multiplication hypothesis was correct then it would be possible to predict the results of

16—P.

repeating the crosses using a second source of white plastids. Since, in the first series of G × W crosses, the green *lamarckiana* plastids were more successful than the green *biennis* plastids when crossed with white *biennis* plastids, he concluded that the green *lamarckiana* plastids must therefore multiply faster than the green *biennis* plastids. Hence, all second series G × W crosses with white *lamarckiana* plastids should produce more variegated seedlings and give a higher variegation rating than the first parallel series of crosses with white *biennis* plastids. As already mentioned, the results of the second series of crosses confirmed the original order of the first series, apart from a few exchanges of neighbouring pairs of species. Moreover, the results of the second series of G × W crosses agreed with the predictions, and thus confirmed that the order of species, according to the percentage of variegated seedlings and the variegation rating, corresponded to the different rates of multiplication of their respective plastids. Furthermore, the second series of crosses improved the earlier analysis by making a much clearer distinction between the species *O. hookeri*, *O. lamarckiana*, and *O. bauri* with the fastest multiplication rates.

VIII.5.ii.b. *Hybrid variegation*

With certain hybrid nuclei the plastids of the mother develop into green chloroplasts but those from the father remain white, or vice versa, so that a hybrid variegation results (see Chapter IX for further details). It is therefore possible to determine the variegation rating for the sum of all the seedlings from one of these crosses, just as it is possible to make this determination for the sorting-out type of variegation. Schötz (1954) reports a number of crosses in which the species presumed to have the slower multiplying plastids were used as the female parents, and the species presumed to have the faster multiplying plastids were used as the male parents. The plastids of the female developed green chloroplasts with the hybrid nucleus, while the plastids from the male remained white. Under these conditions he found that the further apart two species were in their multiplication rates, the higher the variegation rating he obtained. Furthermore, these hybrid variegation ratings showed a good correspondence with the previous sorting-out variegation ratings after making similar crosses. A few other crosses, in which the female instead of the male plastids were unable to green with the hybrid nucleus also agreed with expectation. Hence the results of hybrid variegation add further support to the hypothesis that the plastids are more important than the nucleus in determining the variegation rating of the offspring, and that the plastids have their own specific rates of multiplication.

VIII.5.ii.c.   *Deviations from reciprocal results after reciprocal crosses*

Assuming that the number of plastids transmitted by the pollen is the same for each species, and likewise the much greater number of plastids transmitted by the egg is the same for each species, irrespective of whether the plastids are green or white, and assuming that the green and white plastids mix and sort-out at random, and also multiply at the same rate, then the ratio of green:variegated offspring in one cross should equal the ratio of white:variegated offspring in the reciprocal cross. A comparison of a number of crosses, the results of which are given by Schötz (1954), showed that deviations from this expectation were least when the plastids were most similar, for example when the green and white *biennis* plastids were crossed together, or when two species neighbouring each other in the multiplication scale were crossed. On the other hand, when white *biennis* plastids were crossed with plastids from a green species with a much faster or much slower multiplication rate, then there was a correspondingly large deviation between the proportions of variegated seedlings in reciprocal crosses. These results clearly support the assumption that the plastids have their own specific multiplication rates.

VIII.5.ii.d.   *Rates of sorting-out*

During the course of their further development the variegated seedlings sorted-out to form pure green, pure white, sectorial, and periclinal shoots as expected. Schötz (1958a) found that in plants in which the green and white plastids were presumed to multiply at similar rates, the sorting-out to give pure and chimeral shoots was generally slow, whereas in plants in which the plastids were presumed to multiply at quite different rates sorting-out was generally quick; in fact the greater the difference in the presumed multiplication rates of the two kinds of plastid the more rapid the sorting-out. Now if the two kinds of plastid multiplied at the same rates and sorted-out at random, then the average speed of sorting-out would be the same for all crosses since Schötz believed the contribution of plastids from the two parents to be fairly constant; hence the observations support his assumption that the plastids of different species have their own specific rates of multiplication.

VIII.5.ii.e.   *Mixed cells*

If the variegation rating of the offspring from crosses is dependent upon the differences in multiplication of green and white plastids, then it is to be expected that a corresponding relationship will be shown by the proportions of green:white plastids in mixed cells of the variegated seedlings. Schötz found that the average mixed cell in G × W crosses contained more green than white plastids when the green plastids multiplied faster, and more white than green plastids when white plastids were presumed to multiply faster. To this extent the proportions of plastids in mixed cells supported the multiplication hypothesis, but the differences in the proportions of green:white plastids in mixed cells were far less than he expected to find for good agreement with the hypothesis. The proportions in fact showed far too little deviation from a fifty-fifty distribution, and are thus similar to the later observations of Hagemann in *Antirrhinum* (see VII.5.iv). At the moment the reason for the failure of these counts to agree with expectation is not clear, so it is doubtful if they should be used in evidence either for or against the hypothesis.

VIII.5.iii. ORDER OF PLASTID MULTIPLICATION RATES

As a result of an extensive analysis of his *Oenothera* crossing programme, Schötz came to the tentative conclusion, subject to expected later alterations in the order of neighbouring species, that the species could be arranged in the following order of decreasing plastid multiplication rates: *hookeri > lamarckiana > bauri > rubricaulis > suaveolens > biennis > syrticola > parviflora > rubricuspis > ammophila > atrovirens*. The species *O. blandina* and the hybrid species *O. pictirubata* are not included because they did not contain their own plastids.

Unfortunately, the competitive strengths of plastids from different species were not compared under identical genoms. Yet Schötz concluded that the genom does modify the rate of plastid multiplication to some extent. Hence the different genoms probably had some influence on the suggested order, as Shötz himself was fully aware. Indeed this criticism was confirmed by Kemper (unpublished), who was able to determine the order of certain plastid multiplication rates under identical genoms. She came to the following conclusions:

(1) Under constant ^{h}*hookeri*.^{h}*hookeri* genom the order was: *hookeri > suaveolens > lamarckiana*.

(2) Under constant ^{h}*argillicola*.*gaudens* genom the order was: *bauri > suaveolens > lamarckiana*.

(3) Under constant *pingens*.*gaudens* genom the order was: *franciscana > suaveolens*.

This shows that compared with the finding of Schötz, the order of *bauri* and *lamarckiana* and of *suaveolens* and *lamarckiana* must be reversed.

Now Stubbe concluded after his extensive studies on hybrid variegation (discussed in Chapter IX) among approximately the same range of species as Schötz had used, that the species contain between them five genetically distinct plastoms. Hence one should expect only five groups in regard to plastid multiplication rate. This indeed seems to be the case, for the species containing the fastest multiplying plastids, according to Kemper, are *O. hookeri, franciscana*, and *bauri*, all of which contain plastom I (Table IX.1). Plastom II is contained in *O. suaveolens* and *biennis*, which Schötz found to be similar; plastom III in *O. lamarckiana*; and plastom IV in *O. parviflora, ammophila, atrovirens*, and *syrticola*, all of which Schötz placed at the slowest end of his multiplication scale. Stubbe (1959a, 1960) therefore concluded that the plastid multiplication order, in which one species is given as representing each plastom, should be as follows: *hookeri* (I) > *suaveolens* (II) > *lamarckiana* (III) > *argillicola* (V) > *parviflora* (IV). He later (1963a, 1964) came to the conclusion, however, that the multiplication rates of plastoms II and III are so similar that the order is better represented as:

$$I > II \approx III > V > IV$$

VIII.5.iv. THE RAPID SORTING-OUT OF PLASTIDS

Mixed cells are seldom found later than the cotyledons or first leaves after *Oenothera* crosses showing that sorting-out is very rapid. Yet Schötz has counted an average of 26–31 plastids in the eggs of several species, not to mention the plastids entering from the male parent with the pollen tube. Since there is no reason to think sorting-out is not random, and the multiplication differences are very slight in some crosses, it seems probable that such rapid sorting-out must be due to another cause. Two lines of evidence give an indication as to what this might be:

(1) Curves of the frequencies of the twelve classes of variegation intensities showed that for some crosses an end class, almost all green or almost all white, was unexpectedly missing. This suggested to Schötz that in some crosses the male plastids never succeeded in entering the embryo at all.

(2) According to Renner (1915) the egg becomes flask-shaped after fertilization and then divides into a small terminal cell and a large suspensor cell so that the first division of the embryo is unequal.

The second observation provides the basis for an explanation of the first for assuming that the plastids are very evenly mixed before the first division, it is clear that after the division the number of plastids in the terminal cell would be much fewer than in the suspensor, and there would be a good chance of the male plastids sometimes never entering the terminal cell at all. But it is also possible that the male plastids may enter that part of the egg that is soon to become the suspensor, and if they are slow to circulate to all parts of the egg they may again be cut off from the terminal cell in many cases, and possibly in every case in the crosses between *O. hookeri* and *O. blandina* and the white *biennis* plastids, in which Schötz obtained no variegated seedlings. Or alternatively, so few white plastids may enter the terminal cell that, owing to their slower multiplication, they never reach sufficient numbers to sort-out to give any pure white cells.

VIII.6. Nuclear Gene-induced Plastid Mutations

In contrast to the plants in which sorting-out variegation has arisen by occasional spontaneous plastid mutations in a population, there is another group of plants in which the very much higher plastid mutation rate of many times within an individual is indicative of a nuclear gene-induced plastid mutation. Accordingly, each new mutation is expected to initiate a new multiple cell lineage sorting-out pattern, unless the nuclear gene is sometimes able to induce the mutation of all the plastids in a cell together, when a simple cell lineage would result. The variegation pattern is therefore more complicated than after a spontaneous plastid mutation since it consists of the various stages of sorting-out superimposed on the pattern of new mutations. The breeding behaviour is similarly more complicated since the behaviour of both nucleus and plastid is involved.

VIII.6.i. BREEDING BEHAVIOUR

The breeding behaviour is most easily followed by splitting it into the three stages of selfing, crossing, and segregating, in the order in which they are most likely to be observed.

VIII.6.i.a. *Selfing*

When selfed, the variegated plants do not breed true; instead they usually produce from a few to many white offspring in addition to the variegated, and sometimes a few green offspring are also produced (Table VIII.4). Moreover, the proportions of green, variegated, and white offspring are not characteristic for each plant, but are variable dependent upon the degree of variegation of the seed parent. Thus Hagemann and Scholz (1962) obtained 11·1 per cent white offspring from a phenotypically green seed parent, 14·3 per cent from a weakly variegated seed parent, 25·1 per cent from a medium variegated seed parent, 81·5 per cent from an intensely variegated seed parent, and finally 100 per cent white offspring from the white branch of a varie-

TABLE VIII.4. SAMPLE RESULTS FROM SELFING OR INTERCROSSING VARIEGATED PLANTS, ILLUSTRATING THE SORTING-OUT OF NUCLEAR GENE-INDUCED MUTANT PLASTIDS

Plant and form	Gene symbol	Nos. and percentages of offspring							Authors	Dates
		Green		Variegated		White		Total		
Capsicum annuum	—	358	17·0	1745	83·0*	?	?	2103	Hagiwara, Oomura	1939
Epilobium hirsutum	mp_1	17	1·8	938	98·2*	?	?	955	Michaelis	1965a
Hordeum vulgare Okina-mugi and	—	—	—	335948	95·2	16989	4·8	352937	Só / Imai	1921 / 1928, 35d, 1936b, c
Okina-mugi tricolor	w	22	0·3	871	11·8	6488	87·9	7381	Arnason, Harrington and Friesen	1946
albostrians	as	127	7·2	1146	65·0	489	27·8	1762	Arnason, Walker / Hagemann, Scholz	1949 / 1962
striata-4	—	?	?	?	?	?	?	?	Wettstein, Eriksson	1965b
Nepeta cataria	m	—		216	100·0*	?	?	216	Woods, DuBuy	1951b
Oryza sativa	—	?	4·8	?	30·8	?	64·5	?	Kondô, Takeda, Fujimoto	1927
	—	—		143	38·5	228	61·5	371	Morinaga	1932
	—	?		795	59·2	548	40·8	1343	Pal, Ramanujam	1941
Zea mays iojap	ij	?	?	?	?	?	?	?	Jenkins / Rhoades	1924 / 1943, 46, 50

* Variegated offspring include white seedlings if any. ? = data lacking.

gated seed parent. The sum of their results from selfing weakly, medium, and intensely variegated plants is given in the table. Other workers have also found in their material that the greater the proportion of white tissue in the shoot, the more numerous the white and the fewer the green and variegated seedlings. This correlation between the proportion of white tissue in the female parental shoot and the frequency of white seedlings, corresponds exactly to the finding after spontaneous plastid mutation (see VII.2.i). Clearly the present gene-induced mutant plastids sort-out in the same manner as spontaneously occurring mutant plastids.

Because of the correlation between parent and offspring, the results of selfing are governed by the intensity of variegation of the shoot from which the seeds are taken, making it difficult to compare the results of different workers. Nevertheless, the choice of shoots is governed not only by the observer but primarily by the pattern of mutation and sorting-out of the individual plant. Should plastid mutation occur frequently in embryo development or in the primary growing-point initials, this would give the mutant plastids a good chance to sort-out into pure white cells in the regions of the growing-point, giving rise eventually to intensely variegated and even pure white shoots. Hence a high proportion of white seedlings could be realized. If, on the other hand, plastid mutation was rare in the embryo and primary growing-point initials, sorting-out to give pure white cells in these tissues would be correspondingly rare and consequently few white seedlings would be produced. Bearing in mind these considerations, the very different proportions of white seedlings obtained by different workers from their respective barley mutants (Table VIII.4) is indeed suggestive of different mutation patterns.

The white and more intensely variegated seedlings die. At the other extreme, a few seedlings remain completely green throughout development, yet, when selfed, they produce predominantly variegated and white offspring and again a few greens in proportions similar to those obtained from selfing weakly variegated plants. Evidently these green plants are still homozygous for the major gene which induces plastid mutation, but the genotype sometimes fails to express itself, owing probably to its suppression by the action of minor, modifying genes.

Individual authors have quite naturally expressed their results in their own fashion. This has, however, given rise to an unfortunate tendency to group variegated and white seedlings together, so that it is often not clear whether there were any white seedlings. This applies to the results of selfing, crossing, and segregating. It is a particularly bad omission because the frequency of white seedlings can give us an idea as to the earliness and frequency of plastid mutation. This is, however, not so bad as a complete absence of results in some instances.

It is hoped that by indicating with a question mark in the tables the gaps where data are desirable, future workers will be able to plan their crossing programmes more satisfactorily and so present a more complete picture than has often been the case in the past.

VIII.6.i.b. *Crossing*

Reciprocal crosses show that the nature of the offspring is dependent upon the direction of the cross (Table VIII.5). In most cases, when

TABLE VIII.5. RESULTS OF CROSSES BETWEEN GREEN AND VARIEGATED PLANTS IN WHICH THE VARIEGATION IS CAUSED BY NUCLEAR GENE-INDUCED PLASTID MUTATION

(See also Table VIII.4)

Plant	Authors	Cross	Nos. and percentages of offspring						
			Green		Variegated		White		Total
Capsicum annuum	H and O	G × V	55	100·0	—	—	—	—	55
		V × G	—	—	4	100·0*	?	?	4
Epilobium hirsutum	Michaelis	G × V	1542	99·0	16	1·0	—	—	1558
		V × G	398	42·8	533	57·2*	?	?	931
Hordeum vulgare	Imai	G × V	82	100·0	—	—	—	—	82
		V × G	—	—	47	68·1	22	31·9	69
	A and W	G × V	55	100·0	—	—	—	—	55
		V × G	56	22·4	43	17·2	151	60·4	250
		W branch × G	—	—	—		4	100·0	4
	H and S	G × G branch	57	100·0	—	—	—	—	57
		G × V ,,	37	100·0	—	—	—	—	37
		G × W ,,	11	100·0	—	—	—	—	11
		V × G	23	65·7	1	2·9	11	31·4	35
		W branch × G	—	—	—	—	22	100·0	22
	W and E	G × V	G	100·0	—	—	—	—	?
		V × G	G	?	V	?	?	?	?
Nepeta cataria	W and D	G × V	213	72·9	79	27·1*	?	?	292
		V × G	43	30·7	97	69·3*	?	?	140
Oryza sativa	K, T, and F	G × V	?	?	?	?	?	?	?
		V × G	?	?	V	?	?	?	?
	Morinaga	G × V	G	100·0	—	—	—	—	?
		V × G	?	?	V	?	?	?	?
	P and R	G × V	?	?	?	?	?	?	?
		V × G	2	?	?	?	?	?	?
Zea mays	Jenkins	G × V	?	?	?	?	?	?	?
	Rhoades	V × G	G	?	V	?	W	?	?

* Variegated offspring include white seedlings if any. ? = data lacking, G = green, V = variegated and W = white plant, shoot or offspring.

the female parent is green, all the F_1 offspring are green, whereas when the female parent is variegated, varying proportions of green, variegated, and white offspring are produced. In addition to crosses between variegated and green parents Arnason and Walker (1949) and Hagemann and Scholz (1962) were also able to make the more critical crosses using a pure white shoot of a variegated barley plant. These crosses emphasize the importance of the direction of the cross even more than with the variegated and green crosses. When the white branch was used as pollen parent and the green as the source of the egg Hagemann and Scholz obtained only green offspring. But they and Arnason and Walker, who made only the one cross, both obtained only white offspring when the pure white branch was used as the female parent. These results confirm the permanent change that the plastids have undergone as a result of their mutation. At the same time they show that the white plastids are transmitted to the offspring solely by the female parent and never by the pollen. *Nepeta cataria* is, however, an exception for Woods and DuBuy (1951b) found that the white plastids were transmitted by both parents as shown by the results presented in the table; moreover, the plastid type introduced by the pollen was morphologically recognizable in the variegated offspring thus providing, incidentally, good cytological as well as genetical evidence for the continuity of the plastids. As is so often the case the proportion of white and variegated offspring is higher when the female is the source of white plastids than when the male is the source, indicating a predominantly maternal influence. The cause of the few variegated seedlings produced by the G × V cross in *Epilobium* is not known. It is unlikely that this is due to the male transmission of mutant plastids, because spontaneously occurring mutant plastids are transmitted purely by the female parent.

VIII.6.i.c. *Segregating*

The green F_1 offspring from reciprocal crosses between green and variegated segregate, after selfing, in a Mendelian ratio of 3 green: 1 variegated plus white. Where this has been tested, the F_3 results confirm the F_2 ratio by showing that the green F_2 plants consist of homozygous true-breeding green and heterozygous segregating green families in a ratio of 1:2. The heterozygous greens again produce green and variegated plus white offspring in a Mendelian 3:1 ratio. The results of the F_2 and F_3 segregating families can therefore be combined (Table VIII.6). As we have already seen, the white plastids are permanently changed. Thus the variegation is clearly due to a recessive gene which, when homozygous, induces the mutation of some plastids from green to white. It is interesting to notice that some authors have observed segregation of white offspring as well as variegated. In these cases it must be possible for plastid mutation to take place sufficiently early in embryo development to enable sorting-out to give rise to pure white seedlings. This would necessitate a very rapid rate of sorting-out if

TABLE VIII.6. F_2 and F_3 SEGREGATION FROM SELFING HETEROZYGOUS GREEN OR VARIEGATED F_1 OR F_2 PLANTS OBTAINED FROM CROSSES BETWEEN GREEN AND VARIEGATED PARENTS

(See also Table VIII.5)

Plant	Authors	F_1 or F_2 phenotype	Nos. and percentages of offspring						Total
			Green		Variegated		White		
Capsicum annuum	H and O	green	7479	76·4	2315	23·6*	?	?	9794
		variegated	68	16·9	334	83·1*	?	?	402
Epilobium hirsutum	Michaelis	green	353	79·7	90	20·3*	?	?	443
		variegated	?	?	?	?	?	?	?
Hordeum vulgare	Imai	green	?	?	?	?	?	?	?
		variegated	?	?	?	?	?	?	?
	A and W	green	6571	71·1	2309	25·0	364	3·9	9244
		variegated	330	70·1	99	21·0	42	8·9	471
	H and S	green	5642	79·6	1410	19·9	37	0·5	7089
		variegated	?	?	?	?	?	?	?
	W and E	green	G	?	V	?	46	3·4	1370
		variegated	G	?	V	?	14	4·5	312
Nepeta cataria	W and D	green	1505	74·3	522	25·7*	?	?	2027
		variegated	?	?	?	?	?	?	?
Oryza sativa	K, T and F	green	?	?	?	?	?	?	?
		variegated	?	4·4	?	18·0	?	77·6	?
	Morinaga	green	?	?	?	?	?	?	?
		variegated	—	—	403	45·1	491	54·9	894
	P and R	green	590	76·2	184	23·8*	?	?	774
		variegated	?	?	?	?	?	?	?
Zea mays	Jenkins Rhoades	green	2624	76·5	793	23·1	12	0·4	3429
		variegated	?	?	?	?	?	?	?

* Variegated offspring include white seedlings if any. ? = data lacking.

only one plastid had mutated; it therefore seems possible that all the plastids of a cell are induced to mutate together in these cases, or else some other assumption must probably be made.

The Mendelian segregation after selfing variegated F_1 plants is in *Capsicum* and *Oryza* completely obscured by the sorting-out of plastids which persists irrespective of the genotype. In *Hordeum*, on the other hand, Arnason and Walker presumably selected seed from wholly or predominantly green shoots to give the clear 3:1 segregation from selfing variegated as well as from selfing green heterozygotes.

The earlier suggestion, that differences in the breeding results of different workers with *Hordeum* might be due to differences in the timing and frequency of mutation, is again supported by the higher proportion of white seedlings segregating after selfing green heterozygotes from the strain of Arnason and Walker compared with the strain of Hagemann and Scholz. At the moment, however, we can only note these differences. What is now needed is the opportunity to test by breeding experiments whether the different cases in *Hordeum* and also in *Oryza* are caused by the same or different genes. If it turned out to be the same gene, then any significant differences in the breeding results could probably be attributed to modifying genes in the background genotype.

According to statements of Hagemann (1964) and Edwardson (1965) the influence of other genes in maize has been noted by Mazoti (1949; 1950; 1952; 1954a), who found that the gene R, either homozygous or heterozygous, inhibited the action of the iojap gene (Tables VIII.4, 5, and 6), thereby reducing the frequency of plastid mutation. In other words, there is a nuclear control of the gene that induces the plastids to mutate. Apparently the cytoplasm of the teosinte, *Euchlaena mexicana*, acted in the same way[66].

In conclusion, although the data are incomplete, all of the examples shown in the tables appear to follow the same basic pattern of breeding behaviour, in which a specific nuclear gene induces frequent plastid mutation after which the mutated plastids sort-out quite independently of the genotype and are inherited solely by the mother in some species and by both parents in other species.

VIII.6.ii. DEVELOPMENTAL BEHAVIOUR

VIII.6.ii.a. *Mixed cells*

Following the genic-induction of plastid mutation, it is presumed that the two types of plastid, normal and mutant, sort-out from one another just as after spontaneous plastid mutation. If this is the case, mixed cells should be found in the early stages of sorting-out. These have indeed been observed in *Nepeta* and *Epilobium*. In the remaining examples they have either not been looked for or else they were not found. It should be pointed out, however, that the mode of development of the leaves of grasses such as barley, rice, and maize make it technically more difficult to find mixed cells than from the average dicotyledon leaf.

VIII.6.ii.b. *Stability*

In the Okina-mugi form of barley (Table VIII.4) the nuclear gene induced the frequent mutation of plastids from green to white. In one of these plants a spontaneous plastid mutation from green to yellow also occurred, giving rise to the tricolor, green, yellow, and white form. The variegation pattern was still further complicated by the instability of the yellow plastids. Firstly, in respect of the nuclear gene, the yellow plastids behaved like green ones because the gene frequently induced them to mutate from yellow to white. Secondly, the yellow plastids were also automutable and frequently mutated back to green. The yellow plastid was therefore unstable in both directions and underwent both plastid recovery and plastid deterioration changes (see VIII.7). Phenotypically the yellow lineages were marked by both green and white areas. The mutant white plastids, by contrast, were perfectly stable. The mutation pattern may be represented schematically as follows:

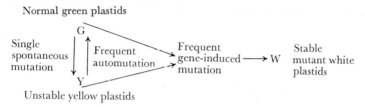

Such an unusual combination of events as in the tricolor barley is rarely found. Nevertheless, secondary plastid changes have been reported elsewhere. According to Woods and DuBuy, the nuclear gene does not always induce the same plastid mutation in *Nepeta cataria*; some of the types produced have already been described (VII.3.ii). Two more types of plastid mutant were called macrograna type 1 and 2, because of the greatly increased size of their grana, compensated for by a decrease in their number. These mutants sorted-out to give olive green areas. In addition small white flecks containing white vacuolate plastids were found within the olive green areas of plants homozygous for the mutation-inducing gene. This suggested that the gene induced a series of changes as follows: Normal plastid → macrograna type 1 or 2 → vacuolate type 1 or 2 plastid. It thus seems as if the mutations can occur in a certain sequence, in which the first mutation conditions the expression of the subsequent mutation. A similar series, green → yellow-green → white, was observed in the variegated *Epilobium*[77].

The gene-induced mutant pale green plastids of *Epilobium* seem to be of a similar kind to the spontaneously occurring yellow plastids of the tricoloured barley, because they also appear to be unstable and frequently mutate back to green. They give rise to numerous green flecks on a pale green to white background, which Michaelis says are less frequent in plants heterozygous for the mutation inducing gene than in homozygous plants. Why this should be so remains unanswered. That this was a true mutation was confirmed by Michaelis finding mixed cells. He also asserts that the green plastids were not always the same as the original wild type plastids, but this opinion is based on minor morphological features of doubtful significance. The new flecks were invariably fairly small showing that the plastid change occurred late in leaf development, and probably corresponded to a particular phase of plastid development.

VIII.7. The Inheritance of Unstable Plastids

VIII.7.i. INITIAL CONCEPTS

Spontaneous defect plastid mutations appear to include a wide variety of phenotypes; for instance, their colour range includes white, cream, yellow, and various shades of green; they may become increasingly normal with age, or they may degenerate either before completing their structural development or after; they may be a light green with plenty of chlorophyll but inviable on their own through their inability to photosynthesize, or they may be a paler shade of green with less chlorophyll yet viable owing to their ability to photosynthesize; they may influence each other within and across cells, or they may have no effect on their neighbours. A similar range of homogeneous chlorophyll deficient phenotypes is brought about by various recessive gene mutants that affect the plastids. In addition, the genes also induce a number of heterogeneously chlorophyll-deficient or variegated pattern mutations in which the irregular development of chlorophyll gives rise to white patches on a green background in the leaves (see Chapter III), or variegation may result from the mutability of the gene itself giving rise to green patches on a white background (see Chapter IV).

Since plastid mutations are able to mimic so many nuclear gene controlled homogeneous chlorophyll deficiencies, it seems quite plausible that plastid mutations could also mimic the heterogeneous chlorophyll deficiencies, thereby producing a variegated phenotype. This concept simply necessitates the existence of mutant plastids that are unstable in development so that they sometimes change from a defect form back to a normal or less defect type—these could be called restitution or recovery changes; or else the plastids change form in the reverse direction from a normal to a defect type, or from one defect type to an even more defect type; these could be called deterioration changes. Or it is still further possible that the plastid changes may proceed stepwise from normal to slightly defect, to extremely defect, or vice versa. The possibility of such plastid changes was considered by Imai (1936b), yet most workers have ignored it, although there is increasing evidence that such changes do in fact take place.

VIII.7.ii. PLASTID RECOVERY CHANGES

Two plants, *Chlorophytum* and *Hosta* (Table VIII.1) are of particular interest. Both possess several variegated forms which are stable periclinal chimeras and which have been maintained in cultivation by vegetative propagation for many years. During this period there must have been many thousands of successive cell divisions so that it would be extremely unlikely for any original mixed cells or pure green cells to be still present in the white tissues. Nevertheless, Yasui (1929) found mixed cells in *Hosta* and also obtained a few variegated seedlings from selfing the white-centred chimera, and from crosses in which this form was used as the female parent. Mixed cells have not been looked for in *Chlorophytum* but a few variegated seedlings were obtained from selfs, and from crosses by Collins (1922) and by Pandey and Blaydes (1957) when a chimerical plant was used as one of the parents. It is thought that the variegated seedlings may be correlated with the occurrence of occasional green flecks which are found in the white tissues of the chimeras. Now these green flecks must occur by occasional spontaneous changes of the plastids from white to green. This would give rise to new mixed cells, from which groups of green cells would arise by a new sorting-out in the leaf; the same change in the germ track would give rise to new mixed eggs, which would sort-out to give the observed variegated seedlings. Variegated or green seedlings appearing to come from the white male parent may in fact come from the chimerical female parent following layer alterations in the formation of the eggs, or they may be unconnected new mutations, or even a trace of male plastid transmission may occur.

In *Pelargonium* most defect plastid mutants give rise to a pure white tissue as found in the cultivar Flower of Spring, yet in the cultivar Dolly Varden tiny green flecks always persist embedded in the white tissue, moreover, the green flecks are also found in the white tissues of variegated offspring after crosses with green plants. Evidently the mutant plastid in Dolly Varden is an unstable type which sporadically reverts to green. Spontaneous plastid mutations that sort-out to give heterogeneous white tissues, which are always sparsely flecked with green have also been found in *Oenothera* (Stubbe, oral communication). Other similar examples which have not been tested, but which may turn out to be plastid-differential chimeras can be found among many ornamental variegated plants.

A spontaneous plastid mutant in the japanese morning glory, *Pharbitis nil*, was observed by Imai (1936b) to sort-out to give a creamish-white tissue with yellow ticks or patches. A sorting-out branch gave green and yellow seedlings and white seedlings with yellow ticks, and a wholly yellow branch gave yellow seedlings. Reciprocal crosses showed that both yellow and white plastids were maternally transmitted. It thus appears that the white plastid was unstable and kept changing to yellow; since the yellow form appeared to be perfectly stable the partial recovery change must be regarded as a mutation. In Imai's terms the original mutation from green to white was spontaneous, but the secondary change from white to yellow was automutable. Imai (1936c) also describes an example, which has already been discussed (VIII.6.ii.b), of a spontaneously occurring yellow plastid mutating to green in *Hordeum vulgare*, and more possible examples are listed in a review paper (1936b).

In many sorting-out plants in *Epilobium* secondary plastid changes have been observed by Michaelis (1962a). In the vast majority of cases the secondary mutation occurred in the cell lineages of the first mutant type. Michaelis could be certain that the change was really a mutation because he sometimes found mixed cells containing all three types of plastid, normal green, yellowish-green, and white, for example. However, he could not be certain whether the second mutant type originated from the first or from a normal plastid. In general, it seemed that the more degenerate was the first mutant type the more frequent was the origin of a second mutant type, which was usually less degenerate than the first.

The sporophytic stage of a variegated form of the fern *Scolopendrium vulgare* was found by Andersson-Köttö (1930; 1931) to consist of a mixture of dark green and pale coloured areas. Sori developed on wholly dark zones gave rise to dark gametophytes while sori developed on variegated zones or wholly pale zones gave a mixture of dark and pale gametophytes. There is no satisfactory evidence of wholly dark zones ever giving rise to any pale gametophytes. Within a sorus individual sporangia produced spores developing exclusively either into dark or into pale gametophytes. No segregation occurred during spore formation in the sporangia where meiosis occurs, which strongly suggests that the observed separation that did take place into dark and pale gametophytes was unconnected with nuclear gene or chromosome segregation. The segregation might therefore be due to the sorting-out of two kinds of plastid, dark and pale, especially as the ratios of dark to pale gametophytes from different wholly pale sori were extremely variable. In addition, some gametophytes were described as intermediate between dark and pale, but they behaved as pale types in breeding experiments.

When selfed or crossed among themselves dark gametophytes gave rise to dark green sporophytes without any recurrence of variegation. Reciprocal crosses between dark and pale gametophytes, both of which were viable, gave rise to variegated sporophytes, as also did selfing or intercrossing pale gametophytes. The gametophytes themselves did not become variegated. The alternation of generations may be summarized schematically as follows:

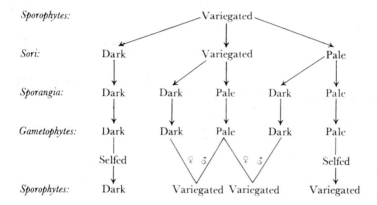

Now a probable interpretation of these observations is that the variegation of the sporophyte is caused by the sorting-out of two types of plastid, dark and pale. The dark green plastids are stable in both gametophytic and sporophytic generations. The pale plastids, by contrast, although stable in the gametophyte frequently mutate to dark plastids in the sporophyte thereby acting, incidentally, as a second cause of variegation:

	Gametophyte		Sporophyte
Plastids:	Dark	→	Dark
	Pale	→	Pale → Dark

Thus the mutation of the unstable pale plastids to the normal dark green type appears to mimic the back-mutation of a recessive nuclear gene to its dominant allele (see Chapter IV). The apparent back-mutation of the yellow plastid to green in *Hordeum vulgare* is similar. It is further interesting to note that if our interpretation of variegation in *Scolopendrium* is correct, then the production of variegated sporophytes from the two reciprocal crosses demonstrates that the plastids must be transmitted by both male and female parents, that is the plastids must be biparentally inherited. As far as is known to the authors there are no other determinations of the mode of plastid inheritance in ferns.

An alternative suggestion made by Darlington (1950) is that the plastid phenotype is controlled not by the plastid itself, but by a plasma-gene, that is another, but as yet morphologically unrecognized extra-nuclear particle. However, this explanation seems the less likely of the two.

17—P.

VIII.7.iii. PLASTID DETERIORATION CHANGES

Nuclear gene-induced plastid deterioration changes from green to white are generally well recognized (VIII.6), but the possibility of similar autonomous plastid deterioration changes has scarcely ever been considered. This has perhaps been due to the almost unchallenged explanation of variegation in *Humulus japonica*. Winge (1917; 1919) found that variegation in *Humulus* was inherited purely by the female parent, yet the green and white parts did not sort-out either during the course of development or in the progeny. The absence of sorting-out convinced him that the variegation must be caused by an abnormality in the cytoplasm and not in the plastids themselves. Ever since, this plant has been repeatedly quoted as the standard example of a variegation caused by a cytoplasmic mutation. In Imai's opinion (1936b; 1937b) the cytoplasm was not defective. He believed that the variegated hop contained two kinds of plastid, a green plastid that was automutable to white and a white plastid that was automutable to green. As evidence for this hypothesis Imai claimed to have observed mixed cells in the leaves. Unfortunately he did not support this claim with any photographs or drawings. Moreover, if mixed cells exist one should expect some degree of sorting-out and yet Imai says there are no intergrades of colour but only sharp divisions between green and white parts. Furthermore it is doubtful if the white plastids are unstable.

Both the explanations of Winge and Imai could be right but neither can be considered to be proved. A third possibility is that the variegation of *Humulus* is due to an unstable plastid that is constantly changing from green to white during the course of development. This suggestion is supported by evidence from the comparable behaviour of other plants. Unfortunately the observations are not as satisfactory as one would like, because the authors were for the most part puzzled by their experimental findings and were at a loss to explain them. Nevertheless the fragments of information, which we will now discuss, all point to the behaviour of unstable mutable plastids.

VIII.7.iii.a. *Sorting-out*

Winge believed that the variegation in *Humulus* could not be due to a plastom mutant because there was no sorting-out. But had he considered the possibility that he was dealing with an unstable plastom he would have realized that sorting-out would only have occurred at the time of origin, whereas the variegated *Humulus* had been propagated by seed for many years. Following a mutation producing an unstable plastid, sorting-out would occur between the normal and unstable plastids. In the original variegated plant most egg cells would contain only normal plastids and would develop into green seedlings. A few eggs, however, would be mixed cells and would contain both normal and unstable plastids. These would sort-out into variegated seedlings which, in turn, would again give rise to the two types of offspring, green and variegated. Finally, other egg cells would develop which had only the unstable plastids and these would give rise to true breeding variegated plants.

The results of a few examples that can be explained on this model are presented in Table VIII.7. In several instances, especially in the

TABLE VIII.7. SUMMARY OF SELECTED BREEDING RESULTS FROM PLANTS IN WHICH THE VARIEGATION IS THOUGHT TO BE CAUSED BY THE BEHAVIOUR OF AN UNSTABLE MUTANT PLASTID

Plant	Self or cross	Nos. offspring			Per cent variegated seedlings	Authors	Dates
		G	V	Total			
Maternal inheritance							
Humulus japonica	G × G	G	—	—	—	Winge	1917, 19
	G × V	G	—	—	—	Imai	1936b, 37b
	V × G	—	V	—	100·0		
	V × V	—	V	—	100·0		
Lycopersicum esculentum	G (pure) self	86	—	86	—	Lesley, Lesley	1942
	G (seg.) self	185	14	199	7·0		
	G (pure) × V	14	—	14			
	G (seg.) × V	104	3	107	2·8		
	V (pure) × G	—	124	124	100·0		
	V (pure) self	—	149	149	100·0		
	V (seg.) self	44	67	111	60·4		
Nicotiana tabacum	G × G	1353	—	1353	—	Edwardson	1965
	G × V	2838	—	2838	—		
	V × G	2074	560	2634	21·3		
	V × V	991	313	1304	24·0		
Plantago major	G (pure) self	G	—	—	—	Kappert	1953
	G (seg.) self	1	112	113	99·1		
	G × V	G	—	—			
	V × G	148	319	467	68·3		
	V (seg.) self	880	1583	2463	64·3		
	V (pure) self	—	1603	1603	100·0		
Triticum vulgare	G self	G	—	—	—	Arnason	1956
	G × V	G	—	—	—		
	V × G	28	48	76	63·2		
	V self	261	236	497	47·5		
Biparental inheritance							
Phaseolus vulgaris	G × V F$_1$	G	1	—	—	Parker	1934
	F$_2$	353	28	381	7·3		
	V × G F$_1$	—	V	—	100·0		
	F$_2$	51	262	313	83·7		
Borrago officinalis	G (pure) self	G	—	—	—	Noack	1931a
	G (seg.) self	112	28	140	20·0		
	G × V	105	103	208	49·5		
	V × G	12	8	20	40·0		
	V (seg.) self	2	10	12	83·3		

tomato, it has been necessary to group the results into the category to which they most likely belong. For instance, it has been necessary to assume that some green families are true-breeding while others are segregating, and in *Plantago* it seems certain that one green family must have been misclassified. In addition, similar results from different years have been added together. When the results are presented in this way, it can be seen that in both *Lycopersicum* and *Plantago* sorting-out has given rise to true-breeding green plants, and segregating and true-breeding variegated plants just as would be expected from the sorting-out of two types of plastid, one stable and the other unstable. In *Triticum* and *Nicotiana* the variegated plants segregated into green and variegated offspring, but true-breeding variegated plants were not obtained. In *Humulus*, on the other hand, only true-breeding variegated plants were found. At first sight the different behaviour of these variegated plants on selfing suggests a lack of similarity between them. But this may not be so. On the contrary, the authors may have studied only certain stages in the sorting-out of an unstable plastid from a mixture of normal and mutant plastids.

VIII.7.iii.b. *Selection of true-breeding variegated plants*

Kappert (1953) found that the original variegated plantain gave mostly green and a few variegated seedlings. The green seedlings bred true. The variegated seedlings again produced green and variegated offspring in varying proportions until, after several generations, Kappert selected a true-breeding line. A true-breeding line was also observed by Lesley and Lesley (1942) in the tomato, but it is not clear how quickly this was achieved since the variegation was not systematically recorded until many years after its origin. Arnason (1956), on the other hand, failed to select a true-breeding line of wheat after two generations. This is, however, not altogether surprising since it may have been impossible to distinguish by eye between a pure variegated plant containing only unstable green plastids and a variegated plant which also contained normal stable green plastids. Only by the chance selection of seed derived from pure germ cells could a true-breeding line be obtained, and as the actual selection was haphazard, and also based on a small number of families, it might well take several generations. There is no record of any sorting-out having occurred in the variegated hop, but this does not mean that we can assume that the variegation arose in one step. On the contrary, it seems quite likely that a similar sorting-out phase would have occurred immediately following the origin of the variegation. But in this case the selection of a true-breeding line was probably made by nurserymen who were selling the seed, because of the plant's ornamental value, long before it was studied by Winge. No attempt appears to have been made to obtain true-breeding variegated lines of *Nicotiana*, *Phaseolus*, and *Borrago*. In addition to these examples, it is worth mentioning that Stubbe (oral communication) has observed what he believes to be the sorting-out of an unstable plastid mutant in an *Oenothera*. Instead of the mutant plastid giving rise to pure white areas, it gave rise only to variegated leaves and shoots.

Kappert, Parker, and Edwardson all consider that the variegation in *Plantago*, *Phaseolus*, and *Nicotiana* respectively is caused by a mutant extra-nuclear particle, but they come to no definite conclusion as to whether the mutation has occurred through a plastom or non-plastom mutation, although Kappert appears to favour the latter alternative. Arnason adopts Imai's reversible plastid mutation hypothesis to account for the absence of white seedlings from his sorting-out wheat plants. But the absence of white seedlings is also to be expected if the unstable plastids never change from green to white in the germ cells, or if the green to white change is a physiological one and not due to mutation. Indeed certain observations in *Humulus* and in *Plantago* suggest that the plastid change is more likely to be physiological than mutational.

VIII.7.iii.c. *Modification of the variegated phenotype*

According to Winge individual hop plants vary from slightly to intensely variegated. Moreover, in some individuals the parts without chlorophyll are most numerous nearest the margin of the leaves and in others nearest the base. This suggests that the plastid change need not always follow cell lineages, which it must do if it is caused by plastid mutation, but need not do if it is a physiological change from green to white. The appearance of variegation is remarkably similar to some of the nuclear gene controlled variegation patterns (see Chapter III). It therefore seems probable that the differences between individuals are similarly due to the effects of modifying genes in the varying genetic backgrounds.

The degree of variegation among plantain seedlings has been shown by Kappert to vary during development and with environmental conditions. Some spring germinated seedlings developed green cotyledons and weakly or strongly variegated first foliage leaves, followed by less variegated leaves and finally wholly green leaves. Other seedlings began the variegation phase slightly later in development and it was less intense. In late autumn the leaves tended to be increasingly variegated and overwintering plants developed almost completely white leaves. If the plants survived, first variegated leaves and then green leaves reappeared during the spring growing season. Genetically green plants remained green throughout the winter. The intensity of variegation of the seedlings appeared to bear no relationship to the intensity of the seed parent, nor were they affected by the pollen parent. Further physiological experiments confirmed that the intensity of variegation was increased by lowering the light intensity and duration, and by lowering the temperature during growth. Furthermore, these three environmental factors appeared not only to affect the behaviour of growing seedlings but also to affect the future behaviour of developing seeds. This was shown by comparing, under uniform growing conditions, the intensity of variegation of seedlings from seeds that had ripened at different times. Seeds that had matured in August gave seedlings with predominantly green cotyledons, whereas those that had matured in December germinated to give seedlings with almost wholly white cotyledons; most of the white seedlings died. Counts of the numbers of plastids in a given area of the white cotyledons showed them to be no fewer than normal so the deficiency must have been connected with a failure to make chlorophyll. Kappert also found that the seeds which had matured under the low light and low temperature conditions of December were considerably underweight compared with the August ripened seeds. He therefore concluded that good light and temperature conditions were necessary for the proper nutrition of the developing embryos and poor nutrition affected their ability to become green, hence their variegation when germinated. These combined physiological and genetical observations in *Plantago* show that by suitably altering the environment one can increase the intensity of variegation of a plant without necessarily producing a corresponding increase in the intensity of variegation of the offspring, which suggests that the green to white plastid changes are phenotypic rather than the result of plastid mutation.

VIII.7.iii.d. *Plastid transmission*

The experiments of Winge, confirmed by Imai, clearly showed that the variegated phenotype in *Humulus* was inherited solely by the female parent; Winge was careful enough to rule out the possibility of apomixis. A similarly purely maternal inheritance was demonstrated by reciprocal crosses between pure green and pure variegated lines of *Lycopersicum*. But the reciprocal crosses in *Plantago*, *Triticum*, and *Nicotiana* between green and variegated plants were less satisfactory since the authors did not use true-breeding variegated plants. Consequently both green and variegated offspring were produced when the variegated plant was used as the female parent (Table VIII.7). Nevertheless, when the green parent was used as the female there were only green offspring demonstrating a purely female inheritance at least in this direction.

Now Edwardson (1965) crossed his variegated tobacco with seven different normal green cultivars and obtained the following results:

V × G (5 cultivars) gave a total of 2074 green : 560 variegated seedlings
V × G (2 cultivars) gave a total of 1049 green : 0 variegated seedlings

In his opinion this result indicated that the first five cultivars contained nuclear genes which permitted the expression of variegation, while the other two cultivars contained nuclear eliminator genes which blocked the expression and transmission of variegation. Unfortunately, this interesting suggestion of the existence of nuclear eliminator genes capable of restoring the mutant plastid to normal cannot be regarded as demonstrated beyond reasonable doubt, because the variegated female parent was not true-breeding. On selfing it gave 991 green : 313 variegated offspring in the first, and 715 green : 64 variegated offspring in the second generation. This segregation is almost certainly due to the sorting-out of two kinds of plastid, the normal stable green plastid and the unstable mutant plastid, which frequently changes to white during development thereby causing the variegation. This means that the V × G crosses are only valid if the eggs actually contained the mutant plastids (see VIII.1.ii), and clearly it is impossible to be certain that they did because the variegated female was not true-breeding. Moreover, the large number of seedlings produced would be no safeguard if these were produced from only a few crosses, as they might have been in *Nicotiana* in which one capsule produces over 500 seeds; Edwardson does not say how many flowers he crossed. As sorting-out was still in progress he may have been fortunate enough to choose some flowers developing in mutant or sorting-out lineages with five cultivar crosses, but unfortunate to choose flowers developing in only normal lineages in crosses with the other two cultivars.

In *Phaseolus*, the F_2 results are seen to produce some plants with the character of the male grandparent (Table VIII.7), which suggested to Parker (1934) that a few extra-nuclear particles were introduced by the male and slowly multiplied unobserved during the F_1 generation, except that one plant was variegated on a single leaf, but which nevertheless occasionally entered the ovules to affect the phenotype of some F_2 plants. Indirect support for the possibility of biparental plastid transmission in *Phaseolus* is given by the frequent pollen transmission of the bean mosaic virus[113]. There is, however, no cause for thinking the present variegation might be the symptom of a virus infection since all attempts to transmit the variegation artificially proved unsuccessful. Reciprocal crosses between green and variegated *Borrago* plants gave both green and variegated offspring suggesting the biparental inheritance of the variegated character. Unfortunately, these crosses are not very conclusive since it is not certain whether or not the green and variegated parents were pure, or whether they both contained a mixture of extra-nuclear particles, which could have been two types of plastid still in the process of sorting-out.

VIII.8. Extra-nuclear Inheritance of Other Characters

The lowest three or four leaves of an *Avena sativa* were found by Ferdinandson and Winge (1930) to develop greenish-brown diffuse spots which gradually became nut-brown with a reddish-brown tinge. Sometimes the elongated spots were arranged in stripes which merged together both longitudinally and laterally. The authors believed that the blotching was not caused by a virus infection although their tests were inadequate to prove this. Their breeding results showed a great variation in the segregation of blotched individuals in which the highest proportion came from those plants in which the blotching had originally been contributed through the egg. In the F_4 generation they succeeded in selecting two families giving wholly blotched offspring. They suggested that a disease factor was in the cytoplasm or in the plastids which was gradually sorting-out. The plastids that carried the disposition to blotching somehow managed to influence the physiology of the whole plant when young causing the disease-like necrotization of the leaf tissue. Emerson (1923) had concluded that a similar blotching in *Zea mays* was caused by a recessive nuclear gene. But Ferdinandsen and Winge believed that his far from satisfactory breeding data could be interpreted in the same way as their *Avena* data. Clearly further work is needed on this problem before any real conclusion can be made.

In another *Avena sativa* the first to third seedling leaves were found by Froier (1948) to have yellow spots in which the plastids appeared to be degenerate. The later leaves were normal green. Reciprocal crosses between green and luteomaculata plants showed that the yellow spotting was transmitted by the female but not by the male parent.

The cotyledons of *Glycine hispida* are green or yellow. Crosses between the two types showed that the seedlings in both first and second generations were the same colour as the original female parent's cotyledons. Terao (1918) and Terao and Nakatomi (1929) therefore concluded that the cotyledon colour was purely maternally inherited.

REFERENCES

1. ÅKERMAN, Å. (1933). *Bot. Notiser.* 255–270
2. ANDERSON, E. G. (1923). *Bot. Gaz.* **76**, 411–418
3. ANDERSSON-KOTTÖ, I. (1930). *Z. Vererbungsl.* **56**, 115–201

4. ANDERSSON-KOTTÖ, I. (1931). *Bibliogr. genet.* **8**, 269–294
5. ARNASON, T. J. (1956). *Canad. J. Bot.* **34**, 801–804
6. ARNASON, T. J., HARRINGTON, J. B. & FRIESEN, H. A. (1946). *Canad. J. Res. C.* **24**, 145–157
7. ARNASON, T. J. & WALKER, G. W. R. (1949). *Canad. J. Res. C.* **27**, 172–178
8. BAUR, E. (1909). *Z. Vererbungsl.* **1**, 330–351
9. BAUR, E. (1910). *Z. Vererbungsl.* **3**, 34–98
10. BAUR, E. (1911a). *Z. Vererbungsl.* **4**, 81–102
11. BAUR, E. (1930). *Einführung in die experimentelle Vererbungslehre.* 7/11. Aufl. Gebrüder Borntraeger, Berlin
12. BROZEK, A. (1923). *Stud. Pl. physiol. Lab. Charles Univ.* **1**, 45–78
13. BROZEK, A. (1926). *J. Hered.* **17**, 113–129
14. BURK, L. G. & GROSSO, J. J. (1963). *J. Hered.* **54**, 23–25
15. BURK, L. G., STEWART, R. N. & DERMEN, H. (1964). *Amer. J. Bot.* **51**, 713–724
16. CHATTAWAY, M. M. & SNOW, R. (1929). *J. Genet.* **21**, 81–83
17. CHITTENDEN, R. J. (1926). *J. Genet.* **16**, 43–61
18. CLAUSEN, J. (1927). *Hereditas* **9**, 245–256
19. CLAUSEN, J. (1930). *Hereditas* **13**, 342–356
20. COLLINS, E. J. (1922). *J. Genet.* **12**, 1–17
21. CORRENS, C. (1909a). *Z. Vererbungsl.* **1**, 291–329
22. CORRENS, C. (1909b). *Z. Vererbungsl.* **2**, 331–340
23. CORRENS, C. (1919b). *S.B. preuss. Akad. Wiss.* 820–857
24. CORRENS, C. (1922). *S.B. preuss. Akad. Wiss.* 460–486
25. CORRENS, C. (1931a). *S.B. preuss. Akad. Wiss.* 203–231
26. CORRENS, C. (1931b). *Z. Vererbungsl.* **59**, 274–280
27. CORRENS, C. edited WETTSTEIN, F. v. (1937). *Nicht mendelnde Vererbung.* Gebrüder Borntraeger, Berlin
28. DALE, E. E. (1930). *Pap. Mich. Acad. Sci.* **13**, 5–8
29. DARLINGTON, C. D. & MATHER, K. (1950). *Genes, Plants and People: Essays on Genetics.* George Allen & Unwin Ltd, London
30. DEMEREC, M. (1927). *Bot. Gaz.* **84**, 139–155
31. DÖBEL, P. & HAGEMANN, R. (1963). *Biol. Zbl.* **82**, 749–751
32. EDWARDSON, J. R. (1965). *Genetics* **52**, 365–370
33. EMERSON, R. A. (1923). *Mem. Cornell agric. Exp. Sta.* **70**
34. FERDINANDSEN, C. & WINGE, Ø. (1930). *Hereditas* **13**, 164–176
35. FROIER, K. (1948). *Hereditas* **34**, 60–82
36. FUNAOKA, S. (1924). *Biol. Zbl.* **44**, 343–384
37. GAIRDNER, A. E. & HALDANE, J. B. S. (1929). *J. Genet.* **21**, 315–325
38. GREGORY, R. P. (1915). *J. Genet.* **4**, 305–321
39. HAAN, H. DE. (1930). *Genetica* **12**, 321–440
40. HAAN, H. DE. (1933). *Bibliogr. genet.* **10**, 357–416
41. HAGEMANN, R. (1960). *Die Kulturpflanze* **8**, 168–184
42. HAGEMANN, R. (1961a). *Die Kulturpflanze* **9**, 163–170
43. HAGEMANN, R. (1964). *Plasmatische Vererbung. Genetik Grundlagen, Ergebnisse und Probleme in Einzeldarstellungen.* Veb Gustav Fischer Verlag, Jena.
44. HAGEMANN, R. (1965). *Genetics Today* **3**, 613–625
45. HAGEMANN, R. & SCHOLZ, F. (1962). *Züchter* **32**, 50–59
46. HAGIWARA, T. & OOMURA, Y. (1939). *Jap. J. Genet.* **15**, 328–330
47. HONING, J. A. (1927). *Genetica* **9**, 1–18
48. HUTCHINS, A. E. & YOUNGNER, V. B. (1952). *Proc. Amer. Soc. Hort. Sci.* **60**, 370–378
49. IMAI, Y. (1928). *Genetics* **13**, 544–562
50. IMAI, Y. (1935a). *J. Genet.* **30**, 1–13

51. IMAI, Y. (1936a). *J. Genet.* **33**, 169–195
52. IMAI, Y. (1936b). *Z. Vererbungsl.* **71**, 61–83
53. IMAI, Y. (1936c). *Genetics* **21**, 752–757
54. IMAI, Y. (1937b). *Z. Vererbungsl.* **73**, 598–600
55. JENKINS, M. T. (1924). *J. Hered.* **15**, 467–472
56. KAPPERT, H. (1953). *Ber. dt. bot. Ges.* **66**, 123–133
57. KARPER, R. E. (1934). *J. Hered.* **25**, 49–54
58. KONDÔ, M., TAKEDA, M. & FUJIMOTO, S. (1927). *Ber. Ohara Inst.* **3**, 291–317
59. LESLEY, J. W. & LESLEY, M. M. (1942). *Genetics* **27**, 550–560
60. LOVE, H. H. & CRAIG, W. T. (1936). *J. Amer. Soc. Agron.* **28**, 1005–1011
61. MALY, R. & WILD, A. (1956). *Z. Vererbungsl.* **87**, 493–496
62. MAZOTI, L. B. (1949). *Cien. e Invest.* **5**, 387–388
63. MAZOTI, L. B. (1950). *Rev. Arg. Agron.* **17**, 145–162
64. MAZOTI, L. B. (1952). *Rev. Arg. Agron.* **19**, 35–38
65. MAZOTI, L. B. (1954a). *Argentina Div. Gen. Invest. Rev. Invest. Agricola* **8**, 175–183
66. MAZOTI, L. B. (1954b). *Argentina Div. Gen. Invest. Rev. Invest. Agricola* **8**, 185–186
67. MICHAELIS, P. (1935). *Planta* **23**, 486–500
68. MICHAELIS, P. (1957a). *Protoplasma* **48**, 403–418
69. MICHAELIS, P. (1957b). *Planta* **50**, 60–106
70. MICHAELIS, P. (1958a). *Planta* **51**, 600–634
71. MICHAELIS, P. (1958b). *Planta* **51**, 722–756
72. MICHAELIS, P. (1959). *Proc. X. Int. Congr. Genet.* **1**, 375–385
73. MICHAELIS, P. (1961a). *Flora* **151**, 162–201
74. MICHAELIS, P. (1962a). *Biol. Zbl.* **81**, 91–128
75. MICHAELIS, P. (1962b). *Planta* **58**, 34–49
76. MICHAELIS, P. (1962c). *Protoplasma* **55**, 177–231
77. MICHAELIS, P. (1965a). *Z. Naturf.* **20**b, 264–267
78. MICHAELIS, P. (1965c). *Flora* **156**, 1–19
79. MIYAKE, K. & IMAI, Y. (1935). *Bot. Gaz.* **96**, 571–574
80. MORINAGA, T. (1932). *Bot. Mag., Tokyo* **46**, 202–207
81. MUNERATI, O. (1928). *Proc. V. Int. Congr. Genet.* **2**, 1137–1142
82. MUNERATI, O. (1942). *Züchter* **14**, 214–215
83. NIJDAM, F. E. (1932). *Genetica* **14**, 161–278
84. NOACK, K. L. (1924). *Verh. phys. -med. Ges. Würzb.* **49**, 45–93
85. NOACK, K. L. (1925). *Verh. phys. -med. Ges. Würzb.* **50**, 47–97
86. NOACK, K. L. (1931a). *Z. Vererbungsl.* **58**, 372–392
87. NOACK, K. L. (1932b). *Z. Vererbungsl.* **63**, 232–255
88. PAL, B. P. & RAMANUJAM, S. (1941). *Indian J. agric. Sci.* **11**, 170–176
89. PANDEY, K. K. & BLAYDES, G. W. (1957). *Ohio J. Sci.* **57**, 135–147
90. PAO, W. K. & LI, H. W. (1946). *J. Amer. Soc. Agron.* **38**, 90–94
91. PARKER, M. C. (1934). *J. Hered.* **25**, 165–170
92. RANDOLPH, L. F. (1922). *Bot. Gaz.* **73**, 337–375
93. RENNER, O. (1915). *Flora* **107**, 115–150
94. RENNER, O. (1924). *Biol. Zbl.* **44**, 309–336
95. RENNER, O. (1929). *Handbuch der Vererbungswissenschaft* Bd. **2A**, 1–161. Eds., E. Baur & M. Hartmann. Gebrüder Borntraeger, Berlin
96. RENNER, O. (1934). *Ber. Math. Phys. Kl. Sächs. Akad. Wiss. Lpz.* **86**, 241–266
97. RENNER, O. (1936). *Flora* **130**, 218–290
98. RENNER, O. (1937b). *Cytologia, Fujii Jubilee* **2**, 644–655
99. RHOADES, M. M. (1943). *Proc. nat. Acad. Sci., Wash.* **29**, 327–329
100. RHOADES, M. M. (1946). *Cold Spr. Harb. Symp. quant. Biol.* **11**, 202–207
101. RHOADES, M. M. (1950). *Proc. nat. Acad. Sci., Wash.* **36**, 634–635
102. RÖBBELEN, G. (1962). *Z. Vererbungsl.* **93**, 25–34

103. ROBERTSON, D. W. (1937). *Genetics* **22**, 104–113
104. ROTH, L. (1927). *Z. Vererbungsl.* **45**, 125–159
105. SCHERZ, W. (1927). *Z. Vererbungsl.* **45**, 1–40
106. SCHLÖSSER, L. A. (1935). *Z. Vererbungsl.* **68**, 222–241
107. SCHÖTZ, F. (1952). *Naturwiss. Rdsch.* **5**, 185–190
108. SCHÖTZ, F. (1954). *Planta* **43**, 182–240
109. SCHÖTZ, F. (1958a). *Planta* **51**, 173–185
110. SCHWEMMLE, J. (1941a). *Z. Vererbungsl.* **79**, 171–187
111. SCHWEMMLE, J., HAUSTEIN, E., STURM, A. & BINDER, M. (1938). *Z. Vererbungsl.* **75**, 358–800
112. SÔ, M. (1921). *Jap. J. Genet.* **1**, 21–36
113. SMITH, K. M. (1957). *A textbook of plant virus diseases.* 2nd ed. J. and A. Churchill Ltd, London
114. STEHLIK, V. (1921). *Z. Zuckerind. csl. Repub.* **45**, 409–414
115. STUBBE, W. (1959a). *Z. Vererbungsl.* **90**, 288–298
116. STUBBE, W. (1960). *Z. Bot.* **48**, 191–218
117. STUBBE, W. (1963a). *Ber. dt. bot. Ges.* **76**, 154–167
118. STUBBE, W. (1964). *Genetica* **35**, 28–33
119. TERAO, H. (1918). *Amer. Nat.* **52**, 51–56
120. TERAO, H. & NAKATOMI, S. (1929). *Jap. J. Genet.* **4**, 64–80
121. TERAO, H. & U, N. (1929). *Jap. J. Genet.* **4**, 86–89
122. TILNEY-BASSETT, R. A. E. (1963a). *Heredity* **18**, 265–285
123. TILNEY-BASSETT, R. A. E. (1963b). *Heredity* **18**, 485–504
124. TILNEY-BASSETT, R. A. E. (1964). *Heredity* **19**, 516–518
125. TILNEY-BASSETT, R. A. E. (1965). *Heredity* **20**, 451–466
126. UFER, M. (1936). *Z. Vererbungsl.* **71**, 281–298
127. UMAR, S. M. (1943). *Indian J. Genet.* **3**, 61–63
128. WETTSTEIN, D. v. & ERIKSSON, G. (1965). *Genetics Today* **3**, 591–610
129. WHITAKER, T. W. (1944). *J. Hered.* **35**, 317–320
130. WILD, A. (1958). *Planta* **50**, 379–387
131. WILD, A. (1960). *Beitr. Biol. Pfl.* **35**, 137–175
132. WINGE, Ø. (1917). *C.r. Trav. Lab. Carlsberg* **13**, 131–275
133. WINGE, Ø. (1919). *C.r. Trav. Lab. Carlsberg* **14**, 1–20
134. WOODS, M. W. & DUBUY, H. G. (1951a). *Amer. J. Bot.* **38**, 419–434
135. WOODS, M. W. & DUBUY, H. G. (1951b). *J. Nat. Cancer Inst.* **11**, 1105–1151
136. YASUI, K. (1929). *Cytologia* **1**, 192–215
137. ZIRKLE, C. (1929). *Bot. Gaz.* **88**, 186–203

CHAPTER IX

Hybrid Variegation

IX.1. The Meaning of Hybrid Variegation

In both wild and cultivated plants crosses between species vary from utter failures to complete successes. Between these extremes a whole range of disturbances may occur to the hybrid, for example the early death of embryos, the failure of seeds to germinate, the development of partial or complete sterility and various degrees of chlorophyll deficiency. In regard to chlorophyll development, crosses between species can produce the following kinds of hybrid offspring:

(1) The offspring are green whichever way the cross is made.

(2) The offspring are chlorophyll deficient whichever way the cross is made.

These two categories are of little interest to us because the reaction of the plastids with the hybrid nucleus is the same for both species, either they become green or they do not. Furthermore, since the reaction of the plastids from both species is the same, it is not possible to tell whether plastid transmission is uniparental or biparental.

(3) The offspring are green from one cross and chlorophyll deficient from the reciprocal cross; the plastids are transmitted only by the female parent. Thus the results of reciprocal crosses between two species A and B can be shown as follows:

$$A♀ \times B♂ \to AB \quad \text{Green hybrid offspring}$$
$$B♀ \times A♂ \to AB \quad \text{Chlorophyll deficient hybrid offspring}$$

In this example the A plastids are able to work efficiently with the hybrid nucleus to develop into normal green chloroplasts, whereas the B plastids are unable to get on with the same hybrid nucleus. Since the nuclear genotype is constant, the difference between the reciprocal crosses must therefore be due to a difference between the extra-nuclear components of the genotype in the two species.

(4) The plastids of one species are able to develop into normal green chloroplasts with the hybrid nucleus, but the plastids of the second species remain chlorophyll deficient, often quite white. The plastids are transmitted predominantly by the female, but the male parent also

268

transmits some plastids. Thus the results of reciprocal crosses between two species A and B would give the following offspring:

A♀ × B♂ → AB   Green + Variegated (green with white flecks) offspring

B♀ × A♂ → AB   White + Variegated (white with green flecks) offspring

Under some circumstances one may even receive from the same cross all three classes of offspring, green, variegated, and white. In this example the A plastids are compatible with the hybrid nucleus and become green, but the B plastids are incompatible and fail to become green. Hence, in the first cross, many offspring are green owing to the sorting-out of the compatible and maternal A plastids, but some become flecked with white owing to the sorting-out of the incompatible white B plastids introduced by the pollen. In the reciprocal cross the situation is reversed.

Now it must be remembered that these variegated plants arise as a result of crossing together two perfectly normal green plants, and do not arise from any kind of Mendelian segregation. The variegation is simply a consequence of hybridization; hence this phenomenon is appropriately called hybrid variegation.

Hybrid chlorophyll deficiency has often been recorded from species crosses, whereas hybrid variegation has been observed less frequently. Nevertheless, in one particular genus, the genus *Oenothera*, hybrid variegation is frequent among interspecific crosses which has led to a very intensive investigation of the phenomenon in particular by Mickan (1935), Renner (1917–1956) and his pupils Stubbe (1953–1965) and Schötz (1952–1965) in the subgenus *Euoenothera*, formerly *Onagra*, and by Schwemmle and colleagues (1935–1965) in the subgenus *Raimannia*, formerly *Euoenothera*. Many species of *Oenothera* have a very special genetical system and this needs to be understood before the interesting features of the hybrid variegation can be described.

IX.2. The Genetic System in Oenothera

IX.2.i. INTERCHANGE HETEROZYGOTES

Many diploid *Oenothera* species are characterized by having from as few as four to as many as all fourteen of their chromosomes linked in a ring or chain at meiosis[10, 11]. They are interchange heterozygotes in which interchanges have taken place between the ends of the seven pairs of chromosomes as in the following diagram of a chain of 14:

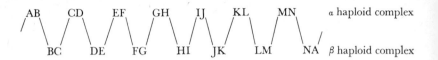

The morphology of each chromosome is extremely similar with a central centromere between two equal length arms. And at meiosis the chiasmata holding the units of the ring together are formed at the tips of each chromosome arm. As a result of this highly symmetrical chromosome arrangement, the ring is usually able to arrange itself on the metaphase spindle in the zig-zag way illustrated so that the alternate chromosomes are regularly distributed at anaphase to opposite poles. Consequently, instead of the chromosomes becoming reshuffled as is normal during meiosis, they separate into the same two groups as had been brought together by the fusion of male and female gametes at the preceding fertilization. Moreover, since there is little recombination between alternate chromosomes, owing to its restriction by the position of the chiasmata to the tips of each chromosome arm, the two groups or complexes of chromosomes remain essentially unchanged by their passage through meiosis. In species which develop a complete ring of fourteen chromosomes, each complex holds together the whole haploid complement of seven chromosomes. But in species forming smaller rings, of eight chromosomes for example, four chromosomes are held together in each haploid complex, while the remaining three pairs of chromosomes become reshuffled at each meiosis. Now each complex has developed its own set of characteristic features, which distinguishes the two complexes of the same species from one another and from the complexes of other species. Hence the two complexes can be designated as α and β or they can each be given their own Latin name, which Renner has done. Thus the two complexes of the species *Oenothera lamarckiana* with a ring of fourteen chromosomes have been named *gaudens* and *velans*, and similarly the complexes of *O. syrticola* are named *rigens* and *curvans*. *O. hookeri*, on the other hand, is a homozygous species and therefore forms no complexes. Nevertheless, because of the widely adopted use of names for the complexes, it has been found convenient to refer to its haploid chromosome set as ʰ*hookeri*. Similarly, each chromosome set of the homozygous species *O. franciscana* is referred to as ʰ*franciscana*.

IX.2.ii. MECHANISMS FOR PRESERVING HETEROZYGOSITY

When a complex heterozygous species is selfed one would expect a Mendelian segregation of 1 : 2 : 1 as in the following example from selfing *O. lamarckiana*:

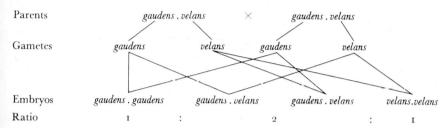

Parents	*gaudens . velans* ×	*gaudens . velans*	
Gametes	*gaudens* *velans*	*gaudens* *velans*	
Embryos	*gaudens . gaudens*	*gaudens . velans*	*gaudens . velans* *velans.velans*
Ratio	1 :	2	: 1

In practice, however, each complex contains recessive lethal factors which prevent the development of the homozygotes, thereby causing the heterozygotes to breed true. Thus each haploid complex is defective in some way or other, but in the heterozygote the defect is covered by its partner.

In certain other hybrid species of *Oenothera*, homozygous embryos are not even formed owing to very effective selection mechanisms operating during the germination of the pollen and the development of the embryo sacs. In *O. syrticola*, for example, the *rigens* complex is able to develop proper embryo sacs but the *curvans* complex fails to do so; in the competition between the two complexes *rigens* wins[43]. Conversely, pollen grains containing the *curvans* complex germinate successfully and fertilize the eggs, but in the competition between the two the *rigens* complex loses[39, 41]. Hence the successful gametic combination is *rigens* ♀ × *curvans* ♂, the combination which ensures the furtherance of the heterozygote and the exclusion of the homozygotes. The two complexes of *O. lamarckiana* are transmitted by both male and female gametes, whereas each complex of *O. syrticola* is transmitted by only one type of gamete. In between we find species such as *O. biennis* in which the *albicans* complex is transmitted only by the egg and the *rubens* complex by both gametes.

IX.3. The Genetic Continuity of the Plastids

IX.3.i. SORTING-OUT

Hybrid variegated *Oenothera* seedlings pass through the stages of fine and coarse variegations followed by the development of pure green, pure white, sectorial, and periclinal shoots in the same manner as variegated *Pelargonium* seedlings and typical sorting-out plants (see Chapters VII and VIII). After *Pelargonium* crosses, Baur (1909) had assumed that the variegation arose by the sorting-out of two genetically and morphologically distinct plastids brought together by the two parents at fertilization; the green plastids came from the female and white plastids from the male parent, or vice versa. It at once appeared to Renner (1922; 1924) that hybrid variegation in *Oenothera* must be due to a similar cause. But in *Oenothera* crosses the two types of plastid revealed their genetical differences only after hybridization, when it was seen that one plastid was able to develop into a normal green chloroplast while the other failed to do so. In other words, the two genetically different plastids which appeared morphologically similar with their respective parent nuclei, became morphologically and physiologically dissimilar, green or white, with the hybrid nucleus.

It can be argued that the varying behaviour of the two plastids is not due to differences within themselves, but rather to differences in some other extra-nuclear particle. But two serious objections can be raised against this. Firstly, the quick sorting-out in variegated *Oenothera* seedlings suggests that a small number of particles is involved, and only the plastids are found in small enough numbers. Secondly, the existence of two morphologically distinct plastids within the same mixed cell was reported by Krumbholz (1925) in variegated cotyledons. Moreover, this has been recently confirmed by Stubbe (1957; 1958) who found mixed cells in the cotyledons and early leaves, and rarely the later leaves of hybrid variegated plants. Hence the morphological observations uphold Renner's hypothesis of two kinds of plastid, which is firmly endorsed by his genetical experiments.

IX.3.ii. INTERACTIONS BETWEEN PLASTIDS AND NUCLEI

IX.3.ii.a. *Genetic variation between plastids*

Renner (1924) found that crosses between *O. hookeri* (*^{h}hookeri.^{h}hookeri*) and *O. lamarckiana* (*gaudens.velans*) gave the following types of offspring:

Cross	F_1 *offspring*
hookeri × *lamarckiana* ♀ Plastids *hookeri*	*^{h}hookeri.gaudens* (green) and *^{h}hookeri.velans* (green + few variegated)
lamarckiana × *hookeri* ♀ Plastids *lamarckiana*	*^{h}hookeri.gaudens* (green) and *^{h}hookeri.velans* (yellow + few variegated)

The hybrids with *hookeri* plastids are mostly green, whereas the same hybrids with *lamarckiana* plastids are partly green and partly yellow. In addition a few of the seedlings are variegated. More precisely, the results show that the *hookeri* plastids develop successfully with both types of hybrid nuclei, while the *lamarckiana* plastids function normally with the *^{h}hookeri.gaudens* nuclear genotype but not with the *^{h}hookeri. velans*. Thus the two plastids, which differ in their reaction with the *^{h}hookeri.velans* nuclear genotype, must themselves differ from one another. Or could the variation be due not to differences in the plastoms, but instead to differences in an alternative extra-nuclear component?

In the cross *O. lamarckiana* × *O. hookeri*, the *lamarckiana* plastids are yellow with the *^{h}hookeri.velans* genotype even though they are still within their own cytoplasm. On the other hand, the *hookeri* plastids, which enter from the male parent and sort-out in the variegated seedlings, develop into functional green chloroplasts with the same *^{h}hookeri.velans* genotype, even though they are now within the foreign *lamarckiana* cytoplasm:

Nucleus:	*^{h}hookeri.velans*	*^{h}hookeri.velans*
Cytoplasm:	*O. lamarckiana*	*O. lamarckiana*
Plastom:	*O. lamarckiana*—yellow	*O. hookeri*—green

Since the cytoplasm as well as the nuclear genotype is constant, the varying reaction of the plastids is clearly due to differences between them. This example is no exception, however, for many other crosses were found by Renner and other workers in which, with a particular nucleus, the plastids of the mother were unable to develop chlorophyll, while the plastids of the father were fully functional. Conversely, other combinations exist in which the plastids from the mother are green and those from the father colourless. What is important is not the direction of the cross but the reaction between the plastids and the nucleus.

IX.3.ii.b. *Reversibility of the physiological reaction*

The surviving variegated seedlings derived from crosses between *O. lamarckiana* and *O. hookeri* sort-out to give pure green or yellow shoots or sectorial and periclinal chimeras, sometimes with yellow and sometimes with green germ layers. If these two types of germ layer are now crossed with the pollen from *O. syrticola* (*rigens♀.curvans♂*) a new genotype is produced which gives the following interesting reaction with the two plastid types:

Green germ layer:

^{h}hookeri.velans (*hookeri* plastids) × *curvans* →
　　　　　　　　　　　　　yellow *^{h}hookeri.curvans* offspring

Yellow germ layer:

^{h}hookeri.velans (*lamarckiana* plastids) × *curvans* →
　　　　　　　　　　　　　green *^{h}hookeri.curvans* offspring

The *hookeri* plastids which were green with the *ʰhookeri.velans* genotype are now yellow with the *ʰhookeri.curvans* genotype. Conversely the *lamarckiana* plastids which were previously yellow are now green. These experiments show that by varying the nuclear genotype the *lamarckiana* plastids changed from green in the original species, *gaudens.velans*, to yellow with the *ʰhookeri.velans* nucleus, and back to green again with the *ʰhookeri.curvans* nucleus. Since the *lamarckiana* plastids were always transmitted through the female, the cytoplasm must have remained fairly constant. Hence the reversible changes in the colour of the plastids must have been caused by their varying physiological interaction with the different nuclei. Again this example is no isolated exception for similar nuclear exchanges with the plastids of other species have shown again and again that the failure of a plastid to make chlorophyll with an incompatible nucleus can always be restored by its return to its own or to another compatible nucleus. In every case the changes in the plastids are clearly reversible.

IX.3.ii.c. *Differential and defect mutations*

In typical sorting-out plants (see Chapters VII and VIII), the first white plastid arises by a new mutation from a normal and potentially green plastid. Experiment shows that this mutation produces a permanent defect in the plastid which prevents it from ever again reacting normally with any nucleus, except by a further mutation. Hence mutations of this kind may be called defect mutations[85]. The difference between the green plastids of *Oenothera* species, on the other hand, must be due to mutations which occurred a long time ago in the course of evolution. Hence Stubbe (1958) has called these differential mutations, and the hybrid variegation that results from crossing certain species is due to the sorting-out of two different plastids, one of which is green and the other white with the hybrid nucleus. But unlike the white defect mutant plastid, the white differential mutant plastid is capable of developing normally again with an appropriate nucleus.

IX.3.iii. PERMANENCE OF PLASTID TYPES

The reversibility of the colour change from green to white and back to green again was found to be a property not only of the *lamarckiana* plastids, but of the plastids of all species. Moreover Renner (1934) was able to show that even after fourteen generations under the influence of a foreign nucleus, *rubens.flavens*, the plastids of *O. syrticola*, *rigens.curvans*, still retained their original behaviour characteristic for the species. An even more striking example has recently been given by Schötz (1962a) in which the plastids of *O. biennis* survived unaltered for twenty generations with an *O. hookeri* nucleus. The synthesis of this combination may be shown schematically as follows:

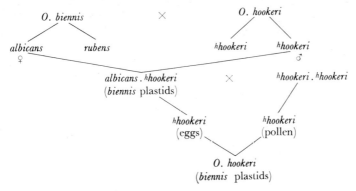

Under the supposition of the genetic autonomy and continuity of the plastids, it is clear that the *biennis* plastids have been inherited only by the mother and have reproduced themselves identically without change.

In criticism of the supposition by Mühlethaler and Bell (1962) that the plastids are derived *de novo* from the egg nucleus following the destruction of the plastids of the previous generation, Schötz (1962a) asks, how do they propose to account for this demonstration of the genetic permanence of the *biennis* plastids? On the basis of the *de novo* theory, first the *albicans*.*hhookeri* nucleus would have to produce new *biennis* plastids after elimination of the old *biennis* plastids, and secondly the *hhookeri*.*hhookeri* nucleus would have to produce repeatedly for twenty generations, instead of its own *hookeri* plastids, the foreign *biennis* plastids; an extremely improbable event. Stubbe (1962) and Haustein (1962) have also criticised Mühlethaler and Bell's hypothesis and have affirmed the genetic continuity of the plastids. Furthermore, contrary to Mühlethaler and Bell's observations, recent electron microscope studies clearly show that at least in some plants the plastids remain in the egg cells as permanent structures at all times and are not eliminated (see I.8).

IX.4. The Evolution of the Subgenus *Euoenothera*

IX.4.i. THE EVALUATION OF TAXONOMIC DATA

The North American *Euoenotheras* have been a difficult group to classify owing to the great variety of forms which grade into one another without clear-cut divisions. Nevertheless, a particularly detailed study of the complicated cytology of this subgenus, stimulated by the early work of Hoeppener and Renner (1929a, b), together with an assessment of morphological, ecological and geographical features, plus attention to the importance of changes from an outbreeding to an inbreeding habit, has enabled Cleland (1957; 1962b; 1964) to present a comprehensive account of the evolutionary history. In his view the present day North American *Euoenotheras* consist of the following ten species which have been derived from successive migrations giving rise to successive populations (Fig. IX.1):

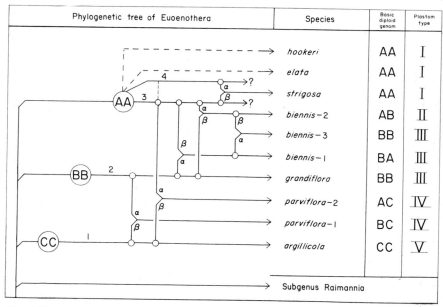

FIG. IX.1. *Phylogenetic tree of the North American species of* Euoenothera. *The successive populations which Cleland believed to have been derived from successive migrations are numbered 1–4; these correspond to the three basic genoms AA, BB, and CC recognized by Stubbe. To each of the ten species of Cleland, one of the six possible diploid genom combinations and one of the five plastom types has been assigned by Stubbe. Redrawn by permission from Stubbe, W.* (1964). Genetica **35**, *28–33. Figure 3, and Martinus Nijhoff, Den Haag*

(1) *O. hookeri* and *O. elata* are two species which retain primitive characters, that is they are open-pollinated, they mostly form seven bivalents at meiosis and the chromosomes do not carry lethal genes. The hookeris either represent the original population of North American *Euoenotheras* or they are a later offshoot which has retained the original characters. The elatas may be closer to the common line from which both South and North American species have sprung.

(2) *O. argillicola* and *O. grandiflora* also retain primitive characters. They are thought to represent relic species of the first and second population spread respectively.

The remaining six species are complex heterozygotes forming large rings at meiosis, usually with all fourteen chromosomes in one ring. They also have self-pollinating flowers and their chromosomes carry lethal genes which prevent the formation of homozygotes.

(3) *O. parviflora* I, in part *biennis* in character, arose as a result of overlapping and consequent hybridization between populations 1 and 2, and *O. parviflora* II, in part *strigosa* in character, by hybridization between populations 1 and 3.

(4) *O. biennis* I and II arose by hybridization between population 2 and a later *strigosa*-like population 3. *O. biennis* III arose by hybridization between *biennis* I and II.

(5) *O. strigosa* is the result of hybridization between population 3, producing the β-*strigosa* complexes, with a later population 4, producing the α-*strigosa* complexes.

This establishment of a sound classification for the North American *Euoenotheras* by standard taxonomic methods is particularly useful to us, because it provides the yardstick by which we can judge the significance of the plastom in evolution, for, as we shall now see, the study of different kinds of plastids has led to a remarkable confirmation of Cleland's conclusions.

IX.4.ii. PERMUTATIONS OF GENOMS AND PLASTOMS

During the course of the very extensive genetical investigations in *Oenothera* over the last fifty years, a number of workers have drawn attention to the occurrence of hybrid chlorophyll deficiency and hybrid variegation following interspecific crosses. Individually the thousands of crosses are not important to us, but the overall results are most interesting and show that some species have one type of plastom and some another, and that altogether there are as many as five genetically different plastoms within the subgenus *Euoenothera*. These plastoms are spread between the fourteen species of Renner's Collection (Table IX.1), most of which originated in Europe. In order to extend the earlier work and to determine the varying degrees of compatibility between the plastoms and the genoms, Stubbe (1959a, b; 1960) synthesized approximately 400 different genom-plastom combinations so as to combine as far as possible each plastom with all available nuclear genoms and each nuclear genom with all available plastoms. He found that in about a third of the combinations the plastids were able to develop into normal green chloroplasts. In the remainder, a wide range of chlorophyll deficiencies were produced which he classified into ten distinct groups (Fig. IX.2).

A comparison of the behaviour of the plastids from the fourteen species with different test-genoms confirmed that in several species the plastids are identical and that there are not more than five wild-type plastoms; these Stubbe designated as follows: *hookeri*-plastom (I); *suaveolens*-plastom (II); *lamarckiana*-plastom (III); *parviflora*-plastom (IV); and *argillicola*-plastom (V), (Table IX.1).

TABLE IX.1. THE DISTRIBUTION OF THE FIVE PLASTOMS WITHIN THE FOURTEEN SPECIES OF *EUOENOTHERA* COLLECTED LARGELY WITHIN EUROPE

By permission, after W. Stubbe, Zeitschrift für Vererbungslehre (*1959*), **90**, *288–298*.
Springer-Verlag, Berlin–Göttingen–Heidelberg

Plastom	Species	Synonyms	Complex combinations
I	*hookeri*	—	ᴴ*hookeri* ☿ . ᴴ*hookeri* ☿
	franciscana	—	ᴴ*franciscana* ☿ . ᴴ*franciscana* ☿
	bauri	*hungarica*	*laxans* ♀ . *undans* ♂
II	*suaveolens*	—	*albicans* ♀ . *flavens* ☿
	biennis	—	*albicans* ♀ . *rubens* ☿
	purpurata	—	ᴴ*purpurata* ☿ . ᴴ*purpurata* ☿
III	*lamarckiana*	—	*gaudens* ☿ . *velans* ☿
	chicaginensis	—	*excellens* ♀ . *punctulans* ♂
IV	*parviflora*	—	*augens* ♀ . *subcurvans* ♂
	ammophila	—	*rigens* ♀ . *percurvans* ♂
	atrovirens	*cruciata*	*pingens* ♀ . *flectens* ♂
	silesiaca	—	*subpingens* ♀ . *subcurvans* ♂
	syrticola	*muricata*	*rigens* ♀ . *curvans* ♂
V	*argillicola*	—	*dilatans* ☿ . *dilatans* ☿

A comparison of the behaviour of the numerous permutations of two haploid genoms from the fourteen species with the five plastoms showed that, allowing for the variability produced by modifying genes, the genoms consist of three similar, but not identical, haploid types which may be called A, B, and C (Table IX.2); these pair to give six diploid genom combinations. Stubbe (1959a, b) has shown that the compatibility relationships between the six diploid genoms and the five plastoms can be conveniently summarized in diagrammatic form (Fig. IX.2). Now, what is so very interesting, is that the three basic genoms recognized by Stubbe from studies of genom-plastom interactions in predominantly European species, clearly correspond to the three main populations recognized by Clcland from an assessment of taxonomical criteria in North American species. This is understandable because the European species are only recently derived from the North American species by migration. Hence studies in European species can be related

TABLE IX.2. DISTRIBUTION OF THE GENOM COMPLEXES AFTER THEIR EFFECT UPON THE GREENING ABILITY OF THE FIVE TYPES OF PLASTOM

*By permission, after W. Stubbe, Zeitschrift für Vererbungslehre (1959), **90**, 288–298. Springer-Verlag, Berlin–Göttingen–Heidelberg*

Genom symbol	Genom complex	Hereditary plastom	Genom symbol	Genom complex	Hereditary plastom
A*	A$_2$	^{h}*franciscana*	I	B	*flavens*	II
		^{h}*hookeri*	I		*rubens*	II
		velans	III		*excellens*	III
					gaudens	III
	A$_1$	*laxans*	I		*augens*	IV
		undans	I		*pingens*	IV
		^{h}*purpurata*	II		*subpingens*	IV
		albicans	II			
		punctulans	III	C	*curvans*	IV
		rigens	IV		*flectens*	IV
					percurvans	IV
					subcurvans	IV
					dilatans	V

*Two distinct subgroups can be recognized within the A genom. They are divided into A$_2$ corresponding to the species *O. hookeri*, and A$_1$ corresponding to the species *O. strigosa* of Cleland's classification.

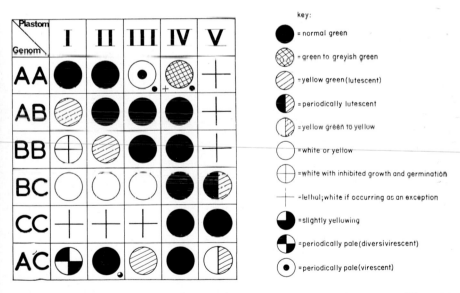

FIG. IX.2. *Compatibility relations between different diploid genoms and plastom types. The use of two signs in some squares depends on slight differences between the A complexes. Redrawn by permission from Stubbe, W. (1964). Genetica 35, 28–33. Figure 4, and Martinus Nijhoff, Den Haag*

to North American species. As a result it has been possible for Stubbe to show that all six possible diploid combinations are represented within the ten species of Cleland, and furthermore, he has been able to assign one of the five plastom types to each species. Thus the connection between the diploid genom complement and the plastom of each species can now be incorporated as an integral part of a phylogenetic tree (Fig. IX.1).

Stubbe's conclusions regarding genom-plastom relationships have been compared with the actual results obtained by Cleland (1935; 1937) and fellow workers[12, 38, 80] from intercrossing North American *Euoenotheras*, and they have been found to be in good agreement. However, not unexpectedly, while agreeing on the numbers of genom classes, Cleland (1962a) does find a few cases in which his results do not fit Stubbe's scheme perfectly, and he expresses doubt on the necessity to distinguish between plastoms II and III, but Stubbe has continued to do so.

IX.4.iii. THE EVALUATION OF THE PLASTOM

Little if any attention has been paid to the role of the plastom in evolution. But in *Oenothera*, at least, Stubbe (1959a, b; 1963a; 1964) has been able to show that this neglect is not justified. For, as we shall now see, the plastom is by no means without evolutionary significance.

IX.4.iii.a. *The oldest plastom*

In all phylogenetic studies it is of great importance to be able either actually to find the oldest ancestor of the family tree, or at least to assess what particular features it must have had. If we accept that today's species evolved from a common ancestor, then today's plastoms must have evolved from the particular plastom possessed by this ancestral type. It is therefore worth inquiring whether there is any evidence for the present-day existence of the ancestral plastom.

The compatibility relations between the different genoms and plastoms shows that of the five plastom types, only plastom IV is compatible with both the B and C genom as well as part of the A genom. It is therefore plausible that the evolution of the three main genoms could have occurred from a common ancestor containing plastom IV. Now the researches of Schötz and others (see VIII.5) have shown that the five plastom types can be arranged in order of multiplication rates as follows: $I > II \approx III > V > IV$. Plastom IV stands out as the type with the slowest multiplication rate, showing it to be the most primitive type. That the slowest plastom must be the most primitive is clear when one realizes that a new plastom mutant would have to be able to multiply faster than the older in order to compete with it successfully in a mixed cell and subsequently to replace it. Hence of the five plastoms in existence today, plastom IV is probably the oldest type, but it is possible that it too may have superseded an even older plastom.

IX.4.iii.b. *The consequences of multiplication differences*

When Stubbe plotted the distribution of the existing ten species among the potentially normal green combinations, he found that not all of the normal green squares were occupied (Fig. IX.3). It is probable

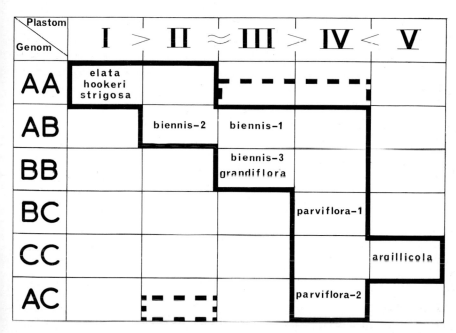

FIG. IX.3. *Distribution of the natural species of* Oenothera, *subgenus* Euoenothera, *among the compatible combinations indicated by the framed squares. The signs between the plastoms I–V refer to the relative multiplication rates of the plastids. Redrawn by permission from Stubbe, W. (1964). Genetica* **35**, *28–33. Figure 5, and Martinus Nijhoff, Den Haag*

that some of these missing combinations existed in the past, because there are still complex heterozygotic species which do possess these plastid types. Moreover, all the gaps are adjoining plastid types with a faster multiplication rate. Hence the former combination AA-II could have been replaced by the faster multiplying plastom I to give the three species with the combination AA-I. Similarly, the combination BB-IV may have been replaced by the faster plastom III to give BB-III, and CC-IV by the faster plastom V to give CC-V. The *biennis* and *grandiflora* species may also have been derived from plastom type IV following the origin of the faster multiplying plastoms II and III. This concept of the replacement of a slower by a faster multiplying plastom is particularly useful for it explains how it is possible for the homozygous species to possess the most primitive genoms AA, BB, and CC without possessing the most primitive plastom IV.

IX.4.iii.c. *The development of functionless pollen*

We have seen earlier that of the two haploid genoms of a complex heterozygote, one frequently functions in the male gamete and the other in the female gamete, thus providing the ideal mechanism for ensuring that all offspring are heterozygous. But how does this mechanism arise? Renner (1919a, b) found from crossing experiments that certain combinations of genoms and plastoms produce living but non-germinating pollen. The development of viable but functionless pollen is clearly a reaction of the male gametophyte with the plastom since there is no correlation between pollen sterility and the presence or absence of chlorophyll deficiency in the parent sporophyte. Furthermore, it seems probable that the inactivation of the pollen is due to the properties of the plastom because in variegated plants containing two types of plastid, the border between the two corresponds to the border between the development of active and the development of inactive pollen[86, 88].

Stubbe (1963a; 1964) suggests that the formation of certain hybrids might result in the production of a heterogamous complex heterozygote according to the following example: If the homozygotes CC-IV and BB-III are crossed together, a typical *parviflora*-1 is produced, namely BC-IV/(III). Plastom III turns white with this diploid genom complex and is therefore of no further importance. It is possible that the combination B-IV will be unable to produce germinable pollen, while C-IV pollen is fully functional. On the other hand, the C-complex may be inactive in the female gametophyte as a result of megaspore competition. Now if the inactivation of one complex in the pollen coincides with the inactivation of the other complex in the embryo sac, the hybrid will be from the very beginning a perfectly heterogamous complex heterozygote, providing the chromosome ring requirements are fulfilled at the same time.

Besides differences in the germination of the pollen, Renner (1919b) also noticed differences in the shape of the starch grains within the pollen. The active pollen usually possessed long, spindle-shaped grains whereas the inactive pollen most frequently possessed abnormal rounder grains. It seems likely that the rounder grain is an expression of the incompatibility between the plastom and the haploid genom, but there does not appear to be any particular meaning to the difference from an evolutionary standpoint.

IX.4.iii.d. *The plastom as a barrier to hybridization*

Hybridization between species carrying different plastoms has shown that in certain combinations the female, and in other combinations the male plastom is unable to develop green chloroplasts with the hybrid nucleus. These combinations can now be predicted from a study of the compatibility chart (Fig. IX.2). The chart also shows that in some combinations neither parent is able to develop normal green chloroplasts with the hybrid nucleus. For example, the reciprocal crosses AB-III × CC-V would be expected to give AC-III/V and BC-III/V embryos. The chart shows that neither plastom III nor plastom V can produce normal green chloroplasts with either the AC or the BC hybrid nucleus and the chlorophyll deficient seedlings would be unlikely to survive in the wild. Similarly, the cross BB-III × CC-V would produce the same BC-III/V hybrid. Hence species with such genom-plastom combinations are genetically isolated from each other, and the plastom differentiation is responsible for the barrier to hybridization.

IX.5. The Physiological Behaviour of Non-harmonious Genom-plastom Combinations

IX.5.i. INHIBITION OF EMBRYO DEVELOPMENT

The compatibility chart (Fig. IX.2) shows that most non-harmonious genom-plastom combinations succeed in producing F_1 seedlings with varying degrees of chlorophyll deficiency. But in the combinations CC-I, CC-II, CC-III and AA-V, AB-V, BB-V and certain AA-IV types the genom-plastom interaction is so severe that it results in an almost complete inhibition of embryo development so that, with rare exceptions, only empty seeds are produced. Nevertheless, Stubbe (1963b) has found it possible to synthesize these lethal combinations, except the particularly lethal AA-IV and AA-V, as chimeras in conjunction with more compatible plastoms introduced through the pollen. For example, the cross AC-II × CC-V has given green-white variegated seedlings having the combination CC-II/V, in which the white tissue is CC-II and the green CC-V. As well as a few chimeras Stubbe obtained many pure green CC-V seedlings, in which the plastids were derived entirely from the father, and many empty seeds. In fact this predominantly paternal plastid inheritance was observed in all the above combinations in which the female plastom was highly incompatible and the male plastom reasonably compatible with the hybrid nucleus. Now a predominantly male inheritance of plastids is quite contrary to the usual rule of a predominantly female plastid inheritance in *Oenothera*. So how can we account for this phenomenon?

The simplest and most likely explanation of these results is that the compatible male plastids overrun the incompatible female plastids in the mixed cells early in embryogenesis owing to their faster multiplication. This would be possible on the assumption that the plastids in extreme genom-plastom combinations are seriously inhibited in their development and division. Moreover, such a plastid inhibition would very likely lead to an inhibition of cell division resulting in the observed early death of the embryos. The introduction of compatible plastids from the male would not alter the inhibited division of the female plastids, but the normal division of the male plastids would allow a normal cell division and hence embryo development would proceed normally, but with male instead of female plastids. The fertilized egg cell would, of course, contain many more female than male plastids; it would only be during the following embryo divisions that their faster multiplication would enable the male plastids to overtake the initial advantage of the female plastids in many embryos. Nevertheless, as the result of chance but favourable sorting-out, some of the female plastids could still be present in mixed cells leading to the formation of the cotyledons and the shoot apex, and these cells would give rise to the variegated seedlings. But if by chance sorting-out all the male plastids were eliminated from the main cell lineage, which would be especially likely in the first few divisions before the advantage of their faster multiplication began to cancel out their initial disadvantage of fewer numbers, then the developing embryo would now have effectively only female plastids and would therefore perish, thus accounting for the many empty seeds observed.

The development of the variegated seedlings is remarkable through demonstrating that, at least after germination, the white tissue is able to grow quite successfully, although of course dependent upon the green tissue of the chimera for its nutrition. Hence the assumed inhibition of plastid and consequently cell division, caused by the lack of harmony between the hybrid nucleus and the incompatible female plastids during early embryogenesis, must have ceased. This suggests that the inhibition is temporary like the periodical bleaching to be found in many hybrids, of which more will be said shortly.

Besides chimeras, Stubbe also obtained a number of so-called 'irregulare' seedlings which are characterized by somewhat deformed leaves owing to an abnormal development of the epidermis. He disagrees with earlier suggestions that the deformity is caused by a dauer-modification of the green tissues. Instead he suggests, from several useful observations, the more likely explanation that these plants are periclinal chimeras with incompatible plastids in the epidermal cells and compatible plastids in the cells of L II and L III. Moreover, in one particularly favourable example he was able to prove the periclinal structure.

IX.5.ii. PERIODICAL CHANGES IN THE INTERACTION BETWEEN NUCLEUS AND PLASTIDS

Hybrid chlorophyll deficient seedlings show every gradation from almost normal green to completely white (Fig. IX.2). The deficiency, however, is not constant, instead many workers[3, 53, 55, 56, 83, 85] observed periodic changes in the intensity of greening during the subsequent development. Under normal daylight most of the weaker seedlings die but Schötz and Reiche (1957) were able to keep many of these alive under weak illumination. Hence, for the first time, the behaviour of a really wide range of hybrids could be followed.

Schötz (1958b; 1959) found that in a great many hybrids the periodical changes caused by the incompatibility between the nucleus and the plastids could be divided into a first green phase, a phase of disturbance called the bleaching phase and a second green phase; during the second green phase further disturbances sometimes occurred. The bleaching phase varied between hybrids both in the time of its onset in the cotyledon, and also in its duration. The bleaching was of two kinds. It either affected only the plastids of newly formed cells, primary action, or it also bleached the green plastids of cells which were already developed before the disturbance set in, secondary action. On the basis of these behavioural differences Schötz has classified the hybrids into the following six types:

(1) The *albivelutina* type: *albicans.velans* with *lamarckiana* plastids.

Immediately after germination the cotyledons are normal green, but within 8–10 days the primary bleaching action sets in and lasts for 2–3 months; there is no secondary bleaching action. All the new tissues formed in this period are pale. During the bleaching period the plastids develop a vacuolar degeneration and become reduced in number per cell, as a result of which the growth of the pale parts is somewhat inhibited as seen particularly clearly in chimeras with a compatible green plastom. After the 11th–12th leaf, the new leaves are perfectly green again and the youngest pale leaves may also turn green showing that the damage to the chloroplasts was not so bad as to be irreversible. In the field the plants are now quite resistant to direct sunlight and are even able to flower in the first year.

(2) The *laxidilatata* type: *laxans.dilitans* with *bauri* plastids.

After germination the cotyledons are normal green, but within 6–10 days the primary bleaching action sets in and affects the still growing base of the cotyledons. The bleaching period lasts only 4–5 days and is followed by the second green period. Since the cotyledons are still growing at the base, the transverse white band developed during the short bleaching period is followed by a basal green zone. During these changes the original green tip of the cotyledons slowly becomes paler owing to a secondary bleaching action until eventually it is hardly distinguishable from the white transverse band; hence the mature cotyledons are divided into a white apex and a green base. During the second green period the leaves are sometimes pale or yellow flecked showing that the nucleus and plastids are still not in perfect harmony with each other. The plants can, however, be grown in the field without too much damage from sunshine, although their growth is not good enough to bring them into flower in the first year.

(3) The *hookericurva* type: *hhookeri.curvans* with *hookeri* plastids.

The cotyledons are green at first but in the second week they begin to lose their colour owing to the onset of a secondary bleaching action. At the same time a primary bleaching action causes the new growth to be pale. At this stage the weakest seedlings die. The survivors enter the second green phase during the development of the first leaves in about the fifth week after germination, consequently these leaves have a pale apex and a green base. All the later leaves are green, but they are sensitive to sunlight and the plants can only be kept alive by growing them under weak illumination.

(4) The *pictirubata* type: *pingens.rubens* with *biennis* plastids.

The cotyledons are green until the bleaching action sets in after five days. The cotyledons then become pale on the margins and base owing to the primary action on the new growth and, at the same time, a secondary bleaching destroys the original green pigmentation causing the cotyledons to become pale all over. At this stage many seedlings die. The survivors enter the second green phase in the course of developing the first pair of leaves, which therefore have a pale apex and a green base. The following leaves are green, but the plants must be grown in weak light to survive.

(5) The *hookeriflexa* type: *hhookeri.flectens* with *hookeri* plastids.

The first green period is completely lacking. Consequently, the cotyledons remain cream or yellow-green or pale green, depending upon the particular hybrid, throughout this initial three-week period of disturbance. During this time most seedlings perish. In the fourth week the new basal cotyledonary growth of the survivors is green, similarly the first and following leaves are green. The plants can be cultivated only under weak illumination.

(6) The *rubiflexa* type: *rubens.flectens* with *biennis* plastids.

The cotyledons are cream owing to the complete absence of the first green period. All the pure seedlings die. But some seedlings may be preserved as chimeras with green *atrovirens* plastids introduced from the pollen. Observations of the white tissues in the chimeras shows that they also fail to develop a second green period. Thus the disharmony between the *biennis* plastids and the *rubens.flectens* nuclear genotype lasts throughout development.

Each of these six groups is representative of many other genom-plastom combinations which Schötz and others have studied. In addition a gene mutant, *O. lamarckiana* mut. *vetaurea*, produces similar periodical changes. A detailed study of this plant showed[59] that the disturbance phase was able to start at quite different times in individual plants, although ending at the same time. In this way a whole series of different bleaching patterns was produced depending upon the stage of growth affected. This led Schötz to conclude that fundamentally the six hybrid groups also differ from each other only by variations in the commencement and duration of the disturbance phase, together with differences between primary and secondary bleaching action. Hence, bearing in mind, as well as these factors, the methods of cotyledonary and leaf growth Schötz was able to develop a general pictorial scheme for all the many variations in the appearance of the bleaching pattern, including both the patterns that he had observed and the theoretical patterns that could be expected. This scheme will clearly be of great value in describing new *Oenothera* hybrids. It may also turn out to be of more general application should similar periodical disturbances between the nucleus and the plastids be found in interspecific hybrids of other genera.

More recently Schötz and Senser have begun to investigate the behaviour of the plastids during the bleaching period in hybrids from the different groups. The *albivelutina* type[79] shows an inhibition of plastid growth together with a hindrance to the normal process of differentiation. There is also an increase in vacuolization, and an inhibition of plastid division which sometimes leads to the development of giant plastids. In addition all cells appear to contain a lesser or greater number of small undifferentiated young plastids, besides fully developed chloroplasts. The combined effect of these processes is to produce cells characterized by a great variety of plastid forms. In the *pictirubata* type[68] plastid development is characterized by an inhibition in the development of the normal number of grana, by the appearance of lipids and by the vacuolization of the plastids which leads to their bursting. Thus the two types so far studied are clearly different from one another, and they also differ from a leaf-bleaching gene mutant, *O. suaveolens* mut 'Weissherz'[61, 67], with which the authors have made comparisons.

Besides these differences in plastid structure and development, Schötz and Bathelt (1964; 1965) have also found differences in the pigment content between the *albivelutina*, the *pictirubata* and the Weissherz types[63]. It will be interesting to see, when more types have been studied, whether or not specific differences in plastid development and pigmentation during the bleaching can be related to any of the six diploid genom combinations, or to any of the five plastoms recognized by Stubbe.

IX.5.iii. PHOTOSTABILITY OF BLEACHING HYBRIDS

The six types of bleaching hybrids were classified by differences between the timing and duration of the bleaching phase and that of the first and second green phases. But there are also important differences between hybrids in the second green phase in regard to the stability of their plastids towards light. Schötz (1958b) recognizes the following four types:

(1) Plants like *O. lamarckiana vetaurea*, *O. albivelutina* (*albicans.velans*) with *lamarckiana* plastids and *O. laxisubcurva* (*laxans.subcurvans*) with *bauri* plastids, which are so photostable that they can be planted outdoors in full sunlight and brought to flower in their first year.

(2) Plants like *O. laxidilata* (*laxans.dilitans*), *O. laxipercurva* (*laxans. percurvans*) and *O. laxicurva* (*laxans.curvans*), all with *bauri* plastids, which also have a high pigment content. They can similarly be planted outdoors without being seriously damaged by the sun. Nevertheless, there are sufficient disturbances between the nucleus and plastids to prevent them from flowering until their second year.

(3) Plants like *O. pictirubata* (*pingens.rubens*) and *O. auctirubata* (*augens.rubens*) with *biennis* plastids, and also *O. hookeriflexa* (*ʰhookeri. flectens*) with *hookeri* plastids, in which the recovery of harmony between nucleus and plastids in the second green period is far from perfect. The young leaves are green and capable of photosynthesis[57, 58], but they become increasingly bleached in sunlight, owing to the breakdown of the plastid grana and lamella structure, until almost white. By this time the leaves are quite inactive. These extremely photolabile forms[24], which are unable to survive in direct sunlight, do, however, remain green in weak light in which they can be kept alive.

(4) Plants like *O. rubiflexa* (*rubens.flectens*) or *O. rubipercurva* (*rubens. percurvans*) with *biennis* plastids, in which the second green period never appears, not even in chimeras. The plastids are evidently upset at a much earlier stage of development than in the first three groups; they are clearly quite incapable of any photosynthesis and, except as chimeras, the plants cannot be kept alive.

IX.5.iv. PHOTOSYNTHETIC ABILITY

Although pale coloured bleaching hybrids with only a little chlorophyll are able to be kept alive in weak light, similar plants containing defect mutant plastids usually die, even if they are actually much greener than the bleaching hybrids. Investigating this curious phenomenon further, Schötz (1955; 1956) found, by manometric determinations of the production of oxygen during daylight, that the bleaching hybrids were able to photosynthesize, whereas the plants with defect mutant plastids were unable to do so. Hence in the case of other plants with defect mutant plastids it is not the shortage of chlorophyll that prevents their survival. Moreover, since under weak illumination there is a demonstrable increase in green coloration, it is doubtful if the primary action of the mutation is to disturb chlorophyll synthesis; it appears to be some other factor connected with photosynthesis that is primarily upset. In a few plastid mutants, however, even this disturbance is not too serious since the plants survive (see VII.2.iii), whereas in a few hybrids the bleaching is so intense that chlorophyll is never formed and the seedlings die.

IX.6. Distinction between the Action of the Plastom and Non-plastom Extra-nuclear Components in the Subgenus *Raimannia*

IX.6.i. SIMILARITIES BETWEEN THE SUBGENERA *RAIMANNIA* AND *EUOENOTHERA*

For over three decades the two species *O. odorata* and *O. berteriana* within the subgenus *Raimannia*, and crosses between them, have been the object of intensive investigations by Schwemmle and his colleagues. Like many of the *Euoenotheras*, the two species are complex heterozygotes with rings of fourteen chromosomes. Their two haploid genoms, which are transmitted by both male and female gametes, have been called v and I from *O. odorata* and B and l from *O. berteriana*[70]. The choice of these letters, which appears to be meaningless, was criticized by Renner (1937b) but unfortunately the classification remains unchanged.

Similar to many reciprocal crosses between species within the subgenus *Euoenothera*, crosses between *O. berteriana* and *O. odorata* produce normal green seedlings when *berteriana* is the mother, but in the reciprocal cross, when *odorata* is the mother, many of the hybrid seedlings are chlorophyll deficient[50, 70]. Moreover, owing to a few plastids being transmitted by the pollen to the egg, some of the hybrid seedlings are variegated[50, 77]. The biparental plastid transmission is also confirmed by the inheritance of mutant plastids[71, 77].

IX.6.ii. SYNTHESIS OF DIFFERENT COMBINATIONS OF GENOM, PLASTOM, AND NON-PLASTOM COMPONENTS

IX.6.ii.a. *Terms and abbreviations*

Ever since they first began their investigations Schwemmle and his colleagues have separated the extra-nuclear components of the cell into the plastids and the plasma. Today the mitochondria have been given a genetic status similar to that of thc plastids in some organisms, so presumably the mitochondriom is included with the plasma in the sense of Schwemmle. In the following account of crossing experiments the plastids or plastom will be abbreviated to Pl., and the plasma, which will be referred to as the cytoplasm, will be abbreviated to Cyt. where appropriate. Also the species *O. berteriana* and *O. odorata* will be abbreviated to *bert.* and *od.* respectively.

IX.6.ii.b. *The initial reciprocal crosses*

After reciprocal crosses between *O. berteriana* and *O. odorata* four hybrid complex combinations are to be expected; lethal factors prevent the development of the homozygotes. In practice, however, all the complexes are not obtained; moreover there are marked reciprocal differences in the nature of the offspring as follows:

(1) *O. berteriana* (B.l)♀ × *O. odorata* (v.I)♂: *bert.* Cyt., *bert.* Pl. The hybrid complex B.v is not formed owing to selective fertilization

> B.I is normal
> l.v is normal
> l.I is normal

whereas in the reciprocal cross:

(2) *O. odorata* (v.I)♀ × *O. berteriana* (B.l)♂: *od.* Cyt., *od.* Pl. The hybrid complex B.v is normal

> B.I is pale green and weak
> l.v is pale green and weak
> l.I is lethal and dies at the embryo stage

Thus in no case do offspring with the same hybrid nucleus behave in the same way after reciprocal crosses. For instance, in the extreme case of the l.I hybrid complex, the offspring are normal with *berteriana* cytoplasm and plastids, but they die during embryo development with *odorata* cytoplasm and plastids, as was also the case in certain incompatible genom-plastom combinations in *Euoenothera*. In fact the l.I hybrid embryos die even if the cytoplasm is from *berteriana* so long as the plastids are from *odorata*[77]; early death of certain hybrid embryos was also observed after crosses between *O. berteriana* or *O. odorata* and *O. hookeri*, that is, after crosses between two subgenera[25]. Hence the varying reaction between the hybrid nucleus and the genetically different plastoms of the two species appears to be the main cause for the reciprocal differences, just as was concluded by Renner for reciprocal differences between interspecific hybrids of *Euoenothera* species.

In addition to the pure green or pale green seedlings, a few variegated offspring are also produced owing to the transmission of plastids by the pollen. For example, the hybrid offspring with the constitution (l.v *bert.* Cyt., *bert.* Pl.) are green, but if in the initial cross a few *odorata* plastids enter into some of the zygotes and subsequently sort-out they produce cells with the constitution (l.v *bert.* Cyt., *od.* Pl.), which are pale green. These hybrid variegated offspring sort-out into pure green, pale green, sectorial, and periclinal shoots during their further growth. Hence the two types can be separated from each other. However, not all the possible combinations of genoms, plastoms, and cytoplasms can be achieved so easily.

IX.6.ii.c. *New plastom–cytoplasm combinations under similar genoms*

By the initial reciprocal crosses all the possible hybrid genom complexes are produced, along with those of the parents, but only certain of the plastom and cytoplasm combinations. For example, in the case of the species *O. odorata* with the v.I genom the following four combinations are possible:

(1) v.I   *od.* Cyt.,   *od.* Pl. (*O. odorata*)
(2) v.I   *od.* Cyt., *bert.* Pl.
(3) v.I *bert.* Cyt.,   *od.* Pl.
(4) v.I *bert.* Cyt., *bert.* Pl.

Of these four combinations, only the first exists to start with, and the remaining three must be synthesized. This may be done by a series of crosses which can be shown schematically as follows, after Arnold (1963):

(2) Synthesis of v.I *od.* Cyt., *bert.* Pl.

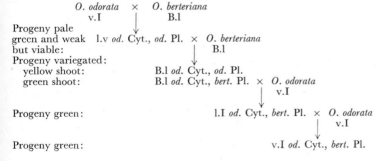

At each step the required progeny must be separated from others that are not needed and which have therefore not been included in the scheme.

(3) Synthesis of v.I *bert.* Cyt., *od.* Pl.

O. berteriana × *O. odorata*
                B.l | v.I
Progeny variegated:
  green shoot: l.v *bert.* Cyt., *bert.* Pl.
  pale green shoot: l.v *bert.* Cyt., *od.* Pl. × *O. odorata*
                                                 | v.I

Progeny green: v.I *bert.* Cyt., *od.* Pl.

Again only the required progeny have been included in the scheme.

(4) Synthesis of v.I *bert.* Cyt., *bert.* Pl.

O. berteriana × *O. odorata*
                B.l | v.I
Progeny variegated:
  pale green shoot: l.v *bert.* Cyt., *od.* Pl.
  green shoot: l.v *bert.* Cyt., *bert.* Pl. × *O. odorata*
                                                   | v.I

Progeny green: v.I *bert.* Cyt., *bert.* Pl.

Again only the required progeny have been included in the scheme.

IX.6.ii.d. *Are the cell components really constant?*

In the four genom–plastom–cytoplasm combinations with the similar genom we may be fairly certain that the plastoms are as stated because the reaction of the *berteriana* and *odorata* plastids with a particular hybrid nucleus is distinct at each stage of the synthesis. But can we be so sure of the constancy of the cytoplasm and the genom?

In synthesizing two of the above genom–plastom–cytoplasm combinations, the required plastids have to be introduced from the pollen parent, and it is probable that some male cytoplasm enters the egg at the same time. Hence the female cytoplasm cannot be assumed to be pure. Nevertheless, since the proportion of plastids from the male is small compared with the proportion of plastids from the female, it may be assumed that the female cytoplasm is at least quantitatively predominant. Moreover no sorting-out of male cytoplasm from female cytoplasm is observed, which suggests that, in those cases in which the male cytoplasm is successfully transmitted, the two cytoplasms mix. It further suggests that the female cytoplasm is also qualitatively predominant. A detailed discussion of this question has been given by Hagemann (1964).

The constancy of the genoms is dependent upon the lack of chromosome reshuffling and gene recombination between the haploid complexes at meiosis. Now the two species *O. berteriana* and *O. odorata* are both complex heterozygotes with all their chromosomes united in a ring of fourteen. Hence there is no chromosome exchange between the complements of their respective haploid complexes, and since chiasmata are restricted to the chromosome ends, gene recombination is extremely limited. Whereas, according to Haustein (1952), the chromosome configurations at meiosis in the four diploid hybrid complexes are as follows:

l.v	14 ring	
B.v	10 + 2 + 2	one ring and two bivalents
B.I	6 + 6 + 2	two rings and one bivalent
l.I	8 + 4 + 2	two rings and one bivalent

This means that in the three hybrids, which do not form a 14-chromosome ring, a reshuffling of chromosomes at meiosis is inevitable. Hence, although it may be still possible for the characteristic features of the complexes to be recognizable, it is not true to say that all the individuals have an identical genom; at best they are only similar. This must clearly be borne in mind when assessing the behaviour of different plastom–cytoplasm combinations under so-called constant genoms.

IX.6.iii. CHARACTERS MODIFIED BY THE PLASTOM AND CYTOPLASM?

IX.6.iii.a. *Leaf shape and dentation*

The species *O. berteriana* (B.l) has a more strongly toothed and somewhat larger leaf than *O. odorata* (v.I). According to Schwemmle (1938; 1941b; 1943) the B.I hybrids between them produced the following leaf shapes:

B.I	*bert.* Cyt.,	*bert.* Pl.	large, strongly toothed leaves
B.I	*od.* Cyt.,	*bert.* Pl.	large, strongly toothed leaves
B.I	*od.* Cyt.,	*od.* Pl.	small, weakly toothed leaves

The same result was achieved even after forming the same hybrids by different parental crosses. Schwemmle therefore concluded that the difference between them was significant and must be due to the varying reaction of the *berteriana* and *odorata* plastids, since varying cytoplasms clearly had no effect. Yet as far as can be judged from published drawings[2, 16, 17, 18, 77] the distinction between *O. berteriana* and *O. odorata* is clear enough, but the differences between the above three B.I hybrid combinations seem to be far less than the differences between their parents. The two hybrids with *berteriana* plastids have leaf sizes and dentation intermediate between that of the two parents; to call them large and strongly toothed like *O. berteriana* seems to be exaggerated. The hybrid with *odorata* plastids does appear to be slightly less toothed and perhaps slightly smaller. But this difference may well be due to the fact that the two hybrids with *berteriana* plastids are green, whereas, owing to the disharmony between the *odorata* plastids and the B.I hybrid nucleus, the third hybrid with *odorata* plastids is pale green. It therefore seems likely that the differences between the two *berteriana*-plastom hybrids and the *odorata*-plastom hybrid may simply be a reflection of the weaker growth of the latter resulting in weaker leaf dentation and smaller leaf size.

Thus the conclusion that the leaf size and dentation is dependent upon the plastom is unconvincing. Moreover a direct influence of the *berteriana* plastids on the leaf does not exist, otherwise plants with the *odorata* complex, v.I, and *berteriana* plastids would be more strongly toothed than pure *odorata* plants with their own *odorata* plastids, which is apparently not the case. The plastom action is therefore explained on the basis that in the B.I hybrid with *berteriana* plastids, a gene of the I-complex, which influences leaf form, is inhibited by the *berteriana* plastom. This enables a gene of the B-complex to act, which causes the strong leaf dentation. In the case of the B.I hybrid with *odorata* plastids the gene of the B-complex is inhibited by the *odorata* plastids, which enables the I complex to cause the weak leaf dentation. This explanation, however, is purely theoretical and it depends on the action of certain hypothetical genes, whose existence has yet to be demonstrated.

IX.6.iii.b. *Hypanthia length*

Parallel to the experiments on leaf dentation, the same plants have been used to determine the hypanthia length of flowers, that is the length of the corolla tube[72, 73, 77]. In one set of measurements, quoted from Hagemann (1964), the following lengths were obtained:

> B.I *bert.* Cyt., *bert.* Pl.   34·3 mm ± 0·1 mm
> B.I *od.* Cyt., *bert.* Pl.   36·5 mm ± 0·1 mm
> B.I *od.* Cyt., *od.* Pl.   38·4 mm ± 0.1 mm

The increase in length between the first and second measurement is attributed to the effect of *odorata* cytoplasm instead of *berteriana* cytoplasm, and the further increase in length between the second and third measurement is attributed to the effect of *odorata* plastids instead of *berteriana* plastids. In other words, both the *odorata* cytoplasm and plastom cause an increase in the hypanthia length. The same set of measurements made in different years showed a similar gradation in hypanthia length between the three B.I hybrids, although the difference between them was not always so great. Comparable measurements with other complex combinations showed that the hypanthia were always longest in plants with an *odorata* cytoplasm. The question again arises, are these differences really significant? This is not easy to answer because the accurate measurement of growth is very difficult, owing to the many environmental factors that affect it. Even two plants of the same clone grown under identical conditions often appear different, for instance, they may not branch at the same nodes, they may not begin flowering at the same time, they may differ in the number of flowers in an inflorescence and so forth. The *Oenothera* plants were not clonal; their genoms were indeed similar but probably not identical. Moreover they were grown outdoors subject to all the effects of a continually changing environment. Hence the hypanthia lengths would be bound to vary as of course they did. It is not so certain, however, that the extent of this variation is taken sufficiently into account in assessing the mean hypanthia length, and it is doubtful if even a difference of as much as 10 per cent is really meaningful for such a plastic factor as growth in length. Finally, if there is a true significant statistical difference, what then is the biological significance?

IX.6.iii.c. *Selective fertilization*

After crosses between *O. berteriana* and *O. odorata* three of the four possible hybrid complexes are formed, but not the B.v hybrid. This is not because B pollen will not germinate; it must do so to give the B.I hybrid. It is also not because the v eggs are lethal; they must be viable to give the I.v hybrid. Hence the failure to give the B.v hybrid is attributed to selective fertilization. It appears that the v eggs will not accept the B pollen, hence the affinity between the two is said to be nil. Now Schwemmle (1952; 1957a, b) and Arnold (1958; 1963) suggest that the different frequencies of fertilization found in different crosses is similarly related to the particular affinities of the male and female gametes for one another, and the measure of fertilization serves as a measure of the affinity.

By making crosses with females having a constant genom, but with all four plastom–cytoplasm combinations, Schwemmle (1957b) was able to determine the effect of the cytoplasm and plastom on the affinity between two complexes. Thus in the following crosses the four types of *O. odorata* (v.I) as mother were crossed with pollen carrying the I complex, firstly with *odorata* cytoplasm and plastids, and secondly with *berteriana* cytoplasm and plastids. Schwemmle obtained the following affinity values:

(1) v eggs for I pollen with (a) *od.* Cyt., *od.* Pl. (b) *bert.* Cyt., *bert.* Pl.
od. Cyt., *od.* Pl. × (a) = 25·0 (28·2–21·9); × (b) = 29·5 (31·4–27·0)
od. Cyt., *bert.* Pl. × (a) = 20·6 (24·7–16·3); × (b) = 21·6 (22·7–20·1)
bert. Cyt., *od.* Pl. × (a) = 21·6 (25·1–19·5); × (b) = 24·1 (27·1–21·6)
bert. Cyt., *bert.* Pl. × (a) = 25·4 (27·6–23·6); × (b) = 28·0 (32·5–24·2)

The affinity is taken as the mean value for the percentage fertilization of v or I eggs by I pollen.

> (2) I eggs for I pollen with (a) *od.* Cyt., *od.* Pl. (b) *bert.* Cyt., *bert.* Pl.
> *od.*   Cyt.,   *od.* Pl. × (a) = 26·8 (29·0–22·1); × (b) = 27·1 (29·0–24·9)
> *od.*   Cyt., *bert.* Pl. × (a) = 25·4 (27·7–23·2); × (b) = 27·3 (29·7–25·4)
> *bert.* Cyt.,   *od.* Pl. × (a) = 26·3 (27·3–24·9); × (b) = 27·0 (29·6–25·2)
> *bert.* Cyt., *bert.* Pl. × (a) = 35·0 (36·1–34·0); × (b) = 35·2 (38·2–30·3)

By comparing various groups of these results certain conclusions have been drawn. For instance, Schwemmle concludes that the affinity of I pollen for v eggs (1) is greater when the I pollen contains the *berteriana* cytoplasm and plastom (b) than when the I pollen contains the *odorata* cytoplasm and plastom (a). This is because each of the four affinity values with *berteriana* is higher than the corresponding values with *odorata* cytoplasm and plastom. A less marked difference in the same direction is shown by the affinity of I pollen for I eggs (2), but this time Schwemmle did not think the difference significant.

Other groups of results may be compared to determine the effect of differences in the plastom under constant genoms and cytoplasms. For example, the affinity of I pollen (a and b) for I eggs (2), when the eggs contain the *berteriana* cytoplasm, is greater if they also contain *berteriana* plastids than if they contain *odorata* plastids, from which it may be concluded that the plastom is one of the factors modifying the affinity of I pollen for I eggs.

Thus in the opinion of Schwemmle and followers, some results show an influence of the male and others an influence of the female plastom and cytoplasm upon the affinity in specific crosses. But are these conclusions really valid?

One's suspicion of the validity of these conclusions is immediately aroused by the fact that other groups of results can be compared which show no differences in the effect of the cytoplasm and plastom upon the affinity. It seems rather illogical that the same factors should sometimes affect the affinity and sometimes not. Doubt is also raised by the method of obtaining the results. If the affinity values are really valid it should be possible for other workers repeating the crosses to obtain the same results. Since fertilization success is known to be a very variable character, this would surely only be possible if each affinity value was based on the full range of variation in fertility, and if the experimental conditions could be matched as closely as possible. Since Schwemmle was obliged to make his pollinations outdoors over a period of many days, the environmental conditions would not have been constant, thus making it all the more important to allow for this by obtaining the fullest range of fertilization values. This could only have been obtained by making a large number of crosses, and not simply by obtaining a large number of seeds from a few crosses. Schwemmle, however, repeated each cross as little as twenty times to obtain twenty capsules, but of these only the ten with the best seed set were taken into consideration. Hence the affinity value was based only on a selected half of an incomplete fertility range derived from too few crosses. There are no grounds for assuming that an inclusion of the ten ignored capsules would have led to the same conclusions in regard to affinity values. Until the experiments have been repeated using more satisfactory methods of scoring, the none-too-large differences in the present affinity values can hardly be regarded as conclusive beyond reasonable doubt.

IX.6.iii.d. *Photoperiodic behaviour and shoot growth*

Oenothera berteriana (B.l) is an obligatory long day plant requiring a light period of at least 14 hours per day, whereas *O. odorata* (v.I) is a facultative long day plant, which is able to flower with a day length as short as six hours.

By comparing forms with one haploid complex in common but differing in the second complex, Schwemmle (1962) found the sequence I-l-v-B, from the weakest to the strongest response, in the genetic control of the long day reaction. In addition, the cytoplasms too influenced the long day reaction. Combined with any of the hybrid complexes, the critical day length was always increased in plants with *berteriana* cytoplasm, whereas it was decreased in plants with *odorata* cytoplasm.

The plastids had no influence on the photoperiodic behaviour, but they did influence the stem growth, which was unaffected by the cytoplasm. The *odorata* plastom caused the development of a longer shoot than the *berteriana* plastom under similar growth conditions.

These conclusions have been accepted by Arnold (1963) and Hagemann (1964) with the reservation that the differences attributed to the cytoplasms and plastoms might in fact be due to differences in the genoms. The different hybrid complexes used in the experiments were obtained from cultures that had been maintained over many years by selfing. Hence the genoms might not have been as constant as it was assumed, owing to the opportunity for chromosome exchange and gene recombination during this period.

IX.6.iii.e. *Seed germination*

In dark experiments, the germination of seeds containing the *odorata* nucleus, v.I, was found to be inferior and slower with *berteriana* plastids than with *odorata* plastids, suggesting an incompatibility between the *odorata* nucleus and the foreign *berteriana* plastom, which inhibited growth. The different cytoplasms did not affect the reaction[78].

After illumination of the seeds from 2 to 10 hours with 300 lux the two types containing *odorata* plastids germinated equally well. Whereas, of the two hybrids containing *berteriana* plastids, the one with *odorata* cytoplasm showed the worst and the other with *berteriana* cytoplasm showed the best germination. From these results it was concluded that the *berteriana* cytoplasm produces a much lower light requirement of the seeds only in combination with *berteriana* plastids. The latter, on the other hand, retarded the process of germination.

These conclusions are based on results which are said to be statistically significant. This is difficult to check, however, since all data are given as percentage germination, and it is not stated how many seeds were sown in each case. Except in crop plants, which have been especially selected for a high germination, germination is frequently very variable and this appears also to be true of *Oenothera*. To what extent the full range of germination variation has been taken into account before assessing the significance of the results in these experiments is not clear. Furthermore, there is no indication as to whether or not the seeds that failed to germinate were good seeds. It seems quite possible that embryo development may have already become inhibited before the seeds were ripe as is found in *Pelargonium*[93], in which case the observed differences would not really be related to germination at all.

We thus see that in all these interesting cases in which Schwemmle and co-workers have attempted to demonstrate an influence of the cytoplasm or plastom, their experiments are not beyond criticism so that the validity of their conclusions is still questionable. As Hagemann (1964) has stated, the most desirable proof would be an independent confirmation of these findings by other workers.

IX.7. Hybrid variegation in other Genera

Hybrid variegation is not a phenomenon restricted to *Oenothera*, it has been found among the progeny of interspecific crosses of at least five other genera, including, in my opinion, the recent results of Moffett (1965) with *Acacia*, and also among the progeny of crosses between different varieties or races in two further species (Table IX.3). Unfortunately, the results have, for the most part, not been stated very clearly so there is little point in giving actual data. Nevertheless, differences in the effective contributions of male and female plastids are apparent. In the interspecific crosses of *Hypericum*, *Rhododendron*, *Silene* and the crosses between the dusky and bright races of *Medicago truncatula* there

TABLE IX.3. LIST OF PLANTS, ADDITIONAL TO *OENOTHERA*, PRODUCING HYBRID VARIEGATION AFTER CROSSING, INDICATING THE EXISTENCE OF AT LEAST TWO TYPES OF PLASTID AND THE BIPARENTAL INHERITANCE OF THESE PLASTIDS

Genus	Species, varieties or races	Authors	Dates
Interspecific crosses			
Acacia	decurrens, mearnsii	Moffett	1965
Hypericum	acutum, montanum, pulchrum, quadrangulum	Farenholz	1927
		Renner	1929
		Noack	1931b; 32a; 34; 1937a, b
		Herbst	1935
Pelargonium	denticulatum, filicifolium	Chittenden	1927
Rhododendron	hortense, japonicum, kaempferi, mucronatum, obtusum, pulchrum, ripense, serpyllifolium, sublanceolatum, transiens, yedoense	Noguchi	1932
Silene	otites, pseudotites	Newton	1931
Intraspecific crosses			
Geranium	bohemicum, bohemicum deprehensum	Dahlgren	1923; 25
Medicago	truncatula: dusky and bright races	Lilienfeld	1962

are always at least two classes of offspring, green and variegated or chlorophyll deficient and variegated, and in *Rhododendron* and *Hypericum* all three classes may occur. In each case, the greater success of the female plastids, indicating a predominantly female plastid contribution, is clear. On the other hand, the *Geranium* and *Pelargonium* crosses gave entirely variegated offspring; even so a reciprocal difference is detectable. The variegation of the offspring is either predominantly green or predominantly white corresponding to the stronger influence of the maternal parent.

These examples thus provide evidence for the evolution of different plastoms in other genera besides *Oenothera*. Moreover, the observations in *Geranium* and *Medicago* indicate the existence of different plastoms within different races of a single species. It seems that the evolution of the plastom may well be more widespread, and perhaps more important for the origin of new species, than has ever been suspected. In addition, the examples extend the list of plants whose plastids are transmitted by both parents, which suggests that a significant contribution of extra-nuclear particles from the male parent in crosses may also be more common than is generally assumed.

REFERENCES

1.   ARNOLD, C. G. (1958). *Ergeb. Biol.* **20**, 67–96
2.   ARNOLD, C. G. (1963). *Ber. dt. bot. Ges.* **76**, 3–12
3.   BAERECKE, M. L. (1944). *Flora* **138**, 57–92
4.   BAUR, E. (1909). *Z. Vererbungsl.* **1**, 330–351
5.   CHITTENDEN, R. J. (1927). *Bibliogr. genet.* **3**, 355–442
6.   CLELAND, R. E. (1935). *Proc. Amer. Philos. Soc.* **75**, 339–429
7.   CLELAND, R. E. (1937). *Proc. Amer. Philos. Soc.* **77**, 477–542
8.   CLELAND, R. E. (1957). *Cytologia* **22**, 5–19
9.   CLELAND, R. E. (1962a). *Planta* **57**, 699–712
10. CLELAND, R. E. (1962b). *Ad. Genet.* **11**, 147–237
11. CLELAND, R. E. (1964). *Proc. Amer. Philos. Soc.* **108**, 88–98
12. CLELAND, R. E. & HAMMOND, B. L. (1950). *Indiana Univ. Publ. Sci. Ser.* **16**, 10–72
13. DAHLGREN, K. V. O. (1923). *Hereditas* **4**, 239–250
14. DAHLGREN, K. V. O. (1925). *Hereditas* **6**, 237–256
15. FARENHOLZ, H. (1927). *Uber Rassen- und Artkreuzungen in der Gattung Hypericum.* Festschrift Schauinsland, Bremen
16. HAGEMANN, R. (1959). *Plasmatische Vererbung.* Die Neue Brehm-Bücherei, Heft 239. A. Ziemsen, Wittenberg-Lutherstadt
17. HAGEMANN, R. (1964). *Plasmatische Vererbung.* Genetik Grundlagen, Ergebnisse und Probleme in Einzeldarstellungen. Veb Gustav Fischer Verlag, Jena
18. HAGEMANN, R. (1965). *Genetics Today* **3**, 613–625
19. HAUSTEIN, E. (1952). *Z. Vererbungsl.* **84**, 417–453
20. HAUSTEIN, E. (1962). *Z. Vererbungsl.* **93**, 531–533
21. HERBST, W. (1935). *Flora* **129**, 235–259
22. HOEPPENER, E. & RENNER, O. (1929a). *Z. Vererbungsl.* **49**, 1–25
23. HOEPPENER, E. & RENNER, O. (1929b). *Bot. Abh.* **15**, 1–86
24. KANDLER, O. & SCHÖTZ, F. (1956). *Z. Naturf.* **11**b, 708–718
25. KISTNER, G. (1955). *Z. Vererbungsl.* **86**, 521–544
26. KRUMBHOLZ, G. (1925). *Jena Z. Naturw.* **62**, 187–260
27. LILIENFELD, F. A. (1962). *Seiken Ziho* **13**, 3–38
28. MICKAN, M. (1935). *Flora* **130**, 1–20
29. MOFFETT, A. A. (1965). *Heredity* **20**, 609–620
30. MÜHLETHALER, K. & BELL, P. R. (1962). *Naturwiss.* **49**, 63–64
31. NEWTON, W. C. F. (1931). *J. Genet.* **24**, 109–120
32. NOACK, K. L. (1931b). *Z. Vererbungsl.* **59**, 77–101
33. NOACK, K. L. (1932a). *Ber. dt. bot. Ges.* **50**, 256–268
34. NOACK, K. L. (1934). *Z. Bot.* **28**, 1–71
35. NOACK, K. L. (1937a). *Z. Vererbungsl.* **73**, 108–130
36. NOACK, K. L. (1937b). *Z. Vererbungsl.* **73**, 373–375
37. NOGUCHI, Y. (1932). *Jap. J. Bot.* **6**, 103–124
38. PREER, L. B. (1950). *Indiana Univ. Publ. Sci. Ser.* **16**, 160–217
39. RENNER, O. (1917a). *Z. Vererbungsl.* **18**, 121–294
40. RENNER, O. (1917b). *Ber. dt. bot. Ges.* **35**, 21–26
41. RENNER, O. (1919a). *Z. Bot.* **11**, 305–380
42. RENNER, O. (1919b). *Ber. dt. bot. Ges.* **37**, 129–135
43. RENNER, O. (1921). *Z. Bot.* **13**, 609–621
44. RENNER, O. (1922). *Z. Vererbungsl.* **27**, 235–237
45. RENNER, O. (1924). *Biol. Zbl.* **44**, 309–336
46. RENNER, O. (1929). *Handbuch der Vererbungswissenschaft.* Bd. 2, A 1–161. Edited by E. Baur & M. Hartmann. Gebrüder Borntraeger, Berlin

47. RENNER, O. (1934). *Ber. Math. Phys. Kl. Sächs. Akad. Wiss. Lpz.* **86**, 241–266
48. RENNER, O. (1936). *Flora* **130**, 218–290
49. RENNER, O. (1937a). *Flora* **131**, 182–226
50. RENNER, O. (1937b). *Cytologia, Fujii Jubilee* **2**, 644–655
51. RENNER, O. (1942). *Ber. dt. bot. Ges.* **60**, 448–486
52. RENNER, O. (1950). *Ber. dt. bot. Ges.* **63**, 129–138
53. RENNER, O. (1952). *S.B. bayer. Akad. Wiss. Math.-naturw.* Kl.: 2 Mai 1952
54. RENNER, O. (1956). *Planta* **47**, 219–254
55. RENNER, O. (1957). *Planta* **48**, 343–392
56. SCHÖTZ, F. (1954). *Planta* **43**, 182–240
57. SCHÖTZ, F. (1955). *Z. Naturf.* **10b**, 100–108
58. SCHÖTZ, F. (1956). *Photogr. Forsch.* **7**, 12–16
59. SCHÖTZ, F. (1958b). *Planta* **52**, 351–392
60. SCHÖTZ, F. (1959). *Photogr. Forsch.* **8**, 65–72
61. SCHÖTZ, F. (1961). *Ber. dt. bot. Ges.* **74**, 215–216
62. SCHÖTZ, F. (1962a). *Planta* **58**, 333–336
63. SCHÖTZ, F. (1962b). *Planta* **58**, 411–434
64. SCHÖTZ, F. & BATHELT, H. (1964). *Planta* **63**, 213–252
65. SCHÖTZ, F. & BATHELT, H. (1965). *Planta* **64**, 330–362
66. SCHÖTZ, F. & REICHE, G. A. (1957). *Z. Naturf.* **12b**, 757–764
67. SCHÖTZ, F. & SENSER, F. (1961). *Planta* **57**, 235–238
68. SCHÖTZ, F. & SENSER, F. (1964). *Planta* **63**, 191–212
69. SCHWEMMLE, B. (1962). *Planta* **58**, 619–646
70. SCHWEMMLE, J. (1935). *Der Erbarzt* **1**, 179–185
71. SCHWEMMLE, J. (1941a). *Z. Vererbungsl.* **79**, 171–187
72. SCHWEMMLE, J. (1941b). *Z. Vererbungsl.* **79**, 321–335
73. SCHWEMMLE, J. (1943). *Flora* **137**, 61–72
74. SCHWEMMLE, J. (1952). *Biol. Zbl.* **71**, 487–499
75. SCHWEMMLE, J. (1957a). *Biol. Zbl.* **76**, 443–453
76. SCHWEMMLE, J. (1957b). *Biol. Zbl.* **76**, 529–549
77. SCHWEMMLE, J., HAUSTEIN, E., STURM, A., & BINDER, M. (1938). *Z. Vererbungsl.* **75**, 358–800
78. SCHWEMMLE, J. & SCHNEIDER, W. (1965). *Planta* **65**, 167–172
79. SENSER, F. & SCHÖTZ, F. (1964). *Planta* **62**, 171–190
80. STINSON, H. T. (1960). *Genetics* **45**, 821–838
81. STUBBE, W. (1953). *Z. Vererbungsl.* **85**, 180–209
82. STUBBE, W. (1954). VIII Congr. int. Bot. Paris. *Compt. rend. des Seanc. et Rapp. et Communic. deposes lors du Congr.* **10**, 129–130
83. STUBBE, W. (1955). *Photogr. u. Wiss.* **4**, 3–8
84. STUBBE, W. (1957). *Ber. dt. bot. Ges.* **70**, 221–226
85. STUBBE, W. (1958). *Z. Vererbungsl.* **89**, 189–203
86. STUBBE, W. (1959a). *Z. Vererbungsl.* **90**, 288–298
87. STUBBE, W. (1959b). *Recent Ad. Bot.* **2**, 1439–1442
88. STUBBE, W. (1960). *Z. Bot.* **48**, 191–218
89. STUBBE, W. (1962). *Z. Vererbungsl.* **93**, 175–176
90. STUBBE, W. (1963a). *Ber. dt. bot. Ges.* **76**, 154–167
91. STUBBE, W. (1963b). *Z. Vererbungsl.* **94**, 392–411
92. STUBBE, W. (1964). *Genetica* **35**, 28–33
93. TILNEY-BASSETT, R. A. E. (1965). *Heredity* **20**, 451–466

CHAPTER X

The Genetic Material of the Plastid

X.1. Introduction

WE HAVE already seen (Chapters I to IX) that on cytological and genetic grounds the idea has arisen that plastids are autonomous, self-replicating bodies. They appear to multiply independently within the cell, each plastid being derived, by division, from a pre-existing plastid. Certain plastid defects are inherited in such a way as to suggest that the mutated genes reside in the plastid rather than in the nucleus. Thus it appears likely that the plastids contain at least some of the genetic information which controls their own growth and multiplication. In this chapter we shall attempt to identify this plastid genetic material.

Two substances are known, in the form of which genetic information can be stored—deoxyribonucleic acid (DNA) and ribonucleic acid (RNA). We shall therefore consider the evidence for the presence of DNA and RNA in plastids.

X.2. Evidence from Light Microscopy

In principle, the simplest way of detecting the presence of nucleic acids in an organelle is to stain the cells with a dye specific for the nucleic acid in question and see if the organelles take up the stain. Chiba (1951) reported that the leaf chloroplasts of *Selaginella savatieri*, *Tradescantia fluminensis*, and *Rhoeo discolor* were stained by the Feulgen method and by methyl green. The staining could not be detected in leaves which had been treated with hot trichloroacetic acid (which removes nucleic acids). The chloroplasts were also stained by pyronin: this staining was abolished by pretreatment with hot trichloroacetic acid, and was reduced by extraction with ribonuclease. He concluded that chloroplasts contained DNA, and possibly RNA. Metzner (1952) reported that chloroplasts of *Agapanthus umbellatus* were stained by the Feulgen

302

procedure and by pyronin and methyl green; no staining was observed in leaves pretreated with hot trichloroacetic acid. It was concluded that the chloroplasts contained both RNA and DNA. Material staining with pyronin has been detected in chloroplasts of *Elodea*[118]: staining was decreased if the cells were first treated with ribonuclease, suggesting that RNA was present. Faint Feulgen staining in chloroplasts of *Beta vulgaris* has been reported[59]: this was not detected in material pretreated with deoxyribonuclease. Littau (1958) was unable to detect DNA by the Feulgen method in chloroplasts of species examined by Chiba and Metzner, but found weak basophilia for azure B, which was abolished by pretreatment with hot trichloroacetic acid. She concluded that these chloroplasts may have contained a small amount of RNA, but did not have enough DNA to be detected by cytochemical methods. Attempts to detect Feulgen-positive material in broad-bean chloroplasts have also failed[114].

There have been reports of the histochemical detection of nucleic acids in the chloroplasts of algae as well as in those of higher plants. Pyronin-staining material which was removed by ribonuclease, and Feulgen-staining material which was removed by deoxyribonuclease, were detected in the chloroplast of *Chlorella vulgaris*[33]: this was taken to indicate the presence of both kinds of nucleic acid. Ris and Plaut (1962) found one or more Feulgen-positive bodies in the chloroplast of *Chlamydomonas moewusii*: similar bodies were seen in *C. reinhardi* and *C. eugametos*. When the cells of *C. moewusii* were treated with ribonuclease to get rid of RNA, and were then stained with acridine orange, fluorescent yellow-green bodies (apart from the nucleus) were seen, and these appeared to be associated with the chloroplast: two such bodies can be seen in a cell in the published photomicrograph. These bodies were thought to be identical with the Feulgen-staining bodies. The presence of DNA in these particles was indicated by the fact that they could not be detected, by Feulgen or acridine-orange staining, in cells treated with deoxyribonuclease. In *Euglena gracilis* an attempt to detect DNA in chloroplasts by the standard Feulgen procedure failed[114]. Also, Givner and Moriber (1964), using a particularly sensitive variation of the Feulgen technique involving fluorescent dyes, were unable to detect any fluorescence outside the nucleus in cells of this alga. Givner and Moriber suggest that either chloroplast DNA is present in a labile form not retained by the standard fixing and staining methods for the Feulgen reaction, or that DNA is not a component of the chloroplast.

Plastids other than the chloroplast have also been examined histochemically for the presence of nucleic acids. Carrot chromoplasts have been reported to be Feulgen-negative but to stain strongly with pyronin[111]. This staining was not observed in chromoplasts pretreated with ribonuclease or hot trichloroacetic acid: the presence of RNA was thus indicated. Basophilic material, removable by ribonuclease, and Feulgen-positive material, removable by deoxyribonuclease, were found in the plastids of *Chlorophytum comosum* and *Helianthus tuberosus*[108]: it was concluded that both RNA and DNA were present. Etioplasts of dark-grown maize seedlings stained intensely with azure B[53]. This staining was abolished by pretreatment with ribonuclease, which indicated that it was due to the presence of RNA. No Feulgen-positive material was detected in these etioplasts.

It is apparent from the foregoing that there is general agreement that histochemical methods indicate the presence of RNA in plastids. As far as DNA is concerned, some workers claim to have detected it, others have failed. In this connection it must be remembered that DNA has to be present in rather high concentrations before it can be readily detected by the standard Feulgen procedure: according to Pollister (1954), in a structure $1\ \mu$ thick, a concentration of at least $6 \cdot 7 \times 10^{-12}$ mg/μ^3 (i.e. about $0 \cdot 67$ per cent of the wet weight or $3 \cdot 3 - 6 \cdot 7$ per cent of the dry weight) is required. As was pointed out by Littau (1958), the amounts of DNA found by analysis of isolated chloroplasts (see X.5) are appreciably lower than the necessary minimum value. It is of interest, here, that even in the nucleus, when this is large so that the DNA concentration is low, there can be difficulty in detecting the presence of DNA histochemically[11]. Also, it may be possible that DNA can be present in high concentration, but in some form which does not take up the Feulgen stain. For instance, there is now evidence[27] that nucleoli contain substantial amounts of DNA: in the case of broad bean nucleoli this may be as high as 37 per cent of the dry weight[70]. However, nucleoli are Feulgen-negative. The absence of Feulgen-staining in plastids, then, is not inconsistent with the presence of DNA in biologically functional quantities.

X.3. Evidence from Electron Microscopy

Electron microscopical techniques, while less specific than histochemical studies with the light microscope, can also be used to locate nucleic acids within the cell. In electron micrographs of *Chlamydomonas reinhardi*, Sager and Palade (1957) observed, within the chloroplast, granules 100–150 Å in diameter. Because of the similarity of these particles to the ribosomes in the cytoplasm, it was suggested that the former might also be ribonucleoprotein particles. Similar ribosome-like particles have been seen in chloroplasts of *Chlamydomonas moewusii*[90], *Ochromonas danica*[34], *Chenopodium album*, *Clivia miniata*[75], spinach[76], maize[53], and oats[44]. Also, ribosome-like particles, about 170 Å in diameter have been observed in the etioplasts of dark-grown maize leaves[53] and oat leaves[45]—see Fig. I.37. These particles could not be found in leaves which had been treated with ribonuclease, indicating that RNA was one of the major constituents. In oat chloroplasts ribosomes are sometimes seen to occur in groups[44]: these may correspond to polyribosomes (ribosomes held together by a molecule of messenger RNA).

Ris and Plaut (1962) found, in cells of *Chlamydomonas moewusii* which had been post-fixed with uranyl acetate (an agent which binds to nucleic acids), low-density areas within the chloroplast which contained fibrils 25–30 Å thick. They reported that in cells which had been pre-treated with deoxyribonuclease the fibrils could no longer be seen. On the basis of this result, and also the similarity of these fibrils to DNA fibres in the nucleoplasm of bacteria, these workers suggested that the fibrils contained DNA. Ris and Plaut also found 25 Å fibrils in the chloroplasts of certain higher plants—*Elodea canadensis*, *Zea mays*, *Helianthus tuberosus*, and in the bryophyte *Anthoceros*. Similar deoxyribonuclease-sensitive fibrils have now been observed in the stroma of chloroplasts of *Phaseolus* and *Beta vulgaris*[59]. In oat chloroplasts, several of these fibril-containing regions may be seen in one section of a chloroplast[44]. Fig. I.37 shows some of these fibres in an etioplast of an oat leaf.

On the basis of electron-microscopical studies, then, it appears that plastids contain RNA in the form of granules similar to ribosomes, and probably also contain DNA.

X.4. Evidence from Autoradiography

Another cytological technique which has been used to detect nucleic acids in plastids is autoradiography. Brachet (1958) reported that after administration of ³H-thymidine to the alga *Acetabularia*, radioactivity could be detected, by the technique of autoradiography, in the chloroplasts. However, since a control with deoxyribonuclease was not carried out, he was not prepared to assume that the incorporation was into DNA. It has also been reported that *Spirogyra*[110] and the fern *Ceratopteris thalictroides*[38] incorporate ³H-thymidine into their chloroplasts. However, in neither case was it shown that the radioactivity could be removed by deoxyribonuclease, so it remains uncertain whether it was in DNA. The importance of this enzymic test for incorporation into DNA is emphasized by recent findings of incorporation of radioactivity from ³H-thymidine into cytoplasmic structures in a form resistant to deoxyribonuclease. Maize leaves were found[62] to incorporate substantial amounts of radioactivity from ³H-thymidine into their chloroplasts, but this radioactivity was not removed by deoxyribonuclease. Cells of *Euglena gracilis* incorporated radioactivity from ³H-thymidine into their cytoplasm[95]: this radioactivity was not removed by deoxyribonuclease, but much of it was removed by ribonuclease.

Wollgiehn and Mothes (1964) have reported that leaf discs of *Nicotiana rustica* incorporate radioactivity from ³H-thymidine into their chloroplasts. Only young, growing leaves and young rooted leaf-cuttings showed this incorporation: mature leaves or old, rooted leaf-cuttings did not. The radioactivity incorporated into chloroplasts was not removed by cold 1·6N perchloric acid or by ribonuclease, indicating that it was not present in the form of RNA. However, the radioactivity was removed by treatment with hot 1·6N perchloric acid or deoxyribonuclease, suggesting that the labelled material was, indeed, DNA. Incorporation of deoxyribonuclease-removable label from ³H-thymidine into chloroplasts has now also been reported for leaves of *Beta vulgaris*[59]. Steffensen and Sheridan (1965) have shown that three species of marine algae, *Dictyota*, *Padina*, and *Bryopsis* incorporated radioactivity from ³H-thymidine into their chloroplasts. The radioactivity was removed by deoxyribonuclease and hot trichloroacetic acid, but not by ribonuclease, indicating that the thymidine had been incorporated into DNA. Surprisingly, there was no incorporation into the nuclei, even though the cells were dividing: to explain this, these authors suggest that in these algae the nucleus does not possess the enzyme thymidine kinase (which is required for utilization of thymidine in DNA synthesis) but that the chloroplasts do. Thymidine incorporation was detectable only in young, dividing chloroplasts; not in the mature non-dividing ones: in the case of *Acetabularia*, it has now been shown (De-Vitry, quoted by Baltus and Brachet, 1963) that most of the radioactivity incorporated from ³H-thymidine into the chloroplasts (see above) can be removed by deoxyribonuclease treatment. Cells of *Euglena gracilis* grown in the presence of ³H-guanine or ³H-adenine incorporated radioactivity into their chloroplasts[96]. Much of this label was removed by treatment of the cells with ribonuclease: however, after this treatment there was still some radioactivity left in the chloroplasts which could be removed by treatment with deoxyribonuclease, suggesting the presence of labelled DNA.

There is some autoradiographic evidence for the presence of DNA in proplastids. Bell (1961) found that when the gametophyte of the fern *Pteridium aquilinum* was supplied with ³H-thymidine during oogenesis, radioactivity occurred throughout the cytoplasm as well as in the nucleus. This radioactivity was removed by deoxyribonuclease, but not by ribonuclease, suggesting that it was in DNA. Electron microscope autoradiography showed that most of the cytoplasmic radioactivity was associated with the proplastids and mitochondria[5]. In the light of the previous finding that the cytoplasmic radioactivity was removed by deoxyribonuclease, it seems likely that the radioactivity in the proplastids corresponded to labelled DNA.

Autoradiography has also been used to detect RNA in plastids. Pieces of leaves of etiolated maize seedlings were found to incorporate radioactivity from ^{3}H-cytidine into their etioplasts[53]: the label was removed by treatment of the leaves with ribonuclease, confirming that it was in RNA. Also, as mentioned previously, much of the radioactivity incorporated from ^{3}H-guanine and ^{3}H-adenine into the chloroplasts of *Euglena gracilis* is removed by ribonuclease[96].

In conclusion, it may be said that autoradiographic studies provide good evidence for the presence of both RNA and DNA in plastids.

X.5. Evidence from Studies on Isolated Plastids

X.5.i. CHEMICAL ESTIMATION OF RNA AND DNA IN PLASTID PREPARATIONS

The method which has been used more than any other for the detection of nucleic acids in plastids is the isolation and chemical analysis of these bodies. The main disadvantage of this approach is that preparations of isolated plastids are usually contaminated by other cell constituents, particularly by nuclei and nuclear fragments. This is particularly likely to be the case for plastids isolated by simple differential centrifugation, the method most commonly used. Nuclear contamination has been demonstrated even in chloroplasts purified repeatedly by this method[116]. Results obtained by workers using differential centrifugation are listed in Table X.1. The content of nucleic acid as a percentage of the dry weight was in some cases taken directly from the published results; in other cases, approximate values were calculated on the basis of other data given in the paper concerned.

Purification methods based on the different densities of the different cellular components are, in general, more satisfactory than differential centrifugation (see I.2.i). Use of a flotation technique to purify spinach and tobacco chloroplasts yielded preparations containing only 0·2 per cent total nucleic acid[54]. Application of high speed density gradient centrifugation to the purification of broad-bean chloroplasts gave preparations containing in the region of 0·1 per cent DNA[58]: no nuclear contamination could be detected cytologically. About a third of this DNA could be removed by repeated density gradient centrifugation:

TABLE X.I. NUCLEIC ACIDS IN PLASTIDS ISOLATED BY DIFFERENTIAL CENTRIFUGATION

Authors	Starting material	Plastid type	% of dry weight of plastid			Comments
			RNA	DNA	Total nucleic acid	
Menke (1938)	Spinach leaves	Chloroplast	—	—	—	Isolated a phosphorus- and pentose-containing protein, thought to be a nucleoprotein
Du Buy and Woods (1943)	Tobacco leaves	Chloroplast	—	—	—	Extracted a nucleoprotein, from which a ribose-containing nucleic acid was isolated
Holden (1952)	Tobacco leaves	Chloroplast	3·0–4·0	0	3·0–4·0	
Parker (1952)	Tobacco leaves	Chloroplast	—	—	—	Nucleic acid shown to yield Adenine, Guanine, Cytidylic acid and Uridylic acid on HCl hydrolysis; therefore RNA
McClendon (1952)	Tobacco leaves	Chloroplast	0·4–2·8	0·6–1·9	1·0–4·7	Nuclei detected in chloroplast fraction, therefore origin of DNA uncertain
Jagendorf and Wildman (1954)	Tobacco leaves	Chloroplast	0·1–0·2	0·2–0·5	0·3–0·7	Nuclei removed by repeated filtration and low-speed centrifugation. Chloroplasts washed repeatedly
Straus (1954)	Carrots	Chromoplast	—	—	0·5	
Smillie (1956a)	Dark-grown pea seedlings	Etioplast	7·2	1·6	8·8	Nuclei detected in plastid fraction, therefore origin of DNA uncertain

Smillie (1956b)	Light-grown pea seedlings	Chloroplast	3·0	0·6	3·6	Published values corrected to allow for removal of lipids
Cooper and Loring (1957)	Tobacco leaves	Chloroplast	2·4	0·6	3·0	
Chiba and Sugahara (1957)	Spinach leaves	Chloroplast	0·4–0·6	0·5–0·9	0·9–1·3	Preparations checked cytologically for freedom from nuclear contamination
	Tobacco leaves	Chloroplast	1·0–1·4	0·7–1·0	1·7–2·4	
Sissakian (1958)	Sugar beet leaves	Chloroplast	0·6–1·7	—	—	Chloroplast RNA content decreased with age of plant
	Tobacco leaves	Chloroplast	1·5–2·8	—	—	
Böttger and Wollgiehn (1958)	*Nicotiana rustica* leaves	Chloroplast	0·8	1·2	2·0	
Kern (1959)	*Cichorium endivia* leaves	Chloroplast	—	—	—	Detected RNA but not DNA
Szarkowski and Golaszewski (1961)	Light-grown rye seedlings	Chloroplast	3·0	—	—	
	Dark-grown rye seedlings	Etioplast	9·0	—	—	
	Light-grown wheat seedlings	Chloroplast	2·7	—	—	
	Dark-grown wheat seedlings	Etioplast	6·3	—	—	

it was not clear whether this fall in DNA content was due to the removal of nuclear material, or simply to leakage from the chloroplasts. The DNA in the broad-bean chloroplasts was identified and estimated by the diphenylamine procedure. At least 62 per cent of this diphenyl-amine-positive material was rendered soluble by treatment with deoxy-ribonuclease, indicating that it was DNA. Chloroplasts purified from spinach leaves by density gradient centrifugation were found to contain 0·1–0·2 per cent DNA[81]. When the purified spinach chloroplasts were deliberately contaminated with nuclei and nuclear fragments and were then re-purified, there was no increase in their DNA content, suggesting that there is little tendency for the chloroplasts to adsorb nuclear material. The absorption spectra of the reaction products of the spinach chloroplast 'DNA' with both diphenylamine and cysteine/sulphuric acid were similar to those given by authentic DNA. Corn leaf chloro-plasts purified by density gradient centrifugation were found to contain about 0·17 per cent DNA and 0·12 per cent RNA[78].

One of the major disadvantages of isolating plastids in aqueous media is that a large part of the water-soluble constituents may be lost (see (I.2.i). Thus, values for nucleic acid contents of plastids prepared in this way might be too low. Some confirmation of this is provided by the observation[6] that spinach chloroplasts prepared in non-aqueous media (which prevent leaching out of soluble constituents—see I.2.i) con-tained as much as 7·5 per cent RNA, which is appreciably higher than the values usually obtained for chloroplasts isolated in aqueous media. The DNA content of these chloroplasts was about 0·4 per cent: no nuclear contamination could be detected cytologically. Other workers have obtained lower values for the RNA content of chloroplasts isolated by this procedure. Chloroplasts isolated in non-aqueous media from rye, broad-bean, tobacco, and spinach leaves[47] contained 1·0–2·5 per cent RNA. Between 17 and 30 per cent of this RNA was not sedimented by centrifugation in the presence of 10^{-2} M $MgCl_2$ for 60 minutes at 100,000 g, suggesting that it was not all ribosomal RNA. Ruppel (1964) reported that chloroplasts of *Allium porrum* and *Antirrhinum majus* obtained by non-aqueous procedures, contained about 1 per cent RNA. After hydrolysis of the whole chloroplasts with concentrated formic acid, no thymine could be detected amongst the purine and pyrimidine bases in the hydrolysate: it was therefore concluded that the chloro-plasts did not contain DNA. More recently, however, Ruppel and van Wyk (1965) have succeeded in detecting DNA in non-aqueously iso-lated chloroplasts of *Antirrhinum majus*, by the diphenylamine procedure, and also by actually isolating the DNA from the chloroplasts. They obtain a DNA content of 0·022–0·025 per cent of the dry weight.

A very direct approach to the problem of avoiding nuclear contami-nation has been used by Gibor and Izawa (1963) and Baltus and

Brachet (1963): they enucleated the giant cells of *Acetabularia* by cutting off the basal third of the cell, and then isolated the chloroplasts from the remainder. Chloroplasts obtained by differential centrifugation were found, by a sensitive fluorometric procedure to contain about one part of DNA for every 5000 parts of protein[37], i.e. the DNA content was about 0·01 per cent: most of this material was rendered soluble by treatment with deoxyribonuclease, confirming that it was DNA. When the chloroplasts were subjected to sucrose density gradient centrifugation the distribution of DNA throughout the gradient correlated well with the distribution of chlorophyll, which is further evidence that the DNA is really in the chloroplasts.

From the results described in this section it appears that RNA can invariably be detected in preparations of isolated plastids. Some of the values reported are very low, going down to about 0·1 per cent; these low values are probably a result of leaching or enzymic degradation of the RNA in chloroplasts isolated in aqueous media. Analyses of chloroplasts isolated in non-aqueous media suggest that the RNA content of chloroplasts is in the region of 1·0–7·5 per cent. Rhodes and Yemm (1963) find 20–30 per cent of the leaf RNA of four-day-old barley seedlings to be associated with the plastids. It is interesting that etioplasts appear to have two to three times as much RNA (per cent of the dry weight) as mature chloroplasts from the same plant[106, 112]. This is in accordance with the observation[53] that in electron micrographs of maize leaves, the ribosome-like particles were present in higher concentration in the etioplasts than in the chloroplasts. The lower overall concentration of RNA in the chloroplasts might simply reflect the fact that they also contain all the proteins and lipids of the photosynthetic apparatus.

Most workers have also found DNA in chloroplast preparations; however Holden (1952), Kern (1959), Menke (1960), and Ruppel (1964) were unable to detect it. A possible explanation of inability to detect DNA in chloroplast preparations in some cases is that the methods used to extract it were inadequate. It has been shown[19, 58] that not all the diphenylamine-positive material in highly purified chloroplasts is liberated by treatment with hot 0·5N perchloric acid (the most commonly used method); it is necessary to use 2N perchloric acid to achieve complete extraction. However, Ruppel (1964) did not use perchloric acid extraction, but instead hydrolysed the whole chloroplast material with anhydrous formic acid, and then attempted to detect thymine in the hydrolysate. The presence of all the other chloroplast components —lipids, proteins, etc.—would tend to produce large amounts of charcoal: a possible explanation of Ruppel's failure to find thymine might be that this base was adsorbed by the charcoal produced in the hydrolysis procedure.

X.5.ii. COMPARISON OF PLASTID- WITH NON-PLASTID NUCLEIC ACIDS

X.5.ii.a. *RNA*

No matter how carefully plastids are purified and checked for contamination, the suspicion will always remain that the nucleic acids in such preparations, particularly when the amount is small, are really nucleic acids from other parts of the cell, either adsorbed onto the plastid surface or present in particles too small to be recognized cytologically. However, if the plastid nucleic acid could be shown to differ from the other cellular nucleic acids in its physical or chemical properties, this would indicate that its presence was not due to contamination.

An indication that plastid RNA might differ in its properties from other cellular RNA was provided by the work of Lyttleton (1962): he found that the total cellular ribosomes of spinach leaves showed two components in the analytical ultracentrifuge, one of these being present in much smaller amounts than the other and sedimenting more slowly. From the chloroplast fraction also he was able to isolate ribosomes, but in the ultracentrifuge these appeared to contain only one component, and this had a sedimentation constant identical with that of the minor, slow-moving ribosome from the whole cells. He concluded that the ribosomes in the chloroplast fraction did, in fact, belong to the chloroplasts, and that the minor component of the total cell ribosomes had also come from the chloroplasts. This conclusion was supported by the fact that in tissues such as roots, which do not contain chloroplasts, only the major, fast-moving ribosome could be detected. Similar results have now been obtained with other plants. Leaves of *Brassica pekinensis* were found to contain two classes of ribosomes, with sedimentation constants 83 S and 68 S: the amount of 68 S type present was 20–35 per cent that of the 83 S ribosomes[21]. Purified chloroplasts contained only the 68 S ribosomes. Also, stems and roots, which lack chloroplasts, contained the 83 S ribosomes but not the 68 S type. It was concluded that the 83 S ribosomes were cytoplasmic ribosomes, and that the 68 S ribosomes were chloroplast ribosomes. Ribosomes with a sedimentation constant ($S_{20,w}$, extrapolated to infinite dilution) of 62 S have been isolated from chloroplasts of pea seedlings[105]. A small amount of a ribosome dimer, sedimentation constant 92 S, was detected. When the Mg^{2+} concentration was reduced from $10^{-2}M$ to $10^{-3}M$, the ribosomes dissociated into subunits with sedimentation constants 46 S and 32 S. The cytoplasmic ribosomes from the pea seedlings had a sedimentation constant of 76 S (dimers, 112 S), with subunits of sedimentation constants 54 S and 38 S. In spinach[107] and tobacco[7] leaves, the chloroplast ribosomes have a sedimentation constant of about 70 S, and the cytoplasmic ribosomes have a sedimentation constant of about 80 S.

Ribosomes differing from cytoplasmic ribosomes have been found in the chloroplasts of an alga as well as in those of higher plants. Brawerman (1962, 1963) isolated ribosomes from chloroplasts of *Euglena gracilis*: these had a sedimentation constant of about 60 S, compared to a value of about 70 S for the cytoplasmic ribosomes[32]. The chloroplast ribosomes appeared to have a higher protein content than the cytoplasmic ribosomes. The RNA isolated from the chloroplast ribosomes consisted of two components, sedimentation constants 14 S and 19 S[16]: the RNA isolated from the cytoplasmic ribosomes consisted of only one component, of sedimentation constant 19 S. The chloroplast and cytoplasmic ribosomes also differed in the base ratio of their RNA: the cytoplasmic ribosomal RNA had a high guanine content, like most ribosomal RNAs, but the chloroplast ribosomal RNA contained more adenine than guanine. The various differences between the chloroplast and cytoplasmic ribosomes of *E. gracilis* are shown in Table X.2. In view of these findings it is a little surprising that Odintsova, Golubeva, and Sissakian (1964) were unable to detect any difference between the base ratio of chloroplast ribosomal RNA and that of cytoplasmic ribosomal RNA in four different higher plant species.

It is clear from the foregoing that the general consensus of opinion, from work on various higher plants, and on *Euglena*, is that the chloroplast ribosomes have a lower sedimentation constant than the cytoplasmic ribosomes from the same cells. In this connection it is interesting that there is some indication from electron micrographs of maize leaves[53] and of *Euglena gracilis* (Dales and Cerami, quoted by Brawerman, 1965) that the ribosomes within the plastids are smaller than those outside. In virtue of their relatively small size and sedimentation con-

TABLE X.2. DIFFERENCES BETWEEN CHLOROPLAST AND CYTOPLASMIC RIBOSOMES OF *EUGLENA GRACILIS*

(*See Brawerman, 1963; Eisenstadt and Brawerman, 1964; Brawerman and Eisenstadt, 1964*)

	Chloroplast ribosomes	Cytoplasmic ribosomes
Sedimentation constant	~60 S	~70 S
RNA/protein	1·3	1·6
Sedimentation constants of RNA components	14 S and 19 S	19 S
Base composition of RNA (moles %)		
Adenine	29·3	22·7
Guanine	27·4	29·5
Cytosine	19·4	27·1
Uracil	23·9	19·6
Pseudo-uridine	Not detected	1·1

stant, chloroplast ribosomes are more similar to those of prokaryotic organisms (bacteria, blue-green algae, etc.) than to the (cytoplasmic) ribosomes of eukaryotes (organisms with a membrane-bounded nucleus, chromosomes, mitotic apparatus, etc.). This is particularly interesting in view of the possibility that chloroplasts may have evolved from symbiotic blue-green algae (see XI.8).

Brawerman and Eisenstadt (1964) have also obtained an RNA component from the soluble fraction (100,000 g supernatant) of the *Euglena* chloroplasts, which has template activity (see XII.6.iii). This RNA has a higher template activity (per mg RNA) than the corresponding cytoplasmic RNA.

X.5.ii.b. *DNA*

The first suggestion of a difference between the properties of plastid DNA and nuclear DNA was the report by Chiba and Sugahara (1957) that substantial amounts of DNA could be extracted from impure tobacco and spinach chloroplasts with 0·5N perchloric acid, but that to liberate DNA from highly purified chloroplasts an acid concentration as high as 2N had to be used. The implication of this finding was that the DNA actually in the chloroplasts was more difficult to extract than the nuclear DNA which contaminated the crude preparations. In confirmation of this it was found[58] in the case of broad-bean leaves, that 97 per cent of the DNA in isolated nuclei was extracted by 0·5N perchloric acid, whereas only 29 per cent of the DNA in the purified chloroplast fraction could be removed in this way, the remainder coming out in 2N perchloric acid.

Another indication of a difference between plastid and nuclear DNA was the report by Iwamura (1960; 1962) of the existence of two kinds of DNA in *Chlorella ellipsoidea*. He found that when a cell homogenate was centrifuged successively at 20,000 g and 105,000 g, most of the DNA was distributed about equally between the 20,000 g pellet and the 105,000 g supernatant. The DNA in the pellet appeared to have a somewhat higher adenine-thymine content than the DNA in the supernatant, and also incorporated ^{32}P-orthophosphate much more rapidly in the light than did the supernatant DNA. In the dark, the DNA in the supernatant incorporated ^{32}P-phosphate more rapidly than that in the pellet. Furthermore, when the cells were pre-labelled with ^{32}P-phosphate and then incubated in the presence of unlabelled phosphate, the specific radioactivity of the pellet DNA rapidly fell, but that of the supernatant DNA did not: this suggested that the pellet DNA undergoes turnover but that the supernatant DNA does not. Since the 20,000 g pellet consisted mainly of chloroplast fragments, Iwamura suggested that the DNA in this fraction might be associated with the chloroplast, and that the DNA in the supernatant might come from the nucleus. The fact that the metabolic activity of the pellet DNA was more dependent on light than was the metabolic activity of the supernatant DNA might also suggest that the former was associated with the chloroplast.

This work was of considerable importance in that it clearly established the existence of at least two kinds of DNA in the cell. However, it must be pointed out that a 20,000 g pellet would certainly contain mitochondria as well as chloroplast fragments. Also, light might be expected to stimulate mitochondrial, as well as chloroplast, metabolism, as a result of the production of oxygen in photosynthesis. Thus while it seems probable, in the light of later work, that the 20,000 g pellet DNA would at least include chloroplast DNA, some more evidence as to the cellular location of these DNA species in *Chlorella* would seem to be desirable.

Rather more direct evidence for a difference in base ratio between nuclear and plastid DNA has come from studies on higher plants and various algae. In the case of broad-bean leaves, it was found[57, 58] that the molar ratio of adenine to guanine was higher (1·67) in DNA from highly purified chloroplasts than in DNA from nuclei (1·54). Chun, Vaughan, and Rich (1963) analysed DNA from spinach and beet leaves by caesium chloride density gradient centrifugation. They found that as well as the major component of density 1·695 (indicating 36 per cent guanine + cytosine, α component) there were two minor components, densities 1·705 (indicating 46 per cent guanine + cytosine, β component) and 1·719 (indicating 60 per cent guanine + cytosine, γ component). When the leaf homogenate was separated into a nuclear fraction and a chloroplast fraction, the former had only the major DNA component but the chloroplasts showed a ten- to thirty-fold enrichment of one or both of the two minor components (Fig. X.1). This suggested that one or other, or both, of these minor DNA components occurred in the chloroplasts. As Fig. X.1 shows, the DNA from the chloroplast fraction still contained a large amount, 50–70 per cent, of the major DNA component, density 1·695: this was probably due to the presence of a certain amount of nuclear material contaminating the chloroplast preparations. Both the minor DNA components appeared to be double-stranded: heat denaturation caused the increase in density, and in absorbance at 260 mμ characteristic of double-helical DNA. The amount of these minor components as a proportion of the total cell DNA seemed to vary from one preparation to another. In some samples of total cell DNA neither the β nor the γ satellite could be detected, indicating that they constituted less than 1–2 per cent of the whole. In one sample of spinach leaf DNA the γ component constituted something in the region of 4 per cent of the total, but the β component was not detected: in DNA from the chloroplast fraction of these leaves, the γ

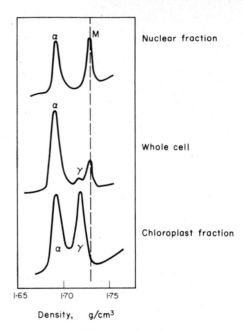

Fig. X.1. *Densitometer tracings of UV-absorption photographs of spinach DNA in the analytical ultracentrifuge, after CsCl equilibrium density gradient centrifugation. By permission, from Chun, E. H. L., Vaughan, M. H. and Rich, A. (1963). J. Mol. Biol. 7, 130–141. α is the major DNA band. γ is one of the satellite DNA bands. M is a band of* Micrococcus lysodeikticus *DNA used as a marker*

component constituted 45 per cent of the DNA present, but the β component was still not detectable. When the β component was detected in DNA from spinach chloroplast preparations it was present in a third to a half of the amount of the γ component: however, in the DNA from a beet chloroplast preparation the β component was present in larger amount than the γ component.

Chun *et al.* also detected a minor DNA component in the algae *Chlamydomonas reinhardi* and *Chlorella ellipsoidea*, but did not attempt to determine its cellular location. In the case of the chlamydomonad, Sager and Ishida (1963) showed that the minor component constituted 6 per cent of the total cell DNA, but about 40 per cent of the DNA in purified chloroplast preparations, suggesting that it originated in the chloroplast. Base analysis of this minor component indicated a GC (guanine + cytosine) content of 39·3 per cent; the major DNA component (presumably from the nucleus) of the cell had a GC content of 62·1 per cent. In *Chlorella ellipsoidea*[20] the minor DNA component had a density of 1·695 (indicating 36 per cent GC) and the major component a density of 1·716 (indicating 57 per cent GC). On the basis of CsCl density gradient centrifugation of ^{32}P-labelled DNA from *C. ellipsoidea*,

Iwamura and Kuwashima (1964) have concluded that this minor component is identical with the DNA component (thought to be chloroplast DNA) showing rapid labelling and turnover, previously described in *Chlorella*[50, 51].

In *Euglena gracilis*, experiments by three independent groups of workers[61, 30, 31, 87, 88, 17] have shown the presence in chloroplasts of a type of DNA with different properties from the nuclear DNA. On CsCl density gradient centrifugation of the total cell DNA, in addition to the main band, presumed to be nuclear in origin, with density 1·706–1·708 (indicating 47–49 per cent GC content), there were two minor, satellite DNA bands, one of density 1·684–1·686 (indicating 24–27 per cent GC content), the other of density 1·690–1·692 (indicating 31–33 per cent GC content). In the DNA obtained from isolated chloroplasts the 1·707 band was still present but the 1·685 component now constituted about 30 per cent of the total DNA, as opposed to only 2 per cent of the total in DNA from whole cells. It was concluded that the 1·685 satellite was, in fact, chloroplast DNA: the continued presence of the 1·707 band was attributed to contamination of the chloroplast preparations by whole cells and/or nuclear material. Both satellite bands were present in the DNA from dark-grown, as well as light-grown cells[31, 88]: it thus appears likely that the 1·685 satellite is present in proplastids as well as in chloroplasts. Nearly all the 1·707 band was removed by lysing the chloroplasts with the surface-active agent sodium deoxycholate, in the presence of magnesium chloride: when this lysate was centrifuged at 23,000 g the DNA in the pellet consisted almost entirely of the 1·685 component[17]. The 1·691 satellite was absent from *Euglena* chloroplasts centrifuged down at 500 g, and appeared to be associated with particles sedimenting at 8,000–40,000 g, suggesting a mitochondrial origin[31]. The base composition of the chloroplast DNA differed from that of the nuclear DNA not only in the ratio of the bases, but also with regard to the presence of 5-methylcytosine: this base was absent from the chloroplast DNA, but present to the extent of 2·3 moles per cent in the nuclear DNA[17, 87]. The behaviour of the chloroplast DNA on heat denaturation, and the fact that its base ratio fitted the base-pairing rule ($G = C$, $A = T$) suggested that it was double-stranded. The molecular weight of the isolated chloroplast DNA was in the same range, 20 to 40 million, as that of the nuclear DNA; in this respect it differed from the 1·691 satellite, which had a molecular weight of only about 3 million[88].

Further evidence for the presence of DNA differing from nuclear DNA in higher plant chloroplasts has been obtained recently. DNA isolated from chloroplasts of *Beta vulgaris* var. cicla was found to contain 30–40 per cent of a type of DNA of a greater density (1·700, suggesting 42 per cent GC content) than that (1·689, suggesting 31 per cent GC content) of the main DNA species (presumed nuclear) of the cell[59].

From chloroplasts of *Antirrhinum majus*, isolated in non-aqueous media, DNA was isolated in which the ratio of (adenine + thymine) to (cytosine + guanine) was 1·65: the value of this ratio in the total (mainly nuclear) DNA of the leaves was 1·49 [94]. It is interesting to compare these values with the A/G ratios obtained for broad bean leaves—1·67 for chloroplast DNA, and 1·54 for nuclear DNA[57, 58]. In the *Antirrhinum* chloroplast DNA the molar ratios of adenine to thymine and cytosine to guanine were approximately unity, but, as was found for *Euglena* chloroplast DNA (see above), 5-methylcytosine was absent (although it was present in the leaf nuclear DNA). DNA isolated from tobacco chloroplasts was shown, by means of the CsCl technique, to consist largely of a component of density 1·703: the main (supposed nuclear) DNA component of the leaves had a density of 1·690[103]. When the young tobacco leaves were allowed to incorporate ³²P-phosphate, a species of DNA was detected which became labelled much more rapidly than the bulk of the cellular DNA. This rapidly labelled DNA had about the same density as the chloroplast DNA, and was therefore thought to be identical with the chloroplast DNA. A further indication that the DNA in the chloroplast fraction was not nuclear DNA was provided by the fact that hybridization experiments showed that the chloroplast DNA had few, if any, major nucleotide sequences in common with the nuclear DNA.

In conclusion, we can say that studies in which the properties of plastid and non-plastid nucleic acids have been compared, strongly indicate that plastids contain their own specific types of RNA and DNA.

X.6. Evidence from Studies on Loss of Chloroplasts

X.6.i. THE BLEACHING OF *EUGLENA GRACILIS*

Another approach to the study of the genetic material of the plastid is to investigate ways in which plastid heredity can be interfered with. Most of the work along these lines has been done with the alga *Euglena gracilis*, an organism that appears to be unique in the ease with which it loses the ability to form chloroplasts. This phenomenon was first observed by Provasoli, Hutner, and Schatz (1948), who found that when *E. gracilis* was grown in medium containing streptomycin, the cells formed no chlorophyll and apparently lacked plastids. The cells still failed to form chlorophyll when subcultured into medium lacking streptomycin and were, in fact, found to have a permanent, hereditary, inability to form chloroplasts. Since then many other treatments have

been found which cause loss of the ability to form chloroplasts in
E. gracilis: growth at high temperatures[83]; non-lethal doses of ultraviolet light[84, 64]; various antibiotics, such as aureomycin[92], erythromycin[29], kanamycin, paromomycin, and neomycin[119]; certain antihistamine drugs such as pyribenzamine[43], methapyrilene, and pyrilamine[119]; various nitrofurans[67]; the amino acid analogue O-methylthreonine[40, 1]; the mutagen N-methyl-N'-nitro-N-nitrosoguanidine[68],
the thymine analogue 5-bromo-uracil[99]; and exposure to extreme
hydrostatic pressure, in the region of 1000 atmospheres[42].

X.6.ii. THE SENSITIVE SITE INVOLVED IN ULTRA-VIOLET-INDUCED BLEACHING

Of all the bleaching agents which have been studied, ultraviolet (UV)-
irradiation is the one which has yielded most information about the
plastid genetic material. The chloroplasts of *Euglena gracilis* are very
much more sensitive to UV than are the cells as a whole. Lyman,
Epstein, and Schiff (1961) found no loss of cell viability at UV doses
which induced loss of chloroplast-forming ability (indicated by formation of white colonies on plating out) in 100 per cent of the cells. Like
UV effects in other biological systems, the bleaching is photoreactivable. To obtain white colonies in the above experiment it was necessary,
after irradiation and plating-out, to grow the cells for five days in the
dark before exposing them to light (to detect ability to form chloroplasts) for a further two days. If the cells were exposed to visible light
throughout the seven days, then the effect of the UV was abolished, all
the colonies being green. Both light-grown and dark-grown cells lost
ability to form chloroplasts on UV treatment, but the light-grown cells
were less sensitive—they required twice as big a dose to produce
100 per cent bleaching as did the dark-grown cells (Fig. X.3). The lower
UV sensitivity of the green cells may be due to shielding of the sensitive
site by the bulk of the chloroplast material.

Lyman *et al.* found the action spectrum of bleaching to have a main
peak in the region of 260 mμ, and a subsidiary one at about 280 mμ
(Fig. X.2), suggesting that the receptor for UV in this system is a
nucleoprotein. This hypothetical nucleoprotein might be situated in the
nucleus or in the cytoplasm. Direct evidence for its location came from
work by Gibor and Granick (1962): they found that irradiation of the
nucleus alone of *E. gracilis*, with a UV microbeam, never resulted in the
appearance of bleached cells; irradiation of the entire cell, or of the
cytoplasm alone, gave rise to a considerable number of bleached
progeny. It thus appears probable that the UV-sensitive site involved
in bleaching is a nucleoprotein situated in the cytoplasm and not in the
nucleus.

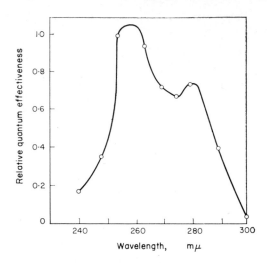

Fig. X.2. *Action spectrum for UV-induced loss of chloroplast-forming ability in* Euglena gracilis (*adapted from Schiff, Epstein, and Lyman, 1961*)

X.6.iii. NUMBER OF SENSITIVE SITES PER CELL— TARGET ANALYSIS

Assuming, then, that the sensitive site is a cytoplasmic nucleoprotein, how many of these nucleoprotein particles are there in a cell? Lyman *et al.* (1961) found that the dose-response curve for ultraviolet bleaching of *E. gracilis* var. bacillaris was of the multi-target type, the apparent target number being in the region of thirty with either light-grown or dark-grown cells (Fig. X.3). This was taken to indicate that there are about thirty particles per cell, all of which must be inactivated to prevent chloroplast formation. Ray (1964) has also obtained a target number of thirty for UV bleaching of cells of the bacillaris strain of *E. gracilis*.

Petropulos (1964) has studied UV-bleaching with cells of the Z strain growing synchronously. With cells taken from the culture at the onset of cell division he obtained a target number of sixty-seven; cells taken during the division period had a slightly higher target number—78— but required about twice the dose (to produce a given percentage of bleached colonies) as the cells sampled before division. The fact that these target numbers are rather more than twice as large as those found by Lyman *et al.* may be due to the difference in culture conditions[80]: Lyman *et al.* grew the cells either in continuous light or continuous darkness, whereas Petropulos alternated 12 hours light with 12 hours darkness, to induce synchronous cell division. The induction of synchronous growth is by itself evidence that the alternate light and dark

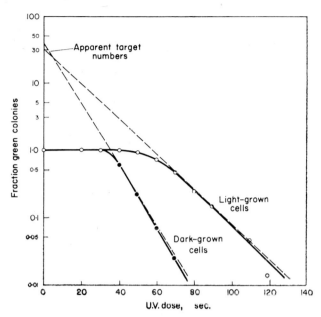

FIG. X.3. *Dose-response curves for UV-induced loss of chloroplast-forming ability (adapted from Lyman et al., 1961)*

treatment has somewhat fundamental effects on cellular organization: it would not, therefore, be surprising if a further consequence of this treatment was, say, a doubling of the number of nucleoprotein particles per cell, assuming the basic number to be in the region of thirty.

Whatever target number is finally arrived at, its interpretation is further complicated by the variation in number of the nucleoprotein particles per cell during the cell division cycle. If, for instance, we take the results of Lyman *et al.*, then the value, thirty, obtained by them presumably represents the average number per cell in the population treated. Since the number of particles per cell will be halved in cell division, then the number must double between one cell division and the next. Thus, if the particles multiply throughout the cell division cycle, then in a typical culture, containing cells of all types from those which have just divided to those about to divide, the number of particles per cell will vary from the post-cell-division number, N, to the pre-cell-division number, $2N$. On this theory, then, the number, thirty, would be somewhere between the post-cell-division number and the pre-cell-division number, i.e. N might be in the region of twenty, and $2N$ about forty. If, however, the number of particles is increased by a rapid doubling at one specific point in the cell division cycle, then other possibilities arise. If the time of doubling is immediately before cell division, then for the greater part of the cell's lifetime, the number of

21—P.

particles per cell remains at the post-cell-division number, i.e. the observed figure, thirty, would represent N; $2N$ therefore being about sixty. If the time of doubling is immediately after cell division, then for the greater part of the division cycle the number of particles per cell is at the pre-cell-division number, i.e. the measured target value, thirty, would be a measure of $2N$, the value of N thus being about fifteen. A doubling time somewhere in the middle of the cell division cycle would mean that the values of N and $2N$ were from fifteen to thirty, and from thirty to sixty, respectively. From the foregoing theoretical discussion it is apparent that an observed target number of thirty indicates that the number of UV-sensitive particles per cell might be anything between fifteen and thirty just after cell division, and between thirty and sixty just before cell division, the actual value depending upon which of the above hypotheses is nearest the truth.

The results of Petropulos, in fact, suggest that the number of UV-sensitive particles doubles immediately after cell division. As mentioned above, cells taken from a culture at the onset of cell division had a target number, for bleaching, of sixty-seven; cells taken about half-way through the division phase had a target number of seventy-eight. In view of the inevitable errors involved in determination of target numbers, the value of seventy-eight is probably not significantly greater than sixty-seven. However, the results do at least suggest that the cells taken half-way through the division phase did not have a lower target number than the cells taken at the onset of division. Now the cell sample taken during the division phase would include a large number of cells which had recently divided: the fact that the average target number was nevertheless just as high as that of the cell sample taken at the onset of division suggests that the number of nucleoprotein particles per cell doubles almost immediately after cell division. This would mean that the number of particles per cell remains constant at the pre-cell-division number, $2N$, from a point in time very shortly after one cell division until the next cell division, i.e. the number per cell is $2N$ for nearly the whole of the cell division cycle. Thus, values of target number obtained with randomly dividing cultures, such as those used by Lyman *et al.*, should correspond to $2N$. Therefore if, for instance, we accept the target number of thirty obtained by Lyman *et al.*, then for most of its division cycle the cell has about thirty nucleoprotein particles: on cell division the number of particles per cell falls to fifteen, but is then quickly restored to thirty.

However, too much weight should not be attached to these calculations because, even apart from the inherent inaccuracy of target number determinations, it is by no means certain that the multi-target hit theory can be applied in this way to the bleaching of *Euglena gracilis*. Ray (1964) has pointed out that if repair of the UV-induced lesions can occur in *Euglena*, as it can in bacteria[102], then the target theory cannot be used in such a straightforward manner.

X.6.iv. NUMBER OF SENSITIVE SITES PER CELL— DILUTION STUDIES

What is it that happens to these nucleoprotein particles as a result of ultraviolet, and other, treatments? An indication of what happens has come from work by Schiff, Lyman, and Epstein (1961) on the photo-reactivation of UV-bleaching. Cells were given a dose of UV sufficient to give 100 per cent white colonies (if plated under non-photoreactivating conditions) and were then kept in the dark, either in growth medium (so that the cells multiplied) or in resting medium (no cellular multiplication). In the case of the non-multiplying culture, the proportion of the cells which could be photoreactivated showed no tendency to diminish with time, being 100 per cent even after five days. However, when the cells were allowed to multiply, the proportion of cells which was photoreactivable began to decrease after 36 hours and fell to zero after five days (Fig. X.4). Schiff *et al.* interpreted this to mean that the effect of UV on the nucleoprotein particles was to prevent them from

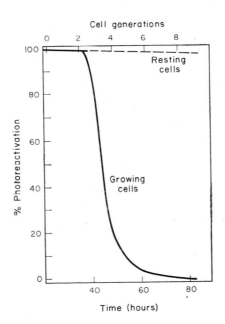

FIG. X.4. *Decay of photoreactivability during cell multiplication (adapted from Schiff, Epstein, and Lyman, 1961).*
   Percentage photoreactivation of non-dividing cells in resting medium--------
   Percentage photoreactivation of cells multiplying in growth medium ————

multiplying, so that they became diluted out from the dividing, but not from the non-dividing, cells.

This assumption, that decay of photoreactivability is due to dilution out of the nucleoprotein particles, provides an alternative method of estimating the number of particles per cell. Schiff *et al.* compared the time course of decay with various theoretical curves obtained by assuming four, eight, ten or twelve photoreactivable particles per cell, with random segregation of these at cellular division. The results of this analysis indicated that about ten units per cell were being diluted out. This value of ten units per cell is smaller than the value obtained by target analysis by a factor of three. In an attempt to reconcile these different findings, these authors suggest that there are, indeed, about thirty nucleoprotein particles in the cell, all of which must be inacti-vated to prevent chloroplast formation, but that these exist in about ten groups of three (there are about ten chloroplasts per cell) each group giving rise to one chloroplast. It is supposed that each group of three particles moves as a unit during cellular multiplication, thus producing the observed dilution kinetics.

Whatever precise value is arrived at for the number of bodies involved, these studies do strongly indicate that UV-bleaching involves inhibition of multiplication, with consequent dilution out, of cyto-plasmic particles. Experiments on streptomycin- and heat-bleaching had already led to similar conclusions. De Deken-Grenson and Messin (1958) exposed cells of *Euglena gracilis* to a high concentration of strepto-mycin and then resuspended the cells in growth medium without the antibiotic. Chlorophyll synthesis ceased for several generations and then resumed again in some, but not all, of the cells. While chloroplast formation was stopped but growth was continuing, samples were taken at intervals and plated out to determine what proportion of the cells still had the ability to give rise to green progeny. Initially, the cells had eight to ten chloroplasts, and it was found that as these were diluted out, there was a rough agreement between the proportion of the cells which had one or more chloroplasts and the proportion which gave rise to green colonies. It was concluded that the ability to form chloroplasts requires the presence of at least one chloroplast in the cell, and that bleaching by streptomycin involves an inhibition of multiplication,and consequent dilution out of the chloroplasts. In the case of heat treat-ment, Brawerman and Chargaff (1960) found that if cells were grown at the bleaching temperature for some time and were then returned to room temperature, the proportion of permanently bleached cells depended upon how fast the cells were allowed to multiply at the lower temperature. Rapidly dividing cells became permanently bleached; cells dividing slowly or not at all regained their ability to form chloro-plasts. These authors suggested that there was a self-duplicating system involved in chloroplast formation, the multiplication of which was inhibited by the bleaching temperature, but could eventually resume when the cells were returned to normal temperature. It was thought to be lost by dilution out if the cells multiplied rapidly before multiplication of the system was resumed. On the basis of the number of cellular divisions at the bleaching temperature required to bring about loss of the ability to form chloroplasts, it was suggested that the number of self-duplicating units per cell might be more than sixty. However, these authors point out that if multiplication of these units was merely slowed down, rather than stopped, at the bleaching temperature, this estimate would be too high.

X.6.v. IS THE DILUTION HYPOTHESIS VALID?

So far, the effects of these three bleaching agents have been interpreted as being due to loss, by dilution out, of cytoplasmic particles. Before we go on to use these findings on bleaching to give us information about the chloroplast genetic material we must consider whether the dilution hypothesis is, in fact, correct. Results casting serious doubts on its validity have been reported by De Deken-Grenson and Godts (1960). Cells of *Euglena gracilis* were briefly exposed to streptomycin as before[26] and then single cells were placed in hanging drops of drug-free medium, and their subsequent fate was followed. As expected on the basis of the previous experiments chlorophyll formation ceased for several generations and then resumed in some, but not all of the cultures. Cultures in which chlorophyll synthesis did not recommence gave rise ultimately, of course, to homogeneously white populations. On the basis of the dilution hypothesis it would be expected that cultures in which chlorophyll synthesis did start again would give rise in some cases to pure green populations, and in others to mixed green and white populations depending upon just how far dilution had proceeded at the time chloroplast formation was resumed. However, this was found not to be the case: all cultures in which chlorophyll synthesis recommenced gave rise, ultimately, to homogeneously green populations. From sixty cells treated with streptomycin, thirteen pure white, forty-seven pure green, and no mixed, cultures were obtained.

Similar experiments were carried out with single cells which had been grown at $34°$, or which had been given a bleaching dose of UV. From forty-one heat-treated cells, twenty-three pure white, sixteen pure green, and two mixed cultures were obtained. From sixteen UV-treated cells, five pure white, seven pure green and four mixed cultures were obtained.

Must we, on the basis of these findings, reject the dilution hypothesis? In the case of UV-bleaching this is not necessary since in that experiment, 25 per cent of the cultures were mixed. Also, after the UV treatment the cells were only grown in the dark for 24 hours to avoid photoreactivation: in fact five days growth in the dark is needed to prevent photoreactivation when the cells are finally grown in the light[101]. In the experiment on heat-bleaching, only two out of forty-one cultures were mixed. However, this experiment differed from the other two in that the organisms were grown under bleaching conditions for a long time (three or four days) before single cells were isolated. Hence it is entirely possible that by this time the chloroplasts, or nucleo-protein particles concerned with chloroplast formation, had been diluted out to such an extent that some of the isolated cells contained them, and others did not. These two types of cell would give rise to green and white cultures respectively. The small proportion of mixed cultures could arise from cases in which an isolated cell, containing one chloroplast or nucleoprotein particle, underwent one cellular division at the lower temperature, before the chloroplast (or particle), had multiplied. Thus, these experiments do not require us to reject the dilution hypothesis for UV- and heat-bleaching.

In the experiment with streptomycin, however, the complete absence of mixed cultures indicates that there was no segregation out of chloro-plast-forming ability within the clone derived from a single treated cell. It appears that the fate of a cell, and all its progeny, was already deter-mined at the time the cell was isolated after its brief exposure to anti-biotic: either chloroplast-forming ability was retained (although its operation was temporarily suspended), or it was lost. A possible explanation of these results could be that at any given moment, all the chloroplasts, or all the nucleoprotein particles controlling chloroplast formation, within a particular cell, might have the same susceptibility to streptomycin. However, at different times within the cellular division cycle, this susceptibility might be greater or lower. The cell sample treated in the experiment was from a normal, logarithmically growing culture, and presumably included cells of all types from those which had just divided to those just about to divide. The period of exposure to drug (two hours) was relatively short, being only about one-twelfth to one-sixth of the generation time. Thus, in some of the cells treated, all the chloroplasts, or nucleoprotein particles, could have been in a state sensitive to streptomycin; in other cells they would be in an insensitive condition. This would account for the all-or-none effect of the drug, the complete loss or complete retention of chloroplast-forming ability. Hence, this experiment does not disprove that in normal cells the ability to make chloroplasts is transmitted by the multiplication and segregation of cytoplasmic particles. However, it does suggest that there may be a difference between the mechanism of streptomycin-bleaching and that of heat- and ultraviolet-bleaching. The latter two are probably due to a temporary inhibition of multiplication of cytoplasmic particles; when the effect of the bleaching agent is overcome by lowering the temperature, or treating with visible light (to photoreactivate) the particles immediately, or after some delay, begin to multiply again, and whether or not bleaching has taken place depends upon how far dilution out has proceeded during the period of blocked particle multiplication. In streptomycin-bleaching, as carried out by De Deken-Grenson and Godts, on the other hand, a brief treatment with a very high concentration of drug would irreversibly block particle multiplication in that fraction of the cells which happened to be in the susceptible state: in the other cells particle multiplication would continue, and any effect on chlorophyll synthesis would be only temporary. If, as is normally done, the organism is allowed to grow for a few generations in the presence of streptomycin, then all the cells will eventually be exposed to the drug during the sensitive part of the division cycle, which would account for the 100 per cent bleaching obtained under those conditions. The theory that the susceptibility of a cell to streptomycin-bleaching varies throughout the division cycle could be tested by using synchronously-growing cells and measuring the proportion of bleached clones produced by brief treatment with antibiotic at different points within the division cycle.

Although the above theoretical treatment does explain the findings of De Deken-Grenson and Godts, there still remains a discrepancy between these results and those obtained previously by De Deken-Grenson and Messin (1958). The experiments with isolated cells suggest that a brief treatment with streptomycin causes immediate loss of chloroplast-forming ability in a proportion of the cells, without any permanent effect on the others. Therefore, if cells so treated are allowed to multiply in the absence of drug, and are plated out at intervals (which is what De Deken-Grenson and Messin did), the proportion of white colonies should remain constant. This, of course, assumes that green and bleached cells multiply at the same rate (De Deken-Grenson and Godts report that this is, in fact, so). However, what actually happened was that the proportion of white colonies steadily increased until it reached nearly 100 per cent. De Deken-Grenson and Godts found that if the experiment was prolonged, then after a while the proportion of white colonies began to fall again, and within anything from three to eight more generations, decreased to between 4 and 20 per cent. To explain this Grenson (1964) suggests that these brief treatments with streptomycin induce a period of genetic instability, during which any radical change in the cell's environment, such as being plated out on solid medium, favours one or other of the alternative stable states, white or green. This period of instability would have two phases, one in which the probability of the white state steadily increased, followed by one in which it decreased.

To explain these results, then, the previous hypothesis might be restated as follows. A brief treatment with a high concentration of streptomycin permanently blocks the multiplication of the cytoplasmic particles concerned with chloroplast formation in that fraction of the cells which are in a susceptible condition; the experiments with isolated cells suggest that, under the conditions used, this fraction is in the region of 20 per cent. In the remaining 80 per cent or so of the cells the particles continue to multiply but, as a result of the streptomycin treatment, are temporarily in an unstable state. The duration of this unstable state might perhaps correspond to the period in which chlorophyll synthesis is halted. If the cells are allowed to go on multiplying in liquid medium, the particles also go on multiplying. If, however, the cells are subjected to a drastic change in culture conditions by being plated out, the particles either cease multiplying altogether (giving rise to a white colony), or revert to their normal state (giving rise to a green colony). It is also necessary to suppose that for some reason the tendency for the particles to stop multiplying when the cells are plated out increases for the first few generations, and then decreases again. It should be noted that this theory is consistent with either a direct, or an indirect effect of streptomycin on the replication of the cytoplasmic nucleoprotein particles (see XV.2.iii for a discussion of the possible mechanism of streptomycin action at the biochemical level).

To sum up, the results of De Deken-Grenson and Godts indicate that the dilution hypothesis in its simplest form is probably not applicable to streptomycin bleaching, and so studies on the time course of this type of bleaching (such as those carried out by De Deken-Grenson and Messin) cannot be used to calculate the number per cell of the cytoplasmic particles involved in chloroplast formation. However, there seems to be no reason why data on UV- and heat-bleaching should not be used for this purpose, since, as we saw above, the findings of De Deken-Grenson and Godts are not inconsistent with a dilution mechanism for these kinds of bleaching.

X.6.vi. THE NUCLEIC ACID COMPONENT OF THE PARTICLE

The evidence which we have discussed so far, indicating that the site of UV-, and possibly other kinds of bleaching, is a cytoplasmic nucleoprotein, is consistent with the nucleic acid component of such a nucleoprotein being either RNA or DNA. We have also seen that the most plausible suggestion as to what happens to the nucleoprotein as a result of the bleaching treatment, is that it is lost from the cells. One of the criteria to use, therefore, in the identification of the nucleoprotein is that it should disappear from the cells as a consequence of the bleaching treatment. A nucleic acid species which disappears from the cells when they are subjected to the bleaching treatment has, in fact, now been discovered.

Green cells of *Euglena gracilis*, as we saw previously, have three (at least) types of DNA, distinguishable on the basis of density: a main band of density 1·707, and two satellite bands, densities 1·685 and 1·691. However, in permanently bleached strains, whether produced by UV, high temperature, or streptomycin treatment, the 1·707 and 1·691 components are present but the 1·685 component is absent[61, 31, 88]. This suggests, although it does not prove, that the 1·685 DNA satellite, possibly in the form of a complex with protein, is the UV-sensitive site involved in bleaching.

If the 1·685 DNA is indeed the chromophore for UV-bleaching, then it is interesting to speculate as to why this cytoplasmic DNA should be so much more sensitive to UV than is the nuclear DNA. That this is so is indicated by the fact that the UV dose required to bring about killing of 90 per cent of the cells is about fifteen times as big as the dose required to bring about bleaching of 90 per cent of the cells[22]. The difference in base ratio between these two kinds of DNA (nuclear DNA has about 52 per cent adenine-thymine content; UV-sensitive satellite DNA has about 74 per cent adenine-thymine content) immediately suggests that the greater sensitivity of the 1·685 satellite is due to its higher thymine content, since UV-damage to DNA is thought to involve formation of dimers between adjacent thymine residues in a given single strand of the DNA[115]. However, while the higher thymine content of the satellite DNA may well contribute to its greater UV-sensitivity, it does not seem sufficient in itself to account for the very large difference observed. If we make the simplifying assumption of random distribution of thymine residues along the DNA chains, then the frequency with which thymine occurs next to thymine in the 1·685 satellite DNA would be only about twice the frequency in the nuclear DNA; but the UV-sensitivities of these DNAs differ by a factor of about 15. The difference in sensitivity might be related to detailed differences in base sequence rather than overall base composition: for instance, the 1·685 DNA might have a relatively long sequence of thymine residues at some point or points in the molecule, so that the increase in probability of UV-damage might be much greater than that suggested by the difference in overall base ratios. However, there are many other possible explanations.

X.6.vii. CONCLUSIONS FROM BLEACHING
EXPERIMENTS

The various studies on bleaching agents which we have considered suggest the following conclusions. That within the cell of *Euglena gracilis* there exist particles of a specific type. These particles probably consist of DNA, possibly complexed with protein. They are present in the cytoplasm but not in the nucleus. The particles are permanently lost from the cell as a result of treatment with UV, heat or streptomycin. When the cells lose the particles they also lose the ability to make chloroplasts. Thus, in view of their probable chemical nature, their cytoplasmic location and their involvement in chloroplast formation, it seems entirely likely that these particles constitute the genetic material of the plastids. This conclusion fits in very satisfactorily with the evidence previously discussed (see X.5.ii), for a physical association between the DNA species in question—the 1·685 satellite—and the chloroplasts.

At this point it is worth mentioning that in higher plants some attempts have been made to induce mutation in the plastid genetic material by means of X-rays, radioactive phosphorus, and other mutagens. Some workers have claimed to have achieved this[60, 74, 91] but others have been unsuccessful[66, 2]. The techniques used generally involve treating the seed with the mutagen, and then attempting to detect mutant plastids in the first or second plant generations after treatment. If a single, mutated, plastid in a cell full of normal plastids, in the embryo, is to become detectable, then during the development of the plant there must arise cells (and cell lineages big enough to see) containing only the mutant plastids. For this to happen the mutant plastids must multiply about as fast as the normal plastids so that there is a reasonable chance of cells containing only mutant plastids arising by the usual sorting-out process (see Chapter VI). Such plastid mutants do exist (see Chapters VI and VII), but if, as seems quite probable, the vast majority of plastid mutations are such as to cause the plastids to multiply more slowly than the wild-type plastids, most plastid mutants will simply never be detected. This might explain the difficulty experienced in artificially producing plastid mutants in higher plants.

X.7. The Nature of the Plastid Genetic Material

On the basis of the histochemical, electron microscopic, and autoradiographic studies with whole cells, and the chemical and other investigations of isolated plastids, it may now be regarded as reasonably certain that plastids contain both RNA and DNA. In principle, the genetic information of the plastid could be stored in either of these components. However, since in all known forms of life other than certain viruses, DNA is the form in which genetic information is stored, it seems very probable that it is the DNA, rather than the RNA, which constitutes the plastid genetic material. This view is supported by the fact that all the chloroplast RNA species which have been examined so far, have turned out to be concerned in the mechanism of protein synthesis (see XII.6.iii). Nevertheless it could be argued that the RNA with template activity (isolated from *Euglena* chloroplasts by Brawerman and Eisenstadt, 1964) might be genetic RNA: if it is, then there should also be a mechanism within the chloroplasts for replicating this RNA—however, Bové, Morel, Bové, and Randot (1965) could detect no RNA-dependent RNA polymerase in chloroplasts from healthy leaves (although such an enzyme was present in chloroplasts of virus-infected plants—see Chapter XII).

Although the plastid DNA seems the more probable candidate for the plastid genetic material, before we assume that it does indeed serve this function, there are certain criteria which must be satisfied. First of all, we might expect the plastid DNA to have the same general physical and chemical properties as genetic DNA from other systems. As we have seen in this chapter, this does seem to be the case: plastid DNA is hydrolysed by deoxyribonuclease but is resistant to alkali[20, 87]; it contains the usual purine and pyrimidine bases[97, 87, 17, 94]; it appears to be double stranded, as indicated by adenine/thymine and cytosine/guanine ratios of unity, and by its increase in optical density at 260 mμ (corresponding to transition from double helix to random coils) at the temperature expected from the known base ratio[20, 30, 17]; it is of high molecular weight (Ray and Hanawalt, 1964, obtained values of 20–40 million, and considered that even these were likely to be under-estimates); it presents a similar appearance in electron micrographs to the DNA in bacterial nucleoplasm[90, 59, 44]; it is susceptible *in vivo* to UV damage, and this damage is photoreactivable[64, 100].

A second condition that we should expect to be fulfilled is that there should be enough DNA in the plastid to contain a useful amount of genetic information; say, at least enough for one structural gene. An analysis of the data shows that there is enough DNA in plastids to contain a large amount of genetic information. We shall confine our attention, here, to the chloroplast, since this is the plastid for which most information is available. The quantity of DNA in a single higher plant chloroplast appears to be in the region of 10^{-15}–10^{-14} g. In the case of broad-bean chloroplasts the lowest value obtained for the DNA content was 0·54 per cent of the chlorophyll content[58]. Assuming the chlorophyll content of the intact chloroplast to be 5 per cent (as for the spinach chloroplast—see Table I.1), then the lowest estimate of the DNA content is 0·027 per cent of the dry weight. If the volume of the broad-bean chloroplast is about the same as that of a tobacco chloroplast, *ca.* 31 $\mu^{3(63)}$, then the dry weight (assuming this to be about 20 per cent of the wet weight) should be in the region of $6·2 \times 10^{-12}$ g. The amount of DNA in a single broad-bean chloroplast may therefore be of the order of 2×10^{-15} g. A figure of about 2×10^{-15} g has been calculated by Gibor and Granick (1964) on the basis of the data of Chun *et al.* (1963) for spinach and beet chloroplasts. Ruppel and van Wyk (1965) have reported a value of $5·6 \times 10^{-15}$ g. for the chloroplast of *Antirrhinum majus*. Amongst the algae, a figure of about 5×10^{-15} g. DNA per chloroplast of *Chlamydomonas reinhardi* may be calculated from the data of Sager and Ishida (1963), and values in the range of 6 to 10×10^{-15} g. have been found for the DNA content of a single chloroplast of *Euglena gracilis*[86,17]. All these values for higher plant and algal chloroplasts are therefore in the range 2 to 10×10^{-15} g. DNA per chloroplast, which is of the order of magnitude of the amount of DNA in a bacterial cell (4×10^9 daltons, or 7×10^{-15} g.—Hershey and Melechen, 1957). A rather lower figure, about 1×10^{-16} g, has been obtained by Gibor and Izawa (1963) for the DNA content of a chloroplast of *Acetabularia mediterranea*. Now, 10^{-15} g of DNA contains about $1·9 \times 10^6$ deoxynucleotides: allowing six deoxynucleotides for one amino acid (three bases per codon, double-stranded DNA), this amount of DNA could therefore code the structure of about 1600 proteins containing, on the average, 200 amino acids each, and so having a molecular weight of *ca.* 27,000. Thus, even 10^{-16} g of DNA, the lowest of the above values, could code for about 160 typical proteins, and the higher values, 2 to 10×10^{-15} g could code for something like 3000 to 16,000 proteins.

However, it must be remembered that there is some evidence that a single chloroplast may contain a number of independent DNA particles or units. Several fibril-containing, nucleoplasm-like regions have been seen in a single section of an oat chloroplast[44]: this suggests that the DNA exists in a number of distinct units, although it is possible that these apparently separate areas might have been connected together in some region of the chloroplast not included in the section. In *Euglena gracilis*, as we have seen, there is some evidence for the presence of about three DNA particles per chloroplast. The different DNA units or particles within a chloroplast may, or may not, be identical. Let us assume, for instance, that there are four physically separate DNA units within a chloroplast. If these four units are identical, we can regard the chloroplast as being, in effect, tetraploid, that is, as possessing four copies of its genome. If, however, all four units are different, then we can regard the chloroplast as being haploid, and as having four 'chromosomes'. If the chloroplast is 'haploid' then the above estimate for the number of proteins that could be coded by chloroplast DNA stands: if, however, the chloroplast is 'polyploid', then the previous estimate of the number of different proteins must be divided by the 'ploidy' of the chloroplast (the number of identical DNA units in a single chloroplast). Since it is still not absolutely certain that there is more than one physically separate DNA unit in a chloroplast, and since, even if there is more than one unit we have no information about whether the units are identical or different, it is clear that we cannot make any absolutely definite statement about the total number of proteins for which the plastid DNA could code. However, on the basis of the evidence that we do have, it would seem reasonable to suppose that the DNA in a single chloroplast could, in principle, contain the information determining the structure of something of the order of 100 to 1000 proteins, and possibly many more. We are not, of course, assuming that this DNA only includes structural genes: regulatory and other genes could also be present; it just happens to be convenient to consider the information content in terms of the equivalent number of protein structural genes.

A third condition that we should expect to be fulfilled, if the chloroplast DNA contains genetic information, is that this DNA should have, associated with it, the same sort of mechanisms for bringing about its genetic effects as are found in other DNA-containing genetic systems. That is, we should expect to find the normal mechanism for making an RNA copy (template RNA) of the DNA, namely, DNA-dependent RNA polymerase. As we shall see later (XII.7) there is now good evidence that chloroplasts do indeed possess this essential component of the genetic process.

From the foregoing discussion it is clear that plastid DNA satisfies at least three of the criteria which we would expect to be satisfied by the plastid genetic material: it is similar in its general properties to genetic DNA from other biological systems, there is enough of it per plastid to contain a substantial amount of genetic information, and it has associated with it the biochemical machinery that it would need if it were to bring about genetic effects. These are not the only criteria which should be satisfied. It would be desirable, for instance, to show that the plastid DNA is stable; that it is replicated and transmitted unaltered to future generations of cells; and that changes in plastid DNA bring about corresponding changes in plastid biochemistry. However, if we assume, on the basis of genetic and cytological studies, that plastids do indeed contain genetic information, then it would seem, on the grounds of the evidence already available, that the plastid DNA is an eminently suitable candidate for the role of the carrier of this genetic information.

An alternative, but perhaps equally valid, way of looking at the results is to say that since we know of no function for DNA other than the storage of genetic information, then the biochemical demonstration of the presence of DNA in plastids is, in itself, direct evidence that plastids contain their own genetic material. The cytological and genetic evidence might then, logically (if not chronologically), be regarded as a confirmation of a conclusion arrived at on purely biochemical grounds.

The conclusion, whichever way we arrive at it, that plastids contain genetic information in the form of DNA is supported by a completely independent line of evidence: that obtained from experiments on bleaching of *Euglena*. As we have seen, these studies suggest that there is in the cytoplasm a specific type of DNA, the presence of which is essential for the formation of chloroplasts. There appear to be several copies of this DNA in any given cell: the number of copies is somewhat uncertain, but there are probably enough to have one copy (and possibly as many as three copies) per plastid.

Taking all this cytological, genetic and biochemical evidence from these first ten chapters together, then, I believe that it is reasonable to conclude that plastids do contain, in the form of DNA, at least some of the genetic information which controls their own growth and multiplication. In the next chapter we shall go on to consider the nature of the genetic information stored in plastid DNA.

REFERENCES

1. AARONSON, S. & BENSKY, B. (1962). *J. Gen. Microbiol.* **27**, 75–98
2. ARNOLD, C. G. & KRESSEL, M. (1965). *Z. Vererbungs.* **96**, 213–216
3. BALTUS, E. & BRACHET, J. (1963). *Biochim. Biophys. Acta* **76**, 490–492
4. BELL, P. R. (1961). *Proc. Roy. Soc. B.* **153**, 421–432
5. BELL, P. R. & MÜHLETHALER, K. (1964). *J. Mol. Biol.* **8**, 853–862
6. BIGGINS, J. & PARK, R. B. (1964). *Nature, Lond.* **203**, 425–426
7. BOARDMAN, N. K., FRANCKI, R. I. B., & WILDMAN, S. G. (1965). *Biochemistry* **4**, 872–876
8. BÖTTGER, I. & WOLLGIEHN, R. (1958). *Flora* **146**, 302
9. BOVÉ, J. M., MOREL, G., BOVÉ, C., & RANDOT, M.-J. In *Symposium on Biochemistry of Chloroplasts (Aberystwyth, 1965).* Ed., T. W. Goodwin. Academic Press, London (in press)
10. BRACHET, J. (1958). *Exp. Cell. Res. Suppl.* **6**, 78–96
11. BRACHET, J. (1962). *J. Cell. Comp. Physiol., Suppl.* **60**, 1
12. BRAWERMAN, G. (1962). *Biochim. Biophys. Acta* **61**, 313
13. BRAWERMAN, G. (1963). *Biochim. Biophys. Acta* **72**, 317–331
14. BRAWERMAN, G. In *Symposium on Biochemistry of Chloroplasts (Aberystwyth, 1965).* Ed., T. W. Goodwin. Academic Press, London (in press)
15. BRAWERMAN, G. & CHARGAFF, E. (1960). *Biochim. Biophys. Acta* **37**, 221–229
16. BRAWERMAN, G. & EISENSTADT, J. (1964a). *J. Mol. Biol.* **10**, 403–411
17. BRAWERMAN, G. & EISENSTADT, J. (1964b). *Biochim. Biophys. Acta* **91**, 477–485
18. CHIBA, Y. (1951). *Cytologia* **16**, 259–264
19. CHIBA, Y. & SUGAHARA, K. (1957). *Arch. Biochem. Biophys.* **71**, 367

20. CHUN, E. H. L., VAUGHAN, M. H. & RICH, A. (1963). *J. Mol. Biol.* **7**, 130–141
21. CLARK, M. F., MATTHEWS, R. E. F. & RALPH, R. K. (1964). *Biochim. Biophys. Acta* **91**, 289–304
22. COOK, J. R. (1963). *Photochem. & Photobiol.* **2**, 407–410
23. COOPER, W. D. & LORING, H. S. (1957). *J. Biol. Chem.* **228**, 813–822
24. DALES, S. & CERAMI, A. (Unpublished.) Quoted by (14)
25. DE DEKEN-GRENSON, M. & GODTS, A. (1960). *Exp. Cell. Res.* **19**, 376
26. DE DEKEN-GRENSON, M. & MESSIN, S. (1958). *Biochim. Biophys. Acta* **27**, 145–155
27. DOUNCE, A. L. (1955). In *The Nucleic Acids*, II. Eds., E. Chargaff & J. N. Davidson. Academic Press, New York, pp. 93–153
28. DU BUY, H. G. & WOODS, M. W. (1943). *Phytopath.* **33**, 766–777
29. EBRINGER, L. (1962). *J. Protozool.* **9**, 373–374
30. EDELMAN, M., COWAN, C. A., EPSTEIN, H. T. & SCHIFF, J. A. (1964). *Proc. Natl. Acad. Sci.* **52**, 1214–1219
31. EDELMAN, M., SCHIFF, J. A. & EPSTEIN, H. T. (1965). *J. Mol. Biol.* **11**, 769–774
32. EISENSTADT, J. M. & BRAWERMAN, G. (1964). *J. Mol. Biol.* **10**, 392–402
33. FLAUMENHAFT, E., CONRAD, S. M. & KATZ, J. J. (1960). *Science* **132**, 892–894
34. GIBBS, S. P. (1962). *J. Cell. Biol.* **15**, 343–361
35. GIBOR, A. & GRANICK, S. (1962). *J. Cell Biol.* **15**, 599–603
36. GIBOR, A. & GRANICK, S. (1964). *Science* **145**, 890–897
37. GIBOR, A. & IZAWA, M. (1963). *Proc. Natl. Acad. Sci.* **50**, 1164–1169
38. GIFFORD, E. M. (1960). *Am. J. Bot.* **47**, 834–837
39. GIVNER, J. & MORIBER, L. G. (1964). *J. Cell Biol.* **23**, 36A
40. GRAY, R. A. & HENDLIN, D. (1962). *Plant Phys.* **37**, 223–227
41. GRENSON, M. (1964). *Int. Rev. Cytol.* **16**, 37–59
42. GROSS, J. A. (1964). *Plant Phys.* **39**, xxxv
43. GROSS, J. A., JAHN, T. L. & BERNSTEIN, E. (1955). *J. Protozool.* **2**, 71–75
44. GUNNING, B. E. S. (1965a). *J. Cell Biol.* **24**, 79–93
45. GUNNING, B. E. S. (1965b). *Protoplasma* **55**, 111–130
46. GYLDENHOLM, A. O. (Unpublished.) Quoted by D. von Wettstein in *Symposium on Biochemistry of Chloroplasts (Aberystwyth, 1965)*. Ed., T. W. Goodwin. Academic Press, London (in press)
47. HEBER, U. (1963). *Planta* **59**, 600–616
48. HERSHEY, A. D. & MELECHEN, N. E. (1957). *Virology* **3**, 207
49. HOLDEN, M. (1952). *Biochem. J.* **51**, 433–442
50. IWAMURA, T. (1960). *Biochim. Biophys. Acta* **42**, 161–163
51. IWAMURA, T. (1962). *Biochim. Biophys. Acta* **61**, 472
52. IWAMURA, T. & KUWASHIMA, S. (1964). *Biochim. Biophys. Acta* **82**, 678–679
53. JACOBSON, A. B., SWIFT, H. & BOGORAD, L. (1963). *J. Cell Biol.* **17**, 557–570
54. JAGENDORF, A. T. (1955). *Plant Phys.* **30**, 138
55. JAGENDORF, A. T. & WILDMAN, S. G. (1954). *Plant Phys.* **29**, 270–279
56. KERN, H. (1959). *Protoplasma* **50**, 505–543
57. KIRK, J. T. O. (1963a). *Biochem. J.* **88**, 45P
58. KIRK, J. T. O. (1963b). *Biochim. Biophys. Acta* **76**, 417–424
59. KISLEV, N., SWIFT, H. & BOGORAD, L. (1965). *J. Cell Biol.* **25**, 327–344
60. KNUDSON, L. (1940). *Bot. Gaz.* **101**, 721–758
61. LEFF, J., MANDEL, M., EPSTEIN, H. T. & SCHIFF, J. A. (1963). *Biochim. Biophys. Res. Commun.* **13**, 126–130
62. LIMA-DE-FARIA, A. & MOSES, M. J. (1965). *Hereditas.* **52**, 367–378
63. LITTAU, V. C. (1958). *Am. J. Bot.* **45**, 45
64. LYMAN, H., EPSTEIN, H. T. & SCHIFF, J. A. (1961). *Biochim. Biophys. Acta* **50**, 301–309

65. LYTTLETON, J. W. (1962). *Exp. Cell. Res.* **26**, 312–317
66. MALY, R. (1958). *Z. Vererbungsl.* **89**, 629–693
67. McCALLA, D. R. (1965a). *J. Protozool.* **12**, 34–41
68. McCALLA, D. R. (1965b). *Science* **148**, 497–499
69. McCLENDON, J. A. (1952). *Am. J. Bot.* **39**, 275
70. McLEISH, J. (1964). *Nature, Lond.* **204**, 36–39
71. MENKE, W. (1938). *Z. phys. chem.* **257**, 43–48
72. MENKE, W. (1960). *Z. Vererbungsl.* **91**, 152–157
73. METZNER, H. (1952). *Biol. Zentr.* **71**, 257–272
74. MICHAELIS, P. (1958). *Planta* **51**, 600–634, 722–756
75. MIKULSKA, E., ODINTSOVA, S. & SISSAKIAN, N. M. (1962). *Naturwiss.* **49**, 549
76. MURAKAMI, S. (1963). *Exp. Cell. Res.* **32**, 398–400
77. ODINTSOVA, M. S., GOLUBEVA, E. V. & SISSAKIAN, N. M. (1964). *Nature, Lond.* **204**, 1090–1091
78. ORTH, G. M. & CORNWELL, D. G. (1963). *Biochim. Biophys. Acta* **71**, 734–736
79. PARKER, G. (1952). *Biochem. J.* **51**, 389–399
80. PETROPULOS, S. F. (1964). *Science* **145**, 392–393
81. POLLARD, C. J. (1964). *Arch. Biochem. Biophys.* **105**, 114–119
82. POLLISTER, A. W. (1955). In *Radiation Biology.* Ed., A. Hollaender, II. McGraw-Hill Book Co. Inc., New York, pp. 203–248
83. PRINGSHEIM, E. G. & PRINGSHEIM, O. (1952). *New Phytol* **51**, 65–76
84. PRINGSHEIM, E. G. (1958). *Rev. Algol.* **4**, 41–56
85. PROVASOLI, L., HUTNER, S. H. & SCHATZ, A. (1948). *Proc. Soc. Exp. Biol. & Med.* **69**, 279–282
86. RAY, D. S. (1964). B. L. Report, No. 125. Stanford University, Stanford, California.
87. RAY, D. S. & HANAWALT, P. C. (1964). *J. Mol. Biol.* **9**, 812–824
88. RAY, D. S. & HANAWALT, P. C. (1965). *J. Mol. Biol.* **11**, 760–768
89. RHODES, M. J. C. & YEMM, E. W. (1963). *Nature, Lond.* **200**, 1077–1080
90. RIS, H. & PLAUT, W. (1962). *J. Cell Biol.* **13**, 383–391
91. RÖBBELEN, G. (1962). *Z. Vererbungsl.* **93**, 25–34
92. ROBBINS, W. T., HERVEY, A. & STEBBINS, M. E. (1953). *Ann. N. Y. Acad. Sci.* **56**, 818–830
93. RUPPEL, H. G. (1964). *Biochim. Biophys. Acta* **80**, 63–72
94. RUPPEL, H. G. & VAN WYK, D. (1965). *Z. Pflanzenphysiol.* **53**, 32–38
95. SAGAN, L. (1965). *J. Protozool.* **12**, 105–109
96. SAGAN, L., BEN-SHAUL, Y., SCHIFF, J. A. & EPSTEIN, H. T. (1964). *J. Cell Biol.* **23**, 81A
97. SAGER, R. & ISHIDA, M. (1963). *Proc. Natl. Acad. Sci.* **50**, 725–730
98. SAGER, R. & PALADE, G. E. (1957). *J. Biophys. Biochem. Cytol.* **3**, 463—488
99. SCHER, S. & COLLINGE, J. C. (1965). *Nature, Lond.* **205**, 828–830
100. SCHIFF, J. A., EPSTEIN, H. T. & LYMAN, H. (1961). *Proc. 3rd Int. Congr. Photobiol.* Eds., B. C. Christensen & B. Buchmann. Elsevier, Amsterdam, pp. 289–292
101. SCHIFF, J. A., LYMAN, H. & EPSTEIN, H. T. (1961). *Biochim. Biophys. Acta* **50**, 310–318
102. SETLOW, R. B. & CARRIER, W. L. (1964). *Proc. Natl. Acad. Sci.* **51**, 226–231
103. SHIPP, W. S., KIERAS, F. J. & HASELKORN, R. (1965). *Proc. Natl. Acad. Sci.* **54**, 207–213
104. SISSAKIAN, N. M. (1958). *Adv. Enz.* **20**, 201–236
105. SISSAKIAN, N. M., FILIPPOVICH, I. I., SVETAILO, E. N. & ALIYEV, R. A. (1965). *Biochim. Biophys. Acta* **95**, 474–485
106. SMILLIE, R. M. (1956). *Austr. J. Biol. Sci.* **9**, 339–346, 347–354
107. SPENCER, D. (1965). *Arch. Biochem. Biophys.* **111**, 381–390

108. SPIEKERMANN, R. (1957). *Protoplasma* **48**, 303–324
109. STEFFENSEN, D. M. & SHERIDAN, W. F. (1965). *J. Cell Biol.* **25**, 619–626
110. STOCKING, C. R. & GIFFORD, E. M. (1959). *Biochem. Biophys. Res. Commun.* **1**, 159–164
111. STRAUS, W. (1954). *Exp. Cell. Res.* **6**, 392–402
112. SZARKOWSKI, J. W. & GOLASZEWSKI, T. (1961). *Naturwiss.* **48**, 457
113. DE VITRY, F. quoted by (3).
114. VOSA, C. & KIRK, J. T. O. (1963). Unpublished
115. WACKER, A. (1963). *Progr. in Nucleic Acid Res.* **1**, 369–399
116. WEIER, T. E. & STOCKING, C. R. (1952). *Am. J. Bot.* **39**, 720
117. WOLLGIEHN, R. & MOTHES, K. (1964). *Exp. Cell. Res.* **35**, 52–57
118. YOSHIDA, Y. (1962). *Protoplasma* **54**, 476–492
119. ZAHALSKY, A. C., HUTNER, S. H., KEANE, M. & BURGER, R. M. (1962). *Archiv. Mikrobiol.* **42**, 46–55

CHAPTER XI

Genetic Control and Plastid Biochemistry

XI.1. Introduction

WHAT is the function of the plastid DNA? Does it contain all the genetic information required for the synthesis of the plastid materials, or is some of this information stored in the nucleus? A possible approach to this problem is to make mutants with aberrant plastids; to carry out biochemical studies on these to identify the lesion—ideally to demonstrate that a particular enzyme is absent or modified; and finally, to determine by genetic experiments whether the inheritance of the defect is Mendelian or non-Mendelian, that is, whether the gene is located in the nucleus or in the cytoplasm. A number of studies along these lines have been carried out and will be described in this chapter.

XI.2. The Control of Chlorophyll Synthesis

Very many mutants of higher plants and algae with lowered chlorophyll content have been described[107, 84, 76, 48, 89, 110]. However, I shall consider only those mutants on which sufficient work has been done to give some indication of the biochemical defect involved and the mode of inheritance. A considerable amount of biochemical research has been carried out by Granick on mutants of *Chlorella* with impaired chlorophyll synthesis (see, for instance, Granick, 1950). Unfortunately, this organism has no sexual mode of reproduction, and therefore it has been impossible to carry out genetic studies. An account of current views on the reactions involved in chlorophyll biosynthesis is given by Granick and Mauzerall (1961) and Bogorad (1965) (see Fig. XII.1).

A mutant of *Chlamydomonas reinhardi* has been found[78] which does not synthesize chlorophyll, but accumulates reddish-brown chlorophyll precursors, amongst which protoporphyrin 9 has been identified spectrophotometrically. On the basis of the frequency of second division

338

segregation of this marker, partial linkage with the centromere was established, and this was taken as evidence for its chromosomal location. A yellow barley mutant, xantha-10, unable to synthesize chlorophyll or protochlorophyll has been described[105,106]; since the mutant could make cytochrome porphyrins, chlorophyll synthesis was thought to be inhibited at some point after protoporphyrin 9. The plastids contained a few large thylakoids, parallel to each other but spaced widely apart. Inheritance of this character was Mendelian. A mutant of *Arabidopsis thaliana* was reported[75] to be able to synthesize protochlorophyll but unable to convert it to chlorophyll. Reduction of protochlorophyllide to chlorophyllide in a homogenate of the mutant would only take place in the presence of an aqueous extract of normal plants, indicating that the mutant was unable to synthesize some substance essential for the reduction process. This mutation was shown to be due to a recessive allele of a single gene, showing normal Mendelian inheritance.

Another barley mutant has been found which has an approximately normal amount of chlorophyll *a*, but is completely lacking in chlorophyll *b*[27]. The character is recessive and is inherited in a normal Mendelian fashion. Interestingly enough this mutant is viable and able to photosynthesize, although the growth rate is lower than that of the wild type[28]. Mutants containing chlorophyll *a* but not chlorophyll *b* have also been found in *Arabidopsis thaliana* and *Pisum sativum*[76,22,67]. In *A. thaliana* a series of mutants with approximately normal amounts of chlorophyll *a*, but with reduced quantities of, or no, chlorophyll *b* have been reported[29]. These were shown to be due to a number of alleles of a single gene: it was possible to assign this gene to one of the known linkage groups.

Genes have been found which appear to affect the timing, rather than the pathway, of chlorophyll synthesis. For instance, a number of so-called 'virescent' mutants of higher plants are known: these differ from wild-type in that although they can synthesize chlorophyll, the synthesis, in the developing plant, takes place a few days later than it does in the wild type. An example is a barley mutant, the seedling of which is pale yellow-green at emergence, but later begins to synthesize chlorophyll, and reaches its maximum level 2–3 days after the normal plant[62]. After four days of growth, when the grana of the normal chloroplasts are well developed, the plastids of the mutant contain no normal thylakoids and grana, but instead have large numbers of vesicles. However, after 12 days the mutant plastids develop into normal chloroplasts with grana. The virescent character is recessive, and is due to a gene on barley chromosome I. A mutant showing the virescent character to an even more marked degree is pale-yellow-1 of maize. When grown in the light the seedlings contain neither chlorophyll *a* nor chlorophyll *b*; when grown in the dark they contain only

10 per cent of the protochlorophyll in the wild-type[38]. The light-grown mutant seedlings also have less carotenes and xanthophylls than the light-grown wild-type; the dark-grown mutant seedlings have less xanthophylls than the dark-grown wild-type, but the same amount of carotenes. After 8 days' growth the mutant block is broken: the mutant seedlings growing in the light begin to accumulate chlorophylls, carotenes, and xanthophylls; the mutant seedlings growing in the dark begin to form protochlorophyll and xanthophylls (but not carotenes).

A gene which may affect the timing of chlorophyll synthesis in the opposite way has been found in the tomato. During the maturation of the tomato fruit, and the differentiation of the chloroplasts into chromoplasts (see XIV.5), chlorophyll synthesis stops, and then the chlorophyll breaks down. However, in the 'green-flesh' (or 'dirty red') mutant, the ripe fruit still contains substantial amounts of chlorophyll, as well as the usual fruit carotenoids[72, 39]. The mutant fruit has at least as much chlorophyllase as the wild-type, which is thought[72] to indicate that impaired degradation of chlorophyll is not responsible for retention of chlorophyll by the mutant. It is thought more likely that in the mutant chlorophyll synthesis is terminated at a later stage in fruit development so that chlorophyll degradation has not gone to completion when the fruit is ripe. Alternatively, the mutation may permit continued synthesis of chlorophyll at a reduced rate even in the ripe fruit. Either way, the mutation is seen as a defect in the mechanism for switching off chlorophyll synthesis. The character is due to a single, recessive factor, inherited in a Mendelian manner; the gene has been given the symbol gf[39]. A single recessive Mendelian factor causing retention of chlorophyll in ripe *Capsicum* fruit has also been found[88].

On the basis of these results it appears likely that at least three of the reactions in chlorophyll synthesis are under nuclear control: a step between protoporphyrin 9 and protochlorophyllide, the conversion of protochlorophyllide to chlorophyllide, and one step which is in the pathway of chlorophyll b synthesis but not that of chlorophyll a synthesis. These conclusion are summarized in Fig. XI.1.

There is also some indication, from studies on the virescent and the green-flesh mutations, that the control of the initiation and termination of chlorophyll synthesis are under nuclear control. However, the true nature of these particular genes is not clear. The virescent barley mutant, for instance, could have a defect in a regulator gene (see XIII.18) concerned with switching on or off the structural genes for one or more of the enzymes of chlorophyll synthesis. The defect would be such that the switching-on of chlorophyll synthesis occurred later than it should. Alternatively, the block might be in the biosynthesis of some amino acid or other essential growth factor (compare with barley mutant, albina-7, XI.6). If the factor was formed by two pathways,

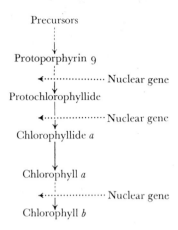

FIG. XI.1. *Nuclear control of chlorophyll synthesis*

one in the mature chloroplast, the other outside the chloroplast, then in the germinating seedling (which initially lacks chloroplasts) the factor would normally be synthesized, to begin with, by the extra-chloroplastic pathway. If there was a partial block (due perhaps to a mutation causing diminished activity of one of the enzymes) in the extra-chloroplastic pathway, then formation of chloroplasts would at first take place relatively slowly, for lack of the essential factor. However, as soon as these slowly developing chloroplasts got to the stage when they began to carry out their own synthesis of this factor (such synthesis might, for instance, be linked to photosynthesis), then there would be a rapid, autocatalytic increase in the rate of chloroplast development, and from then on the plants would grow more or less normally. There are many other possibilities: for instance, Miller and Zalik (1965) have suggested that the virescent mutation causes a change in the protein to which the chlorophyll is bound, so that either the chlorophyll-protein complex is formed at a reduced rate, or it is incorporated into the grana at a reduced rate. The pale-yellow-1 mutation of maize is particularly interesting because it seems to cause a delay in plastid pigment synthesis in the dark as well as in the light. A mutation in a regulator gene is one of the possible explanations.

We can say little about the detailed mode of action of the green-flesh mutation in the tomato, because we know nothing about the mechanism by which chlorophyll synthesis is caused to stop in the ripening fruit. The control could involve inhibition of the activity of one of the enzymes involved in chlorophyll synthesis, or alternatively could be due to inhibition of formation of one of the proteins that are required for chlorophyll synthesis (see Chapter XIII): if the second of these hypotheses is correct, then the green-flesh mutation might be in a regulator gene.

XI.3. The Control of Carotenoid Synthesis

XI.3.i. MUTATIONS AFFECTING THE CAROTENOIDS OF THE CHLOROPLAST

Koski and Smith (1951) showed that an apparently albino mutant of maize (w-3) was, in fact, able to form protochlorophyll and chlorophyll, but that the pigments were bleached on continued illumination. Stanier (1959) suggested that instability of chlorophyll to light was in some cases due to lack of coloured carotenoids. It was shown[1] that this maize mutant was indeed unable to synthesize coloured carotenoids: instead, it accumulated the colourless compound phytoene, thought to be an early carotenoid precursor (see Fig. XII.2). It was suggested that there was a metabolic block between phytoene and coloured carotenoids. The defect was due to a gene on maize chromosome 2[77]. The chlorophyll (or chlorophyllide) formed by this mutant appears to be non-functional since the mutant is unable to carry out photosynthetic $^{14}CO_2$ fixation[56].

Two other photo-sensitive mutants of maize, with blocks in carotenoid synthesis, have now been found[11]. One of these accumulates ζ-carotene, and the other accumulates lycopene. At low light intensities (ca. 30 lux) the chlorophyll content is about 30 per cent of the wild-type level. At higher light intensities the chlorophyll is destroyed. The carotenoids of the mutants are more readily extractable with petrol than are the carotenoids of the wild-type, suggesting that the carotenoids of the mutants are less firmly bound in the chloroplast structure. Both mutations are inherited in a normal Mendelian manner.

A white mutant and a yellow mutant of *Helianthus annuus* which are able to form chlorophyll *a* and chlorophyll *b* in dim light have been found: these pigments are bleached by prolonged exposure to light[101,100,25]. Like the corn variety discussed above, the white mutant has no coloured carotenoids. The yellow mutant has no carotenes but has substantial amounts of xanthophylls which, on the basis of the absorption spectrum, appear to be identical with those of the wild-type. When grown in the dark, the albino mutant forms etioplasts with normal crystalline centres[103,104]. When the leaves have been exposed to light, but before they have bleached, the usual early stages in the metamorphosis of the crystalline centre (breakdown of crystalline structure, dispersion of thylakoids and vesicles in layers throughout the plastids—see XIII.7) take place. There is even formation of some small thylakoid stacks, similar to normal grana. There are also large osmiophilic globuli. During bleaching in continued light, the plastids become amoeboid in shape; the thylakoids swell to produce large vesicles and the grana disintegrate; the globuli disappear. The yellow mutant also forms normal etioplasts when grown in the dark[103, 104]. During exposure to light, but before bleaching has occurred, the etioplasts differentiate in the usual way to form chloroplasts—these contain thylakoids and vesicles, and frequently a few large grana. As a result of the bleaching brought about by continued exposure to light, the chloroplasts become amoeboid, and most of the grana and thylakoids disappear to be replaced by vesicles: an occasional granum may persist. The chloroplasts of the yellow mutant are more resistant to bleaching than those of the white. Both the white and the yellow character show Mendelian inheritance, being controlled by single, recessive factors[100].

The above findings suggest that at least three of the steps of carotenoid synthesis in leaf chloroplasts are under nuclear control: a step between phytoene and ζ-carotene, a reaction immediately or shortly after ζ-carotene, and a step between ζ-carotene and β-carotene (perhaps after lycopene, if this is indeed an intermediate in β-carotene synthesis). These conclusions are shown diagrammatically in Fig. XI.2a.

On the face of it, the results obtained with the yellow *Helianthus* mutant suggest that the nucleus also controls a step which is in the pathway of synthesis of carotenes but not xanthophylls. This is difficult to understand in terms of carotenoid biosynthesis since xanthophylls might be expected to be formed from carotenes. However, another explanation is suggested by the fact that plants grown in the dark have a higher xanthophyll-carotene ratio than plants grown in the light (see I.4.ii). It seems possible that the yellow *Helianthus* mutant has a defect, not in the actual pathway of carotenoid synthesis, but in whatever mechanism it is that switches synthesis towards carotene rather than xanthophyll formation in the light. That is, the mutation might possibly be in a regulator gene.

It is interesting that bleaching of the chlorophyll in strong light is a common feature both of plastom mutants[100, 106] and of those hybrid plants in which there appears to be incompatibility between the plastom and the nuclear genome (see Chapters VII, VIII, and IX). For instance, von Wettstein and Eriksson (1964) have described a white mutant of *Nicotiana tabacum* in which normal chloroplasts are initially formed in the cotyledons and first leaves. As the leaves expand the thylakoids begin to swell and disintegrate, the pigments are destroyed, and eventually large empty plastids containing only a few vacuoles are produced. However, in these cases it seems unlikely that the defect simply involves lack of carotenoids. Certain of the *Oenothera* hybrids

have been shown to contain, prior to bleaching, the usual leaf carotenoids in approximately normal amounts[81,82]. In a plastom mutant
of *Antirrhinum majus* the tendency of the chlorophyll to bleach decreases
as the plant gets older[108].

XI.3.ii. MUTATIONS AFFECTING THE CAROTENOIDS OF CHROMOPLASTS

The chromoplasts of various kinds of fruit, and flower petals, show a
much greater variety in their carotenoid composition than do chloroplasts (see I.6.ii). A certain amount is known about the genetic control
of the formation of these chromoplast carotenoids. The most intensively
studied system of this type is the tomato fruit chromoplast. In the
normal red tomato the major carotenoid is lycopene (87 per cent) and
there is also a small amount (7 per cent) of β-carotene[60]. Several
varieties of tomato are known in which the fruit is of a different colour:
these differ from the wild-type in the amount, and/or kind, of carotenoids present. We shall now discuss these different types of carotenoid
composition, and the way in which they are inherited.

We can say straight away that all the genes discovered so far which
determine tomato fruit colour show normal Mendelian inheritance.
Hurst (1906) showed that red and yellow tomatoes differ at a single
gene. Red tomatoes possess the dominant allele, r^+: yellow tomatoes
are homozygous for the recessive allele, r. This gene is linked to the white
flower (wf) locus on linkage group 2[73]. The r^+/r gene controls the
total amount of carotenoid formed[49], the genotype rr having about
5 per cent of the amount of carotenoids possessed by r^+r^+. It is thought
that this gene controls formation of an enzyme which acts on some
compound prior to phytoene, since this substance does not accumulate
in rr fruit[61]. Another gene which affects the total amount of carotenoids
was discovered by Jenkins and Mackinney (1955). Fruit homozygous
for the recessive allele at are apricot in colour and have only about 10
per cent of the carotenoid content of normal red fruit which possess the
dominant allele, at^+. This gene is not allelic with the r^+/r gene and
differs from it functionally in that $atat$ suppresses lycopene but not β-
carotene formation, whereas rr suppresses both. The at^+/at gene probably also acts at an early stage in biosynthesis.

A third gene which affects the total amount of carotenoids has been
found[93]. This gene differs from the two previously described in that
the mutant allele, hp, increases (by about 100 per cent), rather than
decreases, the total carotenoid content. However, like r and at, hp is
recessive. At first the effect was thought to be due to two genes, but it
was later concluded[94] that only one gene (hp^+/hp) was involved. $hphp$

has been shown[97] to increase the amounts, not only of the final products lycopene and β-carotene, but also of the compounds phytoene and phytofluene, thought to be further back in the synthetic pathway. This suggests that the hp^+/hp gene acts at a stage prior to phytoene.

Another colour variety of tomatoes, tangerine, differs from the red type at a single gene, which was shown[58] to be linked with other loci in linkage group 7. The tangerine fruit are homozygous for the recessive allele, t, and red fruit possess the dominant allele t^+. In fruit of genotype tt, all *trans* lycopene, the major carotenoid of normal red fruit, is largely replaced by prolycopene, which probably contains five to seven *cis* double bonds[112, 50]. Zechmeister and Went (1948) suggested that the gene t^+/t acts by determining the spatial configuration of the lycopene molecule. Mackinney and Jenkins (1952) showed that the more saturated carotenoids, neurosporene and ζ-carotene also accumulated in the tt genotype, and they suggested that the t^+/t gene might control a dehydrogenase involved in the conversion of these carotenoids to lycopene.

Lincoln and Porter (1950) found a new gene which determines whether the major carotenoid of the fruit is lycopene or β-carotene. Normal red high-lycopene fruit are homozygous for the recessive allele, B^+. The orange-coloured, high β-carotene fruit are either homozygous or heterozygous for the dominant allele, B. The total carotenoid content is much the same in the red and orange fruit. The effects of the B^+/B gene are in part governed by a modifier gene, $mo_B{}^+/mo_B$, which is inherited quite independently[98]. In plants homozygous for the recessive allele, mo_B, the carotenoid composition of the fruit is about 90 per cent β-carotene in the presence of B and 90 per cent lycopene in the presence of B^+B^+. However, when $mo_B{}^+$ is present in either homozygous or heterozygous form, the action of B is partially inhibited, and the fruit produce roughly equal quantities of β-carotene and lycopene: $mo_B{}^+$ does not interfere with the action of the allele, B^+, since B^+B^+ fruit still have 90 per cent lycopene in the presence of $mo_B{}^+$. The essential difference between the structures of lycopene and β-carotene is that whereas lycopene has an open chain structure, β-carotene has a ring system at each end: Tomes, Quackenbush, and Kargl (1956) suggest that the function of the allele, B, is to mediate the formation of these β-ionone rings. Goodwin and Jamikorn (1952) found that, in normal red fruit, high temperature inhibits formation of lycopene but not of β-carotene, suggesting that in this fruit β-carotene is not synthesized from lycopene. The enhanced β-carotene synthesis in $hphp$ fruit is also not temperature-sensitive [95], but the increased β-carotene synthesis in fruit containing the B allele is inhibited at $32°$[96]. Tomes (1963) suggested that in tomato fruit there are two separate pathways for β-carotene synthesis: one, temperature-insensitive, in which lycopene is not involved; and another one, temperature-sensitive, in which β-carotene is formed from lycopene or its immediate precursors. The B^+/B gene would thus be concerned with this second pathway.

With regard to the function of the mo_B^+/mo_B gene, it might seem, superficially, that either of the two following explanations is feasible: that the mo_B allele produces something which (in BB fruit) directs carotenoid synthesis mainly towards β-carotene formation, and the mo_B^+ allele is inactive: or that the mo_B^+ allele produces something which (in BB fruit) directs carotenoid synthesis half towards β-carotene, and half towards lycopene, and that the mo_B allele is inactive. However, the fact that mo_B^+ is dominant over mo_B eliminates the first of these hypotheses: it seems likely, therefore, that the mo_B^+ allele is responsible for the production of some compound which has the effect of switching the carotenoid-synthesizing machinery over from making mainly β-carotene to making half β-carotene and half lycopene. This compound could be acting at the metabolic level, perhaps by partially inhibiting the action of one of the enzymes involved in the conversion of lycopene to β-carotene: alternatively it could act at the genetic level, partly repressing formation of one of the enzymes required for the conversion of lycopene to β-carotene. If the latter hypothesis is correct, then mo_B^+/mo_B is, in effect, a regulator gene.

Strains of tomato with a high δ-carotene content have been discovered[71]. The fruit of one such high-delta strain was found to have about 40 per cent less carotenoids than normal tomatoes, and the major component was δ-carotene instead of lycopene[37]. In crosses involving this strain all the F_1 fruits had δ-carotene: in the F_2 generation three-quarters of the plants had fruit with some δ-carotene[95]. These results suggest that the high-delta allele (Del) is dominant: however, quantitative studies imply either incomplete dominance or presence of a modifier gene. Since the δ-carotene molecule probably consists of a lycopene structure with an α-ionone ring at one end[36], it appears likely that the Del^+/Del gene controls an enzyme involved in the closure of this α-ionone ring.

Although all the genes described so far drastically affect the carotenoid composition of the fruit chromoplasts, Mackinney, Rick, and Jenkins (1956) reported that none of them (apart from hp^+/hp and Del^+/Del which were not tested) appear to have any effect on the carotenoids of the leaf chloroplasts. However, these workers found a new gene (ghost) which affects both types of plastid. Seedlings homozygous for the recessive allele gh, start with green cotyledons but rapidly lose chlorophyll in subsequent growth. (See III.2.iii for a detailed account of the effects of this gene on the development of the plant). Grafting of normal scions on $ghgh$ stock frequently induces emergence of shoots from the stock which can flower and set fruit. The mature fruit is slightly yellow due to the non-carotenoid yellow pigment in the skin. The total amount of carotenoids is approximately normal, but practically all of it is phytoene. The leaves of the ghost plants also contain phytoene instead of coloured carotenoids. The biochemical lesion in this tomato mutant may well be the same as that in the maize mutant[1] which was discussed previously.

A gene mutation (lutescent) which appears to affect the timing, rather than the pathway, of synthesis of tomato fruit carotenoids has been described by Mackinney (1952). The mutant has a delay of up to two weeks in lycopene synthesis in the ripening fruit. A rather surprising additional effect of this mutation is to cause premature yellowing of the leaves of the plant. The mutation may perhaps be in a regulator gene concerned with the initiation of chromoplast carotenoid formation. However, other less specific explanations are possible: for instance, the mutation might be having some general inhibitory effect on fruit metabolism so that maturation is retarded.

The results of these investigations on the tomato fruit indicate that eight or more of the processes involved in carotenoid synthesis in the chromoplast are under nuclear control. Exactly which steps are involved is difficult to say, since the precise details of carotenoid biosynthesis are still not entirely certain (for a review of this subject see Goodwin, 1965). However, the conclusions suggested by this work might tentatively be summarized as follows: (1) r^+/r controls formation of an enzyme involved in the synthesis of phytoene, possibly[70] for the condensation of geranylgeranyl pyrophosphate molecules (C_{20}) to phytoene (C_{40}). (2) at^+/at, which has similar effects to r^+/r, acts at a point early in biosynthesis, prior to phytoene. (3) hp^+/hp is probably also concerned with a step in the synthesis of phytoene. (4) gh^+/gh controls formation of an enzyme, probably a dehydrogenase, required for the conversion of phytoene to coloured carotenoids. (5) l^+/l is concerned either with an enzyme which is involved in the oxidation of more saturated carotenoids such as neurosporene or ζ-carotene to lycopene, or with one which determines whether the carotenoids produced shall be all-*trans* or shall contain some *cis* linkages. (6) B^+/B controls an enzyme involved in ring closure of lycopene. (7) mo_{B+}/mo_B modifies the effects of the B^+/B gene, but it is too early to say whether the action is at the metabolic level, or directly on the gene. (8) Del^+/Del controls an enzyme involved in the synthesis of δ-carotene, possibly one required for the formation of an α-ionone ring at the end of the lycopene molecule. Fig. XI.2b shows these relationships in diagrammatic form.

Mutations affecting fruit chromoplast carotenoid formation have also been found in *Capsicum annuum* (the red pepper). Smith (1950) has described a form in which the ripe fruit colour is orange-yellow instead of red. The character appears to be due to a single, recessive Mendelian

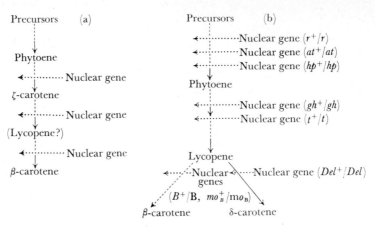

FIG. XI.2. *Nuclear control of carotenoid synthesis.* (*a*) *Chloroplast;* (*b*) *chromoplast* (*tomato*)

factor. The precise nature of the change in carotenoid composition has not yet been investigated, but it seems probable that the total quantity of carotenoids formed is much reduced. Other instances of different colour varieties of *Capsicum*—orange, yellow, and white—have been described[41] and the ultrastructure of the chromoplasts has been examined (Figs. I.42, I.43, and I.44); but genetic studies and complete biochemical analysis have not yet been carried out.

Some nuclear genes affecting carotenoid formation in flower petal chromoplasts are also known. The presence or absence of a carotenoid pigment in flowers of *Cheiranthus cheirii* is governed by a gene Y[83]. Plants homozygous for the recessive allele lack the pigment. In *Eschscholtzia californica* there appears to be a gene affecting the amount of carotenoids formed in the flower, and other genes determining which carotenoids are formed[8]. There is also a gene determining the area of petal containing the pigments: this could be a regulatory gene concerned with the initiation of carotenoid synthesis. In the red flowers of *Mimulus cardinalis*, there are chromoplasts present both in the corolla hairs and in the upper epidermal cells of the corolla: in the pink flowers of *M. lewisii* and hybrids between the two species there are chromoplasts only in the corolla hairs[99, 68]. The absence of chromoplasts from the epidermis is brought about by the presence of one or two dominant alleles of a pair of (Mendelian) genes. One or other, or both, of these genes could be regulatory genes concerned with inducing formation of the enzymes for synthesis of the chromoplast carotenoids. If these are regulatory genes, then the dominant nature of the alleles in *M. lewisii* which repress carotenoid formation would suggest that these alleles are mutations of the 'uninducible' type[33] in which the repressor can no longer combine with the inducer (see XI.8).

XI.4. Genetic Control of Formation of Photosynthetic Apparatus

Another type of mutation which acts on the chloroplast is that which impairs photosynthesis without seriously affecting pigmentation or gross morphology. Several such mutants of the alga *Chlamydomonas reinhardi* have been studied from a genetic and biochemical point of view by Levine and his co-workers. These mutants are referred to as acetate-requiring mutants since, being unable to grow photosynthetically, they must be given an oxidizable carbon source such as acetate.

Three of these mutants, *ac-16*, *ac-115*, and *ac-141*, are unable to carry out the Hill reaction with 2:6-dichlorophenolindophenol (DPIP) or other hydrogen-acceptors. Although extracts of mutant strains will not photoreduce NADP in the presence of their own chloroplast fragments, they are able to do so with spinach chloroplast fragments, indicating that they possess ferredoxin[54]. Furthermore, if provided with reduced 2:6-dichlorophenol-indophenol and ascorbate, extracts of *ac-115* and *ac-141* will photoreduce NADP, without evolution of oxygen[51,52]. This suggests that the later stages of the electron transport pathway from H_2O to NADP, certainly those from chlorophyll a_I onwards (see Fig. I.33), are intact. In *ac-115* and *ac-141* the cytochromes of the chloroplast electron transport system have been shown to be present: cytochrome b_6 in approximately normal amounts; cytochrome f in about twice the amount found in the wild-type[51,87]. Chlorophylls *a* and *b* are present in normal amounts: the carotenoid contents are somewhat low, being 40 per cent, 74 per cent, and 41 per cent of the wild-type levels in *ac-16*, *ac-115*, and *ac-141* respectively, but it is thought that the lowered carotenoid levels could not account for the total inability to photosynthesize[87,43]. If plastoquinone is the immediate hydrogen donor for the photoreduction of DPIP (as suggested by Witt, Müller, and Rumberg, 1963) then the inability of these mutants to reduce this compound suggests that they have a block in the formation of reduced plastoquinone. In fact *ac-115* and *ac-141* have only 20 per cent of the plastoquinone content of the wild type[51]. It may therefore be that these two mutants have defects in plastoquinone synthesis. If this is the explanation then it might seem surprising that the presence of 20 per cent of the normal plastoquinone content does not confer 20 per cent of the normal ability to photoreduce DPIP. One possibility is that the mutants are not making the right kind of plastoquinone: at least four compounds of this type occur in chloroplasts (see Table I.3), and so the mutants may be unable to make just the compound required for this particular photoreduction. Indeed, there is

some indication that one of the chloroplast quinones is missing in
ac-115 and ac-141[87].

All three of these mutations segregate in a normal manner, and it has
proved possible to assign the genes involved to their respective linkage
groups: ac-16, group X; ac-115, group I; ac-141, group III[54]. Since
these mutations are at three different loci it appears likely that they
affect three distinct biochemical processes concerned in photosynthetic
electron transport.

Another acetate-requiring mutant of *Chlamydomonas reinhardi*, ac-21,
is similar to the three described above except that it is able to photoreduce DPIP with evolution of oxygen[54], suggesting that in this case
reduced plastoquinone is being produced normally, and so the block
must be between plastoquinone and NADP. Cytochromes f and b_6 are
present in quantities only slightly lower than normal. Chlorophyll a
and b contents are normal: the carotenoid content is only 37 per cent
of the wild-type value, but this is not considered sufficient to account
for the inability to photosynthesize[87, 43]. Like the others this mutant
can photoreduce NADP in the presence of reduced DPIP and ascorbate.
The block probably, therefore, lies somewhere between plastoquinone
and chlorophyll a_I

The ac-21 mutation segregates in a one-to-one fashion in all crosses
(*Chlamydomonas reinhardi* is haploid) and has been assigned to linkage
group XI[54].

A fifth acetate-requiring mutant, ac-208, is unable to photoreduce
NADP, even in the presence of DPIP and ascorbate. This mutant has
no plastocyanin[21a]. The gene responsible is on Linkage Group III, as
is the ac-141 gene: ac-208 and ac-141 lie about ten map units apart on
opposite sides of the centromere[50a]. Another mutant, ac-206, lacks
cytochrome f; its mode of inheritance has not yet, apparently, been
recorded[21a].

Four further mutants, ac-20, ac-40, ac-46, and ac-59 are unable to
photosynthesize but have the ability to photoreduce NADP, indicating
that the chloroplast electron transport system is functioning. In one of
these, ac-20, the biochemical analysis has proceeded to the stage where
the actual enzyme which is missing is known: it is carboxydismutase[53].
The mode of inheritance of this mutation does not yet appear to have
been recorded. Levine and Volkmann (1961) suggest that the other
three mutants may be blocked in their ability to carry out photosynthetic phosphorylation or in one of the dark reactions of the reductive pentose phosphate pathway. All segregate normally, but so far only
ac-40 has been localized to a linkage group (Group II). Those acetate-
requiring mutants which have been examined with the electron microscope (ac-115, ac-141, and ac-21) have apparently normal chloroplast
structures[50a].

A mutant of a higher plant (*Vicia faba*) with a defect in photosynthesis has also been described by Heber and Gottschalk (1963). This mutant does not evolve oxygen in the light, nor does it fix $^{14}CO_2$ photosynthetically. Isolated chloroplasts do not reduce NADP in the light, but will photoreduce both DPIP and ferricyanide with evolution of oxygen, and can also photophosphorylate in the presence of phenazine methosulphate. Addition of an aqueous extract of spinach chloroplasts does not enable the mutant chloroplasts to photoreduce NADP, indicating that what the mutant lacks is not one of the water-soluble factors of the chloroplast, such as ferredoxin. The ability of the mutant to photoreduce ferricyanide indicates that the electron transport chain is intact from H_2O to component Z, just after chlorophyll a_I (it is thought that ferricyanide is reduced by Z). Heber and Gottschalk suggest that the mutant lacks an insoluble factor which is necessary for transfer of electrons or hydrogen from Z to NADP. The results are consistent with a defect in the flavoprotein which transfers hydrogen from ferredoxin to NADP.

The mutation appears to be due to a single recessive factor, showing normal Mendelian inheritance.

The findings described above suggest that at least nine of the biochemical processes required for photosynthesis are under nuclear control. Three nuclear genes (mutants ac-16, ac-115, and ac-141) may be concerned with the electron transport chain between H_2O and the formation of reduced plastoquinone. These are not necessarily involved with three different electron transport steps: they could, for instance, control three different biosynthetic steps in the formation of one of the electron carriers, such as plastoquinone. The formation of plastocyanin appears to be under the control of a nuclear gene (mutant ac-208). The nucleus appears also to control another electron transport step between plastoquinone and chlorophyll a_I (mutant ac-21), and one between chlorophyll a_I and NADP (Heber and Gottschalk's *Vicia faba* mutant). Three other genes (mutants ac-40, ac-46, and ac-59) may be concerned with steps in photophosphorylation or the pentose phosphate pathway. These conclusions are summarized in Fig. XI.3.

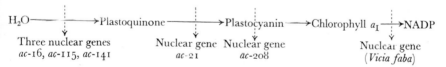

FIG. XI.3. *Nuclear control of formation of photosynthetic electron transport system*

The ability of chloroplasts to photosynthesize can also be affected by plastom mutations. Schötz (1955, 1956) has shown that certain plastom mutants of *Oenothera* are unable to photosynthesize, despite the presence of substantial amounts of chlorophyll in their plastids. However, some *Oenothera* hybrids which, as a result of incompatibility between plastom and nuclear genome (Chapter IX), have even less chlorophyll than the plastom mutants, can nevertheless photosynthesize. Heber (personal communication) has found that the chloroplasts isolated from a plastom mutant of *Vicia faba* have photosynthetic activity, whereas the leaf tissue from which the chloroplasts were isolated apparently had none. This seems to suggest that in the leaves of the plastom mutant there may be present some compound which is inhibiting photosynthesis. This finding is difficult to interpret in terms of the sort of genetic information that one might expect to be present in plastid DNA. One possible line of explanation might be as follows. It seems possible that the pathways of photosynthesis might, like other metabolic pathways, be subject to some system of control to regulate the rate of photosynthesis in accordance with the needs of the cell. In other metabolic pathways, such regulation commonly involves the direct inhibition of the activity of a certain enzyme, or enzymes, by one or more of the metabolites in the pathway. The effect of the plastom mutation in *Vicia faba* might be explained if it caused a change in the structure of the appropriate enzyme, or electron carrier, such that the affinity of the protein for the inhibitory metabolite was much increased, with a consequent inhibition of photosynthesis even at concentrations of metabolite much below the normal inhibitory level. During the process of isolation the chloroplasts would tend to lose the inhibitory metabolite anyway, and so would regain their activity. Another possibility is that the mutation might affect the opening of the stomata.

XI.5. The Control of Plastid Morphogenesis

Since the chlorophylls and the carotenoids make up a substantial proportion of the material of the thylakoids, it is not surprising that mutations which affect the pigments also, as we have seen (XI.2 and XI.3), affect the fine structure of the chloroplast. However, certain mutants are known with chloroplasts which have fairly substantial amounts of pigment but abnormal structures. Von Wettstein (1961) describes two such mutants in barley: *xantha*-3, with chloroplasts having no thylakoids but large globuli, in which it is thought the pigments accumulate, and *xantha*-15, in which granum-like structures are formed but with a larger diameter and greater inter-thylakoid distances than normal grana. *Xantha*-3 has about 12 per cent of the chlorophyll content of the wild-type, and this chlorophyll has a photosynthetic efficiency (μ moles $^{14}CO_2$ fixed/μ mole chlorophyll/hour) which is only 14 per cent of that of the wild type[10]. Both characters show Mendelian inheritance.

These genes may possibly control formation of some chloroplast constituents, other than the pigments, which are important for chloroplast structure. For instance, mutations affecting the thylakoid structural protein might possibly have effects of this type. However, in the case of mutants such as these, which have defective chloroplasts, but for which there is no evidence as to the biochemical nature of the defect, the possibility should be considered that the primary effect of the mutation is on some cellular process other than those specifically belonging to the chloroplast (see next section).

XI.6. Indirect genetic Effects on Plastid Formation

Chloroplasts are sensitive indicators of the state of health of the plant cell: very often amongst the first symptoms of nutrient deficiency, virus infection or other pathological conditions, is a disappearance of chlorophyll in part, or all, of the leaf. It is therefore to be expected that some mutations which act primarily on cellular processes other than those belonging specifically to the chloroplast will affect chloroplast formation. Mutations of this type have, indeed, been found.

Langridge (1958) obtained by X-ray treatment, a mutant of *Arabidopsis thaliana*, the leaves of which were partially or completely lacking in chlorophyll. However, when the plants were supplied with thiamine they became normal: the pyrimidine and thiazole portions of thiamine were ineffective, indicating that the whole molecule was required. A spontaneous mutant of the tomato was also found which lacked chlorophyll, but which was restored to normality by spraying with a solution of thiamine[46]. This mutant responded to pyrimidine alone but not to thiazole alone, indicating that the block was in the formation of pyrimidine. In both the above cases the thiamineless condition appeared to be due to a single, recessive, Mendelian factor.

Inability to synthesize certain amino acids can also cause chlorosis. Two barley mutants of this type are known[9, 102]. One of these, *albina-7*, has only 6·6 per cent of the normal amount of chlorophyll, and the proplastids do not develop into chloroplasts. However, normal formation of chlorophyll and chloroplast structure takes place if the mutant is supplied with aspartic acid. Once the seedling has greened up it will grow normally, without any more aspartic acid being supplied[102]. It seems possible that the block is in the pathway for aspartate synthesis outside the chloroplast: once a chloroplast is formed, it may be that this, by an independent biosynthetic pathway, can supply the cell's requirement for aspartate. The other mutant, *xantha-23*, has about

25 per cent of the chlorophyll content of the wild type and forms chloroplasts containing a few giant grana. When this mutant is supplied with leucine, the chlorophyll content rises to 70 per cent of the wild-type level, and normal chloroplast structures are formed. This mutant is probably blocked in leucine biosynthesis. Both these mutations are due to recessive, Mendelian, factors. Four other chlorophyll-deficient barley mutants have been described[102], which turn green when supplied with a mixture of twenty amino acids, ten vitamins, and adenine. Although the specific compound required was not determined, it seems likely that these also are auxotrophic mutants.

It has been known for over a century that a shortage of iron prevents chlorophyll synthesis. Certain chlorophyll-deficient mutants of higher plants are now known to have defects in their iron metabolism. Holmes and Brown (1955) found that a variety of soybean which was particularly susceptible to chlorosis required a higher concentration of iron than the normal variety: a single recessive gene was responsible. A certain mutation in maize—known as yellow-stripe (ys_1)—produces symptoms similar to those caused by iron deficiency. It was found that if these plants were grown in medium containing iron in the ferrous form, then they produced normal, green leaves; however, if supplied with iron in the ferric form, they showed the yellow-stripe symptoms[3]. Normal plants produced green leaves with either ferric or ferrous iron. It would therefore appear that the yellow-stripe mutation results in an inability to take up ferric iron. When ferric iron was supplied directly to the leaves of the mutant plants the symptoms were overcome: this indicates that the defect in iron metabolism must be sited elsewhere in the plant, possibly in the roots. Another yellow-stripe mutant of maize (ys_3) has been described[2], and this also has a defect in iron metabolism. However, it is believed that in this case the lesion is in the translocation or utilization of iron, not in the absorption by the roots. Both yellow-stripe mutations are due to recessive Mendelian factors.

It is evident from the findings described in this section that mutations which affect plastids are not necessarily directly concerned with plastid formation. Clearly, caution should be exercised before assuming that a mutation which affects the chloroplast must be concerned with the formation of some chloroplast constituent. However, the assumption would seem to be a reasonable one in cases where, for instance, there is accumulation of an intermediate in the biosynthesis of a chloroplast constituent, such as the accumulation of phytoene in the corn mutant, or of protoporphyrin in the *Chlamydomonas* mutant discussed earlier. Again it seems unlikely that defects in the synthesis of amino acids or vitamins can be responsible for cases such as the *Chlamydomonas* photosynthetic mutants, in which the general cell metabolism (as indicated by ability to grow heterotrophically) appears to be unaffected.

XI.7. Effect of loss of Plastid DNA

We have already seen (X.6) that cells of *Euglena gracilis* which have lost the ability to make chloroplasts as a result of treatment with strepto-mycin, high temperature, or UV also lose their chloroplast DNA: at least, they lose most of it—it must be recognized that, with the tech-niques used so far, the possibility of the continued presence of a small proportion, perhaps a few per cent, of the chloroplast DNA, cannot be eliminated. It might therefore seem that one of the most direct ways of determining what information is stored in the plastid DNA would be to attempt to see how much of the information required for making chloroplasts has been lost from these bleached cells. A certain amount of evidence on these points is, in fact, available, but the interpretation of the data is, as we shall see, far from clear.

At the risk of seeming obvious, it can be said that one of the most clear-cut deductions from the bleaching experiments about the function of the plastid DNA is that it is required for the synthesis of more plastid DNA. The fact[16] that irradiation of the nucleus with UV does not cause bleaching (that is, does not cause loss of plastid DNA), whereas irradiation of the cytoplasm does, strongly supports the idea that plastid DNA is formed by replication of pre-existing DNA in the cytoplasm (by implication, in the plastid), and not by replication of DNA in the nucleus. These bleaching experiments thus provide further evidence against the hypothesis of Bell and Mühlethaler (see I.8) that plastids are formed in the nucleus.

There is some evidence that the bleached strains have lost the ability to make chloroplast ribosomes. In his paper on the chloroplast ribo-somes of *Euglena gracilis*[5], Brawerman mentions that there appears to be a small amount of the chloroplast-type ribosomes in dark-grown cells, but none in heat-bleached cells: no further details are given. Also, there is some evidence[34] that enucleated *Acetabularia* have the ability to synthesize RNA, which appears to be ribosomal in type, in their chloroplasts. It therefore seems likely that the chloroplast DNA contains the cistrons which determine the structure of chloroplast ribosomal RNA, although it would be desirable to have much more evidence on this very important point. If chloroplast DNA had no function other than this, then from the known base ratio of *Euglena* chloroplast ribo-somal RNA, as determined by Brawerman (1963), we can calculate that the DNA should have a GC content of 47 per cent. In fact, as we saw earlier (X.5.ii.b), *Euglena* chloroplast DNA has an average GC content of about 25 per cent, so while it could certainly include regions coding for the ribosomal RNA, there must also be other regions having widely different base ratios.

A number of the components of the photosynthetic apparatus have been shown to be absent from bleached strains of *Euglena gracilis*. At least two members of the electron transport chain—plastoquinone[14] and cytochrome-552[111, 69] are absent from bleached cells. Also, streptomycin-bleached cells have been shown to lack at least three of the enzymes of the CO_2 fixation cycle—carboxydismutase, NADP-requiring triose phosphate dehydrogenase[13], and alkaline fructose-1,6-diphosphatase[86]. Superficially this might seem to indicate that the genes determining the structure of these photosynthetic enzymes, or the biosynthetic enzymes required for the biosynthesis of compounds such as plastoquinone, are in the chloroplast DNA. However, it must be pointed out that the absence of these enzymes might merely be an indirect consequence of the lack of chloroplast ribosomes. It should also be remembered that the formation of these enzymes is normally inducible: they are not formed, or are formed only to a small extent, in the dark (Chapter XIII), but synthesis can then be brought about by exposing the cells to light. Therefore, an additional, or alternative, reason for their not being formed might be lack of some component of the inducing system; perhaps chlorophyll or some other chromophore.

A particularly puzzling feature of the bleaching phenomenon is that the ability to synthesize carotenoids and porphyrins varies considerably from one bleached strain to another. The fact that any bleached strain should synthesize plastid components at all might seem surprising in view of the belief that the bleached cells have lost their plastids. However, Lwoff (1950) suggested that these cells must still have some kind of plastid because they are still able to make the polysaccharide paramylon, which, in green cells, is very probably synthesized by the chloroplasts. There is now evidence that this view is correct. De Deken-Grenson (1960) found, on density gradient centrifugation of a homogenate of bleached cells of *E. gracilis*, a yellow layer containing spherical particles which she considered might possibly be residues of plastids. Gibor and Granick (1962b), using phase and fluorescence microscopy, observed small proplastid-like bodies in cells of bleached strains which had been produced by streptomycin-, heat-, or UV-treatment, or which had appeared spontaneously: these bodies contained carotenoids and, under some circumstances, porphyrins. Siegesmund, Rosen, and Gawlik (1962), using electron microscopy, demonstrated the presence of bodies containing numerous concentric lamellae in light-grown cells of a streptomycin-bleached strain; these bodies were absent from normal cells grown in the light. Moriber, Hershenov, Aaronson, and Bensky (1963) examined, by electron microscopy, strains of *E. gracilis* which had been bleached by heat-, UV-, streptomycin-, benadryl-, or O-methylthreonine treatment: in every strain except the streptomycin-bleached one, the cells had bodies in the cytoplasm, similar in size to plastids, and containing lamella- or crista-like structures. The failure of Moriber *et al.* to find 'plastids' in the streptomycin-treated cells is puzzling in the light of the results of Siegesmund *et al.*: in another streptomycin-bleached strain, Dr Juniper and I[40] have observed bodies, somewhat smaller than chloroplasts, containing numerous small vesicles and short lengths of double membrane (Fig. XI.4)—these bodies

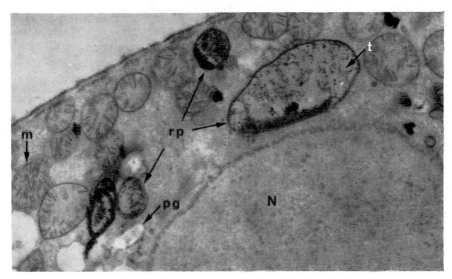

FIG. XI.4. *Plastid-like bodies in a cell of a streptomycin-bleached strain of* Euglena gracilis *(Kirk, J. T. O. and Juniper, B. E., 1963, unpublished).* rp—*organelles that may be residual plastids.* t—*tubules.* pg—*paramylon granule.* m—*mitochondrion.* N—*nucleus*

are absent from normal cells. Taking all the evidence together, it seems likely that these bleached strains of *E. gracilis* do indeed retain a type of plastid. In this connection it is particularly interesting that *Polytoma uvella*, which is generally thought to be a chlamydomonad which has spontaneously lost the ability to form chloroplasts, and which lacks[47] the DNA satellite band that is thought to be the *Chlamydomonas* chloroplast DNA, is still able to form a plastid: this is recognizable as a plastid by virtue of the presence within it of starch grains and eye-spot granules[44]. *Prototheca viformii*, which is thought to be a naturally occurring colourless form of *Chlorella*, also possesses recognizable plastids containing starch grains[63]: it would be of interest to know whether this organism lacks one of the DNA satellite bands that have been observed in *Chlorella*[6, 32].

Granted, then, that most, and probably all, bleached strains retain some kind of plastid, let us now return to the variation in the biosynthetic abilities of these plastids, from one strain to another. With regard to carotenoid synthesis, most strains can form some carotenoids, but the amount and type vary from strain to strain[20, 18]. The carotenoid level is never more than 20 per cent of that in normal cells, and in one strain the pigments appear to be completely absent. Certain carotenoids—phytofluene, ζ-carotene, zeaxanthin, and echinenone—which are absent from green cells, may appear, and a given carotenoid, such as zeaxanthin, may be synthesized by some strains but not by others. So far as ability to form porphyrins in the plastids is concerned, three distinct types of bleached strain have been recognized by Gibor and Granick (1962b): one which accumulates porphyrins (possibly protoporphyrin, detected by fluorescence microscopy) in the light when δ-aminolaevulinic acid (ALA) is supplied; one which accumulates porphyrins in the light even in the absence of ALA; and one which does not accumulate porphyrins whether ALA is supplied or not. Bleached strains of the first type presumably lack an enzyme required for the synthesis of ALA; the fact that they can only proceed as far as porphyrins, even when supplied with ALA, indicates that they also lack one or more of the enzymes required for the conversion of porphyrins to chlorophyll. Strains of the second type have the enzymes for the conversion of ALA to porphyrins but presumably lack one or more of the enzymes for the pathway between porphyrin and chlorophyll. Strains of the third type would appear to have lost the ability to make one or more of the enzymes required for the conversion of ALA to porphyrins: these strains might also lack all the other enzymes of the chlorophyll biosynthetic pathway.

No immediately obvious explanation suggests itself for this variability with regard to carotenoid and porphyrin synthesis. If all the bleached strains have lost all their plastid DNA, then they should all have lost the same biochemical abilities. One possibility is that, as envisaged at the beginning of this section, some of these strains may retain a small amount of plastid DNA, with genes in it for some of the enzymes of chlorophyll or carotenoid synthesis, the difference between the strains perhaps being due to their retaining different segments of the plastid genome. But this hypothesis immediately raises the question of where these enzymes are made. If chloroplast ribosomes are absent, can these enzymes be synthesized by the ribosomes of the cytoplasm? Or, is it possible that the plastid DNA might originally have contained a large number of cistrons for ribosomal RNA, and that the small segment of DNA remaining might include a small number of these cistrons so that a few chloroplast ribosomes could still be made?

Let us assume for the moment that bleached strains may indeed retain a certain amount of plastid DNA, and that the variation from one strain to another is due to different strains having lost different parts of the DNA. To what conclusions does this assumption lead? So far as the first type of bleached strain considered above is concerned, the fact that

its plastids seem to have lost an enzyme required for the synthesis of
ALA and also an enzyme required for the conversion of porphyrins to
chlorophyll, suggests that the structural genes for these two enzymes
are in the plastid DNA: the argument that lack of these enzymes is
merely a consequence of the loss of chloroplast ribosomes seems to be
contradicted by the fact that some plastid enzymes (those for the conversion of ALA to porphyrins) are being synthesized. Also, the argument that the enzymes are not being synthesized because of a fault in
the inducing system seems to be contradicted first by the fact that these
bleached strains still seem to have an inducing system, as indicated by
the fact that growth in the light greatly enhances porphyrin and carotenoid synthesis[17]; and second by the fact that normal cells synthesize
protochlorophyll in the dark, and so the synthesis of the enzymes of this
pathway is not completely dependent upon light induction anyway. In
the case of the second type of bleached strain, the apparent lack of an
enzyme (or enzymes) for the conversion of porphyrins to chlorophyll,
may be taken as further evidence for the conclusion (arrived at from
considering the first type of bleached strain) that the structural gene (or
genes) for this enzyme (or enzymes) is in the plastid DNA. In the case
of the third type of bleached strain, it appears that an enzyme (or
enzymes) required for the conversion of ALA to porphyrins is missing:
however, we cannot deduce from this that the gene for this enzyme is
in the plastid DNA, because there is no evidence that these strains can
form any of the chlorophyll biosynthetic enzymes, and they also appear
to have a much lower ability to form carotenoids than the other strains,
so it seems possible that in these strains the defect may be something
more fundamental, such as the complete absence of chloroplast ribosomes.

The data on the carotenoid composition of different bleached strains
does not lend itself to this sort of analysis. It seems[18] that all those
bleached strains which can make carotenoids at all, can make at least
one of the end-products of the biosynthetic pathway, β-carotene,
although intermediates in the biosynthetic pathway, such as phytofluene and ζ-carotene, do tend to accumulate. The bleached strains also
appear to be able to make xanthophylls, although sometimes only in
trace amounts. In short, none of the strains which have been examined
so far appears to have a definite block at any specific point in the biosynthetic pathway, although considerable derangement of the carotenoid
composition occurs. The strain which completely lacks carotenoids
may have lost, in the plastid DNA, a structural gene for a step in
carotenoid biosynthesis prior to phytoene: however, this is another
case where it seems possible that the inhibition of biosynthesis might be
due to complete loss of chloroplast ribosomes.

Clearly it is very difficult to arrive at any definite conclusions about the information in plastid DNA, on the basis of these studies with bleached strains of *Euglena gracilis*. Some of the evidence suggests that the DNA includes regions determining the structure of chloroplast ribosomal RNA, but, as we have seen, the base ratios indicate that there must be other DNA regions present as well. The data are consistent with these other DNA regions including structural genes concerned with the synthesis of certain photosynthetic enzymes and electron carriers, but, as discussed above, the evidence is equally consistent with these genes being in the nucleus. There is some suggestion, from studies on the ability of bleached strains to synthesize porphyrins, that the plastid DNA contains structural genes for at least two of the enzymes of the biosynthetic pathway of chlorophyll: however, to arrive at this conclusion it was necessary to make certain assumptions, to all of which a considerable degree of uncertainty is attached; consequently this hypothesis can for the moment be regarded as only slightly more probable than the hypothesis that these genes are in the nucleus.

XI.8. General Conclusions

Taking all the evidence, from higher plants and algae, together, we can arrive at the following tentative conclusions. Some of the structural genes for enzymes concerned with synthesis of chlorophylls and carotenoids, and enzymes involved in photosynthesis, are in the nucleus. The genes which determine the structure of chloroplast ribosomal RNA (and perhaps also ribosomal proteins) are probably in the plastid. There is a little evidence that the structural genes for two of the enzymes of chlorophyll synthesis are also in the plastid. There is also some evidence, discussed below, that there is a structural gene for the enzyme thymidine kinase in the plastid. The cellular location of most of the genes determining the structure of plastid enzymes and other proteins is quite unknown: the evidence is consistent with their being in the plastid, or the nucleus, or distributed between the two. The rather meagre evidence so far available on the biochemical characteristics of plastom mutants of higher plants—instability of pigments to light, lack of photosynthetic ability— provides no definite information as to the nature of the genes in the plastid DNA. In the case of the plastom mutant which has chloroplasts inactive in the leaf, but active when isolated, it seems possible (see XI.4) that there might be a defect in the mechanism for regulating photosynthetic activity at the metabolic level. In the case of the plastom mutants the pigments of which are bleached by light (see XI.3) it seems possible that there might be mutations in a plastid gene determining the structure of the thylakoid structural protein to which the pigments are attached. However, these are just speculations, and it is to be hoped that much more biochemical work will be done on these mutants to determine the true nature of the primary lesions.

Even to reach the tentative conclusions above it has been necessary to combine evidence from very different types of plant. To generalize like this might, of course, be quite invalid. It seems entirely possible that there is more information in the plastid DNA of some plants than in others. It is interesting, in this connection, that the amount of DNA in a chloroplast of *Acetabularia* appears to be much less than the amount of DNA in a chloroplast of *Chlamydomonas*, *Euglena*, or a higher plant (X.7). Furthermore, the distribution of information might be different: a gene that is in the plastid in one organism might be in the nucleus in another. There is, in fact, already some evidence that the distribution of genes within the cell can vary from one organism to another. For instance, most plants when supplied with ^{3}H-thymidine, incorporate it into the DNA of their nuclei: some, perhaps most, will also incorporate it into the DNA of their chloroplasts (X.4). However, Steffensen and Sheridan (1965) showed that certain marine algae would incorporate ^{3}H-thymidine into DNA in their chloroplasts but not in their nuclei, even though the cells were dividing at the time. Also, Stocking and Gifford (1959) found that 81 94 per cent of the radioactivity incorporated from ^{3}H-thymidine by *Spirogyra*, was in the chloroplast (although in this case it was not shown that incorporation was into DNA). Steffensen and Sheridan interpret their results as indicating that in these algae the chloroplast DNA contains the gene for thymidine kinase (the first enzyme required in the utilization of thymidine) but the nuclear DNA does not. This would suggest that in those plants which can incorporate thymidine in their chloroplasts and in their nuclei, there is a thymidine kinase gene both in the chloroplast DNA and in the nuclear DNA.

Most of the genes affecting plastids about which we have any definite information appear to be structural genes, that is, genes which determine the amino acid sequence of proteins. But plastid formation must require regulatory genes (see XIII.18) as well: this is indicated by the rapid induction of formation of differentiated kinds of plastid in certain cells under certain conditions—for instance, the formation of chloroplasts that takes place when an etiolated leaf is exposed to the light (Chapter XIII) or the conversion of a chloroplast to a chromoplast in the maturing tissues of various fruits (XIV.5). Already in this chapter we have discussed a number of instances of mutations in nuclear genes which might possibly be regulator genes: examples are the virescent mutation in barley, the green-flesh mutation in the tomato (XI.2), the mo_B and the lutescent mutations in the tomato, and the mutation inhibiting development of chromoplasts in epidermal cells of *Mimulus* petals (XI.3). However, in none of these cases is the evidence sufficiently clear-cut to permit a decision as to whether these genes really are regulator genes. That is, we have in fact no definite information about where in the cell the regulatory genes are situated. The fact that so many of the structural genes appear to be in the nucleus, and also that there is still no absolutely definite example of a structural gene occurring in the plastid, might lead one to the hypothesis that the main function of the plastid DNA is to contain these regulatory genes, and that the nucleus contains all the structural genes. However, if these regulatory genes work in the same way as bacterial regulatory genes are thought to work[33], then loss of plastid DNA would mean that the cell would lose the ability to make the repressors which control the activity of the structural genes in the nucleus. Therefore, cells which have lost their plastid DNA as the result of heat-, streptomycin-, or UV-treatment should carry out an unrestrained synthesis of all chloroplast constituents: however, this is the opposite of what is observed—as we know from studies on *Euglena gracilis,* when cells lose their plastid DNA they in fact stop synthesizing most of their chloroplast constituents. Nevertheless, in favour of this theory it could be argued that these cells are still making all the messenger RNA molecules for these chloroplast proteins, but the proteins are not made because there are no, or perhaps very few, chloroplast ribosomes present to utilize these messenger RNA molecules. But in this case, if the plastids retain any ability to make plastid proteins, then they should make the whole range of plastid proteins, even if only in reduced amounts. However, as we have seen, there are certain bleached strains which can synthesize some plastid proteins (enzymes of carotenoid synthesis, and certain enzymes of the chlorophyll synthetic pathway) but not others. Thus, the simple theory that all the regulatory genes (and genes for plastid ribosomal RNA) are in the plastid, and all the structural genes are in the nucleus, does not seem to fit the data. If we wish to postulate that all the regulatory genes are in the plastid, it seems that we must further suppose that at least some of the structural genes are also in the plastid: this variation of the theory cannot be disproved at the moment, but there is certainly no evidence actually supporting it.

Let us now consider the converse theory to the above, namely that all the structural genes are in the plastid, and all the regulatory genes are in the nucleus. It follows from this hypothesis that all those nuclear mutations which we have hitherto regarded as being in structural genes, are instead in regulator genes. This means that in the case of the corn mutant (XI.3) for example, which has a block in carotenoid synthesis after phytoene, we must suppose that as a result of a mutation in a regulator gene in the nucleus a faulty repressor is made which can no longer combine with the inducer, and which, as a consequence, represses the appropriate structural gene for this carotenoid biosynthetic enzyme in the chloroplast. Mutations of this type are in fact known in bacteria: an example is the 'super-repressed' or 'uninducible' mutation in the regulator gene for β-galactosidase synthesis in *Escherichia coli*[33]. However, the 'uninducible' type of mutation would be dominant when combined with the wild-type allele in a heterozygote, because the faulty repressor would repress the structural gene both on the chromosome which came from the mutant parent, and on that which came from the wild-type parent. But, as we have seen in this chapter, mutations (including the corn mutation) which affect biosynthesis of chloroplast or chromoplast constituents, are generally recessive to the wild type. Therefore, in most cases at any rate, we can reject the hypothesis that mutations causing blockages in biosynthesis of plastid constituents are in regulator genes.

On the whole, then, it seems unlikely that either of these simple hypotheses—that all the regulator genes are in the plastid and all the structural genes in the nucleus, or the converse theory to this—is correct. It seems certain that some of the structural genes are in the nucleus; it seems likely that certain others are in the plastid. The regulator genes could be all in the plastid, or all in the nucleus, or distributed between the two. There is a little evidence suggesting that certain nuclear genes are regulator genes.

It is clear that we still know very little about the function of plastid DNA. We have much more negative information about it than positive information: that is, we can say quite a lot about the genes it does not contain (because they are in the nucleus) but not much about the genes it does contain. However, even such meagre negative evidence as this has certain interesting implications with regard to the evolutionary origin of plastids. It is well known that certain protozoa contain symbiotic blue-green algae, which act, in effect, as the photosynthetic organelles of these protozoa[15]: it has therefore been suggested, originally by Mereschkowski (1905) and Famintzin (1907), and recently by Ris and Plaut (1962) that the chloroplasts (and, by implication, other plastids) of algae and higher plants did, in fact, evolve from such symbiotic cyanophytes. This is a plausible and attractive hypothesis. The plausibility lies to a large extent in the structural similarity between chloroplasts and blue-green algae. These algae have their photosynthetic pigments in thylakoids lying free in the cytoplasm; there is no compartmentation between the photosynthetic apparatus and the rest of the cell. The thylakoids of the blue-green algae are single, in which respect they are similar to the thylakoids of the (supposedly) primitive chloroplasts of the *Rhodophyta*: another similarity is that both the blue-green algal cells, and the red algal chloroplasts, contain biliproteins. Furthermore, as pointed out by Ris and Plaut, the DNA fibre-containing regions of chloroplasts are similar to the nucleoplasm of the blue-green algae. Another reason for the plausibility of the theory is that it seems quite possible, even likely, that the blue-green endosymbionts should, in the course of evolution, lose certain biochemical functions which could be carried out by the host cell, with the result that the symbionts should eventually become unable, as chloroplasts are unable, to grow autotrophically outside the cell. Also, once the symbiont became established, it seems entirely feasible that it should continue its structural evolution to produce the various different kinds of algal chloroplasts and the higher plant chloroplast. One of the attractive features of this theory is that it makes it unnecessary to explain the separate evolution of photosynthetic ability in the prokaryotes (organisms such as bacteria and blue-green algae, with no separate membrane-bounded nucleus, or other organelles) and the eukaryotes (higher organisms, including algae and higher plants, with chromosomes inside a membrane-bounded nucleus, and other membrane-bounded organelles). It also, for instance, explains the presence of chlorophyll *a* and biliproteins in organisms so utterly different in structure and organization as the *Cyanophyta* and the *Rhodophyta* (or *Cryptophyta*).

All things considered then, this hypothesis has a great deal to be said in its favour. However, some of the data we have considered in this chapter are a little difficult to reconcile with this theory. We have seen, for instance, that there is good reason to suppose that at least some of the structural genes concerned with the synthesis of photosynthetic enzymes, and enzymes for chlorophyll and carotenoid formation are now in the nucleus. But when the hypothetical blue-green endosymbiont first became established in its host cell, it presumably carried these genes in its own DNA; that is, the DNA that was to become chloroplast DNA. How is it, then, that these genes are now in the nucleus? It could be argued that these particular genes are for functions which appeared in evolution after the symbiosis commenced. This suggestion would certainly be true for many of the genes concerned with, say, formation of the rather specific kinds of carotenoids found in the chromoplasts of fruit and other specialized higher plant organs. However, this argument would not seem to apply to genes concerned with such fundamental functions as chlorophyll synthesis, or photosynthetic electron transport. If the symbiosis theory of chloroplast evolution is correct, then we must suppose either, that in the course of evolution, DNA from the symbiont has been physically transferred to the nucleus, and become established there, or, that certain genes in the nucleus have evolved to the stage where they can take over the functions of some of the genes in the symbiont. To account for the presence of regulatory genes, for controlling plastid formation, in the nucleus, would be less of a problem: it seems quite plausible that the nucleus should evolve genes for regulating the growth of the symbiont.

The subject of plastid evolution is one that lends itself to much fascinating and enjoyable speculation. To narrow the bounds of such speculation somewhat it is worth pointing out that any theory of plastid evolution must account, not only for the chemistry, morphology, and biochemical abilities of plastids, but also for the distribution within the cell of the genes determining, and regulating, plastid formation.

REFERENCES

1. ANDERSON, I. C. & ROBERTSON, D. S. (1960). *Plant Phys.* **35**, 531–534
2. BELL, W. D. (1961). *Plant Phys.* **36**, xv
3. BELL, W. D., BOGORAD, L. & McILRATH, W. J. (1958). *Bot. Gaz.* **120**, 36–39
4. BOGORAD, L. (1965). In *Chemistry and Biochemistry of Plant Pigments*. Ed., T. W. Goodwin, Academic Press, London, pp. 29–74
5. BRAWERMAN, G. (1963). *Biochim. Biophys. Acta* **72**, 317–331
6. CHUN, E. H. L., VAUGHAN, M. H. & RICH, A. (1963). *J. Mol. Biol.* **7**, 130–141
7. DE DEKEN-GRENSON, M. (1960). *Arch. de Biol.* **71**, 269–341
8. DOUWES, H. (1943). *Genetica* **23**, 353
9. ERIKSSON, H., KAHN, A., WALLES, B. & VON WETTSTEIN, D. (1961). *Ber. Deut. Bot. Ges.* **74**, 221–232
10. FALUDI-DANIEL, A. & GALMICHE, J. (1963). *Hereditas* **50**, 136–138
11. FALUDI-DANIEL, A., LANG, F. & FRADKIN, L. I. In *Symposium on Biochemistry. of Chloroplasts (Aberystwyth, 1965)*. Ed., T. W. Goodwin. Academic Press. London (in press)
12. FAMINTZIN, A. (1907). *Biol. Zentr.* **27**, 353
13. FULLER, R. C. & GIBBS, M. (1959). *Plant Phys.* **34**, 324–329
14. FULLER, R. C., SMILLIE, R. M., RIGOPOULOS, N. & YOUNT, V. (1961). *Arch. Biochem. Biophys.* **95**, 197–202
15. GEITLER, L. (1959). In *Encycl. Plant Phys.* Ed., W. Ruhland. XI. Springer-Verlag, Berlin, pp. 530–545
16. GIBOR, A. & GRANICK, S. (1962a). *J. Cell Biol.* **15**, 599–603
17. GIBOR, A. & GRANICK, S. (1962b). *J. Protozool.* **9**, 327–334
18. GOODWIN, T. W. (1960). In *Comparative Biochemistry of Photoreactive systems*. Ed., M. B. Allen. Academic Press, New York, pp. 1–10
19. GOODWIN. T. W. (1965). In *Chemistry and Biochemistry of Plant Pigments*. Ed., T. W. Goodwin, Academic Press, London, pp. 175–196
20. GOODWIN, T. W. & GROSS, J. A. (1958). *J. Protozool.* **5**, 292–295
21a. GORMAN, D. S. & LEVINE, R. P. (1965). *Proc. Natl. Acad. Sci.* **54**, 1665–1669
21. GOODWIN, T. W. & JAMIKORN, M. (1952). *Nature, Lond.* **170**, 104–105
22. GOTTSCHALK, W. & MULLER, F. (1964). *Planta* **61**, 259–282, **62**, 1–21
23. GRANICK, S. (1950). *Harvey Lectures* **44**, 000
24. GRANICK, S. & MAUZERALL, D. (1961). In *Metabolic Pathways*. Ed., D. M. Greenberg, II. Academic Press, New York, pp. 525–616
25. HABERMANN, H. M. (1960). *Phys. Plant* **13**, 718–725
26. HEBER, U. & GOTTSCHALK, W. (1963). *Z. Naturforsch.* **18b**, 36–44
27. HIGHKIN, H. R. (1950). *Plant Phys.* **25**, 294–306
28. HIGHKIN, H. R. & FRENKEL, A. W. (1962). *Plant Phys.* **37**, 814–820
29. HIRONO, Y. & REDEI, G. P. (1963). *Nature, Lond.* **197**, 1324–1325
30. HOLMES, R. S. & BROWN, J. C. (1955). *Soil. Sci.* **80**, 167–179
31. HURST, C. C. (1906). *Rep. 3rd Int. Congr. Genetics*, pp. 114–129
32. IWAMURA, T. & KUWASHIMA, S. (1964). *Biochim. Biophys. Acta* **82**, 678–679

33.   JACOB, F. & MONOD, J. (1961). *Cold Spring Harbour Symp.* **26**, 193–209
34.   JANOWSKI, M. (1965). *Biochim. Biophys. Acta* **103**, 399–408
35.   JENKINS, J. A. & MACKINNEY, G. (1955). *Genetics* **40**, 715–720
36.   KARGL, T. E. & QUACKENBUSH, F. W. (1960). *Arch. Biochem. Biophys.* **88**, 59–63
37.   KARGL, T. E., QUACKENBUSH, F. W. & TOMES, M. L. (1960). *Proc. Amer. Soc. Hort. Sci.* **75**, 574–578
38.   KAY, R. E. & PHINNEY, B. O. (1956). *Plant Phys.* **31**, 415–420
39.   KERR, E. A. (1956). *Tomato Genetics Coop.* **6**, 17
40.   KIRK, J. T. O. & JUNIPER, B. E. (1963). Unpublished
41.   KIRK, J. T. O. & JUNIPER, B. E. In *Symposium on Biochemistry of Chloroplasts* (*Aberystwyth, 1965*). Ed., T. W. Goodwin, Academic Press, London (in press)
42.   KOSKI, V. M. & SMITH, J. H. C. (1951). *Arch. Biochem. Biophys.* **34**, 189–195
43.   KRINSKY, N. I. & LEVINE, R. P. (1964). *Plant Phys.* **39**, 680–687
44.   LANG, N. J. (1963). *J. Protozool.* **10**, 333–339
45.   LANGRIDGE, J. (1958). *Austr. J. Biol. Sci.* **11**, 58–68
46.   LANGRIDGE, J. & BROCK, R. D. (1961). *Austr. J. Biol. Sci.* **14**, 66–69
47.   LEFF, J., MANDEL, M., EPSTEIN, H. T. & SCHIFF, J. A. (1963). *Biochem. Biophys. Res. Commun.* **13**, 126–130
48.   LEFORT, M. (1957). *Compt. Rend. Acad. Sci.* **245**, 437–440, 718–720
49.   LE ROSEN, A. L., WENT, F. W. & ZECHMEISTER, L. (1941). *Proc. Natl. Acad. Sci.* **27**, 236–242
50.   LE ROSEN, A. L. & ZECHMEISTER, L. (1942). *J. Am. Chem. Soc.* **64**, 1075–1079
50a. LEVINE, R. P. (1963). In *Photosynthetic mechanisms of green plants.* Publ. 1145 NAS-NRC. Washington, D.C., pp. 158–173
51.   LEVINE, R. P. & SMILLIE, R. M. (1962). *Proc. Natl. Acad. Sci.* **48**, 417–421
52.   LEVINE, R. P. & SMILLIE, R. M. (1963). *J. Biol. Chem.* **238**, 4052–4057
53.   LEVINE, R. P. & TOGASAKI, R. K. (1965). *Proc. Natl. Acad. Sci.* **53**, 987–990
54.   LEVINE, R. P. & VOLKMANN, D. (1961). *Biochem. Biophys. Res. Commun.* **6**, 264–269
55.   LINCOLN, R. E. & PORTER, J. W. (1950). *Genetics* **35**, 206–211
56.   LIU, H. Z. & EVERETT, H. L. (1965). *Plant Phys.* **40**, 433–436
57.   LWOFF, A. (1950). *New Phytol.* **49**, 72–80
58.   MACARTHUR, J. W. (1934). *J. Genet.* **29**, 123–133
59.   MACKINNEY, G. (1952). *Ann. Rev. Biochem.* **21**, 473
60.   MACKINNEY, G. & JENKINS, J. A. (1952). *Proc. Natl. Acad. Sci.* **38**, 48–52
61.   MACKINNEY, G., RICK, C. M. & JENKINS, J. A. (1956). *Proc. Natl. Acad. Sci.* **42**, 404–408
62.   MACLACHLAN, S. & ZALIK, S. (1963). *Can. J. Bot.* **41**, 1053–1062
63.   MENKE, W. & FRICKE, B. (1962). *Portugal. Acta Biol. Serie A* **6**, 243–252
64.   MERESCHKOWSKI, O. (1905). *Biol. Zentr.* **25**, 593–602
65.   MILLER, R. A. & ZALIK, S. (1965). *Plant Phys.* **40**, 569–574
66.   MORIBER, L. G., HERSHENOV, B., AARONSON, S. & BENSKY, B. (1963). *J. Protozool.* **10**, 80–86
67.   MÜLLER, F. (1964). *Planta* **63**, 65–82
68.   NOBS, M. A., HIESEY, W. M. & MILNER, H. W. (1964). *Carneg. Inst. Wash. Yearbook* **63**, 432–435
69.   PERINI, F., SCHIFF, J. A. & KAMEN, M. D. (1964). *Biochim. Biophys. Acta* **88**, 91–98
70.   PORTER, J. W. & ANDERSON, D. G. (1962). *Arch. Biochem. Biophys.* **97**, 520–528
71.   PORTER, J. W. & LINCOLN, R. E. (1950). *Arch. Biochem. Biophys.* **27**, 390–403
72.   RAMIREZ, D. A. & TOMES, M. L. (1964). *Bot. Gaz.* **125**, 221–226
73.   RICK, C. M. & BUTLER, L. (1956). *Adv. Genet.* **8**, 267–382

74. Ris, H. & Plaut, W. (1962). *J. Cell Biol.* **13**, 383–391
75. Röbbelen, G. (1956). *Planta* **47**, 532
76. Röbbelen, G. (1957). *Z. Vererbungsl.* **88**, 189–252
77. Robertson, D. S. (1958). *Maize Genetics Coop. Newsletter* **32**, 90
78. Sager, R. (1955). *Genetics* **40**, 476–489
79. Schötz, F. (1955). *Z. Naturforsch.* **10b**, 100–108
80. Schötz, F. (1956). *Photogr. Forsch.* **7**, 12–16
81. Schötz, F. & Bathelt, H. (1964). *Planta* **63**, 213–232, 233–252
82. Schötz, F. & Bathelt, H. (1965). *Planta* **64**, 330–362
83. Scott-Moncrieff, R. (1936). *J. Genet.* **32**, 117
84. Seltmann, H. (1955). *Plant Phys.* **30**, 258–263
85. Siegesmund, K. A., Rosen, W. G. & Gawlik, S. R. (1962). *Am. J. Bot.* **49**, 137–145
86. Smillie, R. (1960). *Nature, Lond.* **187**, 1024–1025
87. Smillie, R. M. & Levine, R. P. (1963). *J. Biol. Chem.* **238**, 4058–4062
88. Smith, P. G. (1950). *J. Hered.* **41**, 138–140
89. Smith, J. H. C., Durham, L. J. & Wurster, C. F. (1959). *Plant Phys.* **34**, 340
90. Stanier, R. Y. (1959). *Brookhaven Symp.* **11**, 43–53
91. Steffensen, D. M. & Sheridan, W. F. (1965). *J. Cell Biol.* **25**, 619–626
92. Stocking, C. R. & Gifford, E. M. (1959). *Biochem. Biophys. Res. Commun.* **1**, 159–164
93. Thompson, A. E. (1955). *Science* **121**, 896
94. Thompson, A. E., Hepler, R. W. & Kerr, E. A. (1962). *Proc. Amer. Soc. Hort. Sci.* **81**, 434–442
95. Tomes, M. L. (1963). *Bot. Gaz.* **124**, 180–185
96. Tomes, M. L., Quackenbush, F. W. & Kargl, T. E. (1956). *Bot. Gaz.* **117**, 248–253
97. Tomes, M. L., Quackenbush, F. W. & Kargl, T. E. (1958). *Bot. Gaz.* **119**, 250–253
98. Tomes, M. L., Quackenbush, F. W. & McQuistan, M. (1954). *Genetics* **39**, 810–817
99. Vickery, R. K. & Olson, R. L. (1956). *J. Hered.* **47**, 195–199
100. Wallace, R. H. & Habermann, H. M. (1959). *Am. J. Bot.* **46**, 157–162
101. Wallace, R. A. & Schwarting, A. E. (1954). *Plant Phys.* **29**, 431
102. Walles, B. (1963). *Hereditas* **50**, 317–344
103. Walles, B. (1965). *Hereditas* **53**, 247–256
104. Walles, B. In *Symposium on Biochemistry of Chloroplasts (Aberystwyth, 1965).* Ed., T. W. Goodwin, Academic Press, London (in press)
105. von Wettstein, D. (1959). *Carneg. Inst. Wash. Yearbook* **58**, 338–339
106. von Wettstein, D. (1961). *Can. J. Bot.* **39**, 1537–1545
106a. von Wettstein, D. & Eriksson, G. In 'Genetics Today'. *Proc. XI Intern. Congr. Genet.*, pp. 591–612
107. Whitaker, T. W. (1952). *Plant Phys.* **27**, 263–268
108. Wild, A. (1960). *Beitr. Biol. Pfl.* **35**, 137–175
109. Witt, H. T., Müller, A. & Rumberg, B. (1963). *Nature, Lond.* **197**, 987–991
110. Wolf, F. T. (1963). *Bull. Torrey Bot. Club.* **90**, 139–143
111. Wolken, J. J. & Gross, J. A. (1963). *J. Protozool.* **10**, 189–194
112. Zechmeister, L., Le Rosen, A. L., Went, F. W. & Pauling, L. (1941). *Proc. Natl. Acad. Sci.* **27**, 668–474
113. Zechmeister, L. & Went, F. W. (1948). *Nature, Lond.* **162**, 847–848

CHAPTER XII

The Biosynthetic Capabilities of Plastids

XII.1. Introduction

INVESTIGATIONS of the sort described in Chapters I to X of this book,
led to the hypothesis that plastids have a kind of autonomy: that they
have continuity from one cell generation to the next, and that they
contain some of their own genetic information, stored in the form of
DNA. The question might now be asked: do plastids, as well as having
some genetic autonomy, have biochemical autonomy? Do they synthesize their own constituents, or are these materials synthesized elsewhere in the cell and then transported into the plastids? In this chapter
we shall consider the question of whether the plastid components are
synthesized within the plastids themselves.

XII.2. Chlorophyll Synthesis

We shall begin with the most conspicuous plastid constituent, chlorophyll. For a full account of the current state of our knowledge of the
biosynthesis of chlorophyll, the reviews by Granick and Mauzerall
(1961) and Bogorad (1965) should be consulted. Fig. XII.1 shows what
is considered[89] to be the probable pathway.

Considering, first, studies with intact cells, it was found by Granick
(1959, 1961a, 1965) that when excised shoots of etiolated barley seedlings were incubated with δ-aminolaevulinic acid overnight in the dark,
large amounts of protoporphyrin accumulated in the lower portions of
the leaves. Under the fluorescence microscope, only the plastids and
mitochondria were seen to have a red fluorescence, indicating that the
protoporphyrin had accumulated in these bodies. In the upper part of
the leaf protochlorophyllide accumulated; so much so that the leaves
were pale green, and intensely fluorescent. The green colour and the
red fluorescence were localized in the plastids. On the basis of an
368

analysis of the wavelengths of the fluorescence emitted by the plastids, it was concluded that Mg protoporphyrin was also present. It thus appears that these plastids contained at least three of the intermediates of chlorophyll synthesis—protoporphyrin, Mg protoporphyrin, and protochlorophyllide. It therefore appears likely that all the steps of chlorophyll synthesis between protoporphyrin and protochlorophyllide actually occur in the plastid: otherwise we have to suppose that intermediates are formed in the plastids, then diffuse out, undergo further change, and diffuse back again, which seems less plausible. The step

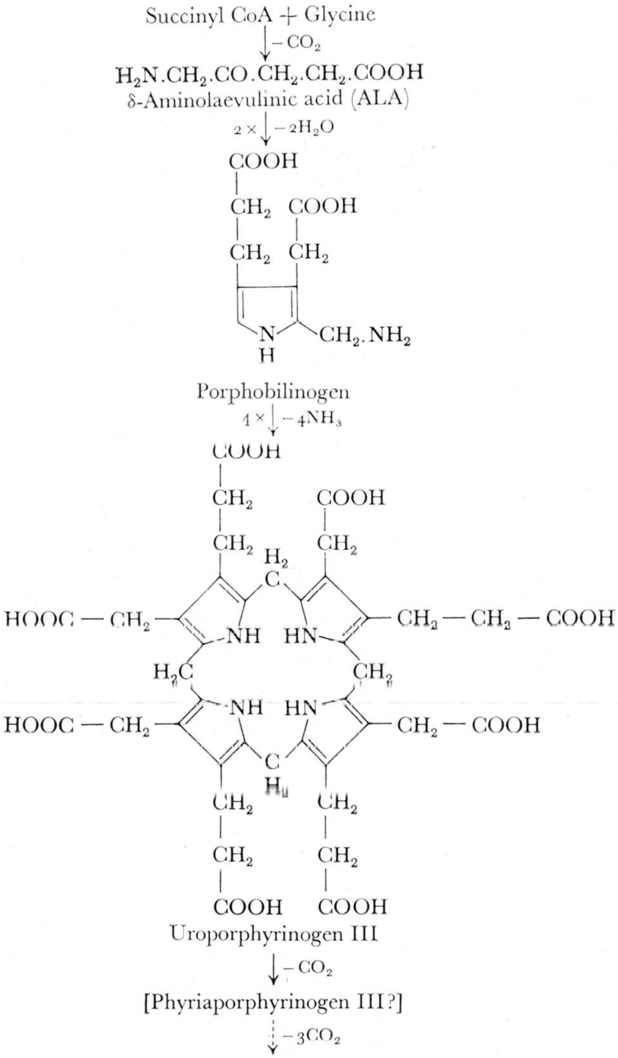

FIG. XII.1. *Biosynthesis of chlorophyll (see Smith and French, 1963; Bogorad, 1965)*

24—P.

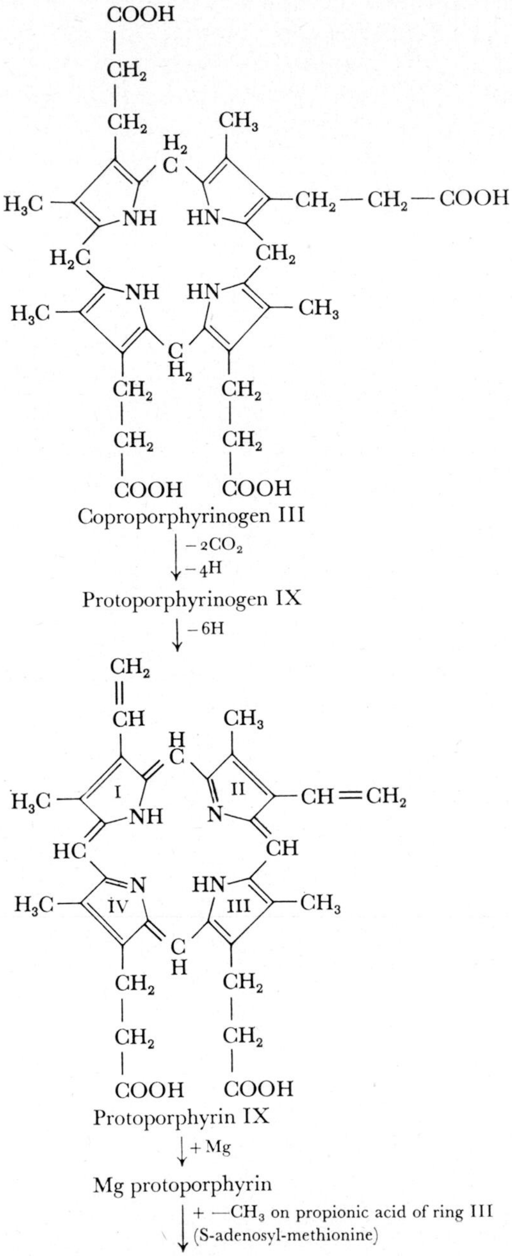

$$COOH$$
$$|$$
$$CH_2$$
$$|$$
$$CH_2 \qquad CH_3$$

Coproporphyrinogen III

$$\downarrow \begin{array}{l} -2CO_2 \\ -4H \end{array}$$

Protoporphyrinogen IX

$$\downarrow -6H$$

Protoporphyrin IX

$$\downarrow +Mg$$

Mg protoporphyrin

$$\downarrow \begin{array}{l} + -CH_3 \text{ on propionic acid of ring III} \\ (\text{S-adenosyl-methionine}) \end{array}$$

FIG. XII.1. (*continued*)

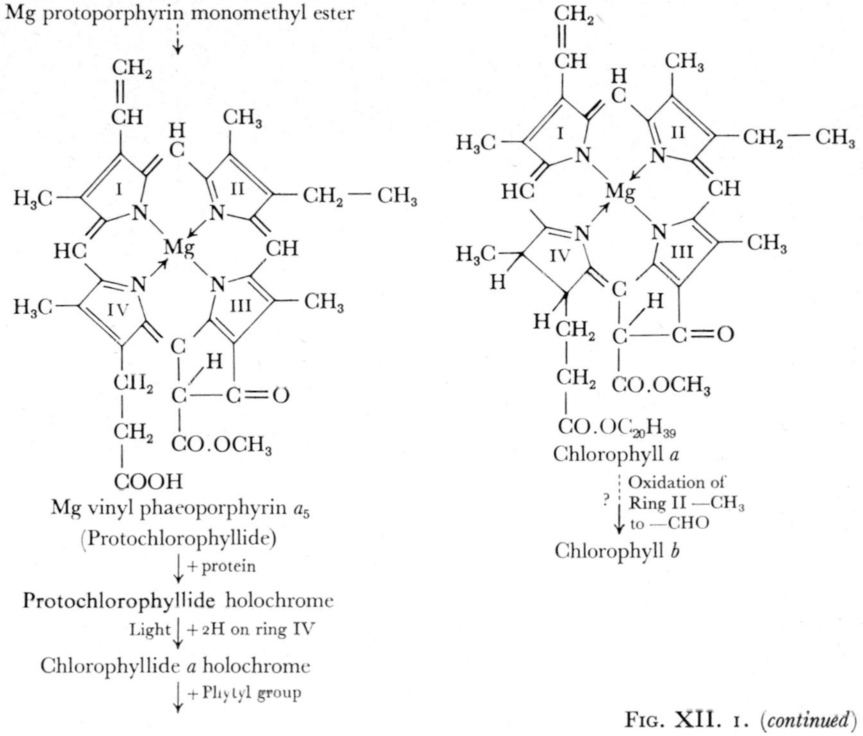

Mg protoporphyrin monomethyl ester

CH_2
||
CH H CH_3
   C

H_3C — I — N — II — CH_2 — CH_3

HC Mg CH

H_3C — IV — N — III — CH_3

C H
CH_2 C — $C=O$
CH_2 $CO.OCH_3$
$COOH$

Mg vinyl phaeoporphyrin a_5
(Protochlorophyllide)

$\downarrow$ + protein

Protochlorophyllide holochrome

Light $\downarrow$ + 2H on ring IV

Chlorophyllide a holochrome

$\downarrow$ + Phytyl group

CH_2
||
CH H CH_3
   C

H_3C — I — N — II — CH_2 — CH_3

HC Mg CH

H_3C — IV — N — III — CH_3
H
H CH_2 C — $C=O$
CH_2 $CO.OCH_3$
$CO.OC_{20}H_{39}$
Chlorophyll a

? Oxidation of Ring II —CH_3 to —CHO

Chlorophyll b

FIG. XII. 1. (continued)

after the formation of protochlorophyllide, its reduction to chloro-phyllide, is known to occur in the plastids. With sufficiently intense light it can take place within a fraction of a second after illumination has begun (XIII.4): thus there is simply not enough time for the proto-chlorophyllide to diffuse out of the chloroplast, be reduced and diffuse back again.

The findings with intact leaves have been supplemented by studies on isolated chloroplasts. Carell and Kahn (1964) have found that chloroplasts of *Euglena gracilis*, purified by density gradient centrifuga-tion, contain 90 per cent of the δ-aminolaevulinic dehydrase activity (the enzyme which converts δ-aminolaevulinic acid to porphobilinogen) of the homogenate. The enzyme appears to be firmly bound to the insoluble portion of the chloroplast (that is the grana) since it is not removed by sonication or osmotic lysis of the chloroplasts. The intact chloroplasts, on incubation with δ-aminolaevulinic acid, also form por-phyrins: these include uroporphyrin and coproporphyrin, but not protoporphyrin. However, after osmotic lysis, the chloroplasts do form protoporphyrin from δ-aminolaevulinic acid. Uroporphyrin, copro-porphyrin and protoporphyrin are also formed when osmotically lysed chloroplasts are incubated with porphobilinogen; however, intact chloroplasts do not appear to metabolize this compound, suggesting that they are impermeable to it.

The conversion of protoporphyrin to protochlorophyllide has not yet been achieved with isolated plastids. However, the conversion of proto-chlorophyllide to chlorophyllide *a* does take place in isolated etioplasts exposed to the light[56]. The last step, the phytylation of chlorophyllide *a* to chlorophyll *a*, may possibly be mediated by the enzyme chloro-phyllase. Normally, the enzyme hydrolyses chlorophyll *a*, but it can also reverse the reaction to some extent[104, 78]. This enzyme is confined to the chloroplasts[57]. However, chlorophyllide phytylation may well be brought about by some enzyme system other than chlorophyllase: nevertheless it still seems very likely, on general grounds, that this last step occurs in the chloroplast.

Summarizing the evidence, then, the work with isolated chloroplasts indicates that they possess the enzymes for converting δ-aminolaevulinic acid to protoporphyrin. The findings with intact leaves suggest that plastids also have the enzymes for converting protoporphyrin to proto-chlorophyllide. The photoconversion of protochlorophyllide to chloro-phyllide *a* is known to occur in the plastid, and it seems virtually certain that the phytylation of chlorophyllide *a* to chlorophyll *a* also occurs in the plastid. Therefore, it seems very likely that the plastid itself carries out the whole sequence of steps in chlorophyll synthesis, from δ-amino-laevulinic acid onwards. Whether δ-aminolaevulinic acid itself is synthesized within the plastids is not known.

XII.3. Carotenoid Synthesis

An account of current views on the biosynthesis of carotenoids may be found in the review by Goodwin (1965a). Fig. XII.2 summarizes the probable pathway.

We shall look first at evidence from work on living cells. Goodwin (1958) found that although excised maize seedlings rapidly incorporated label from ^{14}C-mevalonate into their total unsaponifiable matter, rela-tively little label went into β-carotene, despite the fact that the plants were actively synthesizing β-carotene at the time. With $^{14}CO_2$, on the other hand, there was a very much more rapid incorporation of label into β-carotene. Similar results have been obtained with pine seed-lings[103]: ^{14}C-mevalonate was readily incorporated into sterols but very poorly into β-carotene: $^{14}CO_2$, however, was very readily incor-porated into β-carotene. Goodwin suggests[32, 34] that these results can be explained if β-carotene is synthesized within the chloroplast. The $^{14}CO_2$ is a good precursor because it is being actually fixed by photosynthesis inside the chloroplast; the ^{14}C-mevalonate is a poor precursor, perhaps because it cannot penetrate the chloroplast.

More direct evidence has come from studies on isolated plastids. Shneour and Zabin (1959) reported that a homogenate of tomatoes would incorporate radioactivity from ^{14}C-mevalonate into lycopene in the presence of ATP, pyridine nucleotides, glutathione, Mn^{2+}, and O_2. All the activity of the homogenate was associated with the pellet obtained by centrifugation at 5000 g: this is consistent with the activity being in the chromoplasts. Anderson and Porter (1962) used the particulate fraction obtained by centrifugation of carrot or tomato homogenate at 4000 g: they refer to this as a plastid preparation, and indeed it seems likely that it consists largely of chromoplasts. When the plastids from carrots were incubated with a preparation of ^{14}C-terpenol pyrophosphates, consisting mainly of farnesyl pyrophosphate (C_{15}), there was incorporation of radioactivity into phytoene: this incorporation was stimulated by NADP and by isopentenyl pyrophosphate (C_5). The tomato plastid fraction, under similar conditions incorporated radioactivity mainly into phytoene, but also to a small extent into phytofluene, ζ-carotene, neurosporene, lycopene, γ-carotene, and β-carotene. In further experiments it was found that the specific activities of the polyenes formed decreased in the order—phytoene, phytofluene, ζ-carotene, neurosporene, β-carotene, lycopene, in agreement with the hypothesis that biosynthesis of lycopene proceeds by sequential desaturation of phytoene[8]. The fact that β-carotene had a higher specific activity than the lycopene suggests that, at least in some strains of tomato, β-carotene need not be synthesized from lycopene.

Tomato plastids have also been shown to carry out certain individual steps, or short sequences of steps, in the biosynthetic pathway. A soluble enzyme system has been partially purified from these plastids which, in the presence of Mn^{2+}, Mg^{2+}, NADP, and a sulphydryl reagent will incorporate radioactivity from 4-^{14}C-isopentenyl pyrophosphate into phytoene[51]. Tomato plastids have also been reported to synthesize phytoene from what is thought to be its immediate precursor, geranyl geranyl pyrophosphate[102]. When labelled phytoene was incubated with tomato plastids[7] a small proportion of it was converted to phytofluene. It is also reported[102] that isolated tomato plastids will convert lycopene to γ-, δ-, and β-carotenes. These findings by Porter and co-workers do suggest that tomato (and carrot) chromoplasts have the ability to convert terpenol pyrophosphates to carotenes and carotene precursors. However, some more evidence that the active particles are, in fact, plastids is desirable.

There is some evidence for the presence of enzymes of carotenoid biosynthesis in isolated chloroplasts as well as in chromoplasts. Rogers, Shah, and Goodwin (1965) have shown that *Phaseolus vulgaris* chloro-

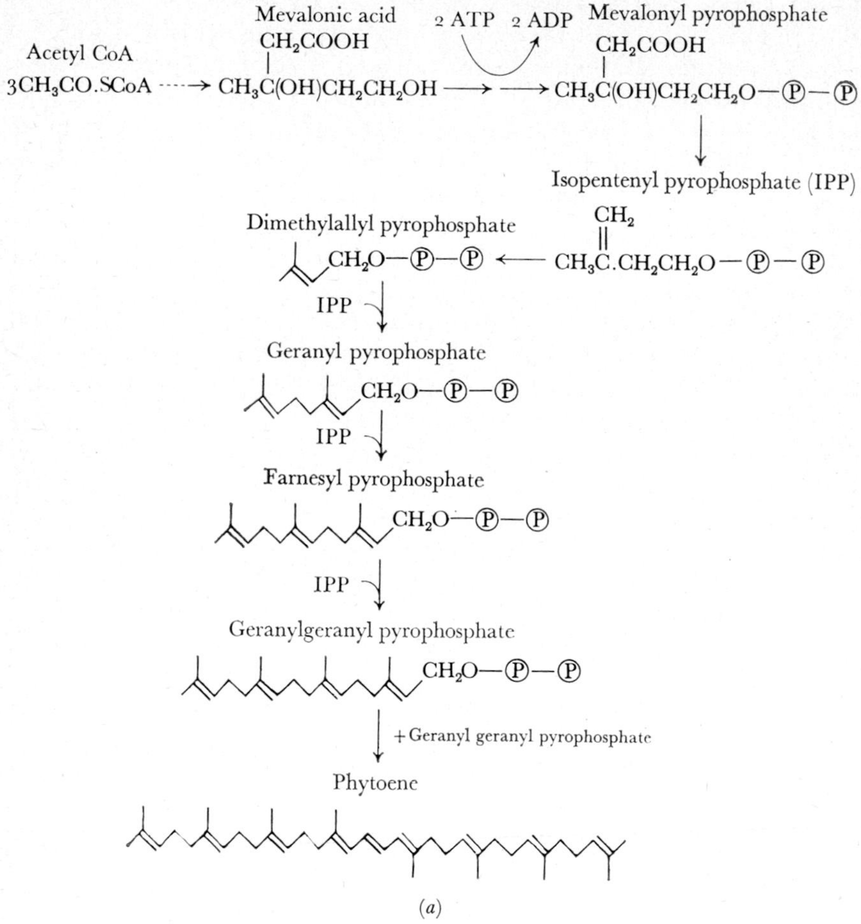

FIG. XII.2. *Biosynthesis of carotenoids (see Goodwin, 1965).*
(*a*) *Biosynthesis of phytoene.* $\textcircled{P}$—*phosphate group.*
(*b*) *Conversion of phytoene to lycopene, β-carotene, and α-carotene*

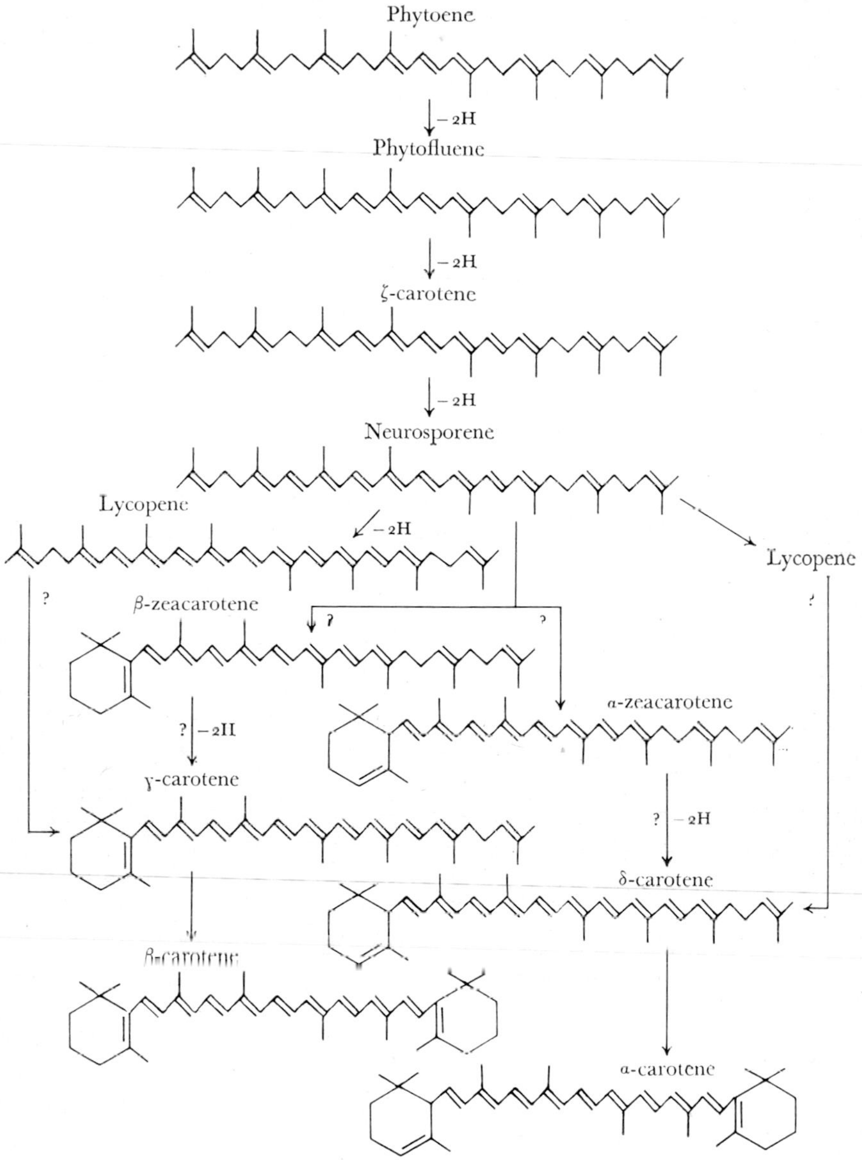

Phytoene

$-2H$

Phytofluene

$-2H$

ζ-carotene

$-2H$

Neurosporene

Lycopene

$-2H$

Lycopene

β-zeacarotene

? | $-2H$

γ-carotene

α-zeacarotene

? | $-2H$

δ-carotene

β-carotene

α-carotene

(b)

plasts contain a mevalonic kinase (phosphorylation is the first step in the synthesis of terpenoids from mevalonate). The activity could only be detected if the chloroplasts were disrupted by ultrasonic or osmotic treatment, which supports Goodwin's hypothesis that exogenous mevalonate is a poor carotenoid precursor in the living cell because it cannot penetrate into the site of carotenoid synthesis within the chloroplast.

Anderson and Porter (1962) reported that isolated spinach chloroplasts would incorporate radioactivity from ^{14}C-terpenol pyrophosphates into phytoene. However, the activity was only about 7 per cent of that of the tomato or carrot plastids, and also required the presence of a soluble enzyme from carrots. Decker and Uehleke (1961) claim that chloroplasts isolated from carrot leaves will convert added ^{14}C-lycopene to β-carotene, and will also convert added ^{14}C-β-carotene to lycopene. In support of this, it has now been reported that isolated spinach chloroplasts will convert lycopene to γ-, δ-, and β-carotenes[102].

The *in vitro* studies, particularly those of the Porter group, and of Shneour and Zabin, taken in conjunction with Goodwin's *in vivo* findings, make it seem probable that in the living cell the complete pathway of carotenoid synthesis takes place within plastids.

XII.4. Terpenoid Side Chain Synthesis

Several chloroplast constituents—chlorophylls *a* and *b*, the plastoquinones, vitamin K_1, α-tocopherol—contain isoprenoid side-chains. Excised maize seedlings in the light incorporate label from $^{14}CO_2$ very rapidly into the phytyl side-chain of the chlorophylls. However, they incorporate virtually no radioactivity into phytol from ^{14}C-mevalonate, despite the fact that this compound is rapidly incorporated into sterols[61, 100]. In pine seedlings also, $^{14}CO_2$ is rapidly incorporated into the chlorophyll phytyl group, whereas ^{14}C-mevalonate is incorporated very poorly into phytol but readily into sterol. Similarly, radioactivity is incorporated into the side-chain of plastoquinone much more rapidly from $^{14}CO_2$ than from ^{14}C-mevalonate, in maize shoots[98]. On the other hand, label is incorporated into the side chain of the mitochondrial quinone, ubiquinone, at a much higher rate from ^{14}C-mevalonate than from $^{14}CO_2$. These findings can be explained by the hypothesis that the side chain of plastoquinone and the phytyl side chain of chlorophyll are synthesized within the chloroplast much more rapidly from the photosynthetically fixed $^{14}CO_2$ than from the exogenous ^{14}C-mevalonate which may penetrate the chloroplast only slowly. The sterols, and the side-chain of ubiquinone, on the other hand, are thought to be synthesized at some other cellular site to which the ^{14}C-mevalonate can penetrate rapidly[35].

Thus, there is some indirect evidence that the terpenoid side chains of chlorophyll and plastoquinone are synthesized in the chloroplast.

XII.5. Synthesis of Fats and other Lipids

XII.5.i. FATTY ACIDS

Fatty acids are, quantitatively, extremely important chloroplast components: they may constitute (in combined form) up to 44 per cent of the chloroplast lipid[21]. Sissakian and Smirnov (1956) found that chloroplasts isolated from sunflower cotyledons would incorporate radioactivity from ^{14}C-acetate into higher fatty acids. This work was continued by Smirnov (1960, 1962) who reported that chloroplasts isolated from spinach or bean leaves also incorporated radioactivity from ^{14}C-acetate into higher fatty acids. The incorporation required the presence of Coenzyme A and Mn^{2+}, and was stimulated by light and by ATP. The characteristics of the system have now been worked out in some detail by other workers using spinach chloroplasts and lettuce chloroplasts.

In the case of spinach chloroplasts[63, 64] incorporation into fatty acids required ATP, Coenzyme A, $NADPH_2$, and Mn^{2+} or Mg^{2+}; synthesis was stimulated by light and by HCO_3^-. The stimulatory effect of light could be largely replaced by adding glucose-6-phosphate: since this compound can serve as a source of reduced NADP, it may be that the main function of light, apart from supplying ATP, is to keep the NADP in its reduced form. Synthesis was also favoured by anaerobic conditions. Incorporation of acetate was inhibited by the biotin-binding protein, avidin, suggesting that biotin is required for fatty-acid synthesis. The chloroplasts also incorporated radioactivity from ^{14}C-malonate into higher fatty acids; this incorporation was not inhibited by avidin. Sulphydryl reagents such as p-chloromercuribenzoate inhibited incorporation of both acetate and malonate. When the chloroplasts were disrupted by osmotic lysis, both the insoluble (grana) and soluble (stroma) fractions were required for fatty acid synthesis. Virtually all the fatty-acid-synthesizing activity of the leaf homogenate was present in the chloroplast fraction.

In the case of lettuce chloroplasts[97, 49, 95] the cofactor requirements for incorporation of acetate into fatty acids were the same as for spinach chloroplasts. In the light, ATP could be replaced by ADP and inorganic phosphate. 3-(p-chlorophenyl)-1,1-dimethylurea, which blocks electron transport, and hence formation of ATP and $NADPH_2$, inhibited fatty acid synthesis. Addition of N-methyl phenazonium methosulphate (which catalyses cyclic, but not non-cyclic photophosphorylation) in the absence of NADP, did not stimulate incorporation, indicating that the function of the NADP is not simply to promote ATP formation. Gas chromatographic analysis of the products showed that radioactivity from ^{14}C-acetate was being incorporated into saturated and mono-unsaturated acids—palmitic, oleic, palmitoleic, stearic, and myristic. There was little, if any, label in the more highly unsaturated fatty acids, linolenic and linoleic, despite the fact that these were the major fatty acid components of these chloroplasts. Furthermore, unlike the intact leaf, the isolated chloroplasts were unable to utilize as substrates the C_8, C_{10}, C_{12}, and C_{14} fatty acids.

More data on the fatty-acid-synthesizing abilities of chloroplasts have appeared recently. Brooks and Stumpf (1965) have obtained a soluble enzyme preparation from lettuce chloroplasts which (in the presence of NADP and glucose-6-phosphate) incorporates radioactivity from ^{14}C-acetyl CoA or 2-^{14}C-malonyl CoA into fatty acids. If a component of a bacterial (*Escherichia coli*) fatty acid synthesis system—the acyl carrier protein (ACP)—is added, then the incorporation from ^{14}C-malonyl CoA, but not that from ^{14}C-acetyl CoA, is very markedly stimulated. In the presence of ACP the incorporation rate is ten times as fast with ^{14}C-malonyl CoA as it is with ^{14}C-acetyl CoA. An ACP-like fraction has been obtained in low concentration from the isolated chloroplasts. It is thought that fatty acid synthesis from malonyl CoA is limited by the amount of ACP present, but that synthesis from acetate or acetyl CoA is limited by the amount of acetyl CoA synthetase and/or the amount of acetyl CoA carboxylase.

Mudd and McManus (1965) have shown that with spinach chloroplasts, if (in the presence of ATP and CoA) glucose-6-phosphate or NADP is omitted, the incorporation of radioactivity from ^{14}C-acetate takes place, not into lipids, but into water-soluble compounds. Also, when both glucose-6-phosphate and NADP are supplied, illumination of the chloroplasts stimulates incorporation into lipid and causes an apparent inhibition of incorporation into water-soluble compounds. With lettuce chloroplasts the stimulatory effect of light on fatty acid formation cannot be replaced by adding large amounts of $NADPH_2$[96]. The fact that light stimulates fatty acid synthesis even when ATP and $NADPH_2$ (or glucose-6-phosphate + NADP) are supplied suggests that light has a stimulatory action over and above that due to the formation of ATP and $NADPH_2$ coupled to photosynthetic electron transport. To explain this, Stumpf and his co-workers[96] suggest that the ACP is in close physical association with the thylakoids of the grana. They further propose that in the dark, the ACP is largely in its disulphide, inactive. form, with the result that lipid synthesis is markedly curtailed. On illumination, the grana would rapidly photoreduce the disulphide form of ACP to the active, thiol form. They postulate that there is a mechanism for reoxidizing ACP to the disulphide form in the dark.

In the earlier work (see above) with lettuce chloroplasts there was virtually no synthesis (from acetate) of the more unsaturated fatty acids, linoleic and linolenic. However, it has now been found[42] that chloroplast fragments from *Chlorella vulgaris* will form linoleic acid and linolenic acid from ^{14}C-oleyl CoA, but not from free ^{14}C-oleic acid. Also, a plastid fraction from immature safflower seeds was shown to convert oleyl CoA to linoleic acid: O_2 was required[60].

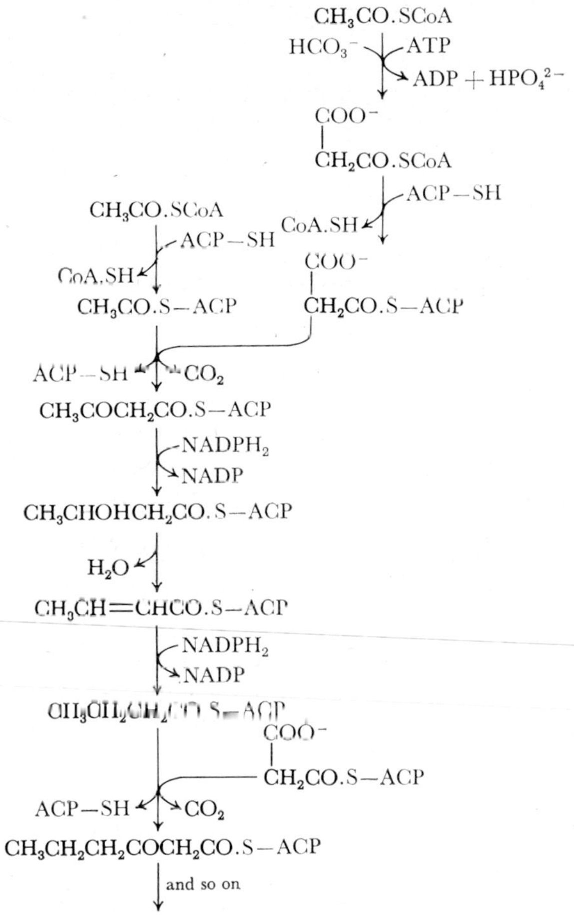

FIG. XII.3. *Biosynthesis of fatty acids (see Lynen, F., Matsuhashi, M., Numa, S., and Schweizer, E. (1963) Biochem. Soc. Symp. 24, 43–55; Vagelos, P. R. (1964) Ann. Rev. Biochem. 33, 139–172; Alberts, A. A., Majerus, P. W., and Vagelos, P. R. (1965) Biochemistry 4, 2265–2274). ACP—Acyl Carrier Protein*

In the light of all this work it appears that chloroplasts do, in fact, synthesize their own fatty acids; indeed, most of the fatty-acid-synthesizing activity of the leaf appears to be carried by the chloroplasts. This is not surprising since most of the fatty acid of the leaf cell is in the chloroplasts. The cofactor requirements of synthesis and the fact that malonate is incorporated too, suggest that the pathway of fatty acid synthesis is similar to that which has been worked out for animal and other cells (Fig. XII.3).

XII.5.ii. OTHER LIPIDS

Most of the chloroplast fatty acid exists in the combined form as part of more complex lipids such as glycerides, phospholipids, and glycolipids. About half the radioactivity from ^{14}C-acetate incorporated by isolated lettuce chloroplasts went into free fatty acids, and another 20 per cent was found in mono-, di-, and tri-glycerides[97]. The rest of the label was in glycolipids and phospholipids. In the spinach chloroplast system, most of the fatty acids formed from ^{14}C-acetate appeared to be in the form of phospholipid[63]. Thus, it appears that the chloroplasts can not only synthesize fatty acids, but also possess the enzymes for introducing fatty acids into glycerides, glycolipids, and phospholipids.

It has also been reported[84] that chloroplasts isolated from sunflower cotyledons incorporate radioactivity from ^{32}P-inorganic phosphate into phospholipid. This suggests that chloroplasts also have the enzymes for introducing the phosphate into phospholipid.

Isolated spinach chloroplasts have been found to incorporate radioactivity from uridinediphospho (UDP) ^{14}C-galactose into material soluble in chloroform, i.e. into a lipid fraction[67]. Incorporation was not affected by light. Uridine triphosphate inhibited the reaction. With UDP-^{14}C-glucose radioactivity was incorporated to about half the extent observed with UDP-^{14}C-galactose: there was effectively no incorporation into lipid when thymidinediphosphogalactose, deoxyuridinediphosphogalactose, adenosinediphosphogalactose, α-galactosyl phosphate, UDP-galacturonic acid, or UDP-pentose (mixture of D-xylose and L-arabinose derivatives), labelled in the sugar moiety, were used as substrates. When an acetone powder of the chloroplasts was prepared, neither the powder nor the components in the acetone filtrate were active alone, but they were active if they were combined together again. Thin-layer chromatography of the chloroform extract at the end of the reaction showed at least eight radioactive products. Three of these were in the approximate area of monogalactosyl distearin, and two in the area of digalactosyl distearin. These results do suggest that chloroplasts have the enzymes for synthesizing glycolipids, but the nature of the reactions involved is far from clear.

From the findings reported in this section, then, it appears that chloroplasts can probably synthesize their own neutral fats (glycerides), phospholipids, and glycolipids, as well as fatty acids.

XII.6. Protein Synthesis

XII.6.i. AMINO ACIDS

Protein is, in terms of quantity at any rate, the major chloroplast component, since it constitutes about 70 per cent of the dry weight of the intact chloroplast (Table I.1). With regard to the site of synthesis of chloroplast protein there are really two questions to be answered: where are the amino acids synthesized, and where are they assembled into protein?

It was shown early on by the Calvin group that certain amino acids —alanine, aspartate, glutamate, and serine—are amongst the first products of photosynthesis with $^{14}CO_2$ by living cells. Smith, Bassham, and Kirk (1961) showed that the rate of synthesis of these amino acids by *Chlorella pyrenoidosa* accounted for at least 32 per cent of all carbon fixation under these steady state conditions: it also accounted for about 62 per cent of all the uptake of NH_4^+ (the sole source of N) by the cells. The primary route for incorporation of the NH_4^+ ions into amino acids in *Chlorella* appears to be the reductive amination of α-ketoglutarate to form glutamic acid[6]. The rate of increase of ^{14}C in these amino acids reached its maximum at the same time as intermediates of the CO_2 fixation cycle became saturated with ^{14}C. This suggests that the immediate precursors of these amino acids are the intermediates of the carbon reduction cycle. From a study of the time course of incorporation into alanine, aspartate, glutamate, and serine, it was concluded that two (or more) distinct pools of these amino acids existed: an 'active' pool, representing 20–50 per cent of the total, which rapidly became labelled, and a more slowly labelled pool. To explain these various findings it was suggested that the rapid synthesis of amino acids in the 'active' pool actually takes place within the chloroplast. The more slowly labelled pool might correspond to the space outside the chloroplast.

This *in vivo* work is to some extent supported by *in vitro* studies: the products of photosynthesis formed from $^{14}CO_2$ by isolated chloroplasts include alanine and aspartate[99]. Also, isolated spinach chloroplasts will incorporate radioactivity from ^{14}C-acetate into an amino acid fraction which includes glutamic acid[63, 65]. In the light of these different findings it therefore appears probable that the chloroplast synthesizes at least some amino acids.

If the chloroplast is to synthesize its own sulphur-containing amino acids then as well as being able to build carbon skeletons it must be able to incorporate sulphur from inorganic sulphate. Chloroplasts appear to be able to carry out at least the first step in this process, since spinach chloroplasts have been shown to have the enzyme which catalyses the formation of adenosine-5'-phosphosulphate from ATP and inorganic sulphate[4]. There is also evidence suggesting that chloroplasts can bring about a light-dependent reduction of the sulphate in 3'-phospho-adenosine-5'-phosphosulphate to sulphite.

XII.6.ii. *IN VIVO* STUDIES ON CHLOROPLAST PROTEIN SYNTHESIS

It was shown by Nichiporovich (1955) that the synthesis of chloroplast proteins in higher plants is greatly accelerated during photosynthesis. The proteins were labelled when $^{14}CO_2$ was administered, but not when ^{14}C-carbohydrates were supplied, suggesting that the accelerated protein synthesis uses intermediates of photosynthetic CO_2 fixation.

If the chloroplast proteins are not synthesized in the chloroplast, then the most likely alternative is that they are synthesized by the cytoplasmic ribosomes, since in animal cells, at any rate, the cytoplasmic ribosomes appear to be the most active protein-synthesizing sites. In order to investigate this possibility, Brachet, Chantrenne, and Vanderhaege (1955) incubated the alga *Acetabularia* for two hours in the light with $^{14}CO_2$, and then isolated the chloroplasts and the microsomal fraction (cytoplasmic ribosomes plus endoplasmic reticulum). They found that the specific radioactivity of the chloroplast protein was 2–3 times as high as that of the microsomal protein. If the chloroplast proteins were synthesized by cytoplasmic ribosomes then the microsomal protein would be expected to have a higher specific activity than the chloroplast protein. These findings therefore support the theory that chloroplast proteins are synthesized in the chloroplast.

A somewhat similar experiment was carried out by Heber (1962) who exposed spinach leaves to $^{14}CO_2$ in the dark for four minutes, and then illuminated the leaves and at intervals of a few minutes, took samples and isolated the chloroplasts, and also the cytoplasmic proteins by a non-aqueous procedure. Radioactivity appeared in the chloroplast protein sooner than it appeared in the cytoplasmic protein, suggesting that the chloroplast protein is, in fact, synthesized in the chloroplast rather than in the cytoplasm.

The same conclusion was reached by Smith et al. (1961) on the basis of their results with *Chlorella*, described above. Since carbon was not only going into the 'active' (supposedly chloroplastic) amino acid pool during steady state photosynthesis, but was also passing through it (i.e. not merely accumulating), and since this carbon was not ending up in the slowly-labelled amino acid pool (supposedly cytoplasmic), it seemed likely that it was being used for protein synthesis inside the chloroplast. From the actual rate at which carbon was passing through this 'active' amino acid pool under these conditions, it appeared that more than 60 per cent of the protein synthesis in *Chlorella* under these conditions took place in the chloroplast.

The data described so far all suggest that in the chloroplast there is active synthesis of protein from photosynthetically fixed CO_2. In view of these findings, some recent results of Parthier (1964), which seem to implicate mitochondria as the primary sites of protein synthesis from $^{14}CO_2$ in leaves, are particularly puzzling. Green leaves of *Nicotiana rustica* were allowed to photosynthesize with $^{14}CO_2$ for 15 minutes in the light, and were then put in the dark. At intervals during the exposure to light, and during the subsequent dark period, the specific radioactivity of the protein in the chloroplasts, mitochondria, ribosomes, and cytoplasmic fraction of the leaf cells was measured. In samples taken at 5, 10, and 15 minutes (during the exposure to light + $^{14}CO_2$), the mitochondrial protein had the highest specific activity, the chloroplast and ribosomal proteins both had specific activities 30–40 per cent lower than the mitochondrial protein, and the cytoplasmic protein had the lowest specific activity of all. The specific activity of the mitochondrial protein continued to increase, and remained higher than that of the other proteins, during the next 18 hours in the dark. The specific activities of the chloroplast and ribosomal proteins eventually (after ca. 8 hours) levelled off at about the same value, a value which, at 18 hours, was only about one sixth that of the mitochondrial protein. The specific activity of the cytoplasmic protein caught up with those of the chloroplast and ribosomal proteins after about three hours in the dark; after 18 hours in the dark the cytoplasmic protein had a specific activity which was about 2·5 times that of the chloroplast and ribosomal proteins. Parthier's results agree with the other results at least to the extent that they provide no evidence for synthesis of chloroplast proteins by cytoplasmic ribosomes. However, the fact that incorporation of radioactivity from $^{14}CO_2$ into mitochondrial protein is apparently more rapid than into chloroplast protein is quite unexpected. Parthier suggests that, as a result of damage to cellular structures, the distribution of incorporated radioactivity between the subcellular fractions may be altered during the isolation procedure. If this is so, then the highly labelled protein in the mitochondrial fraction might, perhaps, have originated in the chloroplasts. An alternative possibility is that some low molecular weight compound, which becomes highly labelled in photosynthesis, is rapidly transported to the mitochondria, and there used as a source of carbon for protein synthesis.

XII.6.iii. PRESENCE OF COMPONENTS OF A PROTEIN SYNTHESIS SYSTEM

Much is now known of the mechanism by which protein is synthesized in the cytoplasm. Detailed accounts may be found in reviews by Hoagland (1960), Gale (1962), Arnstein (1965), and many others. Current views on the reaction sequence involved are summarized in Fig. XII.4. If the plastid can, indeed, synthesize protein, then it might be expected to contain the different catalytic components known to be required for cytoplasmic protein synthesis; unless, of course, plastid proteins are synthesized by a different mechanism, which seems unlikely.

The first step in protein synthesis is the formation of the aminoacyl-AMP compounds from ATP and amino acids, catalysed by the amino acid activating enzymes. Bové and Raacke (1959) measured amino acid activating enzyme activity in various sub-cellular fractions of spinach leaf. Most of the activity was in the final supernatant (after centrifuging down the microsomes) and the chloroplasts. After osmotic lysis and centrifugation of the chloroplasts the activity was found in the supernatant (stroma) but not the pellet (grana). The specific enzyme activity per mg. protein of the chloroplast extract was about the same as that of the final supernatant from the whole homogenate, as measured with an amino acid mixture. However, marked differences were found when the ability of these extracts to activate individual amino acids was tested. In the case of the chloroplast extract, the greatest activity was obtained with tyrosine, followed by methionine and leucine: this order was reversed in the case of the cell supernatant. The high activity of the chloroplast extract and the different relative distribution of individual amino acid activating enzymes in the chloroplast and supernatant fractions make it seem unlikely that the chloroplast activity is due to contamination by cytoplasmic enzymes. In the presence of chloroplast grana and supernatant fractions together, plus cofactors of photophosphorylation, ADP and inorganic phosphate in the light served just as well for amino acid activation as did ATP, indicating that photosynthetically-formed ATP can be used for activation just as effectively as exogenous ATP. Amino acid activating enzymes have also been detected in spinach chloroplasts by Marcus (1959). He found that whereas the cell supernatant was active with lysine but relatively inactive with isoleucine, with the chloroplasts the position was reversed. Spinach chloroplasts prepared by the non-aqueous technique appear

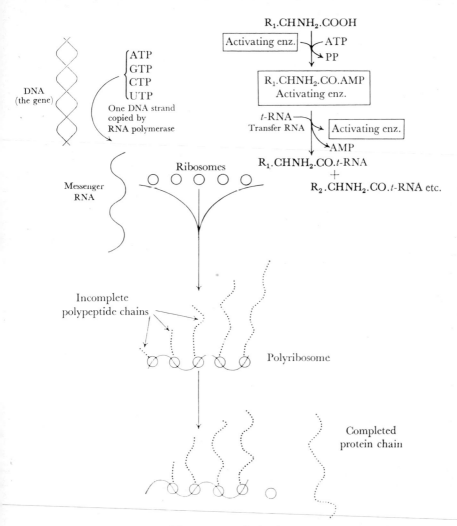

FIG. XII.4. *Biosynthesis of proteins*

to contain 15–40 per cent of the total amino acid activating enzyme activity of the cell[43]. Amino acid activating enzymes have also been found in pea chloroplasts[83].

The next step after formation of the amino acyl-AMP complex is the transference of the amino acid residue to the appropriate transfer-RNA molecule. There is now evidence for the presence of transfer RNA in plastids. Sissakian, Filippovich, Svetailo, and Aliyev (1965) have isolated a low molecular weight RNA from pea seedling chloroplasts. This had a sedimentation constant of 3·2 S, and had the ability to accept amino acids in the presence of amino acid-activating enzymes and

ATP. Similarly, a soluble fraction has been obtained from tobacco leaf chloroplasts which, on incubation with ^{14}C-valine and ATP, gave rise to a product soluble in hot, but not cold, trichloroacetic acid[91]. This radioactive product was probably the valine-transfer RNA complex.

The final stages of protein synthesis, the building up of the poly-peptide chain, occur in the ribosome. As we saw in Chapter X, there is substantial evidence for the presence of ribosomes in plastids. Particles very similar to ribosomes have been seen in electron micrographs of plastids. Particles of the size, centrifugal characteristics, chemical com-position, and properties of ribosomes have been isolated from chloro-plasts of higher plants and algae. Thus on cytological and analytical grounds alone it appears very likely that chloroplasts contain ribosomes.

During protein synthesis in the ribosome, the actual sequence of the amino acids is determined by the template RNA (or messenger RNA) which is itself a copy of the DNA of the gene. Template RNA has been detected in chloroplasts. Brawerman and Eisenstadt (1964) isolated an RNA fraction from chloroplasts of *Euglena gracilis* which stimulated protein synthesis when it was added to a suitable cell-free, protein-synthesizing system from bacteria. The effect did not appear to be due to ribosomal RNA, since the RNA isolated from the soluble fraction (100,000 g supernatant) of broken chloroplasts had nearly three times the stimulatory activity (per mg. RNA) of RNA isolated from the ribosomal fraction (100,000 g pellet). This stimulatory RNA consisted of a major component having a sedimentation constant of 12 S, and a minor component with a sedimentation constant of 22 S.

It is known that in protein synthesis in other systems a given template RNA molecule is usually read simultaneously by a number of ribo-somes: the resulting complex, containing template RNA and a number of ribosomes, is known as a polyribosome. Thus, if chloroplasts contain both template RNA and ribosomes, then we might expect also to find polyribosomes. What appear to be polyribosomes have, in fact, been detected in chloroplasts of *Brassica pekinensis*[19]. The chloroplasts were isolated in the presence of polyvinyl sulphate to inhibit nucleases, and were then disrupted, and the contents analysed by sucrose density gradient centrifugation. As well as the usual 68 S, chloroplast ribosome, band, a broad band of UV-absorbing material, sedimenting more rapidly than single ribosomes, was observed. If the material was treated with ribonuclease before gradient analysis, then the broad band decreased in size, while the 68 S band increased: this is what would be expected if the ribonuclease was liberating single ribosomes from the polyribosomes by degrading the template RNA holding the poly-ribosomes together. There is also some electron microscope evidence for the presence of polyribosomes in plastids. In chloroplasts of leaves of oat[40] and mung bean seedlings (Dr H. Öpik, personal communica-

tion) the ribosomes may often be seen to occur in clusters. These clusters
are probably polyribosomes.

XII.6.iv. PROTEIN SYNTHESIS BY ISOLATED CHLOROPLASTS

It is clear that there is evidence for the presence, within the chloroplasts,
of most of the machinery for protein synthesis. Can isolated chloroplasts
therefore actually carry out protein synthesis? There are now several
reports that they can.

The first paper to appear on this topic was by Stephenson, Thimann,
and Zamecnik (1956). They reported that chloroplasts isolated by
differential centrifugation from tobacco leaves incorporated ^{14}C-leucine
into protein at a rate equivalent to replacement of 1 per cent of the
leucine already present in protein per hour. Incorporation was stimulated by light. This system differed from other cell-free systems for
synthesizing protein in that incorporation was not stimulated by the
addition of ATP, or by a mixture of the other amino acids: a particularly surprising difference was the fact that leucine incorporation was
not inhibited by ribonuclease, even at high concentration. The lack of
effect of ATP and ribonuclease is at variance with more recent results,
and remains unexplained. A little later than these findings appeared,
Sissakian and Filippovich (1957) reported that bean and tobacco leaf
chloroplasts would incorporate ^{14}C-glycine into protein. Incorporation
was stimulated by a mixture of the other amino acids. If the supernatant
left after centrifuging down the chloroplasts from the leaf homogenate
was added back to the chloroplasts, incorporation was about 90 per
cent inhibited: similar observations have now been reported by other
workers[70, 91].

Recently, protein synthesis by isolated chloroplasts of algae and
higher plants has been investigated in some detail by various groups of
workers: we shall now consider their findings. Eisenstadt and Brawerman (1963, 1964, 1965) isolated chloroplasts from *Euglena gracilis* by
differential centrifugation, and purified them by flotation through
75 per cent sucrose. These chloroplasts incorporated ^{14}C-leucine into
protein; this took place most rapidly during the first 15 minutes but
virtually ceased after 30 minutes. Incorporation required ATP plus an
ATP-generating system, and also required exogenous transfer RNA:
under these conditions incorporation was inhibited by light. If the
ATP-generating system was omitted, then in the presence of NADP,
ADP, and KH_2PO_4 (to permit photophosphorylation) light stimulated
the process by about 100 per cent. Incorporation was inhibited by
ribonuclease, puromycin, and chloramphenicol. A high concentration

of actinomycin caused about 10 per cent inhibition: addition of the triphosphates of uridine, cytidine, and guanosine stimulated incorporation slightly, this stimulation being abolished by actinomycin (see XII.7). Addition of a natural messenger RNA preparation stimulated leucine incorporation by 35 per cent. Addition of the synthetic messenger, polyuridylic acid, stimulated phenylalanine incorporation by 100 per cent. Thus, the characteristics of this system are very similar to those of other cell-free, protein-synthesizing systems. The fact that these chloroplasts were prepared from pure cultures of the algae makes it very unlikely that bacterial contamination is responsible for incorporation: however, contamination may be a serious problem when chloroplasts are prepared from leaves which have been stored for some time[3a].

Spencer and Wildman (1964) used the pellet obtained by centrifugation of tobacco leaf homogenate at 1000 g as their experimental material. This was the most active fraction: the 12,000 g and 144,000 g fractions had only 3 and 18 per cent, respectively, of the activity of this fraction, and the final supernatant had no activity. Chloroplasts were by far the major component of the 1000 g fraction, but nuclei were also present together with some small particles of unknown origin. By separating the 1000 g pellet into fractions containing, or not containing, nuclei it was shown that these organelles contributed virtually nothing to the activity. It seems likely, therefore, that it was the chloroplasts which were, in fact, responsible for this activity. The 1000 g pellet incorporated ^{14}C-valine into protein. Incorporation required the presence of ATP plus an ATP-generating system. Omission of a mixture of the other amino acids depressed incorporation by 25 per cent; omission of Mg^{2+} reduced incorporation by 52 per cent; when guanosine triphosphate, uridine triphosphate, and cytidine triphosphate were omitted, incorporation fell by only 8 per cent. The activity was 74 per cent inhibited by 0·2 µg ribonuclease/ml but was only 14 per cent inhibited by deoxyribonuclease at 20 µg/ml. Puromycin at 10 µg/ml and chloramphenicol at 200 µg/ml both inhibited incorporation by 70 per cent; actinomycin D at 20 µg/ml caused only 18 per cent inhibition. Added tobacco mosaic virus RNA did not stimulate incorporation of ^{14}C-valine; however, added polyuridylic acid caused 50–140 per cent stimulation of incorporation of ^{14}C-phenylalanine. During the first five minutes of incubation of the chloroplasts with ^{14}C-valine there was rapid incorporation into a component which was rendered soluble by hot trichloroacetic acid but not by cold trichloroacetic acid. After five minutes the level of radioactivity in this fraction remained constant, although the radioactivity in the hot trichloroacetic-insoluble (protein) fraction continued to increase. This rapidly labelled component is probably amino-acyl-transfer RNA: it accounts for 67 per cent of the incorporated radioactivity at 1 minute, but only 25 per cent after 35

minutes. The enzyme system which incorporated valine into a form
soluble in hot acid, but insoluble in cold, was liberated from the chloroplasts by exposure to hypotonic medium, and 80 per cent of the incorporating activity of the chloroplasts was lost in the process. It is thought
that the amino acid activating enzymes and the transfer RNAs are contained in the chloroplast stroma, and that this is lost on osmotic lysis[26].
This tobacco chloroplast system, then, like the *Euglena* one, has the
characteristics typical of cell-free protein-synthesizing systems.

Similar studies have been carried out on spinach chloroplasts[90]. The
results were much the same as those obtained with tobacco chloroplasts.
In this case, actinomycin D inhibited incorporation by only 4 per cent.
The ATP requirement could be met in the light by supplying ADP,
inorganic phosphate, and pyocyanin (a catalyst of photophosphorylation). Guanosine triphosphate (GTP) was required for activity its
omission caused 61 per cent inhibition of incorporation. Twenty-eight
per cent of the radioactivity incorporated from ^{14}C-valine into protein
could not be sedimented by centrifugation for 60 minutes at 144,000 g.
Of the radioactive material that was sedimented, half could be liberated
into solution by the detergent Triton X-100: this fraction of the radioactivity may be partly in chloroplast structural protein, since this protein is known to be rendered soluble by Triton X-100. The activity of
the spinach chloroplasts fell off markedly with the age of the plant from
which they were isolated: chloroplasts from plants five weeks old had
only 10 per cent of the activity of chloroplasts from plants three weeks old.

Goffeau and Brachet (1965) have studied protein synthesis by chloroplasts isolated from enucleated cells of *Acetabularia mediterranea*. These
rapidly incorporated radioactivity from a ^{14}C-amino acid mixture into
material insoluble in trichloroacetic acid. Incorporation ceased after
about 45 minutes. No significant number of bacteria could be detected
in the chloroplast preparations. ATP stimulated incorporation in the
dark but not in the light, suggesting that in the light the chloroplasts
were making enough ATP for their needs. GTP did not stimulate. After
hydrolysis of the labelled protein, radioactivity could be shown to be
present in at least fifteen of the amino acids. Deoxyribonuclease
(200 μg/ml) had no effect on incorporation: more surprisingly, neither
did ribonuclease (200 μg/ml)—it is thought that the enzyme did not
penetrate the chloroplast membrane. Chloramphenicol (5 μg/ml) and
puromycin (50 μg/ml) each inhibited incorporation by about 50 per
cent. Actinomycin D (50 μg/ml) also inhibited incorporation by about
50 per cent (see XII.7). Neither streptomycin (50 μg/ml) nor penicillin
(50 μg/ml) had any effect.

Russian workers[81, 87] have implicated lipids in protein synthesis by
isolated bean, and other, chloroplasts. They report that during the first
few minutes of incubation the chloroplast lipoproteins took up radio-

active amino acids into both the lipid and protein parts of the molecule. They have detected what they believe to be lipoaminoacid compounds by paper chromatography, and, after incubation of the chloroplasts with ^{14}C-phenylalanine, radioactivity was found in one of these spots. Radioactivity appeared in the lipid and protein moieties of the lipoprotein within seconds, but in the other chloroplast proteins only after a lag period[9]. Puromycin inhibited incorporation into both protein and lipid fractions. When chloroplasts which had already been labelled with ^{14}C-amino acids were incubated for a second time with ^{12}C-amino acids there was a decrease in the radioactivity of the lipids, and an increase in the radioactivity of the protein. When a chloroplast lipid fraction containing ^{14}C-amino acids was incubated with chloroplasts there was transference of radioactivity to chloroplast protein. These workers suggest that the lipid compounds participate in chloroplast protein synthesis.

Protein synthesis studies have now been carried out, not only on the isolated chloroplasts themselves but also on the ribosomes extracted from the chloroplasts. According to Sissakian et al. (1965) the ribosomes isolated from pea chloroplasts were very much more active than the whole chloroplasts at incorporating ^{14}C-glycine into protein. A particularly surprising feature of this work was that the ribosomes were active even in the absence of the usual cofactors of protein synthesis. Addition of ATP and a mixture of the other amino acids had no effect on glycine incorporation. When the ribosomes were dialysed their ability to incorporate glycine into protein fell to only one-tenth of the previous value. The activity was restored to about one-third of the previous level if ATP and an amino acid mixture were added. A further 60 per cent increase in activity was brought about by addition of a 'pH 5 enzyme' fraction from the chloroplasts, which contained amino acid activating enzymes and transfer RNA. Ribonuclease, chloramphenicol, and puromycin all inhibited incorporation. With non-dialysed ribosomes, actinomycin in high concentration (167 μg/ml) inhibited incorporation by 54 per cent (see XII.7). Eisenstadt and Brawerman (1963; 1964) found that ribosomes from Euglena chloroplasts had virtually no ability to incorporate ^{14}C-leucine into protein unless transfer RNA and a cell-supernatant fraction were added, as well as all the usual cofactors of protein synthesis (ATP, GTP, Mg^{2+}, amino acid mixture, etc.). Incorporation was inhibited by ribonuclease, puromycin, and chloramphenicol. Activity was increased nearly five-fold on addition of a natural template RNA preparation: this was a much greater response than that shown by the whole chloroplasts. This suggests that the intact chloroplasts have enough messenger RNA for their needs, but that this is lost on isolation of the ribosomes. When the Euglena chloroplast ribosomes were incubated with RNA from bacteriophage f2, together with the usual *Euglena* supernatant fraction (containing activating enzymes and transfer RNA)[73] there was incorporation of ^{14}C-amino acids into a protein which appeared to be identical with the coat protein of the bacteriophage. This suggests that the *Euglena* chloroplast ribosomes can correctly translate foreign template RNA into protein. App and Jagendorf (1963) isolated ribosomes from spinach chloroplasts: these incorporated radioactive amino acids into protein. Incorporation was enhanced by ATP, GTP, and the pH 5 fraction from the cell supernatant: ribonuclease and chloramphenicol inhibited incorporation. It has been reported[10] that the incorporation of ^{14}C-phenylalanine into protein by spinach chloroplast ribosomes is stimulated by polyuridylic acid; however, this stimulation could only be detected if the ribosomes were pretreated with ribonuclease.

XII.6.v. CONCLUSIONS

In vivo and *in vitro* studies all indicate that chloroplasts can, and do, synthesize protein. It also appears that the mechanism of chloroplast protein synthesis is of the normal type, involving activating enzymes, transfer RNA, ribosomes, and messenger RNA. Just how much of the chloroplast protein is synthesized within the chloroplast is not known for certain, but the work with living cells suggests that most of it is, and indeed on general grounds it seems likely that all of it is. In view of the genetic and other evidence considered in Chapter XI, it seems likely that some of the messenger RNA is synthesized by the nuclear DNA and some by the chloroplast DNA (see next section).

XII.7. Nucleic Acid Synthesis

There is now very good evidence that plastids contain RNA and DNA (see Chapter X). DNA is thought to exert its genetic effects by bringing about the synthesis of RNA. Therefore, quite apart from the presence of RNA in the plastids, the fact that these bodies contain DNA suggests that they should be able to synthesize RNA. The main problem to be overcome in demonstrating RNA synthesis in isolated plastids is the same as that involved in demonstrating the presence of DNA: it is to prove that the results are not due to contaminating nuclear material. Bandurski and Maheshwari (1962) in a study of nucleic acid synthesis by tobacco leaf nuclei mention that the chloroplast fraction, prepared by differential centrifugation, incorporated some radioactivity from ^{14}C-ATP into nucleic acid. However, the presence of DNA in chloroplasts was not established at that time, and the authors did not attempt to determine whether this activity was due to the chloroplasts or to the nuclear material which contaminated the preparation; nor did they infer that chloroplasts could synthesize RNA.

Direct evidence that chloroplasts can synthesize RNA came from experiments on isolated broad-bean chloroplasts[54, 55]. These experiments were part of a study of the function of the DNA which had previously been shown[53] to be present in these chloroplasts. RNA synthesis in nuclei and bacteria is thought to be catalysed by the enzyme RNA polymerase, which uses the four nucleoside triphosphates as substrates in order to make an RNA copy of a DNA template[101, 46, 94, 45, 18]. Accordingly, an attempt was made[54] to detect RNA polymerase activity in broad-bean chloroplasts, rigorously purified by high-speed density gradient centrifugation. When such chloroplasts were incubated with ^{14}C-ATP together with CTP, GTP, and UTP, there was incorporation of radioactivity into material which was insoluble in $0·2$N $HClO_4$ or 67 per cent ethanol. Incorporation proceeded rapidly for about 15 minutes and then levelled off and stopped between 20 and 30 minutes. Incorporation was not stimulated by light. The labelled material was rendered soluble by treatment with $0·5$N $HClO_4$ at 70° for 20 minutes. After incubation with $0·5$N NaOH at 30° for 18 hours, or with 25 µg ribonuclease/ml at 30° for 20 minutes, the material could no longer be precipitated by acid. These data indicate that the radioactivity was being incorporated into a polyribonucleotide. Incorporation was virtually abolished by omission of CTP, GTP, and UTP, and was 90 per cent inhibited by $12·5$ µg deoxyribonuclease/ml. The antibiotic actinomycin D, which inhibits RNA synthesis in vivo[52] and RNA polymerase in vitro[47, 31] by combining with the DNA primer, also inhibited incorporation in the chloroplast preparations. The chloroplast activity required the presence of a divalent cation, such as Mg^{2+} or Mn^{2+}, as do bacterial and nuclear RNA polymerases.

Thus, in all those properties which have been examined (synthesis of polyribonucleotide, requirement for all four nucleoside triphosphates, sensitivity to deoxyribonuclease and actinomycin, requirement for divalent cation) this chloroplast enzyme is very similar to the RNA polymerases which have been found in other biological systems. It therefore seems very likely that the activity is due to an RNA polymerase working with DNA as a template. However, the question of whether this is really a chloroplast enzyme or whether it is due to contaminating nuclear material must now be considered. In an attempt to answer this question, the properties of the enzyme in the chloroplast fraction were compared[54] with those of the enzyme present in the nuclear fraction. A number of distinct differences were found. First of all, the activity of the chloroplast fraction, in terms of rate of incorporation per µg endogenous DNA, was always very much higher (five- to twelve-fold) than that of the nuclear fraction. Secondly, whereas with the chloroplasts, omission of CTP, GTP, and UTP caused 97 per cent inhibition of activity; with the nuclear material, omission of the tri-phosphates either stimulated or caused only a slight inhibition. Thirdly, the nuclear reaction was only about half as sensitive to the inhibitors DNAase and actinomycin as was the chloroplast reaction. Fourthly, the two enzyme preparations responded differently to divalent cations. In the presence of 10mM $MgSO_4$, the further addition of 2mM $MnCl_2$ inhibited the chloroplast activity by 40–49 per cent; the nuclear reaction, on the other hand, was inhibited by only 12–20 per cent. Finally there appeared to be a difference in the base ratios of the RNAs formed by the two preparations[55]. By using ^{14}C-ATP and ^{14}C-GTP it was possible to measure the molar ratio of adenine to guanine incor-porated into the RNA. This was determined by two different techniques, and the mean values of the ratio were 1·56 for the nuclear fraction and 2·02 for the chloroplast fraction. The difference was highly significant, statistically. It is interesting that the RNA made by the chloroplast preparation appears to have a higher adenine to guanine ratio than the RNA made by the nuclear preparation: this is in accordance with the known difference in base ratio of the DNA in these preparations[53]. The existence of all these differences makes it seem unlikely that the incorporation by the chloroplast preparations is due to contaminating nuclear material. The simplest and most probable hypothesis is that the activity represents a chloroplast RNA polymerase working with the chloroplast DNA as a primer.

Evidence has now been obtained for RNA synthesis by chloroplasts isolated from other plants. The fraction sedimenting at 1000 g from tobacco leaf homogenate was found to have the ability to incorporate radioactivity from ^{32}P-ATP and ^{32}P-GTP into RNA[75, 62]; 95 per cent of the RNA-synthesizing activity of the leaf homogenate was present in the 1000 g fraction. The labelled material was rendered soluble by ribonuclease, and the radioactivity remained associated with the RNA fraction during purification by phenol extraction and Sephadex chromatography: thus, it appears that incorporation is indeed into RNA. On alkaline hydrolysis of the reaction product obtained with either ^{32}P-ATP or ^{32}P-GTP, radioactivity was found in all four nucleo-tides. This shows that the labelled product contained ^{32}P-AMP or ^{32}P-GMP in internucleotide linkage with each of the other three nucleo-tides. Incorporation was found to be dependent on the presence of all four nucleoside triphosphates and was inhibited by deoxyribonuclease and actinomycin D, suggesting that the activity was due to a DNA-dependent RNA polymerase. The 1000 g fraction consisted mainly of chloroplasts but also contained nuclei and some smaller particles. When the nuclei were isolated at the end of the incubation, they contained only 5 per cent of the incorporated counts. When the 1000 g pellet was separated into a chloroplast-rich and a nucleus-rich fraction, and each of these was incubated with the appropriate substrates, the 'chloroplast' fraction was found to be much more active than the 'nuclear' fraction. Thus, it appears likely that it is the chloroplasts which make the major contribution to RNA synthesis by the 1000 g fraction.

It has also been reported[74] that chloroplasts isolated from the giant-celled alga *Acetabularia mediterranea* will incorporate ^{14}C-uracil into acid-insoluble material. Incorporation was stimulated 43 per cent by light, and was inhibited by actinomycin D and DNAase. There was also incorporation of radioactivity when the chloroplasts were incubated with all four ribonucleoside triphosphates, labelled with ^{14}C: after alkaline digestion and ion-exchange chromatography of the labelled material the radioactivity coincided with the nucleotide peaks. Since these chloroplasts were obtained from enucleated *Acetabularia* the results presumably cannot be due to nuclear contamination. Isolated chloroplasts of *Acetabularia* have also now been found[29] to incorporate labelled uridine into RNA: this incorporation was inhibited by actinomycin D. These findings suggest that not only do *Acetabularia* chloroplasts have a DNA-dependent RNA polymerase, but that they also have the enzymes for converting uracil and uridine to uridine triphosphate.

Some indirect evidence for DNA-dependent RNA synthesis by chloroplasts is provided by observations on the effect of actinomycin D on chloroplast protein synthesis, described previously. For instance, amino acid incorporation by *Euglena* chloroplasts, in the presence of all four ribonucleoside triphosphates, was 22 per cent inhibited by actinomycin[25]; amino acid incorporation by tobacco chloroplasts was 18 per cent inhibited[91]; amino acid incorporation by *Acetabularia* chloroplasts was 50 per cent inhibited[30]; and amino acid incorporation by un-dialysed ribosomes from pea chloroplasts was 54 per cent inhibited[83]. These results might be taken as evidence that at least a portion of the protein synthesis occurring in isolated chloroplasts makes use of messenger RNA synthesized on a DNA template at the time. However, further evidence on this point would be desirable. It is noteworthy that in the case of spinach chloroplasts when adenosine triphosphate and guanosine triphosphate were already present, the further addition of uridine triphosphate and cytidine triphosphate (which would promote formation of endogenous messenger RNA) did not stimulate protein synthesis: also, actinomycin D at 20 μg/ml caused no significant inhibition of amino acid incorporation[90].

A rather special case of RNA synthesis by chloroplasts is the possible synthesis of viral RNA. There is some electron microscopic evidence for the formation of viruses in chloroplasts[25a, 57a]: in chloroplasts of sugar beet (*Beta vulgaris*) leaves infected with either beets yellows virus or Western yellows virus, about 50 per cent of the chloroplasts in the epidermal cells and a small number of the chloroplasts in the mesophyll contain inclusions, about 1–2 μ across, which at high magnification can be seen to have a regular series of striations. Engelbrecht and Esau (1963) suggest that these inclusions are composed of virus particles.

Zaitlin and Boardman (1958) reported that chloroplasts isolated from tobacco leaves infected with tobacco mosaic virus contained 0·6–4·2 per cent of the infectious particles present in the leaf homogenate. In leaves which had been supplied with ^{14}C-aspartic acid, the viral particles isolated from the chloroplasts had a higher specific radioactivity than viral particles from the supernatant fraction. The difference in specific radioactivity decreased as the time of incubation with ^{14}C-aspartic acid increased. These results are consistent with synthesis of the virus in the chloroplasts, with subsequent release into the cytoplasm.

Matsushita (1965) claims that, 40 hours after inoculation with tobacco mosaic virus, most of the infectivity of a leaf homogenate is in the chloroplasts: thereafter, the infectivity in the chloroplasts decreases and that in the cytoplasm increases. He suggests that the virus may be synthesized in the chloroplasts in the early stages.

In apparent contradiction to the results of Zaitlin and Boardman, and Matsushita are some recent findings by Ralph and Clark (1966). They report that the double-stranded form (the form thought to be involved in virus RNA replication) of tobacco mosaic virus RNA is present in the cytoplasmic fraction, and not the nuclear or chloroplast fractions, of homogenates of infected tobacco leaves. However, in the case of Chinese-cabbage leaves infected with turnip yellow mosaic virus, the double-stranded viral RNA was found in the chloroplast fraction and not in the nuclear or cytoplasmic fractions. Bové, Morel, Bové, and Randot (1965) have studied RNA synthesis in chloroplasts isolated by density gradient centrifugation from healthy leaves, and leaves infected with turnip yellow mosaic virus. In the chloroplasts from normal leaves there appeared to be an RNA polymerase of the normal type, which incorporated radioactivity from ^{32}P-uridine triphosphate in the presence of the other three nucleoside triphosphates into acid-insoluble material: this incorporation was up to 95 per cent inhibited by deoxyribonuclease or actinomycin D. However, in the chloroplasts from virus-infected leaves, about 50 per cent of the RNA synthesis was insensitive to deoxyribonuclease or actinomycin D. Also, a chloroplast band (thought to consist of damaged chloroplasts) which formed higher up in the gradient than the bulk of the chloroplasts, had, when obtained from infected leaves, an RNA polymerase-like activity which was completely insensitive to deoxyribonuclease. The results suggest that in chloroplasts of virus-infected leaves there may be an RNA polymerase whose function it is to replicate the viral RNA; that is, to carry out a type of RNA synthesis which uses an RNA template, and which is, therefore, unaffected by agents such as deoxyribonuclease and actinomycin D, which act specifically on DNA. Thus, there is at least some evidence that the RNA, and possibly also the protein coat, of some plant viruses is synthesized within the chloroplast.

In the light of all this work, then, it appears very likely that chloroplasts can, in fact, synthesize RNA. Whether they synthesize all their own RNA, and the exact nature of the RNA which they synthesize, remains to be determined. DNA synthesis has not yet been demonstrated to occur in isolated chloroplasts. However, since it seems that chloroplasts do contain DNA, and since DNA is thought to be self-replicating in biological systems, generally, it seems probable that chloroplasts can also synthesize DNA. This is supported by Steffensen and Sheridan's observation[92] that certain marine algae incorporate ³H-thymidine into their chloroplast DNA but not their nuclear DNA. The fact that there is no incorporation of this precursor into nuclear DNA indicates that the nuclei cannot use it for DNA synthesis, probably because they lack thymidine kinase. If the nuclei cannot utilize thymidine for DNA synthesis, then the utilization of ³H-thymidine for chloroplast DNA synthesis cannot have taken place in the nucleus. Quantitative studies of the silver grain distribution suggested that the DNA was being synthesized at the edge of the pyrenoid, on either side in a longitudinal direction. When chloroplasts of two of the algae, *Dictyota* and *Padina*, in various stages of division were scored for labelling, the results seemed to indicate that DNA was synthesized only during a certain period of the chloroplast division cycle, analogous to the S period in nuclear division. Mature, non-dividing chloroplasts did not incorporate ³H-thymidine: this suggests that chloroplast DNA does not undergo turnover to any substantial extent. This conclusion is supported by the observation of Wollgiehn and Mothes (1964) that in tobacco, there was no incorporation of ³H-thymidine into chloroplasts in mature leaves. However, there is some suggestion from the work of Iwamura (1960) that chloroplast DNA in *Chlorella* may undergo turnover but, as pointed out previously (see X.5.ii.b), there is a possibility that this DNA may consist, at least in part, of non-chloroplast DNA.

Further evidence relating to the synthesis of DNA in chloroplasts is considered in the next section.

XII.8. Evidence from Enucleated Acetabularia

We have mainly dealt, so far, with investigations of plastid biochemical autonomy carried out with isolated plastids. An alternative approach is to remove some other organelle from the cell and then investigate the biosynthetic abilities of the plastids remaining in the cell. In this way information might be gained as to the extent to which the biosynthetic abilities of the plastids are dependent on that organelle which was removed. The effect of removal of the nucleus on the cell generally, and on the plastids in particular, has been studied in some detail with the alga *Acetabularia*, from which, because of the large cell size, the nucleus may be removed relatively easily. For a full account of this work the excellent review by Hämmerling (1963), a pioneer in this field, should be consulted. The organism consists of a basal rhizoid containing the nucleus, and a stalk 4–6 cm long, with a large cap at the end of the stalk. A segment of the stalk, lacking a nucleus, has the ability to regenerate a new cap. Hämmerling was able to observe directly that the number of chloroplasts increased enormously during regeneration, in fact reaching the same level as in the original cap. Recent studies have shown that the number of chloroplasts in enucleated cells increases by 50–100 per cent in two weeks[76]. These cytological observations have been supported by chemical estimation of the amount of certain chloroplast components. The protein content of the chloroplasts of enucleated segments has been observed to increase by 160 per cent during regeneration[20]; chlorophyll content increased by 87–121 per cent, and the amount of different carotenoids increased by 85–180 per cent[71]. Autoradiography (detection of radioactive leucine incorporation) has also been used to demonstrate the continued synthesis of chloroplast protein in enucleated cells[77].

RNA synthesis by enucleated *Acetabularia* has been studied in some detail by Brachet and his co-workers. An increase in the RNA content of the chloroplast fraction during regeneration of enucleated fragments has been observed[66]: this was balanced by a decrease in the RNA content of the microsomal and supernatant fractions. Furthermore, there was incorporation of ^{14}C-adenine into the RNA of the chloroplast fraction. While these results do suggest that there is synthesis of chloroplast RNA in the enucleated fragments, it must be pointed out that the chloroplast fraction was isolated by centrifugation at 9000 g, and so would be likely to contain mitochondria and possibly some fragments of endoplasmic reticulum. However, the continued synthesis of chloroplast RNA in enucleated cells has been confirmed by the autoradiographic detection of radioactive uridine incorporation in the chloroplasts of such cells; this incorporation was abolished by actinomycin D, indicating that the RNA synthesis was of the DNA-dependent type[77]. Also, enucleated fragments of *Acetabularia mediterranea* incorporated ^{32}P-inorganic phosphate into the RNA of their chloroplast fraction[50]: there appeared to be more than one chloroplast RNA species formed; the base composition of one of these was of the ribosomal RNA type.

There is some evidence for synthesis of chloroplast DNA in enucleated *Acetabularia*. Gibor (1965) grew bacteria-free, enucleated cells in the presence of $^{14}CO_2$ for nine days in the light. From the isolated chloroplasts he obtained a DNA fraction: after CsCl equilibrium density gradient centrifugation of this, the DNA band had a band of radioactivity associated with it. After enzymic hydrolysis of the DNA to the deoxynucleoside level, followed by paper chromatography, some radioactivity could be detected in the purine (but not pyrimidine) deoxynucleosides. Gibor concluded that there are enzymes in the cytoplasm of this alga for the synthesis of deoxynucleotides, and their polymerization to DNA, but that it is not yet established whether all these enzyme systems are localized in the chloroplasts. Further evidence that *Acetabularia* chloroplast DNA is not synthesized in the nucleus is provided by the observation that enucleation does not prevent incorporation of radioactive thymidine (detected by autoradiography) into the chloroplasts[77]. Also, there is some indication[50] that enucleated cells will incorporate ^{32}P-phosphate, not only into RNA, but also into a rather heterogeneous material (in the chloroplasts) which may contain DNA as well as RNA: it is not entirely clear whether the DNA is, in fact, labelled.

The multiplication of the chloroplasts and the increase in chloroplast components in the enucleated segments of *Acetabularia* indicate that the synthesis of chloroplast materials can continue for a long time in the absence of the nucleus. Since all the other cell components are still present, this work cannot be regarded as establishing the biochemical autonomy of the chloroplast, but it does, at least, support this theory.

XII.9. Conclusions

It is apparent from the findings discussed in this chapter that plastids have a high degree of biochemical autonomy. They very probably carry out the complete synthesis of their chlorophylls and carotenoids. They synthesize many, and perhaps all, of their lipids. They can form some amino acids. They appear to synthesize most, and possibly all, of their own proteins. They have the ability to make RNA, and probably also make their own DNA. Thus, these biochemical studies strongly support the concept of the plastid as an autonomous, self-duplicating, body.

REFERENCES

1. ANDERSON, D. G. & PORTER, J. W. (1962). *Arch. Biochem. Biophys.* **97**, 509–519
2. ARNSTEIN, H. R. V. (1965). *Brit. Med. Bull.* **21**, 217–222
3. APP, A. A. & JAGENDORF, A. T. (1963). *Biochim. Biophys. Acta* **76**, 286–292

3a. APP, A. A. & JAGENDORF, A. T. (1964). *Plant Phys.* **39**, 772–776

4. ASAHI, T. (1964). *Biochim. Biophys. Acta* **82**, 58–66

5. BANDURSKI, R. S. & MAHESHWARI, S. C. (1962). *Plant Phys.* **37**, 556–560

6. BASSHAM, J. A. & KIRK, M. (1964). *Biochim. Biophys. Acta* **90**, 553–562

7. BEELER, D. A. & Porter, J. W. (1962). *Biochem. Biophys. Res. Commun.* **8**, 367–371

8. BEELER, D. A. & PORTER, J. W. (1963). *Arch. Biochem. Biophys.* **100**, 167–170

9. BEZINGER, E. N., MOLCHANOV, M. I. & SISSAKIAN, N. M. (1964). *Biokhimiya* (Consultants Bureau transl.) **29**, 641–649

10. BISWAS, S. & BISWAS, B. B. (1965). *Experientia* **21**, 251–253

11. BOGORAD, L. (1965). In *Chemistry and Biochemistry of Plant Pigments*. Ed., T. W. Goodwin, Academic Press, London, pp. 29–74

12. BOVÉ, J. & RAACKE, I. D. (1959). *Arch. Biochem. Biophys.* **85**, 521–531

13. BOVÉ, J. M., MOREL, G., BOVÉ, C. & RANDOT, M.-J. In *Symposium on Biochemistry of Chloroplasts (Aberystwyth, 1965)*. Ed., T. W. Goodwin. Academic Press, London (in press)

14. BRACHET, J., CHANTRENNE, H. & VANDERHAEGE, F. (1955). *Biochim. Biophys. Acta* **18**, 544–563

15. BRAWERMAN, G. & EISENSTADT, J. M. (1964). *J. Mol. Biol.* **10**, 403–411

16. BROOKS, J. L. & STUMPF, P. K. (1965). *Biochim. Biophys. Acta.* **98**, 213–216

17. CARELL, E. F. & KAHN, J. S. (1964). *Arch. Biochem. Biophys.* **108**, 1–6

18. CHAMBERLIN, M. & BERG, P. (1962). *Proc. Natl. Acad. Sci.* **48**, 81–94

19. CLARK, M. F. (1964). *Biochim. Biophys. Acta.* **91**, 671–674

20. CLAUSS, H. (1958). *Planta* **52**, 334–350

21. CROMBIE, W. M. (1958). *J. Exp. Bot.* **9**, 254–261

22. DECKER, K. & UEHLEKE, H. (1961). *Z. Phys. Chem.* **323**, 61–75

23. EISENSTADT, J. M. In *Symposium on Biochemistry of Chloroplasts (Aberystwyth, 1965)*. Ed., T. W. Goodwin. Academic Press, London (in press)

24. EISENSTADT, J. M. & BRAWERMAN, G. (1963). *Biochim. Biophys. Acta.* **76**, 319–321

25. EISENSTADT, J. M. & BRAWERMAN, G. (1964). *J. Mol. Biol.* **10**, 392–402

25a. ENGELBRECHT, A. H. P. & ESAU, K. (1963). *Virology* **21**, 43–47

26. FRANCKI, R. I. B., BOARDMAN, N. K. & WILDMAN, S. G. (1965). *Biochemistry* **4**, 865–872

27. GALE, E. F. (1962). In *The Bacteria*. Eds., I. C. Gunsalus & R. Y. Stanier, III. Academic Press, New York, pp. 471–576

28. GIBOR, A. In *Symposium on Biochemistry of Chloroplasts (Aberystwyth 1965)*. Ed., T. W. Goodwin. Academic Press, London (in press)

29. GIBOR, A. & IZAWA, M. (unpublished). Quoted by Gibor, A. & Granick, S. (1962). *Science* **145**, 890–897

30. GOFFEAU, A. & BRACHET, J. (1965). *Biochim. Biophys. Acta.* **95**, 302–313

31. GOLDBERG, I. H., RABINOWITZ, M. & REICH, E. (1962). *Proc. Natl. Acad. Sci.* **48**, 2094–2101

32. GOODWIN, T. W. (1958). *Biochem. J.* **70**, 612 617

33. GOODWIN, T. W. (1965a). In *Chemistry and Biochemistry of Plant Pigments*. Ed., T. W. Goodwin. Academic Press, London, pp. 175–196

34. GOODWIN, T. W. (1965b). In *Symposium on Biochemistry of Chloroplasts (Aberystwyth, 1965)*. Ed., T. W. Goodwin, Academic Press, London (in press)

35. GOODWIN, T. W. & MERCER, E. I. (1963). In 'The Control of Lipid Metabolism'. *Biochem. Soc. Symp.* **24**. Ed., J. R. Grant. Academic Press, London, pp. 37–41

36. GRANICK, S. (1959). *Plant Phys.* **34**, xviii

37. GRANICK, S. (1961). *Proc. 5th Internat. Congr. Biochem. VI*, 176–186

38. GRANICK, S. In *Symposium on Biochemistry of Chloroplasts (Aberystwyth, 1965)*. Ed., T. W. Goodwin. Academic Press, London (in press)

39. GRANICK, S. & MAUZERALL, D. (1961). In *Metabolic Pathways*. Ed., D. M. Greenberg, II. Academic Press, New York, pp. 525–616

40. GUNNING, B. E. S. (1965). *J. Cell Biol.* **24**, 79–93

41. HAMMERLING, J. (1963). *Ann. Rev. Plant Phys.* **14**, 65–92

42. HARRIS, R. V. & JAMES, A. T. (1965). *Biochem. J.* **94**, 15C–16C

43. HEBER, U. (1962). *Nature, Lond.* **195**, 91–92

44. HOAGLAND, M. B. (1962). In *The Nucleic Acids*. Eds., E. Chargaff & J. N. Davidson. III. Academic Press, New York, pp. 349–408

45. HUANG, R. C., MAHESHWARI, N. & BONNER, J. (1960). *Biochem. Biophys. Res. Commun.* **3**, 689–694

46. HURWITZ, J., BRESLER, A. & DIRINGER, R. (1960). *Biochem. Biophys. Res. Commun.* **3**, 15–19

47. HURWITZ, J., FURTH, J. J., MALAMY, M. & ALEXANDER, M. (1962). *Proc. Natl. Acad. Sci.* **48**, 1222–1230

48. IWAMURA, T. (1960). *Biochim. Biophys. Acta* **42**, 161–163

49. JAMES, A. T. (1963). In 'The Control of Lipid Metabolism'. Ed., J. K. Grant. *Biochem. Soc. Symp.* **24**. Academic Press, London, pp. 17–27

50. JANOWSKI, M. (1965). *Biochim. Biophys. Acta* **103**, 399–408

51. JUNGALWALA, F. B. & PORTER, J. W. (1965). *Plant Phys.* **40**, xviii

52. KIRK, J. M. (1960). *Biochim. Biophys. Acta* **42**, 167–169

53. KIRK, J. T. O. (1963). *Biochim. Biophys. Acta* **76**, 417–424

54. KIRK, J. T. O. (1964a). *Biochem. Biophys. Res. Commun.* **14**, 393–397

55. KIRK, J. T. O. (1964b). *Biochem. Biophys. Res. Commun.* **16**, 233–238

56. KLEIN, S. & POLJAKOFF-MAYBER, A. (1961). *J. Biophys. Biochem. Cytol.* **11**, 433–440

57. KROSSING, G. (1940). *Biochem. Z.* **305**, 359–373

57a. LEYON, H. (1953). *Exp. Cell. Res.* **4**, 362–370

58. MARCUS, A. (1959). *J. Biol. Chem.* **234**, 1238–1240

59. MATSUSHITA, K. (1965). *Plant Cell Phys.* **6**, 1–6

60. MCMAHON, V. & STUMPF, P. K. (1964). *Biochim. Biophys. Acta* **84**, 359–361

61. MERCER, E. I. & GOODWIN, T. W. (1962). *Biochem. J.* **85**, 13P

62. MOYER, R. H., SMITH, R. A., SEMAL, J. & KIM, Y. T. (1964). *Biochim. Biophys. Acta* **91**, 217–222

63. MUDD, J. B. & MCMANUS, T. T. (1962). *J. Biol. Chem.* **237**, 2057–2063

64. MUDD, J. B. & MCMANUS, T. T. (1964). *Plant Phys.* **39**, 115–119

65. MUDD, J. B. & MCMANUS, T. T. (1965). *Plant Phys.* **40**, 340–344

66. NAORA, H., NAORA, H. & BRACHET, J. (1960). *J. Gen. Phys.* **43**, 1083–1102

67. NEUFELD, E. F. & HALL, C. W. (1964). *Biochem. Biophys. Res. Commun.* **14**, 503–508

68. NICHIPOROVICH, A. A. (1955). *1st Geneva Conf. on peaceful uses of Atomic Energy*, paper 697

69. PARTHIER, B. (1964). *Z. Naturforsch.* **19b**, 235–248

70. PARTHIER, B. & WOLLGIEHN, R. (1963). *Naturwiss.* **50**, 598–599

70a. RALPH, R. K. & CLARK, M. F. (1966). *Biochim. Biophys. Acta* **119**, 29–36

71. RICHTER, G. (1958). *Planta* **52**, 259–275

72. ROGERS, L. J., SHAH, S. P. J. & GOODWIN, T. W. In *Symposium on Biochemistry of Chloroplasts (Aberystwyth, 1965)*. Ed., T. W. Goodwin, Academic Press, London (in press)

73. SCHWARTZ, J. H., EISENSTADT, J. M., BRAWERMAN, G. & ZINDER, N. D. (1965). *Proc. Natl. Acad. Sci.* **53**, 195–200

74. SCHWEIGER, H. G. & BERGER, S. (1964). *Biochim. Biophys. Acta* **87**, 533–535

75. SEMAL, J., SPENCER, D., KIM, Y. T. & WILDMAN, S. G. (1964). *Biochim. Biophys. Acta* **91**, 205–216

76. SHEPHARD, D. C. (1965a). *Exp. Cell. Res.* **37**, 93–110

77. SHEPHARD, D. C. (1965b). *Biochim. Biophys. Acta* (in press)

78. SHIMIZU, S. & TAMAKI, E. (1963). *Arch. Biochem. Biophys.* **102**, 152–158

79. SHNEOUR, E. A. & ZABIN, I. (1959). *J. Biol. Chem.* **234**, 770

80. SISSAKIAN, N. M. (1958). *Adv. Enz.* **20**, 201–236

81. SISSAKIAN, N. M., BEZINGER, E. N., MARCHUKAITIS, A. S., MOLCHANOV, M. I., CHIGINEV, V. S. & KOTOVSKAYA, A. P. (1963). *Biokhimiya* (Consultants Bureau transl.) **28**, 262–268

82. SISSAKIAN, N. M. & FILIPPOVICH, I. I. (1957). *Biokhimiya* (Consultants Bureau transl.) **22**, 375–383

83. SISSAKIAN, N. M., FILIPPOVICH, I. I., SVETAILO, E. N. & ALIYEV, K. A. (1965). *Biochim. Biophys. Acta* **95**, 474—485

84. SISSAKIAN, N. M. & SMIRNOV, B. P. (1956). Quoted by Sissakian (1958)

85. SMIRNOV, B. P. (1960). *Biokhimiya* (Consultants Bureau transl.) **25**, 419–426

86. SMIRNOV, B. P. (1962). *Biokhimiya* (Consultants Bureau transl.) **27**, 127–132

87. SMIRNOV, B. P. & RODIONOV, M. A. (1964). *Biokhimiya* (Consultants Bureau (transl.) **29**, 335–340

88. SMITH, D. C., BASSHAM, J. A. & KIRK, M. (1961). *Biochim. Biophys. Acta* **48**, 299–313

89. SMITH, J. H. C. & FRENCH, C. S. (1963). *Ann. Rev. Plant Phys.* **14**, 181–224

90. SPENCER, D. (1965). *Arch. Biochem. Biophys.* **111**, 381–390

91. SPENCER, D. & WILDMAN, S. G. (1964). *Biochemistry* **3**, 954–959

92. STEFFENSEN, D. M. & SHERIDAN, W. F. (1965). *J. Cell. Biol.* **25**, 619–626

93. STEPHENSON, M. L., THIMANN, K. V. & ZAMECNIK, P. C. (1956). *Arch. Biochem. Biophys.* **65**, 194–209

94. STEVENS, A. (1960). *Biochem. Biophys. Res. Commun.* **3**, 92–96

95. STUMPF, P. K., BOVÉ, J. M. & GOFFEAU, A. (1963). *Biochim. Biophys. Acta* **70**, 260–270

96. STUMPF, P. K., BROOKS, J., GALLIARD, T., HAWKE, J. C. & SIMONI, R. In *Symposium on Biochemistry of Chloroplasts (Aberystwyth, 1965)*. Ed., T. W. Goodwin. Academic Press, London (in press)

97. STUMPF, P. K. & JAMES, A. T. (1963). *Biochim. Biophys. Acta* **57**, 400–402

98. THRELFALL, D. R., GRIFFITHS, W. T. & GOODWIN, T. W. (1964). *Biochem. J.* **92**, 56P–57P

99. TOLBERT, N. E. (1959). *Brookhaven Symp.* **11**, 271

100. TREHARNE, K. J., MERCER, E. I. & GOODWIN, T. W. (1964). *Biochem. J.* **90**, 39P–40P

101. WEISS, S. B. (1960). *Proc. Natl. Acad. Sci.* **46**, 1020–1030

102. WELLS, L. W., SCHELBLE, W. J. & PORTER, J. W. (1964). *Fed. Proc.* **23**, 426

103. WIECKOWSKI, S. & GOODWIN, T. W. In *Symposium on Biochemistry of Chloroplasts (Aberystwyth, 1965)*. Ed., T. W. Goodwin, Academic Press, London (in press)

104. WILSTÄTTER, R. & STOLL, A. (1928). *Investigations on chlorophyll*. Science Press, Lancaster, Pa.

105. WOLLGIEHN, R. & MOTHES, K. (1964). *Exp. Cell. Res.* **35**, 52–57

106. ZAITLIN, M. & BOARDMAN, N. K. (1958). *Plant Phys.* **33**, xli

CHAPTER XIII

Growth and Differentiation of Plastids: Part I. Formation of the Chloroplast during Greening of the Etiolated Plant

XIII.1. Introduction

MOST of what we know about the differentiation of the chloroplast has come from studying the formation of chloroplasts as it occurs in etiolated plants exposed to light. We shall, therefore, discuss this process before going on to consider chloroplast formation in the normal green plant.

XIII.2. The Phenomenon of Etiolation

When angiosperm seeds are germinated in the dark, the seedlings possess no chlorophyll, a fact which was first recorded by the great botanist John Ray in 1693[7]. Such plants are called etiolated (*étioler*, to blanch). It is possible that a few angiosperms may have some slight ability to synthesize chlorophyll in the dark: Röbbelen (1956) has reported that etiolated seedlings of *Arabidopsis thaliana* contain a trace of chlorophyll *a*, and it is said[133] that seedlings of the water lotus (*Nelumbo*) form chlorophyll in the absence of light. However, it would be desirable in these cases to have evidence that there was no carry-over of chlorophyll in the seed.

In plants more primitive than flowering plants, the ability to make chlorophyll in the dark is usually, but not invariably, present. Amongst

402

the gymnosperms, seeds of conifers, when germinated in the dark, produce green cotyledons[158]. In the order *Gnetales*, *Ephedra* seeds produce
green cotyledons in the dark[29], but dark-grown seedlings of *Welwitschia*
are colourless[187]. Seeds of *Cycas* and *Zamia* (order *Cycadales*) and of
Gingko (order *Gingkoales*) form no chlorophyll when germinated in the
dark[29,136].

Amongst the Pteridophytes, ferns can make chlorophyll in the
dark[10], and so can *Selaginella* and *Isoetes*[187]. Members of the *Equise-
taceae* do not form chlorophyll in the dark[91].

Bryophytes (mosses) apparently can make chlorophyll in the dark[187].

Most algae synthesize chlorophyll in the dark. *Euglena mesnili*, *E.
gracilis*, and *E. cyclopicola*, however, do not[122,151]. According to
Pringsheim (1948) the *Chrysophyceae* are similar to the *Euglenophyta* in
this respect. Chlorophyll formation in *Ochromonas danica* (*Chrysophyceae*)
is not quite completely blocked in the dark, the cells still make 1–2 per
cent of the chlorophyll that they make in the light[57]. The ability to
form chlorophyll in the absence of light can vary within a single genus:
most species of *Chlorella* are green in the dark, but *Chlorella variegata* and
Chlorella luteo-viridis are not[8,114]. According to Allen (1959) the thermo-
philic alga *Cyanidium caldarium* (*Rhodophyta*) requires light for chlorophyll
formation: however, small amounts of chlorophyll have been found in
dark-grown cells[141].

Plants grown in the absence of light show other abnormalities besides
lack of chlorophyll. Dicotyledons develop elongated stems on which the
leaves have failed to expand, and have rather poorly developed root
systems: monocotyledons produce long, relatively narrow leaves. When
etiolated plants are put in the light, within two or three days they take
on a normal appearance as a result of the leaves expanding and forming
chlorophyll ('greening'). The young leaves of the apex and its region
of elongation become green most rapidly[195].

XIII.3. The Primary Event in the Greening Process

Etiolated leaves are yellow in colour. Pringsheim (1874) extracted such
leaves with alcohol, and in the extract detected an absorption band in
the region of 620–640 mμ: the pigment responsible for this absorption
band he called 'etiolin'. On exposure of etiolated leaves to light, chlorophyll appeared and 'etiolin' disappeared: Monteverde (1893–1894
suggested that this substance was converted to chlorophyll by the action
of light; he renamed it 'protochlorophyll'. Monteverde and Lubimenko, using a microspectroscope, were able to detect the absorption

band of protochlorophyll in the living, etiolated leaf, and to follow the disappearance of this band, and its replacement by the chlorophyll bands on illumination (see Lubimenko, 1928).

At the time that protochlorophyll was first thought to be a precursor of chlorophyll, nothing was known of its chemical structure. Work on the chemistry was facilitated by the discovery[138] that the seed coats of pumpkin seed contained substantial amounts of a greenish pigment similar to protochlorophyll: Noack and Kiessling (1929) purified this substance, and concluded on the basis of its absorption spectrum, and certain other properties, that it was identical with the protochlorophyll of etiolated leaves. Chemical investigation of the pumpkin seed pigment[46, 47] indicated that it was very similar to chlorophyll a, differing only in that it lacked two hydrogen atoms in the 7, 8 position of the ring (see Fig. XII.1). It thus appeared that if protochlorophyll was a precursor of chlorophyll, then the transformation took place by reduction.

However, at this stage it was still not certain that leaf protochlorophyll was identical with pumpkin seed protochlorophyll, or that it was converted to chlorophyll a *in vivo*. This was investigated further by studying the action spectrum for the formation of chlorophyll, i.e. by

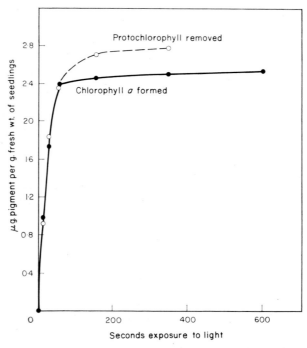

FIG. XIII.1. *Time course of protochlorophyll reduction in corn seedlings. (Redrawn from data of Koski, 1950)*

measuring the effectiveness of light of different wavelengths, and comparing the curve of effectiveness against wavelength with the absorption spectrum of protochlorophyll. An early attempt to do this had been
that of Schmidt (1914): in an action spectrum for chlorophyll formation
in etiolated corn seedlings he found three peaks of effectiveness, at
640, 567, and 450 mμ. A more accurate action spectrum was determined by Frank (1946) using filters with narrow band-width to provide
light of different wavelengths. Using etiolated oat seedlings she found
two major peaks of effectiveness, at 645 and 445 mμ, and two minor
peaks at 575 and 545 mμ. The correspondence between this action
spectrum and the absorption spectrum of pumpkin seed protochlorophyll was taken as evidence that the precursor of chlorophyll in etiolated
plants was identical with the pumpkin seed pigment. A more rigorous
demonstration of the nature of the chlorophyll precursor was carried
out by a group of workers in the Department of Plant Biology, Carnegie
Institute of Washington. For the first time, protochlorophyll was isolated and purified from etiolated leaves[106]: the position of its absorp-

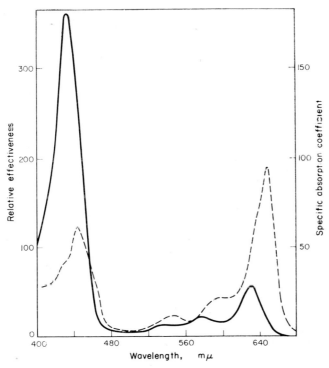

FIG. XIII.2. *Action spectrum for protochlorophyll photoreduction in etiolated corn leaves
compared with protochlorophyll absorption spectrum (adapted from Koski et al., 1951).*
   Action spectrum – – – – – – – – – – – –
   Absorption spectrum of protochlorophyll in methanol —————————————

tion bands agreed with those of pumpkin seed protochlorophyll, and the magnesium content was in good agreement with that calculated from the formula for pumpkin seed protochlorophyll proposed by Fischer and Oestreicher (1940). When dark-grown barley or corn seedlings were illuminated for a short time, for every molecule of protochlorophyll which disappeared, one molecule of chlorophyll appeared[173, 104] —Fig. XIII.1. Finally, a very accurate action spectrum for chlorophyll formation was determined with corn seedlings, using a diffraction grating to provide monochromatic light of different wavelengths: excellent agreement was observed (Fig. XIII.2) between this action spectrum and the absorption spectrum of leaf protochlorophyll[105].

After brief illumination of etiolated seedlings only chlorophyll *a* can be detected; chlorophyll *b* does not appear (Fig. XIII.3) until after the plants have been in the light for one or two hours[164, 67, 104].

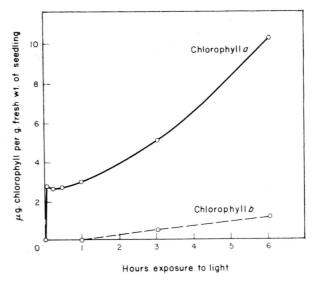

FIG. XIII.3. *Formation of chlorophylls* a *and* b *by etiolated corn seedlings exposed to light (adapted from Koski, 1950)*

XIII.4. Characteristics of Protochlorophyll Photoconversion

The conversion of protochlorophyll to chlorophyll *a* is very rapid[104]: when dark-grown corn seedlings are exposed to white light, at 150 foot-candles, most of the protochlorophyll is transformed to chlorophyll *a* within 60 seconds (Fig. XIII.1). The rate of conversion is directly proportional to the light intensity[180]. With very intense light, provided by an electric flash, the formation of chlorophyll from protochlorophyll, in etiolated barley leaves, is completed within 4 milliseconds after the beginning of one millisecond's illumination[125]. The photoreduction of protochlorophyll in etiolated *Euglena gracilis* appears to be relatively slow; in the experiments of Nishimura and Huzisige (1959), the pigment disappeared in the light with a half-life in the region of 24 minutes. When dark-grown barley leaves are illuminated with light of wavelength 546–589 mμ, the kinetics of transformation are second-order with respect to protochlorophyll concentration: however, with light at 436 mμ the second-order law is not strictly obeyed[180]. The explanation for the second-order kinetics is unknown.

The formation of chlorophyll in the light by etiolated seedlings can take place at temperatures below freezing-point[117]. In etiolated barley leaves there is no transformation of protochlorophyll in the light at −195°, but there is fairly rapid conversion at −70°; the conversion increases in rate and extent with increase in temperature up to 40°[180]. Exposure of leaves to a temperature of 55° for five minutes almost completely destroys their capacity to transform their protochlorophyll.

If the hydrogen atoms used in the reduction of protochlorophyll are derived from water, then it might be expected that the formation of chlorophyll would be accompanied by the liberation of oxygen. To determine whether this was the case, Smith (1951) illuminated etiolated leaves in an atmosphere of hydrogen, and used a very sensitive method (degree of quenching of phosphorescence of trypaflavine) to look for liberation of oxygen. The amount of oxygen evolved was only 2·5 per cent of the quantity calculated from the amount of chlorophyll formed. It therefore appears unlikely that water is the source of hydrogen for the reduction of protochlorophyll.

Although extracted protochlorophyll, dissolved in organic solvents, is not converted to chlorophyll by light, protochlorophyll can be extracted from the cell in a form that does retain the ability to undergo phototransformation. Krasnovsky and Kosobutskaya (1952) obtained cell-free extracts of etiolated bean leaves, in phosphate buffer, which contained protochlorophyll that was converted to chlorophyll in the light. Smith (1952) found that if dark-grown barley leaves were ground in glycerine, all the protochlorophyll was liberated into solution, or suspension; on illumination 70 per cent of it was converted to chlorophyll. Klein and Poljakoff-Mayber (1961) homogenized etiolated bean leaves and showed that the protochlorophyll was present in the isolated plastid fraction.

The active form of protochlorophyll—protochlorophyll holochrome —has been purified and studied by Smith and his co-workers. As purified from etiolated leaves of *Phaseolus vulgaris*, it is a complex of protochlorophyll and protein, of molecular weight estimated by Smith (1960) to be about 700,000, and by Boardman (1962) to be 600,000 ± 50,000. The holochrome particles have a density of 1·16 and appear, in electron micrographs, to be oblate spheroids of uniform size with axial diameters measuring 218, 193, and 93 Å, and having a volume of 2·05 × 10^{-18} cc[181]. Holochrome preparations contain variable amounts of carotenoids[179].

The protochlorophyll holochrome molecule is very similar in its physical properties to Fraction I protein, the protein which carries the carboxydismutase activity of the cell. These two proteins have virtually identical sedimentation constants, diffusion constants, partial specific volumes, and molecular weights, and also have a similar appearance under the electron microscope[13, 14, 193]. Trown (1965) suggests, in view of these similarities, that carboxydismutase, in fact, constitutes the protein moiety of protochlorophyll holochrome. He considers that this view is supported by the fact that carboxydismutase has the ability to bind other molecules to itself. Trown goes so far as to suggest that the binding of the protochlorophyll to the protein may be fortuitous, possibly occurring during the isolation procedure.

There appears to be one protochlorophyll molecule per protein molecule[178, 13], but the mode of the attachment of the protochlorophyll to the protein remains uncertain. Covalent bonding seems unlikely since the pigment can be separated from the protein merely by treatment with certain organic solvents. The fluorescence excited in the proto-chlorophyll holochrome by plane polarized light is itself partially polarized. The extent to which polarization is lost on re-emission depends on a number of factors, one of which is the freedom of rotation possessed by the molecule. From the degree of polarization of the fluorescent light it was concluded[61] that the pigment has partial, but not complete, freedom of rotation within the holochrome. Smith and French (1963) suggest that a type of binding consistent with the results would be attachment to the amino acid side chains of the protein. Transformation is inhibited by increasing pH between 9·16 and 11·92, which might indicate that lysine (pK of ϵ-amino group, 9·4–10·6), cysteine (pK of sulphydryl group, 9·6–10·0), or tyrosine (pK of phenolic group, 9·8–10·4) are involved in protochlorophyll-protein binding; it is thought that the high pH values act by dissociating the pigment from its carrier[179]. Spectral changes in the ultraviolet over this pH range suggest that tyrosine is present and undergoes ionization. Tyrosine is also implicated in binding by the fact that ultraviolet light transforms some of the protochlorophyll[130]: the suggestion is that the tyrosine could transfer its absorbed energy to the protochlorophyll if it was closely associated with the protochlorophyll. However, only 25–30 per cent of the protochlorophyll was transformed in this way, which has been taken to indicate[183] that protochlorophyll is bound to tyrosine on only about 30 per cent of the holochrome particles: on the other particles it might be bound to cysteine or lysine. Protochlorophyll holochrome preparations may be much more heterogeneous than is generally supposed: Capon and Bogorad (1962a), using immunological techniques, detected 8–10 different proteins in a holochrome preparation made by the method of Smith (1959).

In the purified holochrome, 0·6 molecules of protochlorophyll are transformed per quantum of light absorbed[177]. Since this value is close to 0·5, it is possible that two quanta are required to transfer the two hydrogen atoms. However, Smith (1960) considers it more likely that the transformation is a one-quantum process, with an overall efficiency of 0·6.

XIII.5. Different forms of Protochlorophyll

Loeffler (1955) found that a protochlorophyll preparation from etiolated barley seedlings could be separated into two components by paper chromatography. Both compounds had the typical protochlorophyll absorption spectrum, but one was acidic and the other neutral, and they also differed in their solubility properties and their HCl number. Loeffler concluded that the acidic component was magnesium vinyl phaeoporphyrin a_5 (protochlorophyll in which the propionic acid group is not esterified with phytol), and that the neutral component was normal protochlorophyll.

The discovery of two forms of protochlorophyll in the etiolated plant raised the question of whether both forms, or only one, were reduced in the light. If it were the acidic form, then the immediate product of the light reaction would be an acidic form of chlorophyll, lacking the phytyl group; if the neutral form then the neutral, phytylated chlorophyll would be produced. To study this problem Wolff and Price (1957) took advantage of the fact that if these pigments are partitioned between a polar organic solvent (such as aqueous acetone) and a non-polar organic solvent (such as petrol), then the acidic compounds go into the polar phase, and the neutral compounds into the non-polar phase. Dark-grown leaves of *Phaseolus vulgaris* were illuminated for 10 seconds, and the pigments were then extracted and partitioned between the two organic layers as above. Immediately after the illumination, the leaves were found to contain a pigment with the spectrum of chlorophyll *a*, which all went into the polar layer. If, after the illumination, the leaves were incubated in the dark, and extracted at different times, then the absorption spectrum, and the total amount of the chlorophyll-like pigments, remained constant; however, there was a steady decrease in the proportion which went into the polar layer, and a corresponding increase in the proportion which went into the non-polar layer. After 60 minutes practically all the pigment was found in the non-polar layer.

Wolff and Price concluded that in etiolated leaves protochlorophyll exists mainly as the non-esterified form (magnesium vinyl phaeoporphyrin a_5—'protochlorophyllide'). This is reduced in the light to the non-esterified form of chlorophyll a ('chlorophyllide a'), and the chlorophyllide a is then esterified (in the dark or in the light) with phytol to give chlorophyll a. At 0° the leaves were able to carry out the photoreduction of protochlorophyllide, but not the subsequent phytylation.

There is now some uncertainty about the chemical nature of the alkyl group in the neutral form of protochlorophyll that is present in etiolated leaves. Fischer and Rudiger (1959) reported that they were unable to detect phytol in the protochlorophyll from etiolated barley seedlings. However, Godnev, Kaler, and Rotfarb (1961) claimed that they were able to find phytol after alkaline hydrolysis of protochlorophyll from these plants.

The findings of Loeffler, and Wolff and Price, raise certain problems in nomenclature. The word 'protochlorophyll' has been, and is, used in the literature to refer to pigments, found in etiolated leaves, with an absorption maximum (*in vivo* or in the extracted holochrome) at 630–650 mμ, irrespective of whether the pigments are esterified or not. The word 'protochlorophyllide', however, is applied only to the acidic form—magnesium vinyl phaeoporphyrin a_5. In this book, from now on, 'protochlorophyllide' and 'protochlorophyllide ester' will be used for the acidic and neutral forms respectively. 'Protochlorophyll' will be used as a collective term, or when there is some doubt about which pigment is involved. In the isolated holochrome, apparently none of the pigment is esterified[177]: the term 'protochlorophyllide holochrome' will therefore be used.

It is generally accepted that protochlorophyllide constitutes most of the protochlorophyll-type pigments in young etiolated leaves, and that the photoreduction of this provides most, and possibly all, of the chlorophyll-type pigments which appear during a brief illumination. However, it is still not certain whether the protochlorophyllide ester that is present is photoreduced or not. Virgin (1960) investigated the pigments of etiolated wheat leaves, before and after 60 seconds' illumination, by a paper chromatographic technique which separated the alkylated from the non-alkylated pigments. He found that after illumination the protochlorophyllide disappeared to be replaced by chlorophyllide, but there was no change in the spot on the chromatogram attributed to protochlorophyllide ester. This suggests that protochlorophyllide ester is either not photoreduced at all, or is photoreduced very much more slowly than protochlorophyllide. Godnev, Akulovich, and Khoda-sevich (1963) used a solvent partition technique to measure the amount of esterified and non-esterified pigments in etiolated leaves of four plant species, before and after 15 minutes' illumination at 3–5°C. As well as the expected conversion of protochlorophyllide to chlorophyllide, they found that, during the illumination, some protochlorophyllide ester disappeared, and some chlorophyll *a* appeared, and there was fair agreement between the amount of the former disappearing, and of the latter appearing. They concluded that there was indeed photoreduction of protochlorophyllide ester to chlorophyll *a*. However, the partition technique, particularly when (as in this case) ether is used as the non-polar layer instead of petrol, is probably less reliable than the chromatographic technique used by Virgin. Also, the assumption that no phytylation of chlorophyllide could take place in 15 minutes at 3–5°C, may not be valid. The conclusions of Godnev *et al.* would seem to be supported by the report[168] that after one millisecond of intense light about 20 per cent of the chlorophyll-type pigments of etiolated barley leaves are in the esterified form. It thus appears that evidence based on extraction of pigments gives conflicting answers to the question of whether proto-chlorophyllide ester is photoreduced. Further evidence, based on spectroscopic studies on intact leaves, is discussed below.

Different forms of protochlorophyll can be detected in the living leaf as well as in extracts. Shibata (1957) found that young, dark-grown bean leaves had one protochlorophyll absorption peak—at 650 mμ. Older leaves, however, had two peaks—at 650 and 636 mμ. Only the substance having the 650 mμ peak was transformed to chlorophyllide by light. Litvin and Krasnovsky (1957; 1958) measured the fluorescence spectra of etiolated leaves and found two forms of protochlorophyll: one with a fluorescence maximum at 655 mμ which was transformed by light; the other with a fluorescence maximum at 633 mμ which was not transformed. Sironval, Michel-Wolwerz, and Madsen (1965) found that, as in bean leaves, young (7-day) etiolated barley leaves had a protochlorophyll absorption peak at 650 mμ, whereas old (17-day) etiolated barley leaves had a peak at about 635–640 mμ as well as the 650 mμ peak. Associated with the appearance of the 635–640 mμ peak during ageing, there was a corresponding increase in the proportion of the protochlorophyll pigments which were in the esterified form. These authors concluded that the substance responsible for the 650 mμ peak was protochlorophyllide, and the substance responsible for the 635–640 mμ peak was protochlorophyllide ester. If this is so, then it seems quite likely that the protochlorophyll with an *in vivo* absorption peak at 636 mμ, found by Shibata, and the protochlorophyll with an *in vivo* fluorescence maximum at 633 mμ, found by Litvin and Krasnovsky, are both, in fact, protochlorophyllide ester. The fact that neither the proto-chlorophyll with absorption peak at 636 mμ, nor the one with fluores-cence peak at 633 mμ was photoreduced in the light, can then be regarded as further evidence that protochlorophyllide ester is not photo-reduced. Thus it can be said that while there is some experimental support for the idea that protochlorophyllide ester can be photo-reduced, the weight of the evidence is against it. Granick (1961) finds three different kinds of protochlorophyllide in etiolated barley or bean leaves which have been incubated with δ-aminolaevulinic acid. One has an absorption maximum at 650 mμ and is converted by light to chloro-phyllide. Another also has an absorption maximum at 650 mμ but is not transformed in the light. A third kind has an absorption maximum at 631 mμ and is bleached in the light. He suggests that the inactive 650 mμ form may be a holochrome that lacks a reducing constituent.

It is interesting that the position of the *in vivo* absorption peak of proto-chlorophyll in dark-grown barley or bean leaves can be made to shift from 650 to 635 mμ simply by freezing and thawing the leaves[27]. This treatment would not bring about esterification of the protochlorophyllide, so it would seem that the peak can be shifted to shorter wavelengths by purely physical treatments, as well as by formation of protochlorophyll-ide ester. The possible nature of the changes responsible for this shift of the absorption peak are discussed in the next section (XIII.6).

The isolated holochrome preparations may also contain more than one form of protochlorophyll. Krasnovsky, Bystrova, and Sorokina (1961) found both active and inactive forms in a homogenate of etiolated leaves. The active form sedimented more rapidly than the inactive form. Also, as previously mentioned, Smith and French (1963) have suggested that protochlorophyllide is bound to tyrosine on about 30 per cent of the isolated holochrome particles, and to some other amino acid(s) in the remainder. In this connection it is interesting that Boardman (1962b) has suggested that the apparent second-order kinetics of protochlorophyllide photoconversion might be explained by a theory which assumes that the pigment molecules are bound to the protein in two different ways. If both forms of protochlorophyllide are transformed to chlorophyllide by first-order reactions, but at different rates, then by a suitable choice of rate constants the theoretical curve can be fitted to the experimental curve.

XIII.6. The Later Course of Chlorophyll Synthesis

When etiolated leaves are put in the light there is usually, after the rapid reduction of the protochlorophyllide present, a lag phase (Fig.

XIII.3) of one or two hours in which there is little or no chlorophyll synthesis[117, 104]: after this, rapid chlorophyll formation begins, and continues for about two days. This lag does not always occur. Excised leaves of two-, three-, and four-day-old dark-grown seedlings of *Phaseolus vulgaris* synthesized chlorophyll in a linear manner during six hours' exposure to light[169]. However, by the time that the seedlings were seven days old, the leaves showed a lag of 1·5 hours (after reduction of protochlorophyllide) before rapid chlorophyll synthesis started. Freshly excised leaves of etiolated *Phaseolus vulgaris* placed in the light showed only a very short lag (not more than 30 minutes) before the phase of accelerated chlorophyll formation began[215]: but if the excised leaves were kept in the dark for 18 hours after excision, then they had a lag phase of 4–5 hours when finally illuminated. The development of a lag phase in chlorophyll synthesis as seedlings or leaves are aged appears to be due to the loss of some nutrient. The fall in chlorophyll-synthesizing ability of excised leaves during a dark incubation can be prevented by supplying glucose or sucrose, or by leaving a cotyledon attached; the sugars also stimulate protochlorophyllide synthesis in the dark by 350–400 per cent[215]. It is of interest in this connection that, according to Palladin (1923), excised, etiolated bean leaves remained yellow in the light when floated on water, but became green when floated on solutions of sucrose, glucose, raffinose, maltose, or glycerine —it seems likely that he was using old bean leaves with a long lag phase, and that the sugars overcame this lag phase. Too high a concentration of sugar can induce a water deficit, with a consequent inhibition of chlorophyll synthesis; chlorophyll synthesis by pieces of etiolated wheat leaf in the light is 90 per cent inhibited if the tissue is placed in a solution containing 0·6 Molal sucrose or mannitol instead of in water[199a]. Allowing the leaves to dry out slightly has the same effect: a 6 per cent water deficit causes 40 per cent inhibition of chlorophyll synthesis. Water deficit appears to act by diminishing the ability to form proto-chlorophyllide. Normal chlorophyll synthesis is restored when the leaves are immersed in water.

Pre-incubating etiolated leaves in the presence of the porphyrin precursor, δ-aminolaevulinic acid, also abolishes the lag phase in chlorophyll synthesis[169]: this effect may be connected with the fact that during the dark incubation with δ-aminolaevulinic acid, protochlorophyllide and protoporphyrin accumulate[68]. Curiously enough, however, little of this protochlorophyllide is actually transformed when the leaves are put in the light[69, 169], most of it being the form with an *in vivo* absorption peak at 631 mμ (see XIII.5). Nitrogen sources such as casein hydrolysate, an amino acid mixture, or ammonium chloride plus pyridoxamine, are said to shorten the lag period of chlorophyll synthesis in etiolated *Euglena gracilis*[86].

The lag phase of chlorophyll synthesis in dark-grown bean leaves can be abolished not only by added nutrients, but also by giving a small dose of red light, and then incubating in the dark for 5–15 hours[212]. This effect is discussed in more detail in the section on the mechanism of induction of chloroplast formation (XIII.18).

Treatments which shorten the lag phase may also increase the rate of chlorophyll synthesis during the rapid phase. Excised etiolated bean leaves with one cotyledon left attached synthesize chlorophyll nearly twice as rapidly in the light as leaves without a cotyledon[215]. According to Huzisige et al. (1957) casein hydrolysate and certain individual amino acids increase the rate, and final yield, of chlorophyll synthesis in etiolated Euglena gracilis. However, the rate of chlorophyll synthesis by etiolated cells of a different strain of E. gracilis was stimulated not more than 10–15 per cent by addition of an amino acid mixture, ammonium sulphate, peptone, yeast extract, sodium acetate, or a mixture of purines and pyrimidines[97]. Similarly, it has been found[188] that etiolated E. gracilis synthesize chlorophyll at the same rate whether the cells are suspended in growth medium, or in a medium without nutrients. Perhaps different strains of this alga have different amounts of reserve nutrients.

When etiolated bean leaves are illuminated for one minute the chlorophyll that is formed has its absorption peak at 684 mμ[165]. If the leaves are replaced in the dark, then during the next 14 minutes the chlorophyll peak changes to 673 mμ. After 106 minutes in the dark the 673 mμ peak shifts to 677 mμ, the position of the peak of chlorophyll a in normal green leaves or algae. Similar changes were observed in the fluorescence spectra of etiolated leaves exposed to light by Krasnovsky (1960) and his co-workers. The chlorophyll first formed had a fluorescence maximum at 687–690 mμ; this was rapidly converted to a chlorophyll with fluorescence maximum at 680 mμ. As chlorophyll began to accumulate the maximum shifted yet again to 686 mμ. The forms of chlorophyll with fluorescence maxima at 690, 680, and 686 mμ may well correspond to the forms with absorption maxima at 684, 673, and 677 mμ.

Various suggestions have been made as to the nature of the processes responsible for these shifts in the absorption and fluorescence maxima of chlorophyll during the early stages of greening. Granick (1965) has suggested that the shift of the absorption peak from 684 to 673 mμ, found by Shibata, may correspond to separation of chlorophyllide from the holochrome. However, Vorobeva, Bystrova, and Krasnovsky (1963) have reported that when etiolated bean leaves are kept in the dark after a brief exposure to light, there is a rough correspondence between the extent of conversion of chlorophyll-684 (peak actually at 686 mμ) to chlorophyll-673, and the proportion of chlorophyllide a which has been converted to chlorophyll a. They conclude that the conversion of chlorophyll-684 to chlorophyll-673 is, in fact, due to phytylation of the chlorophyllide initially formed. Sironval *et al.* (1965) also find that in etiolated barley leaves incubated in the dark after a brief exposure to light, the time (20 minutes) required for conversion of the 684 mμ form to the 673 mμ form is about the same as the time required for phytylation of the chlorophyllide. They also report that it is possible to detect slight differences in the spectroscopic properties of the extracted pigments, immediately after a flash of light and after a further 20 minutes in the dark: an 80 per cent acetone extract of leaves containing chlorophyll-684 had an absorption peak at 666–667 mμ; an 80 per cent acetone extract of leaves containing chlorophyll-673 had an absorption peak at 665 mμ. This provides further evidence that the 684 to 673 shift corresponds to a chemical change in the chlorophyll. Sironval *et al.* conclude that the shift of absorption peak from 684 to 673 mμ is, in fact, due to esterification of the chlorophyllide. Further evidence in favour of this conclusion is provided by observations on a number of corn mutants which retained the ability to synthesize protochlorophyllide and chlorophyllide, but in which the pigments were bleached by light[182]. It was found that one particular mutant differed from most of the others in that it retained the ability to esterify its chlorophyllide during an incubation in the dark: it also differed from most of the other mutants in that the *in vivo* chlorophyll absorption maximum shifted to shorter wavelengths (682 to 665 mμ) during the 30 minute incubation in the dark. However, while it may well turn out to be true that this spectral shift is due to phytylation, it must be pointed out that similar shifts can be produced by physical treatments which have nothing to do with esterification. For instance, when leaves containing chlorophyll with a peak at 686 mμ are homogenized, the chlorophyll in the homogenate has a peak at 670–672 mμ, even though there is no change in the proportion of chlorophyllide and chlorophyll[201]. Also, Butler and Briggs (1966) found that if etiolated barley or bean leaves were frozen and thawed, then the protochlorophyllide *in vivo* absorption peak shifted from 650 to 635 mμ: on illumination the 635 mμ form was converted to chlorophyllide absorbing at 673 mμ. Also, the isolated protochlorophyllide holochrome had its peak at 635 mμ; on illumination the peak shifted to 672 mμ. Butler and Briggs suggest that it is the aggregation together of the pigment molecules in the crystalline centre of the etioplast that causes the shift of both the protochlorophyllide and chlorophyllide peaks to longer wavelengths. The shift to shorter wavelengths on freezing and thawing, or on incubation in the dark, they attribute to a disaggregation of the pigment molecules due to the disruption of the structure of the crystalline centre. In support of this they point out that dark-grown cells of *Euglena gracilis*, the plastids of which do not have a crystalline centre, do not show the long wavelength-absorbing forms of either the protochlorophyllide or the newly-formed chloro-phyllide. These apparently conflicting theories could, in fact, both be true. It might be, for instance, that the shift of the absorption peak to shorter wavelengths is, indeed, due to disaggregation of the pigment molecules as suggested by Butler and Briggs: but under normal condi-tions it may be necessary for phytylation to occur before this disaggrega-tion can take place. As greening proceeds and chlorophyll accumulates there is, as we have seen, a further shift in the chlorophyll absorption maximum from 673 to 677 mμ, and in the fluorescence maximum, from 680 to 686 mμ. The simple chlorophyll absorption spectrum of the leaf is the sum of the absorption spectra of the different forms of chlorophyll present. The shift of the average absorption peak to longer wavelengths is due to the appearance of forms of chlorophyll which have their absorption maxima at longer wavelengths. Use of derivative spectro-photometry has shown that in etiolated *Phaseolus vulgaris* leaves, after 1·5 to 2 hours' exposure to light, the chlorophyll *a* begins to differentiate into the forms (see I.2.ii.c) with *in vivo* absorption peaks at about 670 and 683 mμ[26]. This 683 mμ-absorbing form, which appears during greening at the time thylakoids begin to form, and which is present in the mature chloroplast, does not show the spectral shift to shorter wave-lengths on freezing and thawing: it is therefore not identical with the 683–685 mμ-absorbing form which appears immediately after illumina-tion of the etiolated leaf[27]. Quite apart from anything else, the form which appears later in greening is presumably phytylated. The appear-ance of these long wavelength absorption peaks may be due to inter-action between the chlorophyll molecules as they begin to aggregate together in the thylakoids. Thus it may be that the chlorophyll-type pigments first of all become less aggregated, possibly as a result of their being phytylated, and then become more aggregated as their concen-tration begins to increase.

A progressive decrease in the extractability of the holochrome during greening was observed by Capon and Bogorad (1962b). From dark-grown leaves of *Phaseolus vulgaris*, three protein fractions were obtained, each of which contained some of the protochlorophyllide holochrome. If the leaves were illuminated for five minutes before harvesting, the holochrome (chlorophyll-containing) was found to have disappeared from one of the fractions. After an hour's illumination the holochrome had nearly all gone from a second fraction also. After three hours illumination no chlorophyll holochrome was found in any of the three protein fractions. These authors suggest that the holochrome may have become incorporated into the plastid structure in such a way as to be unextractable by the method used, or, alternatively, that the pigment may have been dissociated from the protein of the holochrome before being incorporated into the plastid architecture.

The shifts in the absorption and fluorescence spectra, and the decrease in extractibility of holochrome, during greening, all indicate that there are changes in the state of the chlorophyll after it is first formed. Goedheer (1961) has investigated these changes of state by studying the fluorescence yield (the number of light quanta emitted as fluorescence divided by the number of light quanta absorbed) of chlorophyll during greening. When etiolated bean leaves were exposed to light the fluorescence yield immediately after conversion of the protochlorophyllide already present was about 80 per cent of that of chlorophyll a dissolved in methanol. In the first five hours of illumination the relative fluorescence yield fell to 20 per cent, and during the next 19 hours, to 10 per cent. The period of rapid fall of relative fluorescence yield corresponded to the period in which rapid chlorophyll synthesis started. The decrease in fluorescence yield was shown not to be due simply to an alteration of the molecular structure of the chlorophyll, by the fact that there was no change in the fluorescence yield of the extracted pigment during greening.

The changes in chlorophyll fluorescence over shorter periods of time in the dark, after exposure of etiolated leaves to light, were studied by Butler (1961). Dark-grown leaves of *Phaseolus vulgaris* were given a 20-second exposure to light to transform their protochlorophyllide and were then put back in the dark. During the first few minutes an actual increase in the intensity of chlorophyll fluorescence was observed; this corresponded with the shift of the absorption peak of chlorophyll from 685 mμ to 673 mμ. However, after this there was a decrease in the fluorescence yield of chlorophyll. Butler also measured the action spectrum for the excitation of chlorophyll fluorescence at various times during the incubation in the dark. After 30 minutes, bands due to carotenoids were detected in the excitation spectrum, indicating that light energy absorbed by carotenoids was beginning to be transferred to chlorophyll. These bands increased in intensity until about three hours after exposure to light. Butler makes the suggestion that only when chlorophyll is phytylated can it dissolve in the lipid present in the plastid, and come into juxtaposition with the carotenoids: resonance transfer of energy between carotenoids and chlorophyll is then possible.

Changes in the fluorescence properties of the chlorophyll during greening of *Euglena gracilis* have been studied by Brody, Brody, and Levine (1965). Green cells of higher plants and algae possess, as well as the chlorophyll emission band at about 690 mμ, an emission band in the region 710–735 mμ. The 710–735 mμ band becomes much more pronounced if the cells are cooled to $-196°C$. The long wavelength emission band is thought to be due to aggregated chlorophyll molecules, while the 690 mμ band is thought to be due to monomeric chlorophyll molecules[22]. Thus, the ratio of the intensity of emission of the long wavelength band, to that of the short wavelength band, F_A/F_M, should be a measure of the proportion of the chlorophyll which is in the aggregated, rather than the monomeric, form. Brody *et al.* find that when dark-grown cells of *E. gracilis* are incubated in the light, F_A/F_M (measured at $-196°C$) is in the region of 1·0 to 2·5 between 5 and 15 hours. Between 15 and 25 hours, F_A/F_M increases very sharply to about 21. After 25 hours F_A/F_M continues to increase steadily although at a lower rate, reaching a value of 36 after 80 hours in the light. Except for a short lag of about two hours, chlorophyll was synthesized steadily, in a linear fashion, throughout the whole 80 hours. In cells grown in the light, so that the chloroplast was fully developed, F_A/F_M was equal to 257: these light-grown cells had 2·3 times as much chlorophyll as those greened for 80 hours, and it is thought that the greater chlorophyll concentration accounts for the greater value of F_A/F_M. The actual position of the chlorophyll aggregate emission peak moves to longer wavelengths as greening proceeds: after six hours the peak is at about 717 mμ, and after 80 hours approaches the limiting value of 734 mμ. This is thought to be due to increased interaction between the chlorophyll molecules at the higher concentrations. As mentioned above, this shift of the fluorescence maximum to longer wavelengths during later stages of greening, has also been observed for higher plants[107]. The relative fluorescence yield of the *Euglena* cells apparently increased during greening: this is contrary to what Goedheer (1961) found for greening of etiolated bean leaves.

Chlorophyll formation when etiolated leaves are first illuminated is known to take place by photoreduction of protochlorophyllide, but this does not prove that chlorophyll synthesis during the rapid phase takes place by the same route. If etiolated bean leaves which have been allowed to form chlorophyll for two hours in the light are put back in the dark, they soon form substantial amounts of protochlorophyllide[165]. This suggests that chlorophyll could be formed through protochlorophyllide in the rapid phase. Also, the action spectrum for the synthesis of chlorophyll over a long period (96 hours) by dark-grown *Euglena gracilis* resembles the absorption spectrum of protochlorophyll[218]. However, attempts to detect formation of new protochlorophyllide holochrome when partially-greened bean seedlings were returned to the dark failed[115]. Further investigation of this matter is desirable.

In greening of etiolated cells of *E. gracilis*, the highest rate of chlorophyll (and carotenoid) synthesis is brought about by a (white) light intensity of about 100 foot-candles: at intensities higher or lower than this lower rates are obtained[187a].

XIII.7. Ultrastructural Changes during Greening in Angiosperms

When plants are grown in the dark, then during the differentiation of the meristematic cells into leaf cells, the relatively undifferentiated proplastids develop into etioplasts with the characteristic crystalline centres. When the etiolated leaf is exposed to light the etioplasts undergo, during the greening process, a metamorphosis into chloroplasts. The formation of the etioplast was studied, with the electron microscope, by a number of workers, notably Hodge, McLean, and Mercer (1956), Mühlethaler and Frey-Wyssling (1959), and von Wettstein (1959). The differentiation of the etioplast into the chloroplast has been investigated in detail by von Wettstein and his co-workers[205, 41, 200]. However, in much of the early work on these developmental changes, preparation of tissue for electron microscopical examination involved fixation with $KMnO_4$. While these studies have cast a great deal of light on the structural changes involved, there is a possibility that some of the finer details of structure at some stages of development, may be altered by fixation of the material with $KMnO_4$. Fixation of biological material with glutaraldehyde seems to preserve certain cellular structures that are not detected with other fixation techniques. We shall, therefore, in our consideration of the formation of the etioplast, and its further differentiation into the chloroplast, rely heavily on the results obtained by Gunning and Jagoe (1965) with etiolated oat leaves fixed in glutaraldehyde, and post-fixed with osmium tetroxide.

Gunning and Jagoe (1965) find that in oat seedlings growing in the dark, the cells in or near the meristem contain proplastids which, like other proplastids, are relatively undifferentiated, containing just a few single thylakoids. As the meristematic cells develop into the mesophyll cells of the etiolated leaf, these proplastids develop into etioplasts. The first sign of the formation of the crystalline centre is the development of connecting arms between these thylakoids. This process continues until, in the young mesophyll cells, most of the plastids have built up a rather open, somewhat irregular type of lattice. As differentiation proceeds the lattice takes on a more regular crystalline form, so that in the older mesophyll cells, most of the plastids have the typical crystalline centre. Gunning and Jagoe suggest that the crystal lattice is formed by deposition of membranous material around ribosomes; addition of further ribosomes is followed by deposition of more membranes. This theory would account for the presence of a ribosome within each unit cell of the lattice (Fig. I.37). In the earlier work[80, 139, 205] it was reported that during the development of the etioplast, there was an accumulation of vesicles which were produced by invagination of the inner plastid membrane. It was thought that the crystalline centre was formed by fusion of these vesicles. However, in the oat leaves fixed in glutaraldehyde–OsO_4, no stage in which there is a mass of vesicles present was observed[71]. The evidence obtained with glutaraldehyde–OsO_4 does not contradict the suggestion that the membranous material of the crystalline centre originates from the inner plastid membrane. However, this point is still by no means established. In barley seedlings germinating in the dark, fully differentiated etioplasts are present after about 15 days: after 20 days in the dark a few lamellae appear, and these form concentric semicircles at the edge of the crystalline centre, these lamellae being apparently connected to tubes in the crystalline centre[205].

When the etiolated oat leaves are exposed to light at an intensity of 750–1000 foot-candles for five minutes, all the protochlorophyllide is reduced to chlorophyllide. Electron microscopic examination of glutaraldehyde–OsO_4-fixed material shows that in the etioplasts, the order and regularity of the crystalline centre have been largely lost (Fig. XIII.4) although the continuity of the membrane surface is retained[71]. With this particular fixation technique, the transformation of the crystalline centre to a mass of vesicles and elongated tubules, observed by other workers[41, 200, 101] was not seen. Assuming that the fundamental structural change is the same, whether it is seen as a loss of crystalline structure (in glutaraldehyde–OsO_4-fixed material), or as a dissociation into a mass of vesicles ($KMnO_4$-fixed material), then from the work of Eriksson, Kahn, Walles, and von Wettstein (1961), it would appear that this process has a very small energy requirement. Less than 10^4 ergs/cm^2, at 660 mμ, or 445 mμ, is sufficient to transform all the etioplasts in an etiolated bean leaf. Red and blue light are effective in bringing about this transformation, whereas green light, and far-red light are relatively ineffective[200, 101]: this is compatible with protochlorophyllide being the photoreceptor for this process. Although protochlorophyllide reduction takes place at roughly the same time as this structural change, the two processes may not go exactly hand-in-hand. Virgin, Kahn, and von Wettstein (1963) found that an amount of light sufficient to reduce 44 per cent of the protochlorophyllide, brought about no detectable structural change: but a further light dose, which took protochlorophyllide reduction only as far as 61 per cent, brought about the structural change in 99 per cent of the crystalline centres. However, Klein, Bryan, and Bogorad (1964), also using etiolated leaves of *Phaseolus vulgaris*, found that with exposures to red light at a series of different energies, there was a rough parallelism between the proportion of etioplasts which had undergone this structural change, and the proportion of the protochlorophyllide which had been reduced to chlorophyllide. Thus, it is still not entirely clear whether the structural change

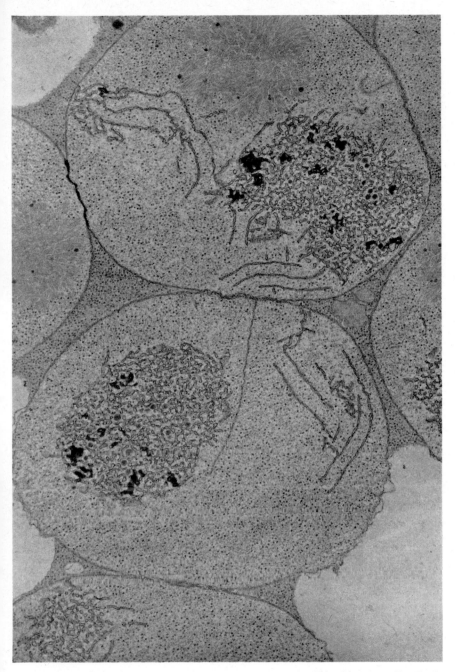

FIG. XIII.4. *First visible change in etioplast structure in light (Gunning, B. E. S., unpublished). Glutaraldehyde–OsO$_4$ fixation. Etiolated oat leaf exposed to light of intensity 750–1000 foot-candles for five minutes. Prolamellar body has lost its crystalline character*

is an immediate and necessary consequence of the photoreduction of protochlorophyllide.

As greening proceeds in the etiolated oat leaves there is an increasing tendency for the tubular connections of the crystalline centre to pinch off, forming a set of two-dimensional, double-membraned sheets (Fig. XIII.5) extending out, roughly parallel to one another, into the stroma[71]. These sheets, or primary lamellae, have many perforations, and so can give the appearance, in section, of rows of vesicles. Fig. XIII.5 shows a plastid in an etiolated oat leaf exposed to light for two hours: the prolamellar body is still detectable, although in a very dis-organized form. The formation of these perforated, double-membraned sheets presumably, then, corresponds to the dispersal of vesicles into concentric layers, previously described by Eriksson et al. (1961), as the second stage of greening in bean leaves. This structural change does not appear to require chlorophyll formation since it is taking place in the lag phase of chlorophyll synthesis[101]. This second stage of the plastid differentiation also requires light, and the rate of extrusion of these perforated sheets into the stroma appears to increase with intensity over the range 75–7500 foot candles[92]. With sufficiently high light intensity this process can take place within a few minutes, suggesting that the necessity for this structural change to take place is not what causes the lag phase in chlorophyll synthesis. This extrusion process will take place, slowly, at a light intensity as low as 2 foot-candles[37], or at a temperature as low as $3°C$[99,41].

The action spectrum for this extrusion, or dispersal, process has a very sharp peak at 450 mμ, with another very small peak at 402 mμ: all other wavelengths in the visible range have only a fraction of the activity of the light at 450 mμ[78]. This suggests that the chromophore for this part of the plastid differentiation is different to that which is responsible for the primary structural change (the 'de-crystallization' of the crystalline centre). The ineffectiveness of red and other long-wavelength light would seem to rule out chlorophyll, protochlorophyll, or phytochrome (see XIII.18) as the pigment responsible. The white mutant of Helianthus which lacks carotenoids can nevertheless carry out this extrusion or dispersal process, indicating that the chromophore in question is not a carotenoid. The low effectiveness of light of wavelength 300–380 mμ is also thought to eliminate compounds such as riboflavin as the photoreceptor[78].

As illumination of the oat seedlings continues, the pores, or perfora-tions, in the double-membraned sheets disappear. There is some sug-gestion that the disappearance of the pores may be correlated in time with the end of the lag period of chlorophyll synthesis. On the basis of rough estimates of the membrane surface present, Gunning and Jagoe (1965) have concluded that by the end of the lag period of greening, no

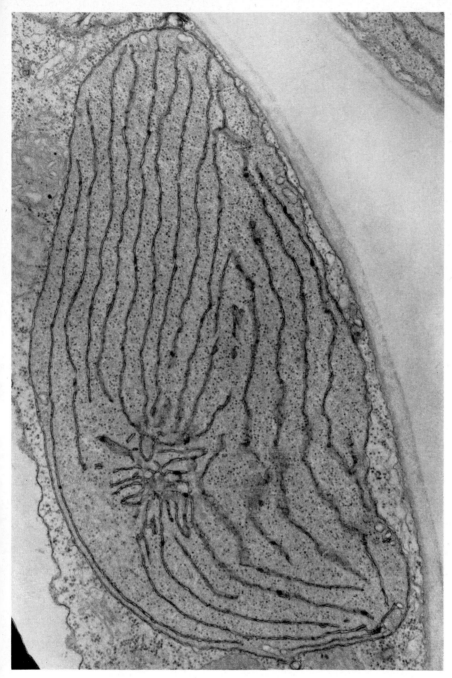

FIG. XIII.5. *Extrusion of primary lamellae (Gunning, B. E. S., unpublished). Glutaralde-hyde–OsO₄ fixation. Plastid of etiolated oat leaf after two hours' light (750–1000 foot-candles). Double-membraned sheets extend from prolamellar body throughout the plastid*

large areas of membrane have been produced *de novo*. This suggests that the membranous structures present in the plastids at this stage have been produced largely by rearrangements of the membranes originally present in the crystalline centre. After the end of the lag phase, as chlorophyll synthesis begins to accelerate, the single double-membraned sheets begin to duplicate themselves, and from here on chlorophyll synthesis seems to go hand-in-hand with formation of thylakoids. Fig. XIII.6 shows a plastid in an etiolated oat leaf after four hours illumination. It can be seen that the primary lamellae have, over certain regions, become double, thus producing, in effect, a 'stack' of two thylakoids. In Fig. XIII.7 it can be seen that after 10 hours' illumination, the duplication process has continued to the stage where there are stacks of three or four thylakoids: it will be noted that the remains of a prolamellar body are still visible; in this particular case the prolamellar body seems to have several osmiophilic globules associated with it. After 20 hours' illumination the grana of the chloroplasts will commonly contain three to eight thylakoids: Fig. XIII.8 shows oat chloroplasts at this stage of development. It can be seen that the grana tend to be arranged in lines, with thylakoids extending from one granum to the next: this linear arrangement of grana may well have something to do with their being formed along the primary lamellae originally extruded from the crystalline centre. Ways in which duplication of thylakoids may occur are discussed in the next chapter (XIV.1.vi).

Differentiation of etioplasts to chloroplasts in mature leaves does not, at any stage, seem to involve plastid division. In etiolated leaves of *Phaseolus vulgaris* exposed to light, the development of the chloroplasts is complete after about 45 hours. Throughout this time, the number of plastids per leaf remains constant at about 2×10^8, indicating that there is no plastid multiplication during chloroplast differentiation[72].

In etiolated leaves of *Phaseolus vulgaris* which have accumulated protochlorophyll as a result of being incubated with δ-aminolaevulinic acid (ALA), the structural changes on illumination differ from those which take place in normal leaves[100]. Such leaves contain several times as much protochlorophyll as normal leaves, and most of this protochlorophyll has its *in vivo* absorption maximum at about 631 mμ: on exposure of the leaves to light this protochlorophyll is destroyed[69], the bleaching process taking three to four hours in white light at 700 foot-candles[100]. The etioplasts of the ALA-treated leaves have an apparently normal fine structure as seen in the electron microscope. Also the initial change in the crystalline centre as a result of 10 seconds' exposure to light, is the same in the treated and normal leaves. However, after 60 minutes' exposure to light, differences become apparent. In the ALA-treated leaves, the prolamellar bodies disappear to be replaced by stacks of ten or more double-membraned lamellae, the

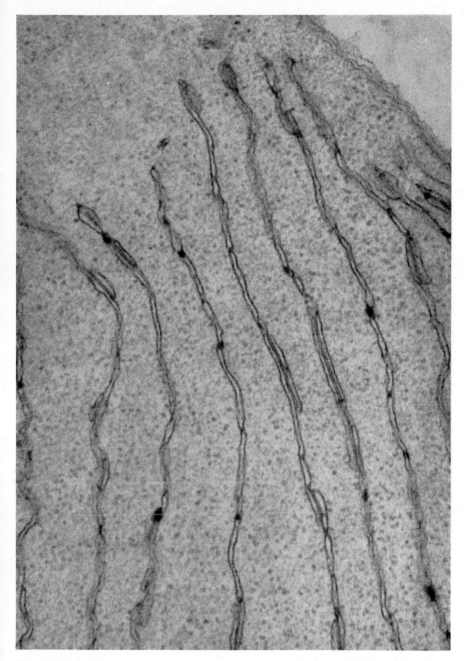

FIG. XIII.6. *First stage of grana formation (Gunning, B. E. S., unpublished). Glutaraldehyde–OsO$_4$ fixation. Plastid of dark-grown oat leaf after four hours' light (750–1000 footcandles). The primary lamellae have become double at various points*

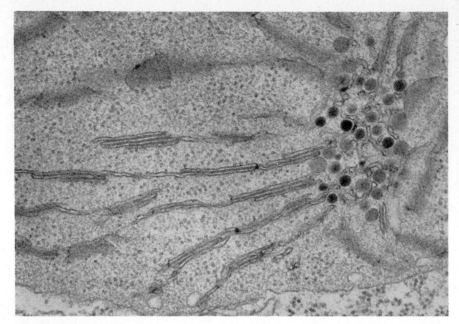

FIG. XIII.7. *Later stage of grana formation (Gunning, B. E. S., unpublished). Glutaralde-hyde–OsO$_4$ fixation. Plastid of dark-grown oat leaf after 10 hours' light (750–1000 foot-candles). Grana containing up to four thylakoids are visible. The remains of the prolamellar body can still be seen*

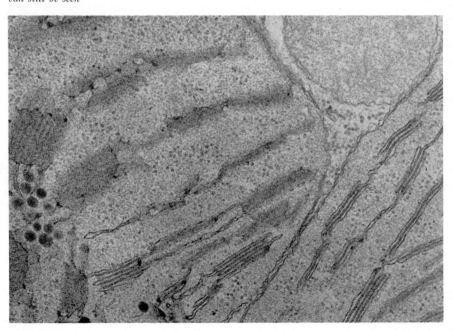

FIG. XIII.8. *Final stages of differentiation of etioplast into chloroplast (Gunning, B. E. S., unpublished). Glutaraldehyde–OsO$_4$ fixation. Plastid of dark-grown oat leaf after 20 hours' illumination (750–1000 foot-candles). Quite large grana, sectioned in various planes*

whole thing looking quite like a stack of thylakoids. Even after three hours' illumination when there are little or no pigments left, these stacks remain. The physical and chemical nature of these granum-like structures is unknown, but their persistence after the pigments have been bleached shows that lamellae of a sort can exist in plastids, even when there are little or no chlorophyll or protochlorophyll pigments present.

The first stage of the differentiation of the etioplast to the chloroplast, the 'de-crystallization' of the crystalline centre, appears to be reversible. When an etiolated oat leaf is given five minutes' exposure to light, and then put back in the dark, re-formation of the regular, crystalline lattice takes place in about 45 minutes[71]: during this time, more protochlorophyllide is being formed. The appearance of the electron micrographs suggests that the greater part of the re-formed crystalline centre is derived from the membranes present in the original lattice. Whether etioplasts whose differentiation towards chloroplasts has proceeded beyond the first step can re-form the normal crystalline centre in the dark is not certain. Some suggestion that the differentiation may be fairly freely reversible is provided by the report[167] that prolamellar bodies may be present in plastids early in the morning, and absent later in the day. Plants grown in the light may form etioplasts in tissues, such as those inside buds[55], or at the base of a barley leaf[219], which receive little illumination.

XIII.8. Ultrastructural Changes during Greening in Algae

Most algae form chlorophyll in the dark. However, both *Euglena gracilis* and *Ochromonas danica* require light for chlorophyll formation, and both have been used for ultrastructural studies of greening.

Dark-grown cells of *E. gracilis* contain proplastids, about 1 μ in diameter, bounded by a double membrane and having little internal structure[9]. Clumps of ribosome-like particles are occasionally seen. After two hours in the light the plastids can be seen to have at least one large invagination extending into the plastid from the inner membrane. These invaginations are not thin tubules, as are found in higher plant proplastids: they look as if a large area of the inner membrane of the plastid was becoming widely separated from the outer membrane. From 4 to 10 hours more membranes can be seen extending into the plastid, and some of these appear to be double. These structures, which in section present the appearance of a double membrane, may correspond to the flattened sacs, or thylakoids, of the higher plant chloroplast. Ben-Shaul, Schiff, and Epstein (1964) suggest that a double-membraned structure is produced by the successive production of two single-membraned invaginations from the same region of the plastid inner surface, with the two single membranes subsequently becoming closely appressed to form a double membrane. From 10 to 96 hours the double membranes inside the plastid increase in number, and also come together in groups of two or three to form thick, compound lamellae.

The increase in number per plastid of the various kinds of membrane is not linear with time. Between 8 and 14 hours, the number of single membranes per plastid suddenly increases by a factor of about 2·5; the number of double membranes per plastid increases approximately fourfold. At the same time the plastid length also increases by a factor of about 2·5. These authors consider that these results support the hypothesis—previously presented on quite different grounds (see X.6.iv)—that the proplastids of dark-grown cells fuse together in groups of three at some time during the formation of chloroplasts in the light. The increase in length would suggest that the fusion of proplastids takes place in a linear sequence.

After 14 hours, formation of lamellae (double membranes) is linear with time, one lamella being produced every 11 hours. Development is complete at about 72 hours, and the lamellae of the mature chloroplast are organized into about 13 compound lamellae, each of which consists of two or three of the simple lamellae (Fig. I.25). The inception of rapid, linear synthesis of chlorophyll corresponds approximately with the beginning of the linear formation of lamellae, i.e. after the sudden increase in the amount of membranous material per plastid, between 8 and 14 hours.

The differentiation of the chloroplast in *Ochromonas danica* appears to follow quite a different pathway[57]. The dark-grown cell contains only one proplastid, unlike *E. gracilis* which has more than 20 proplastids when grown in the dark[40]. Also, Gibbs found that the dark-grown cells always contain some chlorophyll (1–2 per cent of that in light-grown cells) even after repeated sub-culturing in the dark: etiolated *E. gracilis* have protochlorophyll but no chlorophyll[86]. A typical *Ochromonas* proplastid may contain a few small vesicles, a single thylakoid and a large number of dense granules, similar to ribosomes. During the first 12 hours in the light, structures, similar in section to vesicles, appear to align themselves into rows. It may be wondered whether these structures that appear in section to be rows of vesicles, are in fact double-membraned sheets with many pores (see XIII.7). Thylakoids are formed, possibly by fusion of vesicles, or perhaps by the closing up of pores in a double-membraned sheet. However, no evidence was found that vesicles are produced by invagination from the inner plastid membrane, as is thought to happen in higher plants. By 12 hours three to six bands can be seen extending along the plastid, each band consisting of two or three closely appressed thylakoids, or of a single thylakoid. After 48 hours, when the cells have reached 50 per cent of their final chlorophyll content, the chloroplast is full-sized, and contains a normal complement (about ten) of bands, each consisting of three thylakoids. During the next five days the chlorophyll content doubles, but the only apparent structural change is a compression of the thylakoids (the thickness decreases from 180 Å to 130 Å) and a more regular alignment of their membranes.

Another alga in which chlorophyll is not formed in the dark is a mutant of *Chlamydomonas reinhardi*, y^{-}[160]; the wild-type is green both in the light and the dark. When the mutant is grown in the dark it contains protochlorophyll and small amounts of chlorophylls *a* and *b*[159]. This mutant shows a high rate of reversion to wild-type, so the traces of chlorophyll could be due to the presence of a small number of normal cells. The plastid of the dark-grown mutant contains a pyrenoid, starch grains, a few vesicles, and an occasional thylakoid[160, 84]. This plastid (unlike those of etiolated *Euglena* or *Ochromonas*) is about the same size as a mature chloroplast[160]. After two hours' illumination there is little change in the plastid structure, other than possibly an increase in the number of single thylakoids[84]. By the time the cells have been illuminated for three hours the first marked changes appear: long thylakoid-bands, containing two or three thylakoids may be seen to traverse the chloroplast. It seems likely that, as greening continues, the thylakoids continue to multiply, but this process has not been studied in detail.

XIII.9. Carotenoid Formation during Greening

In angiosperms carotenoids, unlike the chlorophylls, are formed in the dark, although to a lesser extent than in the light. The leaves of higher plants grown in the dark contain far more xanthophylls than carotenes (see I.4.ii). However, yellow dark-grown cells of a *y* mutant of *Chlamydomonas reinhardi* (XIII.8) had a lower xanthophyll to carotene ratio than the green, light-grown cells: the total carotenoid content was about 23 per cent of that of the light-grown cells[112].

As might be expected, the exposure of etiolated plants to light initiates a rapid synthesis of carotenoids. Blaauw-Jansen *et al.* (1950) reported that in the case of etiolated oat seedlings, this increase was confined to carotenes. According to Kay and Phinney (1956) the same holds true of etiolated corn seedlings. However, other workers find that etiolated barley[43, 189], *Phaseolus multiflorus*[164], maize[62], *Phaseolus vulgaris*[66], and wheat[213] all synthesize both xanthophylls and carotenes when illuminated. In the case of barley the formation of carotenes, xanthophylls, and chlorophylls appeared to take place roughly in parallel[43]. The percentage increase of carotenes was, of course, much larger than the percentage increase in xanthophylls, because of the much higher starting level of the latter. Goodwin and Phagpolngarm (1960) found that in leaves of dark-grown *Phaseolus vulgaris* the different carotenoid pigments (neoxanthin, lutein, and β-carotene) were synthesized in the light in much the same relative proportions as they occur in the chloroplast.

In the algae, *Euglena gracilis* and *Ochromonas danica*, growth in the dark inhibits carotenoid synthesis as well as chlorophyll synthesis. Etiolated cells of *E. gracilis* have only 5–7 per cent[65, 111], and etiolated cells of *O. danica* have only 4–7 per cent[57] of the carotenoid content of the corresponding cells grown in the light. Krinsky, Gordon, and Stern (1964) find that the major carotenoids present in dark-grown cells of *E. gracilis* are the xanthophylls, antheraxanthin (64 per cent), and zeaxanthin (21·2 per cent): hydroxyechinenone (5·6 per cent), trollein (3·6 per cent), and β-carotene (2·0 per cent) are also present, with traces of echinenone, euglenanone, and cryptoxanthin. When the cells are exposed to light, a linear synthesis of antheraxanthin, β-carotene, trollein, and possibly zeaxanthin, begins immediately (Fig. XIII.9).

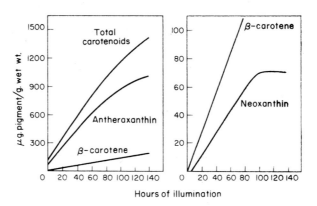

FIG. XIII.9. *Formation of certain carotenoids in dark-grown cells of* Euglena gracilis *exposed to light (adapted from Krinsky et al., 1964)*

Antheraxanthin is synthesized about five times as fast as β-carotene; however, antheraxanthin synthesis ceases after about 100 hours, whereas β-carotene synthesis continues for at least 141 hours. Neoxanthin, which is absent from the dark-grown cells[63, 111] becomes detectable, during greening, at about four hours: its synthesis continues in a linear manner, at rather more than half the rate of β-carotene synthesis, and ceases at about the same time as antheraxanthin synthesis. Krinsky *et al.* suggest that the lag in neoxanthin synthesis may be connected with the fact that there is a lag in the development of photosynthetic ability in greening *E. gracilis*[188]: neoxanthin might be closely related to the photosynthetic system of this organism.

When dark-grown cells of *O. danica* are exposed to light, carotenoid synthesis begins immediately and continues for about five days, by which time the carotenoid content becomes equal to that of light-grown cells[57].

Wolken and Mellon (1956) measured the action spectrum for carotenoid synthesis, over 96-hour periods, in etiolated cells of *E. gracilis* exposed to the light. The spectrum they obtained was similar to the absorption spectrum of protochlorophyll. The meaning of this is not clear. It seems unlikely that the light energy absorbed by protochlorophyll has any direct effect on carotenoid formation. However, chlorophyll synthesis under these conditions was found to have much the same action spectrum, and it might be that carotenoid formation is closely linked to, or dependent upon, chlorophyll synthesis.

XIII.10. Formation of Phycocyanin

The accessory chloroplast pigments, the biliproteins, are found only in the *Rhodophyta*, *Cryptophyta*, and *Cyanophyta* (see I.2.ii.e). *Cyanidium caldarium* (*Rhodophyta?*) contains the biliprotein, phycocyanin: cells of this alga grown in the dark on liquid media, or certain solid media, do not make phycocyanin[1, 141]. Curiously enough, when the cells are grown in the dark on solid medium made up with a certain specific brand of agar, they make phycocyanin: Nichols and Bogorad (1962) suggest that some cofactor or substrate (presumably present in this agar—'Fisher Agar Agar U.S.P.' but not in another agar—'Difco Bacto-agar') can replace the light-mediated reaction in phycocyanin synthesis. When cells grown in the dark on the Difco agar were exposed to light, they synthesized phycocyanin: the action spectrum for this process (actually obtained with a chlorophyll-less mutant of *C. caldarium*) when young cells were used, had maxima at 420 and 550–600 mμ: this suggests that a haem compound is the primary photoreceptor or precursor[141]. In older cells the long-wavelength maximum occupied the range 550–650 mμ, which might indicate that the photoreceptor had been converted to a different form. As mentioned in section XIII.14 there is evidence that there is an increase in some or all of the enzymes required for conversion of δ-aminolaevulinic acid to phycobilin pigments during 24 hours' greening of dark-grown cells in the light.

XIII.11. Formation of Chloroplast Lipids during Greening

Chloroplasts contain large amounts of lipids (about 20 per cent of the dry weight) some of which are peculiar to chloroplasts (see I.2.ii.b). As might be expected, the greening of etiolated plants is accompanied by active lipid synthesis.

When etiolated leaves of *Vicia faba* were allowed to go green, the amount of fatty acids per leaf doubled[34]. Linolenic acid, which is the major fatty acid of the higher plant chloroplast, and which occurs mainly in the chloroplast, made up 72 per cent of the new fatty acids. During greening of etiolated *Phaseolus vulgaris* leaves the relative amounts of palmitic, stearic, oleic, and linoleic acids in the plastids decreased, while the level of linolenic acid increased; that is, the ratios unsaturated/saturated, and C_{18}/C_{16} for the fatty acids increased during greening[202]. Erwin and Bloch (1962) showed that on exposure of dark-grown cells of *Euglena gracilis* to light, the percentage of α-linolenic acid in the total fatty acids rose steadily from 0·6 per cent to 7·8 per cent in 28 hours. This formation of α-linolenic acid appears to be, in part at least, dependent upon photosynthesis: 3-(p-chlorophenyl)-1,1-dimethyl urea, which blocks photosynthetic oxygen evolution, reduces α-linolenic synthesis by etiolated cells of *E. gracilis* in the light[12]. Two of the major fatty acids of etiolated cells of *E. gracilis* are the C_{13} and C_{14} saturated acids[155]: on illumination these rapidly disappear (being nearly all gone in 10 hours), to be replaced by unsaturated fatty acids, mainly C_{16} and C_{18}.

Galactolipids are confined to the chloroplast, and may play a role in the photosynthetic fixation of carbon dioxide (I.2.iv.c). During greening of etiolated leaves of *Phaseolus vulgaris* in the light the galactolipid content of the plastids fell to one-seventh of its original value in 36 hours, during which time the chlorophyll content of the plastids had reached one-third of its final value. After a total of 11 days' illumination, however, the galactolipid content of the plastids was about 8·5 times as high as in the plastids of the dark-grown leaves[202]. The phospholipid content of these plastids had risen by 63 per cent after 36 hours' illumination, and by 94 per cent after 11 days' illumination. When dark-grown cells of *E. gracilis* were exposed to light the galactolipid level increased linearly without a lag phase (unlike chlorophyll content). During the 70 hours required for greening, the galactolipid level rose tenfold[155].

The level of sulpholipids (these are confined to the chloroplast—I.2.ii.b) increased threefold during greening.

The plastoquinones, α-tocopherol and α-tocopherylquinone, are localized in the chloroplast; the plastoquinones are thought to act as carriers in the electron transport system (I.2.iv.b), and tocopheryl-quinones may possibly play a similar role. Dark-grown cells of *E. gracilis* contain only traces of plastoquinone: illumination of such cells was found to result in the synthesis of plastoquinone, α-tocopheryl-quinone, and α-tocopherol, in parallel with chlorophyll formation[190].

There is some evidence that, during the greening of etiolated seedlings in the light, there is a transfer of sterols from other parts of the cell to the developing chloroplasts[64].

XIII.12. Development of Ability to Liberate Oxygen

There are conflicting reports as to whether etiolated plants have the ability to evolve oxygen as soon as they are put in the light. Engelmann (1881) claimed that oxygen was evolved immediately an etiolated *Nasturtium* leaf was illuminated. He detected oxygen by its ability to induce motility in bacteria. Ewart (1895–1897), who used the same technique, reported that cotyledons of etiolated *Helianthus annuus* and *Cucurbita pepo*, at a certain age, showed some evolution of oxygen in the light: older or younger plants were inactive. Primary, simple leaves of dark-grown *Phaseolus multiflorus* showed oxygen production in the light, but younger, trifoliate, leaves did not. Dark-grown leaves of plants with bulbs or rootstocks (such as *Beta vulgaris, Hyacinthus, Allium cepa, Daucus carota*) all showed oxygen evolution in the light: etiolated leaves of certain *Graminae* (*Hordeum distichum, Avena sativa,* and *Zea mays*) were inactive. A criticism that can be made of Ewart's work is that the tissue was exposed to weak light for some minutes while the experiment was being set up. Thus the experiments did not demonstrate oxygen pro-duction *immediately* the etiolated leaves were put in the light: the plants always had at least a few minutes in which to develop photosynthetic activity. More recently Blaauw-Jansen, Kamen, and Thomas (1950) have claimed that etiolated oat seedlings show a very slight oxygen liberation immediately they are exposed to light.

Contrary to the results described above, most modern workers have found that etiolated plants have no ability to liberate oxygen when they are first put in the light. Inman (1935) exposed dark-grown maize leaves to light and used the oxygen-dependent luminescence of lumi-nescent bacteria to detect oxygen production. The first trace of oxygen was found at 135 minutes, by which time the leaves were detectably green. Smith (1954) found that after etiolated barley leaves had been illuminated for 10 minutes they had no significant ability to evolve oxygen (as measured by the phosphorescence-quenching method), although they had chlorophyll *a*, derived from the photoreduction of the protochlorophyllide formed in the dark. Oxygen liberation was detectable at 30 minutes and increased rapidly after this (Fig. XIII.10). In

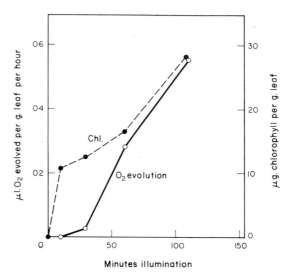

FIG. XIII.10. *Development of oxygen-evolving power and chlorophyll in dark-grown barley leaves exposed to light (adapted from Smith, 1954)*

many instances the leaves aquired the ability to evolve oxygen before they had made any chlorophyll *b*; a similar observation was made by Blaauw-Jansen *et al.* (1950). Gabrielsen, Madsen, and Vejlby (1961) reported that in the case of dark-grown wheat leaves, exposure to light actually increased oxygen consumption at first. Stern, Schiff, and Epstein (1964), using Warburg manometry, found no significant oxygen production by etiolated *Euglena gracilis* until the cells had been illuminated for about eight hours. After this, the ability of the cells to liberate oxygen increased linearly with time, more or less in parallel with formation of chlorophyll and lamellae. The rate of oxygen evolution per unit of chlorophyll was, in fact, highest at about 10 hours. By 20 hours, however, it had fallen by 50 per cent and remained fairly steady from then on. Schiff (1963), using the rather more sensitive oxygen-electrode method, found that steady evolution of oxygen by dark-grown *Euglena gracilis* did not begin until the cells had been exposed to light for four hours. In *E. gracilis* the optimum (white) light intensity for development of ability to liberate O_2 is about 100 foot-candles[187a].

When dark-grown cells of the y^- mutant of *Chlamydomonas reinhardi* (see XIII.8) were exposed to light, the ability to liberate oxygen increased together with chlorophyll content, but reached its final value when the chlorophyll content was only about 50 per cent of the final level[3]. Associated with the absorption of light energy and photolysis of water by chloroplasts, free electrons are produced which can be detected by the technique of electron paramagnetic resonance (EPR) spectroscopy. The dark-grown *C. reinhardi* mutant cells had no photo-induced EPR signal. As the chlorophyll was formed in the light, the EPR signal slowly appeared but lagged behind chlorophyll: half of the final EPR amplitude was produced during the synthesis of the last 15 per cent of the chlorophyll. When cells of another y mutant of *C. reinhardi*, grown in the dark for four days, were exposed to light, there was a low level of oxygen evolution even at the beginning of the illumination[84, 83]. This was not particularly surprising since the cells still had a chlorophyll content which was somewhere in the region of 10 per cent of that of light-grown cells. After a lag period of 1–2 hours, during which there was relatively little change, chlorophyll content and ability to liberate oxygen in the light began to increase rapidly, normal values being restored after 8–10 hours. The ability to liberate oxygen increased more rapidly than did the chlorophyll content: in six hours' illumination, the chlorophyll content increased about sixfold, but the rate of oxygen evolution increased thirtyfold.

The rapidity with which etiolated leaves develop the ability to liberate oxygen appears to depend upon their age. Etiolated leaves from 12-day-old seedlings of *Phaseolus vulgaris* developed much more oxygen-evolving capacity during a given exposure to light than did leaves from 8-day seedlings[21].

When etiolated plants have formed a certain amount of chlorophyll in the light, the ability to liberate oxygen can go on developing, even under conditions which prevent further chlorophyll synthesis. Briggs (1920) allowed dark-grown leaves of *Phaseolus vulgaris*, *Avena sativa*, and *Vicia faba* to become partially green by exposing them to light in air, and then measured their photosynthetic oxygen evolution at daily intervals. The measurements were carried out in an atmosphere of hydrogen and carbon dioxide, and the leaves were kept in the dark between measurements, so that there was no further increase in chlorophyll content. In each case there was a steady increase, over a period of days, in the ability to evolve oxygen. Also, it has been found[176] that when dark-grown barley leaves are illuminated for 5 minutes and then kept in the dark for 110 minutes, they acquire a small but definite capacity for oxygen production.

XIII.13. Development of the Ability to fix Carbon Dioxide

Irving (1910) exposed etiolated shoots of barley and *Vicia faba* to the light for up to 60 hours and at intervals measured their ability to fix carbon dioxide in the light. No assimilation of carbon dioxide was detected in the etiolated leaves, or even in the leaves which had become distinctly green. She found that when the power of photosynthesis did finally develop, it did so very rapidly when the leaves had attained almost a full green colour. Contrary to Irving's results, Wilstätter and Stoll (1918) found that leaves which had developed only a very small proportion of their normal chlorophyll content were able to assimilate the whole of their respiratory carbon dioxide. However, Briggs (1920) points out that whereas Irving measured photosynthesis directly as the leaves greened, Wilstätter and Stoll brought about partial greening and then stored the leaves overnight in darkness before carrying out their measurements. As was discussed in the previous section, leaves which have been exposed to light continue to develop photosynthetic ability (as measured by oxygen liberation) in the dark. Furthermore, the leaves used by Wilstätter and Stoll were older than those used by Irving; a factor which also favours the development of photosynthesis.

Tolbert and Gailey (1955) exposed dark-grown wheat plants to the light, and at intervals measured their ability to incorporate $^{14}CO_2$—a much more sensitive assay for photosynthesis than the methods used by Irving, or Wilstätter and Stoll. Chlorophyll formation showed the usual kinetics—a rapid reduction of protochlorophyllide followed by a lag phase of two or three hours, and then a rapid synthesis of chlorophyll until the normal pigment content had been reached, after one and a half days. There was very little fixation of $^{14}CO_2$ during the first 4–5 hours, i.e. for two hours after rapid chlorophyll synthesis had started. After five hours the rate of fixation began to increase, and continued to increase steadily up to 32 hours, by which time it had reached the normal green plant rate. The rate of fixation of $^{14}CO_2$ increased more rapidly than the chlorophyll content (Fig. XIII.11): this indicates that as greening proceeds, the chlorophyll in the leaf becomes more efficient at promoting photosynthesis. During the first four hours only three compounds were labelled by $^{14}CO_2$ in significant amounts—malic, aspartic, and glutamic acids. At four hours, a small amount of radioactivity was detected in phosphoglyceric acid. At five hours phosphoglyceric acid and alanine were heavily labelled. After five hours ^{14}C appeared in hexose phosphates and sucrose at an increasing rate. Only trace amounts of radioactivity were found in ribulose diphosphate and sedo-

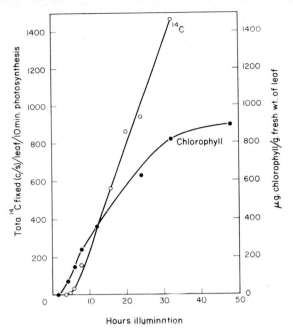

FIG. XIII.11. *Formation of chlorophyll and development of ability to fix $^{14}CO_2$ in dark-grown wheat plants exposed to light (adapted from Tolbert and Gailey, 1955)*

heptulose phosphate at five and six hours; by 25 hours sedoheptulose phosphate had accumulated significant amounts of label, but ribulose diphosphate still contained only traces of ^{14}C. These authors suggest that availability of ribulose diphosphate may be a factor limiting carbon dioxide fixation during greening: spraying the leaves with ribose (which could be converted to ribulose diphosphate) early in the greening process, caused a marked stimulation of $^{14}CO_2$ incorporation. Biggins and Park (1966) have reported a more rapid development of photosynthetic CO_2 fixation during the greening of etiolated barley. Incorporation of $^{14}CO_2$ into phosphoglyceric acid, hexose monophosphates and diphosphates was detectable after one hour's illumination. Radioactivity (8 per cent of total) appeared in sucrose after two hours' illumination; the proportion of the ^{14}C fixed into sucrose increased with time, reaching 18 per cent after three hours in the light.

During the greening of dark-grown cells of *Euglena gracilis*, the ability to fix $^{14}CO_2$ is first detected after six hours in the light[188]. After this lag, fixation increases linearly with time, in parallel with chlorophyll content, lamella formation and oxygen evolution. The optimum light intensity for development of CO_2 fixation capacity is about 100 foot-candles[187a]. When the y^- *Chlamydomonas reinhardi* mutant (see XIII.8) was grown in the dark, the cells fixed $^{14}CO_2$ only into compounds typical of dark carboxylation reactions[3]. The ability to incorporate $^{14}CO_2$ into CO_2 reduction cycle intermediates appeared during the exposure to light, increasing roughly in parallel with chlorophyll content.

As was suggested above, development of the ability to fix carbon dioxide can continue in the dark after a brief exposure to light. Photosynthetic carbon dioxide fixation by etiolated wheat seedlings develops rapidly in intermittent light[53]. If the plants are given four or five light periods followed by dark periods, during a total time of about 50 minutes, carbon dioxide fixation can then be detected in the light. The time taken for photosynthetic ability to appear is about 50 minutes, whether the total previous light exposure is 15 seconds (five three-second exposures) or 8 minutes (four two-minute exposures).

XIII.14. Formation of Chloroplast Enzymes

XIII.14.i. COMPONENTS OF THE ELECTRON TRANSPORT SYSTEM

The chloroplast contains many enzymes, particularly those concerned in photosynthesis. The activity, and hence probably the amount, of these enzymes increases during greening.

We shall first consider the enzymes involved in photosynthetic electron transport, i.e. the enzymes which use light energy to split the water molecule, liberating free oxygen and transferring the hydrogen eventually to NADP, so that it can be used in the reduction of carbon dioxide (see I.2.iv). Smith, French, and Koski (1952) allowed dark-grown barley to green in the light, and at intervals isolated chloroplasts and measured their ability to carry out the Hill reaction (the liberation of oxygen from water in the light) with 2,6-dichlorophenol-indophenol as hydrogen acceptor. Substantial activity was first detected at approximately seven hours, and it continued to increase thereafter until 50 hours. The Hill reaction activity of the chloroplasts was directly proportional to their chlorophyll content. Similarly, during greening of etiolated cells of *Euglena gracilis*, the Hill reaction activity (measured with the above dye) of chloroplast fragments increased in parallel with chlorophyll content of the cells[172, 186].

Anderson and Boardman (1964) measured the photoreduction of ferricyanide by plastids isolated from etiolated bean plants at different times during greening. Reliable evidence for reduction was not obtained until after 6 hours' illumination. Between 6 and 10 hours the rate of reduction per unit chlorophyll nearly doubled, then from 10 to 22 hours the rate per unit chlorophyll fell by about one-third (Fig. XIII.12). Since the chlorophyll content of the whole leaf was rapidly rising between 6 and 22 hours, the total ferricyanide-reducing capacity of the leaf presumably rose continually throughout this period. The finding that the plastids showed the highest photoreduction activity per unit chlorophyll at an early stage in their development (10 hours) is particularly interesting in view of the report by Stern *et al.* (1964), previously mentioned, that during greening of *E. gracilis* the highest rate of oxygen liberation per unit chlorophyll was observed after only 10 hours.

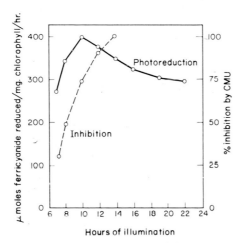

FIG. XIII.12. *Development of Hill reaction activity and changes in sensitivity of this to CMU in plastids isolated from etiolated bean leaves illuminated for various times (adapted from Anderson and Boardman, 1964)*

The Hill reaction of mature chloroplasts is inhibited by 3-(*p*-chlorophenyl)-1,1-dimethyl urea (CMU)[90]. A concentration of this inhibitor which completely blocks the Hill reaction in normal bean leaf chloroplasts had no inhibitory effect whatever on ferricyanide reduction by plastids from etiolated leaves which had been illuminated for six hours. However, plastids isolated at later times showed progressively increasing sensitivity (Fig. XIII.12): after 14 hours' illumination of the leaves, photoreduction by the isolated plastids was completely abolished by the inhibitor. These results suggest that the electron transport pathway in young plastids may not be identical with that in mature chloroplasts[2].

Anderson and Boardman also studied the development of the ability of bean plastids to photoreduce NADP (which is thought to be the natural hydrogen acceptor *in vivo*). Plastids obtained from plants which had been illuminated for eight hours had no ability to reduce this compound in the light. After 16 hours' illumination of the leaves the plastids showed a rate of photoreduction per unit chlorophyll which was about one-third that of mature chloroplasts: after 24 hours the rate per

unit chlorophyll was approximately two-thirds that of mature chloroplasts. It is interesting that the rate of NADP photoreduction was zero
at a time (eight hours) at which the rate of ferricyanide reduction per
unit chlorophyll was nearly maximal. This suggests that the component
of the electron transport pathway which is required for NADP reduction, and which is absent at 8 hours but present at 16 and 24 hours, is
one that is not involved in the photoreduction of ferricyanide.

Butler (1965) has used fluorescence measurements to follow the
development of the photosynthetic electron transport system. The
principle of the method he used is as follows. As we saw in Chapter I
(I.2.iv.b), electron flow in the chloroplast is driven by two light reactions, commonly referred to as Light Reaction I and Light Reaction II.
The pigments contributing energy to Light Reaction I, and the electron
transport components which Light Reaction I primarily affects are
referred to as System I: the pigments contributing energy to Light
Reaction II, and the electron transport components which Light
Reaction II primarily affects are referred to as System II. There is a
form of chlorophyll a which contributes absorbed light energy to Light
Reaction I, and another form which contributes absorbed light energy
to Light Reaction II. The chlorophyll a in System I is assumed to be
non-fluorescent, or weakly fluorescent. The chlorophyll a in System II
is thought to be fluorescent, with a variable yield which depends on the
oxidation state of one of the electron carriers, Q (which might possibly
be plastoquinone). The oxidized form of Q, Q^{ox}, is thought to quench
the fluorescence of System II chlorophyll a, but the reduced form,
Q^{red}, is thought not to quench this fluorescence. Light absorbed by
System II pigments causes the reduction of Q^{ox} to Q^{red}, thus bringing
about an increase in the fluorescence yield of System II chlorophyll a.
Light absorbed by System I pigments causes the oxidation of Q^{red} to
Q^{ox}, via the electron transport chain, bringing about a reduction in the
fluorescence yield. Fig. XIII.13 shows a simplified version of the
electron transport chain in which the relationship of Q to Light
Reactions I and II may be seen. Thus, by investigating the effects, on
fluorescence yield, of actinic light (light intense enough to bring about
photosynthetic effects) absorbed by System I pigments or System II
pigments, it is possible to tell whether System I and System II are in

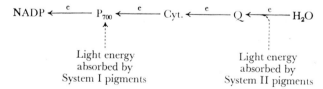

*Fig. XIII.13. Simplified version of photosynthetic electron transport system (adapted from
Butler, 1965)*

operation. Butler used this technique on leaves of dark-grown *Phaseolus vulgaris* exposed to light. During the first 1·5 hours of illumination, actinic light induced no changes in the chlorophyll fluorescence yield, indicating that neither System I nor System II was functioning. During this period the *in vivo* absorption peak of the chlorophyll *a* was at about 670 mμ (presumably after the usual Shibata shift from 684 mμ). After two hours light, there was a slight change in the fluorescence yield in response to actinic light. Chlorophyll *b* was now detectable. At this point (*ca.* the end of the lag phase of chlorophyll synthesis) the chlorophyll *a* was beginning to differentiate into the forms with *in vivo* absorption peaks at 673 and 683 mμ (see XIII.6). Chlorophyll-705, a pigment detected by its fluorescence properties, which Butler considers to be identical with P700 (chlorophyll a_I—see I.2.iv.b), was also first detectable after two hours. All these changes increased markedly on further illumination. The fluorescence yield measurements indicated that System I and System II were active as soon as their pigments appeared. The two pigment systems appeared to become operative at roughly the same time—about two hours. Brody *et al.* (1965), in their fluorescence studies on greening cells of *Euglena gracilis* (XIII.6) found that photosynthetic ability began to rise at about the same time (15 hours' illumination) as the fluorescence from aggregated chlorophyll began its very sharp increase. They believe that the presence of aggregated chlorophyll is a necessary condition for photosynthesis.

As well as these studies on the development of activity of whole sections of the electron transport chain, the synthesis of individual components of the chain has also been examined. Dark-grown cells of *Euglena gracilis* contain only traces of plastoquinone: illumination of such cells results in the synthesis of plastoquinone in parallel with chlorophyll formation[190]. *Euglena* cytochrome-552, which is found only in chloroplasts[171], is absent from etiolated cells[142]. During greening of etiolated cells, cytochrome-552 is formed together with chlorophyll[216, 171]. The molar ratio of chlorophyll to cytochrome-552 is higher at early, than at late, stages of greening[148]: after 4·5 hours' illumination the ratio is 2500: this falls to 945 after 8 hours, and from 25 hours to the completion of greening at 127 hours, remains at a fairly steady level in the region of 350. Another *Euglena* chloroplast cytochrome, of the cytochrome b_6 type, is also synthesized during greening[172].

Ferredoxin appears to be absent from leaves of *Phaseolus vulgaris* grown in the dark[95]: this component is synthesized if the leaves are exposed to light. There is some indication that if the leaves are given a brief exposure to white light (1·5 hours), then they continue to synthesize ferredoxin during a subsequent incubation in the dark. When cells of a *y* mutant of *Chlamydomonas reinhardi* are grown for 96 hours in the dark[83] their chlorophyll content decreases tenfold due to dilution, but their ferredoxin level decreases only threefold (suggesting that there is some synthesis in the dark). When the cells are returned to light, there is a lag period and then, at about the same time as chlorophyll content begins to increase, the ferredoxin level also begins to increase, both reaching values typical of light-grown cells. However, the ratio of ferredoxin activity to chlorophyll is not constant during greening.

Leaves of *Phaseolus vulgaris* grown in the dark were found to have a low, but measurable level of activity of the flavoprotein enzyme which transfers hydrogen from ferredoxin to NADP: after two days, with 10 hours' light each day, the enzyme activity increased by up to fifty-fold[95]. When the leaves were given a brief exposure (1·5 hours) to white light, then during a subsequent two-day incubation in the dark, there was some increase, in the region of threefold, in enzyme activity in the dark, but much less than in the leaves given two 10-hour light periods during the two days. Dark-grown cells of *Euglena gracilis* were found to have substantial levels of this enzyme, about one-quarter to one-third of the level in light-grown cells[116]. When the cells were exposed to light, after a lag period of about 14 hours the enzyme was synthesized in parallel with chlorophyll synthesis. The formation of the enzyme is closely linked to light-driven processes, because when cells growing in the light were put in the dark, the rate of enzyme synthesis immediately fell to the rate typical of cells growing in the dark. It is possible that this enzyme is firmly bound to the thylakoids *in vivo*, and its formation may therefore be closely linked to the formation of the thylakoid membrane, in higher plants at least[95]. In *Euglena*, it would seem that at least some of the enzyme (or another enzyme having similar effects) can exist separately from the thylakoids.

The final acceptor in the electron transport chain is NADP. It is not known whether there is net synthesis *de novo* of NADP in etiolated plants greening in the light. However, when green plants are transferred from darkness to light, it appears that there is a conversion of NAD to NADP[146]. The ratio of $(NADP + NADPH_2)$ to $(NAD + NADH_2)$ is about 0·4 in bean leaves in the dark, and this rises to 2·0 in the light. When the plants are put back in the dark, NADP is re-converted to NAD. In this way the plant ensures that the particular pyridine nucleotide most suitable for the type of metabolism going on, is the one present in the largest amount.

XIII.14.ii. ENZYMES OF CARBON DIOXIDE FIXATION AND OTHER METABOLIC PROCESSES

As well as the electron transport carriers, another group of enzymes, those of the carbon dioxide fixation pathway, is involved in photosynthesis (see I.2.iv.c). The chloroplast enzyme which is thought to carry out the initial reaction with carbon dioxide is carboxydismutase: this catalyses the conversion of one molecule of ribulose diphosphate plus one molecule of carbon dioxide, to two molecules of phosphoglyceric acid. Carboxydismutase appears to be identical with Fraction I protein[204,124]. In dark-grown wheat seedlings the relative amount of Fraction I protein (i.e. as a proportion of the proteins in the extracts) was only about a quarter of the amount in light-grown wheat seedlings; when the etiolated seedlings were put in the light, the relative amount of Fraction I protein increased threefold in 20 hours[123]. Dark-grown barley seedlings have a certain amount of carboxydismutase activity. On exposure of the seedlings to light, the enzyme activity increases five- to sixfold, in a linear manner, in 48 hours[85]. Carboxydismutase activity also increases about fourfold when etiolated bean leaves are exposed to light for 48 hours[128]. Dark-grown cells of *Euglena gracilis* contain about 14 per cent of the carboxydismutase activity of light-grown cells[51]: the activity increases four- to sevenfold during greening in the light[186]. When cells of a *y* mutant of *Chlamydomonas reinhardi* are grown for 96 hours in the dark, the carboxydismutase level decreases threefold, although the chlorophyll content decreases tenfold[83]. When the cells are placed back in the light, carboxydismutase activity begins to increase shortly after the onset of chlorophyll synthesis. A normal level of enzyme activity is regained shortly after the chlorophyll content has once again reached the value found in light-grown cells.

From all these findings it appears that although carboxydismutase does increase in the light, nevertheless plants grown in the dark contain substantial amounts of activity, 14–33 per cent of the activity possessed by green plants.

The phosphoglyceric acid produced by the carboxydismutase reaction is reduced to phosphoglyceraldehyde. One of the enzymes involved is the glyceraldehyde phosphate dehydrogenase (working in reverse) which uses $NADPH_2$ rather than $NADH_2$ as hydrogen donor. This enzyme is located exclusively in the chloroplasts (of higher plant leaves and of *E. gracilis*— see I.2.iv.d), and is present in the leaves and stem of the plant but not in the roots[56]. Pea seedlings grown in the dark do not possess this enzyme, but when such seedlings are placed in the light there is a rapid development of activity which ceases after 48 hours[73]: the enzyme is also formed when etiolated bean leaves are exposed to the light[128]. Dark-grown cells of *E. gracilis* contain none of the NADP-requiring glyceraldehyde phosphate dehydrogenase; when the cells are illuminated enzyme activity appears (Fig. XIII.14) and increases in parallel with chlorophyll[19].

Fuller and Hudock (1965) found that when green cells of a *y* mutant

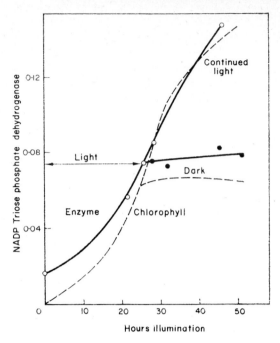

FIG. XIII.14. *Formation of NADP-requiring glyceraldehyde phosphate dehydrogenase by dark-grown cells of* Euglena gracilis *in the light (adapted from Brawerman and Konigsberg, 1960). After ca. 25 hours, one batch of cells returned to the dark.*
Enzyme ——————— Chlorophyll – – – – –

of *Chlamydomonas reinhardi* were put to grow in the dark, the level of NADP-requiring glyceraldehyde phosphate dehydrogenase immediately began to decrease, together with the chlorophyll content: the enzyme activity had completely disappeared after 80 hours. During this time the NAD-requiring glyceraldehyde phosphate dehydrogenase activity per cell increased by about 40 per cent. When the cells were returned to light, then as chlorophyll synthesis recommenced, the NADP-requiring enzyme was formed again and eventually, after about 70 hours, reached twice its normal activity per cell: as this took place, the activity of the NAD-requiring enzyme decreased to the normal level again. The NAD- and NADP-requiring enzymes appear to be similar in their physical properties. In view of this, and in view also of the kinetics of formation of the NADP-requiring enzyme, and decrease in the level of the NAD-requiring enzyme, Fuller and Hudock suggest that these enzymes may be interconvertible: that just as NAD is apparently converted to NADP in the light[146], so NAD-requiring glyceraldehyde phosphate dehydrogenase may be converted to the NADP-requiring enzyme in the light. This view is supported by the observation[128] that in etiolated *Phaseolus* leaves exposed to the light, a concentration of chloramphenicol (an inhibitor of protein synthesis) which abolished the increase in carboxydismutase activity, had no effect on the increase in the NADP-requiring triose phosphate dehydrogenase activity: this could mean that an increase in the activity of this enzyme does not require protein synthesis. In this connection it is interesting that Ziegler and Ziegler (1965) observed a very rapid increase in the activity of NADP-requiring glyceraldehyde phosphate dehydrogenase when green leaves of various plant species were transferred from dark to light. For instance, in the case of *Vicia faba* leaves, the activity of the enzyme increased by 250 per cent in about 20 minutes. When the leaves were transferred from light to dark the activity fell by 67 per cent in about 20 minutes. The extreme rapidity of these changes, and in particular the fact that activity decreases immediately in the dark, makes it seem unlikely that the light-induced increase in enzyme activity is due to net synthesis of the enzyme. Chloramphenicol inhibits the increase in activity by about 50 per cent: Ziegler and Ziegler conclude from this that the increase in activity does indeed involve synthesis of the enzyme. However, a very high concentration of chloramphenicol (2·5 mg/ml) was used, and it seems entirely likely that at this high concentration, chloramphenicol might inhibit other metabolic processes as well as protein synthesis. Fuller and Hudock's hypothesis that NAD-requiring glyceraldehyde phosphate dehydrogenase can be reversibly converted to the NADP-requiring enzyme might well explain these data. Alternatively, it might be that the NADP-requiring enzyme undergoes an allosteric transition from a relatively inactive, to an active, form, as a result of a reaction with some metabolite produced in a light-dependent process. When the leaves are put back in the dark, the concentration of the metabolite falls, and the enzyme reverts to its inactive form. In dark-grown cells of *Euglena gracilis* exposed to light for 25 hours, there is no change in the activity of the NAD-requiring enzyme, although the activity of the NADP-requiring enzyme increases five- to sixfold. Hudock and Fuller (1965) conclude that in this organism there is no conversion of the NAD-requiring enzyme to the NADP-requiring form.

The glyceraldehyde phosphate produced by the above enzyme combines with dihydroxyacetone phosphate, under the influence of the enzyme aldolase, to give fructose-1,6-diphosphate. At least 50 per cent, but probably not more than 80 per cent of this enzyme is localized in the chloroplasts (see I.2.iv.d). The presence of aldolase outside the chloroplasts is to be expected since this enzyme is involved in the non-photosynthetic carbohydrate metabolism of the cells. Similarly, it is not surprising that the enzyme is present in cells of *E. gracilis* grown in the dark[171]. However, whereas Smillie (1963) finds that green cells have only slightly more aldolase than cells grown in the dark with sucrose as carbon source, Spier (1964) finds that cells of *E. gracilis* grown in the dark, with acetate as carbon source, show a thirty- to fortyfold increase in activity when illuminated for 24 hours. This discrepancy may well be due to the different carbon sources used for heterotrophic growth, aldolase perhaps being more necessary for the metabolism of sucrose than for the metabolism of acetate.

Before the fructose-1,6-diphosphate formed by aldolase action can be further metabolized in photosynthesis, its C-1 phosphate must be removed. It is thought that this step is carried out by a fructose diphosphatase with an alkaline pH optimum[152]. This enzyme is confined to the chloroplasts in higher plant leaves and in *E. gracilis*. It is present in pea leaves but not in roots; etiolated pea leaves have less than 5 per cent of the activity of green pea leaves[170]. When dark-grown cells of *E. gracilis* are put in the light, fructose diphosphatase activity increases roughly in parallel with chlorophyll content[4, 171]. The activity per cell increases altogether about fourfold during greening.

The fructose-6-phosphate produced by the action of fructose diphosphatase is converted by various enzymes to a number of other phosphorylated sugars, one of which is ribose-5-phosphate. For this to be transformed into ribulose-1,5-diphosphate (thus completing the cycle by regenerating the CO_2 acceptor) two enzymes are required, one of which is phosphoriboisomerase, which converts ribose-5-phosphate to ribulose-5-phosphate. In *E. gracilis* phosphoriboisomerase is found both in the chloroplasts and in the rest of the cell (Table I.7) Dark-grown barley seedlings were found to have quite high phosphoriboisomerase activity: when the seedlings were exposed to light, after an initial lag period, phosphoriboisomerase activity doubled by 24 hours, and then remained constant[85].

An enzyme which may have a function in photosynthesis is glycollic oxidase, although there is some disagreement as to whether it occurs in the chloroplasts[36, 94]. However, in view of the various theories as to the possible function of this enzyme, it is interesting that its activity increased about fourfold when dark-grown wheat seedlings were exposed to light for 24 hours[191]. An even greater increase was obtained when the seedlings were sprayed with glycollic acid and then incubated in the dark for 24 hours. This might be regarded as a straightforward case of induction of synthesis of an enzyme by its substrate. However, a puzzling feature of these experiments was that just as large an increase in activity was obtained when the sap of etiolated pea plants was incubated with glycollate for 18 hours at 1°. Net synthesis of an enzyme could not take place under such conditions: this might suggest that the increases in enzyme activity were due to activation, by glycollate, of some enzyme precursor. Kuczmak and Tolbert (1962) have found that the increase in activity of the whole leaves, or of the sap, can also be brought about by treatment with flavin mononucleotide. The total enzyme activity which can be revealed by excess flavin mononucleotide is two to three times as great in extracts of green leaves as in extracts of etiolated leaves. There may, therefore, be some actual synthesis, as well as activation of the enzyme precursors during greening.

Another enzyme of glycollic acid metabolism which is present in plants is phosphoglycollate phosphatase, which hydrolyses the phosphate off phosphoglycollic acid. In leaves it appears that at least some of the enzyme may be associated with the chloroplasts[220]. Roots of wheat plants have about one-fifth of the enzyme activity per g. wet weight that etiolated leaves have. The etiolated leaves, in turn, have about one-tenth the activity of green leaves. When etiolated leaves are exposed to light the activity of this enzyme increases, reaching about 30 per cent of the green leaf level in 24 hours[220].

Barley seedlings which have been grown in the dark have a very low level of nitrate reductase activity: this level increases greatly when the seedlings are put in the light[153]. When dark-grown seedlings are exposed to light for a few hours and then returned to darkness, nitrate reductase activity continues to increase for some time.

XIII.14.iii. BIOSYNTHETIC ENZYMES

Chloroplasts contain a number of biosynthetic enzymes (see Chapter XII). Since the rate of synthesis of most, and possibly all, chloroplast components increases from a low level (or zero) at the start of greening to a high, maximum level after some hours greening, then it seems very likely that there is, during greening, synthesis of most, and possibly all, of the enzymes involved in the biosynthesis of these chloroplast components. As far as chlorophyll synthesis is concerned, it is known that a brief exposure to light increases the ability of etiolated leaves to form protochlorophyllide (see XIII.18): this may well be due largely to an increased synthesis of δ-aminolaevulinic acid synthetase. Also when dark-grown cells of a strain of *Cyanidium caldarium* which does not make chlorophyll or phycobilins in the dark, are incubated for 24 hours in the dark with 7×10^{-3}M δ-aminolaevulinic acid, they excrete porphobilinogen, porphyrins, and a phycobilin pigment into the medium[194]. If the cells are first illuminated for 24 hours, then two to three times as much porphyrins and phycobilin are excreted during the incubation with δ-aminolaevulinic acid in the dark. Presumably, therefore, during the 24 hours' illumination there is an increase in some or all of the enzymes involved in the synthesis of these materials from δ-aminolaevulinic acid. The increase in ability to synthesize porphyrins and phycobilin is prevented if chloramphenicol is present during the pre-incubation in the light, suggesting that this increased synthetic ability is indeed due to *de novo* formation of enzymes.

The chloroplast enzyme chlorophyllase hydrolyses chlorophyll *a* to chlorophyllide *a* and phytol, and it can also reverse the reaction to an appreciable extent[211, 166]. It is often assumed that it is chlorophyllase which brings about the phytylation of chlorophyllide *a* to chlorophyll *a* *in vivo*, but this is by no means certain. Dark-grown pea seedlings were found to have only 25 per cent of the chlorophyllase activity of light-grown seedlings: when the etiolated seedlings were exposed to light, the chlorophyllase activity rose in parallel with chlorophyll content, and in two days reached approximately the same level as in the light-grown seedlings[81].

Green cells of *Euglena gracilis* have four times as high a level of the ACP (the Acyl Carrier Protein which functions in fatty acid synthesis— see XII.5.i) as etiolated cells[12]. Also, a soluble enzyme which converts stearyl ACP to oleate (possibly via oleyl ACP) is present in green cells but absent from dark-grown cells. Presumably, therefore, these enzymes would be synthesized during greening of etiolated cells.

It seems very likely that other enzymes concerned with the biosynthesis of plastid materials also increase in the light, but at the moment little evidence is available.

XIII.15. Protein Metabolism during Greening

Approximately 70 per cent of the dry weight of chloroplasts consists of protein, and as much as 75 per cent of the protein of the leaf cell may be found in these organelles (see I.2.ii.a). Mature chloroplasts are larger than etioplasts and so, as might be expected, the greening of etiolated plants involves the synthesis of large amounts of protein. De Deken-Grenson (1954) found that when excised etiolated chicory leaves were exposed to light, the protein content of the isolated plastid fraction increased by 210 per cent in two days: the protein content of the whole leaf rose by about 60 per cent in this time. During the greening of etiolated *Phaseolus vulgaris* leaves, the nitrogen content per plastid increased by 180 per cent in two days[132]. Brawerman and Chargaff (1959) reported that on illumination of dark-grown cells of *Euglena gracilis* suspended in buffered glucose solution, the amount of protein in the plastid fraction rose by 65 per cent in 44 hours; however, in this case the protein content of the whole cells remained constant.

Although greening may be stimulated by the addition of certain nutrients (see XIII.6), it can take place to an appreciable extent in the absence of any external source of carbon or nitrogen; as, for instance, in the case of excised leaves floated on distilled water, or cells of *E. gracilis* suspended in buffer. This raises the question of what is the source (under these conditions) of the amino acids required for the synthesis of all the new chloroplast proteins. In the case of chicory leaves the etiolated cells were found to contain a very large amount of free amino acids, and this decreased by 90 per cent during a two-day incubation in the light: the decrease is sufficient to account for the increase in the protein content of the chloroplasts and other cell fractions[35]. In this instance, therefore, it appears likely that all the amino acids required can be, and are, taken from the pool. Dark-grown cells of *E. gracilis*, however, have only a small quantity of free amino acids in the pool— in the region of 0·9–1·5 μg free amino nitrogen per mg dry weight of cells—and this was found to decrease by only 0·11 μg free amino nitrogen per mg dry weight during a 12-hour incubation in the light[97]. In the course of this incubation 11·4 μg of chlorophyll was synthesized per mg dry weight. Since there was 1·0 μg of chlorophyll per mg dry weight of cells present at the start of the incubation, there would be a total of 12·4 μg of chlorophyll per mg dry weight present at the end of the incubation. This amount of chlorophyll would be expected to have about 170 μg of chloroplast protein associated with it (see Table I.1). By comparison with Brawerman and Chargaff's figures, it seems likely that in such a 12-hour incubation, the protein content of the plastids would have increased by at least 18 per cent: in view of the unusually rapid rate of greening in this particular strain of *E. gracilis*, 18 per cent is probably very much an underestimate in this case. From these data, it may be calculated that associated with the formation of 11·4 μg of chlorophyll, there would be synthesis of at least 26 μg of chloroplast protein, and probably much more. If the amino acids for the synthesis of this protein had been derived solely from the amino acids of the pool, then the free amino nitrogen content of the pool should have fallen by at least 3·20 μg per mg dry weight of cells, which is two or three times greater than the total free amino nitrogen originally present. These results suggest that if amino acids are taken from the pool for the synthesis of chloroplast proteins, then the pool is replenished by the breakdown of other proteins or peptides.

If the amino acids for the synthesis of chloroplast proteins are provided by the breakdown of other proteins, then it might be expected that the protein content of some other cellular fraction(s) would decrease during greening. Brawerman and Chargaff (1959) observed that when dark-grown cells of *E. gracilis* were exposed to light for 44 hours, the increase in the protein content of the plastid fraction was approximately balanced by a decrease in the protein content of the supernatant (after centrifugation at 100,000 g) fraction. These workers also found that the turnover of protein (as measured by the incorporation of ^{14}C-leucine) in the etiolated cells was much greater when they were exposed to light than when they were kept in the dark. However,

29—P.

the stimulatory effect of light on leucine incorporation was no greater in the chloroplast fraction than in any other cell fraction; this was surprising in view of the fact that the chloroplast showed a substantial increase in protein content during greening, whereas none of the other fractions did. To explain these findings, Brawerman and Chargaff tentatively suggested that the increase in chloroplast protein simply involved the transference of intact proteins from other cell fractions to the chloroplasts; that the process did not involve any preferential synthesis of protein in the chloroplasts. However, since this work was done, many reports have appeared of marked increases in the activity of various chloroplast enzymes during the greening of *E. gracilis* and other plants (see XIII.14). These findings suggest that chloroplast formation under these circumstances does involve the synthesis of new proteins. Further evidence that greening in *E. gracilis* requires protein synthesis is provided by the fact that greening is inhibited by antibiotics such as chloramphenicol and actidione, which inhibit protein synthesis (see XV.3). The results of Brawerman and Chargaff might be explained if the occurrence of net protein synthesis in a particular organelle tended to eliminate, or reduce, turnover. Thus the stimulation of leucine incorporation by light in the chloroplasts could be due to net synthesis with little turnover: the stimulation in the other fractions could be due to increased turnover without net synthesis. In this connection it is perhaps relevant that certain non-plastid enzymes are synthesized during the early stages of greening, and are then broken down again (see XIII.17). As far as ^{14}C-leucine incorporation is concerned, this synthesis and breakdown would show up as increased protein turnover in non-plastid cell fractions. Considering all the evidence, it appears most likely that the increase in chloroplast protein in *E. gracilis* is not due to transference of intact proteins from other parts of the cell, but to the breakdown of other cell proteins and the re-utilization of the amino acids produced for the synthesis of chloroplast protein. The fact that the amino acid content of the pool remains fairly constant during greening suggests that the amino acids are re-utilized as soon as they are liberated.

Experiments with antibiotics (see Chapter XV) have yielded some interesting information about the involvement of protein synthesis in the greening process. One conclusion is that chlorophyll synthesis in *Euglena gracilis* at any rate, is completely dependent upon protein synthesis. Concentrations of actidione as low as 3 μg/ml abolish chlorophyll synthesis in dark-grown cells of *E. gracilis* exposed to light[98]. In principle, this might be due to inhibition of formation of enzymes required for chlorophyll synthesis. If this is so then the addition of actidione after greening has commenced should permit chlorophyll synthesis to continue at the same rate (with the enzymes already present), although it should prevent any further acceleration of chlorophyll synthesis. In fact, however, addition of actidione after four hours' greening caused a marked diminution in the rate of chlorophyll synthesis[98]. Similarly, addition of chloramphenicol or puromycin to etiolated bean leaves greening in the light, stops further chlorophyll synthesis even when the antibiotics are not added until the rapid phase of synthesis is under way[54]. To explain their results with bean leaves, Gassman and Bogorad (1965) suggest that the enzymes of δ-aminolaevulinic acid synthesis undergo rapid turnover, so that when they cease to be made, they rapidly disappear from the cell. This hypothesis would certainly explain the bean data, and also the effects of actidione on chlorophyll synthesis in *Euglena*. However, an alternative explanation put forward by Kirk and Allen (1965), is that chlorophyll synthesis requires the formation of some protein in stoichiometric, rather than catalytic (as in the case of an enzyme) amounts. This protein might, for instance, be the protein in the thylakoids to which the chlorophyll is bound: a shortage of this protein might be expected to prevent removal of the chlorophyllide (or chlorophyll, whichever it is) from the protochlorophyllide holochrome protein, thus preventing the holochrome protein from being used for the photoreduction of more protochlorophyllide.

Another conclusion which is suggested by the experiments with actidione, is that carotenoid formation is much less dependent on protein synthesis than is chlorophyll formation. Synthesis of carotenoids by etiolated cells of *Euglena gracilis* in the light is inhibited by actidione, but the inhibition is only about one-third that of chlorophyll synthesis[98]. The inhibition of carotenoid synthesis may well be due to the antibiotic preventing the formation of the enzymes of the carotenoid biosynthetic pathway: it is not surprising that the inhibition is so slight because the etiolated cells must already have enzymes for carotenoid formation, since they form these pigments in the dark as well as in the light. If actidione is added four hours after greening has commenced, there is no actual diminution in carotenoid synthesis; it is, therefore, not necessary to postulate for carotenoid synthesis either that some protein is required in stoichiometric amounts, or that the enzymes are unstable. It seems likely that the carotenoids, unlike the chlorophylls, can accumulate to some extent even when chloroplast protein synthesis is blocked.

XIII.16. Nucleic Acid Metabolism during Greening

Chloroplasts are known to contain substantial amounts of RNA (see Chapter X). It is, therefore, not surprising that there is an increase in the RNA content of plastids during greening. In dark-grown cells of *Euglena gracilis* the isolated plastid fraction was found to contain 11 per cent of the RNA of the cell: after 44 hours in the light, in the absence of external nutrients, this increased to 18 per cent[18]. The total RNA content of the cells did not change during greening under these conditions (no added nutrients). However, in cells of *E. gracilis* illuminated under conditions supporting autotrophic growth (CO_2, nitrogen source, salts supplied) the RNA content increased by 40 per cent in 12 hours, and thereafter remained approximately constant[172].

Pool extracts of etiolated cells of *E. gracilis* have quite a high optical density at 260 mμ: 1 mg dry weight of cells extracted with 1 ml of 0·2N $HClO_4$ gives an OD_{260} of about 0·3[96]. If all the OD_{260} is due to purine and pyrimidine bases, nucleosides, and nucleotides, then there are enough nucleic acid precursors present in the pool to support the synthesis of about 10 μg RNA per mg dry weight of cells, which is in the region of 25 per cent of the normal RNA content of the cells. Thus the increase in plastid RNA which takes place in the absence of added nutrients could possibly be supplied from the RNA precursors already present in the pool. However, when etiolated cells of *E. gracilis* were incubated for 12 hours in the light, under these conditions, there was no fall in the OD_{260} of the pool extracts; indeed there was a rise of about 20 per cent[96, 97]. This might mean that the nucleoside triphosphates used in the synthesis of plastid RNA are synthesized *de novo* from carbohydrates and amino acids rather than from purine- and pyrimidine-containing compounds already in the pool: alternatively, the purine- and pyrimidine-compounds already present might be utilized, but be replaced either by *de novo* synthesis, or by breakdown of other RNA molecules in the cell. It is of interest in this connection that the turnover of the RNA in the dark-grown cells (measured by the incorporation of ^{14}C-adenine) is markedly stimulated—about 80 per cent—by the exposure to light[18]. Also, the ribonuclease activity of dark-grown cells of *E. gracilis* increases about threefold during the first 12 hours of illumination[172]: during the next 36 hours the activity falls to its original level again. The ribonuclease activity might increase in order to break down certain cellular RNA molecules to provide precursors for plastid RNA synthesis. The inhibitory effect of hadacidin (which blocks adenylate synthesis) on greening in *E. gracilis* (XV.3.iv) suggests that much of the adenylic acid required has to be synthesized.

If the etiolated cells of *E. gracilis* are supplied with nitrogenous nutrients during greening, then a greater increase in plastid RNA and protein takes place. Brawerman, Pogo, and Chargaff (1962) found that when cells were incubated in the light with yeast extract and ammonium sulphate, in addition to the usual phosphate buffer, magnesium chloride, and glucose, the RNA content of the plastid fraction and of the combined mitochondrial and microsomal fractions increased rapidly, without any lag, for about 48 hours (Fig. XIII.15). Plastid protein content, on the other hand, showed little increase for about 20 hours, and then rose rapidly between 20 and 60 hours. These workers suggested that the RNA produced in the early stages of chloroplast formation consists mainly of specific ribosomal material necessary for the synthesis of plastid proteins.

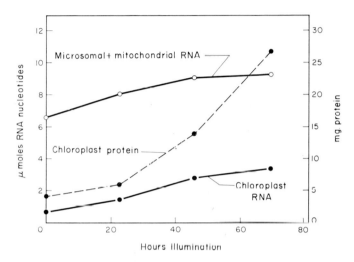

FIG. XIII.15. *Increase in protein and RNA content of some subcellular fractions of dark-grown cells of Euglena gracilis exposed to light in resting medium supplemented with yeast extract and ammonium sulphate (adapted from Brawerman, Pogo, and Chargaff, 1962)*

Some similar studies have now been carried out on higher plants. The RNA content of a single leaf of 16–18-day-old dark-grown *Phaseolus vulgaris* is about 400 μg: during the 45 hours it takes for greening to occur in the light, the RNA content of the leaf rises to about 500 μg[72]. Of the 400 μg RNA present in the etiolated leaf, about 50 μg is associated with the plastids. The RNA content of the plastids remains constant during the first 15 hours of greening. Between 15 and 20 hours, the RNA content of the plastid fraction increases to about 100 μg, and from then on remains more or less constant. The doubling of the plastid RNA content takes place at about the time when the steep increase in rate of chlorophyll synthesis and grana formation begins. Von Wettstein (1965) suggests that this may indicate a doubling of the plastid ribosomes just prior to the synthesis of large amounts of thylakoid material.

The synthesis of types of RNA, other than ribosomal RNA, in etiolated plant cells is also stimulated by light. Sucrose density gradient analysis of RNA isolated from dark-grown cells of *Euglena gracilis* at different times during exposure to light, indicated that there was a marked increase, not only in the amounts of the two species of RNA thought to originate in the ribosomes, but also in the amount of a low molecular weight RNA which might possibly have been transfer RNA[172]. Illumination of etiolated maize leaves increased the incorporation of radioactivity from ^{32}P-phosphate or ^{14}C-uridine into all the RNA species detected by sucrose density gradient analysis[16]: the stimulation of incorporation into plastid RNA was much greater than into cytoplasmic RNA. There are a number of indications that messenger RNA is synthesized in etiolated plants exposed to light. Statistical analysis of electron micrographs of oat leaves has shown that in the etioplasts of the dark-grown plants the ribosomes are distributed essentially at random in the stroma, but after two hours' illumination a large proportion of the ribosomes are in clusters[24]. It seems likely that these ribosomal clusters are polyribosomes formed by attachment of the ribosomes to messenger RNA produced in the light. Also, the ability of ribosome preparations, isolated from dark-grown maize or bean leaves, to carry out protein synthesis *in vitro* was enhanced by 50–200 per cent if the leaves were given 30–60 minutes' exposure to white light, followed by two hours' darkness, before isolation was carried out[208]. The stimulatory effect was observed even when the *in vitro* measurements of protein synthesis were carried out with a supernatant fraction (that is, the source of activating enzymes, transfer RNA etc.) isolated from unilluminated leaves. This shows that it is the ribosomes that are the site of the stimulation. Sucrose density gradient analysis of the ribosome preparations suggested that the increase in activity could be attributed to a small, but consistent, increase in the proportion of polyribosomes present[209]. The light treatment also stimulated incorporation of ^{32}P-phosphate into the RNA of the leaves: this effect accompanied or preceded the increase in ribosome activity[207]. The RNA species, incorporation into which was most stimulated by the light treatment, was an RNA of high specific activity which moved as a diffuse band, of sedimentation constant between 7 S and 18 S, on a sucrose gradient. It is tempting to suppose that this is, or includes, messenger RNA. Red light had about as big a stimulatory effect as white light: blue light was much less effective, and green light had no significant stimulatory action. When the length of the dark incubation before isolation of the ribosomes was varied, it was found with maize that there was only about 8 per cent stimulation 1 hour after the end of the light treatment, 22–35 per cent stimulation 1·5 hours after, and 52–78 per cent stimulation 2 hours after. That is, there is a distinct lag period of about an hour before the stimulatory effect is felt. If the maize plants are kept for a long time in the dark after the illumination then the stimulatory effect decays, disappearing within 40 hours.

It is clear from these various findings that illumination of etiolated leaves causes a marked stimulation of the synthesis of plastid RNA, and possibly also of non-plastid RNA. In particular, it appears that there is formation of plastid ribosomes, and also of the messenger RNA molecules which the ribosomes use as templates for the synthesis of chloroplast proteins. Probably also new transfer RNA molecules are formed to assist in this protein synthesis. That formation of new RNA is absolutely essential for chloroplast formation, and does not merely happen coincidentally, is shown by the fact that agents such as actinomycin and fluorouracil, which specifically inhibit RNA synthesis, also inhibit chloroplast formation (see Chapter XV). Since chloroplast formation is under the control of both plastid and nuclear genes (see Chapter XI) it seems likely that both plastid and nuclear DNA are directing the synthesis of these new messenger RNA molecules. The formation of the plastid ribosomal RNA is probably directed by the plastid DNA (XI.7). Since certain non-plastid proteins are also synthesized during greening (see XIII.17), it seems likely that non-plastid messenger and other RNA species are also formed.

During greening of an etiolated leaf of *Phaseolus vulgaris* the number of plastids per leaf remains constant at about 2×10^{8}[72]. Also, at the end of the greening of a dark-grown cell of *Ochromonas danica*[57] or a dark-grown *y* mutant of *Chlamydomonas reinhardi*[160], there is still only one plastid per cell. During greening of *Euglena gracilis* there may even be a reduction in the number of plastids per cell from about thirty to about ten[9]. Thus, it appears to be generally true that greening of mature, etiolated cells does not involve multiplication of plastids, although it seems possible that there might be some plastid multiplication during greening of young leaves which have not yet formed their full plastid complement. This being so, there would seem to be no reason why greening of mature cells should involve any synthesis of plastid DNA. In accordance with this, no change in the DNA content of the plastid fraction during greening of dark-grown *Phaseolus vulgaris* leaves was detected[72].

XIII.17. Endogenous Energy Sources for Greening

As well as the actual chemical precursors of the proteins, nucleic acids, lipids, and pigments of the chloroplast, the cell requires energy in order to build these precursors up into the finished molecules. The cell gains such energy by oxidizing carbohydrate or lipid, or both. The necessity for oxidative metabolism in greening was demonstrated by Boehm (1865), who showed that etiolated plants would not form chlorophyll if illuminated in an atmosphere of pure nitrogen, hydrogen, or carbon dioxide. Chlorophyll synthesis by dark-grown cells of *Euglena gracilis* in the light occurs at only one-tenth the rate in an atmosphere of nitrogen, as it does in air[172]. Also, compounds which block mitochondrial electron transport or uncouple oxidation from phosphorylation, virtually abolish greening (XV.6). The reserve material of most higher plant seeds is fat, as for instance, in castor oil seeds: in some, however, as in the case of wheat, barley, and maize, the reserve material is polysaccharide. During germination in the dark (or in the light) of those seeds whose reserve is lipid in nature, the fats are converted to carbohydrates, so that in the actual etiolated plant the reserves will be at least partly, and probably mostly, carbohydrate in nature, whatever the reserve material of the seed was. In etiolated corn seedlings, a brief exposure to white light, which initiates plastid development (see next section), was found to cause a 25–73 per cent fall in starch content, during a subsequent 24-hour incubation in the dark[103].

The reserve material in etiolated cells of *Euglena gracilis* is the polysaccharide paramylon: this occurs in large granules which are found outside the plastid. Structurally this substance is a $1:3$-β-glucan[32]. At least 94 per cent of the insoluble carbohydrate (estimated by the anthrone procedure) of the dark-grown cells is found in the paramylon fraction[96], and this polysaccharide accounts for about 50 per cent of the dry weight of the cells[97]. When etiolated cells of *E. gracilis* were allowed to green for six hours in the light, in the absence of a carbon source, the insoluble carbohydrate content (which means, in effect, the paramylon content) of the cells fell by 28 per cent[97]: during the same time in the dark, the paramylon content fell by only 18 per cent, indicating that light increases the rate of paramylon utilization by over 50 per cent. During prolonged incubations in the light (Fig. XIII.16), the paramylon content falls to approximately zero in 24 hours[172].

Smillie, Evans, and Lyman (1964) found that early on in the greening of etiolated cells of *E. gracilis* there was a rapid rise in the levels of one of the enzymes of the hexose monophosphate shunt (glucose-6-phosphate dehydrogenase), and two mitochondrial enzymes: isocitrate dehydrogenase and $NADH_2$-cytochrome reductase. The activities reached a peak after about 12 hours in the light and subsequently declined (Fig. XIII.16). These enzymes are no doubt synthesized in order to permit the speedy utilization of paramylon to supply energy and carbon skeletons for chloroplast formation. It is interesting that the peak of activity of these enzymes comes about half-way through the period of utilization of paramylon (Fig. XIII.16). Smillie *et al.* suggest that the subsequent fall in activity of these enzymes is due to their being broken down to provide amino acids for the synthesis of chloroplast proteins (cf. XIII.15).

The oxidation of paramylon may not be the only source of energy for greening in *E. gracilis*: as mentioned previously (XIII.11) large quantities of C_{13} and C_{14} saturated fatty acids disappear during the first 10 hours of greening[155]. Whether these fatty acids are oxidized, or

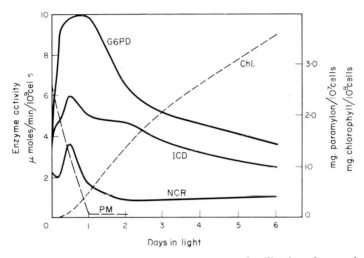

FIG. XIII.16. *Changes in activity of certain enzymes, and utilization of paramylon during greening of etiolated cells of* Euglena gracilis *in the light (adapted from Smillie et al., 1963). G6PD—glucose–6–phosphate dehydrogenase. ICD—isocitrate dehydrogenase. NCR—NADH$_2$ cytochrome reductase. Chl—chlorophyll. PM—paramylon.*

whether the acetyl CoA units produced in their breakdown are used for the synthesis of the new, chloroplast-specific, fatty acids, is not known. A study of the respiratory quotient of *E. gracilis* during greening should cast some light on whether paramylon or fat is the major source of energy under these circumstances.

XIII.18. Mechanism of Induction of Chloroplast Formation

Since the work of Briggs in 1920 (see XIII.9) it had been known that after etiolated leaves had been illuminated for a short time, they could continue to increase their capacity for photosynthesis during a subsequent incubation in the dark. This indicated that the synthesis of some of the enzymes of photosynthesis was triggered off by light but did not require the continued presence of light. In 1956, Withrow, Wolff, and

Price showed that the same was true of some enzyme, or enzymes, involved in chlorophyll synthesis. They used etiolated bean leaves which normally showed a lag of about two hours before rapid chlorophyll synthesis began in the light. If these leaves were given a very small dose of red light, of wavelength about 660 mμ, and were subsequently incubated in the dark for 5–15 hours, then when they were finally exposed to light, rapid chlorophyll synthesis began immediately, without a lag period. Virgin (1957), using dark-grown wheat leaves, investigated the relationship between the length of the dark incubation after the initial light treatment, and the rate of chlorophyll synthesis during the subsequent exposure to light. The optimum dark period was about six hours; with longer incubations the stimulatory effect of the initial dose slowly decreased.

Withrow et al. (1956) found that the effect of the pretreatment with red light could be reversed if it was immediately followed by a dose of far-red light (wavelength greater than 700 mμ). When an 18-hour dark incubation was used the stimulatory effect of red light could be overcome by a far-red treatment applied at anything up to nine hours after the red light[149]. When red and far-red lights were administered alternately a number of times (e.g. red, far-red, red, far-red) it was the type of light given last which determined the rate of chlorophyll synthesis during the subsequent incubation in the light[149, 134]. The stimulatory effect of red light and the antagonistic effect of far-red light applies to the synthesis of chlorophyll b as well as that of chlorophyll a[5]. Virgin (1961) used etiolated wheat leaves to study the action spectrum for the elimination of the lag phase of chlorophyll synthesis by pretreatment with light: the curve had a maximum at 660 mμ with minor shoulders at 540 and 600 mμ. Blue light (400–500 mμ) was relatively ineffective (Fig. XIII.17).

The position of the action spectrum peak and the reversibility of the effect with far-red light indicate that the light receptor responsible for these effects on chlorophyll synthesis is the substance phytochrome. This is a protein pigment, found in higher plants, possibly with a phycobilin type of chromophore, which exists in two forms; one having an absorption maximum at 660 mμ (P_r), and the other having its maximum at 730 mμ (P_{fr}). In the non-irradiated, dark-grown plant, phytochrome consists almost entirely of P_r, which is stable in the dark. P_r is converted by red light (600–700 mμ) to P_{fr}. P_{fr} is converted back to P_r by far-red light (700–800 mμ).

$$P_r \underset{\substack{\text{light, 730m}\mu \\ \text{or} \\ \text{slowly in dark}}}{\overset{\text{light, 660m}\mu}{\rightleftarrows}} P_{fr}$$

P_{fr} is also slowly converted back to P_r in the dark. P_{fr} is the active

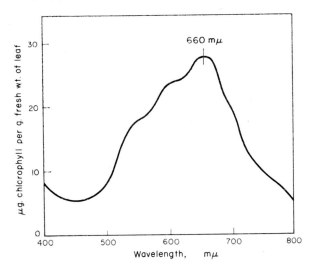

FIG. XIII.17. *Action spectrum for elimination of lag in chlorophyll synthesis (adapted from Virgin, 1961). Dark-grown wheat leaves exposed to monochromatic light of different wavelengths for two minutes and then incubated for five hours in the dark. The leaves were then irradiated with white light for two hours and the amount of chlorophyll formed was measured*

form, and is thought to be an enzyme. As soon as P_{fr} is available to the metabolism of the cell, reactions occur which cannot proceed without P_{fr}, and which finally lead to a variety of observable photomorphogenic responses such as seed germination, expansion of etiolated leaves, anthocyanin synthesis, and photoperiodic flowering response. For a fuller account of this very important subject, see Borthwick and Hendricks (1961), Mohr (1962), Hendricks and Borthwick (1965), Butler, Hendricks, and Siegelman (1965).

There are many possible points in the biosynthesis of chlorophyll at which the phytochrome system might act. When etiolated leaves are illuminated to photoreduce their protochlorophyllide, and are then put back in the dark, protochlorophyll synthesis starts off again[117]. In the case of dark-grown barley leaves, kept in the dark after a very short (0·002 seconds) flash of intense light, or 1 minute weak light, there is a lag phase of 5–10 minutes before protochlorophyll synthesis recommences[6]: the maximum rate of synthesis occurs between about 10 and 20 minutes, and then synthesis stops again after 30 to 40 minutes. The ability of etiolated wheat seedlings to resynthesize protochlorophyll in the dark after a short exposure (15 minutes) to white light to reduce the protochlorophyllide already present was investigated by Virgin (1958). He found that the ability to resynthesize protochlorophyll in the dark was markedly increased if the seedlings were given a three-minute exposure to red light followed by six hours in the dark, before the 15-

minute exposure to white light. In the case of etiolated barley seedlings
re-forming protochlorophyll in the dark after a flash of light, it was
found that leaves which had been given a three-minute exposure to red
light followed by four hours in the dark before the light flash, showed a
shorter (almost non-existent) lag phase in protochlorophyll re-synthesis,
and also a greater final amount of protochlorophyll formed, than leaves
not given the red light pretreatment[6]. Thus the stimulatory effect of
red light pretreatment on chlorophyll synthesis appears to be due to an
effect on protochlorophyllide formation, although additional stimulatory effects on protochlorophyllide reduction, and the subsequent
esterification, cannot be ruled out. It has been reported that in etiolated
seedlings of *Triticum vulgare*, a red light pretreatment stimulates phytylation as well as protochlorophyll synthesis during a subsequent dark
incubation, so that the amount of protochlorophyllide ester increases
more than the amount of free protochlorophyllide[156]: however, no
increase in the rate of phytylation of chlorophyll was detected. The
effects of red light pretreatment may be, in part, mimicked by supplying
the porphyrin precursor, δ-aminolaevulinic acid (ALA). If excised
barley shoots are incubated with this substance for 1–2 days in the dark,
they accumulate protochlorophyllide[68]. Also, if etiolated *Phaseolus
vulgaris* leaves are incubated with ALA in the dark overnight before
being exposed to light, they show no lag phase in chlorophyll synthesis:
red light treatment has no extra stimulatory effect on chlorophyll synthesis in the ALA-treated leaves[169]. Thus it is possible that red light
pretreatment may act by stimulating the synthesis of ALA.

This conclusion can be supported on general grounds. Granick (1965)
has pointed out that the accumulation of protochlorophyllide when
etiolated leaves are supplied with ALA suggests that all the enzymes
involved in the conversion of ALA to protochlorophyllide are present in
non-limiting amounts; that the synthesis of protochlorophyllide in the
dark is normally limited by the low activity of ALA-synthetase. This
being so, then any stimulation of protochlorophyllide synthesis (other
than by actually adding ALA) must presumably involve an increase in
ALA synthetase activity.

This phytochrome-mediated stimulation of protochlorophyllide synthesis appears to take some time to develop. As already noted, after a
pretreatment of etiolated wheat seedlings with light, the shortening of
the lag phase of chlorophyll synthesis during a subsequent illumination
did not reach its maximum value until the seedlings had been incubated
for six hours in the dark after the first light treatment[196]. However,
there is also a very rapid effect of light on protochlorophyllide synthesis:
this is indicated by the fact that an etiolated leaf which has stopped
synthesizing protochlorophyllide, will start off again 5–10 minutes after
its existing protochlorophyllide has been reduced by a flash of light[6].

It thus appears that there are two light-mediated stimulatory effects on protochlorophyllide synthesis: one, a short-term effect, acts to restore (approximately) the level of protochlorophyllide present before the light treatment; the other, a long-term effect, causes the ability to form protochlorophyllide (measured either in terms of protochlorophyllide resynthesis in the dark after a further brief light treatment, or in terms of the ability to synthesize chlorophyll in continuous light) to increase to a level beyond that which is merely required for the restoration of the original protochlorophyllide content.

In both cases it seems likely that the stimulation of protochlorophyllide synthesis involves an increase in ALA synthetase activity. The long-term, phytochrome-mediated effect probably involves an actual increase in the amount of enzyme present. Granick (1965) has suggested that the short-term effect may be due to a temporary lifting of an inhibition of ALA-synthetase: this implies that there is a certain amount of the enzyme present but that it is inactive, as a result of the presence of some inhibitor. If Granick's hypothesis is correct, then the inhibition of ALA synthetase in these etiolated leaves may be an example of the phenomenon of control of a biosynthetic pathway by negative feedback; in which case we would expect the inhibitor to be one of the end products of the biosynthetic pathway. The best candidate for the role of inhibitor would seem to be protochlorophyllide itself[162]. ALA synthetase activity (as measured by protochlorophyllide formation) develops very shortly after the original protochlorophyllide is removed by reduction, and then disappears again when the new protochlorophyllide reaches a certain level.

Pretreatment with red light can also promote the synthesis of other chloroplast constituents. Mego and Jagendorf (1959, 1961) exposed etiolated leaves of Phaseolus vulgaris to red light for two minutes, each day for four days: the leaves were kept in the dark between light treatments. During this period the average diameter of the plastids increased from 3·0 to 4·6 μ (Fig. XIII.18). In leaves which were not exposed to red light, the plastid diameter was only 3·4 μ at the end of the experiment. After 60 minutes' exposure to red light the nitrogen content of the plastids (mainly due to protein) increased by 175 per cent during the next five days in the dark: in untreated leaves the plastid nitrogen content increased by only 21 per cent. Carotenoids and chloroplast lipids were also synthesized in the dark to a greater extent than in untreated leaves. The stimulatory effects of a brief exposure to red light, on plastid growth (Fig. XIII.18) and the synthesis of carotenoids and the nitrogenous components of the plastid, were all diminished if the red-light treatment was immediately followed by exposure to far-red light. Cohen and Goodwin (1962) found that carotenoid synthesis in etiolated maize seedlings in the dark was stimulated

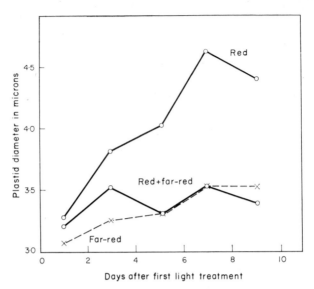

FIG. XIII.18. *Effect of red light pretreatment on plastid growth in dark in etiolated bean leaves (adapted from Mego and Jagendorf, 1961)*

by a brief exposure to red light, and that the effect of red light was over-come by a subsequent treatment with far-red light. The carotenoids synthesized in response to the red light treatment appeared to be the same as those formed by seedlings kept in continual darkness, i.e. mainly xanthophylls. Similar results were obtained with dark-grown pea seedlings[79].

The plastid proteins synthesized in the dark after an exposure to light will include some, and possibly all, of the enzymes involved in photo-synthesis. This is suggested by the work of Briggs (1920), mentioned above, and by the finding of Smith (1954) that etiolated barley leaves have no ability to liberate oxygen after 10 minutes' illumination, but will develop such ability if they are subsequently incubated for 100 minutes in the dark. The effect of light pretreatment on the increase in activity of specific photosynthetic enzymes has also been investigated. Etiolated leaves of *Phaseolus vulgaris* were exposed to red light for five minutes on each of four successive days, and were kept in the dark between each illumination. As a result of this treatment the activity of NADP-linked glyceraldehyde phosphate dehydrogenase in the leaves increased almost as much as it did in leaves subjected to continuous illumination for four days: the activity per leaf was four to five times as great as in leaves kept in the dark all this time[127, 129]. If the leaves were given five minutes' exposure to far-red light after each exposure to red light, the enzyme activity was no higher than in the dark control. How-ever, as previously discussed (XIII.14) there is a possibility that increase in this particular enzyme activity during greening might involve transformation of the NAD-linked enzyme, or conversion of an inactive precursor. Therefore, these findings alone should not be taken as evidence that the red light pretreatment brings about *de novo* synthesis of a specific enzyme. There is some evidence[95] that in etiolated *Phaseolus vulgaris* leaves, ferredoxin is synthesized almost as rapidly in the dark after 1·5 hours' exposure to white light, as it is when the leaves are kept on a 10 hours' light/14 hours' dark régime. The activity of the enzyme (transhydrogenase) which transfers the hydrogen from ferredoxin to NADP increases about threefold during two days in the dark after 1·5 hours' exposure to white light, but this is only a small fraction of the increase in activity (fiftyfold) which takes place during two days of the 10 hours' light/14 hours' dark régime. In the case of these enzymes, it was not determined whether the stimulatory effect of light pretreatment on synthesis was annulled by a subsequent treatment with far-red light.

The breakdown of reserve polysaccharide to provide energy and intermediates for the synthesis of plastid materials, is initiated by a brief exposure to light (see XIII.17). When dark-grown maize leaves were given two 90-second doses of red light during a 24-hour incubation in the dark, the free sugar content fell by 22 per cent, and the starch content by 43 per cent (relative to untreated controls). If the red light treatments were immediately followed by exposure to far-red light only half as much starch, and two-thirds as much sugar, disappeared[103].

From the foregoing evidence it appears that many of the metabolic processes involved in chloroplast formation by the etiolated cell—chlorophyll synthesis, carotenoid synthesis, the formation of photosynthetic enzymes and possibly other chloroplast proteins, utilization of reserve materials—are under the control of the phytochrome system. Whether this is also true of greening in etiolated cells of *E. gracilis* and similar algae is not known. There is some evidence for the presence of the phytochrome system in certain algae: the positive phototactic movement of the chloroplast in *Mougeotia* and *Mesotaenium* (both members of the *Conjugales*) is induced by red light and repressed by far-red light[74, 75]. However, there is no such evidence for the presence of phytochrome in *Euglena*. According to Brawerman and Konigsberg (1960), if, during the greening of dark-grown cells of *E. gracilis*, the light is switched off, then the synthesis of NADP-linked glyceraldehyde phosphate dehydrogenase ceases immediately. This suggests that the continued presence of light is required for formation of this chloroplast enzyme, which is contrary to what was found for a higher plant (see above). One might be tempted to deduce from this that the phytochrome system was not involved in the synthesis of this enzyme in *E. gracilis*. However, according to Spier (1964), in the greening of etiolated cells of *E. gracilis*, the formation of the NADP-linked glyceraldehyde phosphate dehydrogenase, and also of carboxydismutase, in fact continued when the cells were returned to darkness after some hours' exposure to light. After 12 hours in the light the enzymes were synthesized just as fast when the cells were returned to darkness as they were in continued light. However, if the exposure to light was less than 12 hours, the enzymes were synthesized more slowly on withdrawal of light than in continued illumination. While these findings do not provide direct evidence for the presence of the phytochrome system in *Euglena*, they at least cast some doubt on the evidence for its absence.

Some other evidence that in *E. gracilis*, light-induced metabolic changes can continue in the dark, has been reported by Lazzarini and Woodruff (1964). The enzyme that transfers hydrogen from ferredoxin to NADP is synthesized by *Euglena* three to four times as fast in cells growing in the light as in cells growing in the dark. When cells grown in the dark are exposed to light there is a 12-hour lag before the rate of transhydrogenase synthesis reaches the value obtained with cells growing in the light: this is about the same lag period as is required for rapid chlorophyll synthesis to begin. The high rate of transhydrogenase synthesis requires the continued presence of light: if, in a culture growing in the light, the light is switched off, then the rate of synthesis of this enzyme falls to the level typical of cells growing in the dark. If fully etiolated cells growing in the dark are illuminated for one hour with red light, then during a subsequent 12-hours' growth in the dark there is no increase in the rate of transhydrogenase synthesis above the dark rate. However, if the cells are then exposed to continuous white light, the rate of transhydrogenase synthesis changes over to the high value, typical of cultures growing in the light, without the usual 12-hour lag. Thus it appears that a one-hour red light pretreatment causes certain metabolic changes to take place in the dark which bring the cell's ability to synthesize transhydrogenase up to the level characteristic of light-grown cells, so that as soon as light (which is necessary for high rates of synthesis of this enzyme) is supplied, the high rate of synthesis can begin immediately. These workers apparently did not investigate whether this effect of red light was overcome by a subsequent treatment with far-red light, or whether the lag phase of chlorophyll synthesis in *Euglena gracilis* was also abolished by the red light pretreatment. Experiments on the effects of red/far-red light treatment on the lag phase of formation of chlorophyll and other components might provide evidence as to whether *E. gracilis* does possess the phytochrome system.

The appearance of chloroplasts on illumination of dark-grown plants has many of the characteristics of adaptive enzyme formation, which has been studied so extensively in bacteria. The characteristic pigments, lipids and enzymes of the chloroplast are formed in response to a specific outside stimulus. The amount of these enzymes and other substances can increase several-fold in the absence of cell multiplication. The primary stimulus—light—is actually physical, not chemical as is normally the case with formation of adaptive enzymes, but the light will, no doubt, cause the production of specific chemical substances which could act as inducers in the normal way. A further similarity to bacterial adaptive enzyme formation is that formation of chloroplast enzymes and other constituents may be repressed by the addition of substrates which make these enzymes unnecessary. Beijerinck (1904) observed that *Chlorella variegata* had a great tendency to produce chlorotic (without chlorophyll) cells when cultivated on media rich in organic carbon sources. Similarly, Kufferath (1913) found that cells of *Chlorella luteo-viridis* were chlorotic when grown in the light on agar containing 1 per cent glucose or galactose, or 2 per cent sucrose. Fuller and Gibbs (1959) grew *Chlorella variegata* in liquid medium in the light with either carbon dioxide or sodium acetate as carbon source. Under autotrophic conditions normal green cells were formed; however, after several generations under heterotrophic conditions most of the chlorophyll had disappeared, and the cells had lost all their carboxydismutase and NADP-linked glyceraldehyde phosphate dehydrogenase activity. When the organic substrate was removed, carboxydismutase was rapidly formed again[50]. App and Jagendorf (1963) found that the formation of chlorophyll by etiolated cells of *E. gracilis* exposed to light, was inhibited 54 per cent by 0·4 per cent ethanol, 24 per cent by 0·43 per cent malic acid, and 27 per cent by 0·11 per cent sodium acetate. Synthesis of the chloroplast enzyme, alkaline fructose diphosphatase, was inhibited 52, 12, and 28 per cent, respectively, by these three substrates. When cells of *Chlamydomonas mundana* are grown in a medium containing acetate they form chlorophyll, and chloroplast fragments prepared from such cells have about the same ability to carry out the Hill reaction and photophosphorylation as similar cell-free preparations from cells grown in purely inorganic medium[157]. However, these acetate-grown cells have negligible photosynthetic activity as measured by their ability to carry out a light-dependent fixation of CO_2 and liberation of O_2. What the cells appear to lack is certain enzymes of the carbon dioxide fixation cycle. Extracts of the acetate-grown cells have very low levels of carboxydismutase activity compared to extracts of autotrophically-grown cells. Also, an aldolase which is present in the autotrophic cells is absent from the heterotrophic cells, another aldolase with distinctly different properties being present in its place.

In the light of the above findings it appears possible that the mechanism by which the synthesis of chloroplast enzymes and other constituents is controlled is similar to that suggested for the control of bacterial enzyme formation by Jacob and Monod (1961). According to this theory there are two classes of genes: structural genes which deter-

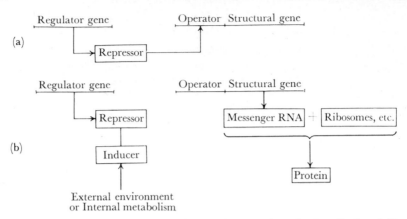

Fig. XIII.19. *Possible mechanism of induction of enzyme formation (see Jacob and Monod, 1961). (a) Repressor combines with operator: structural gene switched off, protein not synthesized. (b) Inducer combines with repressor and prevents it from combining with operator: structural gene switched on, protein synthesized.*

mine the structure of particular proteins, and regulator genes which control the activity of the structural genes. The structural genes act by forming an RNA copy—'messenger RNA'—of the DNA in the gene. The protein whose structure is determined by this gene is then synthesized by a ribosome, which translates the sequence of nucleotides in the messenger RNA into the corresponding sequence of amino acids. The regulator gene is thought to produce a 'repressor' substance: the structure of this is unknown, but it may perhaps be simply the RNA copy of the regulator gene. There are two types of repressor. The first type (Fig. XIII.19) combines directly with a region of the structural gene, known as the 'operator'. The structural gene is thus prevented from acting, and so the enzyme or other protein, whose structure is determined by the gene, is not synthesized. However, the repressor has the ability to combine with certain small molecules (inducers) and the repressor–inducer complex cannot combine with the operator. Thus, in the presence of an inducer the enzyme will be synthesized. An enzyme of this type which is normally not made, but which is synthesized in the presence of a specific inducer is known as an 'inducible' enzyme: an example is β-galactosidase in *Escherichia coli*, the formation of which is induced by a number of different galactosides. It is generally true that only substrates, or substances chemically similar to the substrates, will act as inducers of these enzymes. The second type of repressor (aporepressor) cannot combine directly with the operator, so that the enzyme in question is normally synthesized (Fig. XIII.20). However, this aporepressor has the ability to combine with certain small-molecular-weight compounds (corepressors), and the aporepressor–corepressor complex has the ability to combine with the operator region

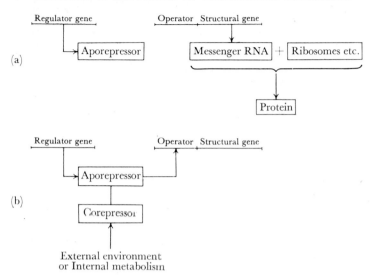

FIG. XIII.20. *Possible mechanism of repression of enzyme formation (see Jacob and Monod, 1961). (a) Aporepressor unable to combine with operator: structural gene switched on, protein synthesized. (b) Corepressor combines with aporepressor, enabling it to combine with operator: structural gene switched off, protein synthesis ceases.*

of the structural gene. Thus, in the presence of a corepressor, the enzyme is not synthesized. An enzyme of this type, which is normally synthesized but whose synthesis can be prevented by the addition of a specific corepressor, is known as a 'repressible' enzyme. Repressible enzymes are usually enzymes involved in the biosynthesis of some essential metabolite, such as an amino acid or a nucleotide, the co-repressor being generally the end product of the synthetic sequence. An example is tryptophan synthetase, the formation of which in bacteria is inhibited by tryptophan.

Another type of enzyme repression—often known as the 'glucose effect'—is found in bacteria. This is the ability of almost any utilizable carbon source to inhibit the synthesis of certain enzymes. It was first discovered by Epps and Gale (1942), who found that glucose inhibited the formation of amino acid deaminases in *E. coli*. It appears[140, 126] that those enzymes, the formation of which is inhibited by glucose, are catabolic enzymes which furnish the cell with products that are also readily obtainable by the metabolism of glucose. Thus the glucose effect is useful to the cell because it involves the inhibition of synthesis of enzymes whose activity does not contribute to the growth of the cell. The mechanism of the glucose effect is not known, but there is some evidence that it differs from the mechanism of enzyme induction and repression suggested by Jacob and Monod (see Magasanik, 1961).

Using the theory of Jacob and Monod, the mechanism of the induction by light of chloroplast formation in etiolated plants might be explained as follows. Many, and perhaps all, of the chloroplast proteins are synthesized in much larger quantities in the light than in the dark. We shall assume that there are two genes concerned with each of these proteins; a structural gene and a regulator gene. Note that a number of different proteins (for instance, the different enzymes of a given bio-synthetic pathway) might be controlled by a single regulator gene, but that each of these proteins will have its own specific structural gene. In the dark-grown cell, the repressors made by the regulatory genes combine with the operator regions of the appropriate structural genes, so that the structural genes are partially, or completely, switched off. It is important to emphasize that the switching-off of the structural genes may be only partial, since some of the chloroplast enzymes, for instance carboxydismutase (see XIII.14), are apparently made in small amounts in the dark. Also, the enzymes involved in the synthesis of carotenoids, and of protochlorophyllide, must be made to some extent in the dark.

In the dark-grown cell of a higher plant, all the phytochrome will be in the P_r form. When the cell is exposed to red light (or to light which includes red light), P_r is converted to P_{fr} and protochlorophyllide to chlorophyllide. Then the P_{fr}, or a substance whose formation is dependent upon P_{fr} (it has been suggested that this form of phytochrome may be an enzyme, possibly involved in acyl transfer or modification— Hendricks and Borthwick, 1965), combines with the repressors of the structural genes for the synthesis of chloroplast proteins and ribosomes, prevents the repressors from combining with their appropriate operators, and thus allows the synthesis of messenger RNA, of chloroplast ribosomal and transfer RNA, and subsequently chloroplast protein. The process could, of course, be more gradual: the primary inducer, whether P_{fr} or a metabolic product of P_{fr}, might de-repress, or induce, only one, or a few, structural genes. Then, perhaps, metabolites formed by the action of enzymes produced by those genes would de-repress other genes, and so on. The synthesis of non-protein chloroplast constituents such as pigments and specific chloroplast lipids, will no doubt begin as soon as the appropriate biosynthetic enzymes have been made. The finding that the formation of chloroplast constituents continues for a long time in the dark after a brief exposure to light may well be connected with the fact that the conversion of P_{fr} back to P_r in darkness is a process that takes a few hours[76]. During these few hours large numbers of messenger RNA molecules and chloroplast ribosomes could be synthesized, and since messenger RNA is probably more stable in higher organisms than in bacteria, synthesis of chloroplast proteins could continue for, perhaps, many hours after all the phytochrome was once again in the form P_r. The prevention of the synthesis of chloroplast constituents when the red light treatment is followed by far-red treatment, is presumably due to the rapid re-conversion of P_{fr} back to P_r, before complete de-repression of genes has taken place.

If the phytochrome-mediated induction of chloroplast formation does involve de-repression of genes, as suggested, then associated with the early stages of chloroplast formation there should be a substantial synthesis of various classes of RNA. As discussed in XIII.16, this does indeed seem to happen. Illumination of etiolated plants stimulates the synthesis of ribosomal RNA and messenger RNA. The stimulation appears to affect both plastid and non-plastid RNA, but is particularly marked in the case of plastid RNA. In the case of the light-induced increase in activity of ribosomes, which may be due to increased messenger RNA synthesis[208, 209, 207], red light was found to be much more effective than blue light, and green light had little or no effect: this is consistent with the chromophore in question being phytochrome. Weidner, Jakobs, and Mohr (1965) have reported that irradiation of etiolated seedlings of *Sinapis alba* with red light causes a marked stimulation of RNA and protein synthesis: this stimulation is abolished by an immediate, subsequent irradiation with far-red light, indicating that phytochrome is the chromophore responsible. Holdgate and Goodwin (1965) were unable to detect any stimulation of RNA synthesis after red light treatment of dark-grown rye seedlings: however, treatment of the seedlings with far-red light seemed to induce a 24-hour lag in RNA synthesis which was not observed in untreated seedlings. Thus, the hypothesis that P_{fr} initiates chloroplast formation by either directly or indirectly de-repressing genes, is consistent with the available evidence, although it is far from proven. Since chloroplast formation is under the control of both chloroplast and nuclear genes, then both nuclear and chloroplast genes will presumably be activated. It is interesting that the phytochrome-induced synthesis of anthocyanins in mustard seedlings (*Sinapis alba*) is inhibited by actinomycin D, an antibiotic which can block the expression of the genes by inhibiting RNA synthesis. While the chloroplasts are not directly concerned with anthocyanin synthesis, this result does, at least, provide evidence for activation of genes by phytochrome in another system[115a].

The induction by light of chloroplast formation in etiolated cells of *Euglena gracilis* and *Ochromonas danica* probably also involves the de-repression of certain genes. However, we cannot say whether phytochrome is involved since it is not known if this pigment is present in these organisms. Even if phytochrome is not present, it is conceivable that the small amount of chlorophyll that is rapidly formed in the light by reduction of the protochlorophyllide present might give rise to metabolic products which would induce the formation of chloroplast proteins in the manner described above. Alternatively, if protochlorophyllide can act as an inhibitor of ALA synthetase—as has been suggested by Schiff and Epstein (1965)—or other enzymes, then removal of protochlorophyllide might set metabolic changes in train that lead to the production of compounds which de-repress the structural genes concerned with chloroplast formation.

The situation in the case of algae which normally make chlorophyll in the dark, but which have mutant forms which only make chlorophyll in the light, may be different. Spier (1964) has obtained a mutant of *Scenedesmus* which, in the dark, makes no chlorophyll but forms normal amounts of carboxydismutase and NADP-requiring glyceraldehyde phosphate dehydrogenase. Thus, the formation of chlorotic cells in the dark may be due, not to repression of enzyme formation, but simply to lack of the ability to carry out the reduction of protochlorophyllide in the dark; that is, the mutation may be in a gene controlling the structure of the protein moiety of the protochlorophyllide holochrome, or the structure of an enzyme which carries out the dark reduction of protochlorophyllide holochrome.

As we have seen previously, there are some strains of *Chlamydomonas reinhardi* which make chlorophyll in the dark, and some (the y strains) which do not (XIII.8). In at least one of the y strains the formation of carboxydismutase, ferredoxin, and NADP-requiring triose phosphate dehydrogenase, as well as that of chlorophyll, is abolished, or greatly diminished in the dark, and induced again in the light[83, 84]. One possible explanation of these data is that the y strains are, in fact, the true wild-types, and that they possess one or more regulatory genes which act by repressing formation of chloroplast proteins in the dark. A strain which makes chlorophyll in the dark might have a mutation in a regulator gene, so that it has lost the ability to repress chloroplast formation in the dark. The suggestion that it is the y strains which are the wild-types, and the strains that make chlorophyll in the dark which are the mutants, gains some support from the fact that at least some of the naturally occurring strains of *C. reinhardi* are, in fact, of the y type. Two strains of this alga which I obtained from the Cambridge Culture Collection of Algae and Protozoa both turned out to consist predominantly of y cells: when the algae were grown on agar plates in the dark, the majority of the colonies in each case were yellow, although there were also a few green colonies.

The inhibitory effects that utilizable carbon sources have on chloroplast formation are reminiscent of the glucose effect in bacteria. Since the cells will have less need of photosynthesis if they have a utilizable carbon source, it will probably be an advantage to them if they can reduce the amount of photosynthetic apparatus which they make. The glucose effect also (see above) appears to involve the inhibition of synthesis of enzymes which are not contributing to the growth of the cell. These considerations might lead one to suppose that the repression of chloroplast formation by carbon sources has the same mechanism as the glucose effect: however, since the mechanism of the glucose effect is quite unknown, such a supposition is of little help. There are many possible mechanisms to choose from. One relatively simple hypothesis can be constructed on the assumption that the primary inducer can exist in an oxidized or a reduced state; only the oxidized form can combine with the repressor, and thus de-repress the structural genes for chloroplast protein formation. Addition of an oxidizable carbon source will shift the redox potential inside the cell towards the reducing side, and thus, perhaps, convert the inducer to its inactive, reduced, form. On the basis of this theory, one might expect that the degree of repression brought about by a carbon source would be a function of the oxygen tension. Also, compounds such as 3-(p-chlorophenyl)-1,1-dimethyl urea which inhibit photosynthetic oxygen evolution, might be expected to repress chloroplast formation. It should, therefore, be possible to test this hypothesis experimentally. It is interesting that carbon source repression of chloroplast formation has so far only been reported for algae; whether similar effects exist in higher plants remains to be seen. As far as chlorophyll synthesis by etiolated leaves is concerned, we know already that sugars tend, if anything, to stimulate (see XIII.6).

REFERENCES

1. ALLEN, M. B. (1959). *Arch. f. Mikrobiol.* **32**, 270–277
2. ANDERSON, J. M. & BOARDMAN, N. K. (1964). *Austr. J. Biol. Sci.* **17**, 93–101
3. ANDROES, G. M., SINGLETON, M. F., BIGGINS, J. & CALVIN, M. (1963). *Biochim. Biophys. Acta* **66**, 180–187
4. APP, A. A. & JAGENDORF A. T. (1963). *J. Protozool.* **10**, 340–343
5. AUGUSTINUSSEN, E. (1964). *Phys. Plant* **17**, 403–406
6. AUGUSTINUSSEN, E. & MADSEN, A. (1965). *Phys. Plant* **18**, 828–837
7. BECK, W. A. (1937). *Plant Phys.* **12**, 885–886
8. BEIJERINCK, M. W. (1904). *Rec. trav. botan. néerl.* **1**, 14–27
9. BEN-SHAUL, Y., SCHIFF, J. A. & EPSTEIN, H. T. (1964). *Plant Phys.* **39**, 231–240
9a. BIGGINS, J. & PARK, R. B. (1966). *Plant Phys.* **41**, 115–118
10. BITTNER, R. (1905). *Ostereich. Bot. Zeit.* Quoted by Stahl (1909).
11. BLAAUW-JANSEN, G., KAMEN, J. G. & THOMAS, J. B. (1950). *Biochim. Biophys. Acta* **5**, 179–185
12. BLOCH, K., CONSTANTOPOULOS, G., KENYON, C. & NAGAI, J. In *Symposium on Biochemistry of Chloroplasts (Aberystwyth, 1965)*. Ed., T. W. Goodwin. Academic Press, London (in press)
13. BOARDMAN, N. K. (1962a). *Biochim. Biophys. Acta* **62**, 63–79
14. BOARDMAN, N. K. (1962b). *Biochim. Biophys. Acta* **64**, 279–293
15. BOEHM, J. A. (1865). *Sitzber. Akad. Wiss. Wien.* **51**, 405–418. Quoted by Smith and Young (1956)
16. BOGORAD, L. & JACOBSON, A. (1965). *Fed. Proc.* **24**, 664

17. BORTHWICK, H. A. & HENDRICKS, S. B. (1961). *Encycl. Plant Phys.* Ed., W. Ruhland. XVI. Springer-Verlag, Berlin, pp. 299–330

18. BRAWERMAN, G. & CHARGAFF, E. (1959). *Biochim. Biophys. Acta* **31**, 164–171

19. BRAWERMAN, G. & KONIGSBERG, N. (1960). *Biochim. Biophys. Acta* **43**, 374–381

20. BRAWERMAN, G., POGO, A. O. & CHARGAFF, E. (1962). *Biochim. Biophys. Acta* **55**, 326–334

21. BRIGGS, G. E. (1920). *Proc. Roy. Soc. B* **91**, 249–268

22. BRODY, S. S. & BRODY, M. (1962). *Trans. Faraday Soc.* **58**, 416–428

23. BRODY, M., BRODY, S. S. & LEVINE, J. H. (1965). *J. Protozool.* **12**, 465–476

24. BROWN, F. A. M. & GUNNING, B. E. S. In *Symposium on Biochemistry of Chloroplasts (Aberystwyth, 1965)*. Ed., T. W. Goodwin. Academic Press, London (in press)

25. BUTLER, W. L. (1961). *Arch. Biochem. Biophys.* **92**, 287–295

26. BUTLER, W. L. (1965). *Biochim. Biophys. Acta* **102**, 1–8

27. BUTLER, W. L. & BRIGGS, W. R. (1965). *Biochim. Biophys. Acta* **112**, 45–53

28. BUTLER, W. L., HENDRICKS, S. B. & SIEGELMAN, H. W. (1965). In *Chemistry and Biochemistry of Plant Pigments*. Ed., T. W. Goodwin, Academic Press, London, pp. 197–210

29. BURGERSTEIN, A. (1900). *Ber. deut. bot. Ges.* Quoted by Stahl (1909)

30. CAPON, B. & BOGORAD, L. (1962a). *Bot. Gaz.* **124**, 128–132

31. CAPON, B. & BOGORAD, L. (1962b). *Bot. Gaz.* **123**, 285–291

32. CLARKE, A. E. & STONE, B. A. (1960). *Biochim. Biophys. Acta* **44**, 161–163

33. COHEN, R. Z. & GOODWIN, T. W. (1962). *Phytochemistry* **1**, 67–72

34. CROMBIE, W. M. (1958). *J. Exp. Bot.* **9**, 254–261

35. DE DEKEN-GRENSON, M. (1954). *Biochim. Biophys. Acta* **14**, 203–211

36. DELAVAN, L. A. & BENSON, A. A. (1959). *Brookhaven Symp. Biol.* **11**, 259–261

37. EILAM, Y. & KLEIN, S. (1962). *J. Cell Biol.* **14**, 169–182

38. ENGELMANN, Th. W. (1881). *Bot. Ztg.* **39**, 440. Quoted by Ewart (1895–97)

39. EPPS, H. M. R. & GALE, E. F. (1942). *Biochem. J.* **36**, 619–623

40. EPSTEIN, H. T. & SCHIFF, J. A. (1961). *J. Protozool.* **8**, 427–432

41. ERIKSSON, G., KAHN, A., WALLES, B. & WETTSTEIN, D. (1961). *Ber. deut. bot. Ges.* **74**, 221–232

42. ERWIN, J. & BLOCH, K. (1962). *Biochem. Biophys. Res. Commun.* **9**, 103–108

43. VON EULER, H. & HELLSTRÖM, H. (1929). *Z. Phys. Chem.* **183**, 177–183

44. EWART, A. J. (1895–97). *J. Linn. Soc. (Bot.)* **31**, 554–576

45. EYSTER, W. H. (1928). *Science* **68**, 569–570

46. FISCHER, H., MITTENZWEI, H. & OESTREICHER, A. (1938). *Z. Phys. Chem.* **257**, IV–VII

47. FISCHER, H. & OESTREICHER, A. (1940). *Z. Phys. Chem.* **262**, 243–269

48. FISCHER, F. G. & RUDIGER, W. (1959). *Annal. Chem.* **627**, 35–46

49. FRANK, S. R. (1946). *J. Gen. Physiol.* **29**, 157–179

50. FULLER, R. C. (1957). In discussion of paper by N. E. Tolbert, in *Research in Photosynthesis*. Ed., H. Gaffron. Interscience, New York, pp. 224–227

51. FULLER, R. C. & GIBBS, M. (1959). *Plant Phys.* **34**, 324–329

52. FULLER, R. C. & HUDOCK, G. A. In *Symposium on Biochemistry of Chloroplasts (Aberystwyth, 1965)*. Ed., T. W. Goodwin. Academic Press, London (in press)

53. GABRIELSEN, E. K., MADSEN, A. & VEJLBY, K. (1961). *Phys. Plant* **14**, 98–110

54. GASSMAN, M. & BOGORAD, L. (1965). *Plant Phys.* **40**, lii

55. GEROLA, F. M. (1959). *Nuovo Giorn. Bot. Ital.* **66**, 506

56. GIBBS, M. (1952). *Nature, Lond.* **170**, 164–165

57. GIBBS, S. P. (1962). *J. Cell Biol.* **15**, 343–361

58. GODNEV, T. N., AKULOVICH, N. K. & KHODASEVICH, E. V. (1963). *Dokl. Akad. Nauk. (biol.) S.S.S.R.* (Consultants Bureau transl.) **150**, 590–593

59. GODNEV, T. N., KALER, V. L. & ROTFARB, R. M. (1961). *Dokl. Akad. Nauk.* (*biol.*) *S.S.S.R.* (Consultants Bureau transl.) **140**, 1445
60. GOEDHEER, J. C. (1961). *Biochim. Biophys. Acta* **51**, 494–504
61. GOEDHEER, J. C. & SMITH, J. H. C. (1959). *Carneg. Inst. Wash. Yearbook* **58**, 334–336
62. GOODWIN, T. W. (1958). *Biochem. J.* **70**, 612–617
63. GOODWIN, T. W. (1960). In *Comparative Biochemistry of Photoreactive systems.* Ed., M. B. Allen. Academic Press, New York, pp. 1–10
64. GOODWIN, T. W. In *Symposium on Biochemistry of Chloroplasts (Aberystwyth, 1965).* Ed., T. W. Goodwin. Academic Press, London (in press)
65. GOODWIN, T. W. & JAMIKORN, M. (1954). *J. Protozool.* **1**, 216
66. GOODWIN, T. W. & PHAGPOLNGARM, S. (1960). *Biochem. J.* **76**, 197–199
67. GOODWIN, R. H. & OWENS, O. H. (1947). *Plant Phys.* **22**, 197–200
68. GRANICK, S. (1959). *Plant Phys.* **34**, xviii
69. GRANICK, S. (1961). *Proc. 5th Intern. Congr. Biochem.* VI, 176–186
70. GRANICK, S. In *Symposium on Biochemistry of Chloroplasts (Aberystwyth, 1965).* Ed., T. W. Goodwin. Academic Press, London (in press)
71. GUNNING, B. E. S. & JAGOE, M. P. In *Symposium on Biochemistry of Chloroplasts (Aberystwyth, 1965).* Ed., T. W. Goodwin. Academic Press, London (in press)
72. GYLDENHOLM, A. O. Quoted by von Wettstein (1965)
73. HAGEMAN, R. A. & ARNON, D. I. (1955). *Arch. Biochem. Biophys.* **57**, 421–436
74. HAUPT, W. (1959). *Planta* **53**, 484–501
75. HAUPT, W. & THIELE, R. (1961). *Planta* **56**, 388–401
76. HENDRICKS, S. B. (1960). *Cold Spring Harbour Symp.* **25**, 245–248
77. HENDRICKS, S. B. & BORTHWICK, H. A. (1965). In *Chemistry and Biochemistry of Plant Pigments.* Ed., T. W. Goodwin, Academic Press, London, pp. 405–439
78. HENNINGSEN, K.-W. In *Symposium on Biochemistry of Chloroplasts (Aberystwyth, 1965).* Ed., T. W. Goodwin. Academic Press, London (in press)
79. HENSHALL, J. D. & GOODWIN, T. W. (1964). *Photochem. & Photobiol.* **3**, 243 247
80. HODGE, A. J., McLEAN, J. D. & MERCER, F. V. (1956). *J. Biophys. Biochem. Cytol.* **2**, 597–607
81. HOLDEN, M. (1961). *Biochem. J.* **78**, 359–364
82. HOLDGATE, D. P. & GOODWIN, T. W. (1965). *Photochem. & Photobiol.* **4**, 1–6
82a. HUDOCK, G. A. & FULLER, R. C. (1965). *Plant Phys.* **40**, 1205–1211
83. HUDOCK, G. A. & LEVINE, R. P. (1964). *Plant Phys.* **39**, 889–897
84. HUDOCK, G. A., McLEOD, G. C., MORAVKOVA-KIELY, J. & LEVINE, R. P. (1964). *Plant Phys.* **39**, 898–903
85. HUFFAKER, R. C., OBERDORF, R. B., KELLER, C. J. & KLEINKOFF, G. E. (1964). *Plant Phys.* **39**, xiv
86. HUZISIGE, H., TERADA, T., NISHIMURA, M. & UEMURA, T. (1957). *Biol J. Okayama Univ.* **3**, 209
87. INMAN, O. L. (1935). *Plant Phys.* **10**, 401–403
88. IRVING, A. A. (1910). *Ann. Bot.* **24**, 805–818
89. JACOB, F. & MONOD, J. (1961). *J. Mol. Biol.* **3**, 318–356
90. JAGENDORF, A. T. & MARGULIES, M. (1960). *Arch. Biochem. Biophys.* **90**, 184–195
91. JOST, L. (1907). *Jost's Plant Physiology.* Transl., R. J. Harvey Gibson. Oxford Univ. Press, Oxford
92. KAHN, A. Quoted by Virgin *et al.* (1963)
93. KAY, R. E. & PHINNEY, B. (1956). *Plant Phys.* **31**, 226–231
94. KEARNEY, P. C. & TOLBERT, N. E. (1962). *Arch. Biochem. Biophys.* **98**, 164–171
95. KEISTER, D. L., JAGENDORF, A. T. & SAN PIETRO, A. (1962). *Biochim. Biophys. Acta* **62**, 332–337
96. KIRK, J. T. O. (1961). *Ph.D. thesis.* Univ. of Cambridge

97. KIRK, J. T. O. (1962). *Biochim. Biophys. Acta* **56**, 139–151
98. KIRK, J. T. O. & ALLEN, R. L. (1965). *Biochim. Biophys. Res. Commun.* **21**, 523–530
99. KLEIN, S. (1960). *J. Biophys. Biochem. Cytol.* **8**, 529–538
100. KLEIN, S. & BOGORAD, L. (1964). *J. Cell Biol.* **22**, 443–451
101. KLEIN, S., BRYAN, G. & BOGORAD, L. (1964). *J. Cell Biol.* **22**, 433–442
102. KLEIN, S. & POLJAKOFF-MAYBER, A. (1961). *J. Biophys. Biochem. Cytol.* **11**, 433–440
103. KLEIN, W. H., PRICE, L. & MITRAKOS, K. (1963). *Photochem. & Photobiol.* **2**, 233–240
104. KOSKI, V. M. (1950). *Arch. Biochem. Biophys.* **29**, 339–343
105. KOSKI, V. M., FRENCH, C. S. & SMITH, J. H. C. (1951). *Arch. Biochem. Biophys.* **31**, 1–17
106. KOSKI, V. M. & SMITH, J. H. C. (1948). *J. Am. Chem. Soc.* **70**, 3558–3562
107. KRASNOVSKY, A. A. (1960). *Ann. Rev. Plant Phys.* **11**, 363–410
108. KRASNOVSKY, A. A. (1961). *Proc. 5th Internat. Congr. Biochem.* Vol. VI. 187–197
109. KRASNOVSKY, A. A., BYSTROVA, M. A. & SOROKINA, A. D. (1961). *Dokl. Akad. Nauk. S.S.S.R.* **136**, 1227–1230. Quoted by Smith and French (1963)
110. KRASNOVSKY, A. A. & KOSOBUTSKAYA, L. M. (1952). *Dokl. Akad. Nauk. S.S.S.R.* **85**, 177–180. Quoted by Shibata (1957)
111. KRINSKY, N. I., Gordon, A. & STERN, A. I. (1964). *Plant Phys.* **39**, 441–445
112. KRINSKY, N. I. & LEVINE, R. P. (1964). *Plant Phys.* **39**, 680–687
113. KUCZMAK, M. & TOLBERT, N. E. (1962). *Plant Phys.* **37**, 729–734
114. KUFFERATH, H. (1913). *Rec. Inst. botan. Leo Errera, Bruxelles*, **9**, 113–119. Quoted by Smith & Young (1956)
115. KUPKE, D. W. (1962). *J. Biol. Chem.* **237**, 3287–3291
115a. LANGE, H. & MOHR, H. (1965). *Planta* **67**, 107–121
116. LAZZARINI, R. A. & WOODRUFF, M. (1964). *Biochim. Biophys. Acta* **79**, 412–415
117. LIRO, J. I. (1909). *Ann. Acad. Sci. Fennicae, Ser. A* **1**, 1–147
118. LITVIN, F. F. & KRASNOVSKY, A. A. (1957). *Dokl. Akad. Nauk. S.S.S.R.* **117**, 106. Quoted by Krasnovsky (1961)
119. LITVIN, F. F. & KRASNOVSKY, A. A. (1958). *Dokl. Akad. Nauk. S.S.S.R.* **120**, 764. Quoted by Krasnovsky (1961)
120. LOEFFLER, J. E. (1955). *Carneg. Inst. Wash. Yearbook.* **54**, 159–160
121. LUBIMENKO, M. V. (1928). *Rev. Gen. Bot.* **40**, 23–29, 88–94, 146–155, 226–243, 303–318, 372–381
122. LWOFF, A. & DUSI, H. (1935). *Compt. Rend. Soc. Biol., Paris* **119**, 1092
123. LYTTLETON, J. W. (1956). *Nature, Lond.* **177**, 283–284
124. LYTTLETON, J. W. & Ts'O, P. O. P. (1958). *Arch. Biochem. Biophys.* **73**, 120–126
125. MADSEN, A. (1963). *Phys. Plant* **16**, 470–473
126. MAGASANIK, B. (1961). *Cold Spring Harbour Symp.* **26**, 249–256
127. MARCUS, A. (1960). *Plant Phys.* **35**, 126–128
128. MARGULIES, M. M. (1964). *Plant Phys.* **39**, 579–585
129. MARGULIES, M. M. (1965). *Plant Phys.* **40**, 57–61
130. McLEOD, G. C. & COOMBER, J. (1960). *Carneg. Inst. Wash. Yearbook* **59**, 324–325
131. MEGO, J. L. & JAGENDORF, A. T. (1959). *Plant Phys.* **34**, xix
132. MEGO, J. L. & JAGENDORF, A. T. (1961). *Biochim. Biophys. Acta* **53**, 237–254
133. MEYER, B. S. & ANDERSON, D. B. *Plant Physiology.* 2nd Ed. 1952. D. Van Nostrand. New York. p. 302
134. MITRAKOS, K. (1961). *Phys. Plant* **14**, 497–503
135. MOHR, H. (1962). *Ann. Rev. Plant Phys.* **13**, 465–488
136. MOLISCH, H. (1889). *Österreich. Bot. Zeit.* Quoted by Stahl (1909)

137. MONTEVERDE, N. A. (1893–94). *Acta Horti Petropolitani* **13**, 201–217. Quoted by Smith & Young (1956)
138. MONTEVERDE, N. & LUBIMENKO, V. N. (1909). *Bull. Jardin Imp. botan. St. Petersbourg.* Quoted by Smith & Young (1956)
139. MÜHLETHALER, K. & FREY-WYSSLING, A. (1959). *J. Biophys. Biochem. Cytol.* **6**, 507–512
140. NEIDHARDT, F. C. & MAGASANIK, B. (1956). *Nature, Lond.* **178**, 801–802
141. NICHOLS, K. E. & BOGORAD, L. (1962). *Bot. Gaz.* **124**, 85–93
142. NISHIMURA, M. (1959). *J. Biochem.* **46**, 219–223
143. NISHIMURA, M. & HUZISIGE, H. (1959). *J. Biochem.* **46**, 225–234
144. NOACK, K. & KIESSLING, W. (1929). *Z. Physiol. Chem.* **182**, 13–49
145. NOACK, K. & KIESSLING, W. (1930). *Z. Physiol. Chem.* **193**, 97–137
146. OGREN, W. L. & KROGMANN, D. W. (1965). *Fed. Proc.* **24**, 608
147. PALLADIN, V. I. (1923). *Plant Physiology.* Ed., B. E. Livingston. Blakiston's Son and Co., Philadelphia, 2nd ed.
148. PERINI, F., SCHIFF, J. A. & KAMEN, M. D. (1964). *Biochim. Biophys. Acta* **88**, 90–98
149. PRICE, L. & KLEIN, W. H. (1961). *Plant Phys.* **36**, 733–755
150. PRINGSHEIM, N. (1874). *Monatsber. Berlin. Akad. Wiss.* Quoted by Eyster (1928)
151. PRINGSHEIM, E. G. (1948). *Biol. Rev.* **23**, 46–61
152. RACKER, E. & SCHROEDER, R. (1958). *Arch. Biochem. Biophys.* **74**, 326–344
153. RITENAUER, G. & HUFFAKER, R. S. (1964). *Plant Phys.* **39**, xx
154. RÖBBELEN, G. (1956). *Planta* **47**, 532
155. ROSENBERG, A. & PECKER, M. (1964). *Biochemistry* **3**, 254–258
156. RUDOLPH, E. (1965). *Planta* **66**, 75–94
157. RUSSELL, G. K. & GIBBS, M. (1964). *Plant Phys.* **39**, xlv
158. SACHS, J. (1859). *Lotos* **9**, 6–14. Quoted by Smith & Young (1956)
159. SAGER, R. (1961). *Carneg. Inst. Wash. Yearbook* **60**, 374–376
160. SAGER, R. & PALADE, G. E. (1954). *Exp. Cell. Res.* **7**, 584–588
161. SCHIFF, J. A. (1963). *Carneg. Inst. Wash. Yearbook* **62**, 375–378
162. SCHIFF, J. A. & EPSTEIN, H. T. In *Symposium on Biochemistry of Chloroplasts* (*Aberystwyth, 1965*). Ed., T. W Goodwin. Academic Press, London (in press)
163. SCHMIDT, A. (1914). *Beitr. Biol. Pflanzen.* **12**, 269–296
164. SEYBOLD, A. & EGLE, K. (1938). *Planta* **28**, 82–123
165. SHIBATA, K. (1957). *J. Biochem.* **44**, 147–173
166. SHIMIZU, S. & TAMAKI, E. (1963). *Arch. Biochem. Biophys.* **102**, 152–158
167. SIGNOL, M. (1961). *Compt. Rend. Acad. Sci.* **252**, 4177
168. SIRONVAL, C., MICHEL-WOLWERZ, M. R. & MADSEN, A. (1965). *Biochim. Biophys. Acta* **94**, 344–354
169. SISLER, E. C. & KLEIN, W. H. (1963). *Phys. Plant* **16**, 315–322
170. SMILLIE, R. (1960). *Nature, Lond.* **187**, 1024–1025
171. SMILLIE, R. M. (1963). *Can. J. Bot.* **41**, 123–154
172. SMILLIE, R. M., EVANS, W. R. & LYMAN, H. (1963). *Brookhaven Symp.* **16**, 88–107
173. SMITH, J. H. C. (1948). *Arch. Biochem. Biophys.* **19**, 449–454
174. SMITH, J. H. C. (1951). *Carneg. Inst. Wash. Yearbook* **50**, 123–124
175. SMITH, J. H. C. (1952). *Carneg. Inst. Wash. Yearbook* **51**, 151–153
176. SMITH, J. H. C. (1954). *Plant Phys.* **29**, 143–148
177. SMITH, J. H. C. (1959). *Brookhaven Symp.* **11**, 296–302
178. SMITH, J. H. C. (1960). In *Comparative Biochemistry of Photoreactive systems.* Ed., M. B. Allen. Academic Press, New York, pp. 257–277
179. SMITH, J. H. C. (1961). In *Biological structure and function.* Eds., T. W. Goodwin & O. Lindberg. Academic Press, London, pp. 325–338
180. SMITH, J. H. C. & BENITEZ, A. (1954). *Plant Phys.* **29**, 135–143

181. SMITH, J. H. C. & COOMBER, J. (1961). *Carneg. Inst. Wash. Yearbook* **60**, 371–374
182. SMITH, J. H. C., DURHAM, L. J. & WURSTER, C. F. (1959). *Plant Phys.* **34**, 340
183. SMITH, J. H. C. & FRENCH, C. S. (1963). *Ann. Rev. Plant. Phys.* **14**, 181–224
184. SMITH, J. H. C., FRENCH, C. S. & KOSKI, V. M. (1952). *Plant Phys.* **27**, 212–213
185. SMITH, J. H. C. & YOUNG, V. M. K. (1956). In *Radiation Biology*. Ed., A. Hollaender. III. McGraw-Hill Book Company Inc., New York, pp. 393–442
186. SPIER, R. (1964). Personal communication
187. STAHL, E. (1909). *Zur Biologie des Chlorophylls*. Gustav Fischer, Jena
187a. STERN, A. I., EPSTEIN, H. T. & SCHIFF, J. A. (1964). *Plant Phys.* **39**, 226–231
188. STERN, A. I., SCHIFF, J. A. & EPSTEIN, H. T. (1964). *Plant Phys.* **39**, 220–226
189. STRAIN, H. H. (1938). *Plant Phys.* **13**, 413–418
190. THRELFALL, D. R. & GOODWIN, T. W. (1964). *Biochem. J.* **90**, 40P
191. TOLBERT, N. E. & COHAN, M. S. (1953). *J. Biol. Chem.* **204**, 639–648
192. TOLBERT, N. E. & GAILEY, F. B. (1955). *Plant Phys.* **30**, 491–499
193. TROWN, P. W. (1965). *Biochemistry* **4**, 908–918
194. TROXLER, R. & BOGORAD, L. In *Symposium on Biochemistry of Chloroplasts (Aberystwyth, 1965)*. Ed., T. W. Goodwin. Academic Press, London (in press)
195. ULEHLA, J. (1961). *Nature, Lond.* **191**, 613–614
196. VIRGIN, H. I. (1957). *Phys. Plant* **10**, 445–453
197. VIRGIN, H. I. (1958). *Phys. Plant* **11**, 347–362
198. VIRGIN, H. I. (1960). *Phys. Plant* **13**, 155–164
199. VIRGIN, H. I. (1961). *Phys. Plant* **14**, 439–452
199a. VIRGIN, H. I. (1965). *Phys. Plant* **18**, 994–1000
199b. VIRGIN, H. I. (1966). *Phys. Plant* **19**, 40–46
200. VIRGIN, H. I., KAHN, A. & VON WETTSTEIN, D. (1963). *Photochem. & Photobiol.* **2**, 83–91
201. VOROBEVA, L. M., BYSTROVA, M. I. & KRASNOVSKII, A. A. (1963). *Biokhimiya* (Consultants Bureau transl.) **28**, 426–433
202. WALLACE, J. W. & NEWMAN, D. W. (1965). *Phytochem.* **4**, 43–47
203. WEIDNER, M., JAKOBS, M. & MOHR, H. (1965). *Z. Naturf.* **20b**, 687–693
204. WEISSBACH, A., HORECKER, B. L. & HURWITZ, J. (1956). *J. Biol. Chem.* **218**, 795–810
205. VON WETTSTEIN, D. (1959). *Brookhaven Symp. Biol.* **11**, 138–159
206. VON WETTSTEIN, D. In *Symposium on Biochemistry of Chloroplasts (Aberystwyth, 1965)*. Ed., T. W. Goodwin. Academic Press, London (in press)
207. WILLIAMS, G. R. (1965). *Plant Phys.* **40**, 1
208. WILLIAMS, G. R. & NOVELLI, G. D. (1964a). *Biochem. Biophys. Res. Commun.* **17**, 23–27
209. WILLIAMS, G. R. & NOVELLI, G. D. (1964b). *Plant Phys.* **39**, li
210. WILSTÄTTER, R. & STOLL, A. (1918). *Untersuchungen über die Assimilation der Kohlensäure*. Julius Springer, Berlin
211. WILSTÄTTER, R. & STOLL, A. (1928). *Investigations on Chlorophyll*. Translated by F. M. Schertz & A. R. Merz. The Science Printing Co., Lancaster, Pa.
212. WITHROW, R. B., WOLFF, J. B. & PRICE, L. (1956). *Plant Phys.* **31**, xiii–xiv
213. WOLF, F. T. (1963). *Plant Phys.* **38**, 649–652
214. WOLFF, J. B. & PRICE, L. (1957). *Arch. Biochem. Biophys.* **72**, 293–301
215. WOLFF, J. B. & PRICE, L. (1960). *J. Biol. Chem.* **235**, 1603–1608
216. WOLKEN, J. J. & GROSS, J. A. (1963). *J. Protozool.* **10**, 189–195
217. WOLKEN, J. J. & MELLON, A. D. (1956). *J. Gen. Physiol.* **39**, 675–685
218. WOLKEN, J. J., MELLON, A. D. & GREENBLATT, C. C. (1955). *J. Protozool.* **2**, 89–96
219. YEMM, E. W. Personal communication
220. YU, Y. L., TOLBERT, N. E. & ORTH, G. M. (1964). *Plant Phys.* **39**, 643–647
221. ZIEGLER, H. & ZIEGLER, I. (1965). *Planta* **65**, 369–380

CHAPTER XIV

The Growth and Differentiation of Plastids: Part II

XIV.1. Chloroplast Formation during normal development of the Green Plant

XIV.1.i. INTRODUCTION

HAVING examined in detail the process of chloroplast formation in dark grown plants exposed to light, we shall now go on to consider the development of the chloroplast as it occurs in plants grown under continuous or intermittent illumination.

XIV.1.ii. CHLOROPHYLL SYNTHESIS

The chlorophyll content $(a+b)$ of leaves of most species of higher plant lies in the range $0\cdot7$–$1\cdot3$ per cent of the dry weight[147, 148]. Since there is little or no chlorophyll in the seed, synthesis of a large amount of chlorophyll must take place during the growth of the plant. When pea plants were grown in soil under normal daylight conditions, the amount of chlorophyll per g fresh weight of leaf was initially low, since the very early development of the immature leaves took place before the plant had emerged from the soil[118]. There was a rapid increase in chlorophyll per g fresh weight between 5 and 9 days after germination, i.e. chlorophyll synthesis was taking place more rapidly than leaf expansion. Between 9 and 12 days after germination chlorophyll synthesis and leaf growth occurred in parallel, so that the amount of chlorophyll per g fresh weight remained approximately constant (Fig. XIV.1). Friend (1961) studying wheat plants growing in the light found that there was no close relationship between chlorophyll content and leaf area or weight, because chlorophyll formation did not take place to any extent until the leaf had become exposed to light by growth through the sheaths of preceding older leaves.

477

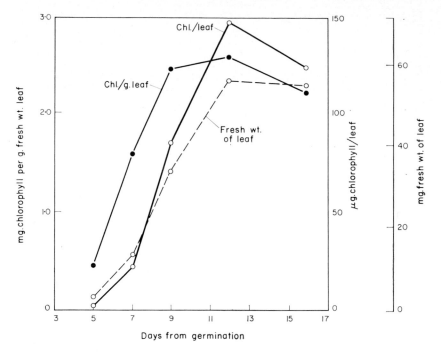

FIG. XIV.1. *Chlorophyll content of pea leaves at various stages of their development (adapted from Smillie and Krotkov, 1961)*

The rate of chlorophyll synthesis per growing leaf increased with temperature over the range 5–20°; there was little change between 20° and 30°, and at 35° the rate of chlorophyll synthesis fell off sharply[37]. There was a marked reduction in leaf area at 30°, compared with 25°, so that the amount of chlorophyll per unit area was about twice as high as it was at 25°[38]. The response to change in light intensity depended upon the temperature. At 10°, 15°, 20°, 25°, and 30° the rate of chlorophyll synthesis increased with light intensity over the range 200–1000 foot-candles. However, when the intensity was raised above 1750 foot-candles the rate of synthesis decreased at 10° and 15°, but increased at 20°, 25°, and 30°. Friend (1960) suggested that the lower temperatures retarded protochlorophyll synthesis but did not affect the light-induced breakdown of chlorophyll.

Amongst higher plants, those species which normally grow in the shade usually have a substantially higher chlorophyll content than those which normally grow in bright sunlight. Three typical shade plants *Aspidistra elatior*, *Tilia parvifolia*, and *Theobroma cacao*, have chlorophyll contents of 0·40, 0·44, and 0·79 per cent of the fresh weight of the leaves respectively: two typical sun species, *Larix europaea*, and *Pinus sylvestris*, have chlorophyll contents of 0·12 and 0·11 per cent, respectively, of the leaf fresh weight[95]. The leaves of shade plants apparently have fewer chloroplasts than those of sun plants, but the chloroplasts of the former are larger, and richer in chlorophyll, than those of the latter.

Amongst the algae it appears to be generally true that when they are grown in the light, the chlorophyll content decreases as the light intensity increases. In the red alga *Porphyridium cruentum*, the concentration of chlorophyll *a* was five times as great in cells grown in white light of low intensity (680 ergs/cm^2/sec) as in cells grown in white light of high intensity (11,400 ergs/cm^2/sec)[18]. In *Euglena gracilis* the chlorophyll content was nearly three times as high in cells grown at 50 foot-candles as it was in cells grown at 1200 foot-candles[19]. In *Chlorella pyrenoidosa* the chlorophyll content of cells grown at a light intensity of 100 foot-candles was about four times as high as in cells grown at an intensity of 1050 foot-candles[133]. Also, in *Acetabularia crenulata* growing on a 16 hour light/8 hour dark régime, the chlorophyll content was three times as high with a light intensity of 50 foot-candles as it was with a light intensity of 450 foot-candles: however, cells grown at 900 foot-candles had about the same chlorophyll content as those grown at 450 foot-candles[130].

Little evidence is available on the effect of wavelength of light on chlorophyll synthesis in growing plants. In the case of barley seedlings, chlorophyll accumulation was found to occur to the same extent in red and green light[82]. In lettuce leaves it is reported that the wavelength has no effect on chlorophyll formation, provided that the incident energy is greater than 20,000 ergs/cm^2/sec[60].

The chlorophyll content of higher plants is affected by daylength. Withrow and Withrow (1949) found that the amount of chlorophyll per unit area, or fresh weight, of growing tomato leaves fell off markedly at daylengths greater than 18 hours. The optimum daylength for chlorophyll content of strawberry leaves is about 13 hours; the amount of chlorophyll per unit area falls off at daylengths greater or less than this[115]. In *Acetabularia crenulata* grown at a given light intensity, 450 foot-candles, the chlorophyll content was about three times as high when the cells were given 8 hours' light per day as when they were given 16 hours' light per day[130]: this inhibitory effect of long light exposures might perhaps be related to the inhibitory effect of high light intensity, mentioned above.

Like other growth processes, chlorophyll synthesis is dependent upon the nutrients available to the plant. Lack of certain nutrients inhibits chlorophyll formation more than leaf expansion, so that the leaves take on a chlorotic, or bleached, appearance. Such chlorosis may be caused by lack of nitrogen, potassium, magnesium, iron, or manganese (see XV.6). As discussed in the previous chapter (XIII.18), certain nutrients, those which are oxidizable carbon sources, can repress chlorophyll formation in certain algae. A particularly interesting example of nutritional control of chlorophyll synthesis is found in *Chlorella protot*thecoides, where there is an interaction between the level of carbon source and the level of nitrogen source[111]. Cells grown in the light in a medium containing 1 per cent glucose and 1 per cent urea, were green (both chlorophylls and carotenoids present); cells grown in a medium containing 1 per cent glucose and 0.5 per cent urea were yellow (only carotenoids present); cells grown in a medium containing 1 per cent glucose and 0.05 per cent urea were white (neither type of pigment present). The important factor seemed to be the urea/glucose ratio rather than the absolute amounts: 0.5 per cent urea + 1 per cent glucose produced yellow cells, but 0.5 per cent urea + 0.1 per cent glucose, or 0.05 per cent urea + 0.01 per cent glucose, produced green cells. The different cell types were interconvertible (in either direction) by simply transferring the cells to new medium with the appropriate urea/glucose ratio. Similar effects were observed if the urea was replaced with other nitrogen sources, such as amino acids or ammonium salts. This phenomenon is discussed in more detail in the next chapter (XV.7.vi).

We shall now consider the question of whether the later stages of chlorophyll synthesis are the same in the normal plant grown in the light as in the dark-grown plant exposed to light. Green plants apparently contain small amounts of protochlorophyll: Smith and Koski (1948) isolated this pigment from mature, green barley leaves. Also, green leaves have the ability to synthesize new protochlorophyll when they are placed in the dark. The fluorescence spectrum of protochlorophyll appears when green sugar-beet leaves are kept in the dark: on illumination the protochlorophyll disappears, indicating that it is the photochemically active form[71]. Using paper chromatography, Virgin (1960) detected protochlorophyllide in green wheat leaves, and showed that the amount increased if the leaves were kept in the dark for five hours. On illumination, this newly-formed protochlorophyllide disappeared, to be replaced by chlorophyllide *a*. During a further incubation in the dark, the chlorophyllide *a* disappeared, probably because it was being phytylated to give chlorophyll *a*. Similar observations have been made with barley leaves[112]. The ability of green wheat leaves to synthesize protochlorophyll in the dark decreased as the plants got older[135]. After about 10 days, when the leaves had completed their growth, there was no formation of protochlorophyll in the dark.

From these studies, involving the direct analysis of pigments, it appears that green leaves have the ability to make protochlorophyllide, to reduce it to chlorophyllide *a* in the light, and they can probably also esterify the chlorophyllide to give chlorophyll. Tracer experiments lead to similar conclusions. Green tobacco leaves in the dark incorporate radioactivity from ^{14}C-δ-amino-laevulinic acid into a substance having the properties of protochlorophyllide[26]. Vlasenok and Shlyk (1963) allowed green barley leaves to incorporate $^{14}CO_2$ for some minutes, and then put the leaves in the dark to allow them to accumulate proto-chlorophyllide. The leaves were briefly exposed to light, to bring about some conversion of the protochlorophyllide, and then returned to the darkness, and samples were taken at intervals for the measurement of the specific radioactivities of the different pigments. The specific activity of protochlorophyllide was the highest, being about twice as high as that of chlorophyllide a, and more than two hundred times that of chlorophyll a. Thus, the order of specific activities is consistent with the supposed biosynthetic sequence. During the subsequent incubation in the dark, the specific activity of chlorophyllide a remained unchanged (although the total amount of this substance decreased) while the specific activity of chlorophyll a rose.

In all these experiments the leaves were incubated in the dark to make them accumulate protochlorophyllide. It might be argued that this is much the same as growing the plants in the dark in the first place, and so it is not surprising that the mechanism of conversion of this protochlorophyllide to chlorophyll during a subsequent illumination is the same as that in the greening of etiolated plants. A more rigorous investigation of the later stages of this pathway has been carried out by Vlasenok, Fradkin, and Shlyk (1965). Green barley seedlings were exposed to $^{14}CO_2$ for 10 minutes, and then allowed to continue growing (in the light) for up to 16 days. At intervals during this time, samples were taken, and the specific activities in the porphyrin rings of proto-chlorophyllide, chlorophyllide a, chlorophyll a, and chlorophyll b were measured. The specific activity of protochlorophyllide rose the most rapidly, reached its peak after about 12 hours, and then rapidly declined. The specific activity of chlorophyllide a reached its highest value (ca. two-thirds that of protochlorophyllide) a few hours after protochlorophyllide, and then also declined rapidly. The specific activity of chlorophyll a rose much more slowly than did that of either of the previous two compounds: the maximum value (about one-fortieth of the maximum value reached by chlorophyllide a) was reached after about one day, and slowly declined during the next 15 days. No protochlorophyllide ester could be detected in extracts of normal green leaves, or in leaves which had been kept in the dark for up to four days, even though a very sensitive fluorescence technique was used: thus protochlorophyllide is the only protochlorophyllic pigment present in green barley leaves. Vlasenok et al. conclude that the later stages of chlorophyll a synthesis in green leaves in the light go according to the sequence:

$$\text{protochlorophyllide} \rightarrow \text{chlorophyllide } a \rightarrow \text{chlorophyll } a$$

Just as chlorophyll *a* is synthesized before chlorophyll *b* during the greening of etiolated leaves, so the radioactive magnesium isotope, ^{28}Mg, is found in chlorophyll *a* sooner than in chlorophyll *b* when young green tobacco shoots are incubated with ^{28}MgCl$_2$ in the light[2]. Also, it has been found by many workers that when higher plants, or algal cells, are supplied with radioactive substrates, the specific activity of chlorophyll *b* rises more slowly, and to a lower final value, than the specific activity of chlorophyll *a*[44, 26, 9, 100, 113, 136]. These findings suggest that in the normal plant grown in the light, chlorophyll *a* is a precursor of chlorophyll *b*. However, it is still possible that chlorophylls *a* and *b* may be formed independently from a close common precursor.

There are conflicting views as to whether there is turnover of the chlorophyll in the leaf once it is formed. Godnev and Shlyk (1956) observed a decrease in the radioactivity of chlorophyll in plants previously given ^{14}CO$_2$ and then transferred to a label-free medium. Duranton *et al.* (1958) found that the specific activity of chlorophyll *a* in tobacco leaves which had been allowed to incorporate ^{14}C-δ-aminolaevulinic acid, fell by about one-third over a 10-day period, although the total amount of chlorophyll *a* remained approximately the same. Sironval (1963) fed young leaves of *Soja hispida* with ^{14}C-δ-aminolaevulinic acid for 24 hours. Maximum incorporation was reached two days after beginning the feeding with the labelled precursor. After this time the radioactivity in both chlorophyll *a* and chlorophyll *b* began to disappear. Sironval calculated that chlorophyll *a* turned over with a half-life of 5·0–6·6 days, and chlorophyll *b* with a half-life of 1·7–5·5 days. However, Roberts and Perkins (1962) could detect no incorporation of radioactivity from ^{14}C-acetate by fully expanded wheat leaves during a four-hour incubation. Similarly, Aronoff (1963) found no incorporation of ^{28}Mg into chlorophyll by mature tobacco leaves during a 22-hour incubation. Roberts and Perkins, and Aronoff concluded that there is no significant turnover of chlorophyll in mature leaves. However, Perkins and Roberts (1963) have now re-investigated the question of chlorophyll turnover in mature leaves using a wider range of plants —four monocotyledon species (lily, oats, *Philodendron*, *Tradescantia*), three dicotyledon species (red clover, *Petunia*, *Geranium*), a gymnosperm (*Picea pungens*), and a fern (*Nephrolepsis exalta*). ^{14}C-acetate or ^{14}C-succinate was fed to leaves of these different plants, and incorporation into the porphyrin ring of chlorophyll *a* and chlorophyll *b* was measured. No incorporation was detected into chlorophylls in the mature leaves of the monocotyledons. However, substantial amounts of radioactivity were incorporated into chlorophylls in the mature leaves of the dicotyledons, the gymnosperm, and the fern. These authors conclude that chlorophyll turnover may indeed occur in mature leaves of these dicotyledon and other species. Thus, the balance of evidence suggests that there is chlorophyll turnover in mature leaves of some species but not others. In the case of wheat, the mature leaves of which do not show chlorophyll turnover, it may be relevant that, as previously noted, the ability to synthesize protochlorophyll is present in young, still-growing, wheat leaves, but not in fully expanded leaves[135].

The problem of chlorophyll turnover is connected with the question of whether there is a diurnal variation in the chlorophyll content of leaves. This is also a matter on which there is a great deal of controversy. An example of a recent report of diurnal variation is the claim by Bukatsch and Rudolph (1963) that leaves of *Rumex alpinus* show a diurnal pigment rhythm, the amplitude of which is 8–11 per cent for chlorophyll *a*, and 5–7 per cent for chlorophyll *b*. The chlorophyll content was said to be highest at noon, and at its lowest in the morning and evening. Another type of diurnal variation was reported by Wieckowski (1963): he found that the chlorophyll content of growing *Phaseolus vulgaris* leaves rose during the day and fell during the night. This type of variation seems quite probable, since it is well known that chlorophyll breaks down in the dark: in corn seedlings, for instance, all the chlorophyll disappears after five days in the dark at $27°$[34]. A recent report of the absence of diurnal variation is that by Wickliff and Aronoff (1962), who found no rise and fall in the chlorophyll content of mature soybean leaves during a 24-hour period; instead there was a slight, but steady, decrease. Bauer (1958) and Seybold and Falk (1959) have reported that the diurnal variation is present in young leaves but not in old leaves. If this difference between old and young leaves is real, it may account for the conflicting reports in the literature. If there is a daily rise and fall (due to destruction in the dark and resynthesis in the light), in the region of 10 per cent, in the chlorophyll content of young leaves of some species, and perhaps even mature leaves of others, then this would provide a mechanism for turnover, i.e. for loss of radioactivity from pre-labelled chlorophyll or acquisition of radioactivity by unlabelled chlorophyll without a gross change in the amount present.

XIV.1.iii. CAROTENOID SYNTHESIS IN THE GREEN PLANT

It has already been noted (XIII.9) that carotenoids are synthesized in the dark. This may account for the finding[58] that when soybeans were germinated in soil in the light, the carotenoid content showed a detectable increase on the fifth day, whereas chlorophyll content did not increase until the eighth day, when the plants were emerging from the soil. As the plant grows and forms chloroplasts naturally the carotenoid content increases steadily. However, the increase in carotenoid content may not keep pace with the expansion of the leaves. For instance, in corn plants the total β-carotene content per plant increased markedly between 45 and 80 days after sowing, but the carotene concentration per g dry weight actually decreased in this time[92]. After 80 days, the total β-carotene content of the plants began to fall again.

Carotenoid synthesis in the green leaf is stimulated by light. Bandurski (1949), using excised bean leaves, found that a light intensity of 600 foot-candles gave the maximum rate of carotenoid synthesis; at intensities higher or lower than this the rate fell off. Variation in light intensity apparently does not affect all carotenoids to the same extent: in corn seedlings, increasing the light intensity to high levels stimulates the synthesis of zeaxanthin and violaxanthin, but reduces formation of β-carotene and lutein[83]. The relative amounts of different carotenoids formed are affected also by temperature: in germinating corn seedlings, low temperatures stimulate zeaxanthin synthesis at the expense of β-carotene[83]. In excised bean leaves, with light at 600 foot-candles, carotenoid synthesis was 40 per cent faster at $35°$ than it was at $26°$[3]. In the mature, green, cell there can be quite rapid changes in carotenoid composition. In leaf discs there is a fairly rapid conversion of violaxanthin to zeaxanthin in the light, which is reversed in the dark[101a, 150a]. Also, in cells of *Euglena gracilis* there is conversion (removal of an epoxide oxygen) of antheraxanthin to zeaxanthin in the light in an atmosphere of nitrogen: if the nitrogen atmosphere is replaced by one of oxygen there is re-conversion of zeaxanthin back to antheraxanthin[63]. Krinsky (1965) suggests that this cyclical oxidation-reduction, zeaxanthin-antheraxanthin interconversion, may provide the mechanism by which carotenoids protect cells against lethal photo-sensitized oxidations, as postulated by Sistrom, Griffiths, and Stanier (1956).

Little is known about the dependence of carotenoid synthesis in higher plants on the wavelength of the light with which they are irradiated. Claes (1965) has studied the wavelength dependence of some of the later stages of carotenoid synthesis in a mutant of *Chlorella vulgaris*. This mutant differs from the wild-type in that it is unable to make the bicyclic carotenoids (molecules with a ring at each end) in the dark: instead it accumulates open-chain C_{40} polyenes. When the dark-grown cells are exposed to the light they start converting these compounds to the cyclic carotenoids. Claes determined the action spectrum for the conversion of the open-chain compounds to cyclic carotenes (α-carotene, β-carotene, β-zeacarotene). No xanthophylls were formed because the experiment was carried out in an atmosphere of nitrogen. The action spectrum for ring closure had its main peak at 670 mμ. The stimulatory effect of light diminished sharply from 670 to 700 mμ, and more slowly from 670 to 500 mμ. There was little synthesis between 500 and 460 mμ. Light of wavelengths between 430 and 400 mμ had about half the stimulatory effect of light at 670 mμ. The stimulatory effect of red light (670 mμ) was not reduced by a simultaneous irradiation with far-red light (727 mμ). Claes concluded that chlorophyll, and not phytochrome, is the chromophore involved.

Like all growth processes, carotenoid synthesis by the developing plant requires nutrients[46, 48]. Lack of iron may affect carotenoid formation more than leaf growth (see XV.7). Carotenoid synthesis by excised bean leaves was stimulated more than 100 per cent by sucrose or glucose in CO_2-poor air: in CO_2-rich air, sucrose had no effect[3]. As mentioned previously, in *Chlorella protothecoides*, carotenoid synthesis, like chlorophyll synthesis, is repressed if the cells are grown in a medium containing a high ratio of glucose to nitrogen source[111]. However, carotenoid synthesis seems to be less sensitive to this type of repression than chlorophyll synthesis: a glucose/urea ratio (by weight) of 2 abolishes chlorophyll synthesis but not carotenoid synthesis: a glucose/urea ratio of 20 stops synthesis of both types of pigment.

Carotenoid content of leaves (like chlorophyll content) has been reported to show a diurnal variation in some species[99]. Carotenoids break down in the dark in excised leaves[3] or in whole plants[34]. Thus, if there really is a diurnal variation in carotenoid content, a mechanism could be provided by breakdown at night followed by resynthesis during the day. The destruction of carotenoids in the dark can be completely prevented by adding glucose[3] or sucrose[34].

XIV.1.iv. CHROMATIC ADAPTATION

Amongst different types of plant the kind of chloroplast pigment present, and the ratio of the various chloroplast pigments to each other, bears some relationship to the light quality (intensity and spectral composition) in the habitat where the plant naturally grows. The nature of the relationship might be summed up by the generalization that those pigments are present which are best suited to absorb, for purposes of photosynthesis, the light available. The standard examples of this relationship are the marine algae. As sunlight passes down through sea water, the light intensity falls off greatly, and also the predominant colour of the light becomes bluish-green: this is due to the fact that red and violet light are lost to a greater extent than the light in the intermediate part of the spectrum[95]. Algae growing in shallow water (for instance, in rock pools) where the light contains the full range of wavelengths, are typically green algae (*Chlorophyta*) whose chlorophyll and carotenoid pigments are able to absorb the red and violet radiation. Algae growing at intermediate depths where blue and green light are predominant, are typically brown algae (*Phaeophyta*), which possess in addition to chlorophyll, the carotenoid fucoxanthin, whose absorption peaks (*in vivo*) are shifted (compared to carotenoids of *Chlorophyta*) away from the violet, and into the blue-green part of the spectrum. Algae growing in deep water, where green light is predominant, are typically red algae (*Rhodophyta*) which possess, in addition to chlorophylls and carotenoids, biliprotein pigments such as phycoerythrin, which are very effective absorbers of green light. When red algal species which naturally occur at different depths are compared, it is found that the phyco-erythrin/chlorophyll ratio increases as the depth of the habitat increases[73]. These phenomena were referred to by Engelmann (1883–1884) as 'complementary chromatic adaptation', because the algae tended to be a colour which was complementary to the colour of the available light.

Chromatic adaptation, as we have discussed it so far, is presumably the result of evolution of the plants to fit their habitats: that is, it has a hereditary basis, these plants having genes which ensure that the appropriate pigments are produced. However, even given a certain genetic disposition in a plant to produce certain types of pigment, the plant still has the ability, to some extent, to vary the ratio of the different kinds of pigment in accordance with the prevailing light quality. Thus, as well as evolutionary chromatic adaptation, there can be physiological chromatic adaptation.

Amongst higher plants we have already seen (XIV.1.ii) that shade species tend to have a higher chlorophyll content than sun species: the high chlorophyll content is of advantage to the shade species since it enables them to absorb a high proportion of the feeble light available; the sun species do not need so much chlorophyll because there is more than enough light available in their habitat. Another difference between shade and sun species is that the former tend to have a higher proportion of their chlorophyll in the *b* form[107, 109]. This might be regarded as chromatic adaptation. The shade plants will normally be growing in the light which has already passed through other foliage. If this other foliage is of a sun species, with a low chlorophyll *b* content, then there may be substantial amounts of light transmitted, of wavelength from 450 to 480 mμ (a part of the spectrum where chlorophyll *b* absorbs but chlorophyll *a* does not). A relatively high proportion of chlorophyll *b* in the shade plant will enable it to use this light more efficiently. The first type of chlorophyll adaptation, the high content of chlorophyll in shade plants, is probably largely genetic rather than physiological: the natural physiological response, in wheat plants at any rate, is for lowered light intensity to produce a lower chlorophyll content[37]. The second type of chlorophyll adaptation, the lower *a/b* ratio in shade plants, may well also be largely genetically determined. However, there is some slight suggestion that there is a physiological mechanism to produce the same effort: Wilstätter and Stoll (1928) found that in a given tree the leaves exposed to the sun might have a somewhat higher (perhaps 30 per cent or so) a/b ratio than leaves in the shade.

There is no evidence that in higher plants the ratio of chlorophylls to carotenoids is affected by chromatic adaptation: there seems to be no particular correlation between the chlorophyll/carotenoid ratio and whether the plant is a sun plant or a shade plant[107, 109]. There is some indication that the xanthophyll/carotene ratio is higher in shade plants[107, 109], but this is unlikely to be anything to do with chromatic adaptation[95]. This effect may have something to do with the fact that the synthesis of a high proportion of carotenes seems to require light: dark-grown plants have a very low proportion of carotenes (I.4.ii).

Amongst the algae, in addition to the genetically-based chromatic adaptation, there is also much physiological chromatic adaptation. In the red algae, plants of a given species show an increase in the concentration of all chloroplast pigments, as the depth at which the plants grow increases[73, 74]. As far as the total amount of chlorophyll is concerned, we saw previously (XIV.1.ii) that it is generally true that in any given alga, the chlorophyll content increases as the light intensity at which the cells were grown decreases. Thus, algae grown at low light intensity have some similarity to shade plants. In at least one alga, *Chlorella vannielii*, it seems that the chlorophyll a to chlorophyll b ratio increases as the light intensity during growth increases: the ratios reported were 2·9 at 100 foot-candles; 3·0 at 300 foot-candles; 3·8 at 900 foot-candles; and 5·0 at 2700 foot-candles[97]. A higher a/b ratio at high light intensity is indeed what might have been expected from the known characteristics of sun species of higher plants. As far as wavelength is concerned, it has been reported[57] that cells of *Chlamydomonas* grown in blue light have a much higher proportion of chlorophyll b to chlorophyll a than cells grown in red or white light. If the blue light used was rich in wavelengths between 450 and 480 mμ, then this might well be genuine chromatic adaptation.

In the red alga, *Porphyridium cruentum*, Brody and Emerson (1959) found that the type of chromatic adaptation that takes place when the cells are grown in light of a particular colour, depends upon the intensity used. Intense green light ($2·5 \times 10^4$ ergs/cm²/sec) increases the ratio of chlorophyll to phycoerythrin, whereas blue light of high intensity ($6·16 \times 10^4$ ergs/cm²/sec) reduces the ratio of chlorophyll to phycoerythrin. This is chromatic adaptation of a non-complementary type. In each case the algae are changing their pigment composition in such a way as to reduce the amount of light absorbed (by making less of that pigment which absorbs the light in question). At light intensities about 1000 times lower (*ca.* 100 ergs/cm²/sec), the effects of the two colours are reversed: blue light increases the proportion of chlorophyll formed, and green light increases the proportion of phycoerythrin. This is true complementary chromatic adaptation: the cells produce more of that pigment which can best absorb the light available. To explain these data, Brody and Emerson suggest that at low light intensities the algae will need to adjust their pigment composition so as to capture as much of the light as possible, but at saturating light intensities will require a pigment composition such as to keep the absorption of light energy down to a level at which the photosynthetic systems can handle it.

XIV.1.v. FORMATION OF OTHER CHLOROPLAST COMPONENTS

During the normal growth of the plant in the light there must be synthesis of all chloroplast components: however, little work has been done so far on the formation of chloroplast lipids, proteins or nucleic acids during the development of the green plant. Bloch, Constantopoulos, Kenyon, and Nagai (1965) found that when *Euglena gracilis* was grown autotrophically at different light intensities, the chlorophyll content of the cells decreased as the light intensity increased, over the range 100–600 foot-candles. The total lipid content of the cells, including the galactoglyceride content, decreased in close parallel with the chlorophyll content. Bloch *et al.* suggest that the morphogenesis of the chloroplast and the synthesis of galactoglycerides occur in synchrony. As the lipid content decreased with increasing light intensity the proportion of monogalactosyl to digalactosyl glyceride increased. Also, as light intensity increased, the proportion of unsaturated fatty acids, particularly α-linolenic and a C_{16} tetraenoic acid, increased in the monogalactosyl fraction but not the digalactosyl fraction. In parallel with the increase in the proportion of α-linolenic acid, the Hill reaction activity of the chloroplasts (measured in terms of the amount of trichlorophenolindophenol reduced/mg chlorophyll/min) also increased.

Protein is the major constituent of the chloroplast. The main increase in chloroplast protein appears to take place during the later stages of leaf growth. When a tobacco leaf expands from one-third its maximum size to its maximum size, the nitrogen content of the chloroplast fraction increases about eighteenfold[50]. Pirson and Böger (1965) have isolated from various green algae (*Chlorella pyrenoidosa*, *Chlorella vulgaris*, *Scenedesmus obliquus*, and *Chlamydomonas reinhardi*) an insoluble chloroplast protein preparation, with the pigments attached, which they believe to consist largely of the chloroplast structural protein. The chlorophyll content of the algae varied from about 8 per cent of the dry weight in cells grown at low light intensity, to about 1 per cent in cells grown at high light intensity. The chlorophyll content of the protein fraction increased as the chlorophyll content of the cells increased. The chlorophyll/nitrogen ratio of the protein fraction varied from about 0·4 in cells with a low chlorophyll content to about 1·6 in cells with a high chlorophyll content. When algae with a low chlorophyll content were put in the dark without a nitrogen source, chlorophyll was synthesized, but the amount of the insoluble protein fraction remained approximately constant. The chlorophyll/nitrogen ratio of the protein fraction increased from 0·41 to 1·04. That is, it appeared as if the newly-synthesized chlorophyll was occupying places on a pre-existent structural protein. When chlorophyll deficiency was induced by lack of nitrogen in the medium, the chlorophyll content of the protein was at the maximum level (chlorophyll/nitrogen = 1·6) even at two very different levels of cellular chlorophyll content, indicating that formation of the protein was inhibited as much as formation of chlorophyll; indeed, in view of the marked dependence of chlorophyll formation on protein synthesis (XIII.15) it seems possible that the lowered chlorophyll content of nitrogen-deficient cells might be due to the lack of chloroplast structural protein. When chlorophyll deficiency was induced by lack of potassium or iron salts in the medium the chlorophyll/nitrogen ratio of the insoluble protein fraction was low, suggesting that lack of these elements inhibits formation of chlorophyll more than formation of chloroplast structural protein. When the potassium- or iron-deficient cells were supplied with potassium or iron, respectively, in dim light, chlorophyll was formed and the chlorophyll/nitrogen ratio of the insoluble protein was restored to the normal level. The general implication of all these results is that formation of chlorophyll is probably limited by the amount of chloroplast structural protein present, but that formation of chloroplast protein is not closely linked to, or limited by, the rate of chlorophyll synthesis. That is, under certain light conditions, or in certain media, chloroplast structural protein can accumulate in excess of the amount required to bind the chlorophyll present.

XIV.1.vi. DEVELOPMENT OF CHLOROPLAST ULTRA-STRUCTURE IN THE GREEN PLANT

The meristematic cells of the shoot contain colourless amoeboid proplastids. These have relatively little internal structure: a few apparently isolated vesicles and thylakoids, and occasional invaginations from the inner plastid membrane (see section I.3 and Fig. I.36). As the meristematic cells begin to differentiate into the mesophyll and palisade cells of the leaf, so the proplastids begin to differentiate into chloroplasts. The following description of this process is based on the electron microscopical studies of many workers, in particular the results of Buvat (1958); Lance (1958); Mühlethaler and Frey-Wyssling (1959); von Wettstein (1959); Gerola, Cristofori, and Dassu (1960); Menke (1960, 1964); Wehrmeyer and Röbbelen (1965).

In the proplastid, as we have mentioned, the inner plastid membrane invaginates, in places, into the stroma of the plastid. In section, these intrusions often appear long and thin, and it is commonly assumed that they are, in fact, tubules. It is entirely possible that some of them may be tubules. However, a section through a double-membraned sheet would have essentially the same appearance as a section through a tubule. Also, some of these intrusions are very long, in the region of 0·5 μ: if they are tubules then it may be wondered why they extend so far without wandering out of the section; if, however, they are fairly wide double-membraned sheets, then this greatly increases the likelihood of their remaining within the section. Thus it seems quite likely that many of these invaginations are not tubules, but are indeed double-membraned sheets, or lamellae. They might be produced by an infolding of the plastid membrane along a line: alternatively they might start off as tubules, and then the tip of the tubule might begin to grow outwards in two dimensions to produce, eventually, a flattened sac, or thylakoid, joined to the inner plastid membrane by a relatively narrow neck. Both of these processes might occur. However, if infolding along a line is the common mechanism, then sections should be found in which the line in the plastid membrane lies within the section; that is, quite wide invaginations should sometimes be seen. Invaginations to be seen in published pictures are narrow at the point where they join on to the plastid membrane: this would seem to favour the second hypothesis, but clearly more information is required.

This process of invagination from the inner membrane continues until there may be many flat sacs, or thylakoids lying in the stroma. Fig. XIV.2 shows a plastid of the leaf meristem of *Oenothera hookeri*[80]. This contains several thylakoids, most of them lying singly in the stroma. Two of the thylakoids can be seen to be joined to the inner plastid membrane: whether the other thylakoids are also joined to the plastid membrane in some region not included in the section, or whether the thylakoid eventually becomes detached from the plastid membrane, is not known.

As differentiation proceeds, the number of thylakoids to be seen in sections of the plastid increases. Also, these thylakoids are now seen to occur almost invariably in stacks of two, three, or more. Fig. XIV.3 shows a plastid which has reached this stage of development in the leaf meristem of *Oenothera hookeri*[80]. As differentiation proceeds further the number of thylakoids in each stack increases until eventually the typical grana (I.2.iii.a) of the mature chloroplast (Fig. I.14) are pro-

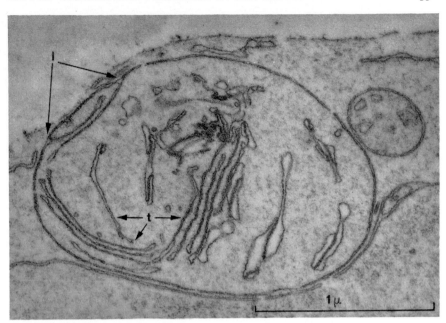

FIG. XIV.2. *Plastid in leaf meristem of* Oenothera hookeri. *By permission, from Menke, W. (1964)* Ber. Deut. Bot. Ges. **77**, *340–354*. i—*invaginations from inner plastid membrane*. t—*single thylakoids*

duced, different grana being connected by thylakoids which pass from one to the other. There are various possible ways in which this multiplication and stacking of thylakoids might occur. One possibility suggested by Menke (1962, 1964) is that, at the edge of a thylakoid, the membrane might begin to invaginate, and grow into and across the intrathylakoid space, eventually fusing with the membrane at the opposite edge: in this way, two separate thylakoids would be produced. Fig. XIV.3 shows a number of thylakoids whose appearance could be a result of the thylakoid membrane invaginating from one edge, almost, but not quite completely, across the intrathylakoid space. However, since there is some evidence (1.2.iii.a) that the intrathylakoid spaces of the different thylakoids of a granum are in communication with each other, it seems possible that the actual fusion process, sealing off the thylakoids from one another, may not take place: that the invagination process might cease before it reaches the opposite side of the thylakoid. In certain sections the two new thylakoids would be seen to be in communication at one edge, but in any section which did not happen to include this region, the thylakoids would appear to be separate.

Wehrmeyer and Röbbelen (1965) have used a pale green mutant of *Arabidopsis thaliana* to study the way in which thylakoid multiplication and stacking occur. This mutant has relatively few thylakoids: these

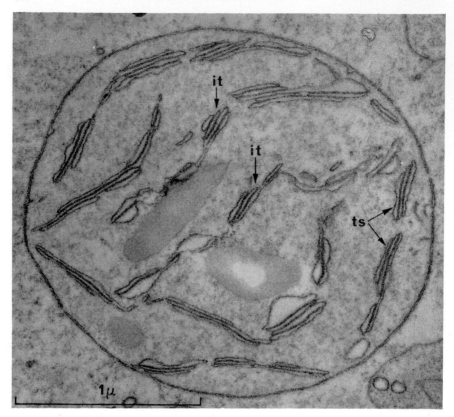

FIG. XIV.3. *Early stage in chloroplast development in leaf meristem of* Oenothera hookeri. *By permission, from Menke, W. (1964). Ber. Deut. Bot. Ges. 77, 340–354. ts—thylakoid stacks. it—invagination into thylakoid*

mainly occur singly, and where there are stacks they consist of only two or three thylakoids so that the interpretation problems are greatly simplified. These authors conclude that as well as invagination, protrusion processes are also involved in granum development. Fig. XIV.4(a) shows a doubling of part of a thylakoid, which might have arisen by invagination. The protrusion process might involve a region of the thylakoid membrane beginning to protrude and then growing out across the surrounding membrane, thus producing another flat sac (thylakoid) lying on top of the original one, and in communication with it at one end. Fig. XIV.4(b) shows such a protrusion. The type of stacking produced by this sort of invagination or protrusion process, Wehrmeyer and Röbbelen call 'conjunctive' stacking (Fig. XIV.4(a), (b), and (c)). Another kind of protrusion process would involve one edge of a thylakoid beginning to grow outwards and then round to one side, so that the new thylakoid material would begin to slide over the old thylakoid material. Fig. XIV.4(d) shows a protrusion of this type: thylakoid stacking produced in this manner Wehrmeyer and Röbbelen refer to as 'disjunctive' stacking. Fig. XIV.4(e) and (f) shows combinations of conjunctive and disjunctive stacking. The appearance in section of thylakoids layered in these ways will, of course, depend upon the precise plane of the section. The structures in Fig. XIV.4(a)–(e) can give six different types of appearance in section, according to where they are cut. Sections cut, as it were, across the page in regions I, II, III, IV, V, or VI will appear as shown in Fig. XIV.5. Sections of all these types were observed in the Arabidopsis mutant, and examination of serial sections supported the three-dimensional interpretations given.

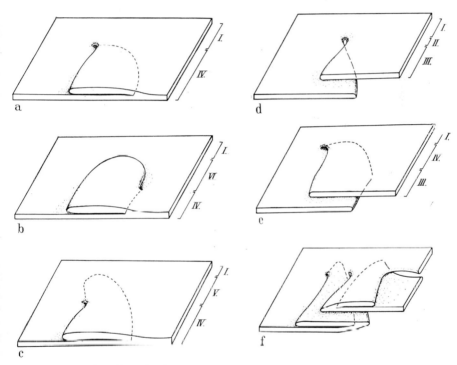

Fig. XIV.4. *Three-dimensional models of different types of thylakoid stacking. By permission, from Wehrmeyer, W. and Röbbelen, G. (1965). Planta **64**, 312–329. Conjunctive (a, b, c), disjunctive (d), and combined conjunctive-disjunctive (e, f), membrane stacking*

It seems entirely plausible that the formation of stacks of thylakoids during chloroplast development should be brought about by the sort of invagination and protrusion processes that we have considered. There also seems to be no reason why in a single, fairly large thylakoid, these processes should not occur in more than one place at once. Alternatively, a thylakoid might grow outwards from one granum to slide over a thylakoid in another granum. By either, or both, of these processes the existence of thylakoids passing from one granum to another could be brought about. Thus, the sort of complicated system of membranes, illustrated in Fig. I.18 could be built up.

This might be regarded as the normal pattern of development of the chloroplast in the growing plant. However, in plants such as barley

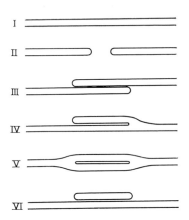

Fig. XIV.5. *Appearance of sections cut across regions I–VI in Fig. XIV.4 (after Wehrmeyer, and Röbbelen, 1965)*

the meristematic region is at the base of the leaf, which is surrounded by the coleoptile or older leaves. Thus, the early development of the chloroplast takes place in dim light or darkness. Consequently, the plastids of such plants pass, in the course of their differentiation to chloroplasts, through a phase in which they have a crystalline centre, even though the plant is grown in the light (Prof. E. W. Yemm, personal communication). In these cases, chloroplast development might be regarded as taking the course—proplastid to etioplast to chloroplast.

In the very young cells of the leaf meristem the number of proplastids per cell is maintained by division of the plastids to keep pace with cell division. In the course of differentiation of the meristematic cells to the mesophyll and palisade cells of the leaf, the number of plastids per cell increases markedly. During the differentiation of the leaf of *Agapanthus umbellatus* the number of plastids per cell increased from about 25 in meristematic cells to 110 in the mature leaf cell[32]. The increase in number is probably less in other species: in the leaf of *Epilobium hirsutum* there are about 31–42 chloroplasts per palisade cell, and about 39–66 per spongy mesophyll cell[81]; for *Ricinus communis* the corresponding figures are about 36 and 20[54]. Increase of ploidy of cells increases the cell size, and also causes a substantial increase in the number of chloroplasts: in *Beta vulgaris*, the normally tetraploid spongy mesophyll cells become largely octoploid in plants which have an extra chromosome II or VIII, and this increase in ploidy is accompanied by increases of up to 60 per cent in the number of chloroplasts per cell[21]. However, whatever the variation from one plant to another, it is generally true that the number of plastids per cell must increase. This is no doubt brought about by the plastids dividing more often than the cells. Michaelis (1962) has reported that the young amoeboid pro-plastids of the meristematic cells of *Epilobium* divide approximately in synchrony, not just within the same cell, but in a number of adjoining cells. Most of the plastid division responsible for the increase in plastid number appears to take place in the very early stages of chloroplast development. During the growth of the tomato leaf from one-third its maximum size to its maximum size, the total number of plastids increases by only about 30 per cent, although the nitrogen content of the chloroplast fraction (determined with tobacco leaves) increases eighteenfold during this stage of leaf development[50]. Although there is little division during the major part of the chloroplast development sequence, occasional divisions of almost mature leaf chloroplasts can apparently take place, as may be seen in Fig. XIV.6[66].

The developmental sequence outlined above was derived from studies on angiosperms. Such detailed information is not yet available on the differentiation of chloroplasts in growing leaves of gymnosperms. Information is also lacking in the case of pteridophytes. However, it has been reported that meristematic cells of *Psilotrum triquetrum*[129] and *Isoetes howellii*[89] contain undifferentiated proplastids, similar in struc-ture to those of angiosperms, and so it seems entirely likely that the process of chloroplast differentiation is very similar to that which takes place in angiosperms. In the case of one fern, *Matteuccia struthiopteris*, the interesting observation has been made that chloroplast division appears not to take place by constriction; the chloroplast is divided by the inward growth of the inner membrane (Fig. XIV.7), thus dividing the chloroplast into two parts[39]. It seems likely that this is followed by separation of the two parts, although such a process was not, in fact, observed. Amongst the bryophytes, chloroplast development has been studied in the meristem of *Anthoceros*[77,146]. The differentiation of this chloroplast starts, as in vascular plants, from a proplastid in the meri-stematic cell. This proplastid has little internal structure: a few thyla-koids and vesicles in the stroma, and some invaginations from the inner plastid membrane[146]. In the early stages of differentiation the number of thylakoids increases, and pairs of thylakoids are seen. The amount of thylakoid material continues to increase until the characteristic *Antho-ceros* chloroplast (Fig. I.19) is produced. On the basis of her studies, Manton (1962) has suggested that the whole system of lamellae in the *Anthoceros* chloroplast is produced by the growth and folding of one

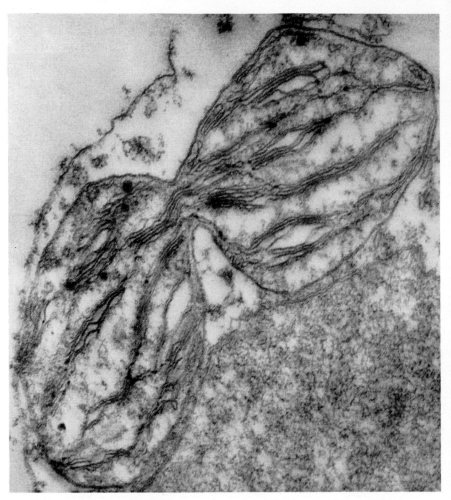

FIG. XIV.6. *Chloroplast of* Chrysanthemum segetum *in course of division. By permission, from Lance, A. (1958). Ann. des. Sci. Nat.* 11e Serie (Bot.) ***19***, *165–202*

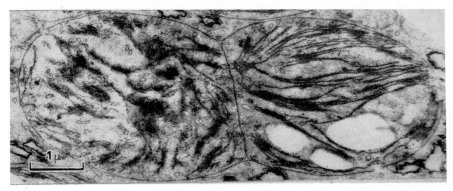

FIG. XIV.7. *Chloroplast of fern in course of division. Reprinted by permission of The Rockefeller University Press from Gantt, E. and Arnott, H. J., J. Cell Biol., November 1963,* ***19***, *No. 2, 446–448. Chloroplast of* Matteuccia struthiopteris *apparently dividing by inward growth of inner plastid membrane*

membrane which is ultimately derived from invaginations protruded into the stroma from the inner plastid membrane.

The chloroplast of the higher plant leaf is an end product. The only further changes it undergoes are degenerative changes (beginning with loss of chlorophyll) when the leaf becomes senescent. When a flower bud begins to form in the axil of a leaf, the cells begin to divide, that is, they become meristematic. Lance-Nougarède (1960) has studied the changes in the structure of the plastids during the initiation of the floral meristem in *Chrysanthemum segetum*. To begin with the plastids exist as chloroplasts, with well-defined grana composed of up to twelve thylakoids. As the cells become meristematic, the amount of lamellar material present begins to decrease. As cell division proceeds the plastids become progressively smaller, and with less and less internal structure, until eventually small, almost completely empty bodies with an occasional invagination from the inner plastid membrane, are produced. Thus, it appears that the differentiation of the proplastid to the chloroplast is not necessarily irreversible: that in certain tissues the chloroplasts can regress to the proplastid state. It seems likely that the same sort of thing may happen when a section of a leaf is made to regenerate a new plant (as can be done with plants such as *Begonia*). Also the changes in the plastid structure observed by Bell and Mühlethaler (1962) in the maturing egg cell of *Pteridium aquilinum*, and interpreted by them as degenerative changes, may in fact be due to the regression of the plastid from the chloroplast stage of development to the proplastid stage of development in preparation for the rapid cell division that will take place after fertilization of the egg. Thus, it may be generally true that whenever a chloroplast-containing plant cell has to start dividing, the chloroplasts revert to proplastids to facilitate the plastid division that must take place if plastid numbers in the cell are to be maintained.

Amongst the algae, chloroplasts are usually derived from pre-existing chloroplasts by division. Von Wettstein (1954) has obtained an electron micrograph of a chloroplast apparently dividing, in the brown alga *Fucus*. Fig. XIV.8(b) shows a dividing chloroplast in a cortical cell of the red alga *Lomentaria baileyana*. Electron micrographs of the dividing chloroplasts of the very small flagellate *Chromulina pusilla* have been published by Manton (1959). Green (1964) has followed division of *Nitella* chloroplasts by microcinephotography, and has published a series of still pictures showing a group of chloroplasts in *Nitella* undergoing division. One complete division cycle of a chloroplast (from fission to fission) took about 22 hours. The chloroplasts appeared to grow in the direction of maximum strain: when a new direction of maximum strain was induced mechanically the chloroplasts elongated in this new direction.

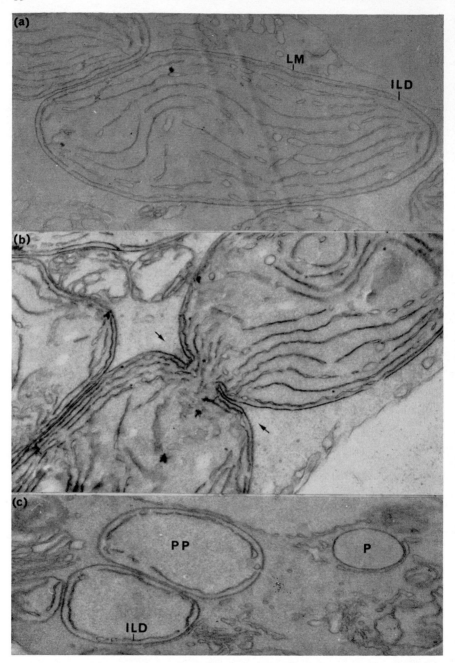

Fig. XIV.8. *Plastids of the red alga,* Lomentaria baileyana. *Reprinted by permission of The Rockefeller University Press from Bouck, G. B., J. Cell. Biol., March (1962),* **12**, *No. 3, 553–569.* (a) *Mature chloroplast.* LM—*limiting membrane.* ILD—*inner limiting thylakoid.* (b) *Chloroplast in course of division.* (c) *Plastids in apical cells.* P—*completely undifferentiated proplastid.* PP—*proplastid which has formed its inner limiting thylakoid*

The disposition of the thylakoid material within the chloroplast is something that varies considerably from one algal group to another (I.2.iii.c). Although quite a lot is known about the structures of the mature chloroplasts, virtually nothing is known about their morphogenesis. In *Chlorella pyrenoidosa*, cells which have a high chlorophyll content as a result of growth at low light intensity, have more numerous and more dense thylakoids in their chloroplasts than cells having a lower chlorophyll content due to growth at high light intensity[133]. In the multicellular algae chloroplasts may be formed from proplastids as well as by division of pre-existing chloroplasts. Bouck (1962) showed that in *L. baileyana*, apical cells contain typical proplastids with little internal structure (Fig. XIV.8(c)). The first structure to appear is that thylakoid which runs round the periphery of the plastid, just underneath, and parallel to, the plastid membrane (this is a feature characteristic of certain algal chloroplasts). As the apical cells differentiate, these proplastids presumably form more thylakoids and develop into mature chloroplasts. The thylakoids may be formed from invaginations of the inner plastid membrane, since a proplastid with such an invagination (similar to those seen in higher plant proplastids) was observed.

As the algal chloroplasts multiply and differentiate, so, of course, must the pyrenoids (when present). In dividing cells of *Scenedesmus quadricauda*, as seen in the light microscope[7], the single pyrenoid seems to disappear between the first and second cleavages, only to reappear again in each of the four daughter cells during their initial elongation. Electron microscope examination[7] showed that in a young cell the pyrenoid had two round or ellipsoidal starch grains, one at each side. As the cell matured the number of starch grains increased from two to many: they also grew laterally and became curved so that they eventually formed a concavo-convex sheath round the pyrenoid. Thylakoids, in groups or bands, grew in round the inner surface of some of these grains and eventually separated them from the pyrenoid. At the same time the shape of the starch grains changed from concavo-convex platelets, to lenticular grains. In this way, eventually, large numbers of starch grains became transferred away from the pyrenoid, in amongst the thylakoid bands. In some cases these grains appeared to be connected to each other by slender starch bridges. The alga *Closterium moniliferum* contains two chloroplasts per cell, each chloroplast with 2–6 pyrenoids. It has been reported[139] that within 36 hours after centrifugation of the cells for 5–10 minutes at 500 g, the average number of pyrenoids per cell increased from 7·9 to 10·7. The maximum number of pyrenoids per cell increased from 12 to 18. Thus, multiplication of pyrenoids might be affected by mechanical strain.

XIV.1.vii. DEVELOPMENT OF PHOTOSYNTHETIC ACTIVITY BY THE GREEN PLANT

According to Briggs (1922), in the case of seedlings of plants such as *Helianthus* and *Cucurbita*, where the first assimilating organ is one that also serves as a storage organ, the photosynthetic activity is fully developed at germination. In plants such as *Phaseolus*, *Ricinus*, and *Zea*, where the seedling develops a specialized photosynthetic organ different from the storage organ, the photosynthetic activity is not developed until some time after germination. As the leaf unfolds and expands, and its chloroplasts develop, the rate of photosynthesis (per unit area) increases: eventually, however, it reaches a maximum value and begins to decrease again. In the case of wheat and linseed, the maximum value is reached after about 70 days[114]. Smillie (1962) found that in young pea plants the photosynthetic rate per leaf, or per gram fresh weight of leaf, reached its maximum 9 days after germination. This maximum was reached while the leaves were still expanding and making chlorophyll. By the time (12 days) the leaves had reached their maximum size and chlorophyll content, the photosynthetic activity had declined somewhat. In *Nicotiana sanderae*, also, the maximum photosynthetic rate (per unit area of leaf) is attained before the leaves have reached their final size[104, 105]. In the case of the *Helianthus* type of plant, although the cotyledons apparently have photosynthetic ability almost as soon as they appear, it seems likely that the new leaves, subsequently produced, would have to develop their powers of photosynthesis in the same way as the leaves of plants of the *Phaseolus* type.

The changes in the photosynthetic activity of developing pea leaves[117] were accompanied by parallel changes in the activity of two chloroplast enzymes—carboxydismutase and photosynthetic pyridine nucleotide reductase (ferredoxin). The activity of two other enzymes believed to be involved in photosynthesis—transketolase and fructose-1, 6-diphosphate aldolase—also increased and decreased together with photosynthetic rate. However, these two enzymes were present in relatively large amounts at a time (5 days) when the photosynthetic rate was still very low. This is not very surprising since transketolase and aldolase, unlike the other two enzymes, are involved in respiratory carbohydrate metabolism as well as in photosynthesis. Hageman and Arnon (1955) found that in pea seedlings germinated in the light, the chloroplast enzyme, NADP-linked glyceraldehyde phosphate dehydrogenase, was only detectable after 10 days. There was a rapid increase in activity between 10 and 15 days. They also made the interesting observation that the newly formed pea seeds had none of this enzyme. Thus, in the life of the plant, from seed to seed, there is a cyclical appearance and disappearance of this enzyme.

In synchronously growing cultures of *Chlorella ellipsoidea*[87] the photosynthetic activity was found to be higher during the growth phase (when the newly liberated autospores were increasing in size) than during the ripening phase (when the grown cells were preparing for cell division). In cells of *Chlorella vulgaris* grown in the light the rate of photosynthetic oxygen production per mg chlorophyll was low in early stages of growth, rose to a maximum after 24 hours, and then declined to the initial low value after 72–90 hours[1a]. These changes were paralleled by changes in the ratio of α-linolenate to chlorophyll. In general the photosynthetic efficiency of the chlorophyll was directly proportional to the magnitude of the α-linolenate/chlorophyll ratio, regardless of whether high values of the ratio were due to high α-linolenate, or low chlorophyll, values. Lövlie and Farfaglio (1965) put single cells of *Euglena gracilis* in growth medium in a Cartesian diver, and measured photosynthetic oxygen production throughout a few division cycles. The increase in oxygen output during the cycle occurred in an approximately sigmoid manner: for instance, in a 16-hour generation time there was little increase in the first two hours, a fairly rapid increase during the next 10 hours, followed by a levelling off during the last four hours and the next cell division. There was some indication that the increase occurred in a small number (about three) distinct steps.

Cells of *Chlorella pyrenoidosa* which have a high chlorophyll content (and more numerous and denser thylakoids) as a result of growth at low light intensities have a higher photosynthetic capacity than normal cells[133]. The amplitudes of various electron spin resonance signals are also different in the high-chlorophyll cells (grown at 100 foot-candles) from what they are in the low-chlorophyll cells (grown at 1050 foot-candles, one quarter as much chlorophyll). The ratio of the light-induced, fast-rise fast-decay signal (signal I) to the broader, slower-decay signal (signal II) is greater in the high-chlorophyll than in the low-chlorophyll cells. The ratio of the Fe^{3+} signal to the Mn^{2+} signal is higher in the high-chlorophyll than in the low-chlorophyll cells. Although the decrease in chlorophyll content caused by high light intensity may reduce the overall photosynthetic capacity, the photosynthetic efficiency of the chlorophyll present may actually increase. In cells of *Euglena gracilis* grown at increasing light intensities, the efficiency of the chloroplast fraction at carrying out the Hill reaction (μ moles trichlorophenolindophenol reduced/mg chlorophyll/minute) increased as the cellular chlorophyll content fell[10].

Development of photosynthetic ability can be affected by the wavelength, as well as the intensity, of the light in which the cells are grown. Cells of *Chlamydomonas* grown in blue light (with a consequent increase in chlorophyll *b* content) incorporated 40–50 per cent of $^{14}CO_2$ radioactivity during a 3–10 minute incubation, into glycollate and related compounds, and 15–25 per cent into citric acid cycle intermediates[57]. The colour of the light (blue, red, or white) during the incubation with $^{14}CO_2$ did not alter the incorporation pattern. Cells grown in red or white light incorporated 40–50 per cent of the ^{14}C into citric acid cycle intermediates, and 5–10 per cent into glycollate products. Sugar phosphates of the CO_2 fixation cycle were labelled by both types of algae. The data indicate that growth of *Chlamydomonas* in blue light not only alters the photosynthetic pigments, but also appears to enhance the ability of the cells to carry out one particular pathway for the utilization of the newly fixed $^{14}CO_2$.

Development of photosynthetic ability by growing algal cells can also be markedly affected by the nutrients in the medium. As we have already seen (XIII.18; XIV.1.ii) the presence of oxidizable carbon sources may markedly repress the formation of certain components of the photosynthetic apparatus.

XIV.2. Chloroplast Formation in Roots and Tubers

XIV.2.i. INTRODUCTION

The great majority of the chloroplasts of the plant are contained in the leaves; some are formed also in stems and immature fruit. Roots and tubers normally contain none: however, under certain circumstances chloroplasts will appear in these tissues.

XIV.2.ii. CHLOROPLAST FORMATION IN ROOTS

When a seed of, say, barley is germinated in the light the newly formed shoot is green but the roots are white, although both organs receive the same illumination. On prolonged illumination of the roots, however, chloroplasts may be formed. Powell (1925) grew sixteen plant species with their roots exposed to light: after two weeks, thirteen species had developed chlorophyll in their roots. The chloroplasts were not uniformly distributed through the different layers of the root: the distribution was constant for a given species, but varied from one species to another. Roots of broad bean, pea, and sunflower are reported to form 5–10 times as much chlorophyll in the light as roots of corn and nasturtium[101]. Gautheret (1932) found that excised roots of barley went green in the light earlier than roots left attached to the plant.

Greening started in the oldest part of the roots and then spread to the younger parts. Formation of chloroplasts in roots of the intact plant was stimulated by glucose and fructose. In wheat and barley roots exposed to light, the chloroplasts are formed in the two innermost layers of the cortex: the capacity for chloroplast formation in wheat root cells is nearly 40 per cent of that of mesophyll cells of the wheat leaf[31]. There is some evidence that the carotenoids formed in root chloroplasts may not be entirely the same as those formed by leaf chloroplasts; Fadeel (1962) found that the carotene and xanthophyll fractions of greening wheat roots each had a peak in the absorption spectrum which was absent from the spectra of the corresponding carotenoid fractions of leaves. In excised wheat roots, blue light is much more effective than red light at bringing about chlorophyll formation: however, the blue light effect is greater if the roots have been pretreated with red light. The action spectrum has a peak at 450 mμ suggesting that the chromophore may be a carotenoid or an iron porphyrin[8a].

Lance-Nougarède and Pilet (1965) have studied the transformation of amyloplasts to chloroplasts in the internal cortex of the root of *Lens culinaris*. These plastids initially (before exposure to light) contain large starch grains (commonly three), a few small vesicles, and a number of invaginations from the inner plastid membrane. After illumination of the roots for six hours there is an increase in the number of invaginations, and also of the number of vesicles. A few double-membraned structures similar to thylakoids appear. After 24 hours' light, the first pairs of appressed thylakoids appear. After 48 hours these two-thylakoid stacks, or grana, are wider and more numerous. After 108 hours' illumination the chloroplasts are nearly fully developed, with grana containing up to seven thylakoids, and some thylakoids extending from one granum to another. Even at this stage the plastids contain large starch granules.

XIV.2.iii. PROTOCHLOROPHYLL FORMATION IN ROOTS

Hejnowicz (1958) found a pigment which he considered to be protochlorophyll in the root tips of all the species (ranging from ferns to angiosperms) he investigated. The pigment was identified as proto chlorophyll on the basis of the fluorescence and absorption spectra of extracts. The pigment disappeared on exposure of the roots to light, but no chlorophyll appeared. Hejnowicz suggested that chlorophyll was formed, but was destroyed by the light. Bjorn (1963) studied the light-induced disappearance of protochlorophyll in corn roots: with low light intensities, a small amount of chlorophyll *a* was formed but later disappeared again. Under high light intensities no chlorophyll could be detected—it was suggested that under these conditions the chlorophyll was being destroyed as soon as it was formed. Most of the protochlorophyll was in the esterified form; there seemed to be a small amount of protochlorophyllide in the apical part of the root. The disappearance of protochlorophyll in the roots had different characteristics from that observed on illumination of etiolated leaves: in the former, the rate was not proportional to light intensity, it did not show second-order kinetics, and it was much slower—the half-life of the protochlorophyll was about five hours in roots, but only about one minute in etiolated leaves illuminated in the same way. A possible explanation of these results might be that the chlorophyll which appears under low illumination is formed by the transformation of the small amount of protochlorophyllide present. The disappearance of the rest of the protochlorophyll might be due simply to photodestruction of the remaining protochlorophyllide ester.

XIV.2.iv. CHLOROPLAST FORMATION IN POTATO TUBERS

It is well known that potatoes turn green on exposure to light for a few days. Quite apart from its theoretical interest, this is an occurrence of some practical importance, since the greening of the potato is accompanied by the formation of toxic amounts of the poisonous alkaloid, solanine[33]. The cells of the tuber contain large amyloplasts. During the greening process these are converted into chloroplasts. In electron micrographs of amyloplasts in the early stages of greening, large vesicles can be seen near the plastid periphery[98]. As chloroplast formation proceeds, these vesicles are replaced by rather vacuolated grana, and eventually by grana of fairly normal appearance. The chloroplasts formed still have very large starch grains. It may be that the large vesicles seen in the early stages are precursors (perhaps vacuolated thylakoids) of the grana, but the precise details of the transformation are not known.

The association of solanine formation with chloroplast formation is particularly interesting. Synthesis of the alkaloid may, however, have no direct connection with the chloroplast; solanine formation might be triggered off by some other photoreceptor system, such as phytochrome.

XIV.3. Chloroplast Formation in the Dark

XIV.3.i. PIGMENT FORMATION IN THE DARK

As was discussed at the beginning of Chapter XIII, gymnosperms and most lower plants can form chlorophyll in the dark. Both chlorophyll *a* and chlorophyll b are formed[107]. However, Lubimenko (1928) showed that in germinating seedlings of *Pinus sylvestris* and *Picea excelsa*, chlorophyll synthesis was two to four times as rapid in the light as it was in the dark. Also, when mature branches of conifers are allowed to form new needles in the dark, these contain almost no chlorophyll[11]. New needles formed by pine saplings in the dark were found to contain only traces of chlorophyll a, chlorophyll b and protochlorophyll[120]. These needles formed chlorophyll only very slowly on illumination.

Pine embryos which have been excised from the megagametophyte can no longer form chlorophyll in the dark, although they will do so in the light[102, 12]. Bogorad (1950) found that even when excised embryos of *Pinus jeffreyi* are supplied with sucrose and a nitrogen source they cannot make chlorophyll in the dark. However, if the seeds are allowed to germinate for six days in the dark, and then the embryos are separated from the megagametophyte, chlorophyll synthesis continues for about two days, but at only a quarter of the normal dark rate. This chlorophyll formation is not stimulated by addition of sucrose and nitrate. Engvild (1964) has reported that a combination of sucrose, urea, and mineral salts does cause some stimulation of chlorophyll synthesis in excised embryos of *P. jeffreyi* in the dark. Addition of a vitamin mixture apparently caused some further stimulation, but an amino acid mixture did not. It appears that chlorophyll synthesis in the dark by this system requires some essential substrates and/or cofactors which are not present in the embryos themselves, but are supplied by the endosperm, and which cannot be completely replaced by exogenous sources of carbon, nitrogen, and vitamins.

The ability of certain plants to form chlorophyll in the dark shows that there must exist a non-photochemical pathway for chlorophyll synthesis. Dark-grown seedlings of *Larix europea* and *Thuja occidentalis*, and pine needles formed in the dark, contain protochlorophyll[74, 120], so it seems likely that protochlorophyllide (or possibly protochlorophyllide ester) is an intermediate in this system: there is presumably an enzymic light-independent mechanism for the reduction of protochlorophyllide. The fact that in excised embryos, and in newly-forming needles on mature branches, chlorophyll is formed in the light but not in the dark, suggests that gymnosperms also possess the photo-chemical pathway for chlorophyll formation. Similarly, it seems likely that those algae which form chlorophyll in the light and in the dark have both pathways, since mutants (of *Chlamydomonas reinhardi* and *Scenedesmus*) which do not make chlorophyll in the dark, can still synthesize it in the light.

The reduction of protochlorophyllide appears to be the only step in chlorophyll synthesis which angiosperms are unable to carry out in the dark. It is well known that they can make protochlorophyllide in the dark; they can synthesize phytol in the dark[45]; and they can attach phytol to chlorophyllide in the dark[150]. Recently, Kupke and Huntington (1963) and Wieckowski (1963) have independently reported that when leaves of *Phaseolus vulgaris* are maintained in the dark for 12 hours, there is an increase in the amount of chlorophyll *a* present, and a corresponding decrease in the amount of chlorophyll *b*. For instance, in one of Kupke and Huntington's experiments, the ratio of chlorophyll *a* to chlorophyll *b* changed from 3·36 to 16·32 during the dark incubation. These changes were not observed with fully expanded leaves, only with young leaves[64]. Both groups of workers suggest that chlorophyll *b* is converted to chlorophyll *a* in darkness. This might at first appear to be in conflict with the conclusion from isotope studies (XIV.1.ii) that chlorophyll *a* is a precursor of chlorophyll *b*. A possible explanation might be that chlorophyll *b* is normally synthesized, in the light, from chlorophyll *a*, but that the conversion of *a* to *b* is reversible, and in darkness the equilibrium tends to shift back towards chlorophyll *a*[145].

$$\text{Protochlorophyllide} \xrightarrow{\text{light}} \text{Chlorophyllide } a \rightarrow$$
$$\text{Chlorophyll } a \underset{\text{dark}}{\overset{\text{light}}{\rightleftharpoons}} \text{Chlorophyll } b$$

Shlyk and Stanishevskaya (1961) believe that there can be conversion of chlorophyll *a* to chlorophyll *b* in the dark: when barley seedlings pre-labelled with $^{14}CO_2$ were put in the dark for four days, the total radioactivity in chlorophyll *a* fell, and that in chlorophyll *b* rose (in both the porphyrin and phytol parts of the molecule).

As might be expected, gymnosperm seedlings form carotenoids as well as chlorophyll in the dark. In *Picea excelsa* seedlings growing in the dark, both xanthophylls and carotenes are formed, but the xanthophylls more rapidly[107].

XIV.3.ii. DEVELOPMENT OF CHLOROPLAST ULTRA-STRUCTURE IN THE DARK

Von Wettstein (1959) found that when seedlings of *Picea* are grown for some time in the light the chloroplasts of the mesophyll of the cotyledons become almost completely filled with starch, with only a few thylakoids present. When these seedlings are put in the dark, the starch breaks down and is rapidly replaced by new thylakoids. During the stage of formation of new thylakoids, the plastid can be seen, in electron micrographs, to contain large numbers of small crystalline centres placed here and there within the ramifying lamellar system (Fig. XIV.9). These crystalline centres may be precursors of the new thylakoids, in the same way as the crystalline centres of etioplasts are thought to act as thylakoid precursors during greening (XIII.7). It is interesting that these spruce chloroplasts appear to contain more than a hundred crystalline centres, whereas angiosperm etioplasts usually possess between one and four.

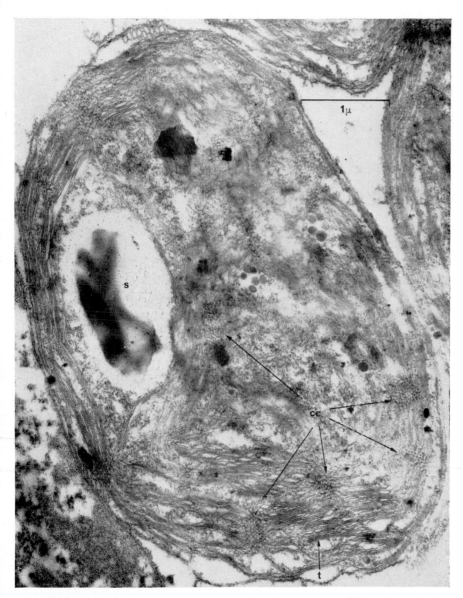

FIG. XIV.9. *Thylakoid formation in the dark in chloroplast of spruce cotyledon. By permission, from von Wettstein, D. (1959). Brookhaven Symp. Biol. 11, 138–159. cc—crystalline centres. t—new thylakoids being formed from crystalline centres. s—starch grain*

XIV.3.iii. DEVELOPMENT OF PHOTOSYNTHETIC ABILITY IN THE DARK

Myers (1940) grew *Chlorella vulgaris* heterotrophically in the dark; he then exposed the cells to light and measured the photosynthetic evolution of oxygen. Oxygen liberation was detectable within one minute, and, indeed, the time course of oxygen evolution was identical with that of cells grown on the same medium in the light. These results indicate that in *Chlorella vulgaris*, at least, the chloroplasts formed in the dark are completely functional, that is, they contain all the enzymes necessary for photosynthesis.

Dark-grown cells of *Chlamydomonas reinhardi* can evolve oxygen in the light, and chloroplast fragments from such cells can photoreduce ferricyanide, but in both cases rates are lower than in the light-grown cells. Also, cells grown in the dark lack an electron paramagnetic resonance signal that is possessed by cells grown in the light[70]. However, on illumination of the dark-grown cells, the rates of oxygen evolution and ferricyanide photoreduction return to normal within 16 minutes. Also, the electron paramagnetic resonance signal returns when the cells are illuminated. The rapidity of these changes make it seem unlikely that they are due to the *de novo* synthesis of chloroplast enzymes: one possibility is that there has to be some light-induced change of the physical state of some, or all, of the chlorophyll molecules before the full rate of photosynthetic electron flow is attained.

Whether the chloroplasts formed in the dark by gymnosperms are completely functional is not known.

XIV.3.iv. GENETIC BASIS FOR FORMATION OF CHLOROPLASTS IN THE DARK

If the formation of the constituents of the chloroplast is, indeed, under the control of regulator genes, as discussed earlier (see XIII.18), then it might seem that the difference between the plants which make chloroplasts in the dark and those which do not, is simply that the former lack some, or all, of the appropriate regulator genes. However, while this may be true in, say, *Chlorella vulgaris*, the situation in some plants of this type appears to be more complex. Organisms which completely lacked these regulator genes would be expected to form chloroplasts under all circumstances, as indeed *Chlorella vulgaris* does. Conifers, on the other hand, while they form chloroplasts in the cotyledons of the developing seedling in the dark, do not form chloroplasts in roots, or in needles newly formed in the dark. Amongst the pteridophytes, *Selaginella* and *Isoetes* make chloroplasts in their leaves in the dark[123] but the meristematic cells contain only a single, colourless plastid[27, 127]. The root cells, and even some of the mature leaf cells of *Isoetes* have colourless plastids. Dark-grown shoots of *Marsilia quadrifolia* have colourless stems but green leaves[123]. It is clear from the above findings that these higher plants can make chloroplasts in the dark, but under certain circumstances will refrain from doing so. A possible explanation would be that these plants do, in fact, have regulator genes concerned with chloroplast formation, but that, unlike the situation in the angiosperms, the inducers (which antagonize the repressors formed by the regulator genes) do not require light for their formation. Thus the structural genes controlling chloroplast formation can be de-repressed in the dark. Perhaps the reason why pine embryos do not form chlorophyll when excised from the megagametophyte, is that the inducer, which is required to de-repress the structural genes, can be supplied only from the endosperm.

The phytochrome system (see XIII.18) may be involved in the control of multiplication of chloroplasts in mosses in the dark. Hahn and Miller (1966) found that in *Polytrichum commune* grown in continuous darkness, the size of the chloroplasts increased but there was no increase in number. In plants grown in continuous white light, or in darkness with 15 minutes red light every six hours, chloroplast multiplication continued. If the plants were exposed to far-red light for 15 minutes after each exposure to red light, then chloroplast multiplication was reduced (but not abolished). The increase in size of the chloroplasts in continuous darkness appeared to be due to accumulation of starch. Phytochrome (P_{fr}) may therefore activate the starch-degrading system as well as chloroplast multiplication.

XIV.4. Development of the Amyloplast

In the meristematic cells of the root, the proplastids have little internal structure; a few isolated vesicles, an occasional invagination from the inner membrane, and perhaps one or two thylakoid-like structures[83, 143]. Sometimes the proplastids contain small starch grains. Some of these plastids appear, in electron micrographs, to be in the process of dividing (Dr B. E. Juniper, personal communication). In the differentiating cells in front of (i.e. the root cap), and behind, the meristematic region, the starch grains grow much larger: this tendency is particularly marked in the root cap, where amyloplasts may be found containing as many as eight starch grains, almost completely filling the interior of the plastid (Fig. I.39). The simplest explanation of the accumulation of starch in the plastids of certain root cells is that sugars are being transported to these cells from the leaves faster than they are being utilized.

We have already seen (XIV.2) that when seeds are germinated in the light the shoots form chloroplasts, but the roots do not (except after a very prolonged illumination). A plausible explanation of this on the genetic level is that certain inducers, formed in the shoots in the light, are not formed by the roots in the light, so that the structural genes for the formation of chloroplast proteins remain repressed. How the plant arranges that the inducers are formed in the shoot but not in the root remains, like most problems in differentiation, a mystery.

XIV.5. Development of Chromoplasts

XIV.5.i. CAROTENOID FORMATION IN FRUIT CHROMOPLASTS

In those fruits, the colour of which is due to chromoplasts, there is a considerable increase in carotenoid content during ripening[46,47]. In the green, unripe fruit, the carotenoids present tend to be those characteristic of the chloroplast, but in the course of ripening, different carotenoids are usually formed, e.g. lycopene in the tomato, and capsanthin in red pepper. In a coloured variety of grapefruit, the first major carotenoid to be formed in the chromoplast is lycopene; later in the season the lycopene content decreases, and the β-carotene content increases[94]. Chlorophyll usually breaks down during the development of the chromoplast: this may occur before, or during, the great increase in carotenoid content. There is a mutant of the red pepper in which chlorophyll does not break down during fruit ripening: the resultant colour (red and green combined) of the fruit is brown[119]. There is a similar mutant of the tomato[96]. It is generally true that chromoplast development in fruit can continue when the fruit is removed from the parent plant, as instanced by the familiar practice of ripening tomatoes indoors.

Like all biological processes, chromoplast development is inhibited by low temperatures, but the effects of higher temperatures may be somewhat complex. In the tomato, formation of lycopene takes place rapidly at temperatures up to 30°, but is markedly inhibited at temperatures above this, so that the fruit becomes yellow rather than red[25]. When the fruits are put back at a temperature of 20°, lycopene formation starts again, and the fruits become red in four or five days. Although lycopene synthesis in the normal red tomato (r^+r^+, see XI.3.ii) is virtually abolished at 37°, β-carotene formation is hardly affected[49]. However, in tomatoes which make large amounts of β-carotene because they are homozygous for the allele B (of the gene B^+/B), β-carotene formation is inhibited at a temperature of $32°$[132]. Thus, in the tomato, the effects of temperature on carotenoid synthesis depend upon the genetic constitution of the plant (see XI.3.ii): the differences may be due to the existence of two different pathways for β-carotene synthesis, lycopene being an intermediate in the temperature-sensitive pathway, but not the other. In the water-melon increasing the temperature from $20°$ to $37°$ does not inhibit lycopene formation[138].

Light is not essential for the development of fruit chromoplasts. However, red varieties of tomato form 40–100 per cent more carotenoid when ripened in the light than they do in the dark: yellow varieties, on the other hand, form less carotenoid in the light than in the dark[121]. According to Nettles, Hall, and Dennison (1955), although total carotenoid content of tomatoes was markedly increased by exposure to light during ripening, carotene content was unaffected. Decomposition of chlorophyll in the ripening tomato is accelerated by light[138]: this may be due to the photodestruction of chlorophyll occurring in addition to the normal decomposition processes.

Oxygen appears to be essential for chromoplast development. Tomatoes form no lycopene when placed in an atmosphere of nitrogen or carbon dioxide[138]. This is not surprising since once the chloroplasts have lost their photosynthetic ability, energy for biosynthesis must be obtained from respiration. Also, carotenoid synthesis is an oxidative process, since it involves the conversion of more saturated to less saturated compounds.

Fruit chromoplast formation does not require that the fruit be intact. Discs excised from the pericarp of *Capsicum annuum* will ripen and form the usual carotenoids when cultured aseptically in aerated liquid media[1]. The most rigorous requirements are an adequate source of carbohydrate and suitable tonicity. The ripening process is relatively insensitive to changes in pH value over the range 6·0 to 8·0. In the presence of an auxin or gibberellin, chlorophyll is preserved and the formation of the chromoplast carotenoids delayed or prevented. Neither kinetin nor benzyladenine has any effect. Exposure to ethylene, which is known to hasten ripening of many kinds of fruit, slightly accelerates the disappearance of chlorophyll and formation of carotenoids in the excised discs.

XIV.5.ii. MORPHOLOGICAL CHANGES DURING FRUIT CHROMOPLAST FORMATION

Many cytological studies have been carried out on the development of chromoplasts. Only a few representative examples will be dealt with here. The paper by Strauss (1953) should be consulted for a review of the earlier work.

Chromoplasts do not always develop from chloroplasts. Guilliermond (1941) carried out light-microscope studies on the transformation of amyloplasts into chromoplasts in the fruit of *Asparagus officinalis*. The starch of the elongated amyloplasts first disappears and then what seem to be colourless vesicles appear. Carotenoid granules are formed around the borders of these vesicles. The plastid also tends to separate into a number of smaller plastids, so that eventually small, rounded, vesiculate chromoplasts are produced. The amoeboid, globule-containing chromoplasts of the epidermis of orange-red berries of *Convallaria majalis* are formed from colourless proplastids[124]. Even in fruits where chromoplasts are normally formed from chloroplasts, chromoplasts can still be produced when chloroplast formation is prevented: if tomato fruits are allowed to form in complete darkness (by covering them up on the vine) chlorophyll never develops—the fruits are at first pure white, and gradually shade into red as they approach maturity[121].

Zurzycki (1954) has studied, with the light microscope, the differentiation of chromoplasts in various types of fruit. The plastids (presumably proplastids) in the ovary cells were small and colourless, or pale green. As the fruit developed, the number of plastids per cell increased from about six to about forty in *Sambucus racemosa*, fifteen to ninety in *Physalis alkekengi*, sixteen to forty-five in *Sorbus aucuparia*, and thirty to one hundred and forty in the tomato. At the same time the plastids increased in size, turned green, and took on the form of normal chloroplasts with distinct grana. As the transformation of chloroplasts into chromoplasts commenced, chlorophyll and grana began to disappear. The subsequent course of chromoplast development differed somewhat in the different species. In *Physalis*, the plastids remained the same shape and size throughout; highly refractive orange grains, $0 \cdot 5 - 1 \cdot 5 \, \mu$ in diameter, then began to appear, at first round the periphery, and eventually in the middle. In the ripe chromoplast, the orange grains were evenly dispersed throughout the colourless stroma of the plastid. In *Sambucus* the plastid became smaller, and almost ball-shaped, and dimly visible granules, about $0 \cdot 3 \, \mu$ in diameter, containing the yellow pigment, appeared. In *Sorbus* the plastids became spindle-shaped: as ripening proceeded further, the spindles became elongated and sharper at the ends. The mature chromoplasts had a faintly fibrous appearance, with the orange colour distributed evenly throughout. In the tomato, first orange grains, and then orange crystals, appeared within a colourless stroma. In the later stages of ripening, the walls of the plastids sometimes disappeared so that long, thin, orange or pink crystals were seen free in the cytoplasm.

Steffen and Walter (1958) have carried out an electron-microscope study on the differentiation of the chloroplast into the chromoplast in fruit of *Solanum capsicastrum*. They found that concomitantly with the disintegration of the grana of the chloroplast, osmiophilic globules appear of diameter from about 0·2 μ down to a tenth, or less, of this (Fig. XIV.10). A stage is reached (yellow colour) in which the internal structure of the plastid consists mainly of these globuli, distributed at random throughout an otherwise electron-transparent stroma. Occasional globuli seem to be drawn out at one, or two points, so that they have the shape of a tadpole, or a spindle: the metamorphosis of the globules appears to continue until, by the time that the yellow-orange stage has been reached, the plastid contents consist mainly of spindle-shaped fibrils, with only a few osmiophilic globuli. In the mature chromoplast the picture is much the same, except that the fibrils are perhaps thinner, and more elongated.

Frey-Wyssling and Kreutzer (1958) found that during ripening of fruit of *Capsicum annuum* the grana of the chloroplasts disintegrated. While this was still happening the bundles of filaments characteristic of the mature chromoplasts (Fig. I.42) began to appear. Eventually, these fibres filled up most of the interior of the plastid. Frey-Wyssling and Kreutzer did not observe osmiophilic globules or tadpole-shaped structures in the chromoplasts they examined. However, Kirk and Juniper (1965) observed large numbers of osmiophilic globules as well as fibres in chromoplasts of another variety of *Capsicum annuum*. Also, some of the fibres had a large osmiophilic swelling (I.6.iii and Fig. I.42): this could represent a stage in the transformation of a globule to a fibre.

The chromoplasts in the rind of the navel orange also develop from chloroplasts. The chloroplasts of the young green fruit are similar in structure to those of leaves[131]. As the fruit ripens, the thylakoid system becomes reduced, then vesiculated, and finally disappears. The large osmiophilic globuli which are initially associated with the thylakoid membranes, increase in size and number. The mature chromoplasts are irregular in shape and contain many large osmiophilic globuli, some starch grains and a small amount of membranous material.

XIV.5.iii. CAROTENOID FORMATION IN FLOWER PETAL CHROMOPLASTS

In those flowers, the colour of which is due to chromoplasts, the carotenoid content of the petals increases from budding up to the formation of the mature flower[151, 69, 59]. The young corolla of *Brugmansia aurea* while it is enclosed within the calyx-tube is green, due to the presence of the normal chloroplast pigments. When it emerges from the calyx it turns greenish-yellow, and then bright yellow, as the chlorophylls are

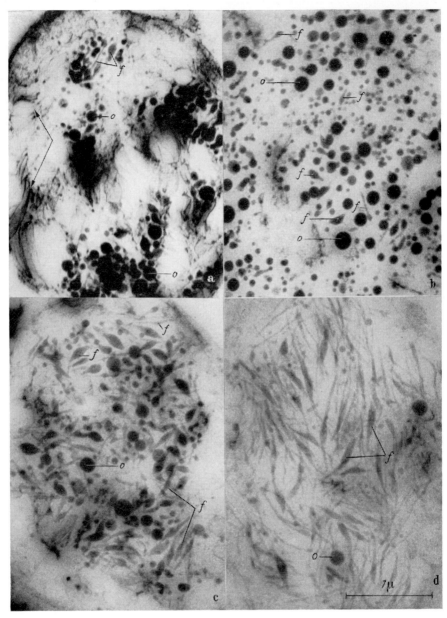

Fig. XIV.10. *Differentiation of chromoplasts in fruit of* Solanum capsicastrum. *By permission, from Steffen, K. and Walter, F. (1958). Planta 50, 640–670. (a) Transition stage between pale green and yellow plastid, with grana disintegrating and osmiophilic globules appearing. (b) Yellow plastid stage. (c) & (d) Yellow-orange stages with numbers of fibrils increasing, and of globules decreasing. o—osmiophilic globules. f—fibrils*

destroyed and carotenoids synthesized. As the corolla matures, part of it becomes deep orange, due to formation of an unidentified red carotenoid[59]. Chlorophyll is not always destroyed in the development of petal chromoplasts: in *Caltha palustris* and *Forsythia intermedia*, the mature flowers (the colour of which is due to carotenoids) still contain appreciable amounts of chlorophyll[106]. The relative amount of different carotenoids synthesized by flowers can vary from one time of year to another: flowers of *Viola tricolor* formed in the spring contain mainly violaxanthin, with only a little auroxanthin, whereas flowers formed in the summer or early autumn contain large amounts of auroxanthin[61]. Carotenoid formation may also be affected by removal of the flowering stem from the plant: carotenoids formed by the flower buds opening on excised stems of *Mimulus longiflorus* consist largely of prolycopene and pro-γ-carotene and other poly-*cis* steroisomers, whereas flowers which develop on the intact plant contain lycopene and β-carotene[103].

XIV.5.iv. MORPHOLOGICAL CHANGES DURING FLOWER CHROMOPLAST FORMATION

According to Geitler (1935), flower petal chromoplasts arise mainly from leucoplasts (colourless plastids), and only exceptionally from chloroplasts. Guilliermond (1941) says that when chromoplasts (of petals or fruit) do not arise by metamorphosis of chloroplasts, they arise from 'chondrioconts' which have first formed starch, i.e. from amyloplasts. For instance, in the petals of *Iris germanica* a yellow pigment (which Guilliermond assumes to be a xanthophyll) appears, in a diffuse state within the amyloplasts. Then the starch disappears and the chromoplasts grow. In many of them large vesicles appear. In the flower of *Clivia nobilis* the starch grains disappear from the amyloplast to be replaced by small grains, and also long needle-shaped crystals, of an orange-red pigment thought to be carotene.

Flowers in which the petal chromoplasts arise from chloroplasts include *Tropaeolum*, *Ranunculus*, and *Lilium tigrinum*[41, 52]. In the case of *Lilium tigrinum* it is the chromoplasts of the mesophyll cells of the petals which arise from chloroplasts: the chromoplasts of the epidermal cells arise from colourless proplastids[124]. In the epidermis of the petals of *Tagetes patula* the chromoplasts arise from proplastids which have begun to go green[124]. Frey-Wyssling and Kreutzer (1958) have studied the transformation of chloroplasts to chromoplasts in *Ranunculus repens*, with the electron microscope. The first change is that homogeneous osmiophilic globuli, up to 0·15 μ in diameter, appear in young chloroplasts or amyloplasts. These increase in size and number while the lamellar structure of the chloroplast disappears. In the mature yellow chromoplast only these droplets remain, lining the inner surface of the plastid membrane.

Young petals of *Spartium junceum* contain partly-differentiated chloroplasts with rather small grana (containing up to four thylakoids): the chloroplasts often contain starch granules[88]. As the petal develops, the lamellar material becomes disorganized and begins to disappear: at the same time, globules, about 1000Å in diameter and faintly osmiophilic, appear. Both these processes continue until eventually all the lamellae have disappeared, and the plastid is almost completely filled with osmiophilic globules which, presumably, contain the carotenoids responsible for the colour of the petals. At this stage the globules are more strongly osmiophilic than they were initially. A mature chromoplast may still contain a large starch grain. The chromoplasts reach this stage of development before the flowers open. After the flowers open the concentration of globules in the chromoplast falls off appreciably. Fig. I.41 shows a chromoplast in the flower at this stage of development.

XIV.5.v. CAROTENOID FORMATION IN ROOT CHROMOPLASTS

The growth of the carrot root is accompanied by the formation of large amounts of α- and β-carotene. Fig. XIV.11 shows the time course of synthesis of carotenes in the developing carrot root[6]. It appears that during the first 25 days, α-carotene is synthesized more rapidly than

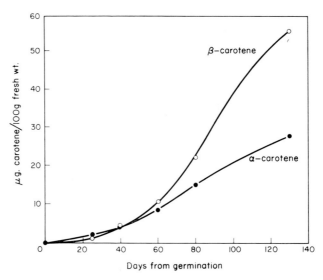

FIG. XIV.11. *Increase in α- and β-carotene content of carrot during growth (plotted from data of Ben-Shaul and Klein, 1965)*

β-carotene, but that β-carotene synthesis then catches up, so that after 130 days, two-thirds of the carotene is β-carotene. The carotenoid concentration reaches a higher level in the phloem than in the xylem[13]. Booth (1951a) found that in the xylem about 70 per cent of the total carotenoid formed consisted of carotenes, the rest of xanthophylls: but in the whole root, 90 per cent of the total carotenoid consists of carotenes[15]. Carotenoid synthesis can continue to some extent when carrots are harvested and stored. The carotenoid content of carrots kept at 6° increased, on the average, by 11 per cent in 60 days[14]: this increase was mainly due to synthesis of xanthophylls, the level of which rose by up to 82 per cent: the carotene content rose only slightly.

XIV.5.vi. MORPHOLOGICAL CHANGES DURING ROOT CHROMOPLAST FORMATION

According to Guilliermond, Mangenot, and Plantefol (1933), the chromoplasts of the carrot are formed from starch-containing 'chondrioconts', i.e. amyloplasts. The starch progressively disappears, to be replaced by a carotene crystal in the form of a needle, a triangular plate, or a spiral ribbon. Eventually the surrounding wall of the plastid disappears, and the carotene crystal is set free in the cytoplasm. More recent light-microscope studies have amplified their findings.

According to Ben-shaul and Klein (1965), in the early stages of root development small colourless vesicles (probably proplastids), 1–2 μ in diameter are observed. These remain colourless while increasing in size to 2–5 μ in diameter. At this stage carotenoid formation becomes detectable, so that yellowish vesicles, 3–5 μ in diameter are seen. As carotenoid formation continues, yellow-orange crystals appear within the 3–5 μ vesicles, between 16 and 28 days after germination. Many of these vesicles contain starch grains, confirming their identification as plastids. Forty-eight to sixty days after germination, in the lower, younger, parts of the root, these plastids containing crystals and some times starch grains are seen. However, in the older cells these plastids have differentiated into either starch-carotene complexes, or free carotene crystals up to 40 μ long; some free starch grains are also seen. The starch-carotene complexes may consist of starch grains embedded within a carotene body, or of a carotene body forming a spiral around the starch grains. The appearance is frequently such as to suggest that the carotenes crystallize around the starch grains. The number of starch grains per complex might be anything from one to ten, or even more. Both the starch and the carotene are presumably formed at the expense of carbohydrate, translocated down from the leaves. There is no obvious necessity, in principle, for starch to be formed before carotene is formed:

this fits in with the observation that not all the plastids in which crystals developed contained starch grains. The simplest hypothesis would be that the sugar translocated from the leaves is used directly for synthesis of both carotene and starch. It is also, of course, possible that some of the starch initially formed might later be broken down and converted to carotene.

In a yellow variety of carrot which produces only about one-eighth the amount of carotene that the normal varieties do, chromoplast development proceeds only as far as the yellowish vesicles. In a white variety of carrot, only the colourless vesicles are formed[6].

According to Steffen and Reck (1964), in certain regions of the carrot (presumably regions exposed to light, near the top) the chromoplasts can be formed from chloroplasts. Carotenoid-containing globuli appear: use of polarization optics indicates that the carotenes in the globuli begin to crystallize. When they become large, the crystals burst through the plastid membrane.

XIV.5.vii. REGULATION OF CHROMOPLAST FORMATION

The phenomenon of chromoplast formation presents a fascinating problem in differentiation. Why is it, for instance, that a chloroplast situated in a leaf cell, will remain a chloroplast, whereas a chloroplast in a ripening fruit on the same plant suddenly begins to synthesize large quantities of new, different carotenoids, and turns into a chromoplast? On the regulator gene hypothesis one would suppose that in the leaf, and in the immature fruit, the structural genes concerned with the formation of those enzymes required for the biosynthesis of the new carotenoids, are repressed. When the fruit has reached a certain stage of development, an inducer (or more than one inducer) is produced, which antagonizes the repressors formed by the regulator genes, thus de-repressing the structural genes. The enzymes are then synthesized, and the specific chromoplast carotenoids begin to appear. The nature of the inducer, and why it appears in the fruit and not in the leaf, is quite unknown. The suggestion that these structural genes are initially dormant, and are then activated is supported by the finding[75] that in the tomato the different alleles of the genes r^+/r, t^+/t, at^+/at, B^+/B, which bring about such drastic changes in the carotenoids of the chromoplasts, have no effect on the carotenoids of the chloroplasts (in the immature fruit, or the leaf) which are the precursors of the chromoplasts. Also, in *Capsicum annuum*, mutations which grossly alter the fruit carotenoid composition, have relatively little effect on the quantity, or the overall absorption spectra, of the leaf carotenoids: one of these varieties (white fruit), in particular, has normal levels of leaf carotenoids, but no detectable carotenoids in the fruit[62]. It seems quite plausible that this strain may have a mutation in a regulator gene, producing an 'uninducible' phenotype; that is, the faulty regulator gene may produce a repressor which does not have the ability to combine with the inducer, with the consequence that some or all of the structural genes for enzymes of fruit carotenoid synthesis remain permanently repressed. An instance where a gene concerned with chromoplast formation may also have an effect on the chloroplast is known in the carrot: strains with white roots have in their leaves a normal β-carotene level, but no α-carotene; in strains with pigmented roots, α-carotene constitutes 13 per cent of the leaf carotenoids[15].

REFERENCES

1. VON ABRAMS, G. J. & PRATT, H. K. (1964). *Plant Phys.* **39**, lxv
1a. APPLEMAN, D., FULCO, A. J. & SHUGARMAN, P. M. (1966). *Plant Phys.* **41**, 136–142
2. ARONOFF, S. (1963). *Plant Phys.* **38**, 628–631
3. BANDURSKI, R. S. (1949). *Bot. Gaz.* **111**, 95–109
4. BAUER, A. (1958). *Planta* **51**, 84–98
5. BELL, P. R. & MÜHLETHALER, K. (1962). *J. Ultrastruct. Res.* **7**, 452–466
6. BEN-SHAUL, Y. & KLEIN, S. (1965). *Bot. Gaz.* **126**, 79–85
7. BISALPUTRA, T. & WEIER, T. E. (1964). *Am. J. Bot.* **51**, 881–892
8. BJÖRN, L. O. (1963). *Phys. Plant* **16**, 142–150
8a. BJÖRN, L. O. (1965). *Phys. Plant.* **18**, 1130–1141
9. BLASS, U., ANDERSON, J. M. & CALVIN, M. (1959). *Plant Phys.* **34**, 329–333
10. BLOCH, K., CONSTANTOPOULOS, G., KENYON, C. & NAGAI, J. In *Symposium on Biochemistry of Chloroplasts (Aberystwyth, 1965)*. Ed., T. W. Goodwin. Academic Press, London (in press)
11. BOEHM, J. A. (1859). *Sitzber. Akad. Wiss. Wien.* **37**, 453–476. Quoted by Smith & Young (1956)
12. BOGORAD, L. (1950). *Bot. Gaz.* **111**, 221–241
13. BOOTH, V. H. (1951a). *J. Sci. Food Agric.* **2**, 350–353
14. BOOTH, V. H. (1951b). *J. Sci. Food Agric.* **2**, 353–358
15. BOOTH, V. H. (1956). *J. Sci. Food Agric.* **7**, 386–389
16. BOUCK, G. B. (1962). *J. Cell Biol.* **12**, 553–569
17. BRIGGS, G. E. (1922). *Proc. Roy. Soc. B* **94**, 12–19
18. BRODY, M. & EMERSON, R. (1959). *Am. J. Bot.* **46**, 433–440
19. BROWN, J. S. (1960). *Carneg. Inst. Wash. Yearbook* **59**, 330
20. BUKATSCH, F. & RUDOLPH, E. (1963). *Photochem. & Photobiol.* **2**, 191–198
21. BUTTERFASS, T. (1964). *Z. Botan.* **52**, 46–77
22. BUVAT, R. (1958). *Ann. des. Sci. Nat. 11e Serie (Bot.)* **19**, 121–161
23. CAPORALI, L. (1959). *Ann. des. Sci. Nat. 11e Serie (Bot.)* **20**, 215–247
24. CLAES, H. In *Symposium on Biochemistry of Chloroplasts (Aberystwyth, 1965)*. Ed., T. W. Goodwin. Academic Press, London (in press)
25. DUGGAR, B. M. (1913). *Washington Univ. Studies* **1**, 22–45
26. DURANTON, J., GALMICHE, J-M. & ROUX, E. (1958). *Compt. Rend. Acad. Sci.* **246**, 992–995
27. EMBERGER, L. (1920–23). Quoted by Guilliermond (1941)
28. ENGELMANN, Th. W. (1883). *Botan. Ztg.* **41**, 18

29. ENGELMANN, Th. W. (1884). *Botan. Ztg.* **42**, 81, 97. Quoted by Rabinowitch (1945)
30. ENGVILD, K. C. (1964). *Phys. Plant* **17**, 866–874
31. FADEEL, A. A. (1962). *Phys. Plant* **15**, 130–147
32. FASSE-FRANZISKET, U. (1956). *Protoplasma* **45**, 195–227
33. FORSYTH, A. A. (1954). *British Poisonous Plants*. Her Majesty's Stationery Office, London
34. FRANK, S. & KENNEY, A. L. (1955). *Plant Phys.* **30**, 413–418
35. FREY-WYSSLING, A. & KREUTZER, E. (1958a). *J. Ultrastruct. Res.* **1**, 397–411
36. FREY-WYSSLING, A. & KREUTZER, E. (1958b). *Planta* **51**, 104–114
37. FRIEND, D. J. C. (1960). *Phys. Plant* **13**, 776–785
38. FRIEND, D. J. C. (1961). *Phys. Plant* **14**, 28–39
39. GANTT, E. & ARNOTT, H. J. (1963). *J. Cell Biol.* **19**, 446–448
40. GAUTHERET, R.-J. (1932). *Compt. Rend. Acad. Sci.* **194**, 1510–1513
41. GEITLER, L. (1935). *Grundriss der Cytologie*. Bornträger, Berlin
42. GEROLA, F. M., CRISTOFORI, F. & DASSU, G. (1960). *Caryologia* **13**, 164–178
43. GODNEV, T. N. & SHLYK, A. A. (1956). *Proc. Int. Conf. Peaceful Uses Atomic Energy*, Geneva **12**, 358
44. GODNEV, T. N. & SHLYK, A. A. (1961). *Proc. 5th Internat. Congr. Biochem.* VI, 163–175
45. GODNEV, T. N., ROTFARB, R. M. & AKULOVICH, N. K. (1963). *Photochem. & Photobiol.* **2**, 119–128
46. GOODWIN, T. W. (1952). *The Comparative Biochemistry of the Carotenoids*. Chapman & Hall, London
47. GOODWIN, T. W. (1958). In *Encycl. Plant Phys.* Ed., W. Ruhland, **X**. Springer-Verlag, Berlin, pp. 186–222
48. GOODWIN, T. W. (1960). In *Encycl. Plant Phys.* Ed., W. Ruhland, V.1. Springer-Verlag, Berlin, pp. 394–443
49. GOODWIN, T. W. & JAMIKORN, M. (1952). *Nature, Lond.* **170**, 104–105
50. GRANICK, S. (1938). *Am. J. Bot.* **25**, 561–567
51. GREEN, P. B. (1964). *Am. J. Bot.* **51**, 334–342
52. GUILLIERMOND, A. (1941). *The cytoplasm of the plant cell*. Transl. by L. R. Atkinson. Chronica Botanica Co., Waltham, Mass.
53. GUILLIERMOND, A., MANGENOT, G. & PLANTEFOL, L. (1933). *Cytologie vegetale*. Quoted by Straus (1953)
54. HABERLANDT, G. (1914). *Physiological Plant Anatomy*. Macmillan, New York
55. HAGEMAN, R. A. & ARNON, D. I. (1955). *Arch. Biochem. Biophys.* **57**, 421–436
55a. HAHN, L. W. & MILLER, J. H. (1966). *Phys. Plant* **19**, 134–141
56. HEJNOWICZ, Z. (1958). *Phys. Plant* **11**, 878–888
57. HESS, J. & TOLBERT, N. E. (1964). *Plant Phys.* **39**, xiv
58. HOLMAN, R. T. (1948). *Arch. Biochem. Biophys.* **17**, 51–57
59. JOSHI, P. C. (1953). *J. Ind. Bot. Soc.* **32**, 17–20
60. KAKHNOVICH, L. V. (1961). *Problems in plant phys. and microbiol. Minsk.* **2**, 78–85; *Biol. Abstr.* **42**, 11698
61. KARRER, P., JUCKER, E., RUTSCHMANN, J. & STEINLIN, K. (1945). *Helv. Chim. Acta* **28**, 1146–1156
62. KIRK, J. T. O. & JUNIPER, B. E. (1965). In *Symposium on Biochemistry of Chloroplasts (Aberystwyth, 1965)*. Ed., T. W. Goodwin. Academic Press, London (in press)
63. KRINSKY, N. I. In *Symposium on Biochemistry of Chloroplasts (Aberystwyth, 1965)*. Ed., T. W. Goodwin. Academic Press, London (in press)
64. KUPKE, D. W. & DORRIER, T. E. (1962). *Plant Phys.* **37**, lxiii
65. KUPKE, D. W. & HUNTINGTON, J. L. (1963). *Science* **140**, 49–51

66. LANCE, A. (1958). *Ann. des. Sci. Nat. 11e Serie (Bot.)* **19**, 165–202
67. LANCE-NOUGARÈDE, A. (1960). *Compt. Rend. Acad. Sci.* **250**, 3371–3373
68. LANCE-NOUGARÈDE, A. & PILET, P.-E. (1965). *Compt. Rend. Acad. Sci.* **260**, 2567–2570
69. LEBEDEV, S. T. & RESHETOVA, G. F. (1949). *Dokl. Akad. Nauk. SSSR.* **66**, 965–967. Quoted by Goodwin (1958)
70. LEVINE, R. P. & PIETTE, L. H. (1962). *Biophys. J.* **2**, 369–379
71. LITVIN, F. F., KRASNOVSKY, A. A. & RIKHIREVA, G. T. (1959). *Dokl. Akad. Nauk. SSSR.* **127**, 699. Quoted by Krasnovsky, A. A. (1960). *Ann. Rev. Plant Phys.* **11**, 363–410
72. LÖVLIE, A. & FARFAGLIO, G. (1965). *Exp. Cell. Res.* **39**, 418–434
73. LUBIMENKO, M. V. (1925). *Compt. Rend. Acad. Sci.* **179**, 1073
74. LUBIMENKO, M. V. (1928). *Rev. Gen. Bot.* **40**, 88–94, 146–155
75. MACKINNEY, G., RICK, C. M. & JENKINS, J. A. (1956). *Proc. Natl. Acad. Sci.* **42**, 404–408
76. MANTON, I. (1959). *J. Marine Biol. Assoc.* (U.K.) **38**, 319–333
77. MANTON, I. (1962). *J. Exp. Bot.* **13**, 325–333
78. MENKE, W. (1960). *Z. Naturforsch.* **15b**, 800–804
79. MENKE, W. (1962). *Ann. Rev. Plant Phys.* **13**, 27–44
80. MENKE, W. (1964). *Ber. Deut. Bot. Ges.* **77**, 340–354
81. MICHAELIS, P. (1962). *Protoplasma* **55**, 177–231
82. MILLER, R. A. & ZALIK, S. (1965). *Plant Phys.* **40**, 569–574
83. MOSTER, J. B. & QUACKENBUSH, F. W. (1952). *Arch. Biochem. Biophys.* **38**, 297–303
84. MÜHLETHALER, K. & FREY-WYSSLING, A. (1959). *J. Biophys. Biochem. Cytol.* **6**, 507–512
85. MYERS, J. (1940). *Plant Phys.* **15**, 575–588
86. NETTLES, V. F., HALL, C. B. & DENNISON, R. A. (1955). *Proc. Am. Soc. Hort. Sci.* **65**, 349 352
87. NIHEI, T., SASA, T., MIYACHI, S., SUZUKI, K. & TAMIYA, H. (1954). *Arch. Mikrobiol.* **21**, 155–164
88. NOUGARÈDE, A. (1964). *Compt. Rend. Acad. Sci.* **258**, 683–685
89. PAOLILLO, D. J. (1962). *Am. J. Bot.* **49**, 590–598
90. PERKINS, II. J. & ROBERTS, D. W. A. (1963). *Can. J. Bot.* **41**, 221–226
91. PIRSON, A. & BÖGER, P. (1965). *Nature, Lond.* **205**, 1129–1130
92. PORTER, J. W., STRONG, F. W., BRINK, R. A. & NEAL, N. R. (1946). *J. Agric. Res.* **72**, 169–187
93. POWELL, D. (1925). *Ann. Bot.* **39**, 503 513
94. PURCELL, A. E., DE GRUY, I, V. & CARRA, J. H. (1962). *Plant Phys.* **37**, xix
95. RABINOWITCH, E. I. (1945). *Photosynthesis.* I. Interscience Publishers Inc., New York
96. RAMIREZ, D. A. & TOMES, M. L. (1964). *Bot. Gaz.* **124**, 221–226
97 REGER, B. J. (1965). *Plant Phys.* **40**, lii
98. DE REZENDE-PINTO, M. C. (1962). *Portug. Acta. Biol.* **VIA**, 239–242
99. ROBERTS, R. A. (1948). *Plant Phys.* **23**, 379–387
100. ROBERTS, D. W. A. & PERKINS, H. J. (1962). *Biochim. Biophys. Acta* **58**, 499–506
101. RUBIN, B. A. & GERMANOVA, R. (1959). *Dokl. Akad. Nauk. SSSR. (Botan)*, AIBS translation, **124**, 57–60
101a. SAPOZHNIKOV, D. I., KRASOVSKAYA, T. A., & MAEVSKAYA, A. N. (1957). *Dokl. Akad. Nauk. SSSR.* **113**, 465
102. SCHMIDT, A. (1924). *Botan. Arch.* **5**, 260–282
103. SCHROEDER, W. A. (1942). *J. Am. Chem. Soc.* **64**, 2510–2511
104. SESTAK, Z. (1963). *Photochem. & Photobiol.* **2**, 101–110

105. SESTAK, Z. & CATSKY, J. (1962). *Biol. Plant* **4**, 131–140
106. SEYBOLD, A. (1953–54). *Sitzber. Heidelberg. Akad. Wiss. Math.-naturw.* Kl 2. Abh. quoted by Paech, K. (1955). *Ann. Rev. Plant Phys.* **6**, 273–298
107. SEYBOLD, A. & EGLE, K. (1938a). *Planta* **28**, 87–123; **29**, 114–118, 119–128
108. SEYBOLD, A. & EGLE, K. (1938b). *Jahrb. wiss. Botan.* **86**, 50–80
109. SEYBOLD, A. & EGLE, K. (1939). *Botan. Arch.* **40**, 560
110. SEYBOLD, A. & FALK, H. (1959). *Planta* **53**, 339–375
111. SHIHIRA-ISHIKAWA, I. & HASE, E. (1964). *Plant & Cell Phys.* **5**, 227–240
112. SHLYK, A. A., KALER, V. L., VLASENOK, L. I. & GAPONENKO, V. I. (1963). *Photochem. & Photobiol.* **2**, 129–148
113. SHLYK, A. A., MIKHAILOVA, S. A., GAPONENKO, V. I. & KUKHTENKO, T. V. (1963). *Fiz. Rastenii.* (Consultants Bureau transl.) **10**, 227–235
113a. SHLYK, A. A. & STANISHEVSKAYA, E. M. (1961). *Dokl. Akad. Nauk.* (AIBS transl.) **144**, 461–464
114. SINGH, B. N. & LAL, K. N. (1935). *Ann. Bot.* **49**, 291–307
115. SIRONVAL, C. (1963). *Photochem. & Photobiol.* **2**, 207–221
116. SISTROM, W. R., GRIFFITHS, M. & STANIER, R. Y. (1956). *J. Cell. Comp. Physiol.* **48**, 473–475
117. SMILLIE, R. M. (1962). *Plant Phys.* **37**, 716–721
118. SMILLIE, R. M. & KROTKOV, G. (1961). *Can. J. Bot.* **39**, 891–900
119. SMITH, P. G. (1950). *J. Hered.* **41**, 138–140
120. SMITH, J. H. C. & KOSKI, V. M. (1948). *Carneg. Inst. Wash. Yearbook* **47**, 93–96
121. SMITH, L. W. & SMITH, O. (1931). *Plant Phys.* **6**, 265–275
122. SMITH, J. H. C. & YOUNG, V. M. K. (1956). In *Radiation Biology*. III. Ed., A. Hollaender. McGraw-Hill Book Co., New York, pp. 393–442
123. STAHL, E. (1909). *Zur Biologie des Chlorophylls*. Gustav Fischer, Jena.
124. STEFFEN, K. (1964). *Planta* **60**, 506–522
125. STEFFEN, K. & RECK, G. (1964). *Planta* **60**, 627–648
126. STEFFEN, K. & WALTER, F. (1958). *Planta* **50**, 640–670
127. STEWART, W. N. (1948). *Bot. Gaz.* **110**, 281–300
128. STRAUS, W. (1953). *Bot. Rev.* **19**, 147–186
129. SUN, C. N. (1961). *Am. J. Bot.* **48**, 311–315
130. TERBORGH, J. & THIMANN, K. V. (1964). *Planta* **63**, 83–98
131. THOMPSON, W. W. (1965). *Am. J. Bot.* **52**, 622
132. TOMES, M. L., QUACKENBUSH, F. W. & KARGL, T. E. (1956). *Bot. Gaz.* **117**, 248–253
133. TREHARNE, R. W., MELTON, C. W. & ROPPEL, R. M. (1964). *J. Mol. Biol.* **10**, 57–62
134. VIRGIN, H. I. (1960). *Phys. Plant* **13**, 155–164
135. VIRGIN, H. I. (1961). *Phys. Plant* **14**, 384–392
136. VLASENOK, L. I., FRADKIN, L. I. & SHLYK, A. A. (1965). *Photochem. & Photobiol.* **4**, 385–389
137. VLASENOK, L. I. & SHLYK, A. A. (1965). *Biokhimiya* (Consultants Bureau transl.) **28**, 44–53
138. VOGELE, A. C. (1937). *Plant Phys.* **12**, 929–955
139. WEBER, C. I. (1965). *Exp. Cell. Res.* **38**, 507–510
140. WEHRMEYER, W. & RÖBBELEN, G. (1965). *Planta* **64**, 312–329
141. VON WETTSTEIN, D. (1954). *Z. Naturforsch.* **9b**, 476–481
142. VON WETTSTEIN, D. (1959). *Brookhaven Symp. Biol.* **11**, 138–159
143. WHALEY, W. G. MOLLENHAUER, H. H. & LEECH, J. H. (1960). *Am. J. Bot.* **47**, 401–419
144. WICKLIFF, J. C. & ARONOFF, S. (1962). *Plant Phys.* **37**, 590–594
145. WIECKOWSKI, S. (1963). *Photochem. & Photobiol.* **2**, 199–205

146. WILSENACH, R. (1963). *J. Cell Biol.* **18**, 419–428
147. WILSTÄTTER, R. & STOLL, A. (1928). *Investigations on chlorophyll.* Science Press, Lancaster, Pa.
148. WILSTÄTTER, R. & STOLL, A. (1918). *Untersuchungen über die Assimilation der Kohlensaure.* Springer, Berlin
149. WITHROW, A. P. & WITHROW, R. B. (1949). *Plant Phys.* **24**, 657–663
150. WOLFF, J. B. & PRICE, L. (1957). *Arch. Biochem. Biophys.* **72**, 293–301
150a. YAMAMOTO, H. Y., NAKAYAMA, T. O. M. & CHICHESTER, C. O. (1962). *Arch. Biochem. Biophys.* **97**, 168
151. ZHUKOVSKII, R. M. & MEDVEDEV, Z. (1949). *Dokl. Akad. Nauk. S.S.S.R.* **66**, 965–967
152. ZURZYCKI, J. (1954). *Acta. Soc. Bot. Polon.* **23**, 161–174

CHAPTER XV

The Inhibition of Plastid Growth

XV.1. Introduction

IN THE previous two chapters we considered the way in which the different kinds of plastid grow and differentiate. Since plastid growth involves the integrated functioning of many different biochemical processes, it is not surprising that it can be inhibited by various substances or treatments which interfere with metabolism. In this chapter we shall consider some of the ways in which plastid development may be inhibited. Since virtually all the work along these lines has been done with the chloroplast, we shall confine our attention to this organelle. We shall be concerned more with direct inhibition of chloroplast growth than with permanent loss of ability to make chloroplasts, which is discussed in more detail in Chapter X. Also, I shall not attempt to deal with the various destructive and inhibitory effects that virus infection can have on chloroplasts.

XV.2. Streptomycin

XV.2.i EFFECT ON HIGHER PLANTS

One of the first antimetabolites to be shown to inhibit chloroplast formation was streptomycin (Fig. XV.1). Von Euler (1947) showed that barley seedlings germinated in a solution of this antibiotic contained neither chlorophyll nor carotenoids; leaves already green were not bleached. Similar results were obtained with *Phleum pratense*[20]. When a 0·2 per cent solution of dihydrostreptomycin was rubbed onto young leaves of *Xanthium*, the leaves continued to grow to their normal size, but formed no chlorophyll[71]: they did form about 10 per cent of their usual carotenoid content. Chlorophyll formation in the dark by seedlings of *Pinus jeffreyi* was also inhibited by streptomycin[17].

524

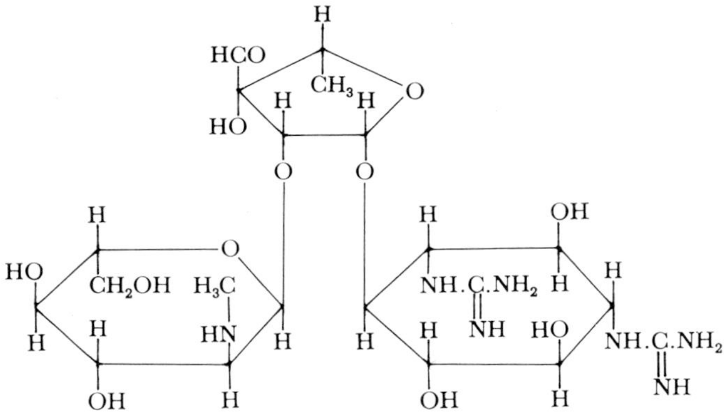

FIG. XV.1. *Streptomycin*

De Deken-Grenson (1955) found, with barley seedlings germinated in the presence of streptomycin, that while most of the leaf was white, the tip was green. The length of the green region decreased accordingly as the concentration of streptomycin in the solution increased, being 20 mm at 0·2 per cent streptomycin, 5 mm at 0·8 per cent streptomycin, and zero at 1·6 per cent streptomycin. If, after three days, the seedlings rendered chlorotic by 0·2 per cent streptomycin were replanted in the absence of antibiotic, then about 11 days later the zone of growth at the base of the plant started to produce green tissue again. Thus, contrary to what happens in *Euglena gracilis* (X.6), streptomycin does not cause permanent loss of ability to make chloroplasts in this higher plant. The inhibitory effect of this drug on chlorophyll formation in barley is overcome by $MnSO_4$ or the ethylenediaminetetraacetic acid chelate of ferric iron[121]. Mn^{2+} ions also overcome the inhibition, by streptomycin, of the growth of *Avena* coleoptile sections[117].

Greening of etiolated leaves is also apparently inhibited by streptomycin: the interior leaves of lettuce, or *Brassica botrytis*, which normally form chloroplasts in the light, do not do so if illuminated while submerged in a solution of the antibiotic[38]. However, streptomycin has no effect even at 20 mg/ml on the photoreduction of protochlorophyllide to chlorophyllide in the isolated holochrome[123].

Signol (1961) has studied the effect of streptomycin on the ultra structure of the leaf plastids of maize seedlings. Bleached leaves with a green tip were used, and the gradation of effect passing from the green part of the leaf through regions of intermediate coloration to the white part was examined. A progressive diminution in the amount of thylakoid material, and an increased disorganization of the granal arrangement, were observed. In a yellow region of the leaf, between the white and the green parts, the plastids contained just one or two granum-like bodies, some of the thylakoids of which were considerably swollen:

there were also many small vesicles dispersed in the stroma. In the completely white part of the leaf, the only structures observable in the plastids were vesicles of various sizes clumped together at one end of the plastid. In barley seedlings germinated in the presence of streptomycin[78], the chloroplasts of the coleoptile, and the white parts of the leaf, contained (as well as starch grains, a number of small vesicles, sometimes in rows, and occasional small thylakoids (Fig. XV.2).

The inhibitory effects of streptomycin on higher plants are by no means confined to the chloroplasts. The drug inhibits the overall growth of barley seedlings (in terms of dry weight) as much in the dark, when chloroplasts are not being formed, as it does in the light[33]. Non-photosynthetic tissue is affected as well as leaves: root growth in germinating seedlings is inhibited, if anything, more than growth of the shoot, and root hair formation is virtually abolished[78]. In an electron microscope investigation of the effects of the drug on non-photosynthetic tissue, Kirk and Juniper (1963) found that the mitochondria in the roots of the treated plants had a drastically altered structure. In the root-cap cells of normal seedlings the mitochondria were typically oval and smooth in outline, with cristae distributed around the periphery. In the root cap cells of seedlings germinated in the presence of streptomycin, the mitochondria were highly variable in shape with irregular outlines; few normal cristae could be seen, and the internal structure consisted of one, two, or three independent lamellae or double-membraned vesicles, which did not appear to be connected to the inner membrane of the mitochondrion (Fig. XV.2). Curiously enough, the root plastids looked much the same in the normal and treated plants, but since these particular plastids have very little internal structure anyway, there is not much scope for expression of structural abnormalities. This effect on mitochondrial structure is particularly interesting because it correlates with the observation, made earlier by Rubin and Ladygina (1957) that barley seedlings germinated in the presence of streptomycin have lower than normal cytochrome oxidase activity.

XV.2.ii. EFFECT ON ALGAE

The first effect of streptomycin on an alga to be discovered was the hereditary loss of ability to make chloroplasts, in *Euglena gracilis*, which was discussed in X.6. As well as this long-term effect of streptomycin some of its direct effects on chloroplast formation in *Euglena gracilis* have been studied. In growing cells the drug does not appear to have any immediate inhibitory effect on chlorophyll synthesis. When cells were exposed to streptomycin for 30 minutes, washed and replaced in fresh growth medium, the subsequent rate of chlorophyll synthesis fell off quite slowly, reaching zero only after two generations[34]. Similarly,

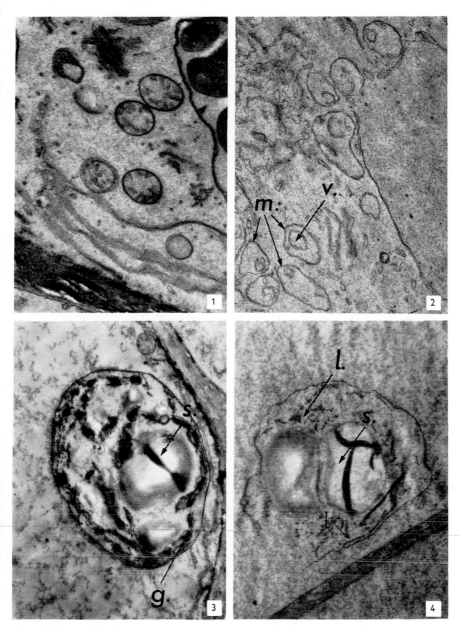

FIG. XV.2. *Effect of streptomycin on formation of chloroplasts and mitochondria in barley.* (*from Kirk, J. T. O. and Juniper, B. E. (1963). Exp. Cell. Res.* **30**, *621–623*). $KMnO_4$ *fixation.* m—*mitochondria.* v—*vesicles.* g—*granum.* s—*starch grain.* l—*lamella.* (*1*) *Root cap cell of normal barley seedling.* (*2*) *Root cap cell of seedling germinated in the presence of streptomycin (4 mg/ml).* (*3*) *Chloroplast in coleoptile of normal seedling.* (*4*) *Plastid in coleoptile of seedling germinated in the presence of streptomycin (4 mg/ml)*

when streptomycin (2 mg/ml) was added to a logarithmically-growing culture of *Euglena gracilis*, chlorophyll formation was hardly affected during the first generation, but fell off rapidly after that[73]. The relative insensitivity of chlorophyll synthesis to streptomycin is a poor guide to the efficacy with which the drug brings about its genetic effects: cells grown in the presence of streptomycin, at one tenth (200 µg/ml) the above concentration, are found to be permanently bleached on sub-culture[74]. The effect on chlorophyll formation in growing cells of *Euglena* is overcome by salts of Ca^{2+}, Mn^{2+}, Sr^{2+}, and Mg^{2+} [118]. The production of colourless mutants by streptomycin is antagonized by Mg^{2+} and also, although less effectively, by the polyamine spermine[125].

As the *Euglena* cells continue to multiply in the presence of this anti-biotic, a progressive disorganization of the regular lamellar system takes place[79]. Recognizable thylakoids are progressively replaced by large numbers of what appear in section to be small vesicles and short tubules. Fig. XV.3 shows a plastid, in an advanced stage of degeneration, from a culture grown for a few generations in the presence of streptomycin. It may be seen that there is still what appears to be a small stack of thylakoids left.

Streptomycin inhibits chloroplast formation in other algae also. *Cyanidium caldarium* will grow in the presence of 1·5 mg drug/ml but the cells are pale yellow in colour[119]: they contain no recognizable chloroplast, but do contain large vacuole-like bodies which might correspond to a plastid without any internal structure. Low concentrations of this antibiotic inhibit chlorophyll formation in *Chlamydomonas reinhardi* in the dark but not in the light[122].

Chloroplast formation by etiolated cells of *Euglena gracilis* exposed to light, under conditions not supporting growth, is also inhibited by streptomycin[65, 74]. A concentration of streptomycin (2 mg/ml) which only has a delayed effect (see above) on chlorophyll synthesis in multi-plying cells, has a more immediate inhibitory effect on chlorophyll and carotenoid synthesis by the non-multiplying, etiolated cells[74]. However, in this system, as with the multiplying cells, chlorophyll synthesis is relatively insensitive (Fig. XV.4) to a concentration of drug (200 µg/ml) which is sufficient to cause permanent loss of chloroplast-forming ability. If the cells are allowed to undergo a few divisions in the presence of streptomycin in the dark before being exposed to light, then much greater inhibitions of chlorophyll synthesis are obtained. When strepto-mycin is supplied only during the light incubation in resting medium, 1–2 mg/ml are required to inhibit chlorophyll synthesis by 50 per cent, but when the drug is supplied during the prior growth in the dark, only 0·1–0·5 µg/ml (during this growth period) are required to cause 50 per cent inhibition of greening during the subsequent light period[94a].

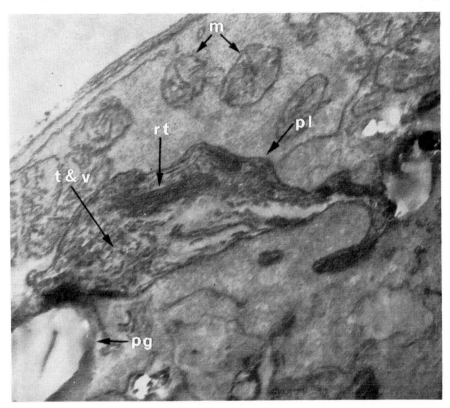

Fig. XV.3. *Disorganization of* Euglena *chloroplast structure after several generations growth in the presence of streptomycin (Kirk, J. T. O. and Juniper, B. E., 1963, unpublished). Cells of E.* gracilis *grown for six days in the light in the presence of streptomycin (600 μg/ml). pl—plastid. rt—residual thylakoids. t & v—tubules and vesicles. m—mitochondria. pg—paramylon granule*

As with higher plants, the effects of streptomycin on algae are by no means confined to the chloroplasts. In some cases cell growth is as sensitive, or nearly as sensitive, as chloroplast formation. *Chlorogonium tetras* is killed by streptomycin at 3 μg/ml and *Chlamydomonas reinhardi* is killed at 10 μg/ml[112]. *Euglena gracilis* is unusual in that it can grow, although rather slowly, in the presence of this drug at a concentration (5 mg/ml) which is many times the concentration required to induce loss of ability to make chloroplasts[111]. The high concentrations of streptomycin (2–4 mg/ml) required to bring about a substantial (> 50 per cent) inhibition of greening in etiolated cells, also have pronounced inhibitory effects on biosynthesis generally. Incorporation of ^{14}C-acetate into cell protein and nucleic acid was inhibited by 60–80 per cent[74]. Incorporation of ^{14}C-leucine into cell protein was 50–60 per cent inhibited (Fig. XV.4) by streptomycin[75]. These inhibitory effects

were almost as great in the dark as they were in the light, indicating
that it is not just synthesis of chloroplast protein and nucleic acid which
is blocked by the antibiotic. The level of free amino acids in the cells
increased in the presence of streptomycin. Incorporation of ^{14}C-acetate
into lipid was only slightly inhibited.

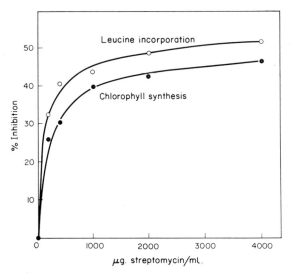

FIG. XV.4. *Effect of streptomycin, at different concentrations, on synthesis of chlorophyll, and
incorporation of ^{14}C-leucine into protein by dark-grown cells of* Euglena gracilis *in the light
(from Kirk, 1961)*

One interesting effect of streptomycin was to cause a 200–300 per
cent increase in the amount of radioactivity incorporated from ^{14}C-
acetate into paramylon, the reserve polysaccharide of *Euglena*[74]. This
effect occurred only in the light. Also the fall in paramylon content
which occurs in cells greening in the light was less in the presence of
streptomycin than in its absence. However, even a high concentration
of the drug (6 mg/ml) had no significant inhibitory or stimulatory
effects on oxidation of simple carbon sources (acetate, ethanol, pro-
pionate), or on endogenous respiration as measured by manometric
techniques[73].

All these effects of streptomycin—on chlorophyll synthesis, carotenoid
synthesis, ^{14}C-acetate incorporation and ^{14}C-leucine incorporation—
were annulled if $MnCl_2$ was added at the same molar concentration as
the drug: $MgCl_2$ was less effective[74, 75]. $CaCl_2$ was as effective an
antagonist as $MnCl_2$ in the case of chlorophyll synthesis (the other processes not being examined in this case).

XV.2.iii. MODE OF ACTION OF STREPTOMYCIN ON CHLOROPLAST FORMATION

Streptomycin is known to combine with and even, under some circumstances, to precipitate, nucleic acids[27]. As far as bacteria are concerned, the most recent evidence indicates that the primary effect of streptomycin is on protein synthesis[56,36,41,42,135]. The sensitive site appears to be the 30 S subunit of the ribosome[31,30]. It appears likely that streptomycin acts by changing the coding properties of codons in the messenger RNA[32]. This can result in inhibition or stimulation of incorporation according to which amino acid and which codon are involved. For instance, the incorporation of phenylalanine into peptide linkage in the presence of the synthetic messenger, polyuridylic acid, is inhibited by streptomycin, whereas the incorporation of isoleucine, leucine, and serine in the presence of polyuridylic acid, are stimulated by the antibiotic. Thus it may be that streptomycin prevents the base sequence—UUU—from coding for phenylalanine, and permits it instead to code for (i.e. direct the incorporation of) the other three amino acids. If, as seems possible, streptomycin could cause some codons to code for no amino acid at all, then the overall inhibitory effect of the drug on protein synthesis, observed with living cells, would be explained. Davies, Gilbert, and Gorini (1964) suggest that the actual lethal effect of streptomycin could be due to the cell being flooded with non-functional proteins.

The inhibitory effect of high concentrations of streptomycin on chloroplast formation in greening cells of *E. gracilis* might perhaps be explained by an effect on protein synthesis at the level of the ribosome. We have already seen that this drug inhibits incorporation of precursors into protein, and in the case of ^{14}C-leucine, this inhibition of incorporation is consistently greater than the inhibition of chlorophyll synthesis[75]. The accumulation of free amino acids is also consistent with this interpretation. The increase in radioactivity of the paramylon in the presence of streptomycin could be due to a feedback inhibition of the utilization of polysaccharide for biosynthesis as a result of the piling up of amino acids and possibly amino acid precursors. In this connection it should be remembered that paramylon utilization is, in fact, diminished by streptomycin. Alternatively, if the acetate carbon is used directly for amino acid synthesis, without being converted to paramylon first, then the labelled intermediates which are not being used for protein synthesis might be converted into polysaccharide. Either way the result is consistent with an inhibition of protein synthesis. The effect on chlorophyll synthesis could be due to inhibition of formation of any of a number of proteins, such as enzymes involved in chlorophyll synthesis, the protein moiety of protochlorophyllide holochrome, the chlorophyll-binding protein of the thylakoids, and so on. The inhibition of carotenoid synthesis might be due to an inhibition of formation of carotenoid biosynthetic enzymes. The inhibition of incorporation into the nucleic acid fraction (which would consist mainly of RNA) is somewhat more difficult to explain, particularly since, in bacteria at any rate, inhibition of protein synthesis by, say, chloramphenicol, does not prevent RNA synthesis[48]. Thus, while an effect on the ribosome can explain most of the effects of streptomycin on greening cells of *E. gracilis*, it does not provide an entirely satisfactory explanation of all of them. The possibility of an additional, or quite a different, action of the antibiotic must be borne in mind.

The general inhibition of growth, the blocking of chloroplast development, and the production of abnormal mitochondria in higher plants grown in the presence of the drug could be explained by an effect on protein synthesis of the type suggested for bacteria. The abnormal structures within the mitochondria (Fig. XV.2) might be formed as a result of the production of proteins with abnormal structures; the lack of cytochrome oxidase activity could be similarly explained. It is not known whether the drug has any effect on nucleic acid synthesis in higher plants as it does in *Euglena*.

Streptomycin is a chelating agent[44, 117]. A plausible explanation of the ability of Mn^{2+} and other cations to overcome the effects of the drug would be that they combine with it to form complexes which do not penetrate the cell, or which do penetrate the cell but are inactive. Alternatively, the ions could act by displacing streptomycin from its site of action (perhaps the ribosome) within the cell.

As we have seen, in *E. gracilis* streptomycin will only bring about substantial biosynthetic effects at a concentration (*ca.* 2 mg/ml) which is about 10 times as high as that (200 µg/ml) which will bring about its genetic effect (loss of ability to make chloroplasts). This suggests that the mechanism of the genetic effect is different from that of the biosynthetic effects: that the genetic effect might be due to direct inhibition of replication of the chloroplast DNA by low concentrations of drug, whereas the biosynthetic effects might be the result of an inhibition of protein synthesis and/or RNA synthesis by high concentrations of drug. However, while the hypothesis that there are two distinct modes of action seems to fit the evidence best, the possibility of a single mode of action must still be considered. For instance, an inhibition of DNA replication could be an indirect result of an effect on protein synthesis. The low concentration of streptomycin which brings about the genetic effect apparently inhibits protein synthesis by only 20 per cent or so[75]. But, although the overall rate of protein synthesis is only slightly reduced, many of the proteins formed could have abnormal structures and be non-functional, as has been suggested in the case of bacteria (see above). Thus, failure of chloroplast DNA replication could follow as a result of formation in the chloroplast of non-functional ribonucleoside triphosphate reductase, thymidylate synthetase, DNA polymerase, or any other enzyme essential for chloroplast DNA synthesis; or it could be a more indirect consequence of the general lethal effects that accumulation of non-functional proteins might have on the chloroplast. The relative insensitivity of cell growth to streptomycin could be due to the cytoplasmic ribosomes being less sensitive to the drug than the chloroplast ribosomes. However, it is perhaps relevant here that the related aminoglycoside antibiotic, spectinomycin, which inhibits protein synthesis in bacteria without, apparently, causing errors in the translation of messenger RNA[31a], is as effective as streptomycin at inducing permanent loss of chloroplasts in *E. gracilis*[124a].

XV.3. Other Antibiotics and Drugs

XV.3.i. CHLORAMPHENICOL

It has been shown by Margulies[83, 84, 85] that the formation of chloroplasts by etiolated leaves of *Phaseolus vulgaris* in the light is partially inhibited by chloramphenicol (Fig. XV.5). The etiolated leaves were

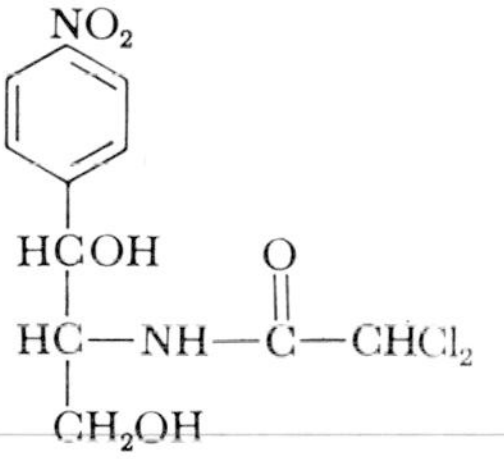

FIG. XV.5. *Chloramphenicol*

placed in water or chloramphenicol solution and illuminated for 24 hours. An inhibition of chlorophyll formation was detectable at 10 μg chloramphenicol/ml, but the curve of inhibition versus concentration levelled off at higher drug concentrations, reaching 60–80 per cent inhibition at 4 mg chloramphenicol/ml (Fig. XV.6). The ratio of chlorophyll *a* to chlorophyll *b* was approximately the same in normal and treated leaves. The ratio of carotenoids to chlorophylls was higher in the treated leaves, suggesting that chloramphenicol inhibits chlorophyll synthesis more than carotenoid synthesis. A study of the action spectra of excitation of chlorophyll fluorescence after two hours' exposure to light indicated that the ability to transfer energy absorbed by carotenoids to chlorophyll developed in chloramphenicol-treated leaves as it did in control leaves. However, with equal amounts of exciting light in the range 420–640 mμ the treated leaves produced twice as much fluorescence as the normal leaves.

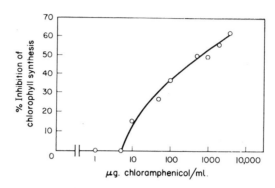

FIG. XV.6. *Effect of chloramphenicol at different concentrations on chlorophyll synthesis by etiolated leaves of* Phaseolus vulgaris *in the light (adapted from Margulies, 1962)*

Leaves which had been illuminated for 24 hours in the presence of 4 mg chloramphenicol/ml had no detectable ability to carry out the photosynthetic fixation of CO_2 even though they had about 40 per cent of the chlorophyll content of leaves illuminated in the absence of drug. Chloramphenicol itself had no direct inhibitory action on photosynthesis. Plastids isolated from the chloramphenicol-treated leaves had only about 10 per cent of the normal ability to carry out the photoreduction of NADP, ferricyanide, or 2,3′,6-trichlorophenol-indophenol, and were also unable to catalyse cyclic photophosphorylation in the presence of phenazine methosulphate. Synthesis of the chloroplast enzyme, NADP-linked glyceraldehyde phosphate dehydrogenase, in the light was not affected by chloramphenicol, but synthesis of another chloroplast enzyme, carboxydismutase, was almost abolished. The increase in total leaf protein that takes place in the greening leaves (on the intact plant) over a 48-hour period was 38 per cent inhibited by chloramphenicol. The increase in plastid protein content that takes place in the light was 50 per cent inhibited by chloramphenicol, so that the plastids finally produced in the presence of antibiotic had 25 per cent less protein per plastid than the plastids formed in control leaves.

It has also been found[124] that when barley seedlings are germinated in the presence of chloramphenicol in the dark, the formation of chlorophyll during a subsequent exposure to light is greatly inhibited. Similarly the formation of one or more of the enzymes involved in CO_2

fixation with ribose-5-phosphate as substrate is inhibited: formation of glycolytic enzymes, however, appears not to be inhibited.

In Margulies' experiments the chloramphenicol was added at the beginning of greening. The drug also inhibits chlorophyll synthesis by the etiolated *Phaseolus* leaves if it is added after the rapid phase of chlorophyll synthesis has started[50]. Chloramphenicol also inhibits chloroplast formation in etiolated cells of *Euglena gracilis* exposed to light[134]. The drug inhibited the synthesis of chlorophyll and of two chloroplast proteins, cytochrome b_6 and cytochrome-552. Incorporation of Mn (an essential thylakoid component) into the chloroplasts was also greatly reduced. Synthesis of two non-chloroplast enzymes, glucose-6-phosphate dehydrogenase and isocitrate dehydrogenase, however, was not affected by chloramphenicol. Incorporation of ^{14}C-leucine into chloroplast protein was more inhibited by chloramphenicol than was incorporation into microsomal or supernatant protein[107]. Further evidence for a relatively specific effect on chloroplast formation is provided by the fact that the growth of cells relying entirely on photosynthetic CO_2 fixation to supply their carbon is drastically inhibited by chloramphenicol, whereas cell growth in media containing oxidizable carbon compounds is relatively insensitive[134]. Parthier (1965a) observed that chloramphenicol inhibited incorporation of ^{35}S-methionine into protein of tobacco leaf discs, to a greater extent in the light than in the dark. He also found that incorporation into chloroplast protein was more inhibited than incorporation into mitochondrial, ribosomal or cytoplasmic protein[102a].

In the alga *Cyanidium caldarium*, the formation of enzymes involved in the synthesis of porphyrins and phycobilins that takes place during a 48-hour illumination of dark-grown cells (XIII.14.iii), is virtually completely inhibited if chloramphenicol ($10^{-3}M$) is present during the illumination[145]. The formation of these enzymes was detected by the ability of the cells to synthesize (and excrete) porphyrins and a phycobilin during a subsequent dark incubation. The synthesis of chlorophyll and phycocyanin during the illumination itself was also completely blocked by chloramphenicol.

In bacteria, chloramphenicol is known to act by inhibiting protein synthesis[49]: it directly inhibits the synthesis of polypeptide by bacterial ribosomes in the presence of synthetic messenger RNA[99] and may possibly be an inhibitor of the peptide bond-forming enzyme[144]. The effects on chloroplast formation can also be explained by an inhibition of synthesis of essential chloroplast proteins. As we have seen, the formation of at least three components of the photosynthetic system—carboxydismutase and two cytochromes—is blocked by the drug: these effects alone would explain the inhibition of development of photosynthetic activity. The inhibition of chlorophyll synthesis could be due to the drug preventing formation of the enzymes involved in chlorophyll biosynthesis. The fact that chloramphenicol stops chlorophyll synthesis in etiolated bean leaves even when added during the rapid phase of greening has been interpreted by Gassman and Bogorad (1965) as being due to an instability of δ-aminolaevulinic acid synthetase: it is supposed that the enzyme undergoes rapid turnover and therefore disappears from the cells as soon as its synthesis is blocked. An alternative explanation is that chloramphenicol inhibits the synthesis of some protein, possibly the chloroplast structural protein, which has to be formed in stoichiometric amounts for chlorophyll synthesis to occur (see XIII.15 and XV.3.ii). The observed inhibition of formation of total plastid protein[84] is also consistent with the hypothesis that the drug acts primarily on protein synthesis, as is the finding that chloramphenicol does not inhibit incorporation of ^{14}C-adenine into RNA in *E. gracilis*[107]. The suggestion that the drug affects synthesis of chloroplast proteins more than synthesis of other cellular proteins[134] is borne out by the observation[35] that incorporation of amino acids into protein by isolated *Euglena* chloroplasts or chloroplast ribosomes is inhibited by chloramphenicol, whereas incorporation by cytoplasmic ribosomes is not.

XV.3.ii. ACTIDIONE

The antibiotic actidione (Fig. XV.7) is a very effective inhibitor of greening in dark-grown cells of *Euglena gracilis* exposed to the light: at drug concentrations of 3 μg/ml and above, chlorophyll formation during a six-hour incubation is virtually abolished[77]. When the antibiotic is

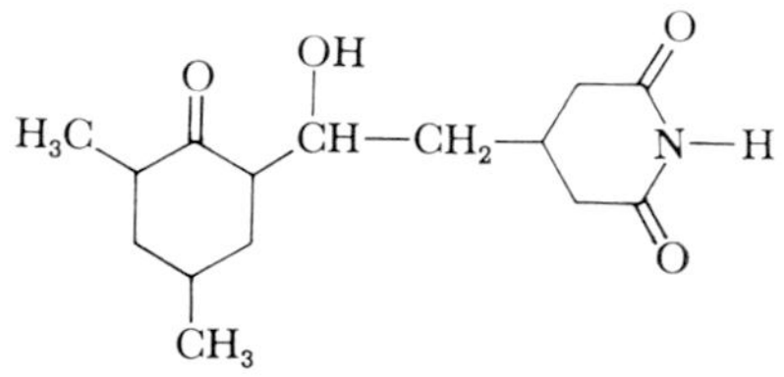

FIG. XV.7. *Actidione*

added four hours after the beginning of the illumination, chlorophyll formation during the next four hours is still drastically inhibited: the cells form only about 40 per cent as much chlorophyll between four and eight hours in the presence of actidione as they do between zero and four hours in its absence; when no actidione is added the amount of chlorophyll synthesized between four and eight hours is substantially higher than that synthesized between zero and four hours.

Carotenoid formation by etiolated cells of *E. gracilis* in the light is much less sensitive to actidione than is chlorophyll synthesis[77]. The time course of pigment synthesis in Fig. XV.8 shows that, at a concentration of actidione which inhibits chlorophyll a synthesis by about 90 per cent, carotenoid synthesis is inhibited by only about 25–50 per cent (the degree of inhibition appearing to increase with time). Increasing the concentration of actidione does not cause any further inhibition of carotenoid synthesis: in a four-hour incubation in the light 10 µg drug/ml causes the same inhibition of carotenoid formation (20–30 per cent) as does 0·32, or 1 µg/ml. When actidione (10 µg/ml) is added to the medium after four hours' greening, there is only a slight inhibition of carotenoid synthesis (about 9 per cent) during the next four hours: since carotenoid synthesis is substantially (*ca.* 70 per cent) faster in the second four-hour period than in the first, the amount of carotenoid formed in the presence of the antibiotic between four and eight hours is greater than the amount made between zero and four hours in the absence of actidione. Thus, addition of actidione after four hours does not cause any actual diminution in the rate of carotenoid formation: this is contrary to what is observed for chlorophyll formation.

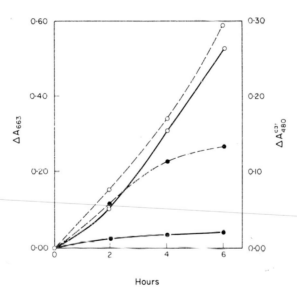

FIG. XV.8. *Time course of effect of actidione on synthesis of chlorophyll* a *and carotenoids by dark-grown cells of* Euglena gracilis *in the light (Kirk, J. T. O. and Allen, R. L., 1965, unpublished). Methods as in Kirk and Allen (1965). Increase in* A_{663} *of acetone extract, due to chlorophyll* a ———. *Increase in* A_{480} *due to carotenoids (corrected for chlorophyll absorption)* - - - - -. *Actidione (1 µg/ml) present* ———●. *Actidione absent* ———○

The effects of actidione on *E. gracilis* are by no means confined to chloroplast formation. Growth of the cells is 97 per cent inhibited at 10 µg actidione/ml, and is completely abolished at concentrations above this[77]. Incorporation of ^{14}C-leucine into protein by the greening cells is severely inhibited by actidone, the inhibition generally being slightly less than the inhibition of chlorophyll synthesis, e.g. at 3–10 μg drug/ml, chlorophyll synthesis is *ca.* 100 per cent inhibited and ^{14}C-leucine incorporation is 70–80 per cent inhibited. Incorporation of ^{14}C-leucine is inhibited to about the same extent by actidone in the dark as it is in the light.

Actidone is known to be a potent inhibitor of protein synthesis in cells of yeast[69,130] and higher animals[13,29]. There is clear evidence that in these organisms the drug acts directly on protein synthesis at the ribosome level[131,147,29,14]. It therefore seems likely that in *Euglena gracilis* also it acts on protein synthesis: this is supported by the finding that the drug inhibits ^{14}C-leucine incorporation. The inhibition of cell multiplication, and the fact that leucine incorporation is inhibited as much by actidone in the dark as in the light, indicate that the drug inhibits the formation of cell proteins generally, not just chloroplast proteins.

The great sensitivity of chlorophyll synthesis to actidone, and the fact that the drug inhibits such synthesis even when it is added some hours after greening has begun, Kirk and Allen (1965) have interpreted (see XIII.15 for a more detailed discussion) as being due to the inhibition, by actidone, of formation of some protein which is required in stoichiometric (as opposed to catalytic) amounts for chlorophyll synthesis. This protein could be the thylakoid structural protein.

XV.3.iii. ACTINOMYCIN D

Chloroplast formation by etiolated cells in the light is partially inhibited by actinomycin D (Fig. XV.9) both in the case of *Euglena gracilis*[106,134,91] and higher plants[18]. Concentrations of actinomycin which inhibit greening of *E. gracilis* inhibit cell growth to at least the same extent; the drug does not cause production of permanently bleached mutants[106,91].

One interesting feature of the effect of actinomycin is that the inhibition of chlorophyll formation appears to be delayed. Pogo and Pogo (1964) incubated dark-grown cells of *E. gracilis* in the presence or absence of actinomycin (10 μg/ml) for 14–16 hours in the dark. The cells were then exposed to light, and chlorophyll synthesis was followed. In the actinomycin-treated cells, chlorophyll formation was almost normal for 12 hours but then fell off very sharply, whereas it continued in the control. There was a similar effect on protein synthesis: incorporation of ^{14}C-leucine by the actinomycin-treated cells in the light was normal for the first nine hours and then ceased, whereas in the un-

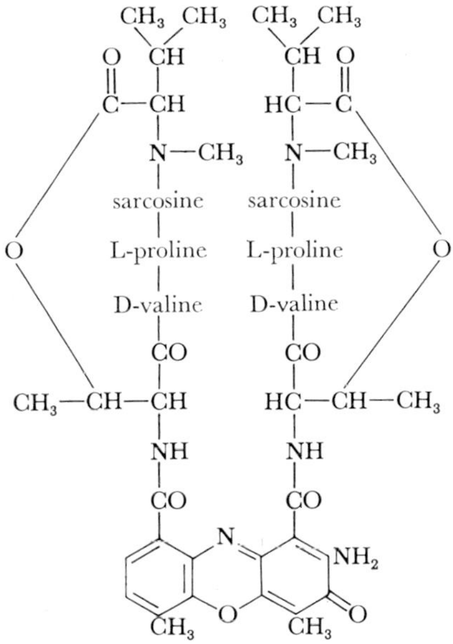

FIG. XV.9. *Actinomycin D*

treated cells it continued. RNA synthesis (as measured by ^{14}C-uracil incorporation) in the light was inhibited without any lag period, the rate in the drug-treated cells being about half that in the control cells. Curiously enough, however, incorporation of ^{14}C-uracil by the actinomycin treated cells continued after incorporation of ^{14}C-leucine had stopped.

Actinomycin D is known to inhibit RNA synthesis *in vivo*[72] and RNA polymerase *in vitro*[64, 52] by combining with the DNA template. The effects on chloroplast formation could certainly be explained by an inhibition of the synthesis of some kind, or kinds, of RNA essential for chloroplast development. The inhibition of ^{14}C-uracil incorporation supports this interpretation. The essential RNA could be messenger RNA to code the structure of chloroplast proteins, or ribosomal RNA to help carry out the synthesis, or both. Since chloroplast formation appears to be under the control of both nuclear and chloroplast DNA (Chapters X and XI), this actinomycin-sensitive RNA synthesis which is essential for chloroplast formation could be taking place in the nucleus or in the chloroplasts, or both. The fact that cell growth is inhibited as much as chloroplast formation shows that the effects are not confined to the chloroplast, and suggests that there is indeed inhibition of nuclear RNA synthesis. Actinomycin is known to inhibit both chloroplast and nuclear RNA polymerases[76].

The delay before protein synthesis stops might perhaps represent the time it takes the cell to use up those messenger RNA molecules which are present before actinomycin is added. The subsequent fall-off in chlorophyll synthesis could perhaps be a consequence of the cessation of protein synthesis: the supply of thylakoid structural protein, or some other essential protein, might have run out.

XV.3.iv. TETRACYCLINES, AND OTHER DRUGS

Growth of *Euglena gracilis* in the presence of a high concentration (5 mg/ml) of aureomycin (chlortetracycline—Fig. XV.10) gave rise to bleached cultures, which, however, reverted to green when transferred to aureomycin-free medium[116]. On plating out it was found that only

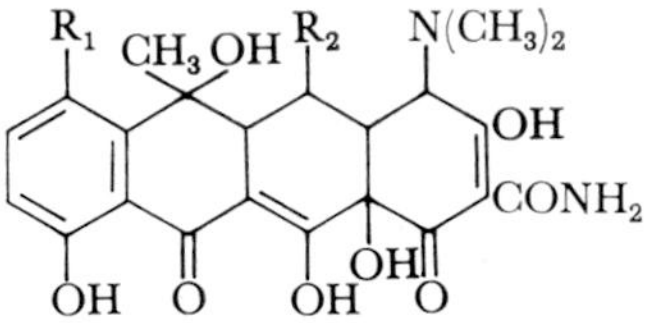

$R_1 = H, R_2 = H.$ Tetracycline
$R_1 = H, R_2 = OH.$ Oxytetracycline
$R_1 = Cl, R_2 = H.$ Chlortetracycline

FIG. XV.10. *Tetracyclines*

12 per cent of the treated cells had lost the ability to form chloroplasts. When seeds of radish or wheat are germinated in solutions containing tetracycline, oxytetracycline, or chlortetracycline (Fig. XV.10) the formation of chlorophyll is somewhat retarded[98]. Chlortetracycline is known to inhibit protein synthesis in bacteria[48]. Evidence obtained with cell-free systems suggests that the tetracyclines act by inhibiting the transfer of amino acids from aminoacyl-transfer RNA to protein in the ribosome[45].

Puromycin (Fig. XV.11) at 5×10^{-4}M inhibits the greening of dark-grown leaves of *Phaseolus vulgaris* exposed to light[50]. This antibiotic also stops chlorophyll synthesis if it is added some time during the rapid phase of greening. Puromycin is known to inhibit protein synthesis at the ribosome level. It may possibly act by substituting for aminoacyl-transfer RNA[153]. It seems likely that it inhibits greening for the same reasons as actidione and chloramphenicol do (XV.3.i and XV.3.ii).

When cucumber seeds were germinated in the presence of 3-(α-imino-ethyl)-5-methyl-tetronic acid (Fig. XV.12) at 100 μg/ml, the seedlings came up yellow[3]: also when bean seedlings were injected with this compound the new leaves produced subsequently were often white. When this compound at 5×10^{-4}M was added to germinating maize seedlings at the time the first leaf had pierced the coleoptile, the second leaf came up white in colour, although with a green tip[132]. An electron microscope examination was carried out of the plastids in

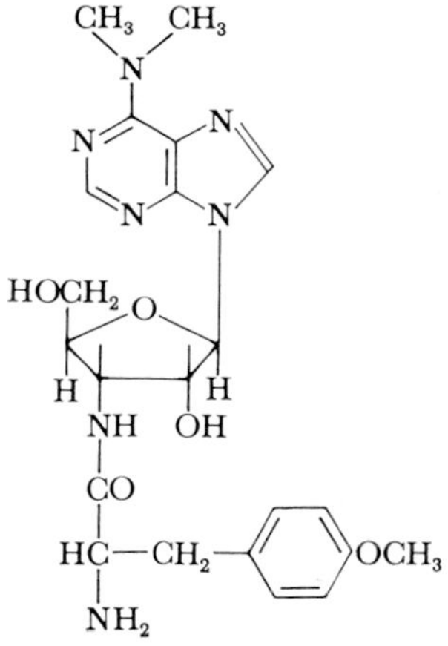

FIG. XV.11. *Puromycin*

different sections of the leaf, from the fully green part to the white part. A progressive diminution in the amount of thylakoid material was observed until finally, in the white part of the leaf, the plastids appeared virtually empty.

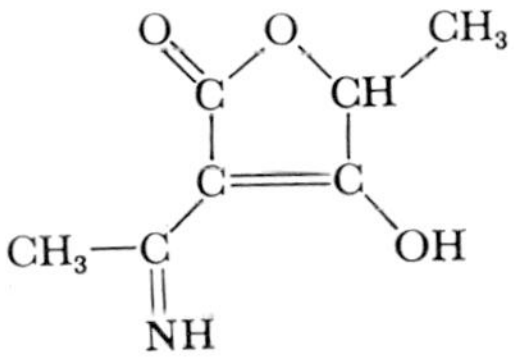

FIG. XV.12. *3-(α-iminoethyl)-5-methyltetronic acid*

All derivatives of 5-nitrofuran which have been tested cause permanent loss of chloroplast-forming ability in *Euglena gracilis*[90]. McCalla (1965) has shown that two of these, nitrofurantoin and 5-nitro-2-furaldehyde also inhibit greening of the etiolated cells in the light. 5-nitro-2-furaldehyde (Fig. XV.13) is the more effective, causing total

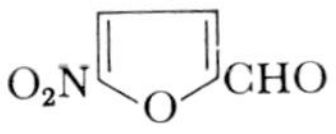

FIG. XV.13. *5-Nitro-2-furaldehyde*

inhibition of chlorophyll synthesis at 10 µg/ml, a concentration which inhibits growth only slightly. An interesting feature of this system is that the concentration at which 5-nitro-2-furaldehyde inhibits greening of etiolated cells is about the same as the concentration at which it causes permanent loss of ability to make chloroplasts: in this respect the compound differs from streptomycin which, as we have seen, has a relatively small effect on greening at concentrations which cause loss of chloroplast-forming ability. McCalla (1965) has suggested that the inhibition of greening by these nitrofurans might have a different mechanism from that by which they cause permanent loss of chloroplasts: the genetic effect could be due to an effect on the chloroplast DNA or DNA-synthesizing system, whereas the inhibition of greening might be a result of the inhibition of carbohydrate metabolism which these compounds are known to induce[22].

Chlorophyll formation by dark-grown cells of *E. gracilis* exposed to light is 50 per cent inhibited by hadacidin (N-formyl-N-hydroxyglycine—Fig. XV.14) at 5×10^{-3}M[93]. Addition of aspartate (10^{-2}M) or adenine (4×10^{-3}M) largely, but not completely, overcame this inhibition; uracil (10^{-2}M) had no effect. The later in the greening process that hadacidin was added, the less was its effect: it brought about no inhibition if added 24 hours after illumination had started, by which time the cells had synthesized only about 16 per cent of their final chlorophyll content. Hadacidin is known to inhibit the synthesis of adenylic acid in ascites tumour cells[129]. It acts by inhibiting the enzyme adenylo-succinate synthetase, which is involved in the conversion of inosinic acid to adenylic acid: the hadacidin competes with aspartic acid (one of the substrates) for the enzyme and its effects are completely overcome by excess aspartic acid[129]. The effects of hadacidin on greening can thus be explained by an inhibition of formation of adenylic acid, with a consequent inhibition of formation of the various kinds of RNA required for chloroplast formation. The antagonistic effect of aspartate and adenine support this interpretation[93].

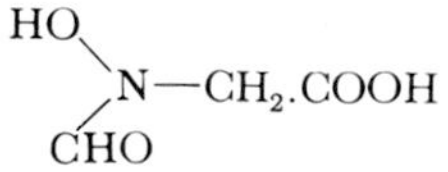

$$\begin{array}{c} \text{HO} \\ \diagdown \\ \diagup \quad \text{N—CH}_2\text{.COOH} \\ \text{CHO} \end{array}$$

FIG. XV.14. *Hadacidin*

When cress (*Lepidium sativum*) seedlings are germinated in solutions containing 10 μg aflatoxin/ml they come up white in colour[127]. Other fungal metabolites—carolic acid, citrinin, frequentin, rugulosin, and terrein—caused production of partially bleached leaves.

As previously mentioned (X.6) permanent loss of ability to form chloroplasts in *E. gracilis* is induced by the streptomycin-type antibiotics kanamycin, paromomycin, and neomycin; by the antihistamine drugs tripelennamine, methapyrilene, and pyrilamine, and by erythromycin. It is not clear whether they have any direct, immediate, effect on the formation of the chloroplast apart from their long-term genetic effects. The permanent bleaching effect of the streptomycin-type antibiotics (and also of streptomycin itself) is overcome by histidine, and also by a mixture of pantothenate, nicotinic acid, and thiamine[154].

Ebringer (1965) has examined a number of macrolide antibiotics for bleaching activity against *Euglena gracilis*. Polyene macrolides, which are active against fungi and yeasts, are highly toxic for *E. gracilis* and could not, therefore, be studied for bleaching action. Ebringer found that all non-polyene macrolides tested which contained an amino sugar moiety bleached *Euglena*: these were erythromycin, carbomycin, tylosin, angolamycin, spiramycin, picromycin, metmycin, oleandomycin, and nineteen antibiotically active modifications of oleandomycin and erythromycin. All these antibiotics, with the exception of picromycin and metmycin, cause permanent bleaching: these two cause only temporary bleaching. All non-polyene macrolides except chalkomycin and lankamycin contain a dimethylaminohexose residue and are consequently of basic character. Chalkomycin and lankamycin are neutral, and do not bleach *E. gracilis* although they have a similar antibacterial spectrum to the rest of these antibiotics. Ebringer points out that the common molecular denominator for bleaching activity among macrolide antibiotics is an aminohexose which is glycosidically linked to the lactone ring of the molecule.

Chlorophyll formation in *E. gracilis* is temporarily arrested by 4-nitro-quinoline-N-oxide[133], which is a carcinogen.

XV.4. Herbicides

XV.4.i. AMITROL

When plants are sprayed with solutions of amitrol (3-amino-1,2,4-triazole—Fig. XV.15) any new leaves formed are chlorotic, but chlorophyll already formed at the time of treatment is apparently not affected[57, 113]. When wheat seedlings are germinated in solutions con-

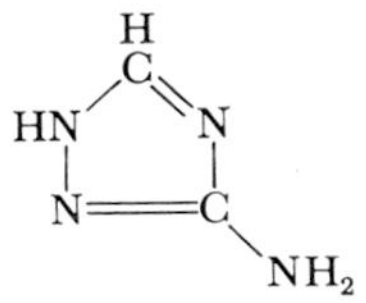

FIG. XV.15. *Amitrol*

taining amitrol at different concentrations, formation of carotenoids is inhibited to about the same extent as formation of chlorophyll, i.e. about 95 per cent at 10^{-4}M amitrol[149]. Similarly, in the algae *Ochromonas danica* and *Euglena gracilis*, amitrol inhibits formation of carotenoids as well as chlorophylls[1]. As well as inhibiting chlorophyll formation in plants growing in the light, amitrol (10^{-4}M) almost abolishes the greening of wheat seedlings grown in the dark and then exposed to light[149]. The photoreduction of protochlorophyllide to chlorophyllide on the protochlorophyllide holochrome is not inhibited by amitrol[97]. The degradation of chlorophyll by plants kept in the dark is not stimulated by amitrol[149].

Light microscopic examination of chlorotic tissue formed in the presence of amitrol indicates that the colourless plastids are few in number, shrunken, and misshapen[113]. An electron microscopic study of wheat seedlings grown in the light in the presence of 10^{-4}M amitrol showed that the plastids either contained membranes concentrically arranged around an electron-dense body, or were highly disorganized, with membranes extending in all directions[10]. The leaf plastids of seedlings grown in the dark in the presence of amitrol had a normal structure, with a typical crystalline centre. When the dark-grown wheat seedlings were exposed to light in the presence of amitrol the crystalline centre persisted for about five hours, and then began to break down[11]: it thus appears that amitrol does not prevent the development of the etioplast, but does inhibit the conversion of the etioplast into a chloroplast in the light, although, as mentioned above, the very first step in this process, the photoreduction of protochlorophyllide, is not inhibited. In the case of the alga *Scenedesmus quadricauda*, the plastids accumulate large amounts of starch when the cells are grown in the presence of amitrol[26].

The effects of amitrol are not confined to the chloroplasts. This herbicide inhibits growth of *Euglena gracilis* and *Ochromonas danica* even under heterotrophic conditions, in which the cells do not need to form chloroplasts anyway[1]. However, growth in general, in the case of wheat seedlings, does appear to be less sensitive to amitrol than chlorophyll synthesis. The accumulation of starch in amitrol-treated cells of *Scenedesmus quadricauda* indicates that the herbicide has little effect on photosynthesis. In barley seedlings, amitrol appears to inhibit incorporation of phosphate into the acid-insoluble fraction (nucleic acids, phosphoproteins, phospholipids) but does not affect incorporation into the intermediates (nucleotides, sugar phosphates) of glycolysis or oxidative phosphorylation[152]. Amitrol can inhibit the growth of non-photosynthetic organisms such as yeast and bacteria[61,148].

A variety of compounds have been reported to overcome the effects of amitrol. The inhibition of chlorophyll formation by 5×10^{-4}M

amitrol in growing tomato leaves was largely overcome by an equimolar concentration of riboflavin, flavin mononucleotide or flavin
adenine dinucleotide[140]: the inhibitory effects on growth were also
partly overcome. In bacteria, the inhibitory effect of amitrol on growth
is reversed by adenine[148]. The inhibition of growth of various yeasts
by amitrol is overcome by histidine[61]. Wolf (1961) reported that the
inhibitory effects of 5 μg/ml amitrol on growth of *Chlorella pyrenoidosa*
were abolished by the purine bases adenine, guanine, hypoxanthine, or
xanthine at 10 μg/ml; uric acid was only slightly less effective. Riboflavin had no antagonistic effect, even in high concentration. However,
in the case of wheat or tomato seedlings germinated in the presence of
10^{-4}M amitrol, the pronounced inhibition of chlorophyll formation
and moderate inhibition of growth were abolished by an equimolar
concentration of riboflavin, flavin mononucleotide or flavin adenine
dinucleotide: the inhibitory effects were not overcome by any of the
above purines, or by histidine, folic acid or xanthopterin. Wolf concluded that the amitrol-sensitive system in *Chlorella* is different to that
in wheat and tomato. In *Ochromonas danica* the inhibition of chlorophyll
formation was overcome by Fe^{2+} or Fe^{3+} (particularly the former), and
by the phospholipid, lecithin[1].

The position with regard to the mode of action of amitrol is far from
clear. It has been variously suggested that it interferes with adenine
synthesis[148] or riboflavin synthesis[139]; that it chelates iron and thereby
inhibits processes (such as chlorophyll synthesis) which require iron[1];
that it interferes with glycine and serine metabolism[25]; that, by virtue
of an interference with adenine metabolism it prevents the formation
of a particular form of phosphorylase[46]. In the case of the yeast,
Saccharomyces cerevisiae, and the bacterium *Salmonella typhimurium*, there
is some quite direct evidence that amitrol interferes with histidine
synthesis[80, 62, 62a]. Cells grown in the presence of amitrol accumulate
one of the intermediates of histidine biosynthesis—imidazoleglycerol
phosphate. Also, the enzyme—imidazoleglycerol phosphate dehydrase
—which acts on this intermediate is apparently inhibited by amitrol,
the herbicide competing with the substrate. Hilton and Kearney (1965)
suggest that protein synthesis, and ultimately growth, is blocked as a
result of the inhibition of histidine synthesis resulting from the inhibition
of this enzyme: the inhibition of RNA synthesis they believe to be an
indirect consequence or possibly[62a] an additional effect on purine
synthesis. Bartels and Wolf (1965) found an accumulation of free amino
acids, and an inhibition of incorporation of ^{14}C-glycine into protein in
wheat seedlings grown in the presence of amitrol in the light, and suggested that protein synthesis was inhibited in the presence of the herbicide. The fact that histidine does not overcome the effects of amitrol on
wheat seedlings[150] may be considered as evidence that in this case

amitrol does not act by inhibiting histidine synthesis: however, it is not certain that the histidine is actually taken up by the wheat plants.

In the case of *Euglena gracilis* there is some evidence that the effect on chloroplast formation is not due to a direct effect on chlorophyll synthesis. When cells which have been grown at a light intensity of 25–50 foot-candles are exposed to light at an intensity of 1500 foot-candles, there is a rapid synthesis of chlorophyll. This synthesis of chlorophyll is not inhibited by amitrol, even at a concentration as high as 3×10^{-3}M[109]. It may be that the cells grown in weak light have an excess of thylakoid structural protein, so that on exposure to high light intensity more chlorophyll can rapidly be synthesized to bind on to this protein. However, when the cells are actually grown in the presence of amitrol it may be that formation of the thylakoid structural protein itself is (either directly or indirectly) inhibited so that chlorophyll formation is inhibited as well.

It is possible that there is more than one mode of action of amitrol as the work of Wolf (above) on *Chlorella* and on wheat and tomato seedlings suggests. The position is complicated still further by the fact that amitrol undergoes extensive metabolism in plants[115, 89]: in bean plants as many as thirteen different compounds may be formed from amitrol[24]. Thus it is entirely possible that the antimetabolic effects of amitrol are due to one or more of the compounds formed from it. At the moment, then, it must be said that the mechanism by which amitrol inhibits chloroplast formation is still unknown.

XV.4.ii. TRIAZINES AND MONURON

Two examples of the symmetrical triazine class of herbicides are simazine and atrazine (Fig. XV.16). The symptoms produced by low concentrations of these compounds (supplied in the culture medium) on

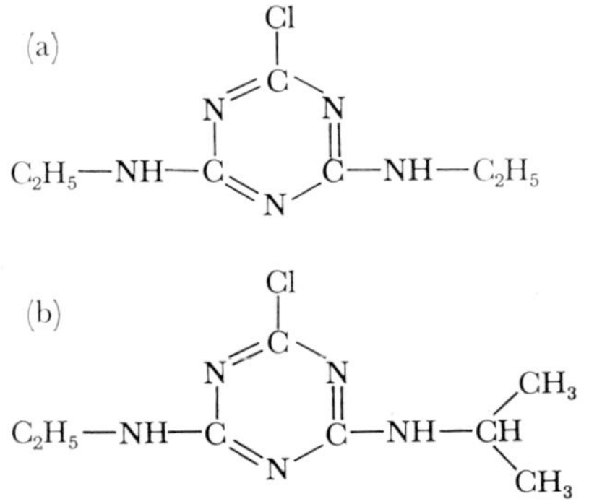

FIG. XV.16. *Triazines.* (*a*) *Simazine;* (*b*) *Atrazine*

Phaseolus vulgaris include interveinal chlorosis in the leaves[7]. Atrazine also diminishes the amount of chlorophyll formed by growing cultures of *Chlorella vulgaris*[6]. Ashton, Gifford, and Bisalputra (1963) found that the leaf chloroplasts of *Phaseolus vulgaris* plants grown in the presence of atrazine in the light become spherical rather than discoid; starch disappears from the lamellar system and the thylakoids of the grana become swollen and ultimately disintegrate. Since atrazine does not affect chloroplast structure in the dark, these authors concluded that atrazine itself is not toxic to the chloroplast, but that toxic substances are formed in the presence of atrazine in the light.

The primary site of action of the symmetrical triazines appears to be the photosynthetic electron transport system. It has been shown[39, 96] that these compounds inhibit the Hill reaction; in the case of isolated barley chloroplasts the inhibition of ferricyanide photoreduction is 50 per cent at 4.6×10^{-6}M[96]. Photosynthetic fixation of $^{14}CO_2$ by intact leaves was almost completely blocked after exposure to simazine for 40 hours[8], presumably as a consequence of the inhibition of electron transport. The supposition that the lethal action of these herbicides is due to their effect on photosynthesis is supported by the fact that if barley plants are made independent of photosynthesis by being supplied with glucose, they can survive and grow in the presence of simazine at a concentration which would otherwise be lethal[96]. The effects on chloroplast structure might well be due, as suggested by Ashton *et al.* (1963), to the accumulation of toxic products in the light: these could be free radicals or other highly reactive compounds produced as a result of the block in electron transport. This view is supported by the observation that atrazine causes more damage when the plants are irradiated with light of wavelengths absorbed by chlorophyll (428 and 658 mμ) than when irradiation is carried out with light of wavelengths (500, 528, 567, and 607 mμ) which are poorly absorbed by chlorophyll[5]. The inhibition of chlorophyll formation, as observed in *Chlorella*[6], might also be, in part, due to the lack of biosynthetic intermediates consequent upon the inhibition of photosynthetic CO_2 fixation.

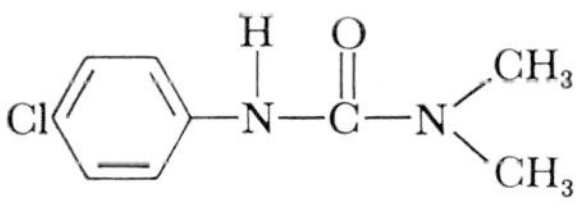

FIG. XV.17. *Monuron*

Monuron, or 3-(*p*-chlorophenyl)-1,1-dimethylurea (Fig. XV.17) has rather similar effects on plants to those produced by triazines: like them, it inhibits photosynthetic electron transport[67]. The toxic effects of this compound on higher plants, and on *Euglena* and *Chlorella* are only obtained in the light[141, 5]. Also, light absorbed by chlorophyll is more effective than light not absorbed by chlorophyll[5]. It therefore seems likely that the damaging effects of monuron on chloroplasts are also due to accumulation of toxic products as a result of the inhibition of photosynthetic electron transport.

XV.5. Protein and Nucleic Acid Precursors

XV.5.i. NATURALLY OCCURRING AMINO ACIDS

There is a pathological condition of tobacco plants known as frenching: in this condition, growth of the terminal bud of the plant slows or stops, and the slowly expanding new leaves develop a network type of chlorosis: these leaves may eventually become strap-shaped[138]. Frenching symptoms have been produced in aseptically-grown seedlings of *Nicotiana rustica* by the addition of the amino acids L-leucine, L-isoleucine, or L-alloisoleucine to the culture medium[137]. L-alloisoleucine was more effective than L-leucine, which in turn was more effective than L-isoleucine; D-leucine, D-isoleucine, and D-alloisoleucine did not cause frenching. A similar condition—yellow strapleaf—the symptoms of which include chlorosis, was induced in *Chrysanthemum* by the application of L-leucine, L-isoleucine, D-isoleucine, or DL-alloisoleucine to the soil around the base of the plant[151]. D-leucine and D-alloisoleucine did not produce this condition. The effects of these amino acids are by no means confined to *Nicotiana* and *Chrysanthemum*: isoleucine was found to produce these symptoms in plants from fifteen out of twenty-two genera tested[151].

The mechanism by which these amino acids induce chlorosis and inhibition of growth is quite unknown. One possibility is that a large concentration of one amino acid might, by feedback inhibition, inhibit the biosynthesis of related amino acids. For instance, in bacteria, leucine and valine have the same biosynthetic pathway as far as α-ketoisovalerate (see review by Umbarger and Davis, 1962). The inhibition of biosynthetic enzymes by the end-product of the biosynthetic pathway is a well-established phenomenon. Thus, if leucine inhibited one of the enzymes prior to α-ketoisovalerate, it would inhibit valine synthesis as well as its own synthesis. Certain of the enzymes of the valine-leucine pathway are also used to catalyse analogous reactions in the isoleucine synthesis pathway[146]. Thus, it seems possible that leucine might also inhibit isoleucine synthesis, or that isoleucine might inhibit leucine and valine synthesis. An inhibition, by a large amount of one amino acid, of the synthesis of one or more other amino acids, would inhibit protein synthesis and might thus explain the interference with growth and chloroplast formation.

An alternative possibility is that a large amount of one amino acid might drive another amino acid out of the cell. For instance, in the bacterium *Escherichia coli*, valine, leucine, and isoleucine have the same uptake mechanism, so that the presence of one of these amino acids interferes with the uptake of another (see review by Képès and Cohen, 1962). Since these amino acids are continually passing in and out of the cell, a large amount of one of them can displace the others from the cell by blocking the uptake but not the exit. If similar mechanisms exist in plant cells, then large amounts of isoleucine might displace valine and leucine from the cells with, again, a consequent inhibition of protein synthesis.

XV.5.ii. O-METHYLTHREONINE

When a 0·1 per cent solution of DL-O-methylthreonine (Fig. XV.18) was applied as a spray, or a soil drench, to young bean or wheat plants the new leaves that formed after treatment contained no chlorophyll[54]; growth was also somewhat inhibited. Inclusion of four to nine times as much DL-isoleucine as O-methylthreonine in the soil drench, abolished the inhibition of growth and chlorophyll formation. Other amino acids —threonine, serine, valine, leucine, and norleucine—did not reverse the

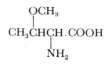

$$
\begin{array}{c}
OCH_3 \\
| \\
CH_3CHCH.COOH \\
| \\
NH_2
\end{array}
$$

Fig. XV.18. *O-methylthreonine*

bleaching effects. O-methylthreonine also inhibited growth and chlorophyll formation in *Euglena gracilis*[54]. In the case of this alga, chlorophyll formation was much more sensitive than growth: concentrations of O-methylthreonine which had little effect on cell multiplication, caused production of cells with no chlorophyll and little, if any, carotenoid[2]. When these cells were subcultured into media not containing the abnormal amino acid, it was found that they had permanently lost the ability to make chloroplasts. The inhibition of chlorophyll formation in *E. gracilis* by O-methylthreonine was overcome by L-isoleucine, L-threonine, L-homoserine, α-aminobutyric acid, and α-ketobutyric acid: α-ketobutyric acid was the most effective. The D-isomers of these amino acids did not act as antagonists.

In ascites tumour cells, O-methylthreonine inhibits the incorporation

of isoleucine into protein; this inhibition is overcome by excess isoleucine[114]. This suggests that O-methylthreonine acts as an analogue
of isoleucine, a view supported by the overall similarity in size and shape
of the two molecules. Since, in *E. gracilis*, isoleucine reverses the effect
of O-methylthreonine, and since the other compounds which reverse
the effects—homoserine, threonine, α-ketobutyric acid, and α-aminobutyric acid—can all be converted to isoleucine within the cell, it seems
quite likely that O-methylthreonine acts as an isoleucine analogue in
this alga, too. The direct inhibition of chloroplast formation could be
due to an inhibition of formation of chloroplast proteins, including
thylakoid structural protein and the enzymes necessary for pigment
synthesis. Alternatively, the O-methylthreonine might not immediately
inhibit protein synthesis but might, by being incorporated in place of
isoleucine, cause the formation of abnormal, non-functional proteins.
The fact that cell multiplication continues at concentrations which
block chloroplast formation could be due to the isoleucine-activating
enzyme in the cytoplasm being better able to distinguish between isoleucine and O-methylthreonine than the corresponding enzyme in the
chloroplasts: this could result in abnormal, O-methylthreonine-contain-
ing proteins being formed in the chloroplasts but not in the cytoplasm.
Alternatively, O-methylthreonine might not actually be activated but
might inhibit the chloroplast isoleucine-activating enzyme but not the
cytoplasmic isoleucine-activating enzyme: in this way the formation of
chloroplast proteins, but not of other cell proteins, would be blocked.
The permanent loss of ability to form chloroplasts, induced by O-
methylthreonine, could be a result of inhibition of replication of chloroplast DNA, due to interference with the formation of one or more of the
enzymes involved in chloroplast DNA synthesis.

On the basis of their observation that α-ketobutyric acid is the most
effective antagonist of O-methylthreonine (being about twice as effective as isoleucine) in *E. gracilis*, Aaronson and Bensky (1962) have suggested that O-methylthreonine acts by interfering with the utilization
of α-ketobutyrate in the synthesis of photosynthetic pigments, and that
isoleucine and the other compounds are effective as antagonists by
virtue of the fact that they can be converted to α-ketobutyrate. While
this possibility must be considered, it should be noted that the fact that
α-ketobutyrate is a better antagonist than isoleucine could possibly be
due to the former compound being more rapidly taken up by the cells.

XV.5.iii. ETHIONINE AND *P*-FLUOROPHENYLALANINE

The rapid formation of chlorophyll that takes place when cells of
Euglena gracilis grown at a light intensity of 50 foot-candles are exposed
to light at 1500 foot-candles, is virtually abolished if the methionine

analogue, ethionine (Fig. XV.19) is added at a concentration of $10^{-4}M^{(109)}$. Ethionine also inhibits chlorophyll (bacteriochlorophyll) synthesis in the photosynthetic bacterium *Rhodopseudomonas spheroides*: in this case it appears likely that ethionine inhibits synthesis by interfering with the formation of the methyl ester group of the chlorophyll[51].

$$CH_3CH_2—S—CH_2CH_2CH.COOH$$
$$\underset{NH_2}{|}$$

FIG. XV.19. *Ethionine*

Thus it may well be that the inhibition of chlorophyll synthesis in *E. gracilis* by ethionine is also due to an effect on methylation. However, ethionine may also have other effects on chloroplast formation: in the case of the alga *Cyanidium caldarium*, ethionine (at $10^{-3}M$) not only inhibits formation of chlorophyll and phycocyanin by dark-grown cells in the light, but also inhibits the development, by these cells, of the ability to convert δ-aminolaevulinic acid to porphyrins, such as coproporphyrin and uroporphyrin, which do not contain the methyl ester group[145]. This suggests that ethionine may perhaps inhibit not only methylation itself, but also the formation of some of the enzymes of chlorophyll synthesis.

For mation of chlorophyll *a* and phycocyanin in the light, by the dark-grown cells of *C. caldarium* is also inhibited by *p*-fluorophenylalanine (an analogue of phenylalanine) at a concentration of $10^{-3}M^{(145)}$. This is probably due to an effect on protein synthesis: either an inhibition of protein synthesis, or the formation of abnormal non-functional protein containing *p*-fluorophenylalanine in place of phenylalanine.

XV.5.iv. 2-THIOURACIL

Heslop-Harrison (1962) found that when leaves of hemp (*Cannabis sativa*) plants were painted daily with a solution containing 100 µg/ml 2-thiouracil (Fig. XV.20), apical growth was progressively arrested, and leaves which expanded after the treatment commenced were chlorotic. The plastids in the chlorotic regions were seen with the light

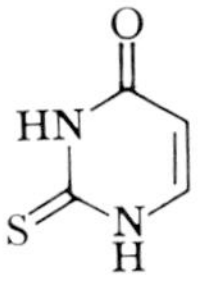

FIG. XV.20. *2-Thiouracil*

microscope to be appreciably narrower than the normal chloroplasts, and appeared to contain local concentrations of yellow pigments, but practically no chlorophyll. Electron microscope examination revealed thylakoid stacks, somewhat similar in appearance to normal grana, but of smaller diameter, containing fewer thylakoids and with fewer thylakoids passing from one granum to another. Also, many of the thylakoids appeared somewhat distended. The osmiophilic globuli present were aggregated together instead of being distributed throughout the stroma as in the normal chloroplast: these aggregates of globuli might possibly correspond to the local concentrations of yellow pigments (presumably carotenoids) seen with the light microscope. This immediate effect of 2-thiouracil on chloroplast formation is thought[58] to be due to a disturbance of RNA metabolism (thiouracil could act as an analogue of uracil) with a consequent inhibition of protein synthesis.

When thiouracil treatment was terminated after 10 days, the plants recovered progressively during the next two weeks, and there was a partial restoration of green colour in the chlorotic zones formed during treatment. During the remaining life of treated plants, chlorotic flecks or streaks appeared intermittently in the leaves. The shapes and positions of these chlorotic regions suggested that the chlorophyll deficiency ran through particular cell lineages and was not the result of local metabolic disturbances. The plastids in these chlorotic regions were smaller than normal chloroplasts and appeared in section to contain large numbers of small vesicles distributed throughout the stroma, and some thylakoid-like structures. What appear to be vesicles are thought, in fact, to be sections of tubes. In some cases the plastid was seen to contain an irregular aggregation of tubules. Heslop-Harrison (1962) suggests that this long-term effect of thiouracil on chloroplast structure has a genetic basis: that there may be mutations in the genetic system of the proplastids in the meristem, followed by the transmission of mixed normal and abnormal plastid populations during the subsequent recovery period. As a result of the random assortment of the two types of plastid at cell division, a cell will occasionally be produced which contains only, or mainly, mutant plastids, and the cell lineages arising from such a cell will give rise to the chlorotic regions.

XV.5.v. 5-FLUOROURACIL AND 5-FLUORODEOXY-URIDINE

Chlorophyll formation by dark-grown cells of *Euglena gracilis* exposed to light, was partially inhibited by 5-fluorouracil (Fig. XV.21): the inhibition reached 50 per cent at 5×10^{-3}M[134]. The fluorouracil was less effective when it was added some hours after greening had commenced: when added at seven hours, this compound had only about half the effect obtained when it was added at the beginning; when added at 19 hours (by which time only about 20 per cent of the final chlorophyll level had been achieved) there was no inhibition of chlorophyll synthesis. Fluorouracil also inhibited synthesis of the chloroplast protein cytochrome-552, in the greening cells: the degree of inhibition was about the same as that of chlorophyll synthesis.

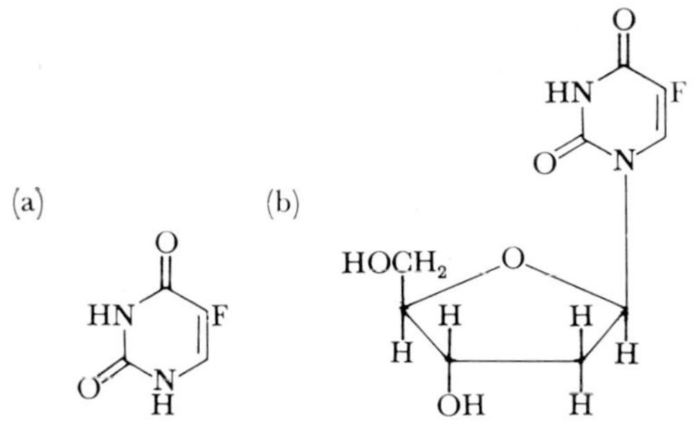

FIG. XV.21. (a) 5-Fluorouracil; (b) 5-Fluorodeoxyuridine

In bacteria, 5-fluorouracil acts as an analogue of uracil: it appears to prevent the formation of functional ribosomes, so that eventually protein synthesis comes to a stop[4]. In *E. gracilis* the inhibitory effect of fluorouracil on chlorophyll formation was abolished by the addition of an equimolar concentration of uracil[134], suggesting that in this organism, too, fluorouracil acts as a uracil analogue. After eight hours' illumination of etiolated cells in the presence of fluorouracil the level of ribosomal RNA, and the amount of ^{14}C-uracil incorporated into ribosomal RNA, were much lower than in cells illuminated in the absence of fluorouracil[134]. The level of soluble RNA, and incorporation into soluble RNA were not affected by fluorouracil. Smillie, Evans, and Lyman (1963) suggest that fluorouracil inhibits chloroplast formation by preventing the synthesis of those new ribosomes (presumably chloroplast ribosomes) which are required for the synthesis of chloroplast proteins.

Van Noort and Wallace (1963) reported that the synthesis of chlorophyll that takes place when iron-deficient (XV.7) plants of *Phaseolus vulgaris* are supplied with iron, was inhibited if the leaves were wetted with solutions of fluorouracil or fluorodeoxyuridine (Fig. XV.21). Fluorouracil at 5×10^{-3}M caused 69 per cent inhibition; fluorodeoxyuridine at 10^{-3}M caused 100 per cent inhibition. The effects of fluorouracil and fluorodeoxyuridine were to a large extent (*ca.* three-quarters) overcome in the presence of an equimolar concentration of thymidine: uridine, however, did not diminish the inhibitory effects of the fluoro-compounds. To explain these results, van Noort and Wallace suggest that the synthesis of chlorophyll under these conditions requires the synthesis of DNA, and that fluorouracil and fluorodeoxyuridine inhibit chlorophyll synthesis by inhibiting the formation of this DNA. Fluorodeoxyuridine is, in fact, known to inhibit DNA synthesis in bacteria by blocking the methylation of deoxyuridylic acid to give thymidylic acid[28].

These findings are extremely puzzling because we know of no reason why recovery of leaves from iron-deficiency should require synthesis of DNA; unless, possibly, there is a diminution of the number of plastids in iron-deficiency, and recovery involves plastid multiplication, as well as growth and chlorophyll formation. It may be wondered whether fluorodeoxyuridine inhibits any other enzymes as well as thymidylate synthetase. It is to be hoped that this very interesting effect will be studied further.

XV.6. General Metabolic Inhibitors

Hydroxylamine hydrochloride, at a concentration of 10^{-3}M, was found to inhibit carotenoid synthesis in excised leaves of *Phaseolus vulgaris* by 74 per cent[9]. Since this concentration of hydroxylamine completely inhibited photosynthesis, it seems likely that the inhibition of carotenoid formation is due to the lack of biosynthetic precursors and energy normally provided by photosynthesis. This interpretation is supported by the fact that when the leaves were supplied with an alternative source of carbon and energy, in the form of 0.15M sucrose, hydroxylamine inhibited carotenoid synthesis by only 36 per cent.

Fluoride is known to induce chlorosis in higher plants. 10^{-3}M sodium fluoride inhibited carotenoid synthesis in excised leaves of *Phaseolus vulgaris* by 29 per cent[9]. The synthesis of chlorophyll *a*, chlorophyll *b*, and carotenoids by excised, etiolated leaves of *Phaseolus vulgaris*, floating on culture solution in the light for four days, was 50 per cent inhibited by 10^{-2}M NaF[92]. Fluoride ion can form complexes with metals such as magnesium, and is known to inhibit many enzymes: it may therefore interfere with chloroplast formation at many different points.

Chlorophyll formation by dark-grown cells of *Euglena gracilis* exposed to the light is about 90 per cent inhibited in the absence of oxygen[134], and is virtually abolished by compounds which block mitochondrial electron transport, or uncouple oxidative phosphorylation (Table XV.1). The effects of these treatments on chloroplast formation may well be due to their interference with production of biosynthetic intermediates (in the citric acid cycle) and energy.

High concentrations of carbon dioxide inhibit greening of etiolated plants in the light[16]. The extent of inhibition varies from species to species, and a concentration sufficient to stop greening in one species might only retard it in another. Steer and Walker (1965) have found

TABLE XV.I. EFFECT OF GENERAL METABOLIC
INHIBITORS ON CHLOROPHYLL SYNTHESIS BY
ETIOLATED CELLS OF *E. GRACILIS*

(*Adapted from Smillie, Evans and Lyman, 1963*)

Inhibitor	Molar concentration	% inhibition of chlorophyll synthesis during three days in the light
Carbonyl cyanide, *m*-chlorophenyl-hydrazone	2×10^{-6}	98
2:4-Dinitrophenol	10^{-5}	99
Sodium azide	10^{-5}	99
Sodium malonate	5×10^{-2}	82
Sodium fluoride	5×10^{-3}	99
Beryllium sulphate	2×10^{-3}	99
Sodium arsenite	10^{-3}	99
Air replaced by atmosphere of N_2	—	88

that the synthesis of chlorophyll by excised, dark-grown barley leaves in the light occurs at only half the rate in an atmosphere containing 20 per cent O_2, 50 per cent N_2, and 30 per cent CO_2 as it does in air. Chlorophyll synthesis in wheat leaves under these conditions is about 70 per cent inhibited: when the CO_2 is removed after three hours, the rate of chlorophyll synthesis rises almost to the normal level. When chlorophyll synthesis is brought about by a series of light flashes (each flash two milliseconds, three minutes' dark after each flash) 30 per cent CO_2 still inhibits: since no photosynthesis would take place under this light régime (only 0·36 seconds' total exposure to light in nine hours) the inhibition of chlorophyll synthesis cannot be due to the known inhibitory effects of CO_2 on photosynthesis. The inhibitory effect of CO_2 on greening is abolished if the barley leaves are supplied with δ-aminolaevulinic acid (0·013M). Steer and Walker conclude that the site of the inhibition is early in chlorophyll synthesis: they point out that high levels of CO_2 are known to inhibit several reactions associated with the citric acid cycle, and this might limit the production of δ-aminolaevulinic acid.

XV.7. Nutritional Deficiencies

XV.7.i. IRON

Like all growth processes, chloroplast formation requires various essential nutrients. Lack of certain nutrients may inhibit the synthesis of certain chloroplast components, particularly chlorophyll, more than the synthesis of other cellular materials. Thus, chlorosis is a common indication of nutritional deficiency in higher plants: a comprehensive account of the effect of inorganic nutrient deficiencies on higher plants may be found in the review by Hewitt (1963). Probably the first nutritional chlorosis to be discovered was that induced by lack of iron. It was shown by Gris in 1844 that when plants were grown in a nutrient solution which lacked iron, then the leaves came up white. If a solution of an inorganic iron salt was painted on the leaf it turned green in two to three days. The iron content of *Euglena gracilis* cells can be adjusted by growth in media containing different concentrations of this element: when such cells are induced to form more chlorophyll by exposure to high light intensities, there is a linear relationship at low iron levels between the rate of chlorophyll synthesis and the cellular iron content[108]. The rate of cell growth is normal at iron levels which permit only one-third the maximum rate of chlorophyll synthesis.

Chlorosis is often observed in plants grown in soil with a high lime content. This type of chlorosis is thought to be, in fact, due to lack of iron. One possibility is that under alkaline conditions, the iron in the soil may be precipitated as a highly insoluble basic ferric hydroxide, and thus rendered unavailable to the plant. Excesses of certain metals, such as manganese, chromium, copper, zinc, cobalt, nickel, and cadmium may induce chlorosis similar to that caused by iron deficiency (see Hewitt, 1963); these effects may, in fact, be due to interference with iron metabolism. Co^{2+} and Zn^{2+} ($6.9 \times 10^{-3}M$) also inhibit greening of etiolated cells of *Euglena gracilis* in the light[74].

Leaves suffering from lime-induced chlorosis contain much higher levels of organic acids, particularly citric, and free amino acids[66]. The accumulation of free amino acids may be a result of a reduction in the formation of chloroplast protein. In *Nicotiana tabacum*, leaves which were not perceptibly chlorotic, taken from iron-deficient plants, incorporated ^{14}C-glycine into protein at a rate 25 per cent lower than that obtained with normal leaves[128]. When chlorotic leaves, with lowered chlorophyll and protein contents, were supplied with iron, the protein content increased together with the chlorophyll content. The protein content of chlorotic leaves of iron-deficient corn plants was 25 per cent lower than that of leaves of normal plants: the protein content of the chloroplast fraction was about 82 per cent lower than in normal plants[103]. However, these chloroplasts were isolated in water and would therefore have lost most of their soluble protein. Plastids of iron-deficient leaves can be seen in electron micrographs to have a greatly reduced content of thylakoid material compared to normal chloroplasts[19]. Thus it seems possible that the chloroplasts from iron-deficient leaves might have a higher proportion of their protein in a soluble form than normal chloroplasts, and therefore might lose a higher proportion of their protein on isolation in aqueous media. Therefore, while it seems likely that there is less chloroplast protein formed, the plastids of iron-deficient leaves may not be as low in protein as the data on corn leaves suggest. There is some indication that formation of chloroplast protein may be less sensitive to iron deficiency than chlorophyll synthesis: in certain unicellular green algae, an insoluble chloroplast protein fraction from iron-deficient cells had a lower chlorophyll/nitrogen ratio than the same fraction from normal cells[105]. When deficient cells were supplied with iron they synthesized chlorophyll until the normal chlorophyll/nitrogen ratio was restored.

In the case of the unicellular green algae (*Chlorella, Scenedesmus, Chlamydomonas*) there is only one chloroplast per cell, so there is no question of a reduction in plastid numbers as a consequence of iron-deficiency. Whether, in a developing leaf, iron-deficiency causes any inhibition of plastid multiplication, as well as reducing the amount of chlorophyll and thylakoid material formed by each plastid, is not known.

Various attempts have been made to discover the reason for the marked effect of iron deficiency on chlorophyll synthesis. Marsh, Evans, and Matrone (1963) found that leaf discs from severely iron-deficient *Vigna sinensis* plants incorporated radioactive δ-aminolaevulinic acid (ALA) into chlorophyll *a* at about the same rate as normal tissue. The incorporation of radioactivity from ^{14}C-α-ketoglutarate into the porphyrin ring of chlorophyll *a*, on the other hand, took place at only about one-twentieth the rate obtained with normal tissue. Also, iron-deficient tissue had lower ability than normal to incorporate radioactivity from ^{14}C-succinate and ^{14}C-citrate into the porphyrin ring of chlorophyll. Since δ-aminolaevulinic acid incorporation is not inhibited, but incorporation of precursors of this compound is, these authors conclude that iron deficiency reduces the rate of synthesis of ALA, and that the inhibition of synthesis of this compound may be sufficient to retard chlorophyll formation. An inhibition of utilization of citric acid cycle intermediates for ALA synthesis might also explain the accumulation of organic acids such as citric acid, in chlorotic tissue. Granick (1965) finds that in etiolated barley leaves, the conversion of ALA to porphyrins, including protochlorophyllide, is stimulated rather than inhibited, by αα-dipyridyl, and pyridyl-2-aldoxime, which chelate iron, suggesting that iron deficiency does not affect the pathway between ALA and protochlorophyllide.

The hypothesis that the inhibition of chlorophyll formation is due to a block before ALA rather than after is supported by the finding that, in moderately iron-deficient cells of *E. gracilis*, in which chlorophyll synthesis was diminished, the activities of δ-aminolaevulinic dehydratase, porphobilinogen deaminase, and those enzymes concerned with the conversion of porphobilinogen to coproporphyrin, were at normal levels[23].

However, some results which are difficult to reconcile with the above theory have been reported by Hsu and Miller (1965). They incubated leaf discs from *Nicotiana tabacum* with ^{14}C-succinate or ^{14}C-ALA. In the dark when no iron salts were added, there was accumulation of ^{14}C-coproporphyrin in the culture medium, whether the leaf discs were from normal or chlorotic (iron-deficient) leaves. This accumulation decreased markedly (with both types of leaf discs) when iron was added to the medium. In the light, the incorporation of these precursors into chlorophyll *a* was greater when the culture medium contained iron, than when it did not, with both normal and chlorotic leaf discs. Hsu and Miller propose that in higher plants the conversion of coproporphyrinogen to protoporphyrin requires iron, and that this iron-sensitive reaction limits chlorophyll synthesis under conditions of iron-deficiency. Thus, while the weight of the evidence seems to indicate that iron-deficiency affects formation of ALA, the results of Hsu and Miller suggest that the sensitive site might be at a later stage in chlorophyll synthesis.

An additional, or alternative, reason why lack of iron should inhibit chloroplast formation is that certain essential chloroplast constituents, for instance ferredoxin and the cytochromes, contain iron. In fact, chloroplasts contain about 82 per cent of the iron of the leaf[81]. Granick (1965) has suggested that chloroplast development might be retarded as a consequence of the inhibition of photosynthesis caused by lack of ferredoxin. When iron-deficient leaves of *Vigna sinensis* are supplied with iron, ferredoxin activity increases together with chlorophyll content[88].

XV.7.ii. MANGANESE

The symptoms of manganese deficiency in higher plants include chlorosis. Leaves of manganese-deficient spinach plants, showing mild chlorosis, contained considerably reduced numbers of chloroplasts[95]. In the chloroplasts of moderately deficient plants there were fewer thylakoids extending from one granum to another, and empty regions appeared in the stroma. In the chloroplasts of more severely deficient plants there were no intergranal thylakoids and the stroma contained numbers of vesicles: the grana became disorganized and appeared as clusters of loosely-connected thylakoids.

The biochemical effects of manganese deficiency are likely to be complex since Mn^{2+} ions are required for various cellular processes. Various enzymes, for instance isocitric dehydrogenase, require Mn^{2+}; this cation may also be required for the stability of plant ribosomes[82]. However, one requirement which might be particularly relevant to the inhibition of chloroplast formation is the requirement for Mn^{2+} in photosynthesis. Manganese deficiency depresses photosynthesis in algae; this depression may be overcome by the addition of Mn^{2+} [104]. Manganese is thought to be involved in the pathway for oxygen evolution[70] and appears to be a component of the thylakoids[101]. *Chlorella pyrenoidosa* requires 10^{-4}M Mn^{2+} for autotrophic growth but only 10^{-7}M for heterotrophic growth[40], suggesting that the photosynthetic system requires higher levels of this cation than do other cellular processes. Thus, photosynthesis is likely to be the first cellular process to be affected by manganese deficiency. Chloroplast formation might be inhibited by the lack of photosynthetically-produced intermediates for the synthesis of chloroplast materials.

XV.7.iii. MAGNESIUM

Since magnesium is a component of the molecules of chlorophylls *a* and *b*, it is not surprising that this element is required for chloroplast formation, quite apart from its essential function in other cellular processes. Chlorosis is one of the first symptoms of magnesium deficiency in higher plants. In leaves of magnesium-deficient plants the chloroplasts form few thylakoids and no proper grana[142]. In the case of the algae, even quite closely related species may react somewhat differently to magnesium deficiency. When *Chlorella pyrenoidosa* was grown in media containing different levels of Mg^{2+} the chlorophyll content of the cells was much the same in all cases[60]; however, the growth of the cells was strictly dependent upon the Mg^{2+} concentration, so that the chlorophyll formed per ml of culture medium increased approximately linearly with Mg^{2+} concentration up to 0·4 μg Mg^{2+}/ml, beyond which there was no further increase. With cells of *Chlorella* Cornell No. 11, on the other hand, the chlorophyll content appeared to depend upon the magnesium concentration in the medium in which they were grown[43]: when the Mg^{2+} content of the medium was raised from 0·02 to 2·0 μg/ml the chlorophyll content of the cells increased twelvefold. The rate of chlorophyll synthesis during short incubations by dark-grown cells of *Euglena gracilis* exposed to the light was found to be only slightly increased by Mg^{2+} [73]: during a six-hour incubation the rate of synthesis was 0·64 μg chlorophyll *a*/mg dry weight of cells/hour in the absence of Mg^{2+} and 20 per cent higher than this in the presence of 10^{-4}M $MgCl_2$. 10^{-3}M $MgCl_2$ stimulated to only the same extent as 10^{-4}M $MgCl_2$; 10^{-5}M $MgCl_2$ had little effect. The cells presumably have an internal pool of Mg which permits them to synthesize some chlorophyll in the absence of exogenous Mg^{2+}. It was found that about 0·94 μg of Mg^{2+} was released from 1·0 mg dry weight of dark-grown cells of *E. gracilis* by 5 per cent trichloroacetic acid[73]—this value is corrected for the small amount of chlorophyll Mg already present. From this amount of Mg, about 35 µg of chlorophyll could, in principle, be made. Nevertheless, in view of the requirement of so many cellular processes for high levels of Mg^{2+}, it seems likely that a more clear-cut requirement for Mg^{2+} in greening might show up in prolonged incubations.

XV.7.iv. NITROGEN

Nitrogen-deficient plants have a lower than normal chlorophyll content. The leaves are pale green: older leaves become yellow-green, and sometimes completely yellow. The chlorophyll content of cells of *Chlorella* Cornell No. 11 was found to be markedly dependent upon the nitrogen content of the growth medium[43]: when the nitrogen content of the medium was raised from 10 to 80 µg/ml, the chlorophyll content of the cells increased thirteenfold. In the leaf plastids of nitrogen-deficient plants the stroma is greatly diminished and the grana thylakoids are swollen and reduced in number[142]. Since nitrogen is an essential component of the chloroplast proteins, chlorophylls, lipids, and nucleic acids, it is, of course, to be expected that lack of this element should depress chloroplast formation. What is rather more interesting, however, is that, as so often seems to be the case, chloroplast formation (or at least, chlorophyll formation) appears to be more sensitive than other cellular processes. This is indicated, for instance, by the finding that in *Chlorella* nitrogen deficiency inhibits chlorophyll formation more than cell growth. This might be because the formation of certain chloroplast components, such as the proteins or the chlorophylls themselves, requires higher levels of nitrogenous intermediates for optimum synthetic rates than does the formation of other cellular components.

XV.7.v. OTHER ELEMENTS

Deficiency of phosphorus or of potassium in higher plants sometimes, but not invariably, causes chlorosis. Apparently normal chloroplasts are formed at first, but then the internal structure begins to degenerate[142]. In the case of phosphorus-deficient plants of *Phaseolus vulgaris*, one of the first detectable changes is an alteration of the thylakoid system. Large stacks of thylakoids are formed, with the thylakoids further apart than in normal grana[143]. In the chloroplasts of more severely deficient leaves, the thylakoids become more loosely organized, or disappear altogether. In plastids with little or no thylakoid material, large osmiophilic globuli accumulate. Thomson, Weier, and Drever (1964) suggest that these globuli are formed of lipid material released by breakdown of the lipoprotein membranes of the thylakoids. It is interesting that phosphorus deficiency appears to allow normal development of chloroplasts, followed by degeneration, rather than inhibiting chloroplast formation from the very beginning. Possibly, the chloroplast structure is unstable owing to the lack of some component such as a phospholipid.

Marschner (1965a, b) grew barley seedlings in the dark either in a medium containing potassium as the monovalent metal ion (2·5 m eq. KNO_3/litre), or in a medium in which 20 per cent of the potassium was replaced by caesium (2·0 m eq. KNO_3 + 0.5 m eq. $CsNO_3$/litre). When the dark-grown plants were illuminated for 11 hours, the amounts of chlorophylls *a* and *b* formed in the Cs-treated plants were about one-third lower than the amounts formed in the normal plants. Large amounts of porphyrins accumulated (more than 60 μg/g fresh weight) in the shoots of the caesium-treated plants. Uroporphyrin constituted 80–90 per cent of these porphyrins; there was little accumulation of coproporphyrin and protoporphyrin. The quantity of porphyrin accumulating was approximately equal to the amount by which chlorophyll synthesized in the normal plants exceeded the chlorophyll synthesized in the caesium-treated plants.

When the caesium-treated plants were put back in the dark for about 13 hours, the porphyrins largely disappeared to be replaced by an approximately equivalent amount of protochlorophyllide. If these plants were then exposed to white light again they suffered severe damage. The damage was dependent upon the wavelength of the light. Five hours' exposure to light at 679 mμ, the absorption peak of chlorophyll, had little effect. However, five hours' illumination with light of wavelength 635 mμ, a wavelength at which inactive protochlorophyll, *in vivo*, absorbs, damaged the plants.

Marschner suggests that caesium inhibits the formation of chlorophyll, but not of porphyrins, in the light, so that chlorophyll synthesis is retarded but porphyrins accumulate. When the plants are put back in the dark, the porphyrins are (perhaps quite slowly) converted to protochlorophyllide, and because of the inhibition of porphyrin synthesis in the dark (XIII.18) no further porphyrins are synthesized. The large amount of protochlorophyllide formed is of the inactive type, which cannot be converted to chlorophyllide (it may be the same as the inactive protochlorophyllide that accumulates in the presence of δ-aminolaevulinic acid) and the light energy it absorbs causes damage to the rest of the cell.

Deficiencies of several other elements, apart from those already dealt with, tend to induce chlorosis in higher plants (see Hewitt, 1963). These elements include sulphur, calcium, copper, zinc, boron, molybdenum, chlorine, and cobalt.

36—P.

XV.7.vi. NUTRITIONAL IMBALANCE

As discussed earlier (XIII.18) chloroplast formation in various algae
can be repressed by certain carbon sources. In one alga, *Chlorella protothecoides*, there are some particularly interesting relationships between
chloroplast formation and the relative amounts of the carbon and nitrogen sources in the medium, which have been studied in some detail by
Hase and his co-workers[3a, 3b, 3c, 3d, 89a, 100a, 128a, 129a]. The general picture is that high ratios of carbon to nitrogen source produce bleached
cells, low ratios produce green cells. If green cells are incubated in the
dark in air in a nitrogen-free medium containing (besides basal mineral
nutrients) either glucose, fructose, galactose, glycerol, or acetate (each
at a concentration of 1 per cent), there is a marked fall in the chlorophyll content of the culture during a 48-hour period: cells incubated
with mineral nutrients alone show no decrease in chlorophyll content.
Glucose, fructose, and acetate all cause about 70 per cent drop in
chlorophyll content, glycerol causes a 50 per cent drop, and galactose,
a 40 per cent drop. Aoki, Matsuka, and Hase (1965) conclude from the
fact that these different carbon sources all bleach, that there is a common intermediate in their metabolic pathways that causes the bleaching. If the glucose is removed from the medium, bleaching continues for
another eight hours before ceasing, suggesting that the bleaching agent
is a metabolic intermediate produced from glucose, the pool of which
is of such a size as to require several hours for depletion. If the incubation in the dark is carried out in an atmosphere of nitrogen instead of
air, there is no loss of chlorophyll. Bleaching ceases immediately if,
during a dark incubation the cells are transferred from air to nitrogen
indicating that an oxygen-requiring step is very directly involved in the
bleaching process. Also, the bleaching that takes place in the dark, in
air, is prevented by dinitrophenol, arsenate, cyanide, and azide, indicating that under these conditions, oxidative phosphorylation is required
for bleaching to occur. Addition of a nitrogen source (0·5 per cent urea)
to the (1 per cent) glucose-containing medium reduces the bleaching from
about 70 per cent destruction of chlorophyll to about 30 per cent destruction: Aoki *et al.* suggest that the active metabolic intermediate produced
from glucose reacts, directly or indirectly, with the nitrogen source and is
thus removed. The fall in chlorophyll content is approximately halved
by dihydrostreptomycin and by actinomycin: the significance of these
findings is far from clear, but they may possibly indicate that synthesis
of protein and of RNA are in some way involved in the bleaching process. During bleaching the amount of the chloroplast sulpholipid in the
cells decreases markedly but the amount of the degradation product,
sulphoquinovosyl glycerol, increases. Shibuya and Hase (1965) suggest

that the sulpholipid is an integral component of the chloroplast struc-ture; that deacylation of the sulpholipid may be a cardinal event in the bleaching process, causing a disintegration of the architecture of the photosynthetic apparatus.

Bleaching (in medium containing 1 per cent glucose but no nitrogen) takes place in the light, in air, as it does in darkness, but the chlorophyll content does not begin to decrease until after a 24-hour lag. There is no bleaching in the light in an atmosphere of nitrogen.

Cells grown under bleaching conditions (1 per cent glucose, 0·1 per cent urea, salts) have no chlorophyll and no photosynthetic activity, but contain large amounts of polysaccharide and lipid. The cell con-tains what looks like a large plastid almost completely full of starch. If these cells are transferred to a medium with a high (0·5 per cent urea) nitrogen content and a low (ca. 0·01 per cent) or zero glucose content, then on incubation in the light, chlorophyll synthesis starts after a lag of 10–15 hours and is still continuing after about 40 hours. Four hours after chlorophyll synthesis has started only chlorophyll a can be found, but 12 hours after the end of the lag phase, both a and b in the usual 3:1 ratio are found. Electron microscope studies have shown that dur-ing the incubation in the light, single thylakoids first become detectable at the end of the lag period of chlorophyll synthesis. By 24 hours, bands containing two, three, or four thylakoids can be seen. Beyond this time the amount of thylakoid material increases steadily until a normal chloroplast is produced. Photosynthetic activity (Hill reaction, $^{14}CO_2$ fixation, photophosphorylation) develops in parallel with chlorophyll content. If the incubation in high-nitrogen medium is carried out in the dark then, after a lag of about 17 hours, chlorophyll synthesis com-mences but the final level (at about 70 hours) is only about one-sixth of that in cells incubated in the light.

Recovery from bleaching can be allowed to take place in two stages. The bleached cells are first transferred to glucose-free medium in the dark, and then after this dark incubation they are supplied with urea and illuminated to induce chloroplast formation. When supplied before exposure to light, 5-fluorouracil strongly inhibits greening: when it is supplied after the beginning of the light incubation the effect is less and decreases as the delay increases. Actinomycin inhibits greening if added during the dark phase but has no effect when present only during the exposure to light. Dihydrostreptomycin has its greatest inhibitory effect when added at the beginning of the dark incubation but still has some (although less) effect when added after 15 hours' exposure to light. Mitomycin C (an inhibitor of DNA synthesis) has no effect on greening. On the basis of these and other results, Hase and co-workers suggest that chloroplast development during recovery from glucose-induced bleaching involves two consecutive phases: an early, light-independent phase, in which RNA and protein synthesis commences, and a further, light-dependent phase, in which chlorophyll is formed, together with more protein, to give the fully organized chloroplast. The chloroplast development does not appear to require the formation of new DNA.

As might be expected, recovery from glucose-induced bleaching is inhibited by glucose itself. When the bleached cells are incubated in the light in medium containing 0·5 per cent urea, increasing concentrations of glucose increase the lag phase, and diminish the rate, of chlorophyll synthesis. For instance, 0·5 per cent glucose increases the lag from about 12 to 20 hours, and diminishes the rate by about 75 per cent. In the presence of 0·1 per cent glucose the amount of RNA synthesized during greening is about half that formed in the absence of glucose. Shihira-Ishikawa and Hase (1965) suggest that glucose (or more likely one of its metabolic products) selectively represses formation of a type of RNA required for chloroplast formation.

In another chlorophycean alga, *Dictyococcus cinnabarinus*, the presence of a sugar in the medium causes, as well as an inhibition of chlorophyll formation, a considerable stimulation of carotenoid production[146a, 34a]. Autotrophically-grown cells are green: when these are inoculated into growth medium containing 2 per cent glucose, and grown on a 12-hour light/12-hour dark régime, the colour of the culture changes gradually from green to yellow to pink, and eventually to an intense orange colour by the time growth is finished. At this stage there is no detectable chlorophyll in the cells.

XV.8. Physical Agents

As we saw previously (X.6) cells of *Euglena gracilis* lose their ability to form chloroplasts on growth at high temperatures. However, the higher temperature does not have much effect on the greening of etiolated cells. The rate of chlorophyll synthesis by dark-grown cells (grown at normal temperature) exposed to the light was only about 25 per cent lower at 34·5° (a temperature which induces permanent bleaching) than it was at room temperature[21]. The complete and permanent loss of chloroplast-forming ability during growth at high temperature takes some time to develop—even after 94 hours' growth at 34·5° the cells will (slowly) regain their normal chlorophyll content when returned to room temperature; however, after 144 hours' growth at 34·5°, they can no longer restore their chlorophyll levels at room temperature[21]. This re-greening by cells grown for a short time at high temperature and then put back at a normal temperature under non-multiplying conditions is inhibited by low concentrations of streptomycin; concentrations of about the level which, in growing cultures, cause loss of ability to form chloroplasts[94]. The inhibition is about 70 per cent for cells grown at high temperature for four days, and about 100 per cent for cells grown at high temperature for five days. This finding is particularly interesting in view of the fact[74], previously discussed, that greening of etiolated cells, grown at normal temperatures is relatively insensitive to streptomycin, being only about 20 per cent inhibited by a concentration which is sufficient to cause loss of ability to form chloroplasts in growing cultures. The results suggest[94] that the streptomycin-sensitive step in the pathway leading to formation of green chloroplasts, is the same as, or occurs after, the step inhibited by growth at high temperature: if streptomycin inhibited at a point before the step blocked by high temperature, then the antibiotic would not inhibit greening.

The exact biochemical mechanism by which growth at high temperature causes loss of ability to make chloroplasts is not known. It does appear that this bleaching treatment, like other bleaching treatments, ultimately causes loss of chloroplast DNA (see X.6): what is not known is how the high temperature brings this about. The inhibition of replication of chloroplast DNA may be a direct, or a very indirect, consequence of growth at high temperature; the evidence available at the moment does not permit us to distinguish between these possibilities.

Although treatment of *Euglena gracilis* with ultraviolet light causes permanent loss of ability to make chloroplasts (see X.6) it appears to have no effect on the greening of etiolated cells. When cells were grown in the dark, given a dose of ultraviolet light sufficient to cause 100 per cent loss of chloroplast-forming ability, and then exposed to red light (red, to avoid photoreactivation of the UV damage), they formed chloroplasts quite normally, as judged by fluorescence microscopy[126]. On plating out, all these cells gave rise to white colonies, indicating that, although they retained the ability to convert those proplastids actually present, to chloroplasts, they could no longer transmit the ability to form chloroplasts to their descendants. It thus appears likely that the effects of UV at these dosages are confined to the replication of the plastid genetic material, and that the biosynthesis of other chloroplast components is not directly affected. A curious effect of ultraviolet light on higher plants is that it may cause disappearance of chloroplasts already there: when leaves of *Phaseolus vulgaris* were irradiated with UV and then placed in the dark, the chloroplasts of the guard cells were found to have completely disappeared after 24 hours[15].

Electromagnetic radiation harder than ultraviolet also interferes with chloroplast formation. Doses of gamma radiation of up to 150 Kr delayed the onset of chlorophyll formation, in etiolated wheat plants exposed to light, by as much as 10 hours[47], although the small amount of protochlorophyllide actually present was, as usual, rapidly converted to chlorophyllide. The chloroplasts finally formed appeared to function normally, since the plants incorporated $^{14}CO_2$ into the usual photosynthetic intermediates. Despite the fact that the chloroplast-forming systems ultimately recovered, the plants nevertheless eventually died, indicating that some other essential cellular component, or process, did not recover. During greening of normal etiolated plants, the ability to fix CO_2 does not appear until some hours after chlorophyll synthesis commences (XIII.13). However, these irradiated plants began to fix $^{14}CO_2$ at about the same time as rapid chlorophyll synthesis started: this suggests that adaptation to photosynthetic CO_2 fixation was in fact taking place during the long lag before chlorophyll synthesis started; that the formation of the enzymes of photosynthesis was less inhibited by the γ-rays than was the formation of the enzymes for chlorophyll biosynthesis. The recovery of the chlorophyll-forming system required light: if the plants were kept in the dark for 6–24 hours after irradiation, and then put in the light, there was still a 10-hour lag before chlorophyll synthesis started. However, continued exposure to light was apparently not required: if the irradiated plants were exposed to light for one hour, and then put in the dark for 9 or 16 hours, they began to synthesize chlorophyll as soon as they were put in the light. It therefore appears that the recovery process, once initiated by light, can continue in the dark: this rather suggests that the phytochrome system may be involved.

Irradiation with X-rays also appears to inhibit greening, but the characteristics of the inhibition appear to be somewhat different from those reported for γ-rays. When excised, etiolated, leaves of *Phaseolus vulgaris* were given X-ray doses of up to 12 Kr, and then exposed to light, the time course of chlorophyll synthesis in the irradiated leaves was similar to that in the unirradiated leaves, but the rate (during the phase of prolonged chlorophyll synthesis) was only about half the normal rate[110]. The actual conversion of the protochlorophyllide already present, to chlorophyllide, was not inhibited. When the plants were illuminated for one minute, to photoreduce their protochlorophyllide, and then put back in the dark for 18 hours to allow them to form more protochlorophyllide, it was found that the irradiated plants had lost the ability to synthesize protochlorophyllide in the dark. When leaves were illuminated for 10 minutes, put in the dark for 10 hours, and then exposed to continuous white light, there was, as is generally found (see XIII.18), a more rapid rate of chlorophyll formation than in plants exposed to continuous light without this light/dark pretreatment. However, the rate of synthesis in the irradiated leaves was still only half that in the unirradiated leaves: that is, there was no evidence for any reversal of the X-ray damage by this light/dark pretreatment.

REFERENCES

1. AARONSON, S. (1960). *J. Protozool.* **7**, 289–293
2. AARONSON, S. & BENSKY B., (1962). *J. Gen. Microbiol.* **27**, 75–98
3. ALAMERCY, J., HAMNER, C. L. & LATUS, M. (1951). *Nature, Lond.* **168**, 85
3a. AOKI, S. & HASE, E. (1964). *Plant & Cell Phys.* **5**, 473–484, 485–493
3b. AOKI, S. & HASE, E. (1965). *Plant & Cell Phys.* **6**, 347–354
3c. AOKI, S., KHAN MATSUBARA, J. & HASE, E. (1965). *Plant & Cell Phys.* **6**, 475–485
3d. AOKI, S., MATSUKA, M. & HASE, E. (1965). *Plant & Cell Phys.* **6**, 487–497
4. ARONSON, A. I. (1961). *Biochim. Biophys. Acta* **49**, 98–107
5. ASHTON, F. M. (1965). *Weeds* **13**, 164–168
6. ASHTON, F. M. & BISALPUTRA, T. (1964). *Plant Phys.* **39**, xxxiii
7. ASHTON, F. M., GIFFORD, E. M. & BISALPUTRA, T. (1963). *Bot. Gaz.* **124**, 329–335, 336–343
8. ASHTON, F. M., ZWEIG, G. & MASON, G. W. (1960). *Weeds* **8**, 448–451
9. BANDURSKI, R. S. (1949). *Bot. Gaz.* **111**, 95–109
10. BARTELS, P. G. (1964). *Plant Phys.* **39**, lxviii
11. BARTELS, P. G. & WEIER, T. E. (1965). *Am. J. Bot.* **52**, 631
12. BARTELS, P. G. & WOLF, F. T. (1965). *Phys. Plant* **18**, 805–812
13. BENNETT, L. L., SMITHERS, D. & WARD, C. T. (1964). *Biochim. Biophys. Acta* **87**, 60
14. BENNETT, L. L., WARD, V. L. & BROCKMANN, R. W. (1965). *Biochim. Biophys. Acta* **103**, 478
15. BLAKELY, L. M. & CHESSIN, M. (1959). *Science* **130**, 500–501
16. BOEHM, J. (1873). *Sitz. Akad. Wiss. Wien.* **68**, 171–184. Quoted by Steer and Walker (1965)
17. BOGORAD, L. (1950). *Am. J. Bot.* **37**, 676
18. BOGORAD, L. & JACOBSON, A. B. (1964). *Biochem. Biophys. Res. Commun.* **14**, 113–117
19. BOGORAD, L., PERES, G., SWIFT, H. & McILRATH, W. J. (1959). *Brookhaven Symp. Biol.* **11**, 132–137
20. BRACCO, M. & VON EULER, H. (1947). *Kem. Arb.* **II**, 10: 4
21. BRAWERMAN, G. & CHARGAFF, E. (1959). *Biochim. Biophys. Acta* **31**, 178–186
22. BUZARD, J. A. (1962). *Giorn., Ital. Chemoterap.* **5**, 1–12
23. CARELL, E. F. & PRICE, C. A. (1965). *Plant Phys.* **40**, 1–7
24. CARTER, M. C. & NAYLOR, A. W. (1960). *Bot. Gaz.* **122**, 138–143
25. CARTER, M. C. & NAYLOR, A. W. (1961). *Phys. Plant* **14**, 62–71
26. CASTELFRANCO, P. & BISALPUTRA, T. (1965). *Am. J. Bot.* **52**, 222–227
27. COHEN, S. S. (1946). *J. Biol. Chem.* **166**, 393
28. COHEN, S. S., FLAKS, J. G., BARNER, H. D., LOEB, M. R. & LICHTENSTEIN, J. (1958). *Proc. Natl. Acad. Sci.* **44**, 1004–1012
29. COLOMBO, B., FELICETTI, L. & BAGLIONI, C. (1965). *Biochem. Biophys. Res. Commun.* **18**, 389–395
30. COX, E. C., WHITE, J. R. & FLAKS, J. G. (1964). *Proc. Natl. Acad. Sci.* **51**, 703–709
31. DAVIES, J. E. (1964). *Proc. Natl. Acad. Sci.* **51**, 659–664
31a. DAVIES, J., ANDERSON, P. & DAVIS, B. D. (1965). *Science* **149**, 1096
32. DAVIES, J., GILBERT, W. & GORINI, L. (1964). *Proc. Natl. Acad. Sci.* **51**, 883–890
33. DE DEKEN-GRENSON, M. (1955). *Biochim. Biophys. Acta* **17**, 35
34. DE DEKEN-GRENSON, M. & MESSIN, S. (1958). *Biochim. Biophys. Acta* **27**, 145–155
34a. DENTICE DI ACCADIA, F., GRIBANOVSKI-SASSU, O., ROMAGNOLI, A. & TUTTO-BELLO, L. (1965). *Nature, Lond.* **208**, 1342–1343

34b. EBRINGER, L. (1965). *Naturwiss.* **52**, 666

35. EISENSTADT, J. M. & BRAWERMAN, G. (1964). *J. Mol. Biol.* **10**, 392–402

36. ERDOS, T. & ULLMANN, A. (1959). *Nature, Lond.* **189**, 618–619

37. VON EULER, H. (1947). *Kem. Arb.* **II.** 9: 1–3

38. VON EULER, H., BRACCO, M. & HELLER, L. (1948). *Compt. Rend. Acad. Sci.* **227**, 16–18

39. EXER, B. (1958). *Experientia* **14**, 136–137

40. EYSTER, C., BROWN, T. E., TANNER, H. A. & HOOD, S. L. (1958). *Plant Phys.* **33**, 235–241

41. FLAKS, J. G., COX, E. C. & WHITE, J. R. (1962). *Biochem. Biophys. Res. Commun.* **7**, 385–389

42. FLAKS, J. G., COX, E. C., WITTING, M. L. & WHITE, J. R. (1962). *Biochem. Biophys. Res. Commun.* **7**, 390–393

43. FLEISCHER, W. E. (1935). *J. Gen. Physiol.* **18**, 573–597

44. FOYE, W. O., LANGE, W. E., SWINTOSKY, J. E., CHAMBERLAIN, R. E. & GUARINI, J. R. (1955). *J. Am. Pharm. Assoc.* **44**, 261–263

45. FRANKLIN, T. J. (1963). *Biochem. J.* **87**, 449–453

46. FREDERICK, J. F. (1963). *Phys. Plant* **16**, 822–827

47. GAILEY, F. B. & TOLBERT, N. E. (1958). *Arch. Biochem. Biophys.* **76**, 188–195

48. GALE, E. F. & FOLKES, J. P. (1953). *Biochem. J.* **53**, 493

49. GALE, E. F. (1963). *Pharmacol. Rev.* **15**, 481–530

50. GASSMAN, M. & BOGORAD, L. (1965). *Plant Physiol.* **40**, lii

51. GIBSON, K. D., NEUBERGER, A. & TAIT, G. H. (1962). *Biochem. J.* **83**, 550–559

52. GOLDBERG, I. H., RABINOWITZ, M. & REICH, E. (1962). *Proc. Natl. Acad. Sci.* **48**, 2094–2101

53. GRANICK, S. In *Symposium on Biochemistry of Chloroplasts (Aberystwyth, 1965)*. Ed., T. W. Goodwin. Academic Press, London (in press)

54. GRAY, R. A. & HENDLIN, D. (1962). *Plant Phys.* **37**, 223–227

55. GRIS, E. (1844). *Compt. Rend. Acad. Sci.* **19**, 1118–1119

56. HAHN, F. E., CIAK, J., WOLFE, A. D., HARTMAN, R. E., ALLISON, J. L. & HARTMAN, R. S. (1962). *Biochim. Biophys. Acta* **61**, 741–749

57. HALL, W. C., JOHNSON, S. P. & LEINWEBER, C. L. (1954). *Texas. Agr. Expt. Sta. Bull.*, 789

58. HESLOP-HARRISON, J. (1962). *Planta* **58**, 237–256

59. HEWITT, E. J. (1963). In *Plant Physiology*. Ed., F. C. Steward. Academic Press, London, pp. 137–360

60. VAN HILLE, J. C. (1938). *Rec. Trav. Botan. Neerl.* **35**, 680–757

61. HILTON, J. (1960). *Weed. Soc. of America, Abstracts*, p. 34

62. HILTON, J. & KEARNEY, P. C. (1965). *Weeds* **13**, 22–25

62a. HILTON, J. L., KEARNEY, P. C. & AMES, B. N. (1965). *Arch. Biochem. Biophys.* **112**, 544–547

63. HSU, W.-P. & MILLER, G. W. (1965). *Biochim. Biophys. Acta* **111**, 393–402

64. HURWITZ, J., FURTH, J. J., MALAMY, M. & ALEXANDER, M. (1962). *Proc. Natl. Acad. Sci.* **48**, 1222–1230

65. HUZISIGE, H., TERADA, T., NISHIMURA, M. & UEMURA, T. (1957). *Biol. J. Okayama. Univ.* **3**, 209

66. ILJIN, W. S. (1951). *Plant & Soil* **3**, 239–256, 339–351

67. JAGENDORF, A. T. & MARGULIES, M. (1960). *Arch. Biochem. Biophys.* **90**, 184–195

68. KEPES, A. & COHEN, G. (1962). In *The Bacteria*. IV. Eds., I. C. Gunsalus & R. Y. Stanier. Academic Press, New York, pp. 179–221

69. KERRIDGE, D. (1958). *J. Gen. Microbiol.* **19**, 497–506

70. KESSLER, E., ARTHUR, W. & BRUGGER, J. E. (1957). *Arch. Biochem. Biophys.* **71**, 326–335
71. KHUDAIRI, A. J. (1961). *Biochim. Biophys. Acta* **46**, 344–354
72. KIRK, J. M. (1960). *Biochim. Biophys. Acta* **42**, 167–169
73. KIRK, J. T. O. (1961). *Ph.D. Thesis.* Cambridge Univ.
74. KIRK, J. T. O. (1962a). *Biochim. Biophys. Acta* **56**, 139–151
75. KIRK, J. T. O. (1962b). *Biochim. Biophys. Acta* **59**, 476–479
76. KIRK, J. T. O. (1964). *Biochem. Biophys. Res. Commun.* **14**, 393–397
77. KIRK, J. T. O. & ALLEN, R. L. (1965). *Biochem. Biophys. Res. Commun.* **21**, 523–530
78. KIRK, J. T. O. & JUNIPER, B. E. (1963). *Exp. Cell. Res.* **30**, 621–623
79. KIRK, J. T. O. & JUNIPER, B. E. (1963). Unpublished
80. KLOPOTOWSKI, T. & WIATER, A. (1965). *Arch. Biochem. Biophys.* **112**, 562–566
81. LIEBICH, H. (1941). *Z. Botan.* **38**, 129–157
82. LYTTLETON, J. W. (1960). *Nature, Lond.* **187**, 1026–1027
83. MARGULIES, M. (1962). *Plant Phys.* **37**, 473–480
84. MARGULIES, M. (1964). *Plant Phys.* **39**, 579–585
85. MARGULIES, M. (1965). *Plant Phys.* **40**, 57–61
86. MARSCHNER, H. (1965). *Flora* **155**, 30–51
87. MARSCHNER, H. (1965). *Flora* **155**, 558–572
88. MARSII, H. V., EVANS, H. J. & MATRONE, G. (1963). *Plant Phys.* **38**, 632–638, 638–642
89. MASSINI, P. (1959). *Biochim. Biophys. Acta* **36**, 444
89a. MATSUKA, M. & HASE, E. (1965). *Plant & Cell Phys.* **6**, 721–741
90. McCALLA, D. R. (1965). *J. Protozool.* **12**, 34–41
91. McCALLA, D. R. & ALLEN, R. K. (1964). *Nature, Lond.* **201**, 504–505
92. McNULTY, I. B. & NEWMAN, D. W. (1961). *Plant Phys.* **36**, 385–388
93. MEGO, J. L. (1964). *Biochim. Biophys. Acta* **79**, 221–225
94. MEGO, J. L. (1964). *Biochim. Biophys. Acta* **88**, 663–665
94a. MEGO, J. L. & BUETOW, D. E. (1966). *J. Protozool.* **13**, 20–23
95. MERCER, F. V., NITTIM, M. & PUSSINGHAM, J. V. (1962) *J. Cell Biol.* **15**, 379–381
96. MORELAND, D. E., GENTNER, W. A., HILTON, J. L. & HILL, K. L. (1959). *Plant Phys.* **34**, 432–435
97. NAYLOR, A. W. (1964). *J. Agric. Food Chem.* **12**, 21–25
98. NÉTIEN, G. & LACHARME, J. (1957). *Compt. Rend. Soc. Biol.* **151**, 127
99. NIRENBERG, M. W. & MATTHAEI, J. H. (1961). *Proc. Natl. Acad. Sci.* **47**, 1588–1602
100. VAN NOORT, D. & WALLACE, E. (1963). *Biochem. Biophys. Res. Commun.* **10**, 109–111
100a. OH-HAMA, T., SHIHIRA-ISHIKAWA, I. & HASE, E. (1965). *Plant & Cell Phys.* **6**, 743–760
101. PARK, R. B. & PON, N. G. (1963). *J. Mol. Biol.* **6**, 105–114
102. PARTHIER, B. (1965a). *Nature, Lond.* **206**, 783–784
102a. PARTHIER, B. (1965b). *Z. Naturf.* **20b**, 1191–1197
103. PERUR, N. G., SMITH, R. L. & WIEBE, H. A. (1961). *Plant Phys.* **36**, 736–739
104. PIRSON, A. (1955). *Ann. Rev. Plant Phys.* **6**, 71–114
105. PIRSON, A. & BÖGER, P. (1965). *Nature, Lond.* **205**, 1129–1130
106. POGO, B. G. T. & POGO, A. O. (1964). *J. Cell Biol.* **22**, 296–301
107. POGO, B. G. T. & POGO, A. O. (1965). *J. Protozool.* **12**, 96–100
108. PRICE, C. A. & CARELL, E. F. (1964). *Plant Phys.* **39**, 862–868
109. PRICE, C. A. & ESTRADA, M.-T., G. (1964). *Weeds* **12**, 234–235
110. PRICE, L. & KLEIN, W. H. (1962). *Radiation Bot.* **1**, 269–275

111. PROVASOLI, L., HUTNER, S. H. & SCHATZ, A. (1948). *Proc. Soc. Exp. Biol. Med.* **69**, 279–282
112. PROVASOLI, L., HUTNER, S. H. & PINTNER, I. J. (1951). *Cold Spring Harbour Symp.* **16**, 113–120
113. PYFROM, H. T., APPLEMAN, D. & HEIM, W. G. (1957). *Plant Phys.* **32**, 674–676
114. RABINOVITZ, M., OLSON, M. E. & GREENBERG, D. M. (1955). *J. Am. Chem. Soc.* **77**, 3109
115. RACUSEN, D. (1958). *Arch. Biochem. Biophys.* **74**, 106–113
116. ROBBINS, W. J., HERVEY, A. & STEBBINS, M. E. (1953). *Ann. N.Y. Acad. Sci.* **56**, 818–830
117. ROSEN, W. G. (1957). *Plant Physiol.* **32**, viii
118. ROSEN, W. G. & GAWLIK, S. R. (1961). *J. Protozool.* **8**, 90–96
119. ROSEN, W. G. & SIEGESMUND, K. A. (1961). *J. Biophys. Biochem. Cytol.* **9**, 910–914
120. RUBIN, B. A. & LADYGINA, M. A. (1957). *Biokhimiya* **22**, 984
121. RUBIN, B. A. & LADYGINA, M. A. (1959). *Dokl. Akad. Nauk. S.S.S.R.* **124**, 64–67
122. SAGER, R. (1961a). *5th Internat. Congr. Biochem. Moscow, Abstract*
123. SAGER, R. (1961b). *Carneg. Inst. Wash. Yearbook* **60**, 374–376
124. SARKISSIAN, I. V. & HUFFAKER, R. C. (1962). *Proc. Natl. Acad. Sci.* **48**, 735–743
124a. SCHER, S. (1966). *Biochem. Biophys. Res. Commun.* **22**, 572–578
125. SCHER, S. & COLLINGE, J. C. (1964). *Plant Phys.* **39**, xxxiv
126. SCHIFF, J. A., LYMAN, H. & EPSTEIN, H. T. (1961). *Biochim. Biophys. Acta* **51**, 340–346
127. SCHOENTAL, R. & WHITE, A. F. (1965). *Nature, Lond.* **205**, 57–58
128. SHETTY, A. S. & MILLER, G. W. (1965). *Plant Phys.* **40**, vi
128a. SHIBUYA, I. & HASE, E. (1965). *Plant & Cell Phys.* **6**, 267–283
129. SHIGEURA, H. T. & GORDON, C. N. (1962). *J. Biol. Chem.* **237**, 1932–1936, 1937–1940
129a. SHIHIRA-ISHIKAWA, I. & HASE, E. (1965). *Plant & Cell Phys.* **6**, 101–110
130. SIEGEL, M. R. & SISLER, H. D. (1964). *Biochim. Biophys. Acta* **87**, 70
131. SIEGEL, M. R. & SISLER, H. D. (1965). *Biochim. Biophys. Acta* **103**, 558–567
132. SIGNOL, M. (1961). *Compt. rend. Acad. Sci.* **252**, 1645–1646, 1993–1995
133. SOLDO, A. Quoted by Zahalsky, A. C., Keane, M. M., Hutner, S. H., Lubart, K. J., Kittrell, M. & Amsterdam, D. (1963). *J. Protozool.* **10**, 421–428
134. SMILLIE, R. M., EVANS, W. R. & LYMAN, H. (1963). *Brookhaven Symp. Biol.* **16**, 88–107
135. SPEYER, J. F., LENGYEL, P. & BASILIO, C. (1962). *Proc. Natl. Acad. Sci.* **48**, 684–686
136. STEER, B. T. & WALKER, D. A. (1965). *Plant Phys.* **40**, 577–581
137. STEINBERG, R. A. (1952). *Plant Phys.* **27**, 302–308
138. STEINBERG, R. A., BOWLING, J. D. & McMURTREY, J. E. (1950). *Plant Phys.* **25**, 279–288
139. SUND, K. A. (1961). *Phys. Plant* **14**, 260–265
140. SUND, K. A., PUTALA, E. C. & LITTLE, H. N. (1960). *J. Agric. Food Chem.* **8**, 210–212
141. SWEETSER, P. B. & TODD, C. W. (1961). *Biochim. Biophys. Acta* **51**, 504–508
142. THOMSON, W. & WEIER, T. E. (1962). *Am. J. Bot.* **49**, 1047–1055
143. THOMSON, W., WEIER, T. E. & DREVER, H. (1964). *Am. J. Bot.* **51**, 933–938
144. TRAUT, R. R. & MONRO, R. E. (1964). *J. Mol. Biol.* **10**, 63–72
145. TROXLER, R. & BOGORAD, L. In *Symposium on Biochemistry of Chloroplasts (Aberystwyth, 1965)*. Ed., T. W. Goodwin. Academic Press, London (in press)
146. UMBARGER, E. & DAVIS, B. D. (1962). In *The Bacteria*. III. Eds., I. C. Gunsalus & R. Y. Stanier. Academic Press, New York, pp. 167–251
146a. WENZINGER, F. (1940). *Thesis*. Geneva, quoted by 34a

147. Wettstein, F. O., Noll. F. & Penman, S. (1964). *Biochim. Biophys. Acta* **87**, 525–528

148. Weyter, F. W. & Broquist, H. P. (1960). *Biochim. Biophys. Acta* **40**, 567–569

149. Wolf, F. T. (1960). *Nature, Lond.* **188**, 164–165

150. Wolf, F. T. (1961). *Plant Phys.* **36**, xxxix

151. Wolz, S. S. & Jackson, C. R. (1961). *Plant Phys.* **36**, 197–201

152. Wort, D. J. & Loughman, B. C. (1961). *Can. J. Bot.* **39**, 339–351

153. Zamecnik, P. C. (1962). *Biochem. J.* **85**, 257–264

154. Zahalsky, A. C., Hutner, S. H., Keane, M. & Burger, R. M. (1962). *Arch. Mikrobiol.* **42**, 46–55

CHAPTER XVI

Conclusions and Discussion

XVI.1. The Nature of Plastids

IN THIS chapter we shall summarize the main conclusions reached in this book, and we shall discuss some of the directions that future research on plastids may take.

In the first section of the book we saw that plastids are a well-defined class of organelles, occurring only in plant cells. Although all the different types of plastids are ontogenetically related, they show very marked differences from one another, in their chemical composition, structure, and function. The chemical components of the chloroplast, the characteristic plastid of leaves and other photosynthetic tissue, are mainly substances involved in the process of photosynthesis—pigments, enzymes, thylakoid structural protein, electron carriers, lipids required for thylakoid membrane structure, and so on. The chemistry of the photosynthetic pigments (except for the biliproteins) is quite well known; also, probably most of the lipid components of the chloroplast have now been identified. However, the chemistry of the chloroplast proteins is still largely unknown, and this is an area where we may hope that modern techniques of protein chemistry will shed a great deal of light in the next few years.

Electron microscopy has told us a great deal about the structure of the chloroplast. The chlorophyll-containing granal system seen by the light microscopist has turned out to consist of a complicated arrangement of flattened, membrane-bounded sacs, the thylakoids, embedded within a matrix, the stroma. The thylakoids contain the pigments and electron carriers; the stroma contains the enzymes of CO_2 fixation. The three-dimensional inter-relationships of the thylakoids, whether they form one ramifying membrane-bounded cavity, or whether there are many distinct cavities, remains to be established. There are indications that we are on the verge of important discoveries on the way in which the different chemical components of the thylakoid are built together to form the thylakoid membrane. It is to be hoped that the different sorts of evidence provided by X-ray diffraction, and the various electron microscopical techniques will be used to give a unified picture, although

572

at the moment there is some degree of conflict between the different interpretations suggested by the different kinds of evidence.

The way in which chloroplasts function, in photosynthesis, is something we have only briefly touched upon in this book. This is a field where the main outlines of the mechanisms are already fairly clear, but it is still not certain which are the important electron carriers, and little is known about the detailed mechanism by which ATP formation is brought about. A field in which a great deal of research remains to be done is in the comparative biochemistry of photosynthesis: the way in which the mechanisms in other groups of algae (having different pigments and also having different photosynthetic end-products, accumulating outside the chloroplasts) differ from those in the *Chlorophyta* and the higher plants.

Proplastids, found in the rapidly dividing, undifferentiated cells of the meristematic regions, are small, relatively empty, undifferentiated bodies which undergo division to keep pace with cell division. They have the ability to develop into the more differentiated kinds of plastid, appropriate to the kind of tissue eventually formed. It seems likely that they also have an important function in the carbohydrate metabolism of the meristematic cell. It is to be hoped that proplastids will be isolated and their biochemical capabilities studied.

Etioplasts are formed in leaves grown in the dark. An etioplast contains one, or a few, crystalline centres—three-dimensional cubic lattices of tubules, which appear to contain the protochlorophyllide, and possibly also the carotenoids of the plastid. Isolation of etioplasts and investigation of the enzymes present, should be a fruitful field of research. The crystalline centres themselves should also be isolated, and their chemical composition studied.

Amyloplasts are plastids the interiors of which are largely filled by starch grains; they are characteristic of storage tissues and cells of the root, particularly the root cap. Their main function (apart, possibly from those in the root cap) is presumably the storage of polysaccharide, and its breakdown when the plant requires it. The isolation, and study of the biochemical capabilities, of intact amyloplasts have yet to be achieved.

Chromoplasts are brightly-coloured, carotenoid-containing plastids, found in many kinds of flower petals, and fruit, the only function of which, so far as we know, is to be seen and to attract the attention of insects and other animals. The carotenoids are contained either in globules, or in fibres (possibly in this case complexed with protein). Once again, relatively little is known about the chemical composition or biochemical capabilities of these plastids. There are so many different kinds of chromoplasts, of various shapes, sizes, and colours, that this is almost virgin territory so far as biochemical research is concerned.

There are various other plastid types—elaioplasts, sterinochloroplasts, proteoplasts—about which we know relatively little at the moment. It is to be hoped that attempts will be made to isolate and study these different kinds of plastid. In particular, the green, but lipid (possibly steroid)-accumulating plastids of certain cacti should be investigated.

Light-microscopic studies over the last 100 years have led to the generally accepted concept that plastids show cytological continuity: that they are never produced *de novo* but are formed only from pre-existing plastids, in the course of both vegetative and sexual reproduction. We have seen that this view has now been questioned by Bell and Mühlethaler, who suggest that in the egg-cell, plastids are indeed formed, *de novo*, by the nucleus. While we, in this book, have concluded that the weight of the evidence contradicts the theory of Bell and Mühlethaler, nevertheless, this question is of such fundamental importance, that much more research, particularly electron microscopic studies on maturing egg-cells, should be carried out to clarify the position once and for all.

XVI.2. Hereditary Properties of Plastids

The nuclei, plastids, and mitochondria are integral and interacting parts of the plant cell such that the normal functioning of each is essential for the proper functioning of the whole. Consequently mutations in one organelle may be reflected in the behaviour of another. This principle is especially apparent in the interactions between the nucleus and plastids. Nuclear gene mutations, stable (Chapter III) or unstable (Chapter IV), and loss of whole or parts of chromosomes (Chapter V), frequently produce changes in the plastid phenotype. The developmental behaviour of the plastids serves as a marker for these changes in the nucleus. Genetic analyses of the nuclear-plastid interactions show that the nuclear genes control numerous steps in the development of plastid structure and the synthesis of plastid pigments; biochemical analysis clarifies the nature of these steps (Chapter XI). Developmental observations show that within individuals the nuclear-plastid interactions vary either in specific areas, producing figurative patterns, or somewhat to completely randomly, producing chlorotic, mosaic, and striped patterns, or even at different stages of the life cycle in the fern *Lastraea atrata*.

The normal development of a young into a mature plastid may well be dependent upon receiving a succession of metabolites produced under nuclear control. This does not mean, however, that the plastid is completely under the control of the nucleus. On the contrary, there is a mass of evidence to show that the plastids contain their own genetic material giving them their own measure of genetic autonomy. After reciprocal crosses between different species of *Oenothera* and other genera (Chapter IX), the frequently varying reaction of the plastids with the same hybrid nucleus indicates that the plastids differ from one another; moreover these differences are fixed, they are permanent over at least twenty generations in *Oenothera*. Such permanent differences in the plastids can only be due to genetic variation resulting from mutation of the plastid genetic material. Furthermore, since the different plastid types are associated with different species and, moreover, the plastids differ not only in their ability to develop into stable chloroplasts with particular test nuclei, but also in other characteristics such as their multiplication rates (Chapter VIII), it is clear that during the evolution of the genus by changes in the nucleus there have also been changes in the plastids. Thus the plastids as well as the nuclei are able to undergo long term evolutionary changes. They are also able to undergo short term changes by mutation.

Detectable spontaneous plastid mutations seem to occur with a low frequency of about once in two thousand plants. Nuclear gene-induced plastid mutations (Chapter VIII) are much more frequent and occur many times within an individual, comparable to the frequency of mutable nuclear genes (Chapter IV). It seems possible that the range of plastid mutation frequencies may be similar to the range of nuclear mutation frequencies due, perhaps, to a common property of a similar genetic material (Chapter X). Furthermore, spontaneous or induced plastid mutations, like nuclear mutations, produce a wide variety of phenotypes. The colour range of the defective mutant plastids includes white, cream, yellow, and various shades of pale green. Some mutant plastids become increasingly normal with age, but others degenerate (Chapter VII). The degeneration of some occurs after cell division has ceased and in others before, which then results in an inhibition of cell division. Some plants with light green mutant plastids are inviable on their own through their inability to photosynthesize, while other plants in which the plastids contain less chlorophyll are nonetheless viable owing to their ability to photosynthesize. Some mutant plastids appear to affect their neighbours within or across cells, while others behave quite independently of one another (Chapter VII). Experiment shows that these various types of behaviour of mutated plastids are independent of the nucleus, hence the differences must lie in the plastids themselves. Plastid mutants also differ in their stability (Chapter VIII). These include plastid types found in barley and probably many other plants which are initially defective, but which appear capable of mutating back to normal, simulating certain mutable nuclear genes (Chapter IV). It would be interesting to know if the frequency of back-mutation of plastid or plastogenes is influenced by temperature in the same way as the back-mutation of nuclear genes. In the fern *Scolopendrium*, a pale plastid which is stable in the gametophyte becomes mutable in the sporophyte, but why this should be is not known and the same is true of many other observations. Yet another kind of plastid is found in wheat, tomato, tobacco, and some other plants which appears to be unstable in the opposite direction. Within an individual the plastid sometimes develops into a normal green chloroplast, but in other areas it is frequently expressed as an underdeveloped white plastid; the two types of plastid expression combine to produce a variegated phenotype similar to many instances of mosaic or striped pattern variegations (Chapter III) produced under the control of mutant nuclear genes.

The existence of different types of nuclear behaviour has long been recognized. By contrast, the existence of so many types of plastid, caused presumably by a corresponding number and variety of plastid mutations, has till now been largely overlooked. In this brief summary and in the main text the multiplicity of plastid mutations has been particularly stressed. The reluctance of so many workers to recognize some of these changes has almost certainly hindered progress in the field of plastid genetics. By drawing attention to their existence now, it is hoped that they will receive much more thorough investigation in the future. If it can be accepted that the plastid contains genetic material, and there is good evidence that it does (Chapter X), there is surely no reason why its behaviour should not be potentially as versatile as the genetic material of the nucleus. Indeed, the variability of plastid mutations demands this. Moreover, the multiplicity and variability of plastid mutations suggests that it is no longer enough to think simply in terms of the plastogene analogous to the nuclear gene: one must also think in terms of the plastid chromosome analogous to the nuclear chromosome. The concept of the plastid chromosome is most useful for it enables one to visualize plastid mutations in the same way as nuclear mutations; how far this is justified remains to be seen. The fact that our present knowledge points in this direction, however, is a measure of how much we have already learnt, and also how much more there is still to be explored in the future. The present time is ripe for a new, widespread and comprehensive series of investigations into the genetic behaviour of the plastids; their present neglect by all but a few workers has continued for too long.

XVI.3. The Biochemistry of Plastid Autonomy and Plastid Growth

In view of the cytological evidence for plastid continuity, and the evidence that plastids have a certain degree of genetic autonomy, it seems likely (as discussed above) that plastids contain at least some of their own genetic information. This genetic information we would expect to be stored in the form of DNA or RNA, and the question of whether these substances are in fact present in plastids has been investigated in detail. Histochemical studies strongly indicate the presence of RNA, and provide a little evidence for the presence of DNA. With the electron microscope, RNA in the form of ribosomes has been detected in plastids, and also, very fine fibres have been observed which appear to contain DNA. Auto-radiographic techniques, combined with appropriate nuclease treatments, have provided evidence for the presence of both DNA and RNA in plastids.

Chemical analysis of isolated plastid preparations almost invariably indicates the presence of both kinds of nucleic acid; however, results of this type are always open to the criticism that the preparations are contaminated by other cellular material. While contamination undoubtedly occurs, the suggestion that it entirely accounts for the presence of nucleic acids in plastid preparations may now be refuted, because the plastid nucleic acids have been shown to differ in certain respects from other cellular nucleic acids. Plastid ribosomes have a lower sedimentation constant than cytoplasmic ribosomes and in one case at least, the plastid ribosomal RNA is known to have a different base ratio from that of the cytoplasmic ribosomal RNA. Plastid DNA has a different base ratio from nuclear DNA, and in two cases it has been shown that the nuclear DNA does, but the plastid DNA does not, contain 5-methylcytosine.

These cytological and chemical studies receive independent support from experiments on the loss of ability to make chloroplasts in the alga, *Euglena gracilis*. These experiments suggest that there is, outside the nucleus, a specific type of DNA, the presence of which is essential for the formation of chloroplasts, and which is lost from the cells as a result of treatment with ultraviolet light, streptomycin, or high temperature.

The evidence, taken all together, firmly establishes that there is both DNA and RNA in plastids: it seems likely that it is the DNA which contains the plastid genetic information. There is still a great deal to be learned about plastid DNA. We do not know whether it is stable or whether it undergoes turnover. It would also be desirable to know whether there is just one, or more than one, copy of the DNA per plastid. Does the plastid 'chromosome' exist as a circle like the bacterial chromosome? Is the absence of 5-methylcytosine a characteristic of plastid DNA from all species? The variation in the amount of DNA per plastid, and the base ratio of the plastid DNA, from one kind of plant to another should also provide a fertile field of study.

The main question to be answered about plastid DNA is, exactly what, in biochemical terms, is its function? It has the right sort of characteristics for genetic DNA: it has the usual chemical properties, it is present in genetically useful amounts, and it has associated with it the machinery (RNA polymerase) for bringing about its genetic effects. Given then, that plastid DNA is genetic DNA, exactly which of the genes concerned in plastid formation does it contain? We are still a long way from answering this question. Most of the genes which affect the plastid that we know about, have turned out to be nuclear genes. There is evidence that at least three of the steps in chlorophyll synthesis, three of the steps of leaf chloroplast carotenoid formation, eight of the reactions in tomato fruit chromoplast carotenoid synthesis, and nine of the biochemical processes, required for photosynthesis, are under nuclear control. So far as the plastid DNA is concerned there is some evidence that it contains the genes for plastid ribosomal RNA, and there is also some indirect evidence that it may contain the genes for two of the enzymes of chlorophyll synthesis, and the gene for the enzyme thymidine kinase. The cellular locations of the majority of the structural genes, and all the regulatory genes, concerned in plastid formation are completely unknown: this is one of the most important problems still to be solved, in plastid biology. More information about the nature of the genes in plastid DNA might come from biochemical studies on plastom mutants of higher plants: this is a field in which relatively little work has been done so far. The distribution of the genetic information between the nucleus and the plastid may have important implications for theories of plastid evolution.

So far as their ability to carry out the synthesis of their own materials is concerned, plastids seem to enjoy a high degree of autonomy. They probably carry out the complete synthesis of their chlorophylls, carotenoids, and lipids, but further evidence for this, particularly the detection of specific enzymes involved in the biosynthetic pathways, would be desirable. There is evidence for the formation of a few amino acids in plastids, but so far as the majority of the 20 amino acids used in the synthesis of plastid proteins is concerned, it is still quite unknown whether they are formed in the plastids or elsewhere in the cell: this is a potentially fruitful field of research in which relatively little has been done so far. It is to be hoped that attempts will be made to detect enzymes of amino acid biosynthesis in isolated plastids. Plastids undoubtedly can, and do, synthesize protein, but it is still not certain whether all plastid proteins are synthesized within the plastid, or whether some are synthesized elsewhere in the cell and transported into the plastids. Plastids can also synthesize RNA, and it seems likely that some of this is messenger RNA, coding the structure of plastid proteins, which is utilized by the plastid ribosomes. However, in view of the evidence that the genes for certain plastid proteins are in the nucleus, it seems possible that some messenger RNA molecules may come to the plastid from the nucleus, and be used by the plastid ribosomes for the synthesis of plastid proteins. Alternatively, these nuclear messenger RNA molecules may be transcribed into protein by the cytoplasmic ribosomes, and the finished proteins, as envisaged above, transported into the plastids. Here then, we have another area in which there is a great deal of research to be done. It seems likely, on various grounds, that plastids also synthesize DNA, but in this case direct evidence, such as, for instance, demonstrating DNA synthesis by isolated plastids, has yet to be obtained. Quite apart from where the actual final polymerization of nucleoside triphosphates to give plastid RNA and DNA takes place, we know very little about where the actual precursors are synthesized. We do not know, for instance, where the synthesis of the purine and pyrimidine bases of the plastid nucleic acids takes place. Whether plastids themselves contain the enzymes for purine and pyrimidine biosynthesis should be investigated. Plastids should also be examined for the presence of enzymes for the later stages in the synthesis of ribonucleoside and deoxyribonucleoside triphosphates: the only evidence available on this matter at the moment comes from reports that isolated *Acetabularia* chloroplasts can incorporate uracil and uridine into RNA. It is clear that while the available evidence does indicate that plastids have considerable biochemical autonomy, there are still large gaps in our knowledge to be filled in.

When meristematic cells differentiate into the specialized cells of the leaf, fruit, root cap or other tissues, so the proplastids differentiate into the type of mature plastid required in that particular tissue. The differentiation of the proplastid to the final plastid may occur directly, or may take place with the intermediate formation of some other, differentiated, kind of plastid. The case of plastid differentiation which has been studied in most detail is the formation of chloroplasts by plants first grown in the dark and then exposed to light. In the leaf cells of angiosperms, grown in the dark, the proplastids develop into etioplasts with their characteristic three-dimensional lattice of tubules (crystalline centre), containing the protochlorophyllide and carotenoids. Exactly how this regular, crystalline structure is built up is still somewhat uncertain. On exposure of the etiolated plant to light, the protochlorophyllide is rapidly converted to chlorophyllide, and then to chlorophyll *a*. A steady synthesis of chlorophylls, carotenoids, specific proteins, nucleic acids, and lipids ensues; the plastid increases in size; the prolamellar body disappears, as the characteristic chloroplast lamellar structure begins to be formed; photosynthetic ability develops, and within about two days a completely functional chloroplast, as found in the normal green leaf, has been formed. The energy, and probably some of the materials for the growth of the chloroplast, are provided by the breakdown of endogenous carbohydrates and/or lipids. A similar course of events, except that no prolamellar body is ever present, is observed when dark-grown cells of the alga, *Euglena gracilis* are exposed to light. In the case of algae such as *E. gracilis* or *Ochromonas danica* the details of the morphogenetic process by which the lamellar system is built up, are still obscure.

Many of the processes involved in chloroplast formation (other than protochlorophyllide reduction) can continue in the dark after a brief exposure to light. It is believed that the phytochrome system is involved in the initiation of chloroplast formation by light but exactly how phytochrome (P_{fr}) brings this about is not known. The adaptive nature of chloroplast formation can be explained in terms of the regulator gene hypothesis, but more evidence for the existence of regulator genes for plastid formation would clearly be desirable. The determination of action spectra for various of the different processes (structural changes, enzyme synthesis, carotenoid synthesis, lipid synthesis, carbohydrate breakdown, etc.) that go on during greening might provide more evidence as to the mechanisms by which light brings about these various effects. The mechanism of nutritional repression of chloroplast formation is also of the greatest interest and should be investigated.

Chloroplast formation during the normal development of the green plant takes place when the meristematic cells of the shoot differentiate into the fully expanded cells of the leaf. Proplastids develop into chloroplasts without the intermediate formation of etioplasts. Formation of chlorophylls and other chloroplast constituents, differentiation of the characteristic lamellar structure, and development of photosynthetic activity takes place at the same time. The details of the morphogenesis of the lamellar system are still uncertain. Also, little is known about the course of synthesis of most chloroplast constituents during the normal development of the green plant, for instance the order in which different components are synthesized, the relationship of such synthesis to the development of chloroplast structure and so on. In particular nothing is known about the mechanism by which the cell ensures that all the different chloroplast components are synthesized in the correct amount. To take one simple example, how does the plant ensure that the ratio of chlorophyll *a* to chlorophyll *b* is about 3·0, and not, say, 0·3, or 30? A related problem is that of the mechanism by which the synthesis of all the chloroplast constituents, either during normal growth of the green plant, or during greening of an etiolated leaf, is eventually brought to a stop. Why, for instance, does chlorophyll synthesis stop? Does it stop when all the available thylakoid structural protein has all its binding sites saturated with chlorophyll, so that newly formed chlorophyllide (or chlorophyll) is not removed from the holochrome protein, with the result that protochlorophyllide accumulates and, perhaps, inhibits δ-aminolaevulinic acid synthetase so that the chlorophyll biosynthetic pathway is switched off? This is certainly one possibility, but even if this is true then we still have to explain why synthesis of thylakoid structural protein stops. Perhaps the structural gene responsible for its synthesis becomes repressed. How does it become repressed? Has the inducer originally involved in de-repressing the gene, disappeared? If so why? Clearly this whole field of the mechanisms by which the synthesis of different chloroplast components are initiated, made to take place at the correct relative rates, and then finally brought to a halt, is one in which research is very much needed.

Formation of chloroplasts in roots and tubers is normally repressed, but will take place on prolonged exposure to light. The mechanism of this repression, and de-repression is also quite unknown.

Many gymnosperms and lower plants can form chloroplasts in the dark. Such plants appear to have both a photochemical and a non-photochemical pathway for chlorophyll formation. We know nothing about the non-photochemical pathway. Chlorophyll synthesis is generally faster in the light. In *Chlorella*, at least, the chloroplasts formed in the dark appear to be completely functional. Gymnosperms and pteridophytes can form chloroplasts in some tissues, but not in others. Thus chloroplast formation can still be regulated in these plants, but the regulatory system must differ in certain respects from that of angiosperms.

In the root, particularly in the cap cells, the proplastids differentiate into amyloplasts, which are packed tightly with starch grains. Whether this accumulation of starch is simply due to the rate of transport of sugar to these cells exceeding the rate of utilization, or whether there is some more specific mechanism acting at the genetic or enzymic level, for ensuring that starch accumulates, is not known.

The development of colour in the maturing fruit or flowers of many plants is due to the formation of chromoplasts. These may be formed from chloroplasts, amyloplasts or proplastids. The grana, or the starch grains, as the case may be, break down and disappear, to be replaced by large amounts of carotenoids, usually of a type not found in the chloroplast itself. Chromoplast formation, like chloroplast formation, is thought to be under the control of regulator genes. Even assuming the regulator gene hypothesis to apply in this case, we still do not know the nature of the inducers which activate the genes concerned in the synthesis of chromoplast carotenoids, nor do we know how it comes about that such inducers are present in the fruit but not, say, in the leaves.

It is quite clear from the foregoing that while we know a certain amount about the chemical and structural changes which accompany the differentiation of the different kinds of plastid, we are, in most cases, almost completely ignorant about the control and regulatory mechanisms by which the plant ensures that a particular type of plastid is made in a particular type of cell. This is a field in which it is to be hoped that much more research will be done.

Many antibiotics and herbicides inhibit chloroplast formation. Some of these, such as chloramphenicol, actidione, and the tetracyclines, probably inhibit chloroplast formation by blocking protein synthesis: streptomycin probably also acts to some extent by interfering with protein synthesis but may have some other mode of action as well. Agents such as actinomycin D, fluorouracil or thiouracil which interfere with RNA synthesis, also inhibit chloroplast formation. The herbicide, amitrol, is a very effective inhibitor of chloroplast formation, but its precise mode of action remains uncertain. Herbicides such as the triazines, or monuron may inhibit chloroplast formation partly because they block photosynthesis, and hence to some extent biosynthesis, but they probably also bring about light-induced damage to the chloroplasts due to the accumulation of toxic intermediates resulting from the inhibition of electron transport. Lack of certain mineral nutrients, particularly iron, inhibits formation of chloroplasts more than it inhibits other cellular processes. Replacement of part of a plant's potassium supply by caesium, causes a partial inhibition of chlorophyll synthesis, resulting in the accumulation of porphyrin precursors. High energy radiation (X-ray and γ-ray) has inhibitory effects on chloroplast formation from some of which the plant may be able to recover. Studies on inhibition of plastid formation, apart from their intrinsic interest, are useful in that they can give us information about the processes involved in plastid growth: for instance, studies with antibiotics have yielded information about the requirement for RNA synthesis during greening, and about the dependence of chlorophyll synthesis on protein synthesis. Specific metabolic inhibitors will continue to be used as tools for studying the mechanisms of plastid formation.

In this chapter we have indicated just some of the very many important questions about plastids that remain to be answered. To attempt to answer these questions will involve a great deal of research by many people for many years to come. Does the importance of the subject warrant the expenditure of such effort? The answer, of course, must be that it does. Plastids are of enormous importance in biology from several different points of view. First of all, thermodynamically speaking at any rate, plastids may be said to form the very basis of biology, in that most forms of life on this planet are ultimately dependent for their energy, and compounds from which to synthesize their cellular material, on the trapping of the sun's energy by chloroplasts and its utilization for the conversion of carbon dioxide to carbohydrate. Secondly, it is the possession of plastids which, at the cellular level, more than anything else distinguishes the Plant Kingdom from the Animal Kingdom. In fact, taxonomically speaking, it might be reasonable to make the presence or absence of plastids the basis for defining an organism as a plant or an animal. Thirdly, plastids are intrinsically, enormously interesting objects for study anyway: they possess a variety of complicated and delicate structures; they contain a very large number of unusual chemical compounds; they carry out intricate metabolic processes; they have mechanisms for converting light energy to chemical energy; they can carry out various long biosynthetic pathways; they show complicated and unusual patterns of inheritance; they provide an ideal system for studying the interaction between an organelle and the rest of the cell. In short plastids are of interest to biologists of all kinds, from the morphologist to the biophysicist.

In addition to the purely academic importance of knowledge about plastids such knowledge is also of considerable practical importance. Virtually all the food eaten by man comes, either directly or indirectly, from plastids. The starch in staple foods such as bread, rice, or potatoes is synthesized by plastids. About 75 per cent of the protein in the herbage eaten by the animals from which we get meat, is leaf chloroplast protein. When the most efficient methods of agriculture are used, the rate of food production may eventually be limited by the photosynthetic efficiency of the chloroplast. Ways (such as, perhaps, artificial production of plastid mutants) may have to be sought for producing more efficient chloroplasts. Breeding programmes may have to be instituted for getting more efficient types of chloroplast, or chloroplasts physiologically more suited to a particular climate, into appropriate crop plants. Ultimately, as the population on this planet increases we may become directly dependent on chloroplasts as our source of protein, instead of wastefully feeding them first to animals to convert them to animal protein. When this situation arrives plants may also have to be bred for the nutritional value, to us, of their chloroplasts. But, whether it be direct, or indirect, the fact remains that man is, and will continue to be, dependent upon plastids in general, and chloroplasts in particular, for the food he eats.

Given, then, the enormous academic and practical importance of plastids, we confidently expect that the many unsolved problems in plastid biology will be vigorously and successfully attacked during the years to come.

Index to Subjects

Index to Taxa

Index to Authors